D1693464

ADC DEUTSCHLAND
ADC GERMANY
2011

ADC DEUTSCHLAND JAHRBUCH 2011
ADC GERMANY ANNUAL 2011

avedition

INHALT
CONTENTS

24	VORWORT PREFACE Jochen Rädeker	524	AGENTUREN UND VERLAGE AGENCIES AND PUBLISHERS
28	ADC GEWINNER NACH KATEGORIEN ADC WINNERS ACCORDING TO CATEGORIES	526	FIRMEN CLIENTS
38	ADC JURY-CHAIRMAN ADC JURY CHAIRMAN Chuck Porter	528	MACHER MAKERS
		536	IMPRESSUM IMPRINT
40	ADC WETTBEWERB 2011 KATEGORIESPONSOREN ADC COMPETITION 2011 CATEGORY SPONSORS	536	DANK ACKNOWLEDGMENTS
44	ARBEITEN WORKS		
468	ADC KUNDE DES JAHRES ADC CUSTOMER OF THE YEAR YVONNE ZIMMERMANN MARC WEEGEN Britta Steffen		
474	ADC EHRENMITGLIED DES JAHRES ADC HONORARY MEMBER OF THE YEAR RAINER BRANDT Lutz Wilde		
480	ADC LEBENSWERK DES JAHRES ADC LIFETIME ACHIEVEMENT REINHARD SIEMES Reinhard Siemes		
484	NACHRUF ZUM TOD VON WALTER LÜRZER OBITUARY ON THE PASSING OF WALTER LÜRZER Hans-Peter Albrecht		
488	NACHRUF ZUM TOD VON REINHARD SIEMES OBITUARY ON THE PASSING OF REINHARD SIEMES Sebastian Turner		
490	NACHRUF ZUM TOD VON KURT WEIDEMANN OBITUARY ON THE PASSING OF KURT WEIDEMANN Jochen Rädeker		
492	ADC DEUTSCHLAND MITGLIEDER ADC GERMANY MEMBERS		
508	ADC DEUTSCHLAND EHRENMITGLIEDER ADC GERMANY HONORARY MEMBERS		
510	ADC DEUTSCHLAND VORSTAND ADC GERMANY BOARD 11.2010–10.2011		
512	ADC DEUTSCHLAND FÖRDERMITGLIEDER ADC GERMANY SUPPORTING MEMBERS		
516	JURYS JURIES		

45 PUNKTE – S. 44
45 POINTS – P. 44

46 WWF
"Save as WWF"

43 PUNKTE – S. 52
43 POINTS – P. 52

54 MERCEDES-BENZ TRANSPORTER
»Meister vs. Meister«

38 PUNKTE — S. 62
38 POINTS — P. 62

33 PUNKTE — S. 70
33 POINTS — P. 70

64   ENTEGA ERNEUERBARE ENERGIE
»Kampagne Denkanstöße«

72   HORNBACH BAUMARKT KAMPAGNE
»Wieviel Wahnsinn steckt in Dir?«

25 PUNKTE – S. 76
25 POINTS – P. 76

78	MULTIPACK "Hidden Heroes"

24 PUNKTE – S. 82
24 POINTS – P. 82

84	BIONADE »Fragen im Raum«
86	KONZERTHAUS DORTMUND SAISONFILM 2010|2011 »Konzertmilch«
88	MODERN MUSIC SCHOOL KAMPAGNE »Talent«

22 PUNKTE – S. 92
22 POINTS – P. 92

20 PUNKTE – S. 98
20 POINTS – P. 98

94   BMW M3 COUPÉ
        »Die BMW Lightwall
        ›Reflexion‹«

96   INITIATIVE VERMISSTE KINDER
        »Deutschland findet euch«

100   HORNBACH BAUMARKT
         »Das grenzenlose Haus«

19 PUNKTE — S. 104
19 POINTS — P. 104

106	LEMONAID JAHRESBERICHT 2010 »Der fairste Jahresbericht der Welt«
108	EXPO 2010, SHANGHAI »Der Deutsche Pavillon«
110	50 JAHRE EDDING »Jubiläumskampagne«

16 PUNKTE — S. 114
16 POINTS — P. 114

116	AMNESTY INTERNATIONAL "Death Penalty"
118	TRANSMEDIALE.11 "Response:ability"
120	SKY BUNDESLIGA »Die Fußballoper«

14 PUNKTE — S. 122
14 POINTS — P. 122

13 PUNKTE — S. 126
13 POINTS — P. 126

124   KONZERTHAUS DORTMUND – EXKLUSIVKÜNSTLER
»Countdown-Orchester«

128   GERMANWINGS
"Planemob"

12 PUNKTE – S. 130
12 POINTS – P. 130

11 PUNKTE – S. 138
11 POINTS – P. 138

132 GRIMM GALLUN HOLTAPPELS
»www.2gh.de«

134 BASISBIBEL
»Kreuzcover«
»Kreuz-Farbschnitt«

136 AUDI A7
»Sportback Live-Plakat«

140 IKEA
»Möbelkunst«

10 PUNKTE — S. 142
10 POINTS — P. 142

144	ARCTIC PAPER "Munken Cube"
146	ZEITMAGAZIN «Mon Dieu! Depardieu!»
148	FERRARI «Coppa di Sicilia»
150	DEUTSCHES SCHAUSPIELHAUS IN HAMBURG »Seit 110 Jahren in der Kritik.«
152	IKEA »Bannerbau«
154	LEGO "Builders of Tomorrow"
156	NIKE FOOTBALL »Der Chip«
158	SERVICEPLAN HAMBURG »Blut, Schweiß und Tränen«

9 PUNKTE — S. 160
9 POINTS — P. 160

162	CARITAS "One Minute of Silence"
163	DAS DEUTSCHE HANDWERK »Die Wirtschaftsmacht. Von nebenan.«
164	HORNBACH BAUMARKT »Ungekürzt«
165	SAP »BIT.CODE – Kunstprojekt und Software-Demo«
166	STAATSTHEATER STUTTGART SCHAUSPIEL »Metropolis Serie« "Corporate Design"

8 PUNKTE — S. 168
8 POINTS — P. 168

170	NIDO MAGAZIN »Jahrgang 2010« »Niedrigenergiespiele« »Ausgabe 6/2010« »Streng sein«

7 PUNKTE — S. 172
7 POINTS — P. 172

174	MERCEDES-BENZ E-KLASSE BAS PLUS "Sorry"
175	DAWANDA "Creating Love – A Communityfilm"
176	FACEBOOK PLACES HIJACK »Erster!«
177	MOTO WAGANARI "Directing Shadows"
178	MERCEDES-BENZ »Sprinter Bewerbung«
179	WIENERS+WIENERS »Selbstübersetzende Mail«
180	GÖRTZ 17 "Shoelace Box"
181	GEGEN STUTTGART 21 »K 21«
182	DIESEL "Be Stupid Facepark"

6 PUNKTE — S. 184
6 POINTS — P. 184

186	STIHL KETTENSÄGE MS 880 »Wikinger«	205	WMF SPARSCHÄLER »Kartoffel, Möhre, Apfel«
187	BUNTSTIFTE VON FABER CASTELL "True Colours"	206	BRAUN SATIN HAIR 5 MULTISTYLER "Hairmoticons"
188	ROLLINGSTONE 'INITIATIVE MONEY FOR MUSIC' »Kopiert ruhig weiter«	207	NATURIA HUNDEFUTTER »Hundefunkspot«
189	SPARKASSE »Synchronsprecher«	208	MISEREOR HILFSWERK "Drive the Mobilombo – Deliver Hope to Africa"
190	MOORMANN KATALOG »Katalog Vol. 3«	209	ROCKET & WINK "Whatever 1st" "At 1st"
191	VERLAG HERMANN SCHMIDT MAINZ »Nea Machina – Die Kreativmaschine«		
192	T.D.G. "Stop The Water While Using Me!"		
193	ZEITMAGAZIN »Typisch jüdisch?«		
194	ZEITMAGAZIN »Wieder alles falsch gemacht«		
195	DIE ZEIT »Grafikseite – Ressort Wissen«		
196	AUDI A1 "Mediawall"		
197	CERN "Universe of Particles"		
198	INSTITUT FÜR STADTGESCHICHTE FRANKFURT »Was die Welt bewegt – Arthur Schopenhauer in Frankfurt«		
199	MAINSHOW SAUDI ARABISCHER PAVILLON, EXPO 2010 "The Treasure"		
200	MAGIC BOX "State Grid Pavilion"		
201	HYPOSWISS PRIVATE BANK KAMPAGNE "Expect the Expected"		
202	PASSIONSSPIELE OBERAMMERGAU SERIE »Passion«		
203	ENTEGA ERNEUERBARE ENERGIE SERIE »Energiemärchen-Kalender«		
204	DEUTSCHER TIERSCHUTZBUND ORIGINAL-KOMPOSITION "A Peace of Mind"		

5 PUNKTE — S. 210
5 POINTS — P. 210

4 PUNKTE — S. 214
4 POINTS — P. 214

212	DAIMLER PRE-SAFE "Transparent Walls"		216	MCFIT »Gib Dich niemals auf.«
213	FEY & CO »lullaland.net«		217	VIVA "ReBrand 2011 'Reel'"
			218	TUI »Donnerwetter Jetter«
			219	EDDING "Digital Highlighter"
			220	VEGETARIERBUND DEUTSCHLAND »Das Kannibalen Restaurant«
			221	ERNTEDANK KREATIVSPEZIALISTEN »Streetview Geburt«
			222	BISCHÖFLICHES HILFSWERK MISEREOR »Buchstabenmailing«
			223	JOBS BEI JUNG VON MATT »Trojanisches Recruiting«
			224	BILD »Das Jahr in Bildern«
			225	RELAUNCH »Cafe Luitpold«
			226	KRAFT FOODS »Kaffee Kategorie«
			227	DU – DAS KULTURMAGAZIN 2010 »Reportage Dezember 2010 Tomi Ungerer«
			228	MOBILITY "Reflective Kinematronic"
			229	MERCEDES-BENZ »Interaktives Präsentationstool – CLS Show Paris 2010«
			230	WELT KOMPAKT »Statusmeldungen«
			231	GREENPEACE SCHWEIZ »Der Zonen Plan«

3 PUNKTE — S. 232
3 POINTS — P. 232

234	FRANKFURTER ALLGEMEINE ZEITUNG »Dahinter steckt immer ein kluger Kopf – Haneke«	253	WAXHOUSE »Waxingkalender«
235	SCHOLZ & FRIENDS »WERU Abschluss-Anzeige«	254	PETER BEHRENS SCHULE DUESSELDORF »Rundgang«
236	BEATE UHSE TV »Kindersicherung«	255	FESTINA PROFUNDO »Die wasserverpackte Taucheruhr«
237	BILD »Bekennerkampagne«	256	THE DELI GARAGE »Backsteine«
238	WELT AM SONNTAG »Sonntagskampagne«	257	FELD HOMMES MAGAZIN »Finale«
239	GOOGLE »Deutsch-Französische Liebe«	258	GOLDEN SECTION GRAPHICS "In Graphics"
240	GOOGLE KAMPAGNE »Das Leben ist eine Suche«	259	MAGAZIN DER BAYERISCHEN STAATSFORSTEN »Bayernwald«
241	SPARKASSE KAMPAGNE »08/15«	260	ZEITMAGAZIN »Es lebe die Einfachheit!«
242	ZDF DAS KLEINE FERNSEHSPIEL »Vorspann ‹Shahada›«	261	ZEITMAGAZIN »Wir machen das Beste aus Ihren Texten«
243	WM DOKUMENTATION »Jeder Glaube hat seine Rituale – die Dokumentation«	262	VICE MAGAZINE »Jahrgang 2010«
244	CBM SPENDENAUFRUF »Spenden«	263	NEON MAGAZIN »Jetzt ist aber Schluss!«
245	1&1 ALL-NET-FLAT KAMPAGNE »Spontan verbunden«	264	STERN MAGAZIN »Das Beben…«
246	ANTIK- & TRÖDELMARKT GARE DU NEUSS KAMPAGNE »An diesem Bahnhof hält die Zeit.«	265	SÜDDEUTSCHE ZEITUNG MAGAZIN »Nur ankommen ist schöner«
247	VERGISS AIDS NICHT "Cock out"	266	SÜDDEUTSCHE ZEITUNG MAGAZIN »Schloss mit lustig«
248	BVB TRIKOT »Kloppo dreht ab«	267	SÜDDEUTSCHE ZEITUNG MAGAZIN »Sieben auf einem Strich«
249	MCCAFÉ »Anna und die Liebe«	268	ZEITMAGAZIN »Leanne Shapton/Was von der Liebe übrig bleibt«
250	AUSSTELLUNGSPUBLIKATION »Zur Nachahmung empfohlen! Expeditionen in Ästhetik und Nachhaltigkeit«	269	WELTGRUPPE »Gesamtauftritt«
251	KOCHBUCH, JOACHIM WISSLER GROUP "JW 4"	270	EXPO PAVILLON 2010 "Urban Planet"
252	TYPOTRON-HEFT 28 »Lokremise«	271	E. BREUNINGER »Weiße Weihnachten 2010«
		272	RUHR.2010 GMBH »Still-Leben Ruhrschnellweg«

2 PUNKTE — S. 284
2 POINTS — P. 284

273	SCHAUSPIEL FRANKFURT »Licht am Ende des Tunnels – Beitrag zur Luminale 2010«		286	VW POLO »Die Recycling-Anzeige«
274	SWISSCOM URBAN HACKING »Wir für die Schweiz«		287	VW POLO BLUEMOTION »Meer«
275	SMART "urban stage"		288	DER SPIEGEL »Perspektiven«
276	DKV REISEKRANKEN-VERSICHERUNG »Reiseartikel aus Absurdistan«		289	MAD MAGAZIN »Glühbirne«
277	LOEWE KAMPAGNE "Individual 3 D"		290	MCDONALD'S KAMPAGNE »Morgenkaffee«
278	AERNOUT OVERBEEKE SERIE "Ndoto, Lengai – Mountain Of God"		291	ABSOLUT VODKA "Made"
279	EIGENWERBUNG SERIE "Lightsounds"		292	MERCEDES-BENZ ALLRAD »Sonntagsfahrer«
280	EIGENWERBUNG SERIE »Torso«		293	VW POLO GTI "Fast Lane – Driven By Fun"
281	MERCEDES-BENZ SERIE »Gesichter der Marke«		294	DIE SAHNESCHNITTE »Ein paar Seiten Radiowerbung für Radiowerbung«
282	MOTOCROSS ENDURO MAGAZIN SERIE "Enduro Untamed"		295	AXE DARK TEMPTATION, UNILEVER DEUTSCHLAND »Adventskalender, 24 mal so unwiderstehlich wie Schokolade«
			296	BIC "Prank"
			297	GÖRTZ SNEAKER-SCHNÜRSENKEL »Vogelhausbuch«
			298	GSK ABTEI »Das Rote-Faden-Buch«
			299	STIHL MOTORSÄGE MS 261 »Die Vorfreude wächst.«
			300	STERN MAGAZIN »Abschied von Vibe«

1 PUNKT — S. 302
1 POINT — P. 302

304	DEUTSCHE BAHN FERNVERKEHR »Deutschland wird kleiner«	324	TOSHIBA "Paper 3D"
305	IGLO DEL MAR CALAMARES »Wo ist eigentlich Paul«	325	VOLKSWAGEN LANE ASSIST »Linien«
306	SIXT »Bruni«	326	KURZFILMAGENTUR HAMBURG »Kurz vor Film – Mehr Vorfilme ins Kino!«
307	ASPIRIN EFFECT »Flughafenkürzel«	327	MEDIA MARKT KAMPAGNE »Billiger geht so!«
308	BERLINER MORGENPOST »Das ist Berlin«	328	AUDI "The Next Big Thing"
309	FRITZ-KOLA »Koffein hochkonzentriert«	329	DIGITAL BOMB "Tron Rap"
310	MERCEDES-BENZ »Gefahren ohne Schrecken«	330	MARSHMALLOW FLUFF "Sticky"
311	MERCEDES-BENZ TRANSPORTER »Die 4x4 Verkehrszeichen«	331	MERCEDES-BENZ FEUERWEHR-FAHRZEUGE »Sirene«
312	VOLKSWAGEN CLASSIC PARTS »Nur ein Volkswagen bleibt ein Volkswagen«	332	SKY HD »Ameisen«
313	VORWERK STAUBSAUGER KOBOLD 140 »Teller«	333	PARSHIP »Amor«
314	LAND BADEN-WÜRTTEMBERG »Die erste Anzeige mit Benzingeruch«	334	DUMMY MAGAZIN «Khowf»
315	DEUTSCHE POST »Alles beginnt mit einem Brief«	335	SPORTJUGEND HESSEN »Helfen ist in Mode«
316	MERCEDES-BENZ »Wackelkontakt«	336	STEPHAN SCHNEIDER 'COLLECTION SS2011' »www.stephanschneider.be«
317	SNICKERS »Du bist nicht du, wenn du hungrig bist/'Peacelord'«	337	IKEA »Billygramm«
318	SMART FORTWO »360°«	338	SONY PLAYSTATION GT5 »Tragt es auf der Strecke aus«
319	MERCEDES-BENZ "The Intelligent Light Billboard"	339	AUDI "Augmented Reality Kalender"
320	SMART FORTWO ELECTRIC DRIVE »Das unsichtbarste Plakat der Welt«	340	LEAGAS DELANEY »Die Copytest App«
321	GOOGLE »Kindertraum«	341	MERCEDES-BENZ SLS AMG »Stuttgarter Sportwagen«
322	JOBSINTOWN.DE »Fischer«	342	SCHÜLER COMMUNITY-CENTER »Schüler Surprise Images«
323	MERCEDES-BENZ »Weihnachtsgruß«	343	IHK FRANKFURT – LICHTSKULPTUR »Puls der Stadt«

344	IKEA KATALOGEINFÜHRUNG 2010/2011 »Der IKEA Katalog kommt nicht allein.«	364	HEIDELBERGER DRUCKMASCHINEN »Aus Respekt vor Dir, Papier.«
345	MCDONALD'S »Nürnburger«	365	LEGO "Signs"
346	PRITT "Paper Gang"	366	OBI MITARBEITERBUCH »40 Jahre OBI«
347	ALL4FAMILY »Memory für Eltern«	367	BIRKHÄUSER "TypoLyrics – The Sound of Fonts"
348	MENSCHENRECHTE (REPORTER OHNE GRENZEN) »Sonderstempel«	368	CHRISTOPHER THOMAS »Passion«
349	DEMNER, MERLICEK & BERGMANN "DMB vs. DDB"	369	COSMIC COLLECTION »Soirée graphique – Ausgabe No.1«
350	STÄDEL MUSEUM »Frankfurt baut das neue Städel«	370	DESIGNFORUM »Wien 2006–2010«
351	FC ST. PAULI »Schädelgenerator«	371	FÖRDERRAUMGESCHICHTEN »Wollen wir einen Raum bieten, in dem man auch scheitern darf?«
352	KOLLE REBBE "The Damn-Hot-Lovely-Christmas-Store"	372	GUM »Magazin für konzeptionelles Gestalten. Ausgabe 11.«
353	SCHOLZ & FRIENDS RECRUITING »Pizza Digitale«	373	JULI GUDEHUS »Das Lesikon der visuellen Kommunikation«
354	SPORTSCHECK – WIR MACHEN SPORT "Sporty Vouchers"	374	STRICHPUNKT DESIGN "It's A Boy – It's A Girl"
355	TAGES ANZEIGER »Dranbleiben 2.0«	375	SUHRKAMP VERLAG »Das Weisse Buch von Rafael Horzon«
356	EXTRA PROFESSIONAL POLAR-FRESH »Minz Tickets«	376	CORPORATE DESIGN »Altes Kloster«
357	IWC SCHAFFHAUSEN »Das erste Bewerbungsbogenpuzzle«	377	CORPORATE DESIGN »Beisser«
358	FRIEDRICHS & FRIENDS "Proofreading Facebook"	378	CORPORATE DESIGN "Community Film"
359	PATTEX KLEBER CLASSIC »Kran«	379	CORPORATE DESIGN »Mutabor«
360	SAW 3D »Kino-Promotion«	380	CORPORATE DESIGN »Restaurant Hoch III Hamburg«
361	TEXTERSCHMIEDE »Guerilla-Funk«	381	AD FONTES – ZU DEN QUELLEN »Jahreskalender 2011«
362	MOORMANN BROSCHÜRE 2010 »In einfachen Verhältnissen«	382	F.A.Z., F.A.S »Der Erste Seite-Kalender«
363	BILEKJAEGER »Hier spricht der Text.«	383	FIFTYFIFTY EDITION »Galerie Plakate«

384	SCHAUSPIELHAUS BOCHUM »Einführungskampagne«	403	DIE ZEIT »Wer wird Präsident?«
385	PANASONIC EVOIA AA-ALKALI-BATTERIE »Die langlebigste Batterie«	404	IN GRAPHICS "Transfer Calligraphy"
386	ROGGENKAMP ORGANICS FRISCHE SUPPEN »Suppentöpfe, ›Hausmacher Art‹«	405	NEON MAGAZIN FEBRUAR 2010 »Lasst sie heulen!«
387	WILD BAG® BOX "Out_Of_Ark"	406	STERN MAGAZIN »Ausbruch ins Leben«
388	THE DELI GARAGE »Lutschwerkzeug«	407	STERN MAGAZIN »Der endlose Krieg«
389	DAS NEUE TESTAMENT ALS MAGAZIN »Ausgabe 1/2010«	408	SÜDDEUTSCHE ZEITUNG MAGAZIN »80 Jahre Helmut Kohl«
390	INTERKANTONALER RÜCKVERSICHERUNGS-VERBAND »100 Jahre IRV«	409	SÜDDEUTSCHE ZEITUNG MAGAZIN »Alle zusammen und jeder für sich«
391	KID'S WEAR MAGAZINE »Vol. 31 Herbst/Winter 2010/11«	410	SÜDDEUTSCHE ZEITUNG MAGAZIN »Da fällt mir Einstein vom Herzen«
392	MAGAZIN DER BAYERISCHEN STAATSFORSTEN »Waldfest«	411	SÜDDEUTSCHE ZEITUNG MAGAZIN »Kunstschuss«
393	NEON MAGAZIN »XXL-Ausgabe – Was bin ich wirklich wert?«	412	ZEITMAGAZIN »Fuchs, du hast die Uhr gestohlen«
394	SLEEK – MAGAZINE FOR ART AND FASHION »#26 ›Flora|Fauna‹«	413	ZEITMAGAZIN »Ich habe einen Traum/Queen Elizabeth II«
395	SÜDDEUTSCHE ZEITUNG MAGAZIN »Edition 46/Menschen. Ein Bilderzyklus von Hans-Peter Feldmann«	414	ZEITMAGAZIN »Ölbilder«
396	SÜDDEUTSCHE ZEITUNG MAGAZIN »Hoffnung?«	415	ZEITMAGAZIN »Schwarz ist das neue Weiß«
397	SÜDDEUTSCHE ZEITUNG MAGAZIN »Solange sie noch leben«	416	ZEITMAGAZIN »Unser Hamlet«
398	VICE MAGAZINE "v7n1 – The Barking Dog Issue"	417	AUDI MAGAZIN "iPad App"
399	DER FREITAG »Nr. 2, 5, 6, 16, 22, 28, 39, 46, 47, 51/52«	418	AUDI MESSAUFTRITT «Mondial de L'Automobile Paris 2010»
400	BERLINER ILLUSTRIRTE ZEITUNG »Kinohauptstadt Berlin: Das Netzwerk«	419	AUDI MESSESTAND CES "Open for the future"
401	BERLINER ILLUSTRIRTE ZEITUNG »Kleine Menschen, große Welt«	420	DESSO, MESSESTAND "Circulation"
402	BERLINER MORGENPOST »Ein einzigartiges Orchester«	421	HASENKOPF MESSESTAND »Hasenkopf entdeckt das Ei des Kolumbus«
		422	PERGAMONMUSEUM BERLIN SONDERAUSSTELLUNG »Die geretteten Götter aus dem Palast vom Tell Halaf«

423	AUDI A7 SPORTBACK »Weltpremiere«	443	BUND FÜR UMWELT UND NATURSCHUTZ DEUTSCHLAND SERIE »5 vor 12«
424	EMMI SCHWEIZ "Lightshow"	444	KULTURSPIEGEL SERIE "Simon Spilsbury"
425	PANASONIC »Barterlass«	445	RADIO MEPHISTO 97.6 SERIE "Heads"
426	ADC »46. Awards Show 2010«	446	STERN MAGAZIN SERIE »Drunter-Welt«
427	75 JAHRE ARAG »Die Geschichte der Versicherung«	447	VW GOLF SERIE »Kein Weg vorbei«
428	AUGSBURGER ALLGEMEINE KAMPAGNE »Weltnachrichten aus der Region«	448	BFF ORIGINALKOMPOSITION »Treppe«
429	DYNAUDIO »Die Nahhörerlebnis-Plakate.«	449	MERCEDES-BENZ E-KLASSE LANG ORIGINALKOMPOSITION "Shadows"
430	FESTOOL PENDELSTICHSÄGE CARVEX PS 400 »Stuttgart 21«	450	VODAFONE MUSIKAUSWAHL "Where are you?"
431	FTD »Kampagne«	451	SP ZÜRICH »Was Zürich braucht.«
432	RITTER SPORT »Kampagne 2010«		
433	SCHEUFELEN »Höchstleistungen«		
434	DAS BRUSTKREBSPROJEKT »Amazonen«		
435	EIGENWERBUNG SERIE »Kulissenbauer«		
436	EIGENWERBUNG SERIE »Seneca tanzt den Ovid«		
437	EIGENWERBUNG SERIE »SLS«		
438	FELD HOMMES MAGAZIN SERIE »Sex Maschine«		
439	ROBERTO SAVIANO, AUTOR GEGEN DIE CAMORRA. SERIE »Ich habe in allen Winkeln der Erde geschrieben…«		
440	STERN MAGAZIN SERIE »Eine verwehte Welt«		
441	TOYOTA AURIS HYBRID SERIE »Perspektivwechsel«		
442	AUDI QUATTRO SERIE »Mechanik und Elektronik innovativ kombiniert«		

VORWORT
PREFACE

JOCHEN RÄDEKER
VORSTANDSSPRECHER DES ADC
ADC SPOKESMAN OF THE BOARD

Liebe Freundinnen und Freunde der Kreativität,

herzlich willkommen im 47. Jahrbuch des Art Directors Club für Deutschland!

Vor Ihnen liegen 536 Seiten, prallvoll mit dem Besten, was im deutschsprachigen Raum an Werbung, Design, Digitalen Medien, Fotografie, Editorial, Illustration und Kommunikation im Raum im vergangenen Jahr entstanden ist.

Der ADC Wettbewerb, im vergangenen Jahr strukturell grundlegend überarbeitet, beweist mit 6.700 eingereichten Einzelarbeiten erneut seine Stellung als Maßstab für kreative, kommerzielle Kommunikation bei Unternehmen und Agenturen.

Die Jury des ADC – mit 325 Jurorinnen und Juroren die größte Kreativjury der Welt – ist bekannt für ihre harte Auswahl der ausgezeichneten Arbeiten, strikt nach den fünf ADC Kriterien:
— Originalität: Ist die Arbeit originär und originell?
— Klarheit: Kommuniziert die Arbeit ihre Inhalte verständlich?
— Kraft: Bewirkt die Arbeit eine Bewusstseinsveränderung?
— Machart: Ist die Arbeit handwerklich überzeugend?
— Freude: Beglückt, berührt oder bereichert die Arbeit?

Nur 338 Arbeiten haben es ins Buch geschafft. Die Jury hat nach dreitägiger Diskussion beim ADC Festival in Frankfurt 1 Grand Prix, 15 goldene, 73 silberne und 131 bronzene Nägel sowie 237 Auszeichnungen verliehen. Damit haben weniger als 7 Prozent aller eingereichten Arbeiten gepunktet – und doch wurde mehr Edelmetall als im vergangenen Jahr vergeben. Was aber nicht an plötzlicher Milde der Juroren, sondern an der nach der Krise fulminant wiedererwachten hohen Qualität deutschsprachiger Kreation liegt. Die Arbeiten sind mutiger, stärker, nachhaltiger, digitaler geworden – und vielfältiger. Oder anders gesagt: Gute Ideen beweisen ihre Funktionsfähigkeit längst nicht mehr nur auf einem Kommunikationskanal. Daher stehen Projekte mit einem integrierten Ansatz auch ganz oben im Ranking – und der Grand Prix ging konsequenterweise an eine Arbeit, die in keine der klassischen Mediengattungen passt, sondern einfach eine neue erfindet.

»Ideen.Durchsetzen.« lautete das Motto des ADC Festivals 2011. In diesem Buch finden Sie eine Fülle großartiger Ideen, die sich durchgesetzt haben: In der Kreation. Beim Kunden. Im Wettbewerb. Ideen, die Motor für die gesamte Wirtschaft sind. Ideen, die nicht nur Freude, sondern auch Ertrag bringen.

Viel Vergnügen, Inspiration und Erfolg für Ihre und mit Ihrer nächsten guten Idee wünscht

Jochen Rädeker
Vorstandssprecher des ADC

Dear Friends of Creativity,

Welcome to the Art Directors Club for Germany's 47th yearbook!

You have in your hands a total of 536 pages, filled to the brim with the best in advertising, design, digital media, photography, editorial, illustration, and communication created last year in German-speaking areas.

Having received over 6,700 individual pieces of work, the ADC Competition, which was completely restructured last year, once again proves its position as the benchmark for creative, commercial communications by companies and agencies.

The ADC jury – comprised of over 325 jurors, making it the largest creative jury in the world – is well-known for its tough selection process, which it carries out strictly according to ADC's five criteria:

— Originality: Is the work original and creative?
— Clarity: Does the work convey its message clearly?
— Power: Does the work cause a change in thinking?
— Workmanship: Is the work well-made?
— Joy: Does the work make you happy, move you, or enrich your life?

Only 338 works made it into the book. After three days of discussion at the ADC Festival in Frankfurt, the jury handed out 1 Grand Prix, 15 gold, 73 silver, and 131 bronze nails, as well as 237 nominations. That means less than 7 percent of all entries scored points – and yet more precious metals were awarded this year than last year. This isn't a reflection of the jury's sudden kindness, but rather of the high quality of German-speaking creations, which roared back to life in spectacular fashion after the global financial crisis. The works became more courageous, more powerful, more effective, more digital – and more diverse. Or, to put it another way: Good ideas have long ceased to demonstrate the extent of their capability in only one medium. That's why projects with an integrated approach also dominate the top of the list – and the Grand Prix was systematically awarded to a work that doesn't fit in any of the classic media categories, but instead simply creates a new one.

The 2011 ADC Festival's slogan is »Ideen.Durchsetzen.« Roughly translated, this means to push through ideas until they catch on and achieve success. And in this book, you'll find a wide range of ideas that did exactly that. During the creative process. With clients. In competition. Ideas that are the driving force behind the entire economy. Ideas that generate feelings of joy and substantial revenues.

I hope you enjoy this book, and that it serves as inspiration for your next successful idea.

Jochen Rädeker
ADC Spokesman of the Board

ADC GEWINNER NACH KATEGORIEN
ADC WINNERS ACCORDING TO CATEGORIES

- GOLD (10 POINTS)
- SILVER (6 POINTS)
- BRONZE (3 POINTS)
- NOMINATION (1 POINT)

CATEGORY		TITLE	PAGE	AWARD
1	Print			
1.1	Single Motif	Sixt «Bruni»	306	●
1.1	Single Motif	Frankfurter Allgemeine Zeitung »Dahinter steckt immer ein kluger Kopf – Haneke«	234	●
1.1	Single Motif	Deutsche Bahn Fernverkehr »Deutschland wird kleiner«	304	●
1.1	Single Motif	VW Polo »Die Recycling-Anzeige«	286	●
1.1	Single Motif	VW Polo BlueMotion »Meer«	287	●
1.1	Single Motif	WMF Sparschäler »Möhre«	205	●
1.1	Single Motif	Scholz & Friends »WERU Abschluss-Anzeige«	235	●
1.1	Single Motif	STIHL Kettensäge MS 880 »Wikinger«	186	●
1.1	Single Motif	Iglo del mar Calamares »Wo ist eigentlich Paul«	305	●
1.2	Campaign	BILD »Bekennerkampagne«	237	●
1.2	Campaign	Lego "Builders of Tomorrow"	154	●
1.2	Campaign	Berliner Morgenpost »Das ist Berlin«	308	●
1.2	Campaign	Mercedes-Benz Transporter »Die 4x4 Verkehrszeichen«	311	●
1.2	Campaign	Das deutsche Handwerk »Die Wirtschaftsmacht. Von nebenan.«	163	●
1.2	Campaign	Aspirin Effect »Flughafenkürzel«	307	●
1.2	Campaign	BIONADE »Fragen im Raum«	84	●
1.2	Campaign	Mercedes-Benz »Gefahren ohne Schrecken«	310	●
1.2	Campaign	WMF Sparschäler »Kartoffel, Möhre, Apfel«	205	●
1.2	Campaign	Beate Uhse TV »Kindersicherung«	236	●
1.2	Campaign	fritz-kola »Koffein hochkonzentriert«	309	●
1.2	Campaign	RollingStone ›Initiative Money for Music‹ »Kopiert ruhig weiter«	188	●
1.2	Campaign	Volkswagen Classic Parts »Nur ein Volkswagen bleibt ein Volkswagen«	312	●
1.2	Campaign	Der Spiegel »Perspektiven«	288	●
1.2	Campaign	Welt am Sonntag »Sonntagskampagne«	238	●
1.2	Campaign	Vorwerk Staubsauger Kobold 140 »Teller«	313	●
1.2	Campaign	Buntstifte von Faber Castell "True Colours"	187	●
1.2	Campaign	Hornbach Baumarkt »Ungekürzt«	164	●
1.2	Campaign	Hornbach Baumarkt »Wahnsinn«	72	●
1.3	Innovative Use of Print	Land Baden-Württemberg »Die erste Anzeige mit Benzingeruch«	314	●
2	Out-of-Home			
2.1	Classic Single Motif	Deutsche Post »Alles beginnt mit einem Brief«	315	●
2.1	Classic Single Motif	BIONADE »Colakinder«	84	●
2.1	Classic Single Motif	BMW M3 Coupé »Die BMW Lightwall ›Reflexion‹«	94	●
2.1	Classic Single Motif	VW Polo »Die Recycling-Anzeige«	286	●
2.1	Classic Single Motif	Snickers »Du bist nicht du, wenn du hungrig bist/ 'Peacelord'«	317	●
2.1	Classic Single Motif	MAD Magazin »Glühbirne«	289	●
2.1	Classic Single Motif	VW Polo BlueMotion »Meer«	287	●
2.1	Classic Single Motif	AUDI A7 »Sportback Live-Plakat«	136	●
2.1	Classic Single Motif	Mercedes-Benz »Wackelkontakt«	316	●
2.2	Classic Campaign	smart fortwo »360°«	318	●
2.2	Classic Campaign	Lego "Builders of Tomorrow"	154	●
2.2	Classic Campaign	BIONADE »Fragen im Raum«	84	●
2.2	Classic Campaign	Mercedes-Benz Transporter Kampagne »Meister vs. Meister«	54	●
2.2	Classic Campaign	McDonald's Kampagne »Morgenkaffee«	290	●
2.2	Classic Campaign	Welt Kompakt »Statusmeldungen«	230	●
2.2	Classic Campaign	Hornbach Baumarkt Kampagne »Wahnsinn«	72	●
2.3	Non-Classic	Serviceplan Hamburg »Blut, Schweiß und Tränen«	158	●
2.3	Non-Classic	ABSOLUT Vodka "Clash Of Words"	291	●
2.3	Non-Classic	smart fortwo electric drive »Das unsichtbarste Plakat der Welt«	320	●
2.3	Non-Classic	ENTEGA Erneuerbare Energie »Der Stromfresser«	64	●
2.3	Non-Classic	BMW M3 Coupé »Die BMW Lightwall ›Reflexion‹«	94	●
2.3	Non-Classic	MAD Magazin »Glühbirne«	289	●
2.3	Non-Classic	AUDI A7 »Sportback Live-Plakat«	136	●
2.3	Non-Classic	Mercedes-Benz »The Intelligent Light Billboard«	319	●
2.3	Non-Classic	Daimler Pre-Safe "Transparent Walls"	212	●
3	Film			
3.1	TV/Cinema Commercial	Lego "Builders of Tomorrow"	154	●
3.1	TV/Cinema Commercial	Hornbach Baumarkt »Das grenzenlose Haus«	100	●
3.1	TV/Cinema Commercial	Amnesty International "Death Penalty"	116	●
3.1	TV/Cinema Commercial	Google »Deutsch-Französische Liebe«	239	●
3.1	TV/Cinema Commercial	jobsintown.de »Fischer«	322	●

CATEGORY		TITLE	PAGE	AWARD
3.1	TV/Cinema Commercial	Braun Satin Hair 5 Multistyler "Hairmoticons"	206	●
3.1	TV/Cinema Commercial	Google »Kindertraum«	321	●
3.1	TV/Cinema Commercial	Deutsches Schauspielhaus in Hamburg »Kritikhagel«	150	●
3.1	TV/Cinema Commercial	Volkswagen Lane Assist »Linien«	325	●
3.1	TV/Cinema Commercial	IKEA »Möbelkunst«	140	●
3.1	TV/Cinema Commercial	Toshiba "Paper 3D"	324	●
3.1	TV/Cinema Commercial	Germanwings "Planemob"	128	●
3.1	TV/Cinema Commercial	Mercedes-Benz Allrad »Sonntagsfahrer«	292	●
3.1	TV/Cinema Commercial	Mercedes-Benz E-Klasse BAS Plus "Sorry"	174	●
3.1	TV/Cinema Commercial	Mercedes-Benz »Weihnachtsgruß«	323	●
3.1	TV/Cinema Commercial	Hornbach Baumarkt »Wieviel Wahnsinn steckt in Dir ('Faces')?«	72	●
3.2	TV/Cinema Campaign	Sparkasse Kampagne »08/15«	241	●
3.2	TV/Cinema Campaign	Media Markt Kampagne »Billiger geht so!«	327	●
3.2	TV/Cinema Campaign	Google Kampagne »Das Leben ist eine Suche«	240	●
3.2	TV/Cinema Campaign	KurzFilmAgentur Hamburg »Kurz vor Film – Mehr Vorfilme ins Kino!«	326	●
3.2	TV/Cinema Campaign	Hornbach Baumarkt Kampagne »Wieviel Wahnsinn steckt in Dir?«	72	●
3.3	Sales Promotion Films	Konzerthaus Dortmund Saisonfilm 2010|2011 »Konzertmilch«	86	●
3.3	Sales Promotion Films	Mercedes-Benz Transporter »Meister vs. Meister«	54	●
3.3	Sales Promotion Films	IKEA »Möbelkunst«	140	●
3.3	Sales Promotion Films	Germanwings "Planemob"	128	●
3.4	Image Films	Hornbach Baumarkt »Das grenzenlose Haus«	100	●
3.5	Internet Films	Hornbach Baumarkt »Das grenzenlose Haus«	100	●
3.5	Internet Films	VW Polo GTI "Fast Lane – Driven By Fun"	293	●
3.5	Internet Films	McFit »Gib Dich niemals auf.«	216	●
3.5	Internet Films	Mercedes-Benz Transporter »Meister vs. Meister«	54	●
3.5	Internet Films	Mercedes-Benz Feuerwehr-Fahrzeuge »Sirene«	331	●
3.5	Internet Films	Marshmallow Fluff "Sticky"	330	●
3.5	Internet Films	Sparkasse »Synchronsprecher«	189	●
3.5	Internet Films	AUDI "The Next Big Thing"	328	●
3.5	Internet Films	Digital Bomb "Tron Rap"	329	●
3.6	TV On-Air Promotion	Sky HD »Ameisen«	332	●
3.6	TV On-Air Promotion	VIVA "ReBrand 2011 – Szeskov"	217	●
3.7	On-Air Design	VIVA "ReBrand 2011 'Reel'"	217	●
3.7	On-Air Design	ZDF ›Das kleine Fernsehspiel‹ »Vorspann ‹Shahada›«	242	●
3.8	Shorts/Special Formats for Moving Pictures	Ferrari «Coppa di Sicilia»	148	●
3.8	Shorts/Special Formats for Moving Pictures	DaWanda "Creating Love – A Communityfilm"	175	●
3.8	Shorts/Special Formats for Moving Pictures	Hornbach Baumarkt »Das grenzenlose Haus«	100	●
3.8	Shorts/Special Formats for Moving Pictures	WM Dokumentation »Jeder Glaube hat seine Rituale – die Dokumentation«	243	●
3.8	Shorts/Special Formats for Moving Pictures	Mercedes-Benz Transporter »Meister vs. Meister«	54	●
3.9	Innovative Use of Film	Daimler Pre-Safe "Transparent Walls"	212	●
4	Film Craft			
4.1	Film Direction	Hornbach Baumarkt »Wieviel Wahnsinn steckt in Dir ('Faces')?«	72	●
4.2	Camera	Hornbach Baumarkt »Wieviel Wahnsinn steckt in Dir ('Faces')?«	72	●
4.3	Cutting	Hornbach Baumarkt »Wieviel Wahnsinn steckt in Dir ('Faces')?«	72	●
4.4	Casting	PARSHIP »Amor«	333	●
4.4	Casting	McFit »Gib Dich niemals auf.«	216	●
4.4	Casting	Mercedes-Benz E-Klasse BAS Plus "Sorry"	174	●
4.6	Motion Graphics and 3D	Amnesty International "Death to Death Penalty"	116	●
5	Audio			
5.1	Radio Commercial	Naturia Hundefutter »Hundefunkspot«	207	●
5.1	Radio Commercial	DUMMY Magazin «Khowf»	334	●
5.1	Radio Commercial	CBM Spendenaufruf »Spenden«	244	●
5.1	Radio Commercial	Modern Music School »Tannenbaum«	88	●
5.1	Radio Commercial	Modern Music School »Trennung«	88	●
5.1	Radio Commercial	Modern Music School »Wandern«	88	●
5.2	Radio Campaign	Antik- & Trödelmarkt Gare du Neuss Kampagne »An diesem Bahnhof hält die Zeit.«	246	●
5.2	Radio Campaign	1&1 All-Net-Flat Kampagne »Spontan verbunden«	245	●

CATEGORY		TITLE	PAGE	AWARD
5.2	Radio Campaign	Modern Music School Kampagne »Talent«	88	●
5.7	Innovative Use of Audio	Sky Bundesliga »Die Fußballoper«	120	●
5.7	Innovative Use of Audio	Die Sahneschnitte »Ein paar Seiten Radiowerbung für Radiowerbung«	294	●
5.7	Innovative Use of Audio	Naturia Hundefutter »Hundefunkspot«	207	●
5.7	Innovative Use of Audio	Konzerthaus Dortmund Saisonfilm 2010|2011 »Konzertmilch«	86	●
6	Audio Craft			
6.1	Radio Direction	Modern Music School »Talent«	88	●
7	Digital Media			
7.1	Websites	Moto Waganari "Directing Shadows"	177	●
7.1	Websites	Sportjugend Hessen »Helfen ist in Mode«	335	●
7.1	Websites	Stephan Schneider 'Collection SS2011' »www.stephanschneider.be«	336	●
7.2	Microsites	AXE Dark Temptation, Unilever Deutschland »Adventskalender, 24 mal so unwiderstehlich wie Schokolade«	295	●
7.2	Microsites	MISEREOR Hilfsorganisation "Drive the Mobilombo – Deliver Hope to Africa"	208	●
7.2	Microsites	Multipack "Hidden Heroes"	78	○
7.2	Microsites	Fey & Co »lullaland.net«	213	●
7.2	Microsites	edding Webspecial "Wall of Fame"	110	●
7.3	Social Media	IKEA »Billygramm«	337	●
7.3	Social Media	Nike Football »Der Chip«	156	●
7.3	Social Media	Deutschland-findet-euch »Die Suche auf Facebook«	96	◐
7.3	Social Media	edding "Digital Highlighter"	219	●
7.3	Social Media	Sony PlayStation GT5 »Tragt es auf der Strecke aus«	338	●
7.3	Social Media	edding Webspecial "Wall of Fame"	110	◐
7.4	Mobile	AUDI »Augmented Reality Kalender«	339	●
7.4	Mobile	Leagas Delaney »Die Copytest App«	340	●
7.4	Mobile	TUI »Donnerwetter Jetter«	218	◐
7.4	Mobile	Facebook Places Hijack »Erster!«	176	○
7.5	Online Advertising	IKEA »Bannerbau«	152	●
7.5	Online Advertising	edding "Digital Highlighter"	219	●
7.5	Online Advertising	BIC "Prank"	296	●
7.5	Online Advertising	WWF "Save as WWF"	46	○
7.5	Online Advertising	Schüler Community-Center »Schüler Surprise Images«	342	●
7.5	Online Advertising	Mercedes-Benz SLS AMG »Stuttgarter Sportwagen«	341	●
7.6	E-Mail	WIENERS + WIENERS »Selbstübersetzende Mail«	179	●
7.7	Viral	Vegetarierbund Deutschland »Das Kannibalen Restaurant«	220	◐
7.7	Viral	WWF "Save as WWF"	46	○
7.7	Viral	Erntedank Kreativspezialisten »Streetview Geburt«	221	●
7.8	Digital Media Environment Design	Deutscher Pavillon EXPO 2010 »Die Kugel von balancity«	108	○
7.8	Digital Media Environment Design	IHK Frankfurt – Lichtskulptur »Puls der Stadt«	343	●
7.8	Digital Media Environment Design	Mobility "Reflective Kinematronic"	228	●
7.9	Digital Campaigns	IKEA »Bannerbau«	152	●
7.9	Digital Campaigns	Vergiss Aids nicht "Cock out"	247	◐
7.9	Digital Campaigns	Nike Football »Der Chip«	156	●
7.9	Digital Campaigns	IKEA Katalogeinführung 2010/2011 »Der IKEA Katalog kommt nicht allein.«	344	●
7.9	Digital Campaigns	Deutschland findet euch »Die Online-Suche«	96	●
7.9	Digital Campaigns	VW Polo GTI "Fast Lane – Driven By Fun"	293	●
7.9	Digital Campaigns	Mercedes-Benz Transporter »Meister vs. Meister«	54	○
7.9	Digital Campaigns	McDonald's »Nürnburger«	345	●
7.9	Digital Campaigns	Caritas "One Minute of Silence"	162	◐
7.9	Digital Campaigns	Pritt "Paper Gang"	346	●
8	Digital Media Craft			
8.1	Motion Design	Moto Waganari "Directing Shadows"	177	●
8.1	Motion Design	Multipack "Hidden Heroes"	78	◐
8.1	Motion Design	Grimm Gallun Holtappels »www.2gh.de«	132	○
8.2	Interface/Navigation	Deutscher Pavillon EXPO 2010 »Die Kugel von balancity«	108	●
8.2	Interface/Navigation	Moto Waganari "Directing Shadows"	177	●
8.2	Interface/Navigation	Multipack "Hidden Heroes"	78	○
8.2	Interface/Navigation	Fey & Co »lullaland.net«	213	●

CATEGORY		TITLE	PAGE	AWARD
8.2	Interface/Navigation	Grimm Gallun Holtappels »www.2gh.de«	132	⚪
8.3	Innovative Technologies	Deutscher Pavillon EXPO 2010 »Die Kugel von balancity«	108	🟤
8.3	Innovative Technologies	Facebook Places Hijack »Erster!«	176	🔴
8.4	Sound Design	Multipack "Hidden Heroes"	78	🔴
8.4	Sound Design	Fey & Co »lullaland.net«	213	🟤
9	Dialog Marketing			
9.2	Dialog Mail	Kraft Foods »Kaffee Kategorie«	226	🔴
9.2	Dialog Mail	all4family »Memory für Eltern«	347	🔴
9.2	Dialog Mail	Menschenrechte (Reporter ohne Grenzen) »Sonderstempel«	348	🔴
9.2	Dialog Mail	Mercedes-Benz »Sprinter Bewerbung«	178	⚪
9.3	Dialog Broadcast	DaWanda "Creating Love – A Communityfilm"	175	🔴
9.3	Dialog Broadcast	BVB Trikot »Kloppo dreht ab«	248	🟤
9.4	Dialog Digital	IKEA »Bannerbau«	152	🟤
9.4	Dialog Digital	WWF "Save as WWF"	46	🟤
9.4	Dialog Digital	WIENERS + WIENERS »Selbstübersetzende Mail«	179	⚪
9.4	Dialog Digital	edding Webspecial "Wall of Fame"	110	🔴
9.5	Dialog Mobile Marketing	Misereror Hilfswerk "Drive the Mobilombo – Deliver Hope to Africa"	208	🟤
9.5	Dialog Mobile Marketing	Deutschland findet euch »Vermisst-App«	96	🔴
9.6	Dialog Cross-Media Campaigns	Greenpeace Schweiz »Der Zonen Plan«	231	🔴
9.6	Dialog Cross-Media Campaigns	Initiative vermisste Kinder »Deutschland findet euch«	96	🟤
9.6	Dialog Cross-Media Campaigns	Demner, Merlicek & Bergmann »DMB vs. DDB«	349	🔴
9.6	Dialog Cross-Media Campaigns	Städel Museum »Frankfurt baut das neue Städel«	350	🔴
9.6	Dialog Cross-Media Campaigns	Konzerthaus Dortmund Saisonfilm 2010|2011 »Konzertmilch«	86	🟤
9.6	Dialog Cross-Media Campaigns	Mercedes-Benz Transporter »Meister vs. Meister«	54	🟡
9.6	Dialog Cross-Media Campaigns	Caritas "One Minute of Silence"	162	🟤
9.7	Dialog Social Media Campaigns	Vegetarierbund Deutschland »Das Kannibalen Restaurant«	220	🔴
9.7	Dialog Social Media Campaigns	Nike Football »Der Chip«	156	⚪
9.7	Dialog Social Media Campaigns	FC St. Pauli »Schädelgenerator«	351	🔴
9.8	Dialog Alternative	IKEA »Möbelkunst«	140	🔴
9.8	Dialog Alternative	Scholz & Friends Recruiting «Pizza Digitale»	353	🔴
9.8	Dialog Alternative	Kolle Rebbe "The Damn-Hot-Lovely-Christmas-Store"	352	🔴
9.8	Dialog Alternative	Jobs bei Jung von Matt »Trojanisches Recruiting«	223	🔴
10	Promotion			
10.1	Activities	Konzerthaus Dortmund – Exklusivkünstler »Countdown-Orchester«	124	🔴
10.1	Activities	Sky Bundesliga »Die Fußballoper«	120	🔴
10.1	Activities	Tages Anzeiger »Dranbleiben 2.0«	355	🔴
10.1	Activities	Konzerthaus Dortmund Saisonfilm 2010|2011 »Konzertmilch«	86	⚪
10.1	Activities	Mercedes-Benz Transporter »Meister vs. Meister«	54	⚪
10.1	Activities	Caritas "One Minute of Silence"	162	🟤
10.1	Activities	Germanwings "Planemob"	128	🟤
10.1	Activities	BIC "Prank"	296	🔴
10.1	Activities	WWF "Save as WWF"	46	⚪
10.1	Activities	SportScheck – Wir machen Sport "Sporty Vouchers"	354	🔴
10.1	Activities	Erntedank Kreativspezialisten »Streetview Geburt«	221	🔴
10.1	Activities	Daimler Pre-Safe "Transparent Walls"	212	🔴
10.1	Activities	Deutschland findet euch »vermisstes Einlaufkind«	96	⚪
10.2	Means	Bischöfliches Hilfswerk MISEREOR »Buchstabenmailing«	222	🟤
10.2	Means	IWC Schaffhausen »Das erste Bewerbungsbogenpuzzle«	357	🔴
10.2	Means	TUI »Donnerwetter Jetter«	218	🔴
10.2	Means	Extra Professional Polar-Fresh »Minz Tickets«	356	🔴
11	Media			
11	Media	McCafé »Anna und die Liebe«	249	🟤
11	Media	IKEA »Bannerbau«	152	🔴
11	Media	BMW M3 Coupé »Die BMW Lightwall ›Reflexion‹«	94	⚪
11	Media	Sky Bundesliga »Die Fußballoper«	120	⚪
11	Media	Texterschmiede »Guerilla-Funk«	361	🔴
11	Media	ENTEGA Erneuerbare Energie »Kampagne Denkanstöße«	64	⚪
11	Media	Saw 3D »Kino-Promotion«	360	🔴
11	Media	Konzerthaus Dortmund Saisonfilm 2010|2011 »Konzertmilch«	86	🟡
11	Media	Pattex Kleber Classic »Kran«	359	🔴

CATEGORY		TITLE	PAGE	AWARD
11	Media	IKEA »Möbelkunst«	140	●
11	Media	Germanwings "Planemob"	128	●
11	Media	Friedrichs & Friends "Proofreading Facebook"	358	●
11	Media	Jobs bei Jung von Matt »Trojanisches Recruiting«	223	●
12	Literature			
12.1	Advertising Brochures	BILD »Das Jahr in Bildern«	224	●
12.1	Advertising Brochures	Moormann Broschüre 2010 »In einfachen Verhältnissen«	362	●
12.1	Advertising Brochures	edding »Markenbuch«	110	●
12.1	Advertising Brochures	Görtz Sneaker-Schnürsenkel »Vogelhausbuch«	297	●
12.2	Image/Information Brochures	Heidelberger Druckmaschinen »Aus Respekt vor Dir, Papier.«	364	●
12.2	Image/Information Brochures	GSK Abtei »Das Rote-Faden-Buch«	298	●
12.2	Image/Information Brochures	ENTEGA Erneuerbare Energie »Denkanstöße Magazin 03«	64	●
12.2	Image/Information Brochures	LemonAid Jahresbericht 2010 »Der fairste Jahresbericht der Welt«	106	●
12.2	Image/Information Brochures	bilekjaeger »Hier spricht der Text.«	363	●
12.2	Image/Information Brochures	Rocket & Wink "Whatever 1st"	209	●
12.3	Catalogs	Moormann Katalog »Katalog Vol. 3«	190	●
12.3	Catalogs	Lego "Signs"	365	●
12.3	Catalogs	Ausstellungspublikation »Zur Nachahmung empfohlen! Expeditionen in Ästhetik und Nachhaltigkeit«	250	●
12.4	Reports	OBI Mitarbeiterbuch »40 Jahre OBI«	366	●
12.4	Reports	LemonAid Jahresbericht 2010 »Der fairste Jahresbericht der Welt«	106	●
12.5	Books	Juli Gudehus »Das Lesikon der visuellen Kommunikation«	372	●
12.5	Books	Strichpunkt Design "It's A Boy – It's A Girl"	374	●
12.5	Books	Kochbuch, Joachim Wissler Group »JW 4"	251	●
12.5	Books	Typotron-Heft 28 »Lokremise«	252	●
12.5	Books	GUM »Magazin für konzeptionelles Gestalten. Ausgabe 11.«	372	●
12.5	Books	Verlag Hermann Schmidt Mainz »Nea Machina – Die Kreativmaschine«	191	●
12.5	Books	Christopher Thomas »Passion«	368	●
12.5	Books	cosmic collection »Soirée graphique – Ausgabe No.1«	369	●
12.5	Books	birkhäuser "TypoLyrics – The Sound of Fonts"	367	●
12.5	Books	Görtz Sneaker-Schnürsenkel »Vogelhausbuch«	297	●
12.5	Books	designforum »Wien 2006–2010«	370	●
12.5	Books	förderraumgeschichten »Wollen wir einen Raum bieten, in dem man auch scheitern darf?«	371	●
12.7	Book Jackets/Covers	Suhrkamp Verlag »›Das Weisse Buch‹ von Rafael Horzon«	375	●
12.7	Book Jackets/Covers	BasisBibel »Kreuzcover«	134	●
13	Corporate Design			
13.1	Corporate Design	Corporate Design »Altes Kloster«	376	●
13.1	Corporate Design	Corporate Design »Beisser«	377	●
13.1	Corporate Design	Relaunch »Cafe Luitpold«	225	●
13.1	Corporate Design	Corporate Design "Community Film"	378	●
13.1	Corporate Design	Corporate Design »Mutabor«	379	●
13.1	Corporate Design	Corporate Design Kopfbahnhof 21 »Nein zu Stuttgart 21«	181	●
13.1	Corporate Design	Transmediale.11 "Response:ability"	118	●
13.1	Corporate Design	Corporate Design »Restaurant Hoch III Hamburg«	380	●
13.1	Corporate Design	Corporate Desgin »Staatstheater Stuttgart Schauspiel«	166	●
13.1	Corporate Design	T.D.G. "Stop The Water While Using Me!"	192	●
13.2	Individual Graphics	Whatever "At 1st"	209	●
13.2	Individual Graphics	SAP »BIT.CODE – Kunstprojekt und Software-Demo«	165	●
13.2	Individual Graphics	Serviceplan Hamburg »Blut, Schweiß und Tränen«	158	●
13.2	Individual Graphics	BIONADE »Fragen im Raum«	84	●
13.2	Individual Graphics	Mercedes-Benz »Sprinter Bewerbung«	178	●
13.2	Individual Graphics	edding Webspecial "Wall of Fame"	110	●
13.3	Calendars	AXE Dark Temptation, Unilever Deutschland »Adventskalender, 24 mal so unwiderstehlich wie Schokolade«	295	●
13.3	Calendars	F.A.Z., F.A.S »Der Erste Seite-Kalender«	382	●
13.3	Calendars	Kraft Foods »Der geheimnisvolle Kaffee Kalender«	226	●
13.3	Calendars	STIHL Motorsäge MS 261 »Die Vorfreude wächst.«	299	●
13.3	Calendars	Ad fontes – zu den Quellen »Jahreskalender 2011«	381	●
13.3	Calendars	WaXhouse »Waxingkalender«	253	●
13.4	Art/Culture/Event Posters	Schauspielhaus Bochum »Einführungskampagne«	384	●

CATEGORY		TITLE	PAGE	AWARD
13.4	Art/Culture/Event Posters	fiftyfifty Edition »Galerie Plakate«	383	●
13.4	Art/Culture/Event Posters	Staatstheater Stuttgart Schauspiel »Metropolis Serie«	166	●
13.4	Art/Culture/Event Posters	Transmediale.11 "Response:ability"	118	●
13.4	Art/Culture/Event Posters	Peter Behrens Schule Düsseldorf »Rundgang«	254	●
13.4	Art/Culture/Event Posters	Deutsches Schauspielhaus in Hamburg »Seit 110 Jahren in der Kritik.«	150	●
13.5	Packaging	Neuentwicklung und Redesign »Cafe Luitpold«	225	●
13.5	Packaging	Panasonic EVOIA AA-Alkali-Batterie »Die langlebigste Batterie«	385	●
13.5	Packaging	Festina Profundo »Die wasserverpackte Taucheruhr«	255	●
13.5	Packaging	Wild Bag® Box "Out_Of_Ark"	387	●
13.5	Packaging	Görtz 17 "Shoelace Box"	180	●
13.5	Packaging	Roggenkamp Organics Frische Suppen »Suppentöpfe ›Hausmacher Art‹«	386	●
13.6	Product Design	The Deli Garage »Backsteine«	256	●
13.6	Product Design	BasisBibel »Kreuz-Farbschnitt«	134	●
13.6	Product Design	The Deli Garage »Lutschwerkzeug«	388	●
13.6	Product Design	Arctic Paper "Munken Cube"	144	●
13.6	Product Design	Görtz 17 "Shoelace Box"	180	●
14	Editorial			
14.1	Print/Issue	sleek – magazine for art and fashion »#26 ›Flora|Fauna‹«	394	●
14.1	Print/Issue	Interkantonaler Rückversicherungsverband »100 Jahre IRV«	390	●
14.1	Print/Issue	Das neue Testament als Magazin »Ausgabe 1/2010«	389	●
14.1	Print/Issue	NIDO Magazin »Ausgabe 6/2010«	170	●
14.1	Print/Issue	Magazin der Bayerischen Staatsforsten »Bayernwald«	259	●
14.1	Print/Issue	Süddeutsche Zeitung Magazin »Edition 46/Menschen. Ein Bilderzyklus von Hans-Peter Feldmann«	395	●
14.1	Print/Issue	ZEITmagazin »Es lebe die Einfachheit!«	260	●
14.1	Print/Issue	Feld Hommes Magazin »Finale«	257	●
14.1	Print/Issue	Süddeutsche Zeitung Magazin »Hoffnung?«	396	●
14.1	Print/Issue	Golden Section Graphics "In Graphics"	258	●
14.1	Print/Issue	Süddeutsche Zeitung Magazin »Solange sie noch leben«	397	●
14.1	Print/Issue	ZEITmagazin »Typisch jüdisch?«	193	●
14.1	Print/Issue	VICE Magazine "v7n1 – The Barking Dog Issue"	398	●
14.1	Print/Issue	kid's wear Magazine »Vol. 31 Herbst/Winter 2010/11«	391	●
14.1	Print/Issue	Magazin der Bayerischen Staatsforsten »Waldfest«	392	●
14.1	Print/Issue	ZEITmagazin »Wieder alles falsch gemacht«	194	●
14.1	Print/Issue	ZEITmagazin »Wir machen das Beste aus Ihren Texten«	261	●
14.1	Print/Issue	NEON Magazin »XXL-Ausgabe – Was bin ich wirklich wert?«	393	●
14.2	Print/Year's Issue	Du Das Kulturmagazin 2010 »Jahrgang 2010«	262	●
14.2	Print/Year's Issue	NIDO Magazin »Jahrgang 2010«	170	●
14.2	Print/Year's Issue	VICE Magazine »Jahrgang 2010«	262	●
14.2	Print/Year's Issue	der Freitag »Nr. 2, 5, 6, 16, 22, 28, 39, 46, 47, 51/52«	399	●
14.3	Print/Individual Work	Süddeutsche Zeitung Magazin »80 Jahre Helmut Kohl«	408	●
14.3	Print/Individual Work	stern Magazin »Abschied von Vibe«	300	●
14.3	Print/Individual Work	Süddeutsche Zeitung Magazin »Alle zusammen und jeder für sich«	409	●
14.3	Print/Individual Work	stern Magazin »Ausbruch ins Leben«	406	●
14.3	Print/Individual Work	Süddeutsche Zeitung Magazin »Da fällt mir Einstein vom Herzen«	410	●
14.3	Print/Individual Work	stern Magazin »Das Beben…«	264	●
14.3	Print/Individual Work	stern Magazin »Der endlose Krieg«	407	●
14.3	Print/Individual Work	Berliner Morgenpost »Ein einzigartiges Orchester«	402	●
14.3	Print/Individual Work	ZEITmagazin »Fuchs, du hast die Uhr gestohlen«	412	●
14.3	Print/Individual Work	DIE ZEIT »Grafikseite – Ressort Wissen«	195	●
14.3	Print/Individual Work	ZEITmagazin »Ich habe einen Traum/Queen Elizabeth II«	413	●
14.3	Print/Individual Work	NEON Magazin »Jetzt ist aber Schluss!«	263	●
14.3	Print/Individual Work	Berliner Illustrirte Zeitung »Kinohauptstadt Berlin: Das Netzwerk«	400	●
14.3	Print/Individual Work	Berliner Illustrirte Zeitung »Kleine Menschen, große Welt«	401	●
14.3	Print/Individual Work	Süddeutsche Zeitung Magazin »Kunstschuss«	411	●
14.3	Print/Individual Work	NEON Magazin Februar 2010 »Lasst sie heulen!«	405	●
14.3	Print/Individual Work	ZEITmagazin »Leanne Shapton/Was von der Liebe übrig bleibt«	268	●
14.3	Print/Individual Work	ZEITmagazin «Mon Dieu! Depardieu!»	146	●
14.3	Print/Individual Work	NIDO Magazin »Niedrigenergiespiele«	170	●

CATEGORY		TITLE	PAGE	AWARD
14.3	Print/Individual Work	Süddeutsche Zeitung Magazin »Nur ankommen ist schöner«	265	●
14.3	Print/Individual Work	ZEITmagazin »Ölbilder«	414	●
14.3	Print/Individual Work	Du Das Kulturmagazin 2010 »Reportage Dezember 2010 Tomi Ungerer«	227	●
14.3	Print/Individual Work	Süddeutsche Zeitung Magazin »Schloss mit lustig«	266	●
14.3	Print/Individual Work	ZEITmagazin »Schwarz ist das neue Weiß«	415	●
14.3	Print/Individual Work	Süddeutsche Zeitung Magazin »Sieben auf einem Strich«	267	●
14.3	Print/Individual Work	In Graphics "Transfer Calligraphy"	404	●
14.3	Print/Individual Work	ZEITmagazin »Unser Hamlet«	416	●
14.3	Print/Individual Work	Die ZEIT »Wer wird Präsident?«	403	●
14.4	Multimedia/Integrated Concept	Weltgruppe »Gesamtauftritt«	269	●
14.4	Multimedia/Integrated Concept	AUDI Magazin "iPad App"	417	●
15	Environmental Design			
15	Environmental Design	ENTEGA Erneuerbare Energie »Café Endlager«	64	●
15	Environmental Design	DESSO, Messestand "Circulation"	420	●
15	Environmental Design	EXPO 2010, Shanghai »Der Deutsche Pavillon«	108	●
15	Environmental Design	ENTEGA Erneuerbare Energie »Der Stromfresser«	64	●
15	Environmental Design	Pergamonmuseum Berlin Sonderausstellung »Die geretteten Götter aus dem Palast vom Tell Halaf«	422	●
15	Environmental Design	Hasenkopf Messestand »Hasenkopf entdeckt das Ei des Kolumbus«	421	●
15	Environmental Design	Gegen Stuttgart 21 »K 21«	181	●
15	Environmental Design	AUDI A1 "Mediawall"	196	●
15	Environmental Design	AUDI Messauftritt «Mondial de L'Automobile Paris 2010»	418	●
15	Environmental Design	AUDI Messestand CES "Open for the future"	419	●
15	Environmental Design	Mobility "Reflective Kinematronic"	228	●
15	Environmental Design	Magic Box "State Grid Pavilion"	200	●
15	Environmental Design	Mainshow Saudi Arabischer Pavillon, EXPO 2010 "The Treasure"	199	●
15	Environmental Design	CERN "Universe of Particles"	197	●
15	Environmental Design	EXPO Pavillon 2010 "Urban Planet"	270	●
15	Environmental Design	Institut für Stadtgeschichte Frankfurt »Was die Welt bewegt – Arthur Schopenhauer in Frankfurt«	198	●
16	Environmental Design Craft			
16.2	Media Design and Integration	Mercedes-Benz »Interaktives Präsentationstool – CLS Show Paris 2010«	229	●
16.2	Media Design and Integration	E. Breuninger »Weiße Weihnachten 2010«	271	●
16.3	Lighting Design, Sound Design	Konzerthaus Dortmund – Exklusivkünstler »Countdown-Orchester«	124	●
17	Events			
17	Events	Panasonic »Barterlass«	425	●
17	Events	Diesel "Be Stupid Facepark"	182	●
17	Events	ENTEGA Erneuerbare Energie »Café Endlager«	64	●
17	Events	Konzerthaus Dortmund – Exklusivkünstler »Countdown-Orchester«	124	●
17	Events	Schauspiel Frankfurt »Licht am Ende des Tunnels – Beitrag zur Luminale 2010«	273	●
17	Events	Emmi Schweiz "Lightshow"	424	●
17	Events	Mercedes-Benz Transporter »Meister vs. Meister«	54	●
17	Events	balancity – Der Deutsche Pavillon EXPO 2010, Shanghai »Show in der Energiezentrale«	108	●
17	Events	RUHR.2010 GmbH »Still-Leben Ruhrschnellweg«	272	●
17	Events	AUDI A7 Sportback »Weltpremiere«	423	●
17	Events	Swisscom Urban Hacking »Wir für die Schweiz«	274	●
18	Events Craft			
18.1	Dramaturgy	ADC »46. Awards Show 2010«	426	●
18.2	Media Design and Integration	Mercedes-Benz »Interaktives Präsentationstool – CLS Show Paris 2010«	229	●
18.3	Lighting, Music, Sound	Konzerthaus Dortmund – Exklusivkünstler »Countdown-Orchester«	124	●
18.4	Set Design/Architecture	Diesel "Be Stupid Facepark"	182	●
18.4	Set Design/Architecture	smart "urban stage"	275	●
19	Copy			
19	Copy	75 Jahre ARAG »Die Geschichte der Versicherung«	427	●
19	Copy	Dynaudio »Die Nahhörerlebnis-Plakate.«	429	●

CATEGORY		TITLE	PAGE	AWARD
19	Copy	STIHL Motorsäge MS 261 Kampagne »Die Vorfreude wächst.«	299	🔴
19	Copy	Das deutsche Handwerk Kampagne »Die Wirtschaftsmacht. Von nebenan.«	163	🟤
19	Copy	Die Sahneschnitte »Ein paar Seiten Radiowerbung für Radiowerbung«	294	🔴
19	Copy	Hyposwiss Private Bank Kampagne "Expect the Expected"	201	⚪
19	Copy	BIONADE »Fragen im Raum – Anzeigen, Plakate«	84	🔴
19	Copy	BIONADE »Fragen im Raum – Microsite«	84	🟤
19	Copy	FTD »Kampagne«	431	🔴
19	Copy	Ritter Sport »Kampagne 2010«	432	🔴
19	Copy	Mercedes-Benz Transporter Kampagne »Meister vs. Meister«	54	🔴
19	Copy	DKV Reisekrankenversicherung »Reiseartikel aus Absurdistan«	276	🟤
19	Copy	Deutsches Schauspielhaus in Hamburg Kampagne »Seit 110 Jahren in der Kritik.«	150	🟤
19	Copy	Welt Kompakt »Statusmeldungen«	230	🟤
19	Copy	Festool Pendelstichsäge CARVEX PS 400 »Stuttgart 21«	430	🔴
19	Copy	Hornbach Baumarkt Kampagne »Ungekürzt«	164	🟤
19	Copy	Augsburger Allgemeine Kampagne »Weltnachrichten aus der Region«	428	🔴
20	Typography			
20	Typography	SAP »BIT.CODE – Kunstprojekt und Software-Demo«	165	🟤
20	Typography	Serviceplan Hamburg – Eigenwerbung »Blut, Schweiß und Tränen«	158	🔴
20	Typography	Bischöfliches Hilfswerk MISEREOR »Buchstabenmailing«	222	🔴
20	Typography	BILD »Das Jahr in Bildern«	224	🔴
20	Typography	GSK Abtei »Das Rote-Faden-Buch«	298	🔴
20	Typography	LemonAid Jahresbericht 2010 »Der fairste Jahresbericht der Welt«	106	⚪
20	Typography	BMW M3 Coupé »Die BMW Lightwall ›Reflexion‹«	94	🟤
20	Typography	Scheufelen »Höchstleistungen«	433	🔴
20	Typography	Loewe Kampagne "Individual 3 D"	277	🟤
21	Photography			
21	Photography	stern Magazin »Abschied von Vibe«	300	🔴
21	Photography	Das Brustkrebsprojekt »Amazonen«	434	🔴
21	Photography	stern Magazin Serie »Eine verwehte Welt«	440	🔴
21	Photography	Mercedes-Benz Serie »Gesichter der Marke«	281	🟤
21	Photography	Roberto Saviano, Autor gegen die Camorra. Serie »Ich habe in allen Winkeln der Erde geschrieben…«	439	🔴
21	Photography	Eigenwerbung Serie »Kulissenbauer«	435	🔴
21	Photography	Eigenwerbung Serie "Lightsounds"	279	🟤
21	Photography	Aernout Overbeeke Serie "Ndoto, Lengai – Mountain Of God"	278	🟤
21	Photography	Passionsspiele Oberammergau Serie »Passion«	202	⚪
21	Photography	Toyota Auris Hybrid Serie »Perspektivwechsel«	441	🔴
21	Photography	Eigenwerbung Serie »Seneca tanzt den Ovid«	436	🔴
21	Photography	Feld Hommes Magazin Serie »Sex Maschine«	438	🔴
21	Photography	Eigenwerbung Serie »SLS«	437	🔴
21	Photography	NIDO Magazin Serie »Streng sein«	170	🔴
21	Photography	Eigenwerbung Serie »Torso«	280	🟤
22	Illustration			
22	Illustration	Bund für Umwelt und Naturschutz Deutschland Serie »5 vor 12«	443	🔴
22	Illustration	stern Magazin Serie »Drunter-Welt«	446	🔴
22	Illustration	Motocross Enduro Magazin Serie "Enduro Untamed"	282	🟤
22	Illustration	ENTEGA Erneuerbare Energie Serie »Energiemärchen-Kalender«	203	⚪
22	Illustration	Radio Mephisto 97.6 Serie "Heads"	445	🔴
22	Illustration	VW Golf Serie »Kein Weg vorbei«	447	🔴
22	Illustration	AUDI quattro Serie »Mechanik und Elektronik innovativ kombiniert«	442	🔴
22	Illustration	McDonald's Serie »Morgenkaffee«	290	🔴
22	Illustration	SPIEGEL-Verlag Rudolf Augstein Serie »Perspektiven«	289	🔴
22	Illustration	Deutsches Schauspielhaus in Hamburg Serie »Seit 110 Jahren in der Kritik.«	150	🟤
22	Illustration	KulturSPIEGEL Serie "Simon Spilsbury"	444	🔴

CATEGORY		TITLE	PAGE	AWARD
23	Music and Sound			
23	Music and Sound	Deutscher Tierschutzbund Originalkomposition "A Peace of Mind"	204	●
23	Music and Sound	Konzerthaus Dortmund – Exklusivkünstler Originalkomposition »Countdown-Orchester«	124	●
23	Music and Sound	Hornbach Baumarkt Musikauswahl »Das grenzenlose Haus«	100	●
23	Music and Sound	Sky Bundesliga Originalkomposition »Die Fußballoper«	120	●
23	Music and Sound	Braun Satin Hair 5 Multistyler Musikauswahl "Hairmoticons"	206	●
23	Music and Sound	Mercedes-Benz E-Klasse Lang Originalkomposition "Shadows"	449	●
23	Music and Sound	Mercedes-Benz Allrad Musikauswahl »Sonntagsfahrer«	292	●
23	Music and Sound	Modern Music School Sounddesign »Talent«	88	●
23	Music and Sound	BFF Originalkomposition »Treppe«	448	●
23	Music and Sound	Vodafone Musikauswahl "Where are you?"	450	●
23	Music and Sound	Hornbach Baumarkt Sounddesign »Wieviel Wahnsinn steckt in Dir? ('Faces')«	72	●
24	Integrated Campaigns			
24	Integrated Campaigns	Hornbach Baumarkt »Das grenzenlose Haus«	100	●
24	Integrated Campaigns	Greenpeace Schweiz »Der Zonen Plan«	231	●
24	Integrated Campaigns	Initiative Vermisste Kinder »Deutschland findet euch«	96	●
24	Integrated Campaigns	50 Jahre edding »Jubiläumskampagne«	110	●
24	Integrated Campaigns	ENTEGA Erneuerbare Energie »Kampagne Denkanstöße«	64	●
24	Integrated Campaigns	Konzerthaus Dortmund Saisonfilm 2010|2011 »Konzertmilch«	86	●
24	Integrated Campaigns	ABSOLUT Vodka "Made"	291	●
24	Integrated Campaigns	Mercedes-Benz Transporter »Meister vs. Meister«	54	●
24	Integrated Campaigns	SP Zürich »Was Zürich braucht.«	451	●

ADC JURY-CHAIRMAN
ADC JURY CHAIRMAN

CHUCK PORTER
ADC JURY-CHAIRMAN
ADC JURY CHAIRMAN

Wow. Diese Show war besser als erwartet, und ich hatte einiges erwartet. Erstens hatte ich den Eindruck, dass die Organisation und das Management der Show unglaublich reibungslos und sorgfältig geklappt haben. Das ist eine große Show, und für gewöhnlich muss man mit mindestens ein paar großen Problemen rechnen. Falls es während der Jurierung Probleme gegeben hat, habe ich sie zu keinem Zeitpunkt bemerkt. Was ich gesehen habe, war ein Team aus absoluten Profis, die für einen planmäßigen Ablauf gesorgt haben, unerschütterliche Integrität und Fairness bewiesen haben und der künstlerischen Vision treu geblieben sind, die diesen Wettbewerb zu etwas Besonderem macht. Und das sage ich nicht nur, weil die Versorgung mit Brezeln, Wurst und Bier jeden Nachmittag so gut gewesen ist.

Zweitens war, und das ist sogar noch wichtiger, meiner Ansicht nach das Niveau der Arbeiten überragend. Ich war nicht überrascht über die außerordentlich große Kreativität des Designs – das ist etwas, wofür Deutschland schon immer bekannt war. Aber so viele wirklich wunderschöne Arbeiten zu sehen, ist für mich immer eine Freude. Auch war mir klar, dass es phantastische Film- und Printarbeiten geben würde, was auch der Fall war. Was mich richtig überrascht hat, war die große Anzahl an wirklich originellen und innovativen Ideen – nicht einfach nur großartigen Anzeigen, sondern neuen Herangehensweisen an Marken und Produkte. Ich habe Arbeiten gesehen, die das Potenzial hatten, die Welt zu verändern. Ich denke, der „Best of Show"-Sieger war ein echtes gedankliches Meisterwerk, aber es gab auch andere Meisterwerke und die Wahl fiel schwer.

Für mich war all dies eine unvergessliche und aufschlussreiche Erfahrung. Ich hoffe, dass ich vielleicht ein weiteres Mal eingeladen werde – wenn ich verspreche, fließend deutsch zu lernen.

Wow. This show was really more than I expected, and I expected a lot. First, I thought the organization and management of the show was amazingly smooth and thorough. This is a big show, and usually you can anticipate at least a few big problems. If there were problems during this judging, I never saw them. What I saw was a group of consummate professionals who kept everything on schedule, maintained an unwavering level of integrity and fairness, and stayed true to the artistic vision that makes these awards special. And I would say that even if they hadn't so thoughtfully provided pret-zels, wurst and beer every afternoon.

Second, and even more important in my judgment, the level of work was superb. I wasn't surprised to see the extraordinary standard of creativity in design – it's something that Germany has always been known for. Still, seeing so much really beautiful work is always a joy. I also knew there would be wonderful work in film and print, and there was. What really did surprise me were the number of truly original and innovative ideas – not just great ads, but new ways of looking at brands and products. I saw work that had the potential to change the world. I believe the best of show winner was genuinely a masterpiece of thinking, but there were other masterpieces as well and it definitely wasn't an easy choice to make.

For me, the whole experience was memorable and edifying. I'm hoping that, if I promise to become fluent in German, perhaps I'll be invited to return.

ADC WETTBEWERB 2011 KATEGORIESPONSOREN
ADC COMPETITION 2011 CATEGORY SPONSORS

KLASSISCHE MEDIEN
CLASSICAL MEDIA
Print
Print

Diese Kategorie wird gesponsert von
This category is sponsored by

KLASSISCHE MEDIEN
CLASSICAL MEDIA
Out-of-Home
Out-of-Home

Diese Kategorie wird gesponsert von
This category is sponsored by

FOCUS

FAW | FACHVERBAND AUSSENWERBUNG E.V.

KLASSISCHE MEDIEN
CLASSICAL MEDIA
Film
Film
TV/Kino Einzelspot/ Kampagne
TV/Cinema Commercial/ Campaign

Diese Kategorie wird gesponsert von
This category is sponsored by

WERBEWEISCHER
WERBUNG IM KINO

CRAFT
CRAFT
Text
Copy

Diese Kategorie wird gesponsert von
This category is sponsored by

WIENERS+WIENERS
Übersetzen · Adaptieren · Korrigieren

CRAFT
CRAFT
Typografie
Typography

Diese Kategorie wird gesponsert von
This category is sponsored by

APPEL GROUP.
BERLIN DÜSSELDORF FRANKFURT HAMBURG MÜNCHEN STUTTGART

PUNKTE
POINTS

GOLD
DIGITALE MEDIEN
DIGITAL MEDIA
- Digitale Medien
- Online-Werbemaßnahmen
- Digital Media
- Online Advertising

SILVER
DIALOGMARKETING/ PROMOTION/MEDIA
DIALOG MARKETING/ PROMOTION/MEDIA
- Promotion
- Aktivitäten
- Promotion
- Aktivitäten

SILVER
DIGITALE MEDIEN
DIGITAL MEDIA
- Digitale Medien
- Viral
- Digital Media
- Viral

BRONZE
DIALOGMARKETING/ PROMOTION/MEDIA
DIALOG MARKETING/ PROMOTION/MEDIA
- Dialogmarketing
- Dialog Digital
- Dialog Marketing
- Dialog Digital

WWF
"Save as WWF"

Lead Agency
  Jung von Matt AG
Contributing Agencies
  Jung von Matt/Fleet,
  Jung von Matt/next,
  Dederichs Reinecke & Partner,
  Portrix.net,
  7 Seas,
  White Horse Music
Client
  WWF Deutschland
Executive Creative Direction
  Doerte Spengler-Ahrens,
  Jan Rexhausen,
  Armin Jochum
Creative Direction
  Doerte Spengler-Ahrens,
  Jan Rexhausen
Art Direction
  Michael Kittel
Client Consulting
  Jose Luis Carretero Lopez,
  Miriam Paneth,
  Benjamin Wenke
Camera
  Jesse Rosten
Copy
  Michael Kittel,
  Henning Müller-Dannhausen,
  Lisa Glock
Cutting
  Florian Panier
Film Production
  Florian Panier
Graphic Design
  Alexander Norvilas
Idea
  Michael Kittel
Illustration
  Michael Kittel
Music Composition
  Schumann Bach,
  White Horse Music
Production
  Florian Paul (7 Seas)
Programming
  Knud Alex Müller (Portrix.net),
  Florian Paul (7 Seas),
  Lana Nugent (7 Seas)
Speaker
  Klaas Nocken
Technical Conception
  Simone Bitzer
Technical Implementation
  Michael Behrens,
  Sven Loskill,
  Tom Schallberger,
  Michael Seifert,
  Franziska Löffler,
  Simone Bitzer,
  Susanne zu Eicken,
  GoSign Media

Wie kann man den bewussten Umgang mit Papier fördern? Und im Idealfall nicht nur das Bewusstsein, sondern auch das Handeln verändern? Mit einem neuen, grünen Dateiformat: WWF – ein Dateiformat, das man definitiv nicht ausdrucken kann. Mit jedem gespeicherten WWF, jedem per E-Mail verschickten WWF und jedem "SAVE AS WWF"-Button verbreitet sich das WWF immer weiter um die ganze Welt. www.saveaswwf.com

How can we become more aware of how we use paper? And ideally, not only change our awareness, but also our behaviour? With a new, green file format: WWF – the format that you definitely cannot print out. With every saved WWF file, every WWF sent via e-mail and every "save as WWF" button, WWF is spread even further throughout the world. www.saveaswwf.com

Das erste grüne Dateiformat der Welt: das WWF.

Millionen von Quadratmetern Regenwald werden jedes Jahr abgeholzt. Nur für Papier.
Papier, mit dem überall auf der Welt sinnlos Dokumente ausgedruckt werden.
Wir wollten das unnötige Ausdrucken stoppen und den bewussten Umgang mit Papier starten.

Deshalb haben wir ein neues, grünes Dateiformat erfunden: Das WWF.
Ein Dateiformat, das man definitiv nicht ausdrucken kann. Eine simple Idee, die Bäume rettet.
Jeder Einzelne und jedes Unternehmen konnte durch Nutzen und Verbreiten des WWF Formats einen aktiven Beitrag zum Umweltschutz leisten.
Hier ist nicht schlaue Kommunikation das Produkt, sondern ein schlaues Produkt macht die Kommunikation. **Unsere große Botschaft:**

SAVE AS WWF, SAVE A TREE

Was ist das WWF?

Das erste grüne Dateiformat, das man definitiv nicht ausdrucken kann.

Was bringt es der Umwelt?

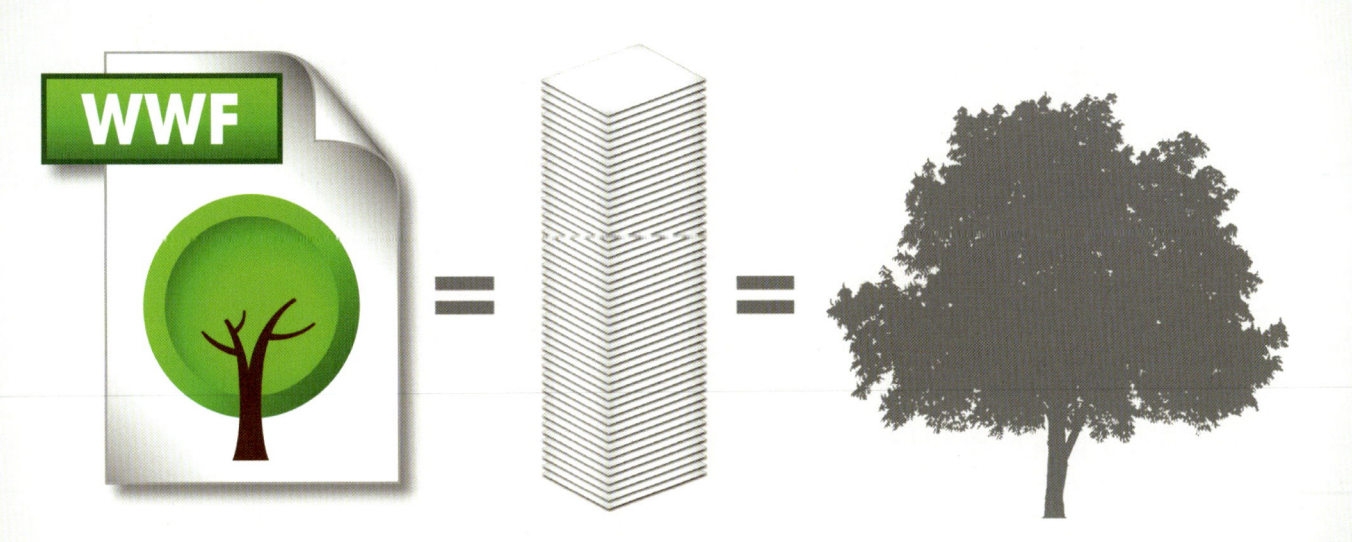

Ein WWF kann so viele Seiten enthalten, wie aus einem ganzen Baum gewonnen werden können. Mit einem einzigen WWF kann man also einen ganzen Baum retten.

Wie funktioniert das WWF?

Einfach die kostenlose WWF Software für PC und MAC auf www.saveaswwf.com downloaden, installieren und mit einem Klick viele andere Dateiformate in das WWF-Format umwandeln.

Um die Empfänger eines verschickten WWFs über unser grünes Dateiformat zu informieren und mit ihnen in Dialog zu treten, fungiert die letzte Seite eines jeden WWF Dokuments als Response-Element mit Erklärungstext und Verweis auf die Website.

Wie verbreitet sich das WWF?

Mit jedem gespeicherten WWF, jedem per E-Mail verschickten WWF und jedem WWF Button auf Websites verbreitet sich das WWF immer weiter um die ganze Welt.

Und wen interessiert das?

Wenige Tage nach Kampagnenstart war das WWF DAS Thema in den News, Tweets und Blogs der Welt. Nach vier Wochen hatte die Website bereits 200.000 Besucher aus 183 Ländern und die Software wurde über 30.000 mal heruntergeladen. Und das war erst der Anfang.

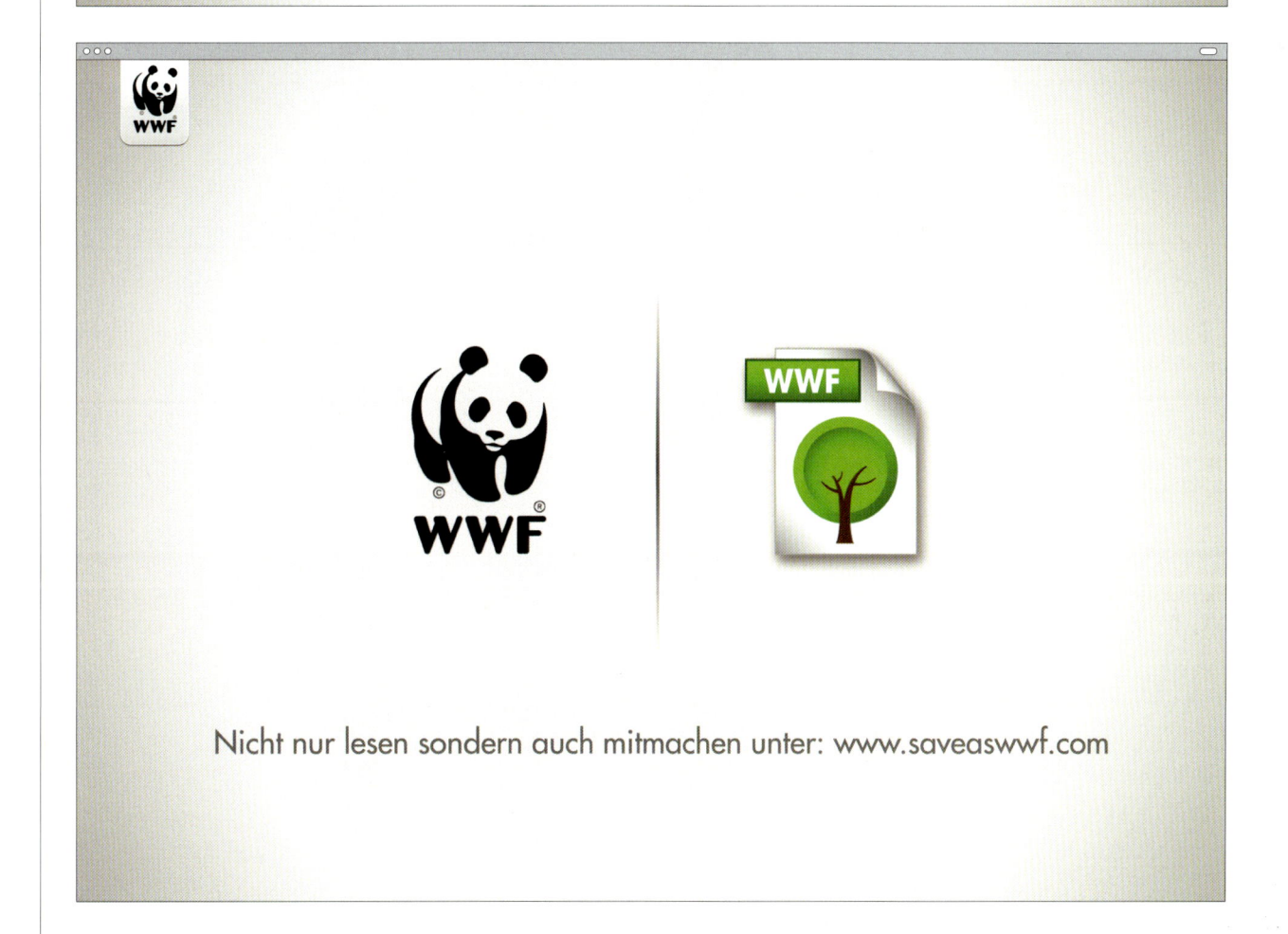

Nicht nur lesen sondern auch mitmachen unter: www.saveaswwf.com

3 PUNKTE
POINTS

● GOLD
DIALOGMARKETING/
PROMOTION/MEDIA
DIALOG MARKETING/
PROMOTION/MEDIA
- Dialogmarketing
- Dialog Crossmediale Kampagnen
- Dialog Marketing
- Dialog Cross-Media Campaigns

● SILVER
DIALOGMARKETING/
PROMOTION/MEDIA
DIALOG MARKETING/
PROMOTION/MEDIA
- Promotion Aktivitäten
- Promotion Activities

● SILVER
GANZHEITLICHE KOMMUNIKATION
INTEGRATED CAMPAIGNS
- Ganzheitliche Kommunikation
- Integrated Campaigns

● SILVER
KLASSISCHE MEDIEN
CLASSICAL MEDIA
- Film
- Kurzfilme/Sonderformate für Bewegtbild
- Film
- Shorts/Special Formats for Moving Pictures

● SILVER
DIGITALE MEDIEN
DIGITAL MEDIA
- Digitale Medien
- Digitale Kampagnen
- Digital Media
- Digital Campaigns

● BRONZE
KLASSISCHE MEDIEN
CLASSICAL MEDIA
- Film
- Filme für Verkaufsförderung
- Film
- TV/Sales Promotion Films

● BRONZE
KLASSISCHE MEDIEN
CLASSICAL MEDIA
- Film
- Internetfilme
- Film
- Internet Films

● NOMINATION
RÄUMLICHE INSZENIERUNG
SPATIAL SCENE-SETTING
- Events
- Events

● NOMINATION
CRAFT
CRAFT
- Text
- Copy

● NOMINATION
KLASSISCHE MEDIEN
CLASSICAL MEDIA
- Out-of-Home
- Klassisch Kampagne
- Out-of-Home
- Classic Campaign

MERCEDES-BENZ TRANSPORTER
»Meister vs. Meister«

Lead Agency
   Scholz & Friends
Client
   Daimler AG
Marketing Direction
   Nicole Baldisweiler
Advertising Direction
   Lutz Wienstroth
Executive Creative Direction
   Martin Pross,
   Matthias Spaetgens
Creative Direction
   Robert Krause,
   Philipp Wöhler
Art Direction
   Jörg Waschescio,
   Jens Stein,
   Melanie Specht,
   Stefan Schuster,
   Patricia Stolz,
   Florian Hucker
Client Consulting
   Stefanie Wurst,
   Ellen Staudenmayer,
   Vera Krauße,
   Anna Gabriel,
   Ulf Cerning,
   Josef-Konstantin Schulte
Strategic Planning
   Malte Fischer,
   Nicolas Schindler,
   Mario Gamper
Agency Production
   Benito Schumacher,
   Diana Wuttge,
   Katharina Meyer
Art Buying
   Kirsten Rendtel
Audio Production
   Studio Funk
Camera
   Philipp Kirsamer,
   Felix Leibert
Chief Editing
   Dominik Thesing
Copy
   Stefan Lenz,
   Christian Brandes,
   Tobias Deitert,
   Johannes Vogl,
   Folke Renken
Cutting
   Daniel Klessig,
   Marty Schenk,
   Rain Kencana
Editing
   Dominik Thesing,
   Anke Oßwald,
   Sandro Krauss,
   Christian Wahl,
   Philip Gursch,
   Rebecca Kircher
Film Direction
   Johannes Grebert,
   Philipp Stölzl
Film Production
   Bigfish Filmproduktion GmbH
Image Editing
   Appel Grafik,
   blink imaging
Image Processing
   Appel Grafik,
   blink imaging
Media
   Mediaedge,
   Maria Bruns,
   Alexa Montag
Photography
   Nikolas Schmidt-Burgk,
   Tino Pohlmann,
   Frithjof Ohm,
   Nico Hesselmann
Postproduction
   Das Werk
Radio Production
   Hastings Music GmbH,
   Studio Funk
Technical Implementation
   Scholz & Friends Brand Affairs
Other
   Communication Agency:
   deepblue networks AG
   Editing: Dominik Thesing,
   Anke Oßwald,
   Sandro Krauss,
   Christian Wahl,
   Philip Gursch
   Event: Jürgen Lange,
   Florian Mildner

In einer Aktion von Mercedes-Benz Transporter können sich Handwerksmeister online um ein Spiel gegen ein Allstar-Team aus ehemaligen Fußballwelt- und -europameistern bewerben: Vier Teams dürfen DFB-Legenden auf ihrem lokalen Fußballplatz herausfordern. Das Ergebnis: über 7.500 Online-Bewerbungen, 15.000 Zuschauer, 640 Reportagen in TV, Radio und Presse, 500.000 Klicks auf der Kampagnenwebsite und ein glückliches Gewinnerteam. Ein einstündiges Roadmovie, das die ganze Meister-vs.-Meister-Tour im Internet erzählt, wollen über 300.000 Menschen sehen.

In an action from Mercedes-Benz Transporter, master-craftsmen can apply via Internet to play against an all-star team of former World and European football champions. Four teams are able to challenge the DFB legends on their home pitches. The result: over 7,500 online-applications, 15,000 spectators, 640 TV, radio and press reports, 500,000 clicks on the campaign website and one lucky winner team. At the end, a one-hour roadmovie documents the whole »Meister vs. Meister« tour on the Internet and is watched by over 300,000 people.

43

Meister vs. Meister

DFB-ALLSTARS

GERÜSTBAU J. MOTZKAU

Sonntag, 30. Mai, ab 11 Uhr – Stadion Sonnenblume, Velbert

Mercedes-Benz

Sepp Maier

Halb Mensch, halb Reflex.

„Die Katze von Anzing." Geboren am 28. Februar 1944 in Metten, Niederbayern. 14 Jahre lang hielt der Rekordtorhüter den Kasten des FC Bayern München blitzsauber. Dabei gönnte er sich genauso wenig wie seinen Gegnern: Von 473 Spielen absolvierte er 442 ohne Unterbrechung. Maier ist einfach immer da – links, rechts, oben, unten. Mit ihm zwischen den Pfosten bekommt der Begriff Strafraum eine ganz neue Bedeutung. Fehler darfst du dir nicht erlauben – mit einem Lächeln auf den Lippen rächt der Meister der abgefangenen Flanke jede Unachtsamkeit. Man hat ihn mit Messern beworfen, mit Enten versucht, ihn vom Spiel abzulenken. Vergeblich. Als Nationalkeeper wurde er Welt- und Europameister, mit dem FC Bayern sammelte er mehr Pokale, als auf eine Seitenlinie passen. Wenn er im Tor steht, heißt es: Schuhe aus! Der 16-Meter-Raum ist sein Wohnzimmer.

www.meister-vs-meister.de   Mercedes-Benz

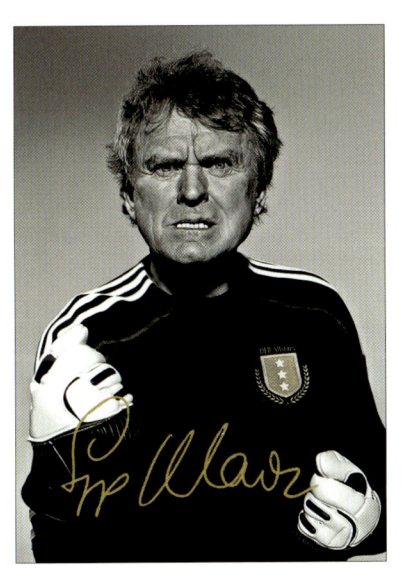

Uwe Schmidt

Sein erstes Kuscheltier war eine Plüschaxt.

„Der Gladiator." Geboren am 30.5.1960 in Wuppertal. Ein Raubein, wie es im Buche steht. Uwe Schmidt erkämpft sich nicht nur Bälle, sondern auch Gegner. Wenn man den Wuppertaler Obermonteur erst mal von der Leine lässt, dann ist er bissig wie eine tollwütige Königskobra. Im defensiven Mittelfeld beheimatet, hält der Mann mit der Statur eines griechischen Halbgottes hauptsächlich seinen offensiveren Mitspielern den Rücken frei. Nebenbei lässt er Gegner immer wieder an der Grasnarbe riechen, um dann wie aus dem Nichts den entscheidenden Impuls für den nächsten Konter zu geben. Spieler wie Uwe Schmidt bleiben seltener als Zuschauern als den gegnerischen Mannschaftsärzten in Erinnerung. Aber sie machen ein Team komplett. Und berüchtigt.

www.meister-vs-meister.de   Mercedes-Benz

DACHDECKEREI WENDT,
NEUMÜNSTER

PGH WURSTWAREN,
SCHÖNEBECK

GERÜSTBAU MOTZKAU,
VELBERT

INSTALLATEURE DÜRR & FEIL,
ELLWANGEN

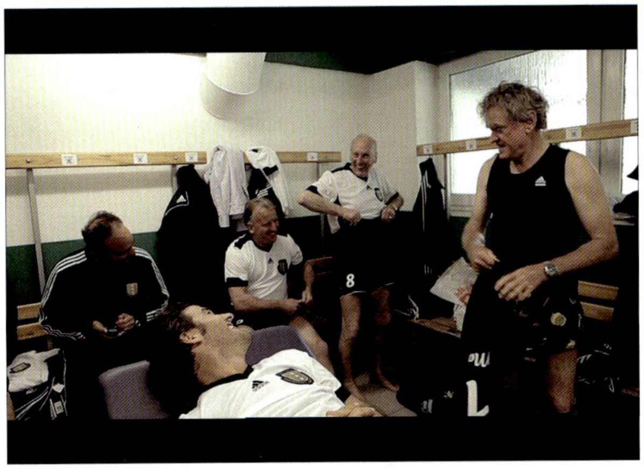
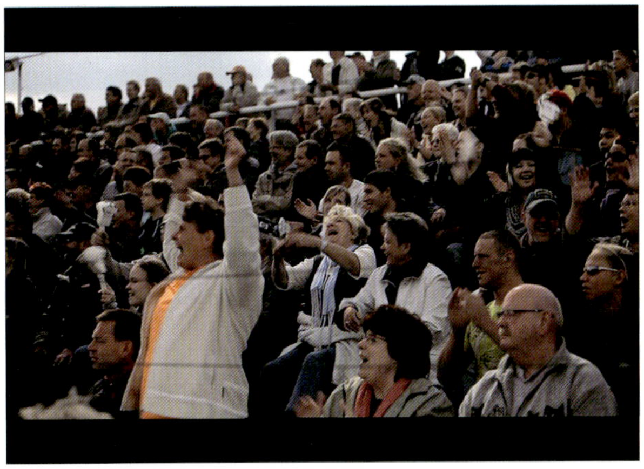

43

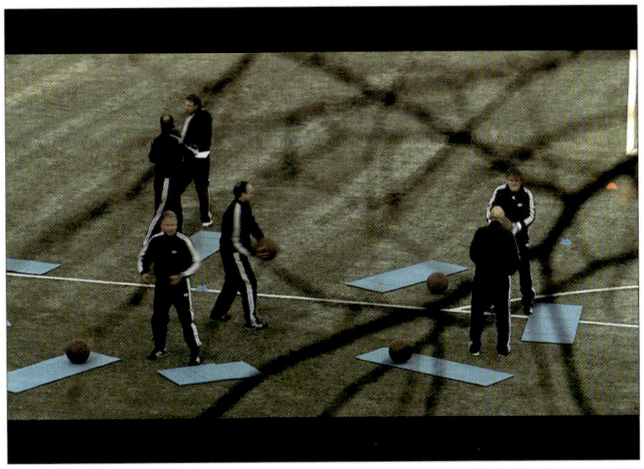
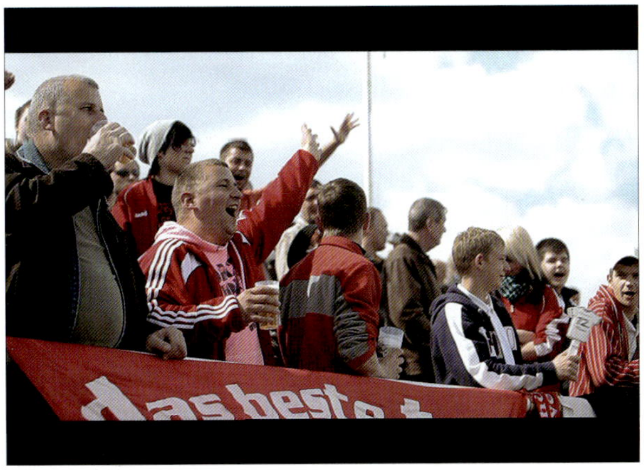
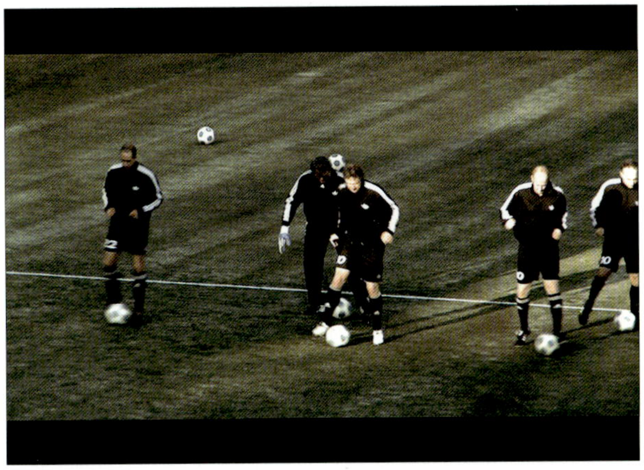
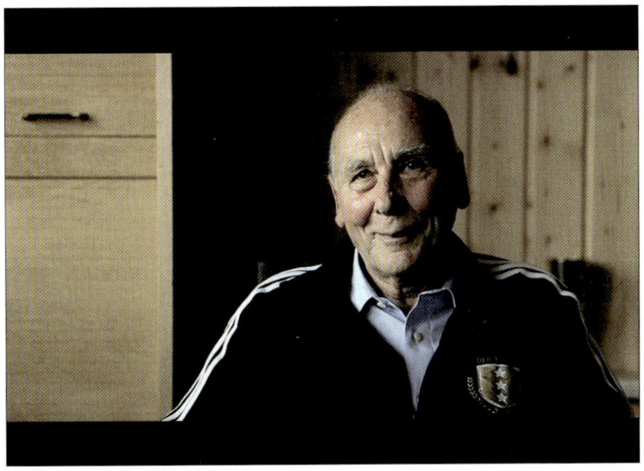
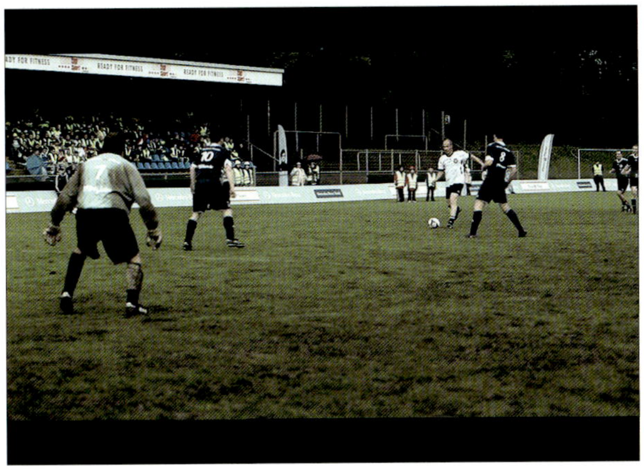

Die DFB-Allstars fordern Deutschlands Handwerker heraus.

6 gegen 5 Millionen.

Mercedes-Benz Transporter präsentiert

Treten Sie mit Ihren Kollegen gegen die Legenden des deutschen Fußballs an.

www.meister-vs-meister.de

Mercedes-Benz

Der Wettkampf | Die Meister | Für Fans | Video & Fotos

DFB-Allstars, aufgepasst!

Wir nehmen die Herausforderung an!

FC Birbaum & CO	Die Weltmeister...	Deinzerteam	Rennert - Kicker	Die Flintstones	Bald fertig
Torjäger-Meister	Die Bunzelmänner	Himmelsstürmer	The Hammers	Gauchos 1	1. FC Boymann L...
Der Schalkner M...	1.FC Maria hilf	Die Billis	Lacklerprofis	Polymold GmbH &...	Scherrer
Eutiner-Löwen	Team Frankenluk	Die Kugelstumper	Sutum Allstars	Dream-Team Mark...	Hade Holzbau
SKV Intering	Fliesen-Arts Dr...	Schienbein 04	Schlossi Bürger	Berenbold Kickers	Mächtig Starke ...
Die Rauswerfer	Podlech 2010	Holledauer Drea...	Sengger Gebäude...	Lukeske Dachhasen	Real Forstwolfe...
Autohaus Hellw...	Die Grünen Meister	Eisbernd Bauunt...	Domeler Warriors	SG Einhelzer	Holzwürmer Johann
Calmus GmbH	Solartechnik Th...	FC Sturmtief Sc...	Werbetechnik La...	Tischlerei Lüdke	Team 10.000-Volt

(Mehr zum Team)

YouTube

Die Rückkehr der Legenden

jokerooDOTcom 10 Videos Abonnieren

1:14 / 1:16

Mag ich | Hinzufügen zu | Weiterleiten | Einbetten

125.495

Alle Kommentare (23) — Alle anzeigen

Best of Deutschland ist das von Basler mal abgesehen nicht. Aber wenigstens solide. Die Franzosen wollen Eric Cantona ins rennen schicken, der ja für Geld bekanntlich alles macht.
Fussballchecker335 vor 11 Monaten

von der Aufstellung her siehts nachm Kleinfeldturnier aus
Poohbearparty vor 11 Monaten

Vielleicht die letzte Möglichkeit richtige Fußballer wie Mario Basler und Jürgen Kohler nochmal in Aktion zu sehen. Irgendwann haben wir Chips im Ball, Sensoren an der Grundlinie und was weiß ich nicht noch fürn Scheiß. Sind so und so nur noch Ballerinas aufm Feld.
pimpinpancho vor 11 Monaten

Kohler 4 Ever !!!! Borussia rulezzzzzzzzz
tiegerhut vor 11 Monaten

MB hat auf jeden Fall die gleichen Lactat Werte wie ne Flasche Becks.
conny030 vor 11 Monaten

Wie geil. Der Doppelherz-Cup. Was hat eigentlich Sepp Meier für Lactat-Werte?
famkleinehingen vor 11 Monaten

Wie geil! Ichg steh auf Stefan Beinlich!
TheAnka1701 vor 11 Monaten

Romario kommt für die Selecao, mehr weiß ich aber auch net.
filigrantechniker76 vor 11 Monaten

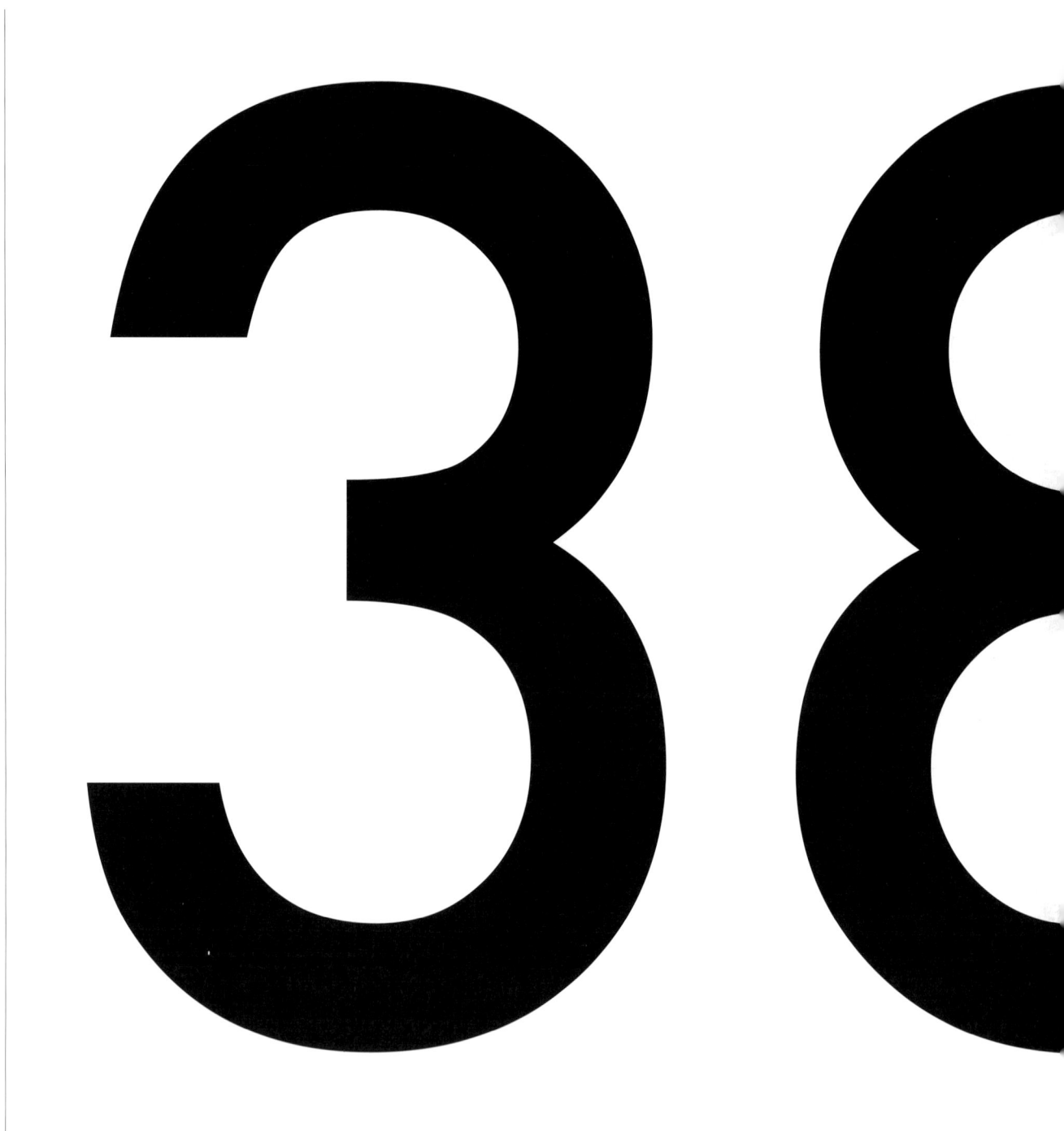

38

PUNKTE
POINTS

GOLD
KLASSISCHE MEDIEN
CLASSICAL MEDIA
- Out-of-Home
- Nicht-Klassisch
- Out-of-Home
- Non-Classic

SILVER
GANZHEITLICHE
KOMMUNIKATION
INTEGRATED CAMPAIGNS
- Ganzheitliche Kommunikation
- Integrated Campaigns

SILVER
DESIGN
DESIGN
- Literatur
- Image-/Informations-broschüren
- Literature
- Image/Information Brochures

SILVER
DIALOGMARKETING/
PROMOTION/MEDIA
DIALOG MARKETING/
PROMOTION/MEDIA
- Media
- Media

SILVER
RÄUMLICHE INSZENIERUNG
SPATIAL SCENE-SETTING
- Kommunikation im Raum
- Environmental Design

BRONZE
RÄUMLICHE INSZENIERUNG
SPATIAL SCENE-SETTING
- Kommunikation im Raum
- Environmental Design

NOMINATION
RÄUMLICHE INSZENIERUNG
SPATIAL SCENE-SETTING
- Events
- Events

ENTEGA ERNEUERBARE ENERGIE
»Kampagne Denkanstöße«

Lead Agency
  DDB Tribal Group
Contributing Agencies
  trigger happy productions
Client
  ENTEGA VERTRIEB GMBH
Marketing Direction
  Dr. Karoline Haderer
Advertising Direction
  Sandra Schamber
Executive Creative Direction
  CCO: Eric Schoeffler
  ECD: Stefan Schulte,
  Bastian Meneses von Arnim
Creative Direction
  Ludwig Berndl,
  Kristoffer Heilemann,
  Ralf Schmerberg
  Digital Director:
  Achim Weber
  Managing Director:
  Andreas Poulionakis
Art Direction
  Judith Baumgartner,
  Lars Buri,
  Sebastian Jerez,
  Marian Grabmayer,
  Chan-Young Ramert,
  Michael Janke,
  Cathrin Ciuraj,
  Petra Langhammer
Client Consulting
  Ann-Katrin Schelkmann,
  Caroline Sturm,
  Sebastian Neumann
Strategic Planning
  Christina Keller,
  Andreas Butterbrodt
Agency Production
  Barbara Simon
Architecture/Scenography
  Construction:
  Studio Babelsberg
Artist
  Isabel Ott
Audio Production
  Hastings Audio Network Berlin,
  Studio Funk Berlin
Consulting
  Project Management:
  Bella Sahin,
  Mathias Westebbe,
  Felix Vogler,
  Cornell Henze
  Client Service Director:
  Anke Peters,
  Matthias Meusel
  Project Management:
  Snowman Demonstration:
  Cornell Henze,
  Bella Sahin
  Cafe Endlager:
  Cornell Henze,
  Bella Sahin
  Power Guzzler:
  Bella Sahin,
  Mathias Westebbe
  Editing:
  Isabelle Erler
Copy
  Mona Sibai,
  Nina Faulhaber,
  Res Matthys,
  Edgar Linscheid,
  Antje Gerwien,
  Lennart Frank,
  Ludwig Berndl
Design
  Archive Images:
  Stephan Gessler,
  Anne Gold,
  Duane Hanson,
  Martin Johnson Heade,
  Chris Jordan,
  Sebastian Krawinkel,
  Thomas Meyer,
  Holger Mette,
  Julian Röder,
  Linn Schröder,
  Mike Sinclair
Editing
  Chief Editing:
  Ralf Grauel
  Final Editing:
  Matthias Sommer
  Editing:
  Isabelle Erler
Film Direction
  Ralf Schmerberg
Final Artwork
  Other Artists:
  Silvana Toneva,
  Ole Wulfert,
  Antonio Tiller
Graphic Design
  Sebastian Jerez,
  Steffen Boseckert,
  Mattias Nygard,
  Christophe-Claude Bugetti,
  Tim Kremer
Idea
  Ralf Schmerberg
Illustration
  Daniel Stolle
Image Editing
  Tobias Kruse,
  Maria Leutner
Image Processing
  Lithography/Pre-Press:
  max-color
Media
  PR: Bureau N,
  Snowman Demonstration:
  Johanssen+Kretschmer
Music Composition
  Snowman Demonstration:
  Dragan Espenschied
Photography
  Dennis De La Haye,
  Max Merz,
  Sven Glage,
  Szymon Plewa,
  Grover Schrayer,
  Rachel de Joode,
  Peter Lorenz,
  Katja Renner,
  Ljupcho Temelkovski,
  Stephan Vens
Printing
  Druckhaus Spandau
  Lithography:
  twentyfour seven creative media services
Production
  trigger happy productions
  Executive Production:
  Stephan Vens,
  Eva Maier-Schönung
  Production:
  Nani Miliane Meimeth
  Assistance Production:
  Nicolas Blankenhorn,
  Josefine Bothe,
  Mindpirates
Programming
  Mindpirates
Publishing House
  trigger happy productions,
  Mindpirates
Sound Design
  Lukas Walter,
  Lars Gelhausen,
  Nina Steiger,
  Claudia Hesse
Trade Fair Construction
  Curating Café Endlager:
  Dr. Carola Dürr,
  Ralf Schmerberg
Typography
  PR: Bureau N
Other
  Production Design:
  Snowman Demonstration:
  Peter Weber
  Cafe Endlager:
  Peter Weber
  Power Guzzler:
  Sebastian Krawinkel
  Controlling:
  Uta Abt
  Stuntman:
  Luca Pasini
  Artists:
  Dirk Behrend,
  Hans Harrow-Sandmann,
  Roby Horsley,
  Filippo Martelli,
  Dario Niederprüm,
  Juri Nöldge,
  Isabel Ott,
  Paul Ott,
  Greta Schmerberg-Davila,
  souziehaas,
  Alexander Tiller

Um den Ökostromanbieter Entega bundesweit bekannt zu machen, gingen wir einen neuen Weg der Kommunikation. Nachhaltiges Engagement nicht behaupten, sondern beweisen – das ist die Idee der Kampagne Denkanstöße. Die temporäre Kunstausstellung »Café Endlager« und die Installation »Stromfresser« aus alten Kühlschränken widmeten sich den Themen Atomkraft und Energieverschwendung. Das weltweite Medienecho und über 75.000 Besucher verbreiteten die Botschaft.

To raise awareness for the green energy provider Entega, we chose a new way of communication. The goal of the campaign "Food for Thought" was to place crucial topics in society and thereby prove sustained commitment. The temporary art exhibition »Café Endlager« and the »Stromfresser« (power guzzler) made of old refrigerators helped understand the topics nuclear energy and energy waste. Over 75,000 visitors and a worldwide media response spread the message.

38

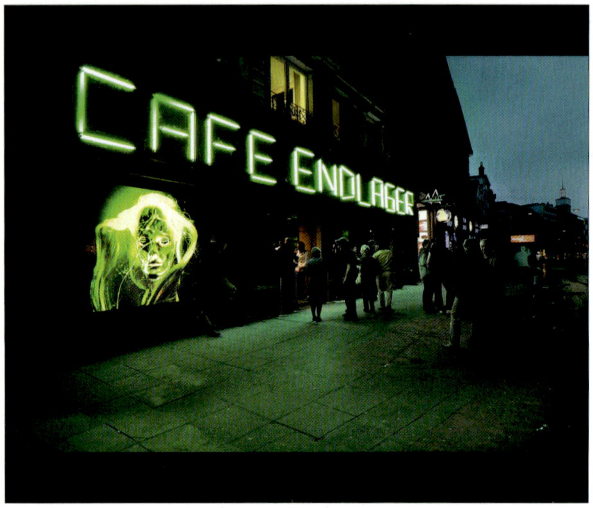

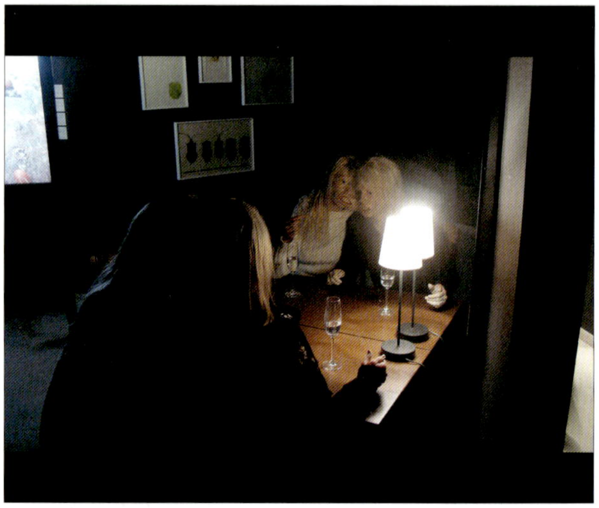

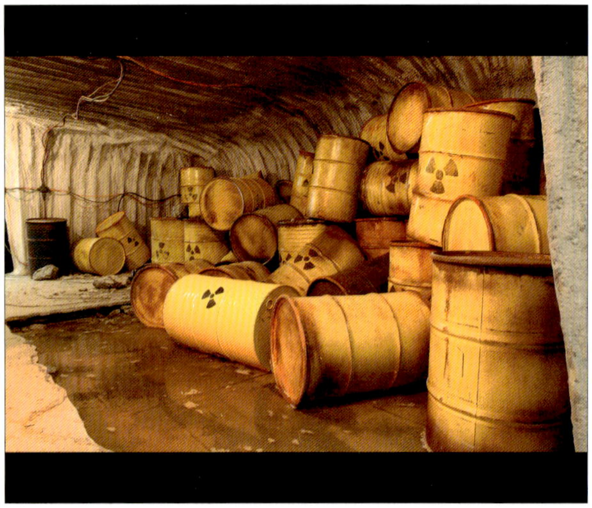

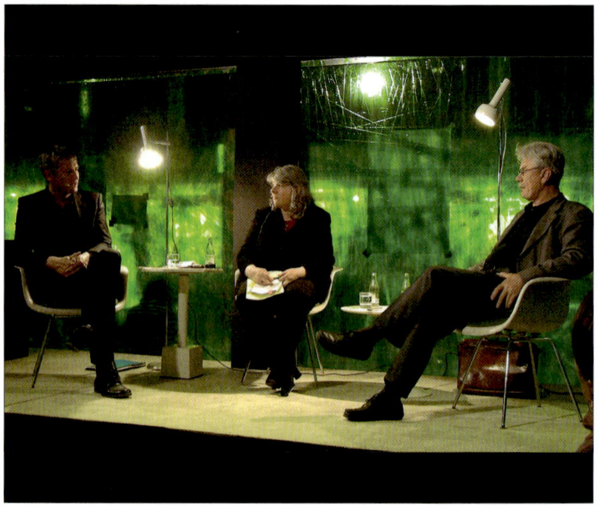

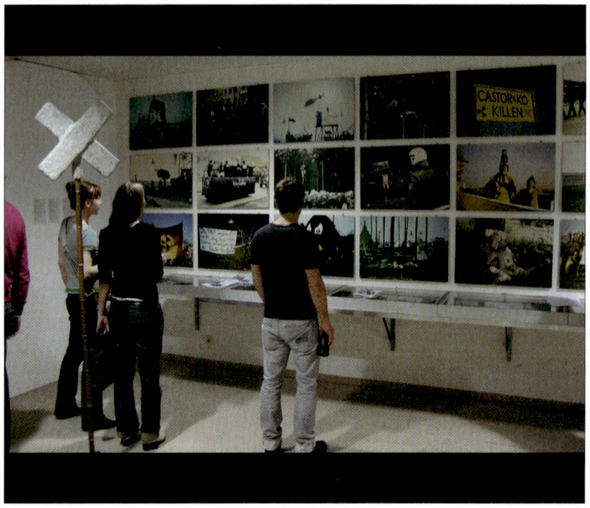

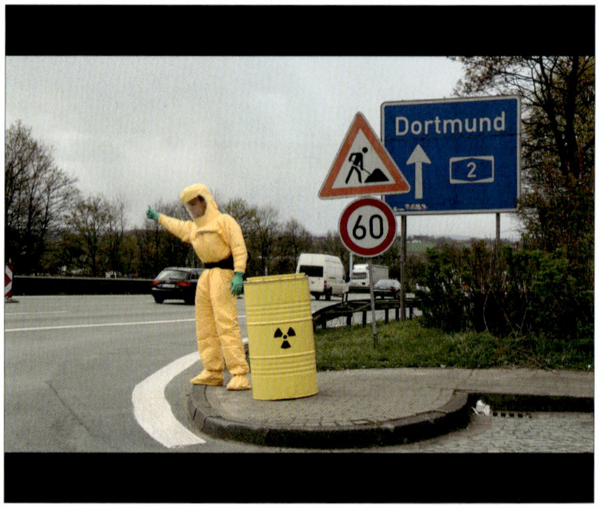

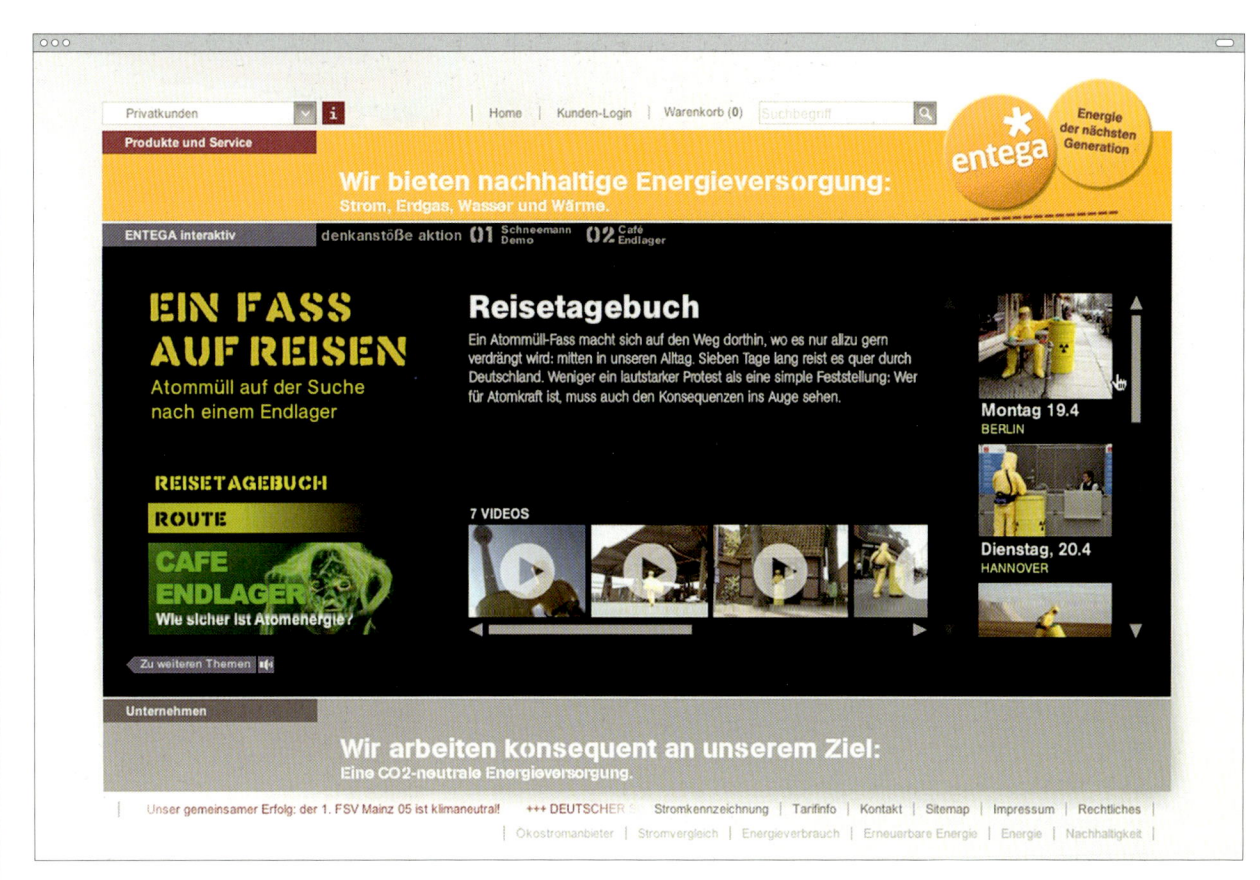

EIN FASS AUF REISEN
Atommüll auf der Suche nach einem Endlager

Reisetagebuch
Ein Atommüll-Fass macht sich auf den Weg dorthin, wo es nur allzu gern verdrängt wird: mitten in unseren Alltag. Sieben Tage lang reist es quer durch Deutschland. Weniger ein lautstarker Protest als eine simple Feststellung: Wer für Atomkraft ist, muss auch den Konsequenzen ins Auge sehen.

Vergeudet, verwüstet, vernichtet

Der Kapitalismus ist die größte Verschwendungsmaschine, die der Mensch je erfunden hat. Er verschleudert nicht nur die natürlichen Ressourcen unseres Planeten, sondern verursacht auch enorme soziale Kosten. Ein Plädoyer für das Ende eines verhängnisvollen Wirtschaftsmodells. *Von Susan George*

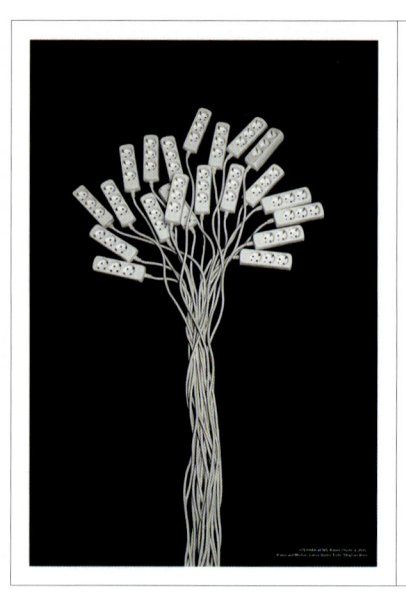

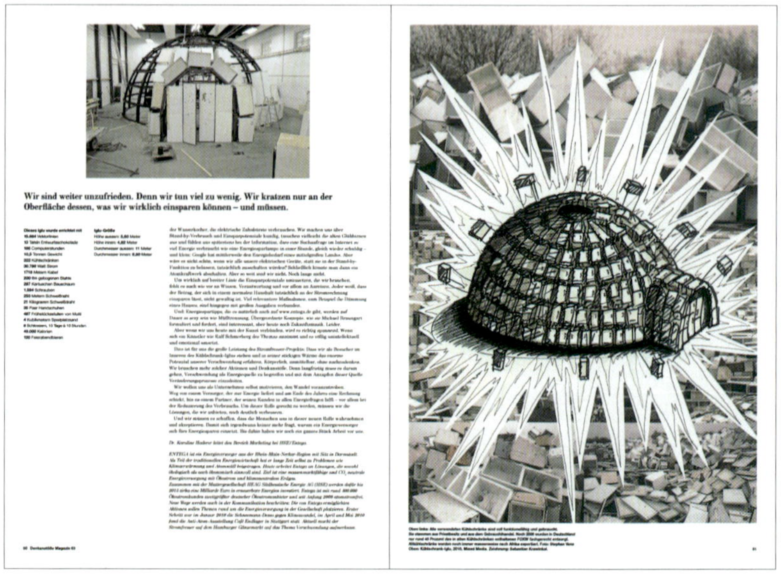

Energie, Gesellschaft und Wandel
denkanstöße
ermöglicht von
entega
Energie der nächsten Generation
DOSSIER
Standhaft nur in stetem Wandel?
Gespräche über Gesellschaft und Veränderung
In dieser Woche:
Der Künstler Johannes Stüttgen
KULTUR
Verschwendung als Stütze der Gesellschaft?
Ein Beitrag zur Kulturgeschichte der Verschwendung
mehr Artikel
GESELLSCHAFT
Religion und Umweltethik
Teil 2: Über buddhistische, hinduistische und daoistische
MAGAZIN 3 2 1
DENKANSTÖSSE MAGAZIN 03
VERSCHWENDUNG
IST DIE GRÖSSTE ENERGIEQUELLE
VIDEOS
UTOPIA KONFERENZ
Utopia Konferenz 2010
... mehr
DENKANSTOSS NR. 3
Der "Stromfresser"
... mehr
TABLE OF FREE VOICES ON RELIGION
Table of Free Voices über Natur, Ökonomie und Religion
... mehr

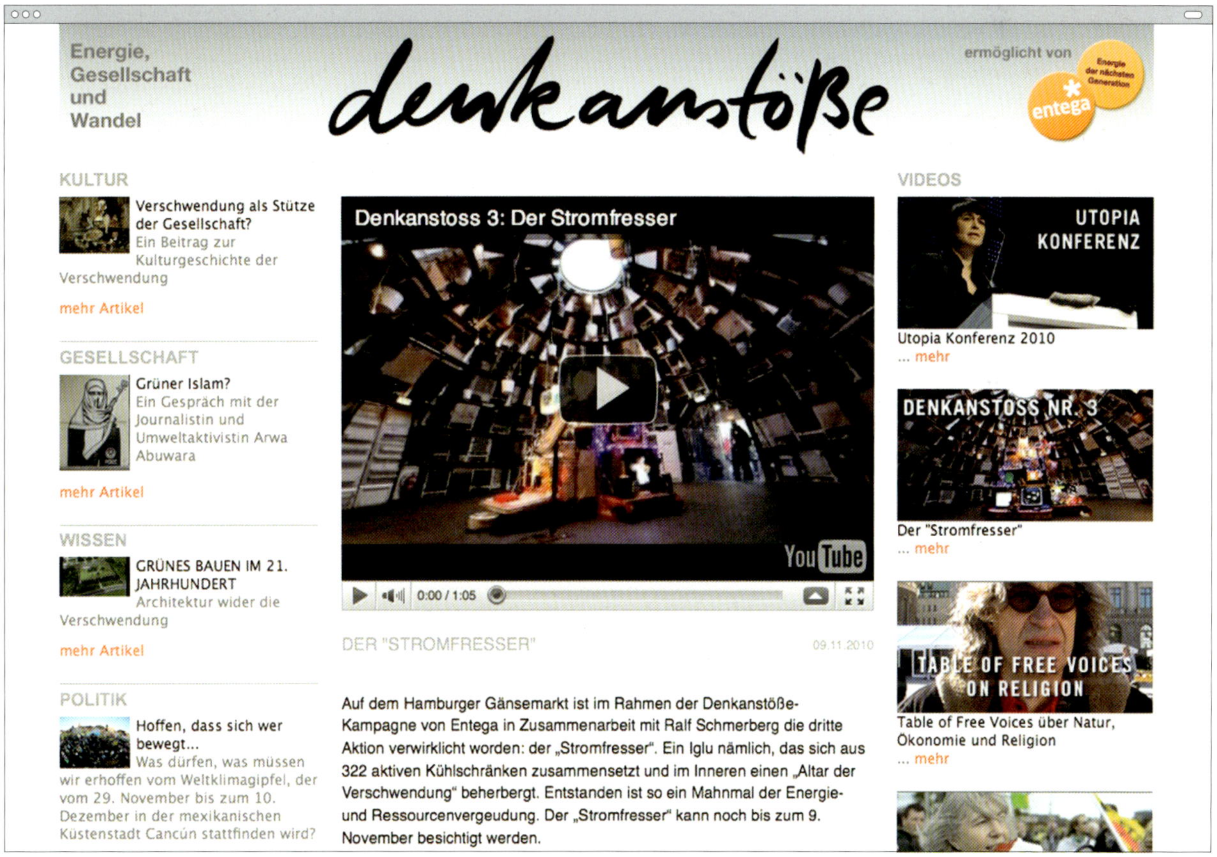
Energie, Gesellschaft und Wandel
denkanstöße
ermöglicht von
entega
Energie der nächsten Generation
KULTUR
Verschwendung als Stütze der Gesellschaft?
Ein Beitrag zur Kulturgeschichte der Verschwendung
mehr Artikel
GESELLSCHAFT
Grüner Islam?
Ein Gespräch mit der Journalistin und Umweltaktivistin Arwa Abuwara
mehr Artikel
WISSEN
GRÜNES BAUEN IM 21. JAHRHUNDERT
Architektur wider die Verschwendung
mehr Artikel
POLITIK
Hoffen, dass sich wer bewegt...
Was dürfen, was müssen wir erhoffen vom Weltklimagipfel, der vom 29. November bis zum 10. Dezember in der mexikanischen Küstenstadt Cancún stattfinden wird?
Denkanstoss 3: Der Stromfresser
YouTube
0:00 / 1:05
DER "STROMFRESSER"
09.11.2010
Auf dem Hamburger Gänsemarkt ist im Rahmen der Denkanstöße-Kampagne von Entega in Zusammenarbeit mit Ralf Schmerberg die dritte Aktion verwirklicht worden: der „Stromfresser". Ein Iglu nämlich, das sich aus 322 aktiven Kühlschränken zusammensetzt und im Inneren einen „Altar der Verschwendung" beherbergt. Entstanden ist so ein Mahnmal der Energie- und Ressourcenvergeudung. Der „Stromfresser" kann noch bis zum 9. November besichtigt werden.
VIDEOS
UTOPIA KONFERENZ
Utopia Konferenz 2010
... mehr
DENKANSTOSS NR. 3
Der "Stromfresser"
... mehr
TABLE OF FREE VOICES ON RELIGION
Table of Free Voices über Natur, Ökonomie und Religion
... mehr

38

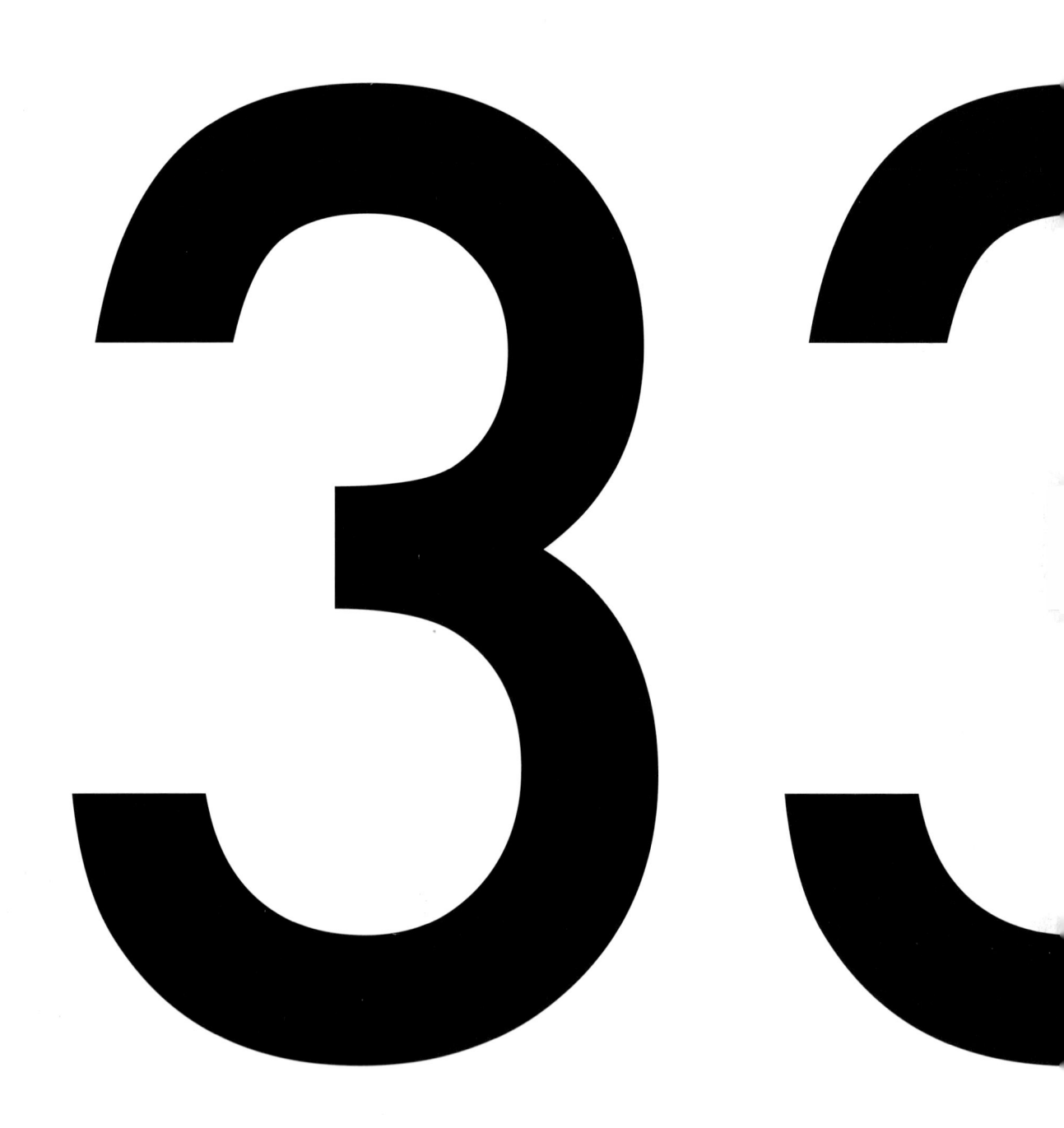

PUNKTE
POINTS

GOLD
KLASSISCHE MEDIEN
CLASSICAL MEDIA
  Film
  TV/Kino Einzelspot
  Film
  TV/Cinema Commercial

SILVER
KLASSISCHE MEDIEN
CLASSICAL MEDIA
  Film Craft
  Schnitt
  Film Craft
  Cutting

SILVER
KLASSISCHE MEDIEN
CLASSICAL MEDIA
  Film
  TV/Kino Kampagne
  Film
  TV/Cinema Campaign

BRONZE
KLASSISCHE MEDIEN
CLASSICAL MEDIA
  Film Craft
  Regie
  Film Craft
  Film Direction

BRONZE
KLASSISCHE MEDIEN
CLASSICAL MEDIA
  Film Craft
  Kamera
  Film Craft
  Camera

BRONZE
CRAFT
CRAFT
  Musik und Sound
  Music and Sound

NOMINATION
KLASSISCHE MEDIEN
CLASSICAL MEDIA
  Print
  Kampagne
  Print
  Campaign

NOMINATION
KLASSISCHE MEDIEN
CLASSICAL MEDIA
  Out-of-Home
  Klassisch Kampagne
  Out-of-Home
  Classic Campaign

HORNBACH BAUMARKT
KAMPAGNE
  »Wieviel Wahnsinn steckt in Dir?«

Lead Agency
  HEIMAT, Berlin
Client
  Hornbach Baumarkt AG
Marketing Direction
  Frank Sahler
Advertising Direction
  Sylvia Späthe
Executive Creative Direction
  Guido Heffels
Creative Direction
  Guido Heffels,
  Matthias Storath
Art Direction
  Hendrik Schweder,
  Teresa Jung,
  Susanna Fill,
  Alexander Stauss
Client Consulting
  Maik Richter,
  Mark Hassan,
  Nicole Varga,
  Daniela Strauss
Strategic Planning
  Matthias von Bechtolsheim
Agency Production
  Kerstin Heffels
Art Buying
  Jessica Valin
Audio Production
  Soundsquare,
  Prague
Camera
  Stepan Kucera
Copy
  Guido Heffels,
  Matthias Storath,
  Mirjam Kundt,
  Kai Abd-EL Salam,
  Laura Müller-Rossbach
Cutting
  Guido Notari@Damaso
  Queirazza, Milan
Film Direction
  Martin Krejci
Film Production
  Stink GmbH, Berlin
Image Processing
  twentyfour seven, Berlin
Media
  Crossmedia, Duesseldorf
Photography
  Daniel Sommer
Production
  Jan Dressler (Executive Production)
Sound Design
  Viktor Ekrt@Soundsquare,
  Prague

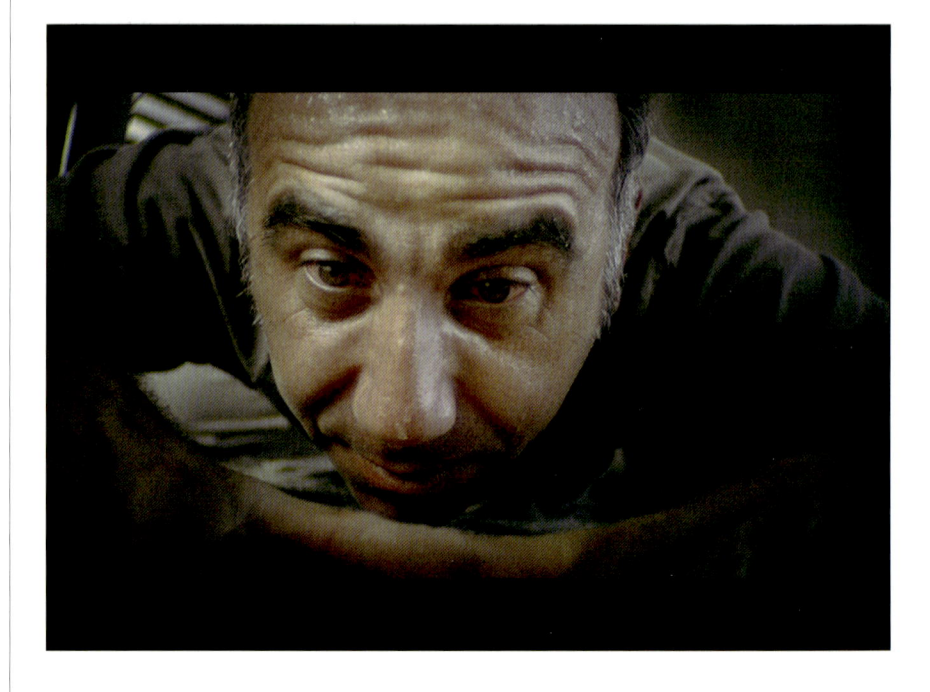

Hornbach "Faces". Der Film dokumentiert die ganze Bandbreite der mit einem echten Projekt einhergehenden Emotionen – von Leidenschaft über Frustration bis Stolz. Zupackend und ehrlich inszeniert in einer künstlerischen Collage aus Close-up-Sequenzen: Entschlossene Gesichter, pulsierende Adern, konzentrierte Blicke und bebende Muskeln. Am Ende steht die Frage: »Wieviel Wahnsinn steckt in Dir?«. Die beiden Filme "Cow" und "Faces" zeigen die Leidenschaft und den Wahnsinn, die Heimwerker brauchen, um auch die ganz großen Projekte umzusetzen.

Hornbach "Faces". The film shows the whole range of emotions that come out of doing real DIY projects: Passion, frustration, pride, joy. Grippingly staged in an artistic montage of close up sequences: Hell-bent facial expressions, pulsating veins, concentrated looks and trembling muscles – ending with the question: "How much madness are you made of?". The two spots "Cow" and "Faces" communicate the passion and the madness every DIY person needs to tackle big projects.

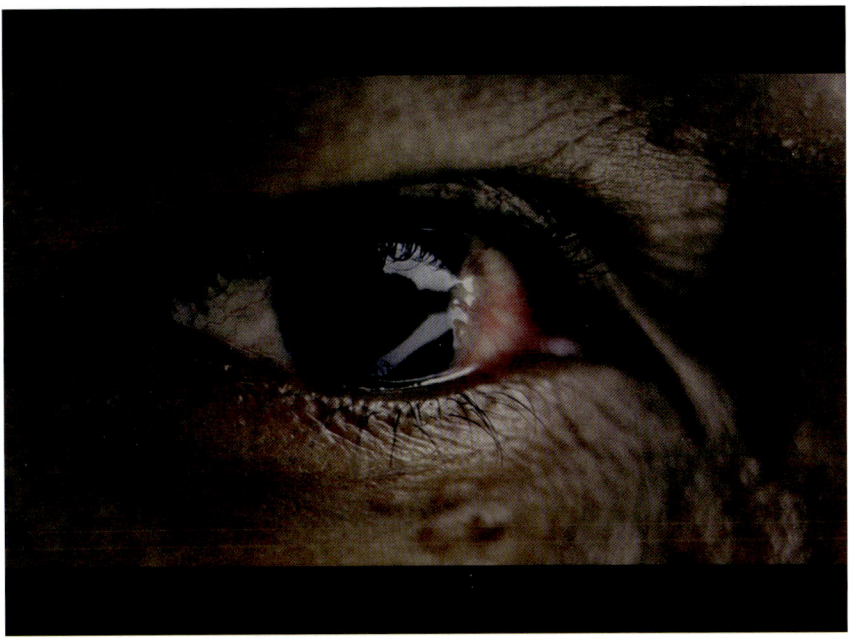

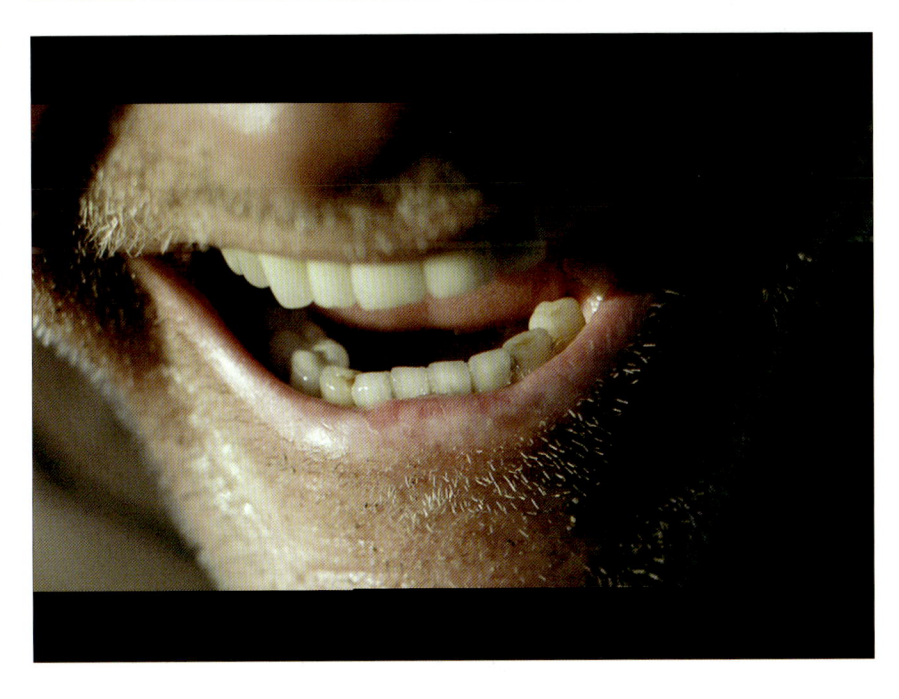

33

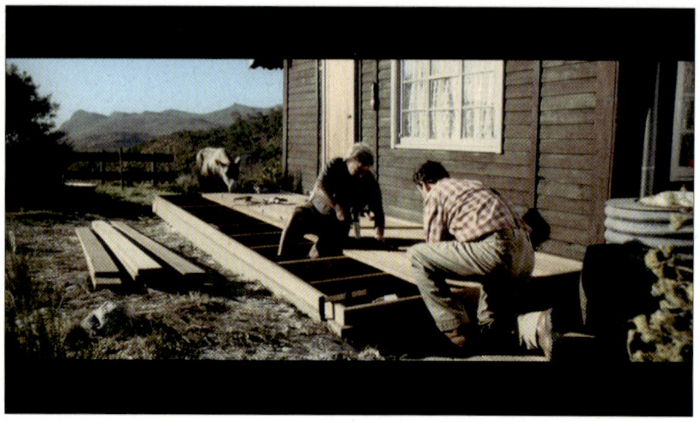

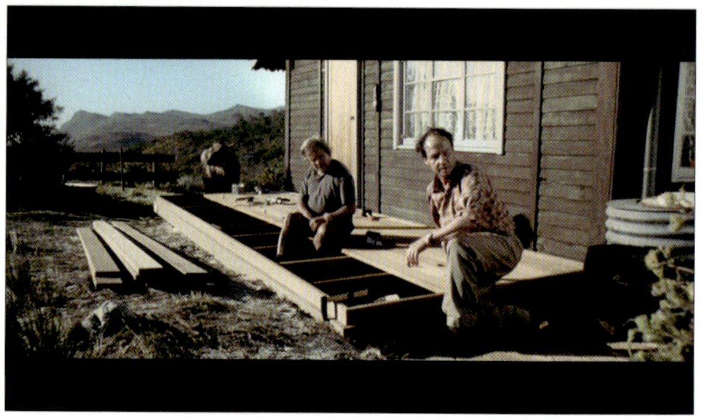

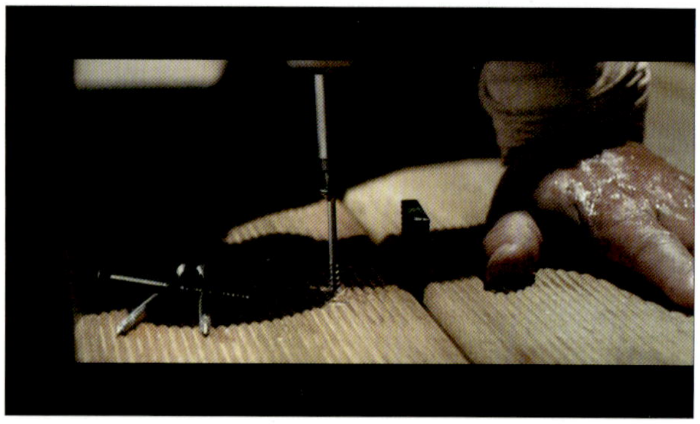

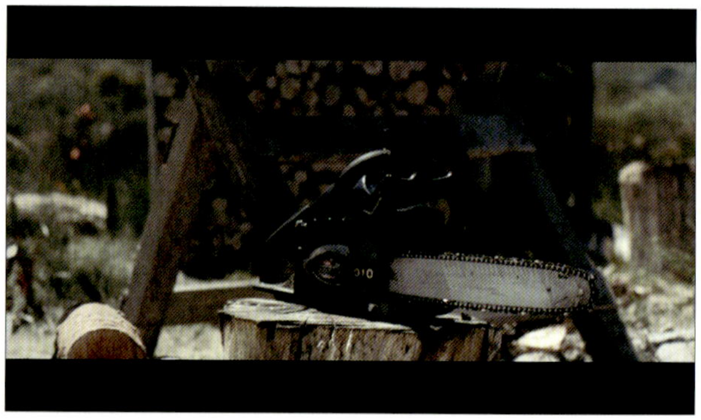

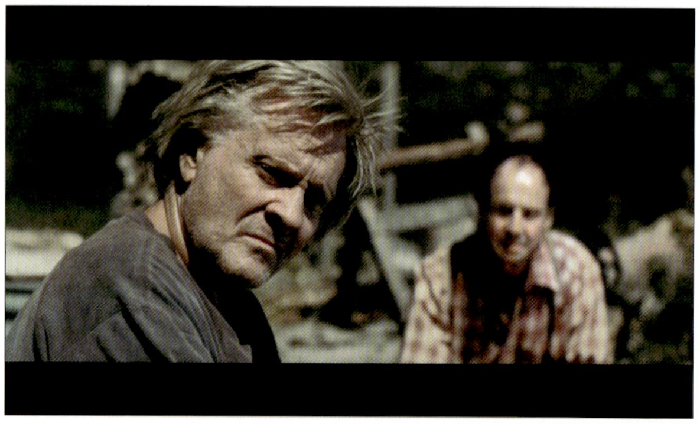

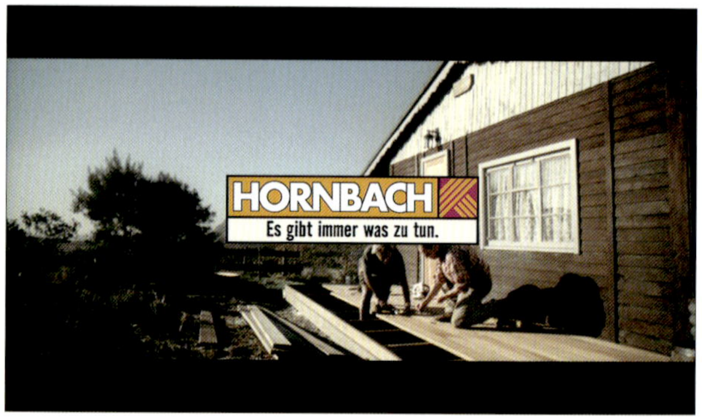

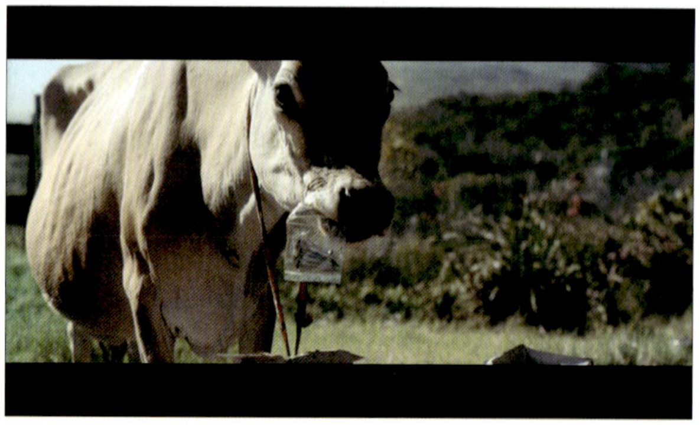

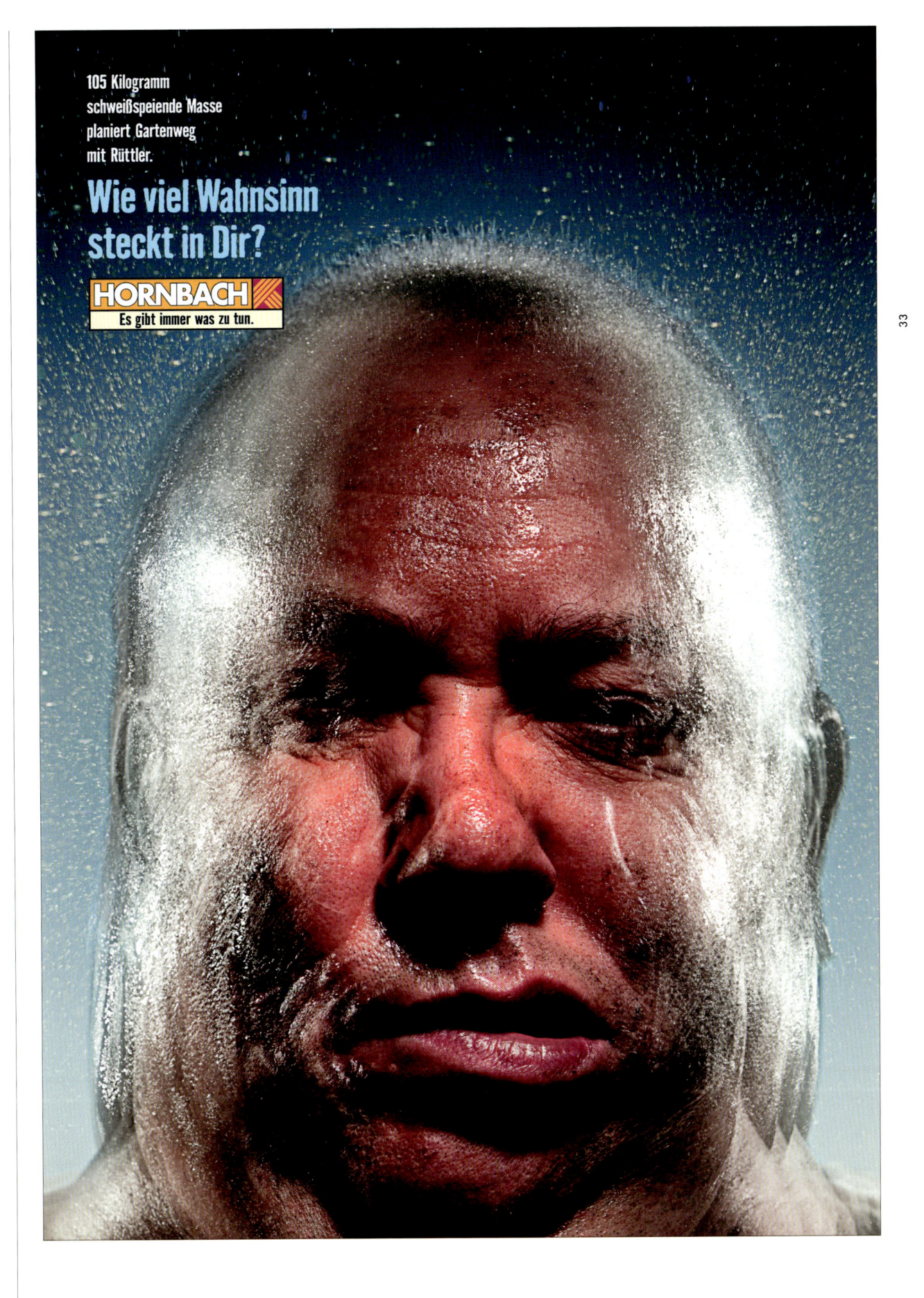

105 Kilogramm
schweißspeiende Masse
planiert Gartenweg
mit Rüttler.

Wie viel Wahnsinn steckt in Dir?

HORNBACH
Es gibt immer was zu tun.

25

PUNKTE
POINTS

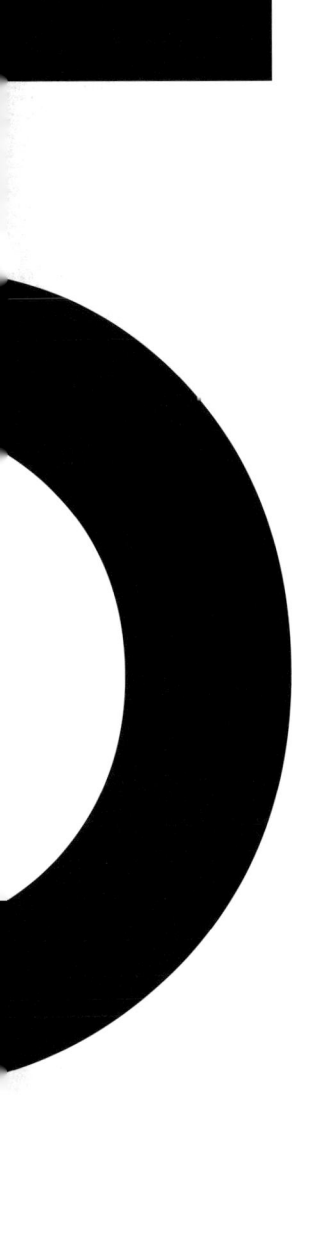

GOLD
DIGITALE MEDIEN
DIGITAL MEDIA
  Digitale Medien Craft
  Motiondesign
  Digital Media Craft
  Motion Design

SILVER
DIGITALE MEDIEN
DIGITAL MEDIA
  Digitale Medien Craft
  Interface/Navigation
  Digital Media Craft
  Interface/Navigation

SILVER
DIGITALE MEDIEN
DIGITAL MEDIA
  Digitale Medien
  Microsites
  Digital Media
  Microsites

BRONZE
DIGITALE MEDIEN
DIGITAL MEDIA
  Digitale Medien Craft
  Sounddesign
  Digital Media Craft
  Sound Design

MULTIPACK
  "Hidden Heroes"

Lead Agency
  Grimm Gallun Holtappels
  Werbeagentur GmbH & Co. KG
Contributing Agencies
  Büro Rempen GmbH
  (Prof. Thomas Rempen,
  Uwe Stoklossa)
Client
  Hi-Cone, a division of ITW
  ESPAÑA, S.A.
Marketing Direction
  Hans-Jürgen Meyer
Advertising Direction
  Hans-Jürgen Meyer
Executive Creative Direction
  Florian Grimm,
  Nils Gallun
Creative Direction
  Matthias M. Müller
Art Direction
  Matthias M. Müller,
  Tobias Mausolf
Client Consulting
  Torben Erhorn, Ute Klemp
Audio Production
  BLUWI Music and Sound
  Design
Design
  Pascal Czerlinski
Graphic Design
  Matthias M. Müller,
  Tobias Mausolf,
  Pascal Czerlinski,
  Ole Warns,
  Christian Rieger,
  Alexander Milde
Interface/Navigation
  Matthias M. Müller,
  Matthias Schulz
Motion Design
  Matthias Schulz
Programming
  Matthias Schulz
Sound Design
  BLUWI

Die Ausstellung »Heimliche Helden. Das Genie alltäglicher Dinge« des Vitra Design Museums in Kooperation mit Hi-Cone beschäftigt sich mit der Geschichte und den Geschichten der Alltagshelden. Die parallel entwickelte Website präsentiert ein neues mediengerechtes Interface für eine Ausstellung im Internet und greift dabei das Raumerlebnis durch überraschende Wechsel zwischen 2 D und 3 D auf.

The exhibition "Hidden Heroes. The genius of everyday things" of the Vitra Design Museum in cooperation with Hi-Cone is devoted to the history and stories behind everyday objects. The website designed parallel to this presents a new, media-oriented interface for an exhibition on the Internet, continuing the experience of space with surprising alternation of 2 D and 3 D.

FLIP-FLOPS

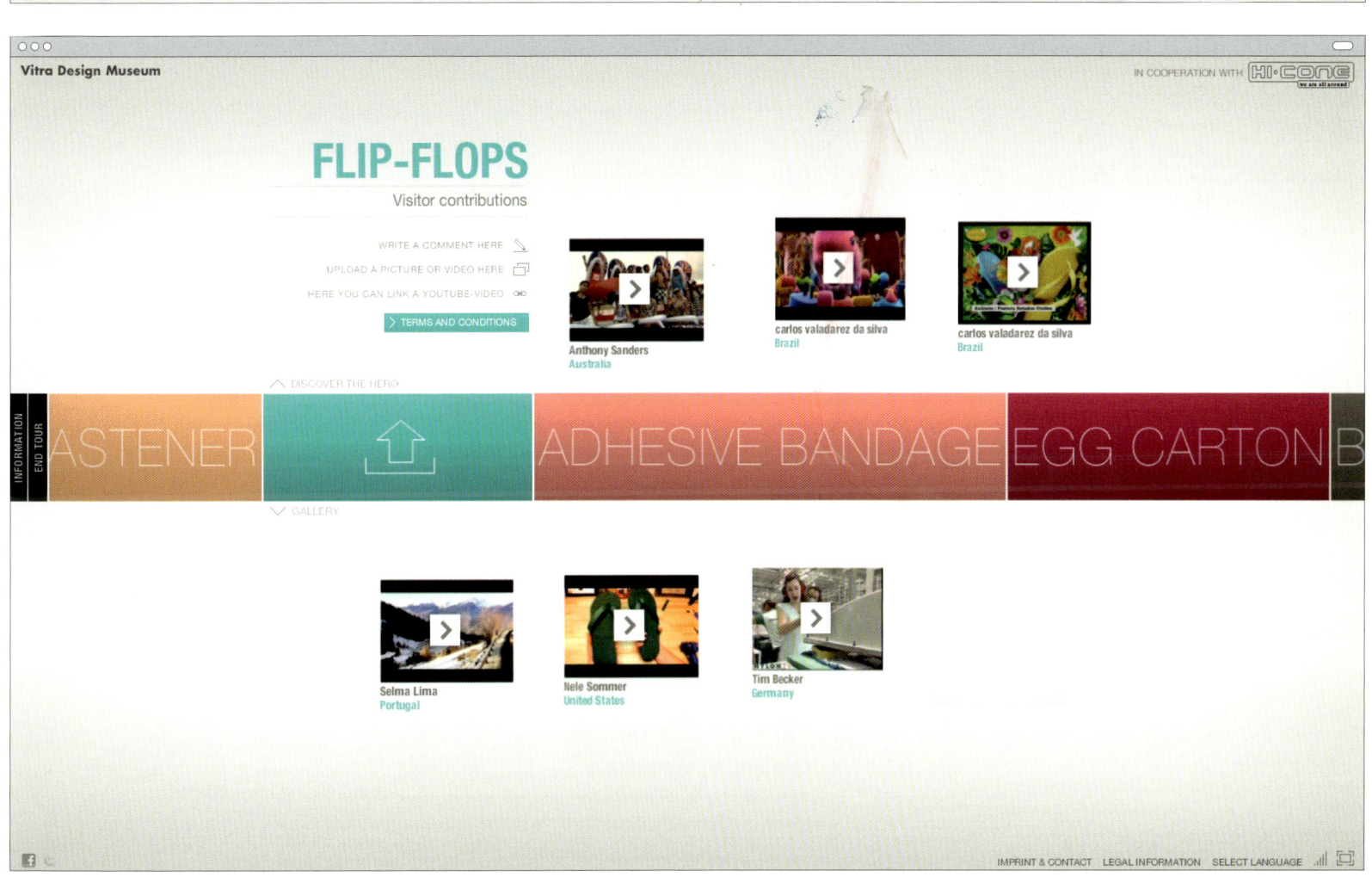

Visitor contributions

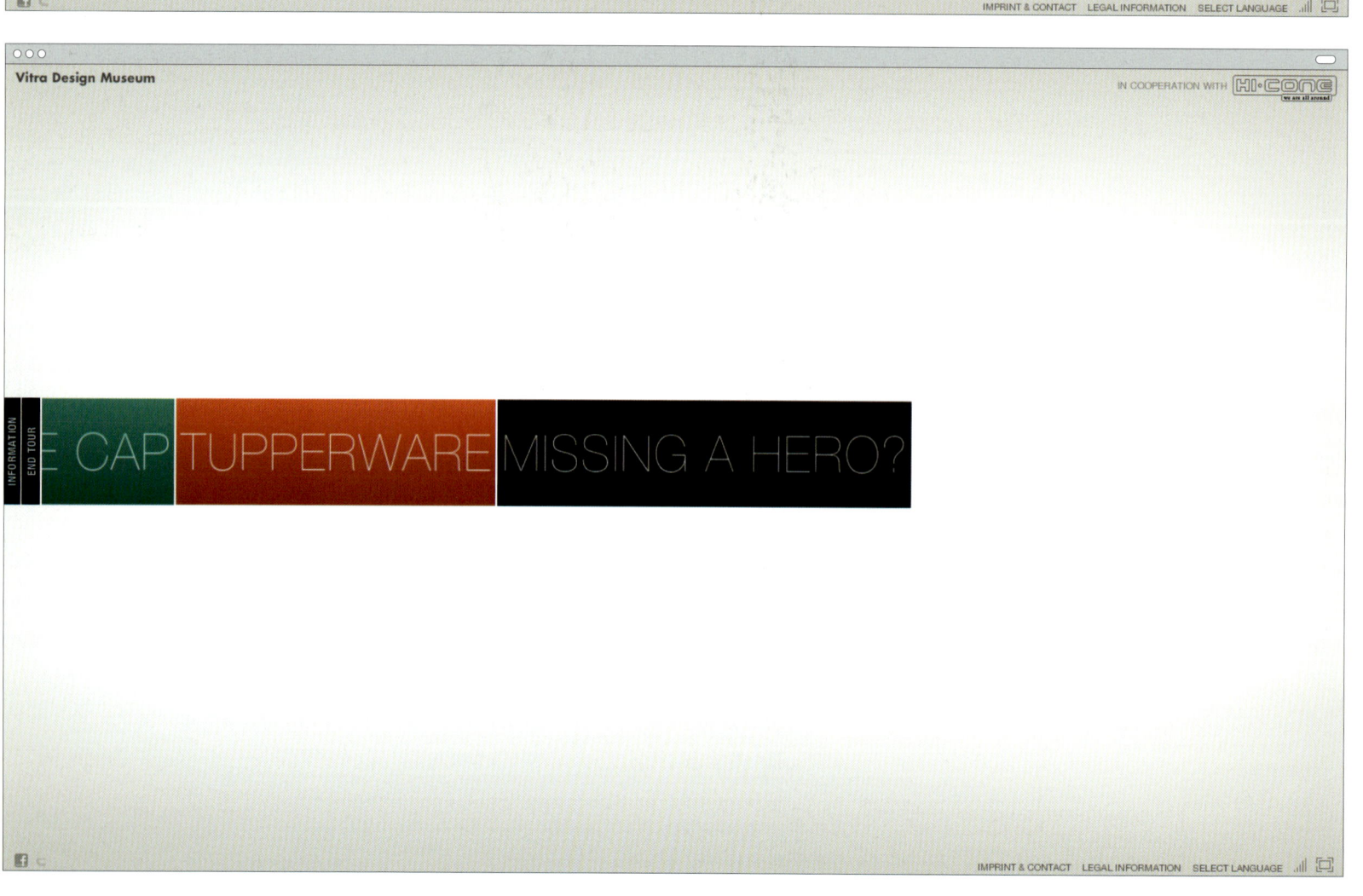

Vitra Design Museum

IN COOPERATION WITH HI·CONE

OVERVIEW

BANDAGE   TISSUE ZIP

INFORMATION
END TOUR

VISITOR CONTRIBUTIONS

IMPRINT & CONTACT   LEGAL INFORMATION   SELECT LANGUAGE

Vitra Design Museum

IN COOPERATION WITH HI·CONE

INFORMATION
END TOUR

E CAP TUPPERWARE MISSING A HERO?

IMPRINT & CONTACT   LEGAL INFORMATION   SELECT LANGUAGE

25

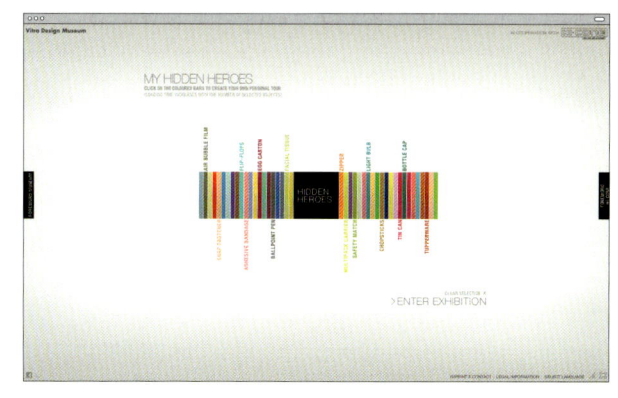

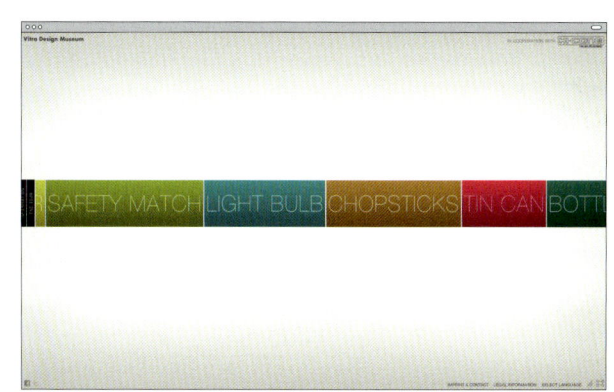

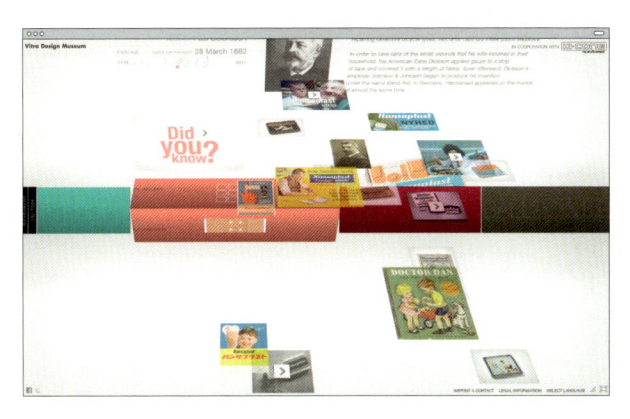

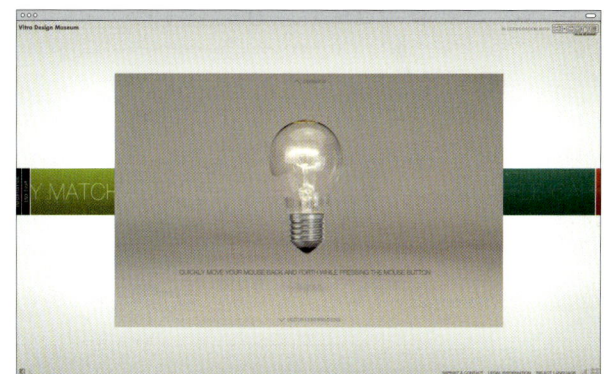

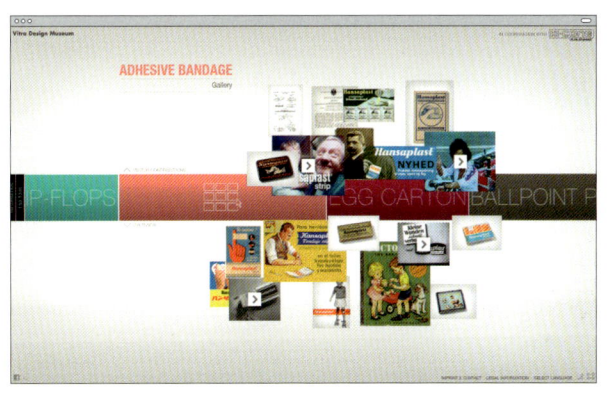

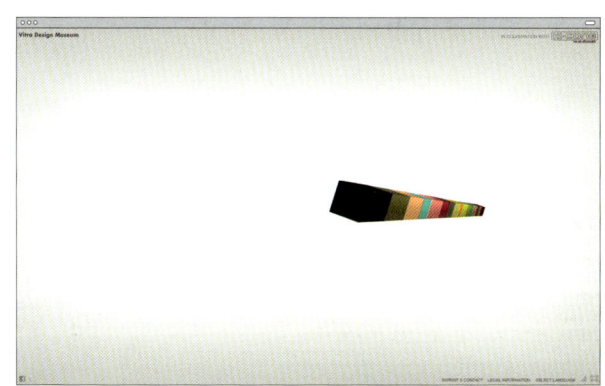

24

PUNKTE
POINTS

GOLD
KLASSISCHE MEDIEN
CLASSICAL MEDIA
- Out-of-Home
- Klassisch Kampagne
- Out-of-Home
- Classic Campaign

SILVER
KLASSISCHE MEDIEN
CLASSICAL MEDIA
- Print
- Kampagne
- Print
- Campaign

BRONZE
KLASSISCHE MEDIEN
CLASSICAL MEDIA
- Out-of-Home
- Klassisch Einzelmotiv
- Out-of-Home
- Classic Single Motif

BRONZE
CRAFT
CRAFT
- Text
- Copy

NOMINATION
DESIGN
DESIGN
- Design
- Grafische Einzelarbeiten
- Design
- Individual Graphics

NOMINATION
CRAFT
CRAFT
- Text
- Copy

BIONADE
»Fragen im Raum«

Lead Agency
  Kolle Rebbe GmbH
Client
  BIONADE GmbH
Marketing Direction
  Wolfgang Blum
Creative Direction
  Stefan Wübbe,
  Rolf Leger
Art Direction
  Rolf Leger,
  Jörg Dittmann,
  Thomas Knüwer,
  Michael Füsslin
Client Consulting
  Inken Schulz
Strategic Planning
  Dominic Veken
Art Buying
  Katrin Grün
Copy
  Stefan Wübbe,
  Florian Ludwig,
  Bijan Farsijani,
  Oliver Ramm,
  Ansgar Böhme,
  Sascha Petersen
Final Artwork
  Maik Spreen
Idea
  Stefan Wübbe
Image Processing
  recom GmbH & Co. KG
Photography
  Packshot:
  Oliver Schwarzwald,
  Forest Motive:
  Michael Schnabel
Printing
  Ellerhold Witten GmbH
Production
  Martin Lühe

Bionade bleibt dabei, nicht über das Produkt, sondern über eine Lebenshaltung für die Marke zu werben. 2010 stellt Bionade Fragen in den Raum. Genauer gesagt in die Natur. Es sind Fragen zu unserem Leben, unserer Gesellschaft und unserer Umwelt. Die Kampagne ist ein Statement für das Nachdenken – gegen die Gedankenlosigkeit.

Contrary to all expectations, the campaign strategy Bionade adopted in 2010 stuck to using values and lifestyles – not products – to advertise the brand. Bionade throws out questions in the room. Or, to be more precise, into nature. Questions about our lives and our attitude to society, nature and the environment. The campaign is a declaration of reflection – and against thoughtlessness.

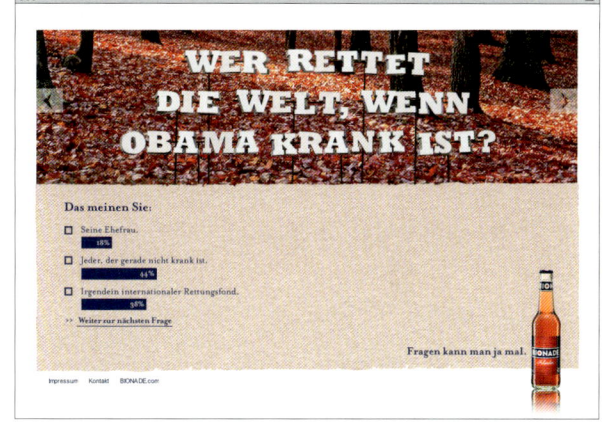

GOLD
DIALOGMARKETING/
PROMOTION/MEDIA
DIALOG MARKETING/
PROMOTION/MEDIA
  Media
  Media

SILVER
DIALOGMARKETING/
PROMOTION/MEDIA
DIALOG MARKETING/
PROMOTION/MEDIA
  Promotion
  Aktivitäten
  Promotion
  Activities

BRONZE
GANZHEITLICHE
KOMMUNIKATION
INTEGRATED CAMPAIGNS
  Ganzheitliche Kommunikation
  Integrated Campaigns

BRONZE
DIALOGMARKETING/
PROMOTION/MEDIA
DIALOG MARKETING/
PROMOTION/MEDIA
  Dialogmarketing
  Dialog Crossmediale
  Kampagnen
  Dialog Marketing
  Dialog Cross-Media
  Campaigns

NOMINATION
KLASSISCHE MEDIEN
CLASSICAL MEDIA
  Film
  Filme für Verkaufsförderung
  Film
  TV/Sales Promotion Films

NOMINATION
KLASSISCHE MEDIEN
CLASSICAL MEDIA
  Audio
  Innovative Nutzung von Audio
  Audio
  Innovative Use of Audio

KONZERTHAUS DORTMUND
SAISONFILM 2010|2011
»Konzertmilch«

Lead Agency
  Jung von Matt AG
Contributing Agencies
  Jung von Matt/Elbe GmbH
Client
  Konzerthaus Dortmund GmbH
Marketing Direction
  Anne-Katrin Röhm
Executive Creative Direction
  Sascha Hanke
Creative Direction
  Tobias Grimm,
  Jens Pfau,
  Jo Marie Farwick
Art Direction
  Damjan Pita
Client Consulting
  Jochen Schwarz,
  Dajana Crantz,
  Marijke Fisser
Strategic Planning
  Liane Siebenhaar
Agency Production
  Meike van Meegen
Audio Production
  Infected Postproduction GmbH
Camera
  Silvio Helbig
Consulting
  Mhoch4 GmbH & Co. KG
Copy
  Henning Robert,
  Jan-Hendrik Scholz
Cutting
  Tobias Suhm,
  Niels Münter
Film Direction
  Silvio Helbig
Film Production
  Markenfilm GmbH & Co. KG
Graphic Design
  Sven Gabriel,
  Christoph Mäder,
  Nicolas Schmidt-Fitzner
Music Composition
  Joseph Haydn
Postproduction
  Infected Postproduction GmbH,
  VCC Agency für Postproduction
Production
  Johannes Bittel,
  Claudia Westermann,
  Markenfilm GmbH & Co. KG
Sound Engineering
  Mikis Meyer
Other
  Production: Johannes Bittel,
  Claudia Westermann
  Direction: Benedikt Stampa

Wir machten den Menschen die neue Saison im Konzerthaus Dortmund auf außergewöhnliche Weise schmackhaft: mit Milch. Es ist wissenschaftlich erwiesen, dass Klassik die Milchproduktion von Kühen positiv beeinflusst. Deshalb spielten wir Kühen die Musik der neuen Saison vor und brachten die Milch als »Konzertmilch Dortmund« in den Handel. Musik zum Schmecken – so hat man Klassik noch nie erlebt.

We're getting people interested in the Dortmund Concert Hall's new season in an unusual way: with milk. It's scientifically proven that classical music has a positive impact on cows' milk production. That's why we played the music from the new season to cows and then sold their milk as "Dortmund Concert Milk". Music you can taste – you've never experienced classical music like this before.

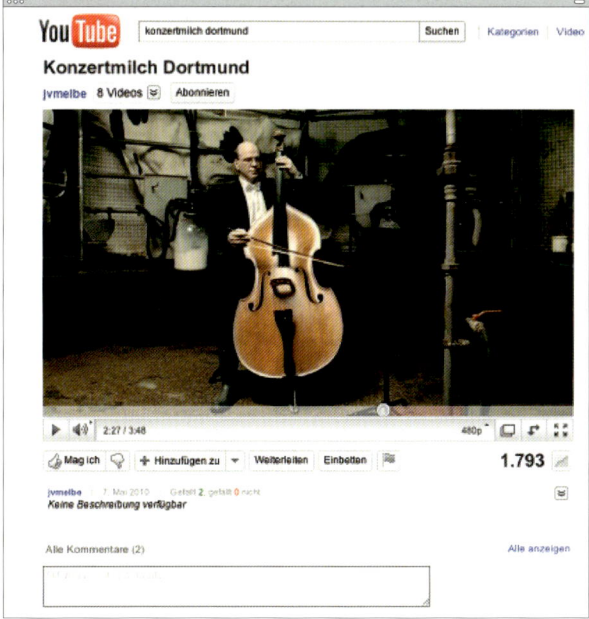

●
GOLD
KLASSISCHE MEDIEN
CLASSICAL MEDIA
  Audio
  Radio Einzelspot
  Audio
  Radio Commercial

●
SILVER
KLASSISCHE MEDIEN
CLASSICAL MEDIA
  Audio
  Radio Kampagne
  Audio
  Radio Campaign

●
BRONZE
KLASSISCHE MEDIEN
CLASSICAL MEDIA
  Audio
  Radio Einzelspot
  Audio
  Radio Commercial

●
BRONZE
KLASSISCHE MEDIEN
CLASSICAL MEDIA
  Audio
  Radio Einzelspot
  Audio
  Radio Commercial

●
NOMINATION
KLASSISCHE MEDIEN
CLASSICAL MEDIA
  Audio Craft
  Regie
  Audio Craft
  Radio Direction

●
NOMINATION
CRAFT
CRAFT
  Musik und Sound
  Music and Sound

MODERN MUSIC SCHOOL
KAMPAGNE
  »Talent«

Lead Agency
  Grabarz & Partner
Client
  Modern Music School
Marketing Direction
  Hans-Peter Becker
Executive Creative Direction
  Ralf Heuel
Creative Direction
  Ralf Heuel
Client Consulting
  Ina Bach,
  Nils Rüsenberg
  Executive Direction Consulting:
  Thomas Eickhoff
Audio Production
  Studio Funk,
  Hamburg
Copy
  Ralf Heuel,
  Christian Möhler,
  Verena Bartholdt,
  Heiner Twenhäfel
Radio Direction
  Torsten Hennings,
  Ralf Heuel
Radio Production
  Studio Funk,
  Hamburg
Sound Design
  Supreme Music,
  Studio Funk, Hamburg
Sound Engineering
  Torsten Hennings
Other
  Record Label:
  Supreme Music
  Music Composition:
  Supreme Music
  Publishing House:
  Edition So Supreme,
  Emi Music Publishing

Für die Modern Music School entwickelten wir eine Funkkampagne, die humorvoll zeigt, dass in manchen Menschen viel musikalisches Talent steckt. Jeder Spot beginnt mit einer Szene, in der wir eine Person in einer konkreten Situation erleben. Exakt dieselbe Szene spielt sich dann nochmals ab, allerdings mit instrumentaler Unterstützung. Das Ergebnis ist eine absolut bühnenreife Performance.

We developed a radio campaign for the Modern Music School that shows in a humorous way how much musical talent lies undiscovered in so many people. Each ad begins with a scene in which listeners are introduced to a person in a particular situation. Precisely the same scene is then repeated, but this time with instrumental backing. The result is a performance that is absolutely stage-worthy.

AUDIO

DER FUNKSPOT »TRENNUNG«.

SFX:
Schulhofatmosphäre.

JUNGER MANN, LÄSSIG:
»Hi Ina: Ich wollt' dir nur sagen. Ich hab mich in 'ne andere verknallt. Es ist Schluss!«

JUNGE FRAU, WEINERLICH:
»Das kannst du doch nicht machen, wir sind vier Jahre zusammen … Ich liebe dich doch so … und … DU BIST SO GEMEIN!«

OFF, TROCKEN:
»Du hast viel mehr Talent als du denkst.«

SFX:
Wir hören Deutschrock à la Silbermond. Dazu genau den Text der jungen Frau von oben: »Das kannst du doch nicht machen, wir sind vier Jahre zusammen … Ich liebe dich doch so … und … DU BIST SO GEMEIN!«

OFF, TROCKEN:
»Komm zur Modern Music School. Über 60 Mal in Deutschland. www.modernmusicschool.de.«

DER FUNKSPOT »TANNENBAUM«.

SFX:
> Winter, im Wald.

(JUNGE FRAU, HILFLOS:)
> »Schatz, weißt du wirklich, wie man mit so einer Kettensäge umgeht? Wir könnten den Tannenbaum doch sonst auch einfach im Baumarkt kaufen ...?«

JUNGER MANN, LÄSSIG:
> »Kleines, echte Männer sägen so ein Bäumchen selbst!«

SFX:
> Kettensäge wird angeworfen. Wir hören ein bisschen Sägen, dann wie die Kettensäge abrutscht und der Mann sich in den Fuß sägt. Dann den sehr lauten Schrei des Mannes: »Aaaaaaaaahhhhhhhhhhhh!«

JUNGE FRAU, ERSCHROCKEN:
> »Oh Gott!«

DER JUNGE MAN FLUCHT SCHMERZERFÜLLT:
> »Fuuuuck! Fuuuuuuuuck! Fuuuuuuuuuuck!«

OFF, TROCKEN:
> »Du hast viel mehr Talent als du denkst.«

SFX:
> Wir hören laute gitarrenlastige Heavy-Metal-Musik. Dazu ertönt exakt der gleiche Schrei von gerade noch mal:
> »Aaaaaaaaahhhhhhhhhhhh! Fuuuuck! Fuuuuuuuuck! Fuuuuuuuuuuck!«

OFF, TROCKEN:
> »Komm zur Modern Music School. Über 60 Mal in Deutschland. www.modernmusicschool.de.«

DER FUNKSPOT »WANDERN«.

(SFX:)
    Naturatmosphäre, Bergidylle.

(JUNGER MANN, FRUSTRIERT:)
    »Ah Mist, ich wette, genau an dieser Weggabelung waren wir schon mal.«

(JUNGE FRAU:)
    »Na klasse! Bergwandern – tolle Idee von dir. Es wird dunkel und mir ist kalt.«

(JUNGER MANN:)
    »Warte mal! … (er ruft laut, Echo) … Hallllooooo? Ist da jemannnnd? Kann uns irgend jemand höööören?«

(OFF, TROCKEN:)
    »Du hast viel mehr Talent als Du denkst.«

(SFX:)
    Wir hören stumpfen Techno à la Scooter. Dazu genau den Text des jungen Mannes von oben, mit genau dem gleichen Echo: »Hallllooooo? Ist da jemannnnd? Kann uns irgend jemand höööören? Halloooo? Ist da jemannnnd? …«

(OFF, TROCKEN:)
    »Komm zur Modern Music School. Über 60 Mal in Deutschland. www.modernmusicschool.de.«

22

PUNKTE
POINTS

● GOLD
KLASSISCHE MEDIEN
CLASSICAL MEDIA
  Out-of-Home
  Klassisch Einzelmotiv
  Out-of-Home
  Classic Single Motif

● SILVER
DIALOGMARKETING/
PROMOTION/MEDIA
DIALOG MARKETING/
PROMOTION/MEDIA
  Media
  Media

● BRONZE
KLASSISCHE MEDIEN
CLASSICAL MEDIA
  Out-of-Home
  Nicht-Klassisch
  Out-of-Home
  Non-Classic

● BRONZE
CRAFT
CRAFT
  Typografie
  Typography

BMW M3 COUPÉ
  »Die BMW Lightwall
  ›Reflexion‹«

Lead Agency
  serviceplan
Client
  BMW AG Deutschland
Marketing Direction
  Manfred Bräunl
Advertising Direction
  Dr. Hans-Peter Ketterl
Executive Creative Direction
  Alexander Schill
Creative Direction
  Maik Kaehler,
  Christoph Nann
Art Direction
  Roman Becker,
  Savina Mokreva,
  Manuel Wolff
Client Consulting
  Michael Falkensteiner
Copy
  Andreas Schriewer
Typography
  Andreas Schriewer

Für das BMW M3 Coupé, ein Auto, das über Grenzen hinausgeht, entwickelten wir ein Poster, das über Grenzen hinausgeht. Wir schrieben eine Headline mit halben Buchstaben – erst durch ihre Reflexion auf dem glänzenden Steinboden wird sie vollständig. Das Ergebnis: doppelte Mediafläche und doppelte Aufmerksamkeit – kostenlos.

For the BMW M3 coupé, a car that exceeds limits, we created a billboard that exceeds limits. We designed a headline out of half letters. To complete them we used their reflection on the shiny floor. The result: we doubled the media space for free. We doubled the attention for free.

SILVER
GANZHEITLICHE KOMMUNI-
KATION
INTEGRATED CAMPAIGNS
  Ganzheitliche Kommunikation
  Integrated Campaigns

SILVER
DIALOGMARKETING/
PROMOTION/MEDIA
DIALOG MARKETING/
PROMOTION/MEDIA
  Promotion
  Aktivitäten
  Promotion
  Activities

BRONZE
DIALOGMARKETING/
PROMOTION/MEDIA
DIALOG MARKETING/
PROMOTION/MEDIA
  Dialogmarketing
  Dialog Mobile Marketing
  Dialog Marketing
  Dialog Mobile Marketing

BRONZE
DIGITALE MEDIEN
DIGITAL MEDIA
  Digitale Medien
  Social Media
  Digital Media
  Social Media

BRONZE
DIALOGMARKETING/
PROMOTION/MEDIA
DIALOG MARKETING/
PROMOTION/MEDIA
  Dialogmarketing
  Dialog Crossmediale
  Kampagnen
  Dialog Marketing
  Dialog Cross-Media
  Campaigns

NOMINATION
DIGITALE MEDIEN
DIGITAL MEDIA
  Digitale Medien
  Digitale Kampagnen
  Digital Media
  Digital Campaigns

INITIATIVE VERMISSTE KINDER
»Deutschland findet euch«

Lead Agency
  kempertrautmann gmbh
Contributing Agencies
  fischerappelt AG,
  Blue Mars GmbH
Client
  Initiative vermisste Kinder
Marketing Direction
  Lars Bruhns
Creative Direction
  Marcell Francke,
  Patrick Matthiensen
Art Direction
  Leif Johannsen,
  Bruno Luglio
Client Consulting
  Marcell Francke,
  Patrick Matthiensen
Concept
  Marcell Francke,
  Leif Johannsen,
  Patrick Matthiensen,
  Sebastian Merget,
  Stefan Walz
Consulting
  Carolin Panier,
  Biljana Retzlek,
  Moritz Fürste,
  Dorothea Feurer
Copy
  Sebastian Merget
Graphic Design
  Bruno Luglio,
  Leif Johannsen,
  Patrick Schroer
Idea
  Marcell Francke,
  Patrick Matthiensen,
  Leif Johannsen,
  Sebastian Merget
Interactive Production
  Mathias Muck
Production
  cmp, Alexander Kate
Programming
  Blue Mars GmbH,
  Thomas Kiesl
Technical Conception
  Blue Mars GmbH
Technical Implementation
  Blue Mars GmbH
Other
  Processing: nhb video GmbH

Jedes Jahr werden in Deutschland mehr als 100.000 Kinder als vermisst gemeldet. Um die Suche schneller und effizienter zu machen, starteten wir für die »Initiative Vermisste Kinder« eine einzigartige Suchaktion: »Deutschland findet euch«. Um die größte Suchmannschaft Deutschlands aufzubauen, nutzten wir die Kraft des populärsten Social Networks der Welt: Facebook. Zur mobilen Unterstützung der Suchenden entwickelten wir zusätzlich die »Vermisst«-App. Diverse medienübergreifende Maßnahmen vergrößerten die Plattform und machten sie schlagkräftiger. Der Kick-off: Beim Spiel FC Bayern München vs. Real Madrid betraten die Spieler das Feld, wie gewohnt mit einem Kind an der Hand. Bis auf einen: er hielt stattdessen das Bild eines vermissten Kindes.

Every year, more than 100,000 children are reported missing in Germany. On behalf of »Initiative Vermisste Kinder«, we launched the campaign »Deutschland findet euch« (Germany will find you), where everybody can play an active role in the search. By using a range of tools, we raised awareness for the campaign and brought together a search party. To get as many people involved as possible, we created a Facebook page, which we promoted through diverse digital channels, and developed Germany's first mobile search tool for finding missing children: the »Vermisst« App. The kick-off: FC Bayern Munich vs Real Madrid. As always, the players ran onto the pitch, each accompanied by a child. Except for one, who carried a picture of a missing child instead.

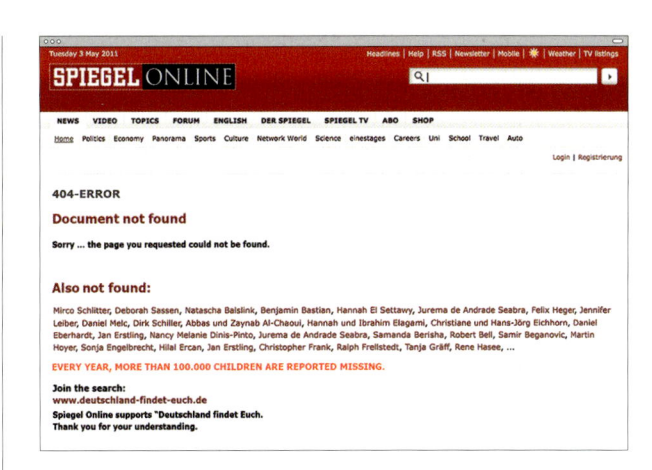

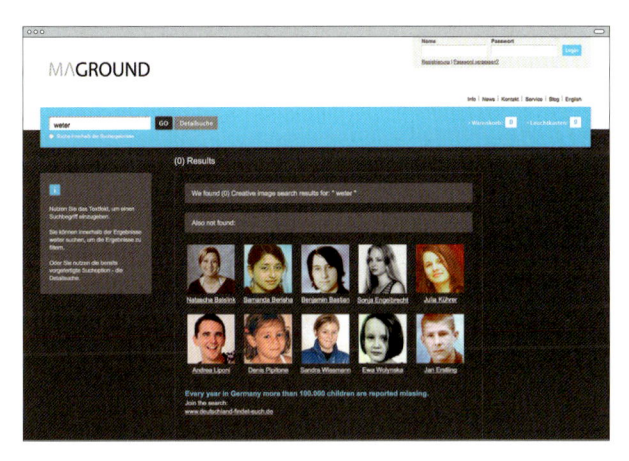

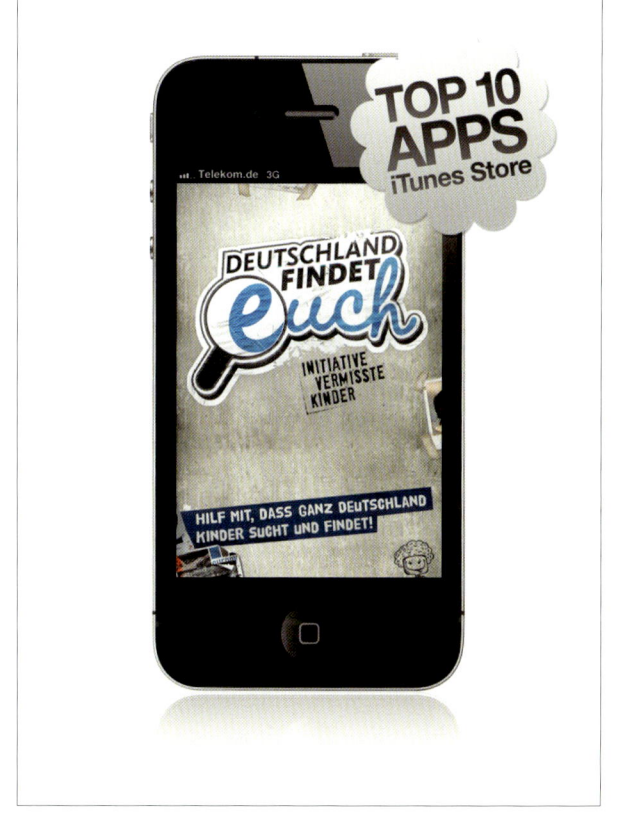

PUNKTE
POINTS

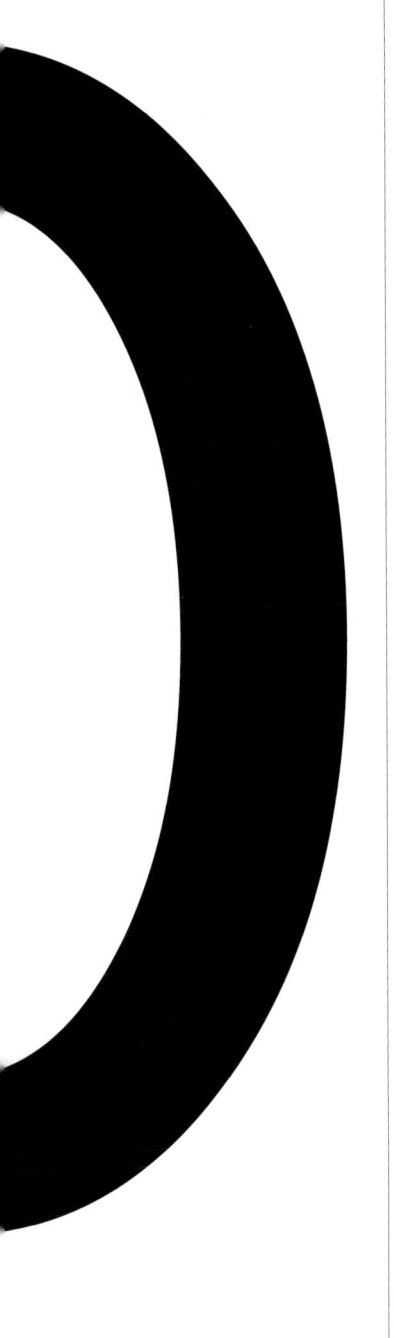

● SILVER
KLASSISCHE MEDIEN
CLASSICAL MEDIA
- Film
- TV/Kino Einzelspot
- Film
- TV/Cinema Commercial

● SILVER
KLASSISCHE MEDIEN
CLASSICAL MEDIA
- Film
- Filme für Unternehmensdarstellungen
- Film
- TV/Image Films

● BRONZE
GANZHEITLICHE KOMMUNIKATION
INTEGRATED CAMPAIGNS
- Ganzheitliche Kommunikation
- Integrated Campaigns

● BRONZE
CRAFT
CRAFT
- Musik und Sound
- Music and Sound

● NOMINATION
KLASSISCHE MEDIEN
CLASSICAL MEDIA
- Film
- Internetfilme
- Film
- Internet Films

● NOMINATION
KLASSISCHE MEDIEN
CLASSICAL MEDIA
- Film
- Kurzfilme/Sonderformate für Bewegtbild
- Film
- Shorts/Special Formats for Moving Pictures

HORNBACH BAUMARKT
»Das grenzenlose Haus«

Lead Agency
  HEIMAT, Berlin
Client
  Hornbach Baumarkt AG
Marketing Direction
  Frank Sahler
Advertising Direction
  Sylvia Späthe
Executive Creative Direction
  Guido Heffels
Creative Direction
  Guido Heffels,
  Matthias Storath
Art Direction
  Myles Lord,
  Jue Alt,
  Hendrik Schweder,
  Frank Hose,
  Teresa Jung,
  Susanna Fill,
  Maria Botsch
Client Consulting
  Maik Richter,
  Mark Hassan,
  Nicole Varga
Strategic Planning
  Matthias von Bechtolsheim
Agency Production
  Kerstin Heffels
Art Buying
  Jessica Valin
Audio Production
  Audioforce, Berlin
Camera
  Jallo Faber
Copy
  Mirjam Kundt,
  Woof Wan-Bau
Cutting
  Paul Hardcastle
Film Direction
  Joji Koyama aka Woof Wan-Bau
Film Production
  Radical.media GmbH, Berlin
Idea
  Heimat, Berlin
Illustration
  Doc Robert
Image Processing
  Twentyfour Seven, Berlin
Media
  Crossmedia, Duesseldorf
Music Composition
  Martin Landquist, Stockholm
Music Selection
  Martin Landquist, Stockholm
Printing
  Seltmann+Söhne
Production
  Christiane Dressler (Executive Production),
  Christoph Petzenhauser (Production)
Publishing House
  Seltmann+Söhne
Screen Design
  BBDO Proximity, Frankfurt
Sound Design
  Audioforce, Berlin

Hornbach »Das grenzenlose Haus«. Ein rund zehnminütiger märchenhafter Kurzfilm bildet das Herzstück der kanalübergreifenden Kampagne. Die Geschichte: Ein Mann zieht in eine winzige, halb verfallene Hütte. Von den Nachbarn mit Argwohn beäugt, baut er sie zu einer immer größer werdenden, phantasievollen Villa aus: dem »grenzenlosen Haus«. Begleitende Maßnahmen: ein Kinderbuch, ein Facebook-Sequel, eine DVD als Beileger in einer Programmzeitschrift und ein Printauftritt in bekannten Tageszeitungen und Magazinen.

Hornbach "The Infinite House". The centerpiece of the multi-channel campaign is a fairytale-like 10-minute short film. The storyline: A man moves in a tiny, run-down hut. Eyed by his suspicious neighbours, he renovates and expands the hut and step-by-step turns it into a fanciful villa – "The Infinite House".

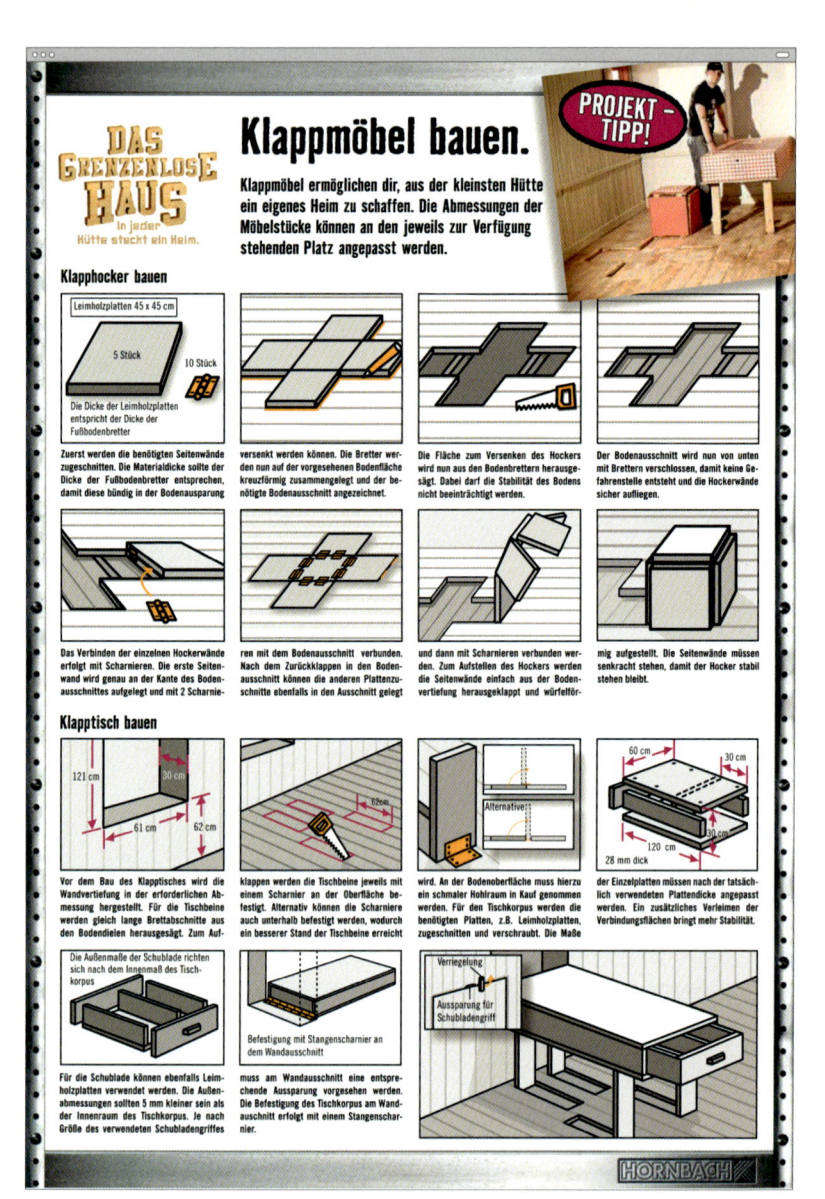

DAS GRENZENLOSE HAUS
In jeder Hütte steckt ein Heim.

Klappmöbel bauen.

PROJEKT-TIPP!

Klappmöbel ermöglichen dir, aus der kleinsten Hütte ein eigenes Heim zu schaffen. Die Abmessungen der Möbelstücke können an den jeweils zur Verfügung stehenden Platz angepasst werden.

Klapphocker bauen

Leimholzplatten 45 x 45 cm
5 Stück — 10 Stück
Die Dicke der Leimholzplatten entspricht der Dicke der Fußbodenbretter.

Zuerst werden die benötigten Seitenwände zugeschnitten. Die Materialdicke sollte der Dicke der Fußbodenbretter entsprechen, damit diese bündig in der Bodenaussparung versenkt werden können. Die Bretter werden nun auf der vorgesehenen Bodenfläche kreuzförmig zusammengelegt und der benötigte Bodenausschnitt angezeichnet.

Die Fläche zum Versenken des Hockers wird nun aus den Bodenbrettern herausgesägt. Dabei darf die Stabilität des Bodens nicht beeinträchtigt werden.

Der Bodenausschnitt wird nun von unten mit Brettern verschlossen, damit keine Gefahrenstelle entsteht und die Hockerwände sicher aufliegen.

Das Verbinden der einzelnen Hockerwände erfolgt mit Scharnieren. Die erste Seitenwand wird genau an die Kante des Bodenausschnittes aufgelegt und mit 2 Scharnieren mit dem Bodenausschnitt verbunden. Nach dem Zurückklappen in den Bodenausschnitt können die anderen Plattenzuschnitte ebenfalls in den Ausschnitt gelegt und dann mit Scharnieren verbunden werden. Zum Aufstellen des Hockers werden die Seitenwände einfach aus der Bodenvertiefung herausgeklappt und würfelförmig aufgestellt. Die Seitenwände müssen senkrecht stehen, damit der Hocker stabil stehen bleibt.

Klapptisch bauen

121 cm · 30 cm · 61 cm · 62 cm · 62 cm · 60 cm · 30 cm · 120 cm · 30 cm · 28 mm dick

Vor dem Bau des Klapptisches wird die Wandvertiefung in der erforderlichen Abmessung hergestellt. Für die Tischbeine werden gleich lange Brettabschnitte aus den Bodendielen herausgesägt. Zum Aufklappen werden die Tischbeine jeweils mit einem Scharnier an der Oberfläche befestigt. Alternativ können die Scharniere auch unterhalb befestigt werden, wodurch ein besserer Stand der Tischbeine erreicht wird. An der Bodenoberfläche muss hierzu ein schmaler Hohlraum in Kauf genommen werden. Für den Tischkorpus werden die benötigten Platten, z.B. Leimholzplatten, zugeschnitten und verschraubt. Die Maße der Einzelplatten müssen nach der tatsächlich verwendeten Plattendicke angepasst werden. Ein zusätzliches Verleimen der Verbindungsflächen bringt mehr Stabilität.

Die Außenmaße der Schublade richten sich nach dem Innenmaß des Tischkorpus.

Verriegelung · Aussparung für Schubladengriff · Befestigung mit Stangenscharnier an dem Wandausschnitt

Für die Schublade können ebenfalls Leimholzplatten verwendet werden. Die Außenabmessungen sollten 5 mm kleiner sein als der Innenraum des Tischkorpus. Je nach Größe des verwendeten Schubladengriffes muss am Wandausschnitt eine entsprechende Aussparung vorgesehen werden. Die Befestigung des Tischkorpus am Wandausschnitt erfolgt mit einem Stangenscharnier.

HORNBACH

HORNBACH YippieYeah auf Facebook — Gefällt mir · 8 Tsd

Der Kurzfilm
Hornbach-Projekte
Gewinnspiel
Das Making-of
Das Kinderbuch
Projekt Klappmöbel

Die Geschichte geht weiter. Triff alle Charaktere aus dem Kurzfilm auf Facebook!

Yippie! Hornbach jetzt auch bei: Facebook · Twitter · YouTube · Impressum

---

Thomas Kraft Tipp: Wenn ihr eh gerade Fliesen macht, baut doch noch eine Fußbodenheizung ein.
4. September 2010 um 13:21 · Gefällt mir · Kommentieren

Heinrich Grums Fußbodenheizung. Das ist doch teurer, unnützer Luxus. Und macht Schweissfüße.
4. September 2010 um 13:23 · Gefällt mir · Melden

Thomas Kraft Wärme steigt nach oben, also ist eine Heizung auf dem Boden ziemlich nützlich. Die spart Energie und Geld.
4. September 2010 um 13:24 · Gefällt mir · Melden

Heinrich Grums Na gut, aber beim Einbau kommt man ins Schwitzen!
4. September 2010 um 13:25 · Gefällt mir · Melden

Thomas Kraft Stimmt nicht. Nimm dir doch einfach mal das Projektbuch (Projektbroschüre) zu Hand. Aber pass auf, dass Du dich nicht verhebst.
http://www.amazon.de/gibt-immer-was-tun-Hornbach-Projekt-Buch/dp/3766717081/ref=sr_1_1?ie=UTF8&s=books&qid=128205...

Mehr anzeigen
4. September 2010 um 13:29 · Gefällt mir · Melden

Schreibe einen Kommentar ...

103

19

PUNKTE
POINTS

● GOLD
DESIGN
DESIGN
  Literatur
  Berichte
  Literature
  Reports

● SILVER
CRAFT
CRAFT
  Typografie
  Typography

● BRONZE
DESIGN
DESIGN
  Literatur
  Image-/Informations-
  broschüren
  Literature
  Image/Information Brochures

LEMONAID JAHRESBERICHT 2010
  »Der fairste Jahresbericht der Welt«

Lead Agency
  Jung von Matt AG
Client
  LemonAid Beverages GmbH
Marketing Direction
  Jakob Berndt
Executive Creative Direction
  Wolf Heumann
Creative Direction
  Peter Kirchhoff
Art Direction
  Annika Frey
Client Consulting
  Antje Lindenberg
Copy
  Christina Drescher,
  Peter Kirchhoff
Design
  Annika Frey,
  Katja Kirchner
Graphic Design
  Katja Kirchner
Illustration
  Annika Frey
Photography
  Stefanie Bütow,
  Johann Cohrs
Production
  Christian Will
Typography
  Annika Frey,
  Katja Kirchner

DER FAIRSTE JAHRESBERICHT 2010
33 SEITEN GERECHTIGKEIT ZUM NACHSCHLAGEN.

LEMONAID BEVERAGES GMBH

WIR MACHEN KEINE UNTERSCHIEDE – WEDER ZWISCHEN ÜBERSCHRIFT UND TEXT, NOCH ZWISCHEN PLANTAGENARBEITER UND GESCHÄFTSFÜHRER.

KLASSISCHE GESCHÄFTSMODELLE VERFOLGEN NUR EIN EINZIGES ZIEL: PROFIT. LEMONAID BEVERAGES IST ANDERS. STATT JEDER MARKTLÜCKE HINTERHER ZU RENNEN, GEHT ES EHER DARUM, EINEN BEITRAG ZU LEISTEN, DER DEN SOZIALEN WANDEL AKTIV MITGESTALTET. GENAUER: ES GEHT UM SOCIAL BUSINESS. WIR, DIE GRÜNDER DIESES START-UPS, WOLLEN VOR ALLEM REGIONEN UNTERSTÜTZEN, DIE SONST VOM INTERNATIONALEN HANDEL BENACHTEILIGT WERDEN. SCHON UNSERE ERSTEN SCHRITTE ENTSPRACHEN NICHT DEN GÄNGIGEN KONVENTIONEN: STATT IN TEUREN CHEMIE-LABORS KÜNSTLICHE SUBSTANZEN ZUSAMMEN ZU MIXEN, EXPERIMENTIERTEN WIR MIT NATÜRLICHEN PRODUKTEN IN UNSERER WG-KÜCHE. DABEI LEITETE UNS VOR ALLEM EIN GEDANKE: DIE WELT EIN WENIG GERECHTER MACHEN. DAS ERGEBNIS WAREN NACHHALTIG PRODUZIERTE SZENEGETRÄNKE BESTEHEND AUS FAIR GEHANDELTEN ROHSTOFFEN.

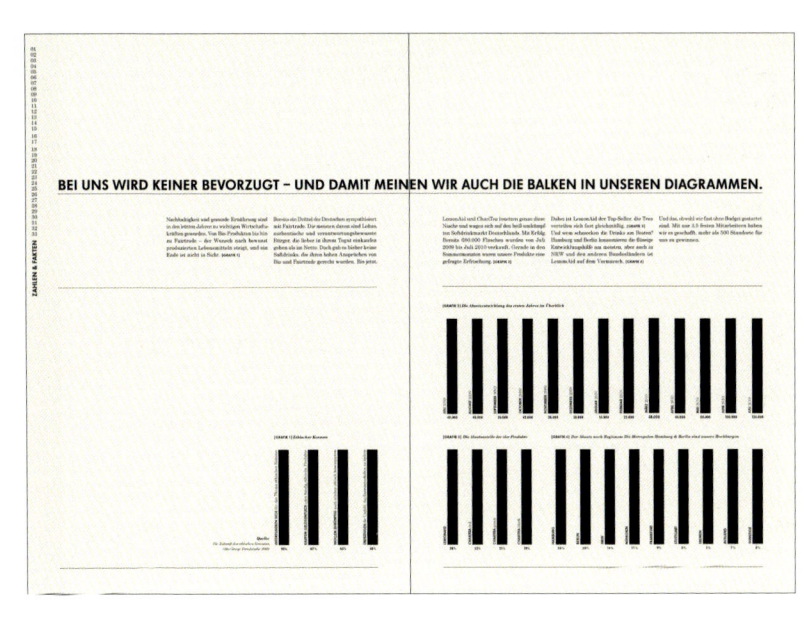

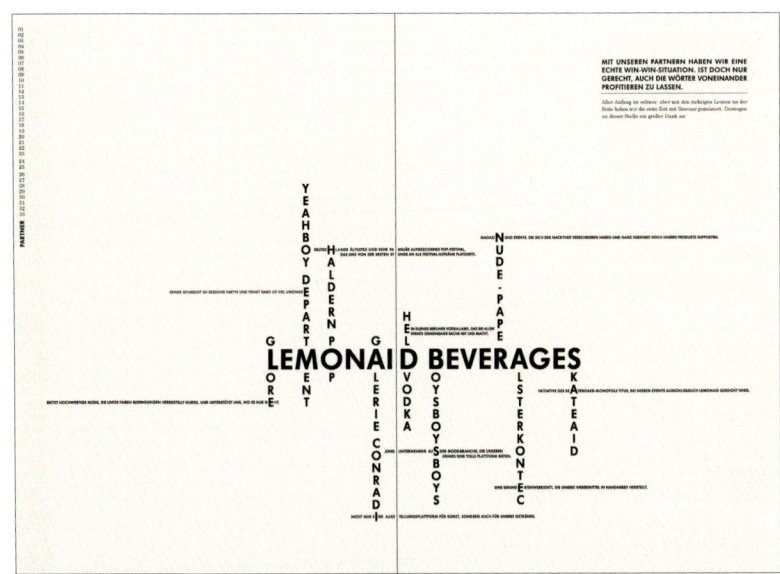

BEI UNS WIRD KEINER BEVORZUGT – UND DAMIT MEINEN WIR AUCH DIE BALKEN IN UNSEREN DIAGRAMMEN.

DIE ZUTATEN FÜR UNSERE PRODUKTE BEZIEHEN WIR ZU 100%* *bis auf Wasser AUS FAIREM HANDEL – UND WEIL WIR AUCH SONST NIEMANDEN BENACHTEILIGEN WOLLEN, DARF DER STERNCHENTEXT AUCH MAL IN DER ÜBERSCHRIFT STEHEN.

MIT UNSEREN PARTNERN HABEN WIR EINE ECHTE WIN-WIN-SITUATION. IST DOCH NUR GERECHT, AUCH DIE WÖRTER VONEINANDER PROFITIEREN ZU LASSEN.

LEMONAID BEVERAGES

WARUM WIR DIESE SEITE NEGATIV GESTALTEN?

NA, WEIL DIE PRESSESTIMMEN SCHON SO POSITIV SIND.

107

○ SILVER
DIGITALE MEDIEN
DIGITAL MEDIA
  Digitale Medien
  Digitale Medienformate im Raum
  Digital Media
  Digital Media Environment Design

○ SILVER
RÄUMLICHE INSZENIERUNG
SPATIAL SCENE-SETTING
  Kommunikation im Raum
  Environmental Design

● BRONZE
RÄUMLICHE INSZENIERUNG
SPATIAL SCENE-SETTING
  Events
  Events

● BRONZE
DIGITALE MEDIEN
DIGITAL MEDIA
  Digitale Medien Craft
  Innovative Technologien
  Digital Media Craft
  Innovative Technologies

● NOMINATION
DIGITALE MEDIEN
DIGITAL MEDIA
  Digitale Medien Craft
  Interface/Navigation
  Digital Media Craft
  Interface/Navigation

EXPO 2010, SHANGHAI
»Der Deutsche Pavillon«

Lead Agency
  Milla & Partner/
  Schmidhuber + Partner/
  Nüssli (Deutschland) GmbH
Contributing Agencies
  Schmidhuber + Partner,
  Milla & Partner,
  Nüssli (Deutschland) GmbH
Client
  Bundesministerium für Wirtschaft und Technologie represented by Koelnmesse International GmbH
Executive Creative Direction
  Peter Redlin (M&P),
  Lennart Wiechell (S+P)
Creative Direction
  Peter Redlin (M&P),
  Lennart Wiechell (S+P)
Film Production
  emenes, Stuttgart
Innovative Technologies
  Milla & Partner,
  Universität Stuttgart
Interface Navigation
  Milla & Partner,
  Universität Stuttgart
Trade Fair Construction
  Nüssli (Deutschland) GmbH

"balancity", der Deutsche Pavillon auf der Expo 2010, widmet sich dem Gleichgewicht einer nachhaltigen, lebenswerten Stadt. Die begehbare Raumskulptur drückt das Thema architektonisch aus: Nur gemeinsam halten die Baukörper die Balance, formen Räume und Landschaften. Darin erleben Besucher Lösungen zu urbanen Herausforderungen "made in Germany". Höhepunkt ist die interaktive Kugel-Show: Die riesige, mit über 400.000 LEDs besetzte Kugel hängt in einem theaterähnlichen Raum und zeigt emotionale Bilder einer lebenswerten Stadt der Zukunft. 600 Besucher blicken von drei Galerien auf das interaktive Exponat, das sie durch lautes Rufen mittels Sprachsteuerung bewegen können.

"balancity", the German Pavilion at Shanghai Expo 2010, is devoted to the "balance" of a sustainable city. As a walk-through sculpture, balance is expressed as an interplay between the separate construction elements, which hold each other in perfect equilibrium forming exhibition spaces and landscapes. A journey shows solutions concerning urban challenges "made in Germany". Final highlight is the show with an interactive sphere: Fitted with 400,000 LEDs, it hangs in a dome-like theater, showing pictures of a sustainable city in balance. 600 people, spread across three galleries, experience how to set the sphere in motion simply with their calls. Its mechanics are controlled by acoustic assessment.

● SILVER
DESIGN
DESIGN
- Design
  Grafische Einzelarbeiten
- Design
  Individual Graphics

● BRONZE
DESIGN
DESIGN
- Literatur
  Produkt-/Werbebroschüren
- Literature
  Advertising Brochures

● BRONZE
GANZHEITLICHE KOMMUNI-
KATION
INTEGRATED CAMPAIGNS
- Ganzheitliche Kommunikation
- Integrated Campaigns

● BRONZE
DIGITALE MEDIEN
DIGITAL MEDIA
- Digitale Medien
  Microsites
- Digital Media
  Microsites

● BRONZE
DIGITALE MEDIEN
DIGITAL MEDIA
- Digitale Medien
  Social Media
- Digital Media
  Social Media

● NOMINATION
DIALOGMARKETING/
PROMOTION/MEDIA
DIALOG MARKETING/
PROMOTION/MEDIA
- Dialogmarketing
  Dialog Digital
- Dialog Marketing
  Dialog Digital

---

50 JAHRE EDDING
»Jubiläumskampagne«

Lead Agency
  kempertrautmann gmbh
Client
  edding International GmbH
Marketing Direction
  Per Ledermann
Advertising Direction
  Angelika Schuhmacher,
  Andreas Baxmann
Creative Direction
  Gerrit Zinke,
  Jens Theil,
  Mieke Haase (Book),
  Simon Jasper Philipp,
  Christoph Gähwiler,
  Stefan Walz,
  Christian Fritsche
Art Direction
  Florian Schimmer (Book),
  Simon Jasper Philipp,
  Stefan Walz (Online)
Client Consulting
  Andrea Bison,
  Niklas Kruchten,
  Thomas Dirfard,
  Dorothea Feurer,
  Jan Rütten (Book),
  Elisabeth Einhaus (Online)
Animation/Visual Effects/Special Effects
  Liga_01 Computerfilm GmbH
  (Pen Animations)
Art Buying
  Susi Kastner-Linke,
  Lina Eggers
Audio Production
  Supreme Music Gbr
Computer Animation
  Liga_01 Computerfilm GmbH
  (Pen Animations)
Concept
  Simon Jasper Philipp,
  Christoph Gähwiler,
  Stefan Walz,
  Wolf Nöding,
  Carsten Fischer,
  Alexander El Meligi,
  Florian Schimmer,
  Michael Götz,
  Florian Wögerer
Consulting
  Dorothea Feurer
Copy
  Michael Götz,
  Heiko Franzgrote,
  Johannes L'Hoest,
  Alexander Lipp (Book),
  Christoph Gähwiler,
  Samuel Weiß (Online)
Final Artwork
  Produktionsbüro Romey von Malottky GmbH
Graphic Design
  Bastian Adam,
  Karola Korten (Book),
  David Scherer,
  Tobias Lehment (Online)
Idea
  Florian Schimmer,
  Michael Götz
Illustration
  Romy Blümel/2 Agenten,
  John Langdon/Ambigramm (Book),
  Mirko Reisser,
  Various Users (Online)
Image Processing
  flavouredgreen/PX Group GmbH
Interface/Navigation
  Simon Jasper Philipp,
  Stefan Walz,
  Alexander El Meligi,
  Florian Wögerer
Motion Design
  Liga_01 Computerfilm GmbH,
  demodern | digital design studio
Motion Graphics and 3D
  Liga_01 Computerfilm GmbH,
  demodern | digital design studio
Photography
  Sarah Illenberger/emeisdeubel (Book),
  Nordstern Studio (Online),
  Supreme Music Gbr
Postproduction
  flavouredgreen/PX Group GmbH,
  Liga_01 Computerfilm GmbH
Printing
  Beisner Druck
Production
  demodern | digital design studio,
  Produktionsbüro Romey von Malottky GmbH
Programming
  demodern | digital design studio
Publishing House
  Production: Produktionsbüro Romey von Malottky GmbH
Screen Design
  Tobias Lehment,
  David Scherer
Sound Design
  Supreme Music Gbr
Technical Conception
  demodern | digital design studio
Technical Implementation
  demodern | digital design studio
Technical Installation
  demodern | digital design studio
Other
  Facebook Production:
  Christian Pappas,
  Florian Wögerer

Diese Jubiläumskampagne zieht durch, was 1960 zum ersten Mal mit einem Edding gezogen wurde: eine Linie. Ihren Anfang nahm sie in einem Markenbuch. Weiter gezogen wurde sie auf der Edding "Wall of Fame" – dem Webspecial der Kampagne. Und zwar von zehntausenden Menschen aus der ganzen Welt. Outdoor-Projektionen machten die Seite zum Live-Event – die Linie fand ihren Weg zurück in die reale Welt.

An anniversary campaign which is centered around "the line" – to draw it, people have been using Edding pens ever since 1960. It all started with a brand book aimed at edding fans and partners. The idea was then further developed by tens of thousands of users from all around the world on the "Wall of Fame", the campaign microsite. Outdoor projections turned the "Wall" into a stage and a live event.

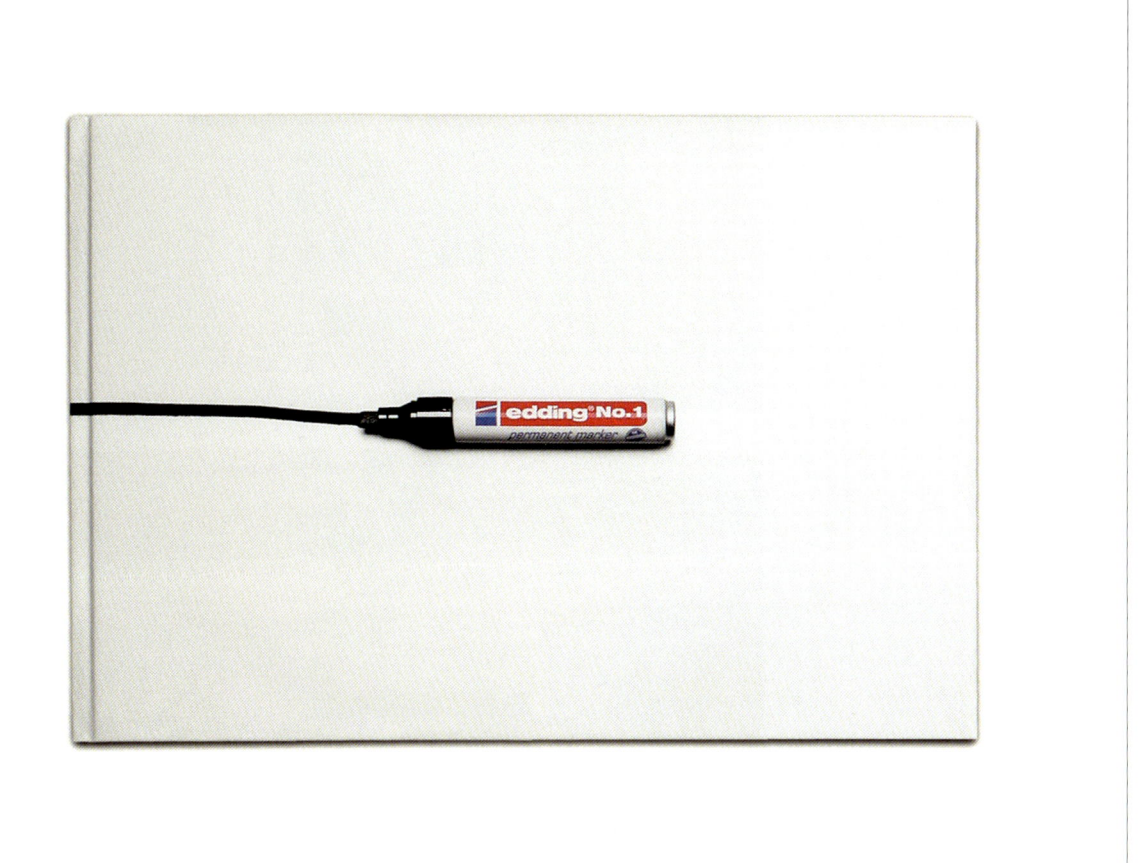

19

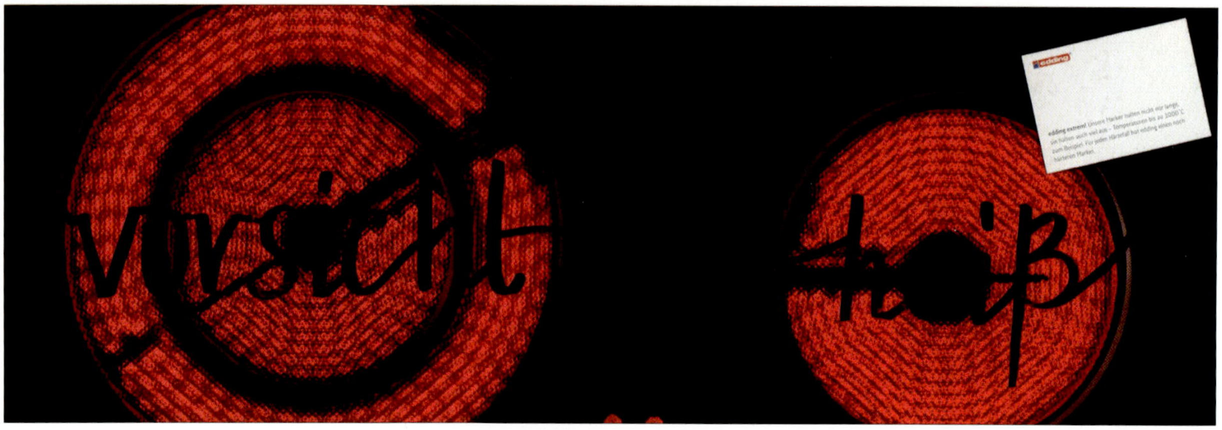

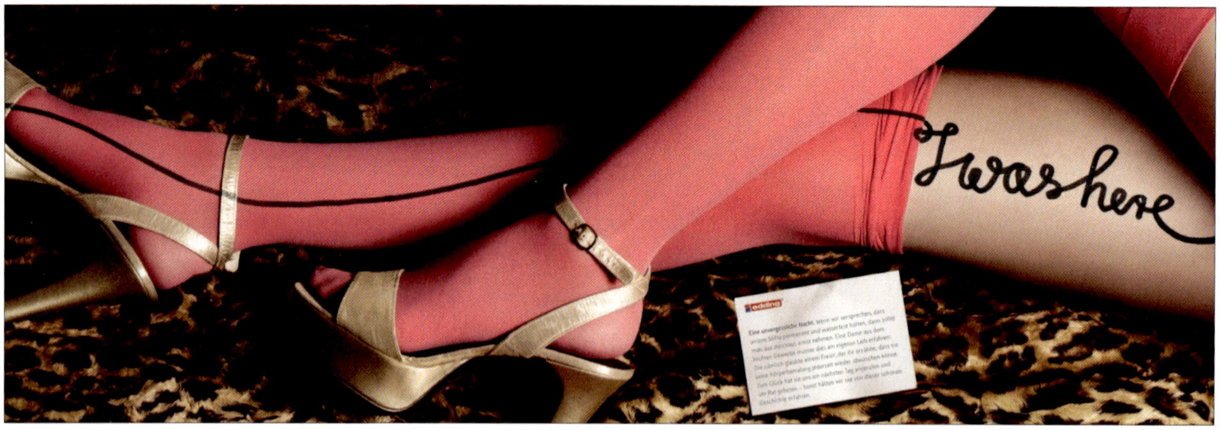

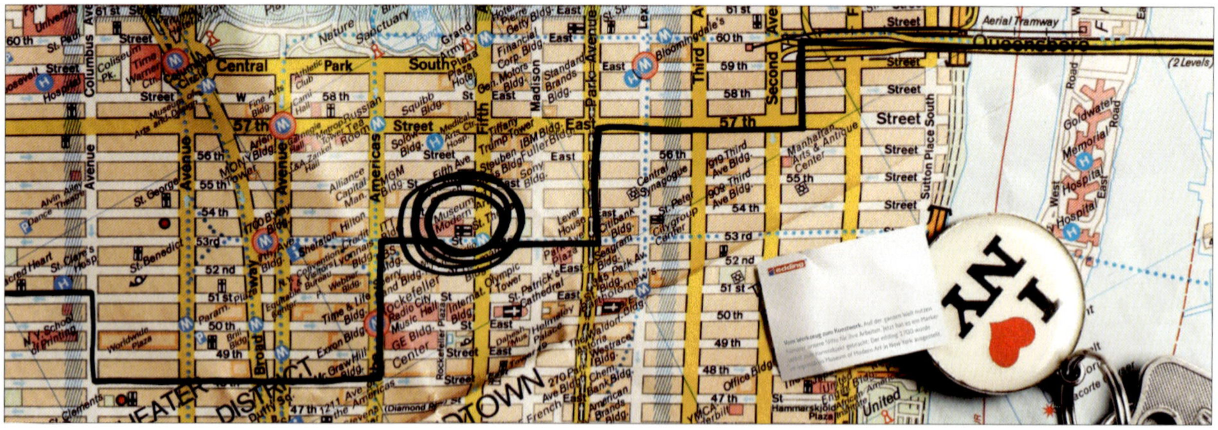

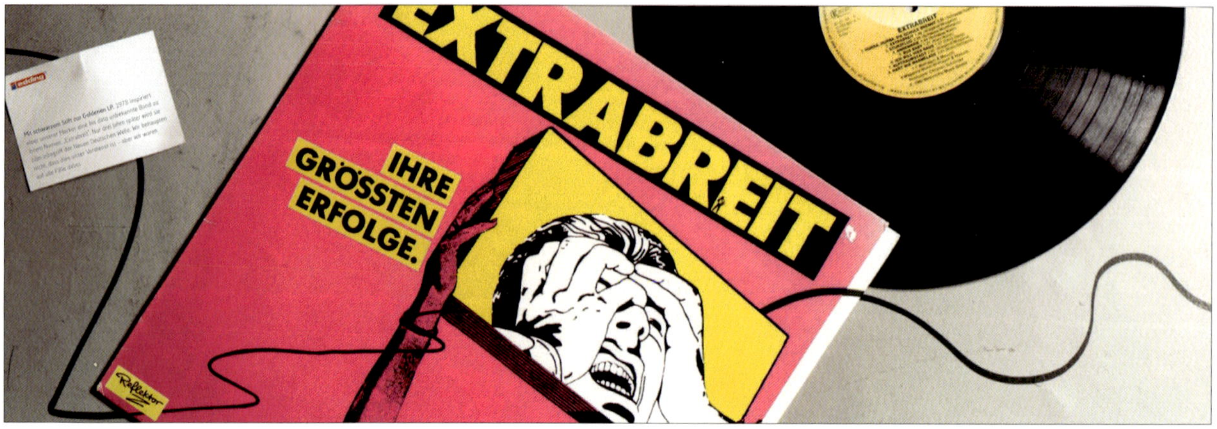

DRAWING HERE
Peter Pen
edding 3300
permanent marker

edding
Übertragung von der Wall of Fame! LIVE
Graffiti Artist DAIM
WALL-OF-FAME.COM
RESTAURANT

SHARE
No.1
3000
3300
500
550
400
404
This edding is free.
DRAW SOMETHING

19

16

PUNKTE
POINTS

● GOLD
KLASSISCHE MEDIEN
CLASSICAL MEDIA
   Film
   TV/Kino Einzelspot
   Film
   TV/Cinema Commercial

● SILVER
KLASSISCHE MEDIEN
CLASSICAL MEDIA
   Film Craft
   Motion Graphics und 3D
   Film Craft
   Motion Graphics and 3D

AMNESTY INTERNATIONAL
"Death Penalty"

Lead Agency
   TBWA Paris
Client
   Amnesty International France
Executive Creative Direction
   Eric Holden,
   Rémi Noël
Creative Direction
   Eric Holden,
   Rémi Noël
Art Direction
   Philippe Taroux
Client Consulting
   Account Super: Anne Vincent,
   Account Management:
   Anne-Laure Brunner
Agency Production
   Maxime Boiron
Copy
   Benoît Leroux
Film Production
   Warm & Fuzzy
Motion Graphics and 3D
   Pleix/Digital District
Production
   Edward Grann,
   Jean Ozannat
Sound Design
   Artist/Song Title:
   Carly Comando – Everyday

139 COUNTRIES HAVE WIPED OUT THE DEATH PENALTY.
ONLY 58 ARE LEFT TO CONVINCE.

● GOLD
DESIGN
DESIGN
　Design
　　Corporate Design
　Design
　　Corporate Design

● SILVER
DESIGN
DESIGN
　Design
　　Kunst-/Kultur-/
　　Veranstaltungsplakate
　Design
　　Art/Culture/Event Posters

TRANSMEDIALE.11
　"Response:ability"

Lead Agency
　® ruddigkeit corporate ideas
Contributing Agencies
　MFO Berlin, Achter April
　Stuttgart
Client
　Kulturprojekte Berlin
　Transmediale
Marketing Direction
　Filippo Giannetta
Advertising Direction
　Stephen Kovats
Executive Creative Direction
　Raban Ruddigkeit
Creative Direction
　Raban Ruddigkeit
Art Direction
　Dirk Heider,
　Kristina Brasseler,
　Gianna Pfeifer
Agency Production
　Lasse Noerbaek
Animation/Visual Effects/
Special Effects
　Emilia Forstreuter,
　Marcel Weber,
　Michael Fragstein,
　Moritz Reichartz
Audio Production
　Sam Spreckley,
　Marc Fragstein
Film Production
　Turan Tehrani,
　Julia Schlingmann,
　Anna Göhrig,
　Benjamin Wieg,
　Ulé Barcelos
Printing
　Druckerei Seltmann
Production
　Lasse Noerbaeck
Other
　Marc Bieling,
　Christian Vogel (Wall AG)

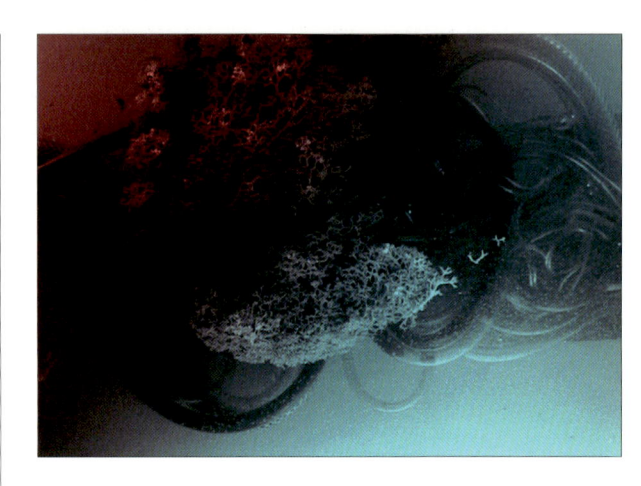

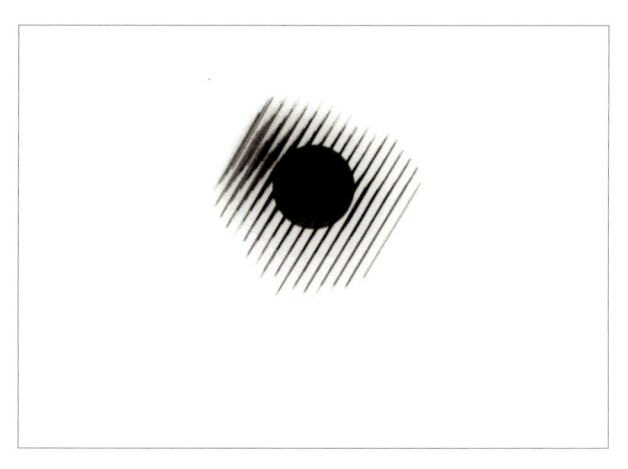

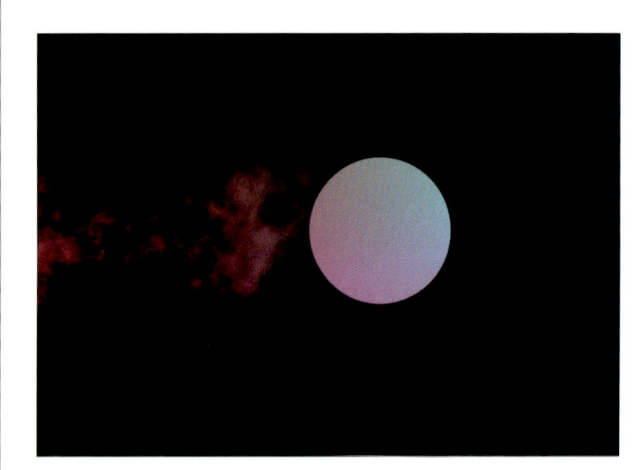

Das Design für die Transmediale basiert auf der Einfachheit eines Punktes und eines Striches bzw. auf 0 und 1. Diese sind ebenso die Basis des Binärsystems wie der menschlichen DNA und verdeutlichen so die Schnittstelle zwischen Mensch und Computer. Ein Code, aus dem sich unzählige Worte und Bilder ergeben, die das Thema des Kunst- und Medienfestivals facettenreich illustrieren.

The design for Transmediale is inspired by the simplicity of one line and one dot as in the 1 and the 0: the basic pattern of the binary system and the DNA. Thus, a code connecting man and machine and allowing for infinite words and images.

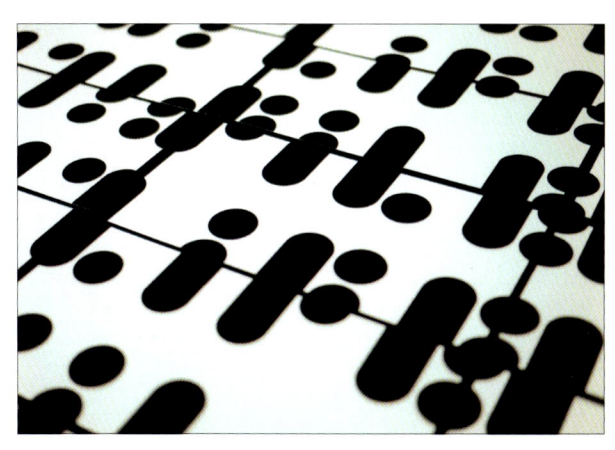

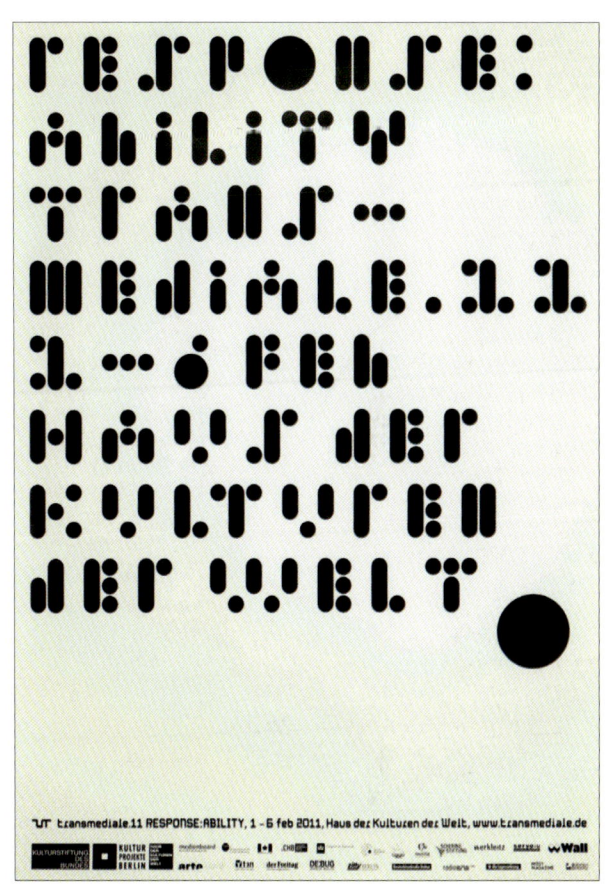

● SILVER
DIALOGMARKETING/
PROMOTION/MEDIA
DIALOG MARKETING/
PROMOTION/MEDIA
- Media
- Media

● SILVER
CRAFT
CRAFT
- Musik und Sound
- Music and Sound

● BRONZE
KLASSISCHE MEDIEN
CLASSICAL MEDIA
- Audio
- Innovative Nutzung von Audio
- Audio
- Innovative Use of Audio

● NOMINATION
DIALOGMARKETING/
PROMOTION/MEDIA
DIALOG MARKETING/
PROMOTION/MEDIA
- Promotion
- Aktivitäten
- Promotion
- Activities

SKY BUNDESLIGA
»Die Fußballoper«

Lead Agency
  Serviceplan
Client
  Sky Deutschland Fernsehen GmbH & Co. KG
Executive Creative Direction
  Alexander Schill
Creative Direction
  Christoph Everke,
  Matthias Mittermüller,
  Tim Strathus
Art Direction
  Matthias Mittermüller,
  Monika Steiner,
  Basma Attalla
Client Consulting
  Diana Günder,
  Marco Wendt
Audio Production
  Sky Deutschland Fernsehen GmbH & Co. KG
Camera
  Roman Lipah
Copy
  Tim Strathus,
  Juliana Hirsing,
  Tobias Blineder
Film Direction/Radio Direction
  Alexander Geissler
Film Production
  Sky Deutschland Fernsehen GmbH & Co. KG
Illustration
  Christoph Mittermüller
Music Composition
  Michael Armann
Sound Design
  La Triviata: Andreas Dellert,
  Benno Vogel,
  Michael Armann,
  Sybilla Duffe,
  Verena Barth

Die Aufgabe: Mit Sky das Besondere sehen – für seine Hauptsparte machte Sky ein Fußballspiel zur Oper! Idee: Ein Opern-Ensemble verwandelte das Spiel Bayern München gegen Schalke 04 zur Fußballoper. Jede Handlung, jeder Gedanke der Spieler wurde live besungen und auf einem zweiten Kanal ausgestrahlt. Ergebnis: Sky verzeichnete über 1.000.000 Zuschauer und weltweite Presse nach Abpfiff.

Task: See something special on Sky. Therefore, Sky made football a great opera! Idea: An opera ensemble transformed the match Bayern Munich vs Schalke 04 into a football opera. The players: their thoughts and actions are expressed in beautiful tones on a second channel. Result: Sky records over 1,000,000 viewers and worldwide press after the final whistle.

14

PUNKTE
POINTS

● SILVER
RÄUMLICHE INSZENIERUNG
SPATIAL SCENE-SETTING
  Events
  Events

● BRONZE
RÄUMLICHE INSZENIERUNG
SPATIAL SCENE-SETTING
  Events Craft
  Licht, Musik, Sound
  Events Craft
  Lighting, Music, Sound

● BRONZE
CRAFT
CRAFT
  Musik und Sound
  Music and Sound

● NOMINATION
DIALOGMARKETING/
PROMOTION/MEDIA
DIALOG MARKETING/
PROMOTION/MEDIA
  Promotion
  Aktivitäten
  Promotion
  Activities

● NOMINATION
RÄUMLICHE INSZENIERUNG
SPATIAL SCENE-SETTING
  Kommunikation im Raum Craft
  Lichtdesign, Sounddesign
  Environmental Design Craft
  Lighting Design, Sound Design

KONZERTHAUS DORTMUND –
EXKLUSIVKÜNSTLER
»Countdown-Orchester«

Lead Agency
  Jung von Matt AG
Contributing Agencies
  Jung von Matt/Elbe GmbH
Client
  Konzerthaus Dortmund GmbH
Marketing Direction
  Anne-Katrin Röhm
Executive Creative Direction
  Sascha Hanke,
  Norman Störl
Creative Direction
  Jo Marie Farwick,
  Tobias Grimm,
  Jens Pfau
Art Direction
  Nicolas Schmidt-Fitzner
Client Consulting
  Jochen Schwarz,
  Dajana Crantz,
  Marijke Fisser
Audio Production
  bauhouse
Consulting
  Mhoch4 GmbH & Co. KG
Copy
  Jan-Hendrik Scholz
Cutting
  Niels Münter
IT Direction
  Jan Beckmann
Lighting Design/Sound Design
  Clemens Wittkowski,
  Fabian Grobe (bauhouse)
Lighting/Music/Sound
  Clemens Wittkowski,
  Fabian Grobe (bauhouse)
Music Composition
  bauhouse with Max Renne
Production
  STINK GmbH (Nils Schwemer,
  Steffen Leiser)
Radio Direction
  Clemens Wittkowski,
  Fabian Grobe (bauhouse)
Other
  Direction: Benedikt Stampa
  Orchestra: The Powertones

Wir begeisterten Dortmund und alle Klassikfreunde mit dem ersten lebendigen Uhrwerk der Welt: Zwölf Musiker spielten gemeinsam 21.600 Takte und 86.400 Einzeltöne – vom 13. September um 20.00 Uhr bis zur Saisoneröffnung 24 Stunden später. Ein musikalischer Countdown, der die dreijährige exklusive Residenz des Star-Dirigenten Esa-Pekka Salonen am Konzerthaus Dortmund einleitete.

We created the first living clockwork in the world: 12 musicians played 21,600 bars and 86,400 individual notes from a custom-composed score on a stage in front of the Dortmund Concert Hall. For 24 hours in a row. This unique musical countdown experiment marked the beginning of the three year residency of star conductor Esa-Pekka Salonen.

13

PUNKTE
POINTS

● SILVER
KLASSISCHE MEDIEN
CLASSICAL MEDIA
  Film
  TV/Kino Einzelspot
  Film
  TV/Cinema Commercial

● BRONZE
DIALOGMARKETING/
PROMOTION/MEDIA
DIALOG MARKETING/
PROMOTION/MEDIA
  Promotion
  Aktivitäten
  Promotion
  Activities

● BRONZE
KLASSISCHE MEDIEN
CLASSICAL MEDIA
  Film
  Filme für Verkaufsförderung
  Film
  TV/Sales Promotion Films

● NOMINATION
DIALOGMARKETING/
PROMOTION/MEDIA
DIALOG MARKETING/
PROMOTION/MEDIA
  Media
  Media

GERMANWINGS
  "Planemob"

Lead Agency
  Lukas Lindemann Rosinski
  GmbH
Client
  Germanwings GmbH
Marketing Direction
  Thomas Labonde
Advertising Direction
  Sandra Friedrich
Executive Creative Direction
  Bernhard Lukas,
  Arno Lindemann
Creative Direction
  Bernhard Lukas,
  Arno Lindemann
Art Direction
  Michael Mackens
Client Consulting
  Daniela Stephan,
  Anika Zocholl
Copy
  Tim Esser,
  Jan Hoffmeister
Graphic Design
  Sön Becker,
  David Soukup,
  Hannah Ziegler
Media
  Mindshare GmbH

Germanwings bietet mehr Komfort, mehr Service und weniger versteckte Kosten als andere Budget-Fluggesellschaften. Ziel war es, diese Vorteile gegenüber anderen Wettbewerbern herauszustellen. Wir buchten Flüge beim größten Konkurrenten und starteten mit ein paar Papp-Schildern die erste Guerilla-Kampagne über den Wolken: den "Planemob"! Resultat: Über 600.000 Views und jede Menge Buzz im Internet.

The budget-airline market is highly competitive. One benefit of flying with Germanwings: Reserved seats at no extra charge. The aim was to highlight this benefit. We went where our arguments would be immediately obvious: aboard the flights of the largest competitor. There we started the first airborne guerrilla campaign: the Planemob! Result: More than 600,000 views and a lot of buzz on the Internet.

12

PUNKTE
POINTS

●
SILVER
DIGITALE MEDIEN
DIGITAL MEDIA
  Digitale Medien Craft
   Motiondesign
  Digital Media Craft
   Motion Design

●
SILVER
DIGITALE MEDIEN
DIGITAL MEDIA
  Digitale Medien Craft
   Interface/Navigation
  Digital Media Craft
   Interface/Navigation

———
GRIMM GALLUN HOLTAPPELS
»www.2gh.de«

Lead Agency
  Grimm Gallun Holtappels
  Werbeagentur GmbH & Co. KG
Client
  Grimm Gallun Holtappels
  Werbeagentur GmbH & Co. KG
Creative Direction
  Nils Gallun,
  Florian Grimm,
  Matthias M. Müller
Art Direction
  Matthias M. Müller,
  Matthias Netzberger
Interface Navigation
  Matthias Schulz
Motion Design
  Matthias Schulz

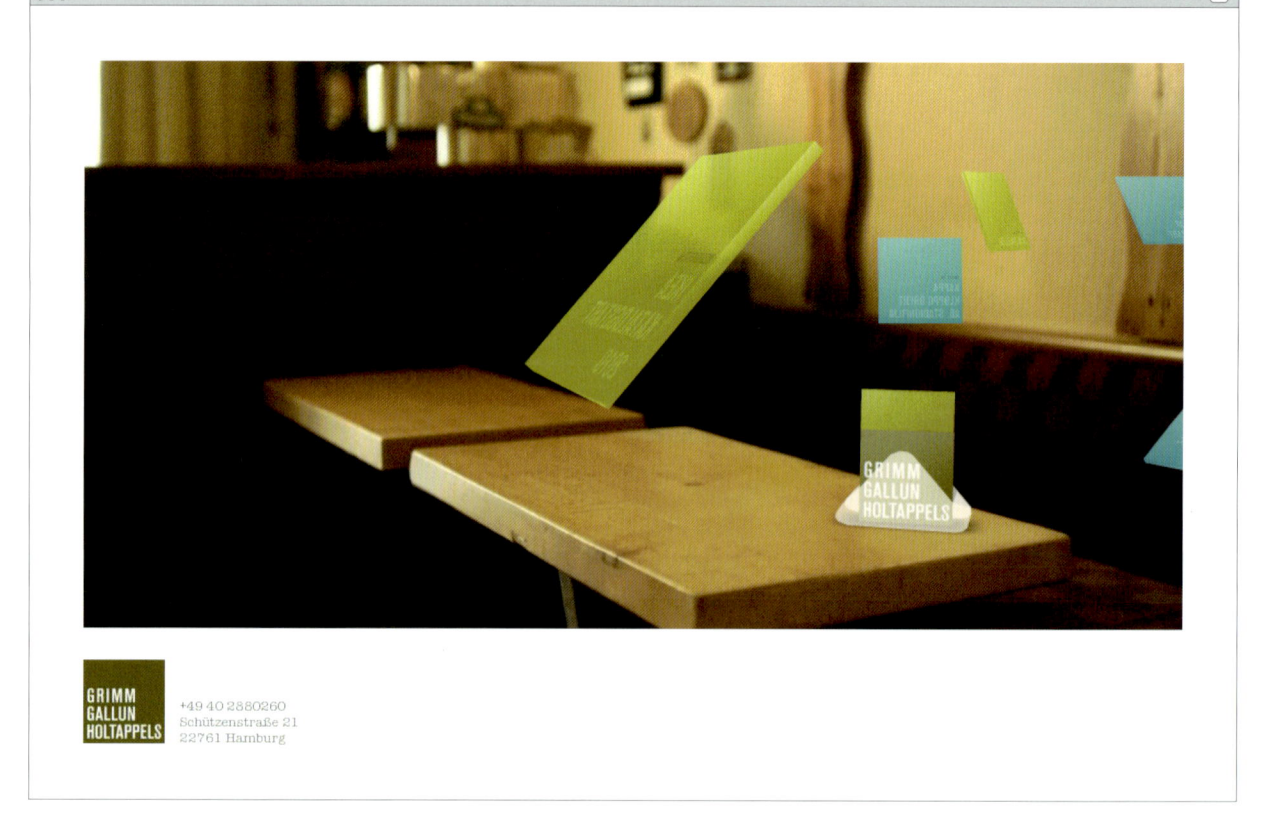

Mit unserem Online-Auftritt wollen wir sowohl Kunden als auch Branchengenossen begeistern und unsere Fähigkeiten in Sachen Kreation online präsentieren. Dafür haben wir eine Seite entwickelt, die sowohl formal/ästhetisch überrascht und Spaß macht als auch technisch an die derzeitigen Limits des Machbaren stößt. In unserer Agentur hat alles seinen Ursprung in unserer eigenen Kneipe.

We want our online appearance to delight our customers and our colleagues in the industry, and to present our abilities in online creation. We have developed a site that is of formal and aesthetic appeal and that also reaches the boundaries of what is currently technically feasible. Another point to be considered is that in our agency, everything starts in our own pub.

● SILVER
DESIGN
DESIGN
 Literatur
 Buchumschläge/-titel
 Literature
 Book Jackets/Covers

● SILVER
DESIGN
DESIGN
 Design
 Produktdesign
 Design
 Product Design

BASISBIBEL
 »Kreuzcover«
 »Kreuz-Farbschnitt«

Lead Agency
 gobasil GmbH
Client
 Stiftung Deutsche Bibel-
 gesellschaft
Marketing Direction
 Florian Theuerkauff
Executive Creative Direction
 Eva Jung,
 Nico Mühlan
Creative Direction
 Eva Jung,
 Nico Mühlan
Art Direction
 Oliver Popke
Client Consulting
 Eva Jung,
 Nico Mühlan
Copy
 Eva Jung
Design
 Oliver Popke
Publishing House
 Stiftung Deutsche Bibel-
 gesellschaft

Die Basisbibel ist die erste deutsche Bibelübersetzung, die den Lesebedürfnissen des 21. Jahrhunderts gerecht wird: Nah am Urtext, prägnant in der Sprache und crossmedial vernetzt. Die Bibel benutzt klare Sätze und eine durchgehend rhythmische Sprache. Das konsequente Design erscheint in fünf Sonderfarben mit partiellem Farbschnitt, der so im Buchhandel noch nie zu sehen war.

The „BasisBibel" is the first German bible translation which does justice to the needs of the reader of the 21st century: Close to the original text, clear and concise in its use of language and crossmedially linked. The outstanding consistently designed Bible is published in five colors with partial edge colouring – something unprecedented in the book trade to date.

●
SILVER
KLASSISCHE MEDIEN
CLASSICAL MEDIA
  Out-of-Home
  Klassisch Einzelmotiv
  Out-of-Home
  Classic Single Motif

●
SILVER
KLASSISCHE MEDIEN
CLASSICAL MEDIA
  Out-of-Home
  Nicht-Klassisch
  Out-of-Home
  Non-Classic

AUDI A7
»Sportback Live-Plakat«

Lead Agency
  kempertrautmann west gmbh
Client
  Audi AG
Marketing Direction
  Hans-Peter Kleebinder
Advertising Direction
  Peter Zieten,
  Silvia Chudalla
Executive Creative Direction
  Kai Röffen
Creative Direction
  Fabian Kirner
Art Direction
  Rilana von Werne
Client Consulting
  Jan Rütten,
  Hendrik Heine,
  Niklas Kruchten
Art Buying
  Susi Kastner-Linke
Copy
  Michael Manke,
  Stefano Sciolti
Film Production
  Felipe Ascacibar,
  Kai Branss
Graphic Design
  Bastian Adam
Illustration
  Oliver Kray
Postproduction
  Pirates'n Paradise
Production
  Produktionsbüro Romey von
  Malottky GmbH
Other
  Music: Thomas Kisser, s12
  Sound: 3Klang

Audi
Vorsprung durch Technik
Nichts ist inspirierender
als ein weißes Blatt Papier.
Es ist die Chance, etwas
Einzigartiges zu kreieren.
Der Audi A7 Sportback.
www.audi.de/a7

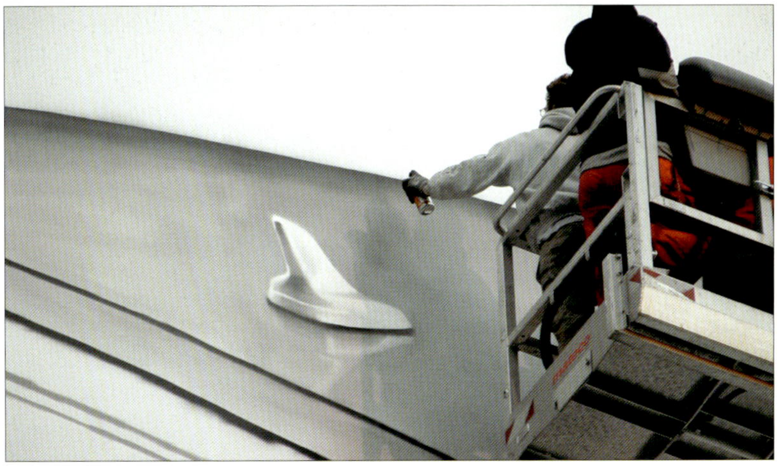

miet...
mateco
WT 370

12

11

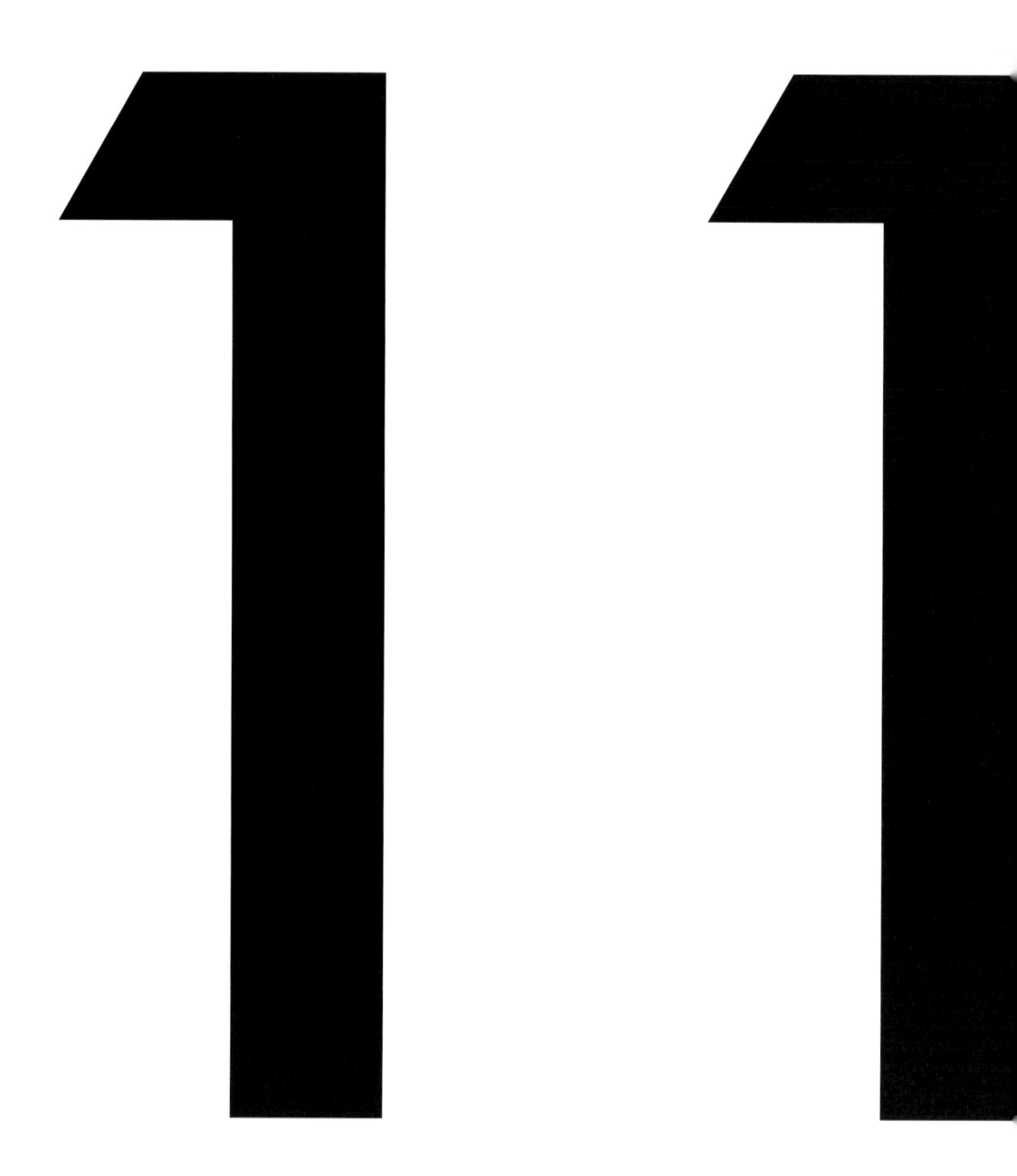

PUNKTE
POINTS

● SILVER
KLASSISCHE MEDIEN
CLASSICAL MEDIA
　Film
　　Filme für Verkaufsförderung
　Film
　　TV/Sales Promotion Films

● BRONZE
DIALOGMARKETING/
PROMOTION/MEDIA
DIALOG MARKETING/
PROMOTION/MEDIA
　Media
　Media

● NOMINATION
KLASSISCHE MEDIEN
CLASSICAL MEDIA
　Film
　　TV/Kino Einzelspot
　Film
　　TV/Cinema Commercial

● NOMINATION
DIALOGMARKETING/
PROMOTION/MEDIA
DIALOG MARKETING/
PROMOTION/MEDIA
　Dialogmarketing
　　Dialog Alternative
　Dialog Marketing
　　Dialog Alternative

IKEA
　»Möbelkunst«

Lead Agency
　Grabarz & Partner,
　Lukas Lindemann Rosinski
Client
　IKEA Deutschland GmbH & Co. KG
Marketing Direction
　Claudia Willvonseder (Marketing Management)
Advertising Direction
　Hendrik Zimmer (Head of Advertising)
Executive Creative Direction
　Ralf Heuel,
　Arno Lindemann
Creative Direction
　Tom Hauser
Art Direction
　Moritz Tolle,
　Oliver Brkitsch,
　Jan Wölfel,
　Stefan Schömbs,
　Tim Hartwig
Client Consulting
　Denise Ewald,
　Franziska Mattes,
　Laura Becker
Animation/Visual Effects/Special Effects
　Sven Schönmann
Copy
　Tom Hauser,
　André Hennen,
　Heiko Notter
Cutting
　Josch Kretzschmar,
　Sabine Panek,
　Dennis Riebenstahl
Film Direction
　Silvio Helbig
Film Production
　Joschmid! Filmproduktion GmbH
Graphic Design
　Josefine Nitsch
Postproduction
　Slaughterhouse Hamburg
Production
　Joschmid! Filmproduktion GmbH
Sound Design
　Thomas Nitzsche
Other
　Production: Jürgen Joppen
　Music: Massive Music Amsterdam
　Composer: Joep Beving
　Postproduction: Andi Mall, Gwen Teichmann
　Sound Studio: Hahn Nitzsche
　Dummy: Arndt von Hoff
　Production: Natalie Buba, Tanja Bruhn

IKEA hat sehr schöne Möbel zum Selbst-Zusammenbauen. Aber nicht jeder baut seine Möbel gern selbst auf. Aus diesem Grund bietet IKEA einen Aufbauservice an, der das professionell und günstig erledigt. Ein avantgardistischer Film wirbt auf ungewöhnliche Weise für diesen Service. Indem er faszinierende Möbelskulpturen zeigt, die sich als falsch aufgebaute IKEA Produkte entpuppen. Im Museum für Kunst und Gewerbe in Hamburg fand 2010 die Ausstellung Fenomen IKEA statt. Zwischen regulären Exponaten waren faszinierende Skulpturen platziert – aus falsch zusammengebauten IKEA Möbeln. Schilder warben für den Montageservice.

IKEA has beautiful furniture that can be self-assembled. But not everyone enjoys assembling furniture. That's why IKEA offers a service that does this in a professional and affordable way. A film advertised the IKEA Assembly Service by showing fascinating furniture sculptures, which were actually completely wrongly assembled IKEA furniture. At the Fenomen IKEA exhibition in Hamburg, we surprised visitors with a truly avant-garde idea: IKEA Furniture Art. Next to regular exhibition pieces, we placed fascinating sculptures – made of wrongly assembled IKEA furniture. Banners resolved the idea in a charming way and advertised the IKEA assembly service.

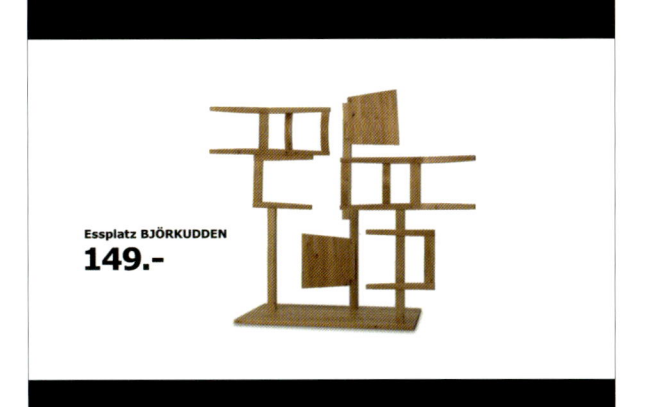

10

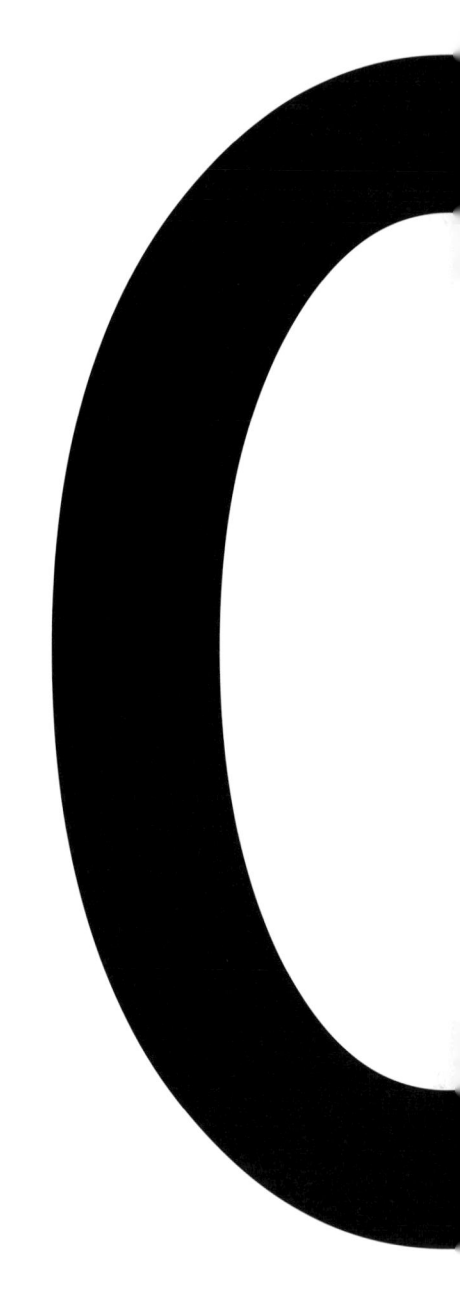

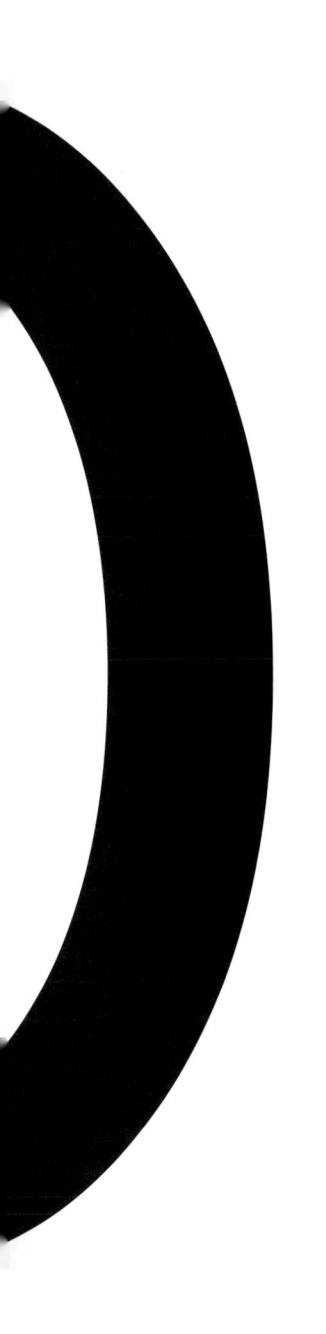

PUNKTE
POINTS

GOLD
DESIGN
DESIGN
  Design
  Produktdesign
  Design
  Product Design

ARCTIC PAPER
"Munken Cube"

Lead Agency
  JUNO
Client
  Arctic Paper
Executive Creative Direction
  Björn Lux,
  Wolfgang Greter,
  Frank Wache
Creative Direction
  Björn Lux,
  Wolfgang Greter
Printing
  eurodruck, Eurocaribe Druck und Verlag GmbH

Der Papierhersteller Arctic Paper und die Möbelmarke E15 wollen durch ungewöhnliche Kommunikationsmaßnahmen bekannter werden und ihr Image festigen. Juno erfindet mit dem Munken Cube ein Designobjekt, über das man spricht. Denn seine pure Machart aus Papier und Holz ist anders und bietet Freidenkern viel – als verformbare Skulptur, inspirierendes Arbeitsinstrument, schönes Konzeptmöbel.

Arctic Paper, producer of graphic fine-paper and furniture brand E15 want to strengthen their image and become even better known through unusual communication. Juno invents the Munken Cube, a design object which is talked about. Because its pure and radical paper and wood nature is different and offers the open minded many ways to use it: as shapeable sculpture, work tool or concept furniture.

GOLD
EDITORIAL
EDITORIAL
Editorial
Print/Einzelleistung
Editorial
Print/Individual Work

ZEITMAGAZIN
«Mon Dieu! Depardieu!»

Lead Agency
 ZEITmagazin
Client
 DIE ZEIT
Creative Direction
 Mirko Borsche
Art Direction
 Katja Kollmann
Chief Editing
 Christoph Amend
Graphic Design
 Nina Bengtson,
 Jasmin Müller-Stoy,
 Mirko Merkel
Image Editing
 Michael Biedowicz,
 Andreas Wellnitz
Image Processing
 Twentyfour Seven Creative
 Media Services GmbH
Photography
 Jonas Unger
Publishing House
 Zeitverlag Gerd Bucerius
 GmbH & Co. KG

ZEIT MAGAZIN

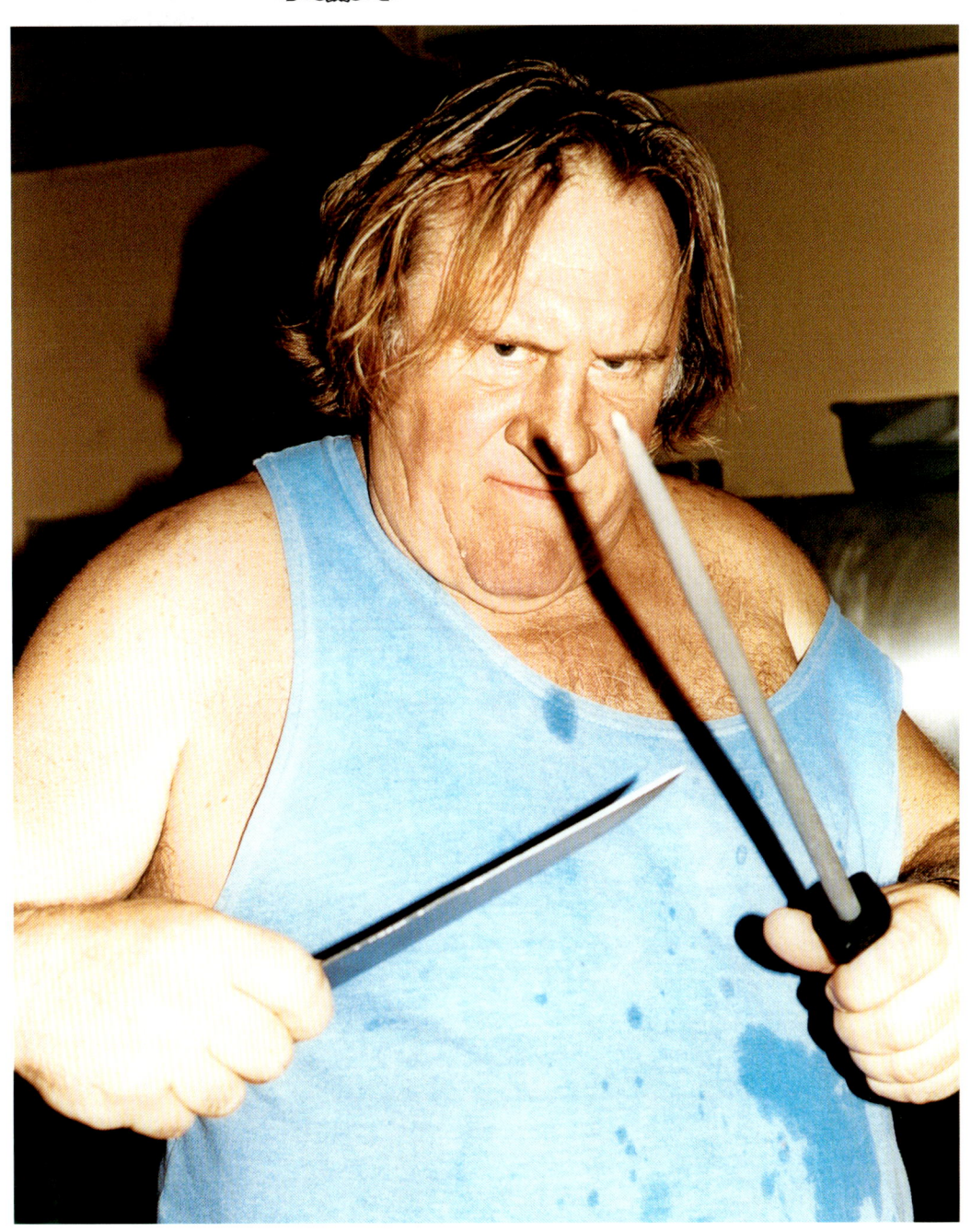

AAAH! GÉRARD!

ZU BESUCH AUF DEM WEINGUT VON FRANKREICHS GRÖSSTEM STAR

GOLD
KLASSISCHE MEDIEN
CLASSICAL MEDIA
Film
Kurzfilme/Sonderformate
für Bewegtbild
Film
Shorts/Special Formats
for Moving Pictures

FERRARI
 «Coppa di Sicilia»

Lead Agency
 Jack Rouse Associates
Client
 ALDAR Properties PJSC +
 Ferrari SPA
Marketing Direction
 Antonio Ghini
Advertising Direction
 Michele Pignatti
Creative Direction
 Randy Smith
Agency Production
 Anita Daugherty
Camera
 Jan Velicky
Cutting
 Filip Malasek E.C.
Film Direction/Radio Direction
 Ivan Zacharias
Film Production
 Group.IE GmbH in Co-production with Stink, London
Music Composition
 Varhan Orchestrovich Bauer
Postproduction
 Robota
Production
 Mark Gläser,
 Nick Landon

«Coppa di Sicilia» wurde exklusiv für das Cinema Maranello in dem 2010 neu eröffneten Themenpark Ferrari World in Abu Dhabi produziert und lässt den Zuschauer an dem glamourösen und intensiven Straßenrennen der 20er-Jahre teilhaben. Atmen Sie die Bergluft, hören Sie die Gänge schleifen und fühlen Sie den Staub, wenn die klassischen Rennwagen und ihre Fahrer sich diesem wagemutigen Rennen stellen.

«Coppa di Sicilia» has been exclusively produced for the Cinema Maranello in the Ferrari World Abu Dhabi, which opened in 2010. The audience virtually takes part in the as glamorous as intense road race in the early 1920s. You can almost breathe the mountain air as you can hear the gears shift and feel the dust, when the brave pilots meet the challenge of the venturous race in the fastest cars of their time.

- **BRONZE**
  DESIGN
  DESIGN
  Design
  Kunst-/Kultur-/
  Veranstaltungsplakate
  Design
  Art/Culture/Event Posters

- **BRONZE**
  CRAFT
  CRAFT
  Text
  Copy

- **BRONZE**
  CRAFT
  CRAFT
  Illustration
  Illustration

- **NOMINATION**
  KLASSISCHE MEDIEN
  CLASSICAL MEDIA
  Film
  TV/Kino Einzelspot
  Film
  TV/Cinema Commercial

DEUTSCHES SCHAUSPIELHAUS IN HAMBURG
»Seit 110 Jahren in der Kritik.«

Lead Agency
  Leagas Delaney Hamburg GmbH
Client
  Deutsches Schauspielhaus in Hamburg
Marketing Direction
  Olaf Bargheer,
  Uwe Heinrichs
Executive Creative Direction
  Hermann Waterkamp,
  Stefan Zschaler
Creative Direction
  Oliver Grandt,
  Willy Kaussen,
  Hermann Waterkamp
Art Direction
  Patrik Hartmann
Client Consulting
  Tjarko Horstmann,
  Heinke Kraack
Strategic Planning
  Simone Sauvigny
Agency Production
  Patrick Plogstedt,
  Katrin Wilken
Camera
  Timo Fritsche
Computer Animation
  Robert Rhee,
  Johannes Lippert,
  Sebastian Spitze,
  Axel Schmidt,
  Rafael Ahamad
Copy
  Michael Okun
Film Direction
  Michael Reissinger
Film Production
  Leagas Delaney Production,
  Pixelbutik by Deli Pictures
Final Artwork
  Dennis van Leeuwen,
  Kim-Fabien Eisenberg
Graphic Design
  Björn Byns,
  Sona Krude,
  Michael Reissinger,
  Björn Byns
Idea
  Michael Okun,
  Patrik Hartmann
Illustration
  Patrik Hartmann,
  Björn Byns,
  Sona Krude
Image Processing
  Dennis van Leeuwen,
  Kim-Fabien Eisenberg
Motion Graphics and 3D
  Stefan Rüffer,
  Thomas Volkmann,
  Malte Sarnes,
  Johannes Lippert
Music Composition
  BLUWI Music and Sound Design,
  Timo Blunck,
  Stefan Will,
  Marco Dreckkötter
Postproduction
  Deli Pictures,
  Bianca Mack
Production
  Sven Schmiede,
  Leagas Delaney Production,
  Pixelbutik by Deli Pictures
Screen Design
  Michael Reissinger
Sound Design
  BLUWI Music und Sound Design,
  Timo Blunck,
  Stefan Will,
  Marco Dreckkötter
Sound Engineering
  BLUWI Music and Sound Design,
  Timo Blunck,
  Stefan Will,
  Marco Dreckkötter
Typography
  Sona Krude

Das Deutsche Schauspielhaus hat in seiner langen Geschichte die Kritiker und das Publikum mit seinen gewagten Inszenierungen, ungewöhnlichen Interpretationen und provozierenden Vorstellungen immer wieder gegen sich aufgebracht. Das Jubiläum ist ein willkommener Anlass, die umstrittene Stellung des Theaters in der Stadt zu zelebrieren.

Throughout the long and vibrant history of the Hamburg Theatre, it has stirred critics and audiences alike with its adventurous productions, unusual interpretations and provocative performances. The Jubilee will be a fantastic occasion designed to celebrate the theatre's radical social standing and place in Hamburg's cultural heart.

● BRONZE
DIGITALE MEDIEN
DIGITAL MEDIA
  Digitale Medien
  Digitale Kampagnen
  Digital Media
  Digital Campaigns

● BRONZE
DIALOGMARKETING/
PROMOTION/MEDIA
DIALOG MARKETING/
PROMOTION/MEDIA
  Dialogmarketing
  Dialog Digital
  Dialog Marketing
  Dialog Digital

● BRONZE
DIGITALE MEDIEN
DIGITAL MEDIA
  Digitale Medien
  Online-Werbemaßnahmen
  Digital Media
  Online Advertising

● NOMINATION
DIALOGMARKETING/
PROMOTION/MEDIA
DIALOG MARKETING/
PROMOTION/MEDIA
  Media
  Media

IKEA
  »Bannerbau«

Lead Agency
  Grabarz & Partner
Client
  IKEA Deutschland GmbH & Co. KG
Marketing Direction
  Claudia Willvonseder (Marketing Management)
Advertising Direction
  Hendrik Zimmer (Head of Advertising)
Executive Creative Direction
  Ralf Heuel
Creative Direction
  Tom Hauser
Art Direction
  Oliver Zboralski
Client Consulting
  Denise Ewald,
  Franziska Mattes,
  Laura Becker
Copy
  Constantin Sossidi
Graphic Design
  Eike Fietje,
  Milena Pfannkuche
Production
  Erste Elf
Technical Direction
  Holger Knauer
Other
  Art Direction/Online:
  Per Wolter
  Flash/Animation:
  Matthias Mach
  Project Management:
  Jan Luebcke

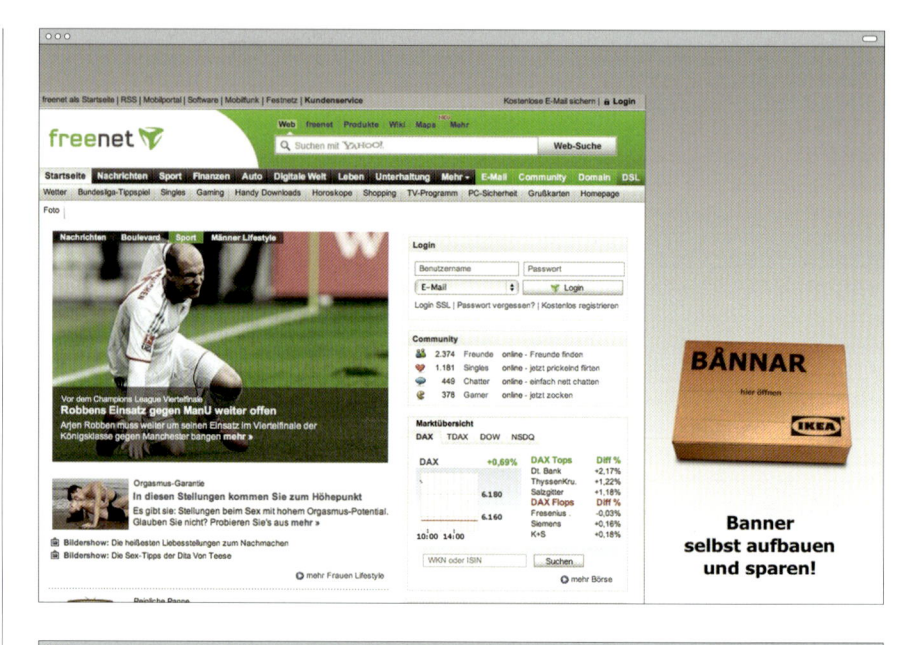

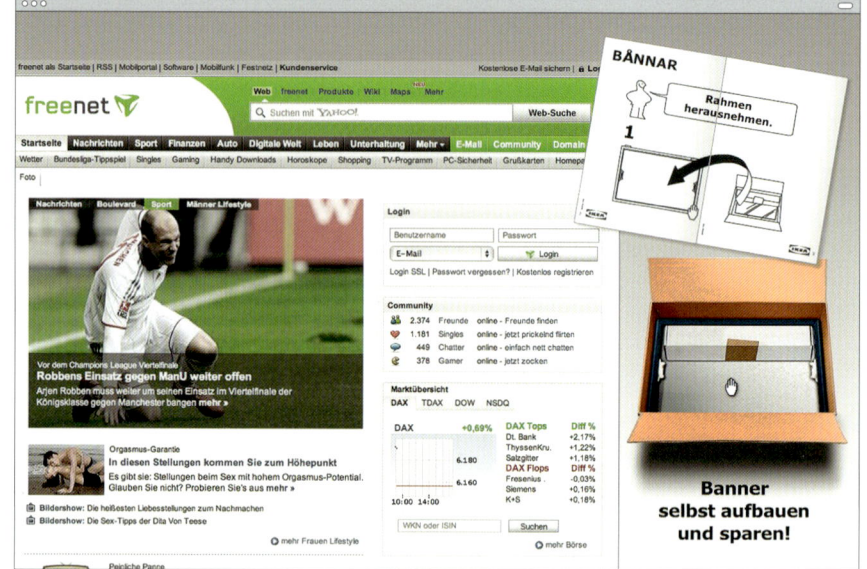

Mit Bannern, die der User selbst zusammenbauen konnte, machten wir spielerisch auf Angebote im Online-Store sowie auf das eigentliche IKEA Prinzip aufmerksam: Weil jeder seine Möbel selbst zusammenbaut, ist bei IKEA alles so schön günstig. Nach der Montage des Banners wurde der Preis des Produktes gesenkt und mit nur einem Klick gelangte der User direkt zum IKEA Online-Store.

With banners that can be self-assembled, we wanted to communicate the IKEA philosophy in a playful way: saving money by assembling things themselves. Each banner showed the IKEA Flatpack containing all the parts along with assembly instructions for putting it together. Once completed, the price was lowered and the visitor could then directly go on visit the IKEA online store.

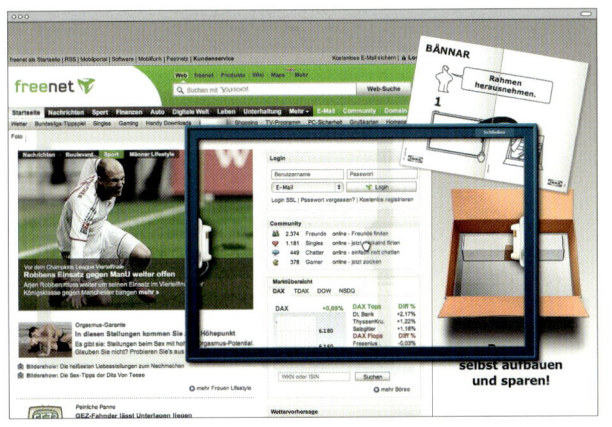

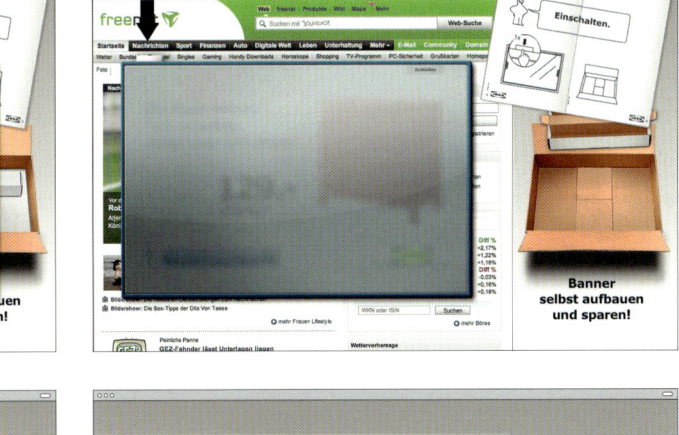

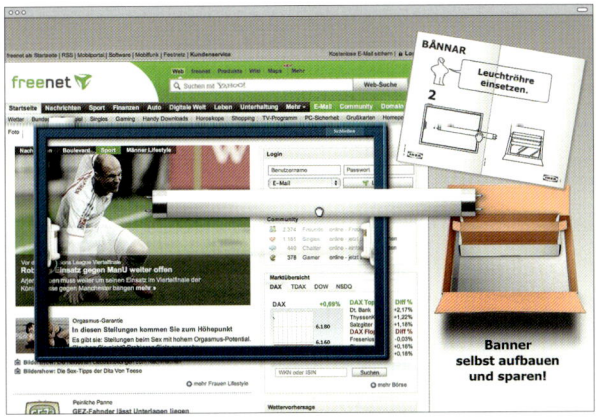

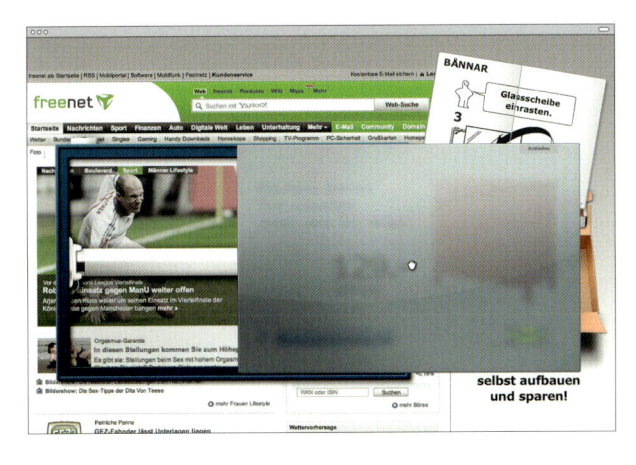

● SILVER
KLASSISCHE MEDIEN
CLASSICAL MEDIA
  Print
  Kampagne
  Print
  Campaign

● BRONZE
KLASSISCHE MEDIEN
CLASSICAL MEDIA
  Out-of-Home
  Klassisch Kampagne
  Out-of-Home
  Classic Campaign

● NOMINATION
KLASSISCHE MEDIEN
CLASSICAL MEDIA
  Film
  TV/Kino Einzelspot
  Film
  TV/Cinema Commercial

LEGO
  "Builders of Tomorrow"

Lead Agency
  Serviceplan
Client
  LEGO GmbH
Marketing Direction
  Christian Korbes
Executive Creative Direction
  Alexander Schill,
  Matthias Harbeck
Creative Direction
  Oliver Palmer
Art Direction
  Sandra Loibl,
  Julia Koch
Client Consulting
  Monika Klingenfuß,
  Denise Mancinone
Copy
  Frank Seiler
Film Direction
  Susanne Dittrich
Film Production
  Embassy of Dreams Film-
  produktion GmbH
Graphic Design
  Franz Röppischer
Photography
  Susanne Dittrich
Production
  Alexa Günther,
  Sebastian Eberhard,
  Igor Patalas
Sound Design
  m-sound

Die Baumeister von morgen sind die Lego-Baumeister von heute. Und gestern! Denn Lego ist und war schon immer das Spielzeug der Vordenker, der Smarten und Kreativen. Derjenigen, die ihrer Zeit schon immer weit voraus waren.

The builders of tomorrow are the Lego builders of today. And yesterday! Lego is and has always been the toy of the smart and creative ones. Those who have always been one step ahead.

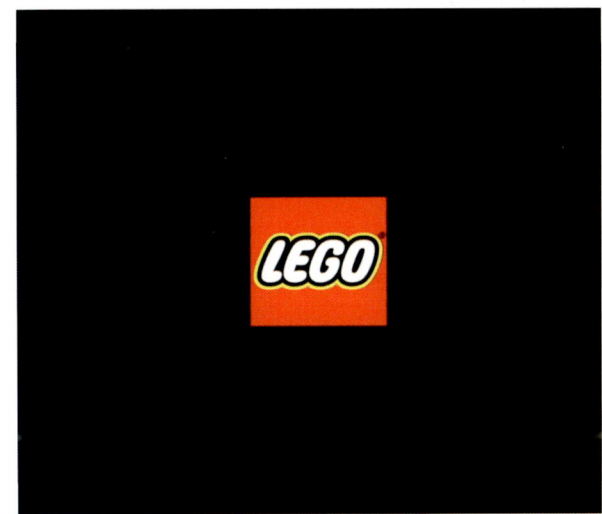

Builders of Tomorrow.

LEGO

SILVER
DIALOGMARKETING/
PROMOTION/MEDIA
DIALOG MARKETING/
PROMOTION/MEDIA
- Dialogmarketing
- Dialog Social Media
- Kampagnen
- Dialog Marketing
- Dialog Social Media
- Campaigns

BRONZE
DIGITALE MEDIEN
DIGITAL MEDIA
- Digitale Medien
- Digitale Kampagnen
- Digital Media
- Digital Campaigns

NOMINATION
DIGITALE MEDIEN
DIGITAL MEDIA
- Digitale Medien
- Social Media
- Digital Media
- Social Media

NIKE FOOTBALL
»Der Chip«

Lead Agency
 Kolle Rebbe GmbH
Client
 Nike Deutschland
Marketing Direction
 Oliver Eckart
Executive Creative Direction
 Stefan Kolle
Creative Direction
 Justin Landon,
 Florian Ludwig
Art Direction
 Felix Schulz,
 Jörg Dittmann
Client Consulting
 Markus Drühe,
 Florian Völlmecke
Agency Production
 Lars Wiepking
Copy
 Florian Ludwig,
 Malik Benamara
Cutting
 Kristin Ließ
Design
 Felix Schulz
Film Direction
 Kai Zastrow (Shylo)
Film Production
 Shylo
Idea
 Felix Schulz
Production
 Powerflasher GmbH
Sound Design
 Robert Jähnert
Other
 Concept: Tobias Wortmann
 Direction: Kai Zastrow (Shylo)

Mit der Social Media Promotion "The Chip" wandte sich Nike Football im Vorfeld der WM 2010 an die Facebook Community. Fußballfans erhielten die Chance, den Nationalspieler und Nike Athleten Mesut Özil auf einzigartige Weise ins Turnier zu begleiten – mit ihren anfeuernden Worten auf einem Microchip in dessen Schuh. Über eine Facebook-App konnten Fans Botschaften auf den Chip speichern.

Nike Football gave fans the once-in-a-lifetime opportunity to take part in the historic moments of the World Cup. The fans "stood on the pitch" with Mesut Özil with their words of encouragement on a microchip implanted in his shoe. With the help of Facebook, fans could save their message directly on the chip. All that was necessary: becoming a fan of the Nike Football Germany fanpage.

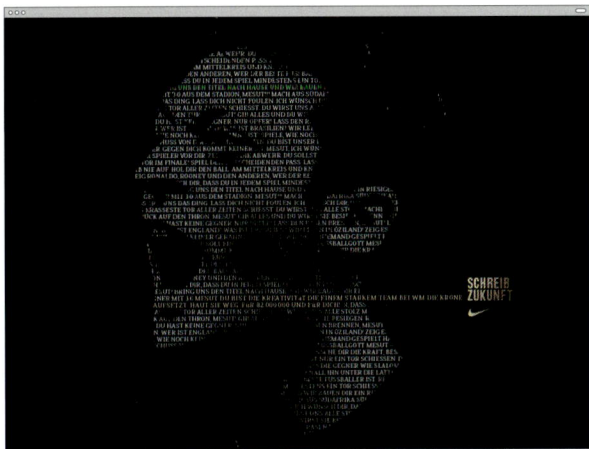

● SILVER
KLASSISCHE MEDIEN
CLASSICAL MEDIA
  Out-of-Home
  Nicht-Klassisch
  Out-of-Home
  Non-Classic

● BRONZE
DESIGN
DESIGN
  Design
  Grafische Einzelarbeiten
  Design
  Individual Graphics

● NOMINATION
CRAFT
CRAFT
  Typografie
  Typography

SERVICEPLAN HAMBURG
»Blut, Schweiß und Tränen«

Lead Agency
  serviceplan
Contributing Agencies
  plan.net
Client
  serviceplan campaign hamburg
Marketing Direction
  Stephanie Kramer
Executive Creative Direction
  Alexander Schill
Creative Direction
  Christoph Nann,
  Maik Kaehler
Art Direction
  Manuel Wolff,
  Savina Mokreva
Client Consulting
  Michael Falkensteiner
Graphic Design
  Maren Wandersleben,
  Christoff Strukamp,
  Christoph Kueckner
Typography
  Maik Kaehler
Other
  Programming: Steffen Knoblich

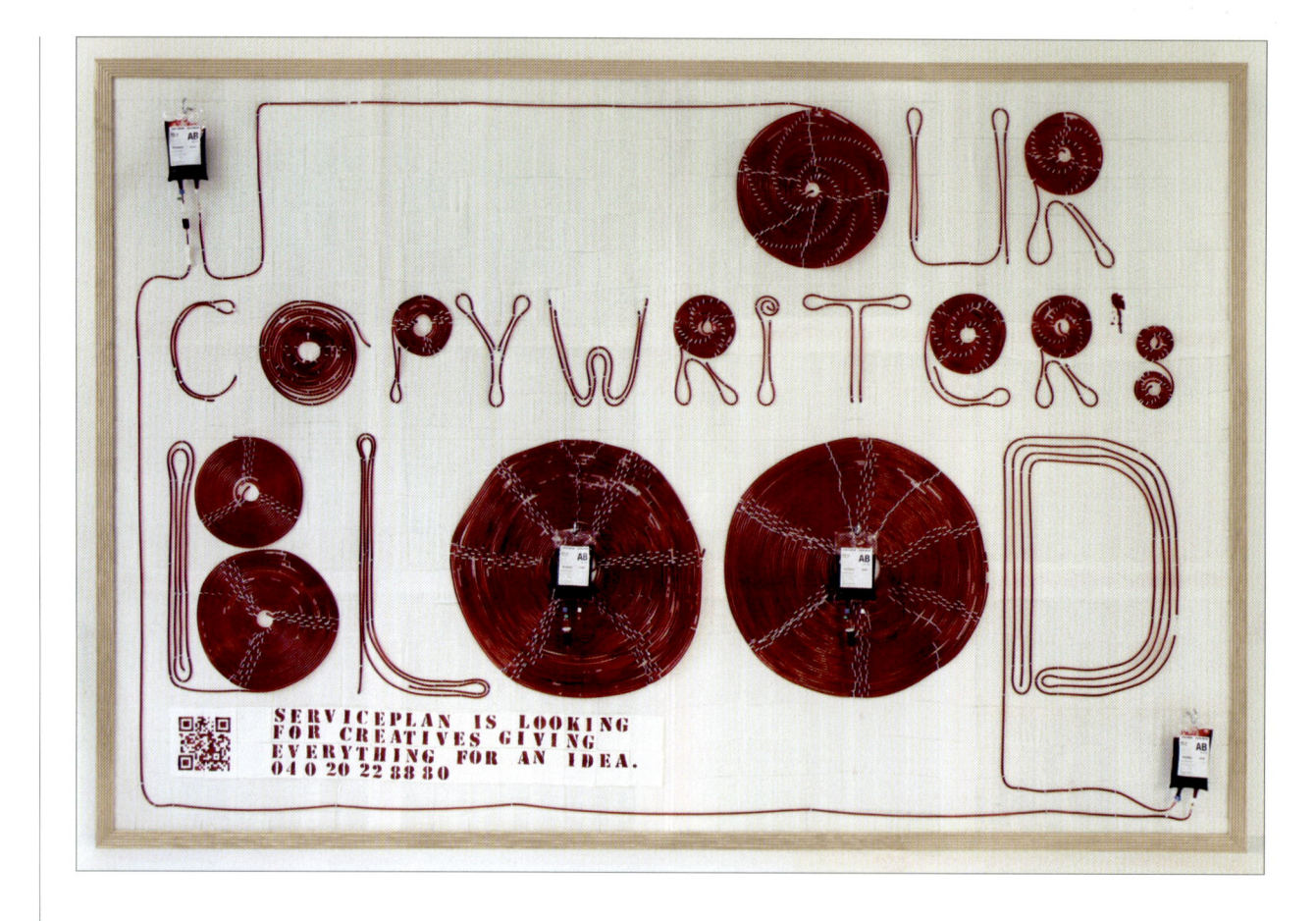

Serviceplan braucht Kreative, die für eine gute Idee alles geben – das heißt: Blut, Schweiß und Tränen. Um diese Aussage zu kommunizieren, haben wir Plakate aus genau diesen Rohstoffen gemacht.

Serviceplan needs creatives, who give everything for a good idea – meaning: blood, sweat and tears. To communicate this message, we made posters out of these materials.

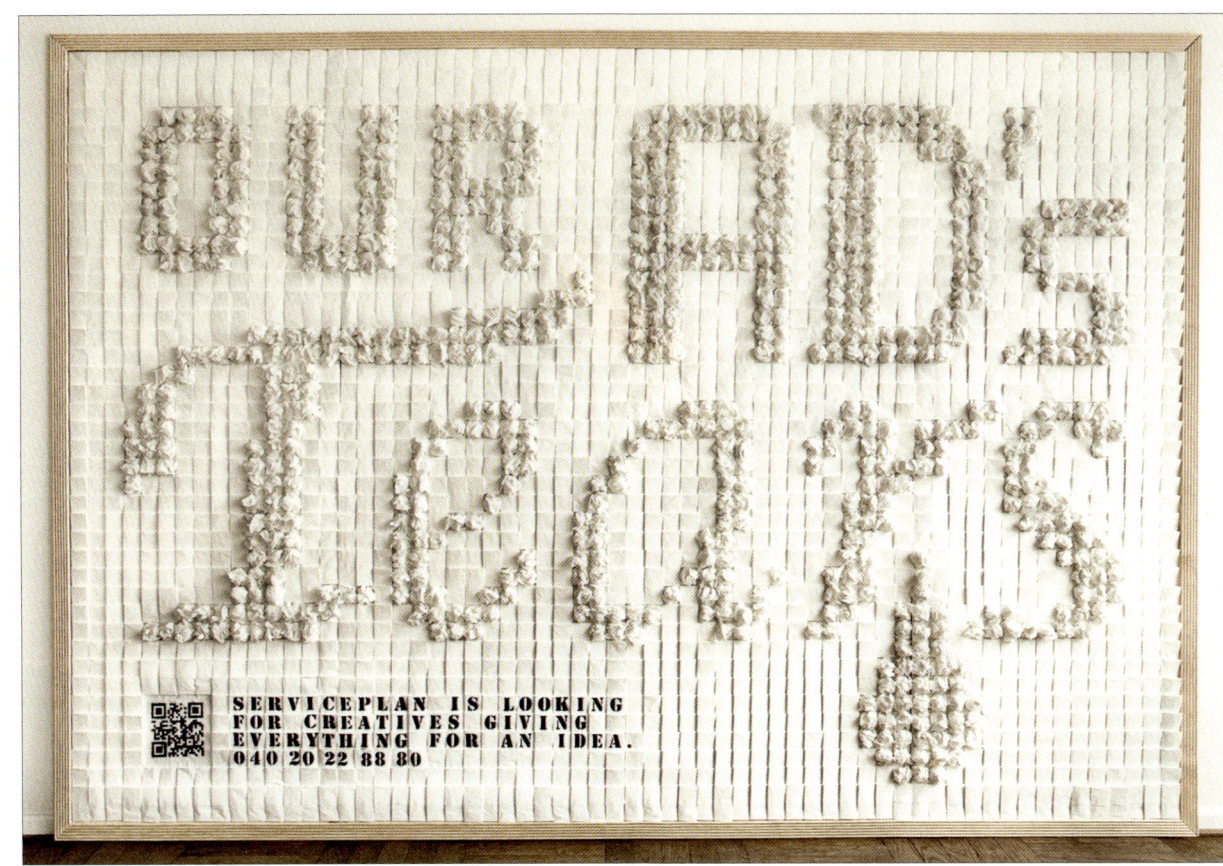

9

PUNKTE
POINTS

● BRONZE
DIGITALE MEDIEN
DIGITAL MEDIA
  Digitale Medien
  Digitale Kampagnen
  Digital Media
  Digital Campaigns

● BRONZE
DIALOGMARKETING/
PROMOTION/MEDIA
DIALOG MARKETING/
PROMOTION/MEDIA
  Promotion
  Aktivitäten
  Promotion
  Aktivitäten

● BRONZE
DIALOGMARKETING/
PROMOTION/MEDIA
DIALOG MARKETING/
PROMOTION/MEDIA
  Dialogmarketing
  Dialog Crossmediale
  Kampagnen
  Dialog Marketing
  Dialog Cross-Media
  Campaigns

CARITAS
  "One Minute of Silence"

Lead Agency
  Jung von Matt/Limmat
Client
  Caritas
Marketing Direction
  Jörg Arnold
Advertising Direction
  Andriu Deflorin
Executive Creative Direction
  Alexander Jaggy
Creative Direction
  Lukas Frei
Art Direction
  Fernando Perez
Client Consulting
  Martin Samsel,
  Sebastian Durband,
  Roman Meister,
  Andrea Gnädinger,
  Remo Brunner,
  Daniel Nessler
Strategic Planning
  Martin Samsel
Agency Production
  Ilonka Galliard
Copy
  Livio Dainese
Graphic Design
  Christina Baeriswyl
Production
  Südlich-t
Programming
  Pascal Beyeler
Publishing House
  Universal Music

Nach dem Erdbeben von Haiti lancierten Caritas und Universal Music "One Minute of Silence for Haiti". Eine Schweigeminute in Form einer leeren Musikdatei im Gedenken an die Opfer. Eine Mikrospende, bereit zum Download auf Musikplattformen. Die Aktion fand ihren Weg in die Medien. Popstars wurden zu Promotern. Radios spielten die Schweigeminute. Sie half mit, Haiti nicht zu schnell zu vergessen.

After the earthquake in Haiti, Caritas and Universal music launched "One Minute of Silence for Haiti" – an empty music track made in memory of the victims. It was available on several online music platforms and served as a micro donation. With pop stars promoting it and radio stations playing it, the campaign found its way into the media and helped us all to not forget Haiti too soon.

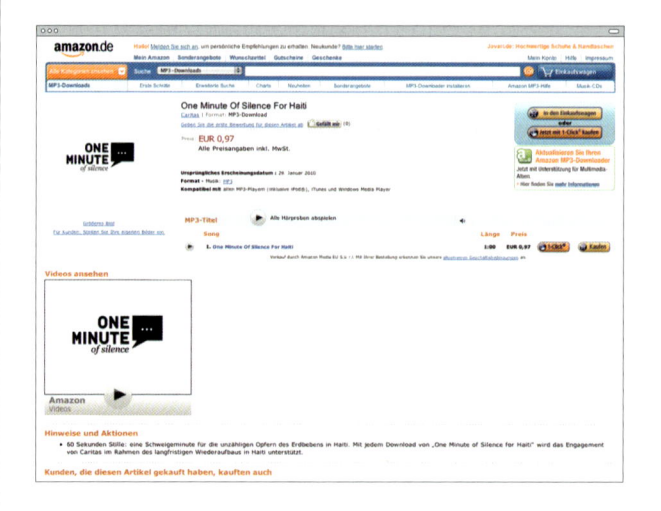

● SILVER
KLASSISCHE MEDIEN
CLASSICAL MEDIA
  Print
  Kampagne
  Print
  Campaign

● BRONZE
CRAFT
CRAFT
  Text
  Copy

DAS DEUTSCHE HANDWERK
  »Die Wirtschaftsmacht. Von nebenan.«

Lead Agency
  Scholz & Friends
Client
  Deutscher Handwerkskammertag (DHKT)
Marketing Direction
  Stefan Koenen
Executive Creative Direction
  Martin Pross,
  Matthias Spaetgens
Creative Direction
  Mathias Rebmann,
  Florian Schwalme,
  Oliver Handlos
Art Direction
  Felix Roy,
  Michael Schmidt
Client Consulting
  Benjamin Baader,
  Sven Weiche,
  Jana Bähr
Copy
  Mateo Sacchetti,
  Caspar Heuss,
  Momme Clausen,
  Edgar Linscheid,
  Nils Tscharnke
Graphic Design
  Patrick Vogel,
  Ines Gerlach

163

SILVER
KLASSISCHE MEDIEN
CLASSICAL MEDIA
 Print
 Kampagne
 Print
 Campaign

BRONZE
CRAFT
CRAFT
 Text
 Copy

HORNBACH BAUMARKT
»Ungekürzt«

Lead Agency
 HEIMAT, Berlin
Client
 Hornbach Baumarkt AG
Marketing Direction
 Frank Sahler
Advertising Direction
 Tina Heinz
Executive Creative Direction
 Guido Heffels
Creative Direction
 Guido Heffels,
 Matthias Storath
Art Direction
 Michael Dunlap,
 Benjamin Mohr,
 Myles Lord
Client Consulting
 Maik Richter,
 Mark Hassan,
 Daniela Strauss
Strategic Planning
 Matthias von Bechtolsheim
Art Buying
 Jessica Valin
Copy
 Guido Heffels,
 Matthias Storath,
 Mirjam Kundt
Final Artwork
 twentyfour seven, Berlin
Image Processing
 twentyfour seven, Berlin
Media
 Crossmedia, Duesseldorf
Photography
 Reinhard Hunger

○ SILVER
DESIGN
DESIGN
  Design
  Grafische Einzelarbeiten
  Design
  Individual Graphics

● BRONZE
CRAFT
CRAFT
  Typografie
  Typography

SAP
  »BIT.CODE – Kunstprojekt und Software-Demo«

Lead Agency
  Ogilvy Frankfurt
Client
  SAP Deutschland
Marketing Direction
  Barbara Windisch
Executive Creative Direction
  Dr. Stephan Vogel
Creative Direction
  Peter Strauss
Art Direction
  Christian Leithner
Client Consulting
  Veronika Sikvolgyi
Strategic Planning
  Co-Founder/Organisation:
  Victoria&Albert Museum,
  London
Design
  Artist: Julius Popp
Typography
  Artist: Julius Popp
Other
  Co-Founder/Organisation:
  Victoria & Albert Museum,
  London

Gemeinsam mit dem Victoria & Albert Museum beauftragte SAP den Leipziger Künstler Julius Popp, ein Kunstwerk zum Thema Datenflut zu gestalten. So entstand bit.code, eine Mischung aus monumentalem Schiebepuzzle und mechanischem Display. Zur Steuerung dient dabei SAP Software, die in Echtzeit besonders relevante Begriffe aus dem Internet filtert.

Commissioned by SAP and the Victoria & Albert Museum, Julius Popp created "bit.code". The machine uses SAP software to filter keywords from the Internet, which then appear on a huge mechanical display comprised of moving black and white chain links.

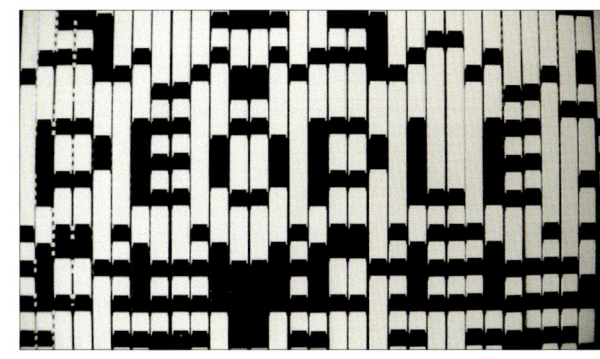

165

● SILVER
DESIGN
DESIGN
   Design
   Kunst-/Kultur-/
   Veranstaltungsplakate
   Design
   Art/Culture/Event Posters

● BRONZE
DESIGN
DESIGN
   Design
   Corporate Design
   Design
   Corporate Design

STAATSTHEATER STUTTGART
SCHAUSPIEL
   »Metropolis Serie«
   "Corporate Design"

Lead Agency
   Strichpunkt Design
Client
   Staatstheater Stuttgart
   Schauspiel
Marketing Direction
   Ingrid Trobitz
Executive Creative Direction
   Kirsten Dietz,
   Jochen Rädeker
Creative Direction
   Kirsten Dietz
Art Direction
   Julia Ochsenhirt
Client Consulting
   Alexandra Storr
Strategic Planning
   Kirsten Dietz,
   Jochen Rädeker
Concept
   Strichpunkt Design
Design
   Strichpunkt Design,
   Christopher Biel,
   Kirsten Dietz,
   Julia Ochsenhirt
Final Artwork
   Thomas Langanki
Graphic Design
   Strichpunkt Design
Illustration
   Strichpunkt Design
Typography
   Strichpunkt Design

Das Stuttgarter Schauspiel zieht aufgrund der Sanierung des Staatstheaters für eine Spielzeit in eine ehemalige Autowerkstatt und eröffnet gleichzeitig eine weitere neue Spielstätte fernab der Innenstadt, das »Nord«. Um die neuen Spielstätten deutlich ins Bewusstsein der Öffentlichkeit zu bringen, wird das Corporate Design umfassend überarbeitet und in Richtung eines Off-Theaters verändert.

Due to renovations at the Staatstheater (state theater), the Stuttgart Schauspiel (Stuttgart playhouse) is moving to a former car workshop for one season and, at the same time, opening a further new venue outside the city center, the »Nord«. In order to bring the new venues clearly into public consciousness, the corporate design has been comprehensively reworked and given an off-theater touch.

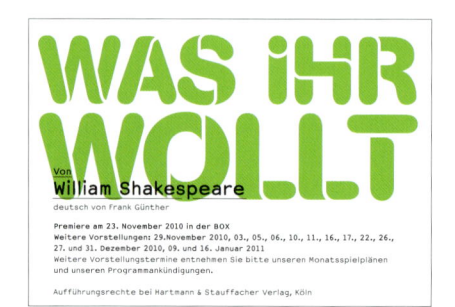

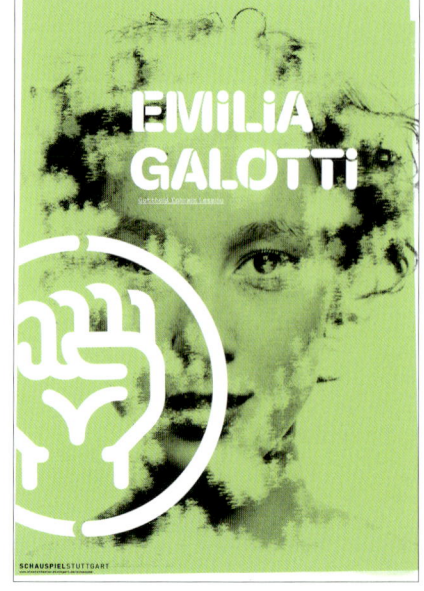

8

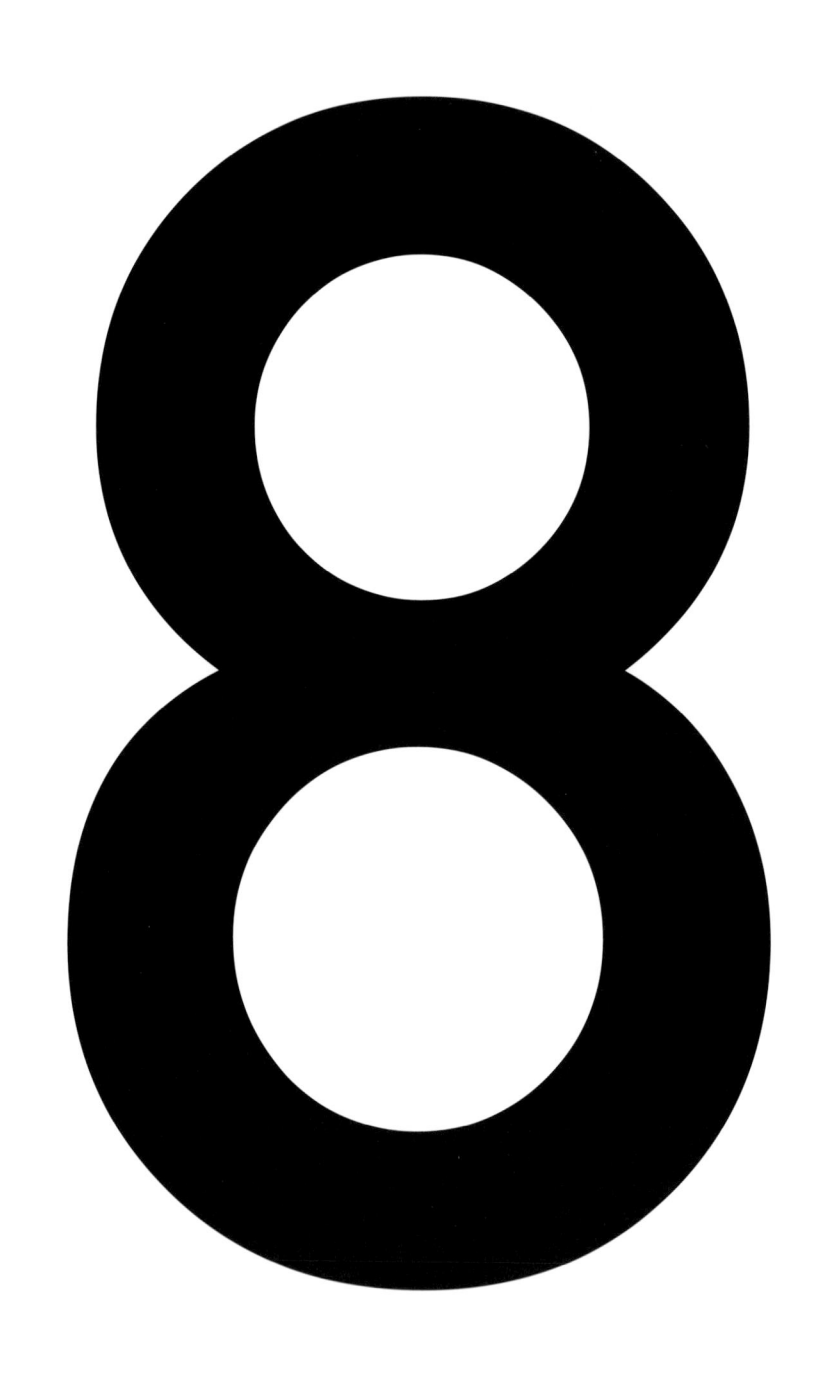

PUNKTE
POINTS

● **BRONZE**
EDITORIAL
EDITORIAL
  Editorial
  Print/Jahrgang
  Editorial
  Print/Year's Issue

● **BRONZE**
EDITORIAL
EDITORIAL
  Editorial
  Print/Einzelleistung
  Editorial
  Print/Individual Work

● **NOMINATION**
EDITORIAL
EDITORIAL
  Editorial
  Print/Ausgabe
  Editorial
  Print/Issue

● **NOMINATION**
CRAFT
CRAFT
  Fotografie
  Photography

NIDO MAGAZIN
  »Jahrgang 2010«
  »Niedrigenergiespiele«
  »Ausgabe 6/2010«
  »Streng sein«

Lead Agency
  Redaktion NIDO
Client
  NEON Magazin GmbH
Marketing Direction
  Antje Schlünder
Executive Creative Direction
  Thomas Lindner,
  Andreas Petzold
Art Direction
  Tom Ising
Chief Editing
  Michael Ebert,
  Timm Klotzek
Copy
  Paul-Philipp Hanske
Editing
  Patrick Bauer,
  Marc Deckert (Editor-in-Chief),
  Paul-Philipp Hanske,
  Maike Rohlfing,
  Julia Rothhaas,
  Benedikt Sarreiter,
  Alex Schmid,
  Vera Schroeder (Deputy Chief Editing),
  Kerstin Seidel,
  Sandra Stolle
Graphic Design
  Franziska Kronast,
  Axel Lauer
Illustration
  Various
Image Editing
  Yvonne Bauer (Director of Photography),
  Nina Banneyer,
  Gregor Wilhelm
Photography
  Julia Meister and Giovanni de Paulis,
  Silke Weinsheimer,
  Various
Printing
  Mohn Media GmbH
Publishing House
  NEON Magazin GmbH/
  Gruner+Jahr AG & Co KG
Other
  Styling: Syria Bellisario

7

PUNKTE
POINTS

○ SILVER
KLASSISCHE MEDIEN
CLASSICAL MEDIA
  Film
    TV/Kino Einzelspot
  Film
    TV/Cinema Commercial

● NOMINATION
KLASSISCHE MEDIEN
CLASSICAL MEDIA
  Film Craft
    Casting
  Film Craft
    Casting

MERCEDES-BENZ E-KLASSE BAS PLUS
  "Sorry"

Lead Agency
  Jung von Matt AG
Client
  Daimler AG
Marketing Direction
  Lüder Fromm,
  Anders-Sundt Jensen
Advertising Direction
  Jochen Schmidt,
  Damir Maric,
  Kai Köpf
Creative Direction
  Michael Ohanian,
  Jacques Pense
Art Direction
  Robert Herter
Client Consulting
  Florian Schramm,
  Sven Dörrenbächer,
  Sonja Stockmann
Agency Production
  Vanessa Fischbeck
Camera
  Marc Achenbach
Casting
  element-e Filmproduktion
  GmbH/Silja Uckert
Copy
  Robert Herter
Cutting
  firsteight, Timo Fritsche
Film Direction
  Alex Feil
Film Production
  element-e Filmproduktion
  GmbH/Bernd T. Hoefflin
Idea
  Robert Herter
Music Composition
  Supreme Music,
  Maximilian Olowinsky,
  Felix Müller,
  Florian Lakenmacher
Postproduction
  firsteight/Acht Frankfurt
Sound Design
  A.R.T. Studios/Ben Meinhof

Ein Mann fährt in einem Mercedes durch den Wald. Plötzlich taucht neben ihm der leibhaftige Tod auf und sagt in sarkastischem Ton: "sorry". Da passiert es: Das Auto fährt auf ein umgekipptes Baufahrzeug zu und bremst gerade noch rechtzeitig ab. Nach einer kurzen Schrecksekunde antwortet der Fahrer bissig: "Sorry". (Super:) Erkennt Gefahren und verstärkt die Bremskraft. Der Bremsassistent Plus.

A man is driving a Mercedes. Suddenly, the Grim Reaper appears next to him. He looks to the shocked driver and sarcastically says "sorry". The car heads straight for an overturned construction vehicle and manages to stop. After a second of shock, the driver turns to the Reaper and caustically replies "sorry". (Chart:) Senses danger and increases braking power. Brake Assist Plus.

SILVER
KLASSISCHE MEDIEN
CLASSICAL MEDIA
   Film
   Kurzfilme/Sonderformate für Bewegtbild
   Film
   Shorts/Special Formats for Moving Pictures

NOMINATION
DIALOGMARKETING/ PROMOTION/MEDIA
DIALOG MARKETING/ PROMOTION/MEDIA
   Dialogmarketing
   Dialog Broadcast
   Dialog Marketing
   Dialog Broadcast

DAWANDA
   "Creating Love – A Communityfilm"

Lead Agency
   WE DO communication GmbH GWA
Client
   DaWanda GmbH
Marketing Direction
   Christiane Thom
Executive Creative Direction
   Prof. Christoph M. Scheller
Creative Direction
   Thomas Avenhaus
Art Direction
   Fabian Jung,
   Sebastian Kamp,
   Anja Diezel
Client Consulting
   Cécile Engelen
Strategic Planning
   Prof. Christoph M. Scheller
Agency Production
   Cécile Engelen
Computer Animation
   Christoph Wanja
Concept
   Fabian Jung,
   Sebastian Kamp
Consulting
   gregor c. blach
Copy
   Felix Wetzel
Cutting
   Oskar Ziemba
Design
   DaWanda Community
Film Production
   WE DO communication GmbH GWA
Graphic Design
   DaWanda Community
Idea
   Fabian Jung,
   Sebastian Kamp
Illustration
   Pia Marecki
IT Direction
   Andreas Maser
Motion Graphics and 3D
   Christoph Wanja
Postproduction
   Oskar Ziemba
Programming
   Christoph Wanja
Sound Design
   Oskar Ziemba
Technical Conception
   Andreas Maser
Technical Direction
   Andreas Maser

Dawanda, der Online-Marktplatz für Unikate und Selbstgemachtes, ruft seine Community dazu auf, ein Stück handgemachter Kommunikation zu gestalten: 1.620 Kreative aus über 30 Ländern schaffen gemeinsam ein visuelles Feuerwerk aus ebenso vielen Einzelbildern, die als animierter und komplett User-generierter Kurzfilm mit einem Augenzwinkern erzählen, wie Dinge mit Liebe gemacht werden.

Dawanda, the online market for one-of-a-kind and handmade pieces called on its users to design a piece of "crafted communication". 1,620 designers from more than 30 countries created a visual piece of art comprised of just as many individual frames. Knitted together, these frames make for an animated, exclusively user-generated short film that shows with a wink how things are made with love.

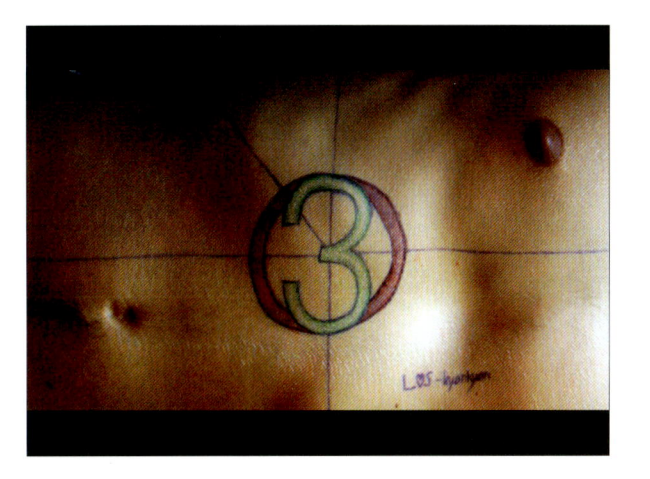

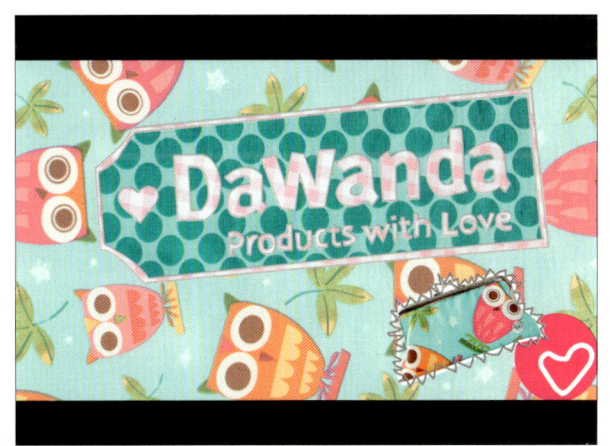

**SILVER
DIGITALE MEDIEN
DIGITAL MEDIA**
 Digitale Medien
 Mobile
 Digital Media
 Mobile

**NOMINATION
DIGITALE MEDIEN
DIGITAL MEDIA**
 Digitale Medien Craft
 Innovative Technologien
 Digital Media Craft
 Innovative Technologies

FACEBOOK PLACES HIJACK
 »Erster!«

Lead Agency
 Jung von Matt AG
Client
 Jung von Matt AG
Creative Direction
 Kai Heuser,
 Michael Ohanian
Copy
 Gün Aydemir
Idea
 Kai Heuser,
 Gün Aydemir
Innovative Technology
 Gün Aydemir,
 Kai Heuser

Wir nutzten einen technischen Trick, um die "Places" unserer Mitbewerber noch vor dem Start des Dienstes auf Facebook anzulegen und dort eine Nachricht zu hinterlassen. Zum offiziellen Deutschlandstart von "Places" checkten die Kreativen in ihren Agenturen ein und wurden dort von unserer Botschaft erwartet: »Erster! Wärt ihr auch gern? Dann checkt ein bei jvm-neckar.de/jobs, wir suchen neue Köpfe.«

Using a simple technical trick, we created our competitors "places" on Facebook before the service started in Germany. Three months later, "places" started officially and creatives who checked into their agencies received our message: First! Want to join? Check in at www.jvm-neckar.de/jobs, we are hiring.

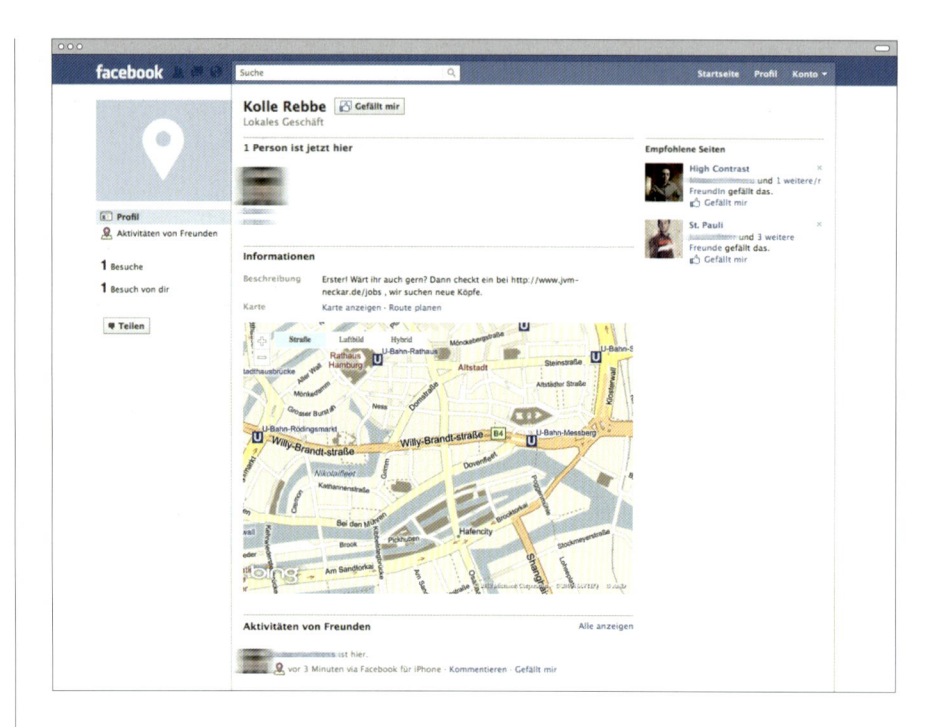

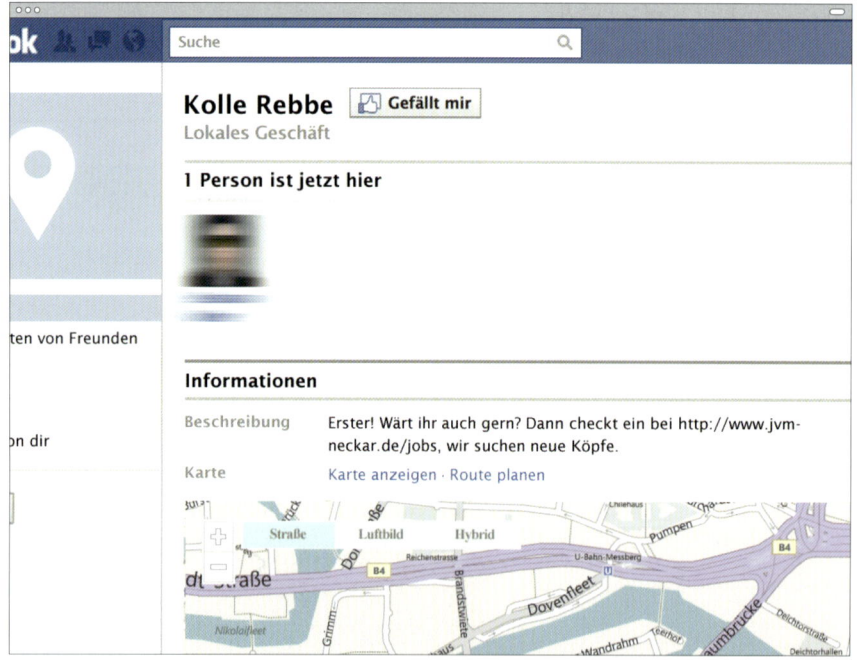

● **BRONZE**
DIGITALE MEDIEN
DIGITAL MEDIA
  Digitale Medien Craft
  Motiondesign
  Digital Media Craft
  Motion Design

● **BRONZE**
DIGITALE MEDIEN
DIGITAL MEDIA
  Digitale Medien Craft
  Interface/Navigation
  Digital Media Craft
  Interface/Navigation

● **NOMINATION**
DIGITALE MEDIEN
DIGITAL MEDIA
  Digitale Medien
  Websites
  Digital Media
  Websites

MOTO WAGANARI
  "Directing Shadows"

Lead Agency
  Ogilvy Frankfurt
Client
  Moto Waganari
Executive Creative Direction
  Michael Kutschinski
Creative Direction
  Uwe Jakob,
  Dr. Ulf Schmidt
Art Direction
  Uwe Jakob
Strategic Planning
  Project Management:
  Jens Steffen, Uwe Jakob
Computer Animation
  Jens Steffen,
  Ralf Zimmermann
Copy
  Dr. Ulf Schmidt
Idea
  Uwe Jakob,
  Jens Steffen
Interface Navigation
  Uwe Jakob,
  Jens Steffen,
  Ralf Zimmermann
Motion Design
  Uwe Jakob,
  Jens Steffen,
  Ralf Zimmermann
Programming
  Jens Steffen,
  Ralf Zimmermann,
  Frank Schwarzhoff,
  Isabell Grasshoff
Sound Design
  Lars Kellner, Sinus AV Studio
Other
  Project Management:
  Jens Steffen, Uwe Jakob

Um die filigranen Plastiken von Moto Waganari am zweidimensionalen Screen interaktiv zu präsentieren und zu verkaufen, eröffneten wir "Directing Shadows", die interaktive Lichtgalerie. Per Feuerzeug oder Handy-Display steuert der User über seine Webcam das Licht und wird zum Regisseur eines Licht-, Schatten- und Klangspiels. Er hört Kommentare des Künstlers und kann die Skulpturen direkt bestellen.

Only with light and space, the filigree sculptures of the Japanese artist Moto Waganari become a real artistic experience. Therefore, we built "Directing Shadows," the interactive light gallery. Take your lighter or your phone display, hold it in front of your webcam. The light beam on the website reacts to your movements. Immerse into the play of light and shadow and hear the artist's comments.

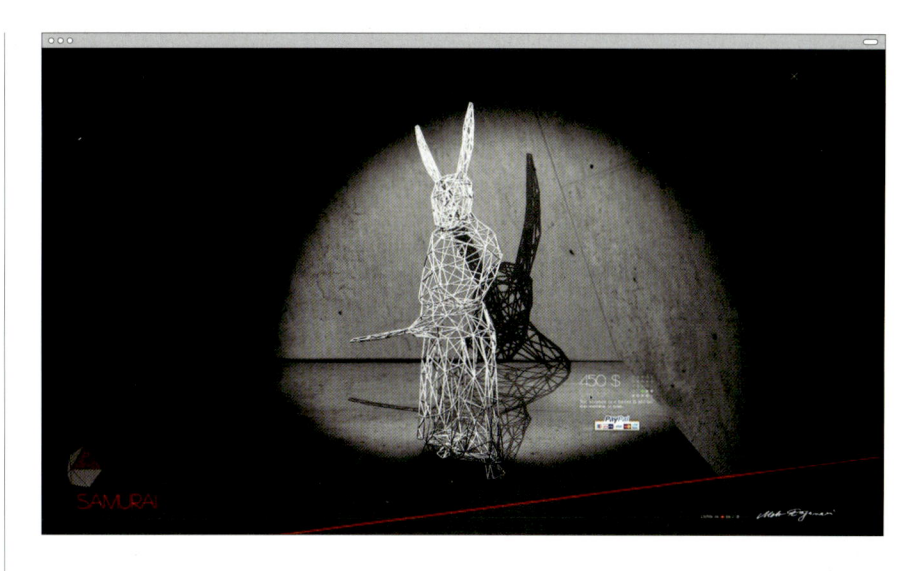

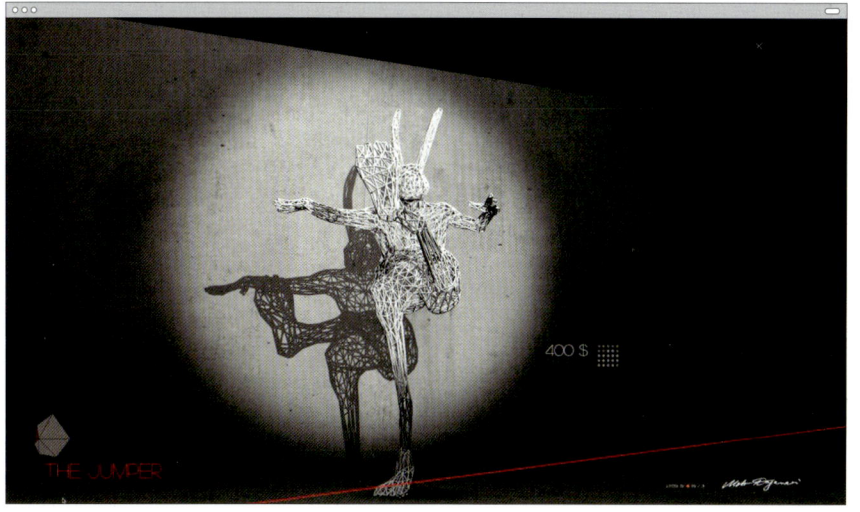

SILVER
DIALOGMARKETING/
PROMOTION/MEDIA
DIALOG MARKETING/
PROMOTION/MEDIA
 Dialogmarketing
 Dialog Mail
 Dialog Marketing
 Dialog Mail

NOMINATION
DESIGN
DESIGN
 Design
 Grafische Einzelarbeiten
 Design
 Individual Graphics

MERCEDES-BENZ
 »Sprinter Bewerbung«

Lead Agency
 Lukas Lindemann Rosinski GmbH
Client
 Daimler AG
Marketing Direction
 Andrés Orejón
Advertising Direction
 Till Wartenberg
Executive Creative Direction
 Arno Lindemann,
 Bernhard Lukas
Creative Direction
 Thomas Heyen,
 Markus Kremer,
 Jakob Kriwat
Art Direction
 Markus Kremer,
 Damian Kuczmierczyk
Client Consulting
 Konstanze Kievenheim,
 Jascha Oevermann
Agency Production
 Martin Schön (Markenfilm Crossing)
Copy
 Thomas Heyen
Film Direction
 Marc Bethke
Film Production
 Markenfilm Crossing
Graphic Design
 Victor Aloji
Production
 Thomas Beecken
Other
 Timo Schwarz (DoP)

Der Sprinter: bester Arbeiter fürs Unternehmen. Und wer in Unternehmen arbeiten will, muss sich persönlich bewerben. Wir erfanden den ersten Reifen mit Typografie-Profil. Mit echtem Matsch auf seinem Reifen »schrieb« der Sprinter seine Bewerbungen einfach selbst. Über einen Link auf eine Microsite konnten die angeschriebenen Unternehmen die Entstehung der Bewerbung nachvollziehen.

The Sprinter is one of the best workers a company could have. However, before you can work in a company, you have to apply for a job. So the Sprinter did: he wrote his own letter of application with specially made tires. Each letter of application came with a link to a campaign microsite, providing video evidence that the Sprinter really had written the application itself.

SILVER
DIALOGMARKETING/
PROMOTION/MEDIA
DIALOG MARKETING/
PROMOTION/MEDIA
   Dialogmarketing
   Dialog Digital
   Dialog Marketing
   Dialog Digital

NOMINATION
DIGITALE MEDIEN
DIGITAL MEDIA
   Digitale Medien
   E-Mail
   Digital Media
   E-Mail

WIENERS+WIENERS
   »Selbstübersetzende Mail«

Lead Agency
   Grabarz & Partner
Client
   WIENERS+WIENERS GmbH
Marketing Direction
   Tina Berns
Advertising Direction
   Managing Director:
   Ralf Wieners
Executive Creative Direction
   Ralf Heuel
Creative Direction
   Djik Ouchiian,
   Martin Grass
Art Direction
   Thorsten Sievering
Client Consulting
   Ina Bach,
   Nils Rüsenberg,
   Executive Direction Consulting:
   Thomas Eickhoff
Copy
   Gregor Willimski,
   Max Benrath,
   Andreas Schriewer
Other
   Flash Development:
   Veronika Ziegler,
   Sebastian Fiedler

Der extrem schnelle Übersetzungsservice von Wieners+Wieners sollte beworben werden. Idee: Wir entwickelten das erste Mailing der Welt, das sich selbst übersetzt. Öffnete der Empfänger die E-Mail, verwandelte sich das deutschsprachige Anschreiben – Wort für Wort und von links nach rechts – automatisch ins Englische. Botschaft: Keiner übersetzt schneller.

The extremely fast translation service provided by Wieners+Wieners needed to be advertised. The idea: we developed the world's first e-mail that translates itself. When the recipient opens the e-mail, the German message transforms automatically – word for word from left to right – into English. The message: No one translates faster.

● SILVER
DESIGN
DESIGN
  Design
  Packaging
  Design
  Packaging

● NOMINATION
DESIGN
DESIGN
  Design
  Produktdesign
  Design
  Product Design

GÖRTZ 17
"Shoelace Box"

Lead Agency
  loved gmbh
Contributing Agencies
  kempertrautmann gmbh
Client
  Görtz GmbH,
  Görtz 17 GmbH
Marketing Direction
  Michael Jacobs
Creative Direction
  Tim Belser,
  Heiko Freyland
Client Consulting
  Dr. Michael Trautmann
Copy
  Heiko Freyland
Design
  Tim Belser,
  Heiko Freyland
Graphic Design
  Christiane Eckhardt
Photography
  Peter Rüssmann
Production
  Alexander Kate (Cross Marketing Produktion GmbH)

Der erste Schuhkarton, für den keine Einkaufstüte benötigt wird. Die puristische Gestaltung legt den Fokus auf die Tragegriffe, die sich entfernen und als zusätzliches Paar Schnürsenkel verwenden lassen. Die Serie umfasst fünf Designs, farblich abgestimmt auf die Converse Kollektion von Görtz 17.

The first recyclable shoebox that makes the plastic bag unnecessary. Its minimalist design draws attention to the handles, which can be removed and used as an extra pair of shoelaces. The series consists of five colour-coordinated designs that match Görtz 17's Converse collection perfectly .

● SILVER
RÄUMLICHE INSZENIERUNG
SPATIAL SCENE-SETTING
   Kommunikation im Raum
   Environmental Design

● NOMINATION
DESIGN
DESIGN
   Design
   Corporate Design
   Design
   Corporate Design

GEGEN STUTTGART 21
»K 21«

Lead Agency
   Stuttgart Citizens
Client
   Stuttgart Citizens
Marketing Direction
   Stuttgart Citizens
Advertising Direction
   Stuttgart Citizens
Creative Direction
   Stuttgart Citizens
Art Direction
   Stuttgart Citizens
Strategic Planning
   Stuttgart Citizens
Agency Production
   Stuttgart Citizens
Animation/Visual Effects/
Special Effects
   Stuttgart Citizens
Architecture
   Stuttgart Citizens
Architecture/Scenography
   Stuttgart Citizens
Art Buying
   Stuttgart Citizens
Artist
   Stuttgart Citizens
Audio Production
   Stuttgart Citizens
Computer Animation
   Stuttgart Citizens
Concept
   Stuttgart Citizens
Consulting
   Stuttgart Citizens
Copy
   Stuttgart Citizens
Design
   Stuttgart Citizens
Editing and Copywriting
   Stuttgart Citizens
Exhibit Design
   Stuttgart Citizens
Film Production
   Stuttgart Citizens
Final Artwork
   Stuttgart Citizens
Graphic Design
   Stuttgart Citizens
Idea
   Stuttgart Citizens
Illustration
   Stuttgart Citizens
Image Editing
   Stuttgart Citizens
Image Processing
   Stuttgart Citizens
Interactive Production
   Stuttgart Citizens
Media Systems
   Stuttgart Citizens
Motion Graphics and 3D
   Stuttgart Citizens
Photography
   Stuttgart Citizens
Production
   Stuttgart Citizens
Technical Implementation
   Stuttgart Citizens
Technical Installation
   Stuttgart Citizens
Typography
   Stuttgart Citizens

Der Widerstand gegen Stuttgart 21 beginnt im Oktober 2009 mit vier Leuten. Ein Jahr später sind es 100.000. Kaum ein räumliches Zeichen hat in den letzten zwölf Monaten eine größere Medienpräsenz ausgelöst als der Bauzaun am Nordflügel des Stuttgarter Bahnhofs. Dahinter stehen kein Kunde, kein Auftrag, keine Agentur, keine Kampagne, kein Etat, sondern tausende Stuttgarter Bürger. Kommunikation auf allen Kanälen. Der Widerstand gegen Stuttgart 21 geht weiter.

Resistance to Stuttgart 21 began in October 2009 with just four people, one year later there were 100,000. Few barriers have generated a larger media presence in the past twelve months than the building site fence at the north wing of Stuttgart main station. There is no client, no assignment, no agency, no campaign and no budget behind it, but thousands of Stuttgart citizens. Communication across all channels. The resistance to Stuttgart 21 goes on.

SILVER
RÄUMLICHE INSZENIERUNG
SPATIAL SCENE-SETTING
  Events
  Events

NOMINATION
RÄUMLICHE INSZENIERUNG
SPATIAL SCENE-SETTING
  Events Craft
  Setdesign/Architektur
  Events Craft
  Set Design/Architecture

DIESEL
  "Be Stupid Facepark"

Lead Agency
  DDB Tribal Group
Contributing Agencies
  Nowadays GmbH & Co. KG,
  Parasol Island GmbH
Client
  Diesel Deutschland GmbH
Marketing Direction
  Christina Käßhöfer
Executive Creative Direction
  Eric Schoeffler
Creative Direction
  Dennis May, Dan Strasser
Art Direction
  Franziska Scholz,
  Dominika Zajac,
  Chris Bueltmann,
  Mihai Botarel,
  Tobias Hecking
Client Consulting
  Sönke Bruns, Marco Diel
Agency Production
  Johannes Haverkamp,
  Jankel Huppertz
Camera
  Dennis Guth, Lars Romanti
Copy
  Mihai Botarel,
  Tobias Hecking
Film Direction
  Alexander Eckert,
  Matthias Freier
Film Production
  Parasol Island GmbH
  (Sebastian Druschel,
  Sara Dadras)
Production
  Nowadays GmbH & Co. KG
  (Marielle Jaquier, Tatjana Volk)
Programming
  Dennis Markgraf,
  Roland Loesslein,
  Alexander Valentin
Screen Design
  Alexander Lenz, Regina Rebele
Set Design/Architecture
  Marielle Jaquier, Tatjana Volk,
  Dennis May, Dan Strasser,
  Franziska Scholz,
  Dominika Zajac,
  Chris Bueltmann
Other
  Dennis Guth, Stephan Krause

2010 brachten wir Diesels "Be stupid"-Philosophie ins echte Leben. Mit Facepark. Einem anti-digitalen Event, das Elemente aus dem Internet analog in einen Park brachte; Pappprofilwände, analoge Kommentar-, Gefällt-mir- und Anstups-Funktionen, Spiele, Gruppen, Youtube-Player und andere Elemente ließen Menschen erleben, dass es besser ist, sein Leben im Park als vor einem Bildschirm zu verschwenden.

In 2010, we brought Diesel's "Be stupid" philosophy to real life. With Facepark. An anti-digital event that brought elements from the Internet into a park in an analog way; cardboard profilewalls, analog comment, like and poke functions, games, groups, a Youtube player and other elements let people experience that it's better to waste one's life in the park than in front of a screen.

6

PUNKTE
POINTS

SILVER
KLASSISCHE MEDIEN
CLASSICAL MEDIA
  Print
  Einzelmotiv
  Print
  Single Motif

STIHL KETTENSÄGE MS 880
»Wikinger«

Lead Agency
  Scholz & Friends
Client
  ANDREAS STIHL AG &
  Co. KG
Marketing Direction
  Jürgen Fitting
Advertising Direction
  Norbert Blania
Executive Creative Direction
  Martin Pross,
  Matthias Spaetgens
Creative Direction
  Michael Winterhagen
Art Direction
  Philipp Weber
Client Consulting
  Benjamin Baader,
  Sven Weiche,
  Albert Petzold
Copy
  Felix John
Illustration
  recomCGI
Image Processing
  recomPOST

SILVER
KLASSISCHE MEDIEN
CLASSICAL MEDIA
　Print
　Kampagne
　Print
　Campaign

BUNTSTIFTE VON FABER CASTELL
　"True Colours"

Lead Agency
　Serviceplan
Client
　A. W. Faber-Castell Vertrieb GmbH
Marketing Direction
　Hannelore Warning
Executive Creative Direction
　Alexander Schill,
　Matthias Harbeck
Creative Direction
　Oliver Palmer
Art Direction
　Andreas Balog
Client Consulting
　Sandra Robert,
　Alex Wieland
Copy
　Nicolas Becker,
　Lorenz Langgartner
Graphic Design
　Marijo Sanje

SILVER
KLASSISCHE MEDIEN
CLASSICAL MEDIA
  Print
  Kampagne
  Print
  Campaign

ROLLINGSTONE 'INITIATIVE MONEY FOR MUSIC'
»Kopiert ruhig weiter«

Lead Agency
  Ogilvy Frankfurt
Client
  Axel Springer Mediahouse
  Berlin GmbH
Marketing Direction
  Rainer Schmidt
Executive Creative Direction
  Dr. Stephan Vogel
Creative Direction
  Helmut Meyer
Art Direction
  Eva Stetefeld
Client Consulting
  Dr. Stephan Vogel
Art Buying
  Christina Hufgard
Consulting
  Peter Heinlein
Copy
  Taner Ercan,
  Dr. Stephan Vogel
Other
  Project Consulting:
  Georg Fechner

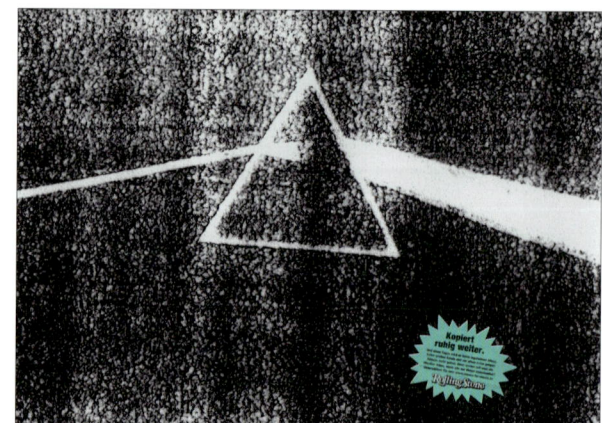

SILVER
KLASSISCHE MEDIEN
CLASSICAL MEDIA
Film
Internetfilme
Film
Internet Films

SPARKASSE
»Synchronsprecher«

Lead Agency
　Jung von Matt AG
Client
　DSV
Marketing Direction
　Dr. Lothar Weissenberger
Advertising Direction
　Dr. Lothar Weissenberger
Executive Creative Direction
　Mathias Stiller,
　Wolfgang Schneider
Creative Direction
　Jan Harbeck,
　David Mously
Art Direction
　Daniel Haschtmann
Client Consulting
　Helen Seife,
　Philip Rother
Agency Production
　Julia Cramer
Camera
　Jens Schwengel
Copy
　David Missing
Cutting
　Tom Henze
Film Direction
　Tom Henze
Film Production
　Radical Media Berlin
Idea
　David Missing
Postproduction
　NHB Studios Berlin
Production
　Christiane Dresser,
　Caroline Kousidonis
Sound Engineering
　Andy Schlegel
Speakers
　Kena Amoa,
　Daniela Reidies,
　Jürgen Vogel

Um die »Mission Finanzcheck«-Kampagne mit Jürgen Vogel aufmerksamkeitsstark ins Netz zu verlängern, enthüllten wir im Stil einer Dokumentation Vogels größtes Geheimnis: Seit einem Unfall hat er eine Frauenstimme und lässt sich in allen Lebenslagen von einem Sprecher synchronisieren. Wir zeigten das harte Los dieses Mannes, der dank des Sparkassen-Finanzchecks den Absprung vom Job schaffte.

The Sparkasse »Mission Finanzcheck« campaign featured famous German actor Jürgen Vogel. As a viral add-on to the campaign, we created a mockumentary-style viral, which uncovers Vogel's biggest secret: his squeaky female voice. Our film tells the story of a man that Vogel employs as voice-over actor to keep his secret under wraps.

SILVER
DESIGN
DESIGN
Literatur
Kataloge
Literature
Catalogs

MOORMANN KATALOG
»Katalog Vol. 3«

Lead Agency
  Jäger & Jäger
Client
  Nils Holger Moormann GmbH
Marketing Direction
  Nicole Christof
Agency Production
  Jäger & Jäger
Publishing House
  Verlag Hermann Schmidt Mainz

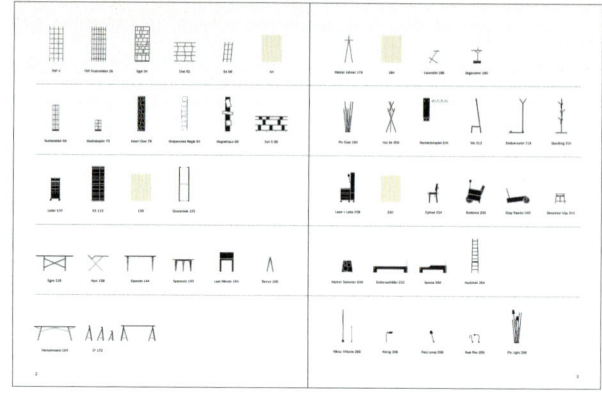

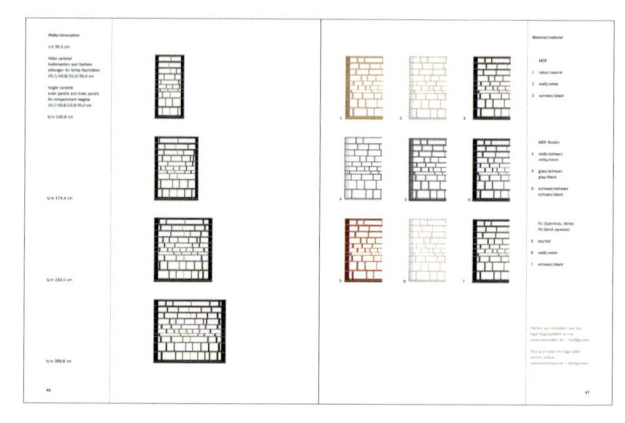

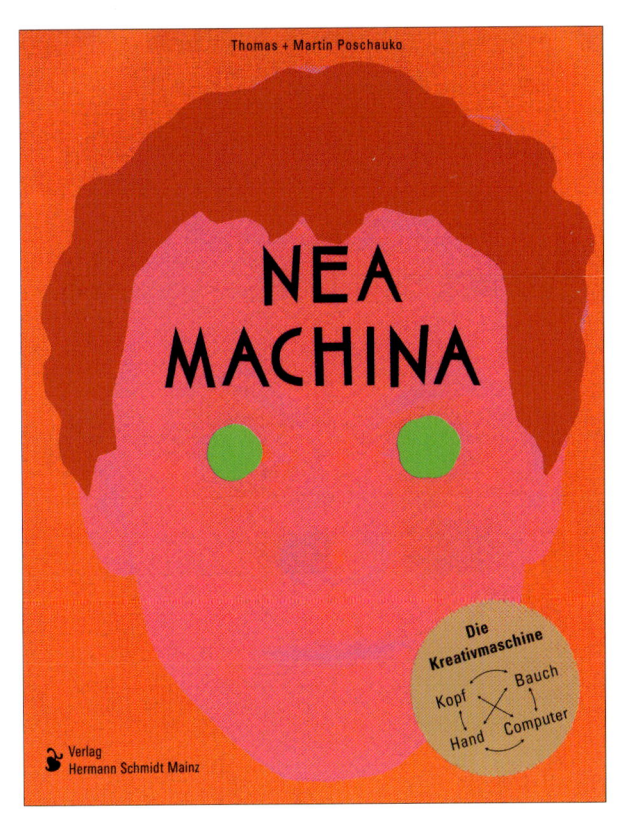

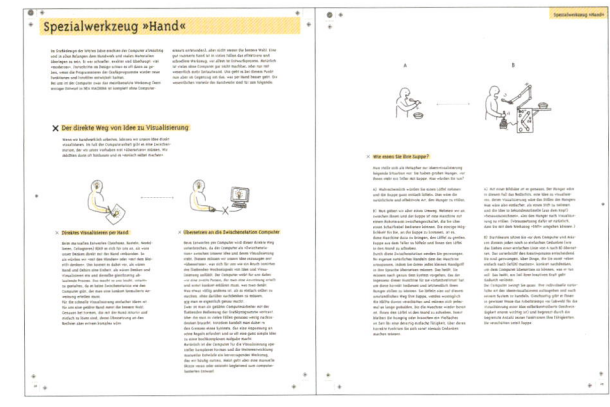

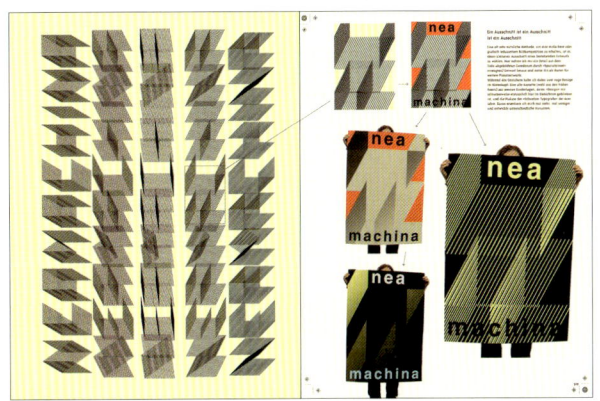

SILVER
DESIGN
DESIGN
Literatur
Bücher
Literature
Books

VERLAG HERMANN SCHMIDT MAINZ
 »Nea Machina –
 Die Kreativmaschine«

Lead Agency
    Verlag Hermann Schmidt Mainz
Client
    Verlag Hermann Schmidt Mainz
Marketing Direction
    Karin Schmidt-Friderichs
Advertising Direction
    Karin Schmidt-Friderichs
Creative Direction
    Bertram Schmidt-Friderichs
Art Direction
    Thomas and Martin Poschauko
Concept
    Karin and Bertram Schmidt-
    Friderichs,
    Thomas and Martin Poschauko
Design
    Thomas and Martin Poschauko
Graphic Design
    Thomas and Martin Poschauko
Idea
    Thomas and Martin Poschauko
Photography
    Thomas and Martin Poschauko
Printing
    Universitaetsdruckerei
    H. Schmidt, Mainz
Publishing House
    Verlag Hermann Schmidt Mainz
Typography
    Thomas and Martin Poschauko

191

● SILVER
DESIGN
DESIGN
  Design
  Corporate Design
  Design
  Corporate Design

T.D.G.
"Stop The Water
While Using Me!"

Lead Agency
  Kolle Rebbe/KOREFE
Client
  T.D.G. Vertriebs
  GmbH & Co. KG
Marketing Direction
  Felix Negwer
Creative Direction
  Katrin Oeding
Art Direction
  Christian Doering
Client Consulting
  Marie Steinhoff
Art Buying
  Emanuel Mugrauer
Copy
  Till Grabsch
Graphic Design
  Ana Magalhaes
Photography
  Imke Jansen
Production
  Produktionsbüro
  Romey von Malottky GmbH
Typography
  Ana Magalhaes

Die Pflegeserie "Stop The Water While Using Me!" ist durch und durch bioverträglich. Von der umweltfreundlichen Produktion über das Verpackungsdesign bis zum finalen Produkt. Das extrem reduzierte Erscheinungsbild der Marke soll diesem Anspruch in allen Bereichen gerecht werden.

"Stop The Water While Using Me!" is a high-quality range of cosmetics that meet the increasing requirements of an ecologically aware society. The products set new standards in environmental protection and awareness. The range is thoroughly eco-friendly – from environmentally friendly manufacturing through to the design of the packaging right up to the finished product.

192

SILVER
EDITORIAL
EDITORIAL
Editorial
Print/Ausgabe
Editorial
Print/Issue

ZEITMAGAZIN
»Typisch jüdisch?«

Lead Agency
  ZEITmagazin
Client
  DIE ZEIT
Creative Direction
  Mirko Borsche
Art Direction
  Katja Kollmann
Chief Editing
  Christoph Amend
Graphic Design
  Nina Bengtson,
  Jasmin Müller-Stoy
Image Editing
  Michael Biedowicz,
  Andreas Wellnitz
Image Processing
  Twentyfour Seven Creative
  Media Services GmbH
Publishing House
  Zeitverlag Gerd Bucerius
  GmbH & Co. KG

193

SILVER
EDITORIAL
EDITORIAL
 Editorial
 Print/Ausgabe
 Editorial
 Print/Issue

ZEITMAGAZIN
 »Wieder alles falsch gemacht«

Lead Agency
 ZEITmagazin
Client
 DIE ZEIT
Creative Direction
 Mirko Borsche
Art Direction
 Katja Kollmann
Chief Editing
 Christoph Amend
Graphic Design
 Nina Bengtson,
 Jasmin Müller-Stoy,
 Mirko Merkel
Image Editing
 Michael Biedowicz,
 Andreas Wellnitz
Image Processing
 Twentyfour Seven Creative
 Media Services GmbH
Publishing House
 Zeitverlag Gerd Bucerius
 GmbH & Co. KG

SILVER
EDITORIAL
EDITORIAL
    Editorial
    Print/Einzelleistung
    Editorial
    Print/Individual Work

DIE ZEIT
    »Grafikseite – Ressort Wissen«

Lead Agency
    DIE ZEIT
Client
    DIE ZEIT
Art Direction
    Haika Hinze
Illustration
    Mona Lisa:
    Katrin Guddat
    Ersatzteile Mensch:
    Martin Burgdorff
    Tierliebe: Niels Schröder
    Parasiten: Martin Burgdorff
    Fußball: Wieslav Smetek
    Todsünden: Anne Gerdes
    Mücken: Helen Gruber
Image Editing
    Ellen Dietrich
Infographics
    Nuller Jahre: Julika Altmann
    Geben: Christoph Drösser
    Giga Liner: Torsten Laß
    Mikrobenzoo: Martin Burgdorff
Publishing House
    Zeitverlag Gerd Bucerius
    GmbH & Co. KG

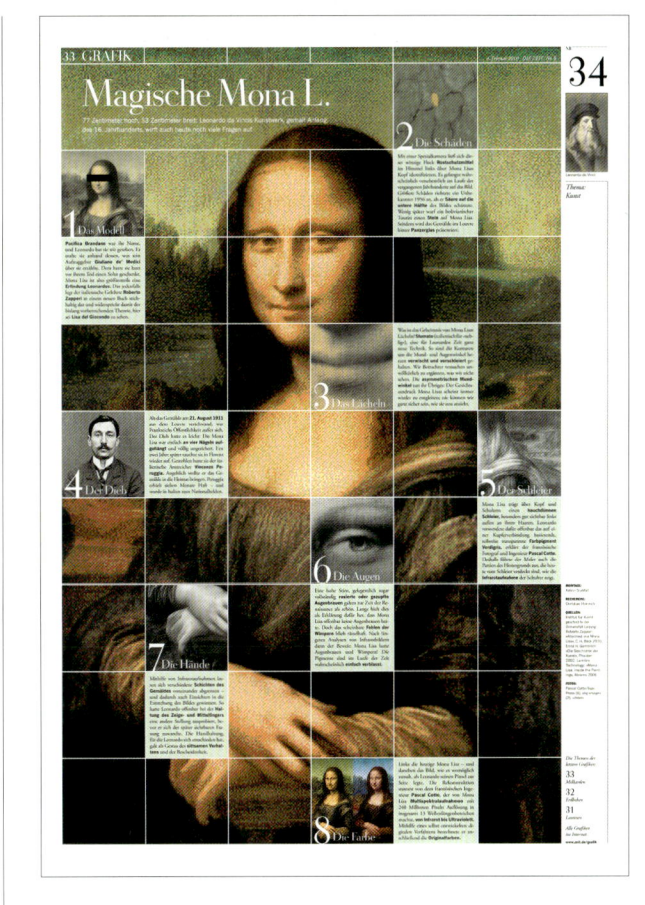

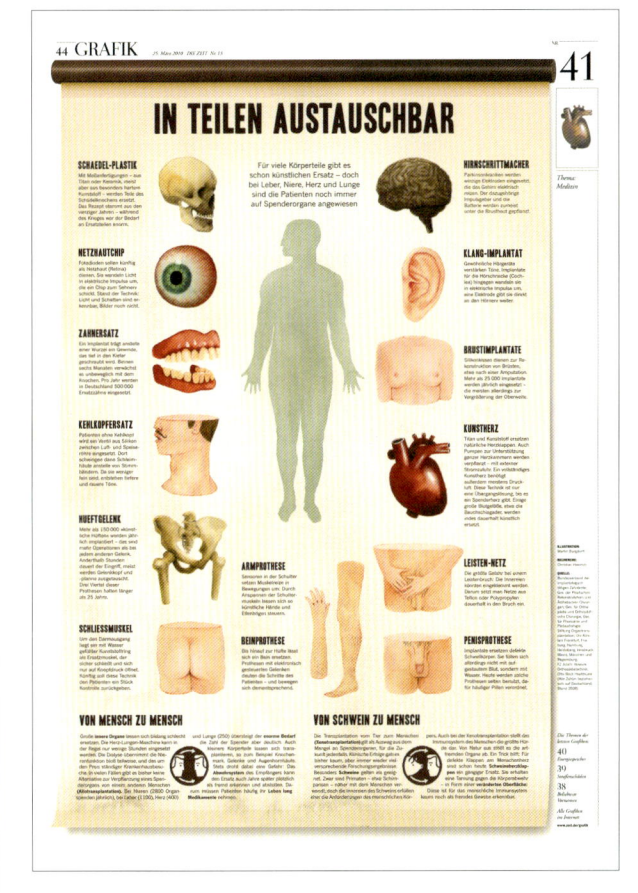

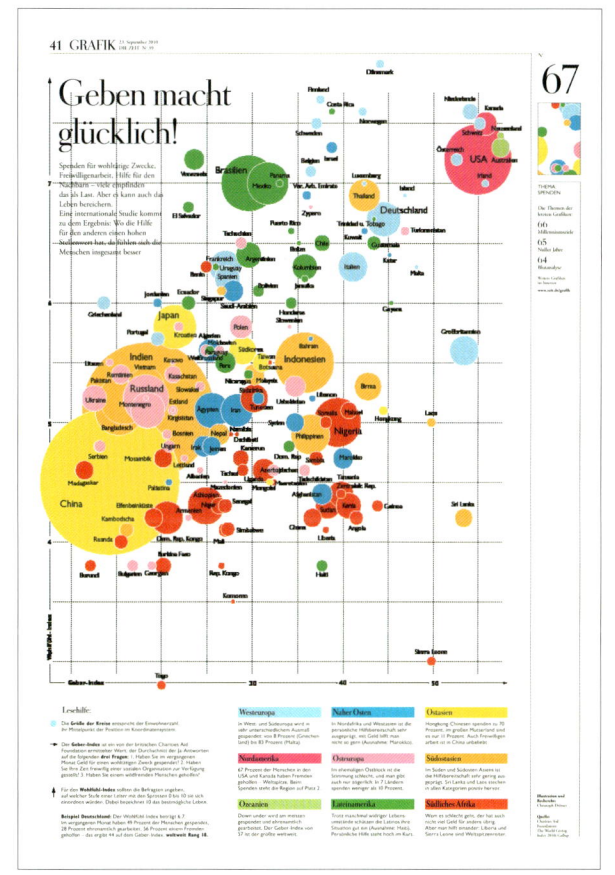

SILVER
RÄUMLICHE INSZENIERUNG
SPATIAL SCENE-SETTING
Kommunikation im Raum
Environmental Design

AUDI A1
"Mediawall"

Lead Agency
  Mutabor Design GmbH
Contributing Agencies
  Schmidhuber und Partner GbR,
  Munich (Concept, Architecture)
Client
  Audi AG
Marketing Direction
  Bernhard Neumann
Creative Direction
  Johannes Plass,
  Ben Kunze
Art Direction
  Malte Schweers,
  Alexander Hanowski
Client Consulting
  Alexandra Steinert
Animation/Visual Effects/Special
Effects
  Mitra Navab-Pour,
  Johannes Kollender
Graphic Design
  Sarah Gossner,
  Kai Riemland,
  Maxie Pantel,
  Patrick Molinari,
  Martin Oberhäuser
Programming
  Stephan Huber

Auf dem Internationalen Automobil-Salon Genf 2010 präsentiert Audi sein neuestes Modell, den Audi A1, mit dem Claim: »Der nächste große Audi«. Zentrum des Standes ist eine komplexe kinetische und mediale Inszenierung: die A1 Mediawall. Verfahrbare LED-Segmente und integrierte verschließbare Fahrzeugboxen erzeugen sich stetig verändernde, überraschende Welten und Perspektiven.

At the Geneva International Motorshow 2010, Audi presented and promoted its latest model, the Audi A1, with the claim "The next big Audi". The centerpiece of the stand was a complex kinetic and media-based presentation: the A1 Mediawall. Manoeuvrable LED segments and integrated closable vehicle boxes created constantly changing and surprising worlds and perspectives.

SILVER
RÄUMLICHE INSZENIERUNG
SPATIAL SCENE-SETTING
Kommunikation im Raum
Environmental Design

CERN
"Universe of Particles"

Lead Agency
  ATELIER BRÜCKNER
Client
  CERN
Creative Direction
  Prof. Uwe R. Brückner
Art Direction
  Matt Schwab
Architecture/Scenography
  Atelier Brückner
Film Production
  Tamschick Media+Space
Graphic Design
  Atelier Brückner,
  Jana Fröhlich
Lighting Design
  Atelier Derrer
Media Design and Integration
  iart interactive ag
Sound Design
  Bluwi

Die Ausstellung ermöglicht emotionalen Zugang zur komplexen Forschungsarbeit, die im CERN geleistet wird. Im contentgenerierten "Universe of Particles" bieten Displays und Medienstationen – eingebettet in sphärische Formen – Informationen on Demand. Highlight ist die Mainshow: durch dreidimensionale Film-, Sound- und Lichtchoreographie wird der Ausstellungsraum selbst zum Exponat.

The exhibition provides emotional access to the complex research work taking place at CERN. A content-generated room, the "Universe of Particles", offers displays and media stations integrated into spherical forms, which provide information on demand. Highlight of the staged free-flow exhibition is the mainshow: Via film, sound and lighting choreography, the exhibition becomes an exhibit itself.

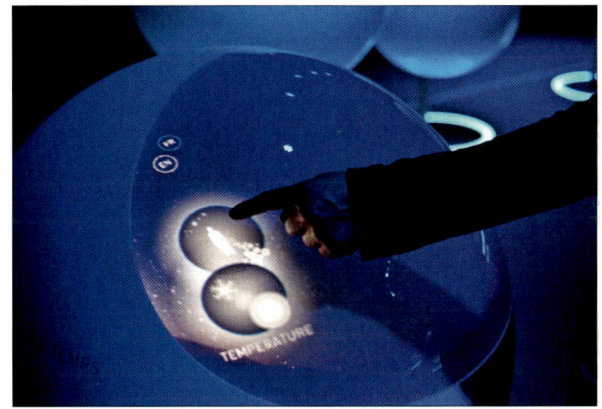

SILVER
RÄUMLICHE INSZENIERUNG
SPATIAL SCENE-SETTING
Kommunikation im Raum
Environmental Design

INSTITUT FÜR STADT-
GESCHICHTE FRANKFURT
»Was die Welt bewegt –
Arthur Schopenhauer in
Frankfurt«

Lead Agency
   Atelier Markgraph
   (Spacial Concept, Exhibition
   Design, Print Measures)
Client
   Institut für Stadtgeschichte
   Frankfurt

Zum 150. Todestag Arthur Schopenhauers lenkt eine Ausstellung in Frankfurt den Blick auf den großen Vordenker und weckt eine neue Lust am philosophischen Denken. Ein begehbares organisches Netzwerk setzt Schopenhauers Modell des vernetzten Denkens räumlich um. In zwölf Themenräumen lässt die Ausstellung Philosophie und Leben des Wahlfrankfurters lebendig werden. Philosophie ohne Berührungsangst.

To mark the 150th anniversary of the death of Arthur Schopenhauer, an exhibition directs attention to the pioneering thinker and kindle fresh pleasure in philosophical thinking. A walk-through organic network lends form and shape to Schopenhauer's model of networked thinking. In twelve theme rooms, the exhibition brings to life the philosophy and life of the man who made Frankfurt his home. Hands-on philosophy.

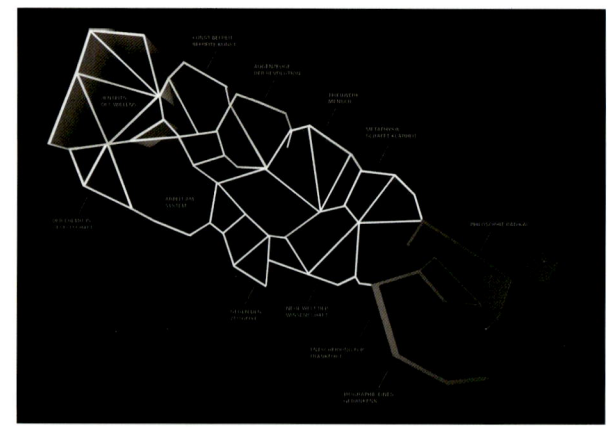

**SILVER
RÄUMLICHE INSZENIERUNG
SPATIAL SCENE-SETTING**
Kommunikation im Raum
Environmental Design

**MAINSHOW SAUDI
ARABISCHER PAVILLON,
EXPO 2010**
"The Treasure"

Lead Agency
GENERAL DE PRODUCCIONES Y DISEÑO, S.A. Sevilla with Tamschick Media+Space GmbH, Berlin
Contributing Agencies
BLUWI, Hamburg/m box bewegtbild GmbH, Berlin
Client
Saudi Expo 2010 Commission, Ministry of Municipal and Rural Affairs, Saudi Arabia
Creative Direction
Boris Micka (GPD S.A.), Marc Tamschick (TMS)
Art Direction
Marcel Schobel (m box bewegtbild GmbH, Berlin)
Agency Production
Nina Hüskes (Tamschick Media+Space GmbH, Berlin)
Audio Production
Stefan Will (BLUWI Music & Sound Design, Hamburg)
Concept
Boris Micka (GPD S.A.), Marc Tamschick (TMS)
Design
Tamschick Media+Space GmbH, Berlin with m box bewegtbild GmbH, Berlin
Film Direction
Boris Micka (GPD S.A.), Marc Tamschick (TMS)
Film Production
Tamschick Media+Space GmbH, Berlin
Idea
Boris Micka (GPD S.A.), Marc Tamschick (TMS)
Media Systems
Skyskan Inc. Europe
Motion Graphics and 3D
m box bewegtbild GmbH, Berlin
Photography
Max Piquel
Production
Tamschick Media+Space GmbH, Berlin
Sound Design
Stefan Will (BLUWI Music & Sound Design, Hamburg)
Technical Implementation
Skyskan Inc. Europe

Im Inneren des Saudi-Arabischen Pavillons auf der Expo Shanghai gleitet der Besucher wie auf einem fliegenden Teppich über die konkave, den gesamten Boden umfassende 1.600m² große Projektionsfläche. Ausgehend vom tiefsten Punkt des Raumes fließen Bildcollagen aus grafischen Formen, orientalischen Mustern und Filmmotiven in den Raum und schaffen eine emotionale poetische Hommage an Saudi-Arabien.

Inside the Saudi Arabian Pavilion, the visitors glide over the 1,600m² concave projection surface, which encompasses the entire floor, like on a magic carpet. Compositions of floral forms, oriental patterns and poetic images of Saudi Arabia proceed from the room's deepest point to fill the floor and walls in their entirety. An overwhelming poetic homage to the Saudi Arabian country and its people.

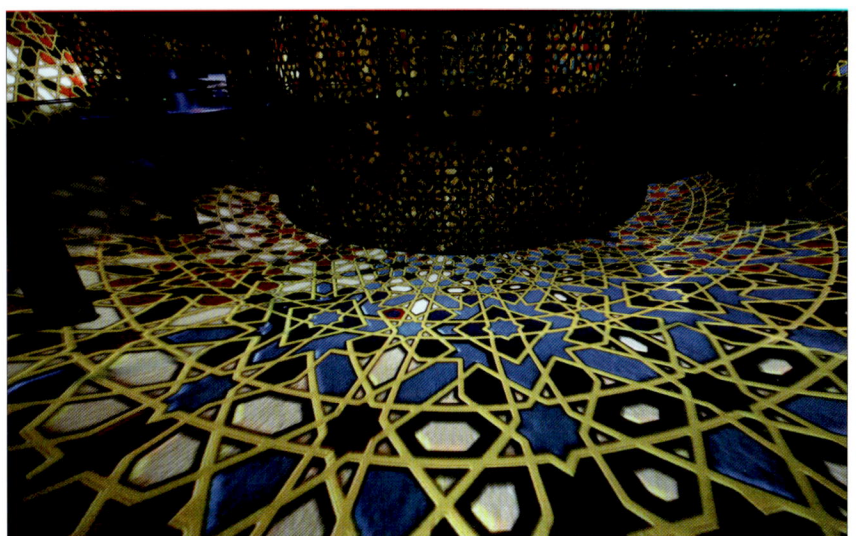

SILVER
RÄUMLICHE INSZENIERUNG
SPATIAL SCENE-SETTING
Kommunikation im Raum
Environmental Design

MAGIC BOX
"State Grid Pavilion"

Lead Agency
 ATELIER BRÜCKNER
Client
 SGCC (State Grid Corporation of China)
Marketing Direction
 IBM China Company Limited, Shanghai
Creative Direction
 Prof. Uwe R. Brückner
Art Direction
 Dominik Hegemann
Architecture/Scenography
 Atelier Brückner
Film Direction
 Marc Tamschick,
 Tamschick Media+Space
Film Production
 m box bewegtbild
Sound Design
 Idee und Klang

Der State Grid Pavillon auf der Expo Shanghai 2010 vermittelt Aufgaben und Visionen des nationalen Energielieferanten SGCC. Im Inneren erlebt der Besucher eine filmische Rauminszenierung: Sechsseitig wird er umspielt von imaginären Welten, die im Hinblick auf das Expo-Motto "Better City – Better Life" die Verbesserung städtischer Lebensqualität mittels ressourcenschonender Energieübertragung zeigen.

Task of the State Grid Pavilion at the Expo Shanghai 2010 is to transport visions and functions of the Chinese energy provider SGCC. Inside, the visitor experiences a 720° screening combined with a three-dimensional sound space. According to the Expo's motto "Better City – Better Life", striking images show how responsible usage of energy resources will improve life in the cites.

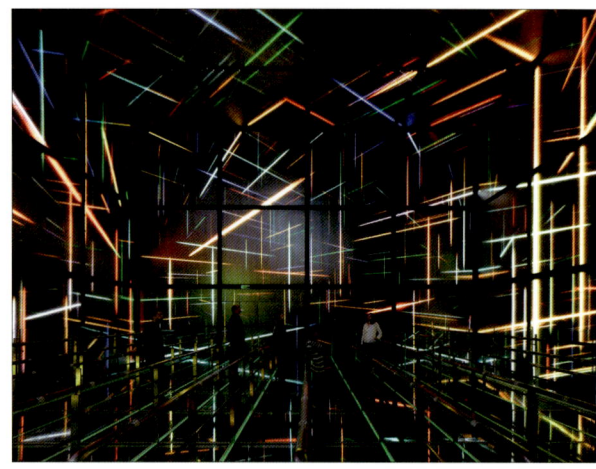

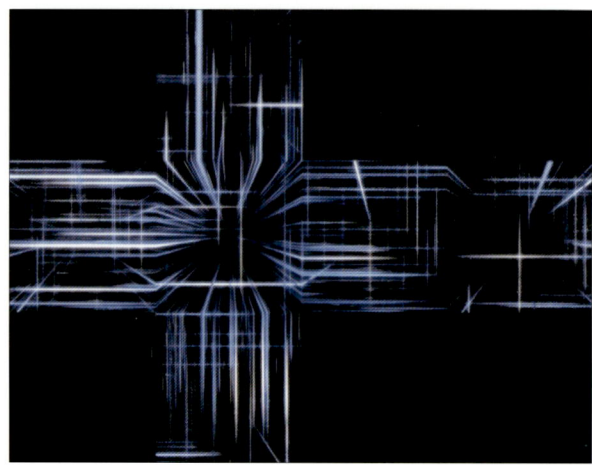

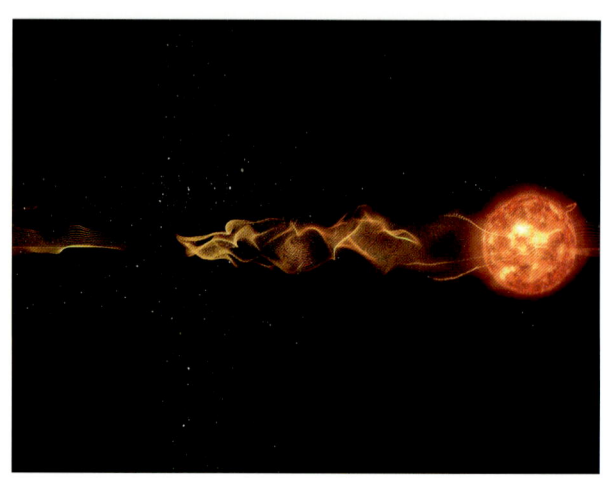

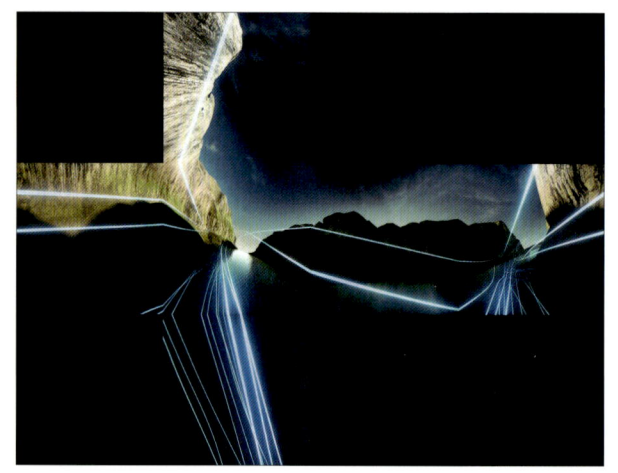

SILVER
CRAFT
CRAFT
Text
Copy

—

HYPOSWISS PRIVATE BANK
KAMPAGNE
 "Expect the Expected"

Lead Agency
  walker
Client
  Hyposwiss Private Bank
Creative Direction
  Pius Walker
Art Direction
  Stefanie Huber,
  Golf Nuntawat
Client Consulting
  Lisa Binkert,
  Cornelia Nünlist
Copy
  Martin Arnold,
  Heinz Helle,
  Henning Müller-Dannhausen

"It will never be about you and us. It will always be about your money."

HYPOSWISS PRIVATE BANK
Expect the expected

"Promises are overrated."

HYPOSWISS PRIVATE BANK
Expect the expected

"If you look at a risk in a positive way, it is still a risk."

HYPOSWISS PRIVATE BANK
Expect the expected

"The safest way to make money is to work for it."

HYPOSWISS PRIVATE BANK
Expect the expected

SILVER
CRAFT
CRAFT
　Fotografie
　Photography

PASSIONSSPIELE
OBERAMMERGAU SERIE
　»Passion«

Lead Agency
　Anzinger | Wüschner | Rasp
　Agentur für Kommunikation
　GmbH
Client
　Passionsspiele Oberammergau
Marketing Direction
　Frederik Mayet
Advertising Direction
　Frederik Mayet
Executive Creative Direction
　Markus Rasp
Creative Direction
　Markus Rasp
Art Direction
　Daniel Pietsch,
　Sabine Düe
Client Consulting
　Ira Stehmann
Strategic Planning
　Ira Stehmann
Copy
　Christian Stückl,
　Ludwig Mödl,
　Petra Giloy-Hirtz
Photography
　Christopher Thomas

SILVER
CRAFT
CRAFT
Illustration
Illustration

ENTEGA ERNEUERBARE
ENERGIE SERIE
»Energiemärchen-Kalender«

Lead Agency
  DDB Tribal Group
Client
  ENTEGA VERTRIEB GmbH
Marketing Direction
  Dr. Karoline Haderer
Advertising Direction
  Isabell Höppler
Executive Creative Direction
  CCO: Eric Schoeffler
  ECD: Stefan Schulte,
  Bastian Meneses von Arnim
Creative Direction
  Kristoffer Heilemann,
  Ludwig Berndl
Art Direction
  Lars Buri,
  Chan-Young Ramert
Graphic Design:
  Christophe-Claude Bugetti
Idea:
  Tim Kremer
Client Consulting
  Caroline Sturm,
  Sebastian Neumann
  Managing Director:
  Andreas Poulionakis
Copy
  Nina Faulhaber,
  Ludwig Berndl,
  Mona Sibai,
  Lennart Frank,
  Res Matthys,
  Antje Gerwien
Illustration
  Chris Buzelli

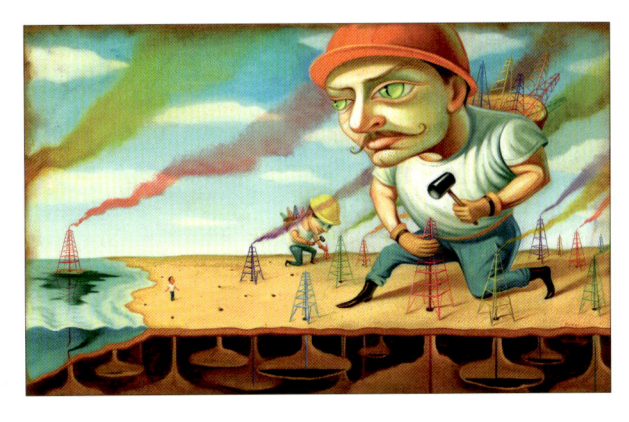

SILVER
CRAFT
CRAFT
Musik und Sound
Music and Sound

DEUTSCHER TIERSCHUTZBUND
ORIGINALKOMPOSITION
"A Peace of Mind"

Lead Agency
　Grey Worldwide GmbH
Client
　Deutscher Tierschutzbund e.V.
　Bundesgeschäftsstelle
Marketing Direction
　Marius Tünte
Executive Creative Direction
　Andreas Henke,
　Sacha Reeb
Creative Direction
　Moritz Grub,
　Regner Lotz
Art Direction
　Regner Lotz
Client Consulting
　Sandra Lehrenfeld
Audio Production
　BLUWI Music & Sound Design
Copy
　Moritz Grub
Music Composition
　Fritz Rating

　Kommunizieren, was Tiere nicht sagen können. Die Welt davon in Kenntnis setzen, was im Kopf eines gequälten Tieres vorgeht. Und das auf eine Art und Weise, die nicht ignoriert werden kann. Mit einer Kampagne, die die mentalen Wunden zeigt, die Versuchstieren zugefügt werden. Eine Kampagne, die zeigt, dass Tierversuche immer Schmerz und Leid bedeuten.

　Communicate what animals can't. Inform the world of the horrors that take place inside a tortured animal's head. And do it in a way that can't and won't be ignored. With a campaign that shows the mental scars that are inflicted on test animals. A campaign that makes people understand that animal testing always means pain and suffering.

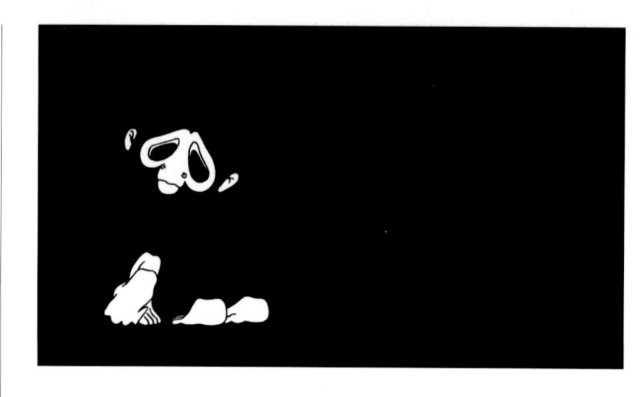

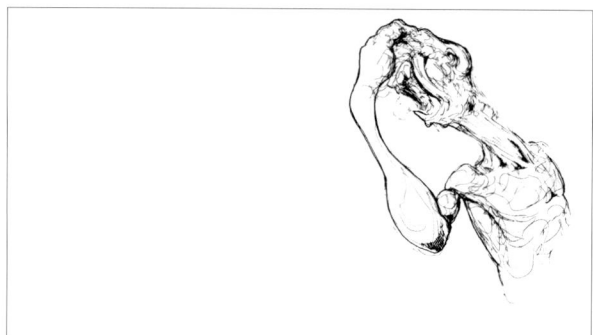

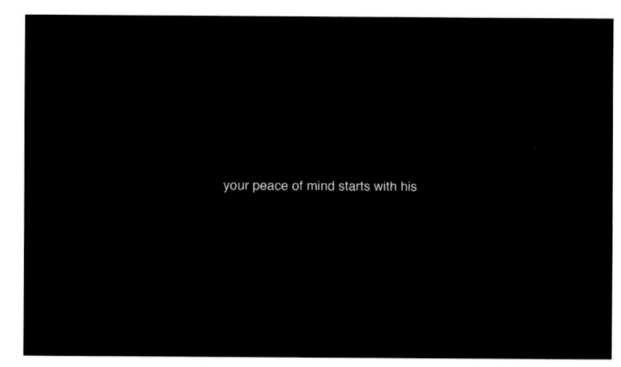

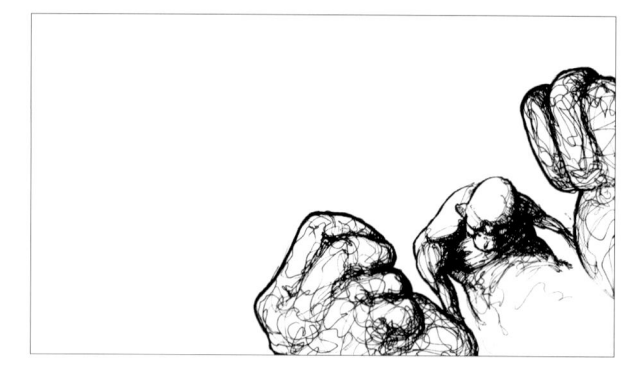

- **BRONZE**
KLASSISCHE MEDIEN
CLASSICAL MEDIA
  Print
  Einzelmotiv
  Print
  Single Motif

- **BRONZE**
KLASSISCHE MEDIEN
CLASSICAL MEDIA
  Print
  Kampagne
  Print
  Campaign

WMF SPARSCHÄLER
  »Kartoffel, Möhre, Apfel«

Lead Agency
  KNSK Werbeagentur GmbH
Client
  WMF AG
Marketing Direction
  Stefan Kellerer
Advertising Direction
  Stephen Schuster
Executive Creative Direction
  Detmar Karpinski
Creative Direction
  Ulrike Wegert,
  Tim Krink
Art Direction
  Julian Heidt,
  Thomas Thiele
Client Consulting
  Kirsten Kohls
Art Buying
  Julia Gaentzsch
Copy
  Dieter Kolaja
Final Artwork
  Julia Klaas,
  Marco Reuke
Graphic Design
  Julian Heidt,
  Albert Bauer Companies,
  Sarah Stowasser
Idea
  Julian Heidt
Illustration
  Julian Heidt,
  Albert Bauer Companies
Image Processing
  Albert Bauer Companies
Photography
  Peter Backens
Postproduction
  Albert Bauer Companies
Typography
  Julian Heidt

205

● **BRONZE**
KLASSISCHE MEDIEN
CLASSICAL MEDIA
  Film
  TV/Kino Einzelspot
  Film
  TV/Cinema Commercial

● **BRONZE**
CRAFT
CRAFT
  Musik und Sound
  Music and Sound

**BRAUN SATIN HAIR 5
MULTISTYLER**
  "Hairmoticons"

Lead Agency
  BBDO Proximity GmbH,
  Duesseldorf
Client
  Braun GmbH
Executive Creative Direction
  Christian Mommertz,
  Wolfgang Schneider
Creative Direction
  Christian Mommertz,
  Steffen Gentis
Art Direction
  Stephan Eichler,
  Philipp Alings
Client Consulting
  Phoebe Moll
Agency Production
  Steffen Gentis
Audio Production
  Studio Funk GmbH,
  Duesseldorf
Copy
  Christopher Fink
Cutting
  Florian Alt,
  Markus Jäschke
Film Direction
  Christian Mommertz,
  Steffen Gentis
Film Production
  VCC GmbH, Duesseldorf,
  CGI: Das Werk, Duesseldorf
Music Composition
  Leroy Anderson
Music Selection
  Christian Mommertz
Other
  Music Publisher:
  EMI Music Publishing

Emoticons haben sich in unserer Kommunikation etabliert – und jetzt sind sie auch nicht mehr kahl. Wie im »echten Leben« lässt sich mit den Hairmoticons die eigene Stimmung nun auch über die Frisur ausdrücken. Und das ist es, was der Film zeigt: verschiedenste Hairmoticons zu der unverwechselbaren Musik von Leroy Andersons "The Typewriter" – denn es gibt einfach so viele Styles für jede Stimmung.

Emoticons are established in our communication – and now they are not bald anymore. With the Hairmoticons you can express your personal mood additionally with an individual hairstyle – like in "real" life. And that is what the film shows: different Hairmoticons to the distinctive sound of Leroy Anderson's "The Typewriter" – because there are so many styles for any mood.

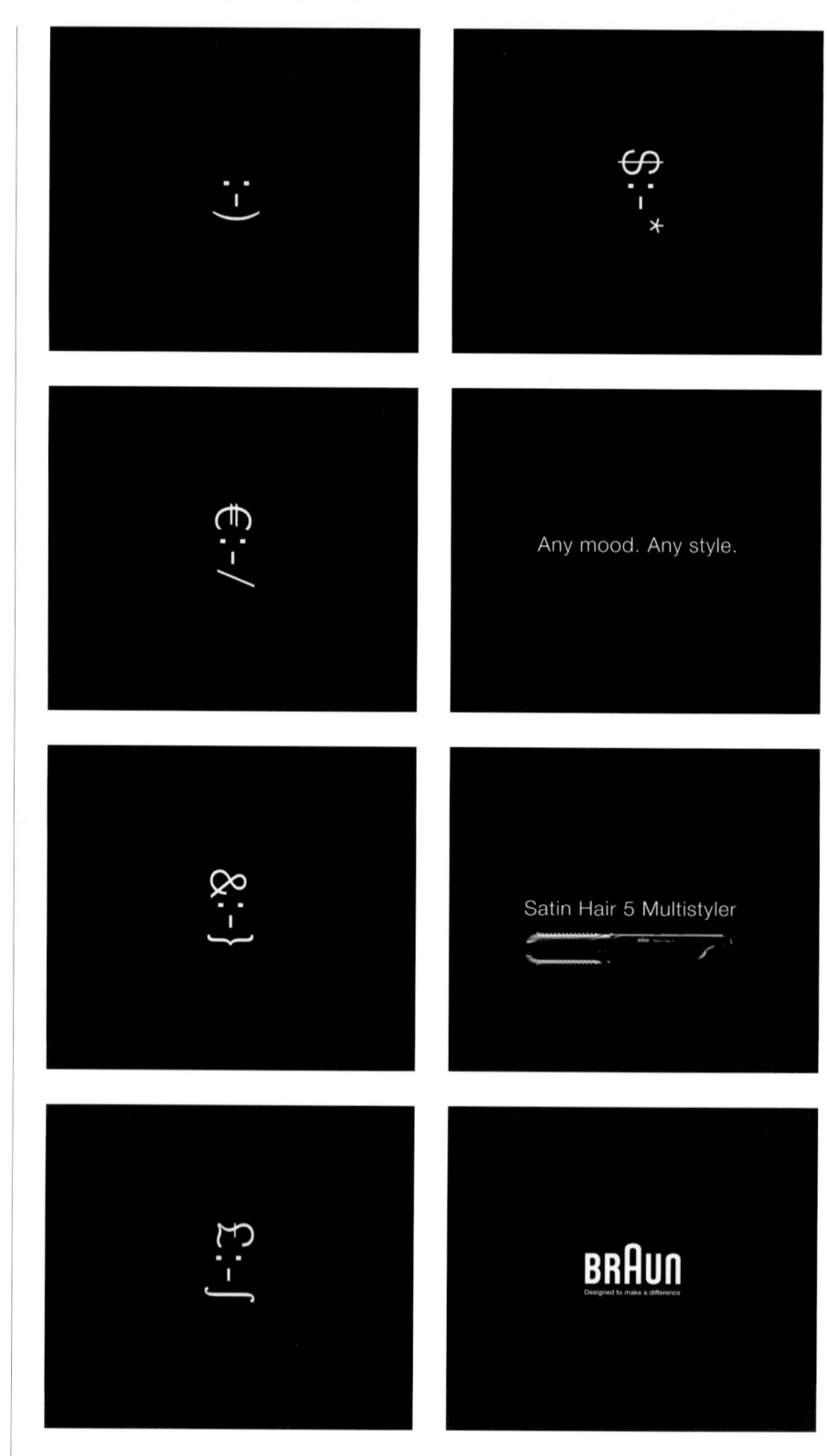

206

● BRONZE
KLASSISCHE MEDIEN
CLASSICAL MEDIA
Audio
Radio Einzelspot
Audio
Radio Commercial

● BRONZE
KLASSISCHE MEDIEN
CLASSICAL MEDIA
Audio
Innovative Nutzung von Audio
Audio
Innovative Use of Audio

NATURIA HUNDEFUTTER
»Hundefunkspot«

Lead Agency
  Grabarz & Partner
Client
  Galaxxy-Pet Food GmbH
Marketing Direction
  Carsten Isernhagen
Advertising Direction
  Carsten Isernhagen
Executive Creative Direction
  Ralf Heuel
Creative Direction
  Ralf Heuel,
  Tom Hauser
Art Direction
  Jan Wölfel
Client Consulting
  Denise Ewald
Audio Production
  Studio Funk, Hamburg
Copy
  André Hennen
Production
  Film Production: The Shack
Radio Direction
  Torsten Hennings,
  Ralf Heuel
Sound Engineering
  Torsten Hennings

AUDIO

NATURIA HUNDEFUNKSPOT

»Die NATURIA Hundeforschung hat herausgefunden, dass bei vielen Hunden allein die Erwähnung des Namens NATURIA Hundefutter körperliche Reaktionen auslöst: Sie spitzen die Ohren, fangen dümmlich an zu sabbern oder verhalten sich sonst wie anormal, sobald sie den Namen NATURIA Hundefutter hören. Die Ursache: Hunde können nicht sprechen. Daher weist Ihr Hund Sie mit den ihm von der Natur gegebenen Mitteln darauf hin, dass NATURIA Hundefutter das Hundefutter seiner Wahl ist. Sollte ihr Hund gerade oben beschriebene Auffälligkeiten zeigen, will er Ihnen sagen: ›Kauf NATURIA Hundefutter. Ich weiß nicht, wie ich es sonst ausdrücken soll. Tut mir leid. Ich bin ein Hund. Ich kann nicht sprechen. Ich kann nur die Ohren spitzen, dümmlich sabbern oder mich sonst wie anormal verhalten, wenn ich den Namen NATURIA Hundefutter höre.‹ Danke für die Aufmerksamkeit sagt: NATURIA Hundefutter.«

● **BRONZE**
DIGITALE MEDIEN
DIGITAL MEDIA
  Digitale Medien
  Microsites
  Digital Media
  Microsites

● **BRONZE**
DIALOGMARKETING/
PROMOTION/MEDIA
DIALOG MARKETING/
PROMOTION/MEDIA
  Dialogmarketing
  Dialog Mobile Marketing
  Dialog Marketing
  Dialog Mobile Marketing

MISEREOR HILFSWERK
  "Drive the Mobilombo –
  Deliver Hope to Africa"

Lead Agency
  Kolle Rebbe GmbH
Client
  Bischöfliches Hilfswerk
  MISEREOR e.V.
Marketing Direction
  Michael Kleine
Advertising Direction
  Elisabeth Kleffer
Executive Creative Direction
  Stefan Kolle
Creative Direction
  Justin Landon,
  Lorenz Ritter,
  Sven Klohk
Art Direction
  Felix Schulz,
  Michael Matthias
Client Consulting
  Guido Block,
  Jessica Gustafsson
Copy
  Malik Benamara
Cutting
  Kristin Ließ
Film Production
  The Shack
Idea
  Felix Schulz,
  Michael Matthias
Illustration
  Michael Matthias
Programming
  Tobias Böhning
Sound Design
  Robert Jähnert
Typography
  HVD Fonts
Other
  Speakers:
  Konrad Peschman, Alan Orpin
  Sound Engineering:
  Konrad Peschman,
  Tobias Sauer
  Concept:
  Felix Schulz, Grit Hornich
  Design: Johannes Widmer
  Graphic Design: Peter Fehler

Mobilombo.org ist eine interaktive Spendenhotline. Jeder Anruf treibt einen Miniatur-Truck, das Mobilombo, an und spendet automatisch 2 Euro an ein Hilfsprojekt in Südafrika, dem Ziel der Reise. Das Mobilombo wird von einem Handy mit Vibrationsalarm angetrieben, das auf dem schrägen Set hinabrutscht. Die Reise von Aachen nach Südafrika ist Live im Netz zu verfolgen.

Mobilombo.org is an interactive charity hotline. Whenever a visitor calls, it powers a miniature truck, the Mobilombo, and automatically donates 2 euros to a relief project in South Africa, the truck's final destination. The engine is built using a mobile phone with a vibration alarm. The drive is broadcasted live on the Internet – accompanied by Twitter, Facebook & Co.

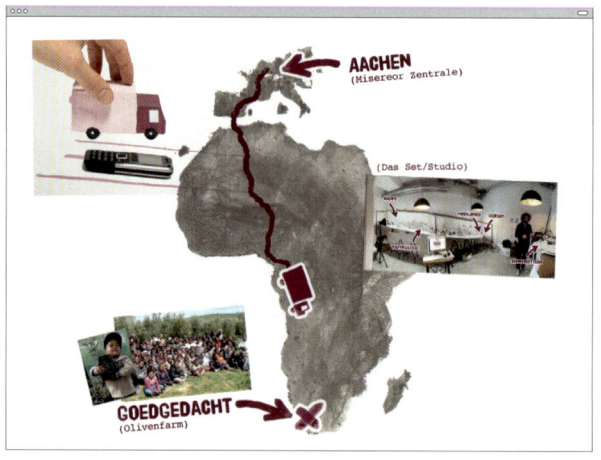

● **BRONZE**
DESIGN
DESIGN
Literatur
Image-/Informations-
broschüren
Literature
Image/Information Brochures

● **BRONZE**
DESIGN
DESIGN
Design
Grafische Einzelarbeiten
Design
Individual Graphics

ROCKET & WINK
"Whatever 1st"
"At 1st"

Lead Agency
  Rocket & Wink
Client
  Rocket & Wink
Executive Creative Direction
  Dr. Gerald Rocketson,
  Petronius Amund Wink
Creative Direction
  Rocket & Wink
Concept
  Rocket & Wink
Design
  Rocket & Wink
Idea
  Rocket & Wink
Illustration
  Rocket & Wink
Printing
  Seltmann GmbH
  Druckereibetriebe
Publishing House
  seltmann+söhne
Typography
  Rocket & Wink

"Whatever" ist ein monothematisches Magazin des neu gegründeten Hamburger Design-Teams Rocket & Wink. Es dient als Portfolio- und Ideensammlung. Alle Illustrationen, Produkte und Ideen sind speziell für die jeweilige Ausgabe entwickelt worden und zeigen das Spektrum von Rocket & Wink. In der ersten Ausgabe "At First" dreht sich alles um das Thema Anfänge.

"Whatever" is a monothematic magazine by newly established design team Rocket & Wink. It serves as a portfolio and collection of ideas. All illustrations, products and ideas are specially designed for the particular issue and show the spectrum of Rocket & Wink. The first edition "At First" is all about beginnings.

209

5

PUNKTE
POINTS

● BRONZE
KLASSISCHE MEDIEN
CLASSICAL MEDIA
  Out-of-Home
  Nicht-Klassisch
  Out-of-Home
  Non-Classic

● NOMINATION
DIALOGMARKETING /
PROMOTION / MEDIA
DIALOG MARKETING /
PROMOTION / MEDIA
  Promotion
  Aktivitäten
  Promotion
  Activities

● NOMINATION
KLASSISCHE MEDIEN
CLASSICAL MEDIA
  Film
  Innovative Nutzung von Film
  Film
  Innovative Use of Film

DAIMLER PRE-SAFE
"Transparent Walls"

Lead Agency
  Jung von Matt AG
Client
  Daimler AG
Marketing Direction
  Anders-Sundt Jensen,
  Lüder Fromm
Advertising Direction
  Damir Maric,
  Lena Ernst
Executive Creative Direction
  Sascha Hanke
Creative Direction
  Jo Marie Farwick,
  Jens Pfau,
  Tobias Grimm
Art Direction
  Alphons Conzen,
  Frederico Gasparian,
  Benjamin Busse,
  Damjan Pita
Client Consulting
  Sven Dörrenbächer,
  Dajana Crantz,
  Marijke Fisser
Agency Production
  Jannik Endemann
Copy
  Frederico Gasparian,
  Florian Hoffmann,
  Henning Robert,
  Jan-Hendrik Scholz
Film Direction
  Mortimer Hochberg
Film Production
  Erste Liebe Filmproduktion
  GmbH
Graphic Design
  Samuel Huber

Interactive Production
  Sascha Kurfiss
IT Direction
  Sascha Kurfiss
Media Systems
  Gahrens & Battermann GmbH
Production
  Justin Mundhenke
Technical Direction
  Habib Breitkreuz
Technical Implementation
  Martin Heesch,
  Jens Gröger
Technical Installation
  Bernhard Waack
Other
  Technology:
  Bernhard Waack,
  Martin Heesch,
  Jens Gröger,
  Habib Breitkreuz

Um das Sicherheitssystem Pre-Safe von Mercedes-Benz zu demonstrieren, filmten wir schlecht einsehbare Straßen und projizierten sie auf die Häuserwände davor. So konnten Verkehrsteilnehmer durch die Häuserwände »hindurchschauen« und nahende Gefahren rechtzeitig erkennen. Eine Werbemaßnahme also, die nicht nur Pre-Safe erklärte, sondern auch den Verkehr ein wenig sicherer machte.

To demonstrate the Pre-Safe Mercedes-Benz safety system, we filmed streets with bad visibility at dangerous intersections and projected the images onto the buildings in front of them. This way, everyone was literally able to "see through" the walls and identify dangers just in time. A unique advertising effort which not only explained Pre-Safe, but also made traffic a little bit safer.

● BRONZE
DIGITALE MEDIEN
DIGITAL MEDIA
　Digitale Medien Craft
　Sounddesign
　Digital Media Craft
　Sound Design

● NOMINATION
DIGITALE MEDIEN
DIGITAL MEDIA
　Digitale Medien
　Microsites
　Digital Media
　Microsites

● NOMINATION
DIGITALE MEDIEN
DIGITAL MEDIA
　Digitale Medien Craft
　Interface/Navigation
　Digital Media Craft
　Interface/Navigation

FEY & CO
»lullaland.net«

Lead Agency
　Jung von Matt AG
Client
　Fey & Co.
Marketing Direction
　Michael Böhm
Executive Creative Direction
　Sascha Hanke,
　Norman Störl
Creative Direction
　Jo Marie Farwick,
　Nicole Holzenkamp,
　Arne Habermann
Art Direction
　David Aufdembrinke,
　Johannes Schubert,
　Annabel Schubert
Client Consulting
　Sascha Kurfiss, Annette Krebs,
　Yves Zeh
Concept
　Björn-Arne Lange, Johannes
　Schubert, Annabel Schubert
Copy
　Katharina Schmitt
Design
　Michael Blendow,
　Silja Schulwitz
Graphic Design
　Kay Potthoff,
　Benjamin Wild
Interface Navigation
　David Aufdembrinke
Motion Graphics and 3D
　Malte Rehde, Oliver Kossatz
Programming
　Markenfilm Crossing GmbH,
　Benjamin Herholz,
　Konrad Gulla
Sound Design
　Klaas Nocken
　(White Horse Music)

Die ersten melodischen Tweets der Welt. Bei Matratzenhersteller Fey & Co. dreht sich alles um den perfekten Schlaf. Und weil Fey & Co. aus jeder guten Nacht eine sehr gute Nacht machen will, sammeln wir weltweit alle Gute-Nacht-Wünsche von Twitter und wandeln sie in individuelle Schlaflieder um. So entsteht eine weltweit einzigartige, riesige Sammlung von Tweet-Melodien: www.lullaland.net

The first melodic tweets in the world. At mattress manufacturer Fey & Co., everything revolves around the perfect night's sleep. And because Fey & Co. want to turn every good night into a great night, we're collecting good-night wishes on Twitter from all over the world and are turning them into personal lullabies. The result is a huge collection of tweet melodies like nothing else in the world.

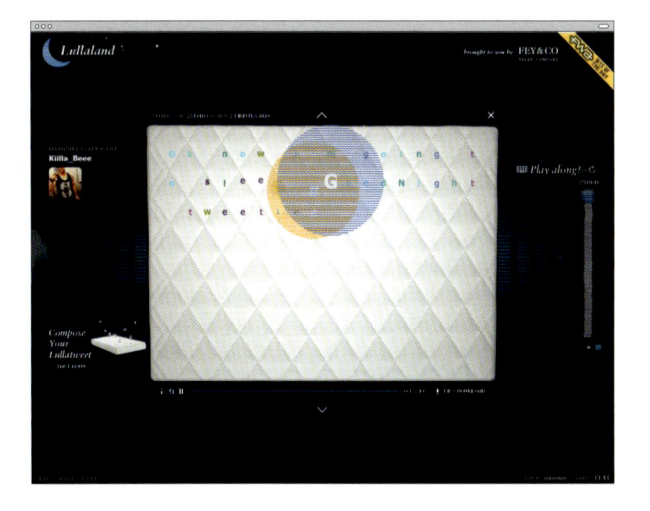

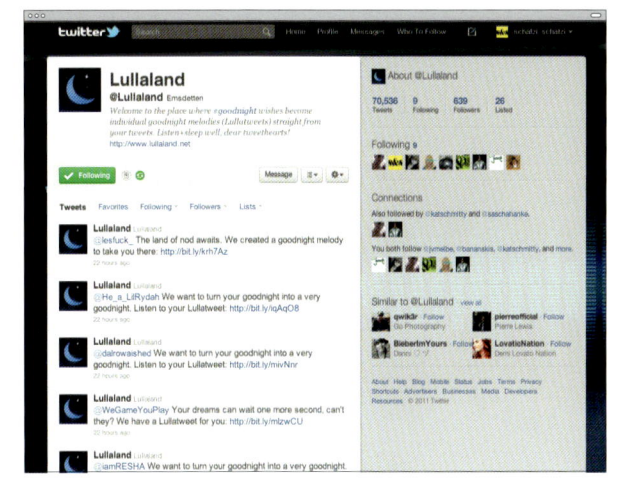

4

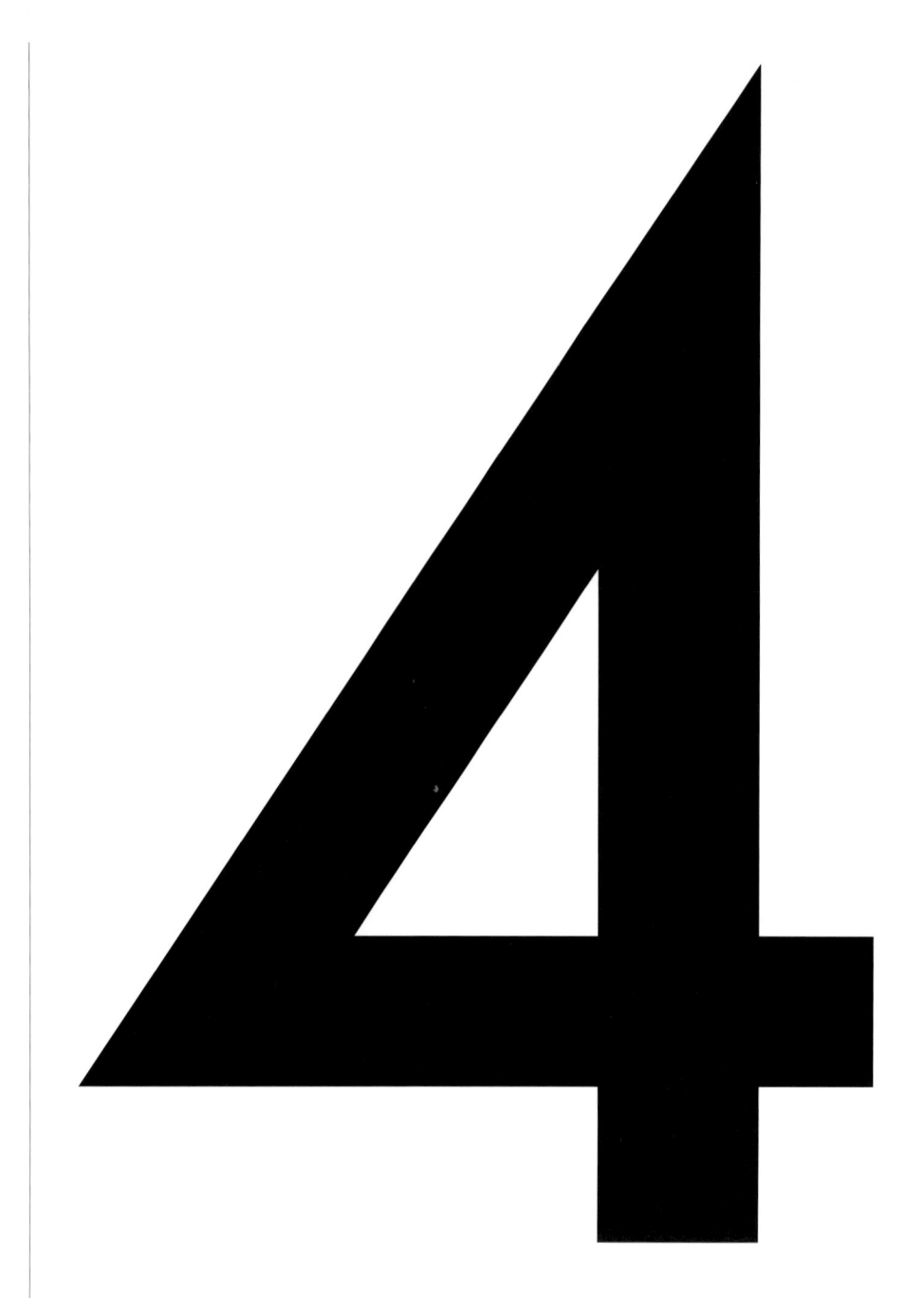

PUNKTE
POINTS

● **BRONZE**
KLASSISCHE MEDIEN
CLASSICAL MEDIA
　Film
　Internetfilme
　Film
　Internet Films

● **NOMINATION**
KLASSISCHE MEDIEN
CLASSICAL MEDIA
　Film Craft
　Casting
　Film Craft
　Casting

MCFIT
　»Gib Dich niemals auf.«

Lead Agency
　HEIMAT, Berlin
Client
　McFit GmbH
Marketing Direction
　Dr. Björn Schultheiss
Advertising Direction
　Anja Tillack
Executive Creative Direction
　Guido Heffels
Creative Direction
　Guido Heffels,
　Myles Lord,
　Ole Vinck
Art Direction
　Michael Dunlap,
　Matthias Walter
Client Consulting
　Mark Hassan
Strategic Planning
　Matthias von Bechtolsheim
Agency Production
　Kerstin Heffels
Audio Production
　Loft Tonstudios Berlin GmbH
Camera
　Jean Louis Bompoint
Casting
　Partizan GmbH, Berlin
Copy
　Stephen Quell,
　Siyamak Seyedasgari,
　Nico Beyer
Cutting
　Tom Seil
Film Direction
　Nico Beyer
Film Production
　Partizan GmbH, Berlin
Music Composition
　Mosermeyer
Production
　Moritz Merkel,
　Svenja Babucke
Screen Design
　Venim GmbH
Sound Design
　Loft Tonstudios Berlin
　GmbH/Mosermeyer

Der dokumentarisch gedrehte Film zeigt, was passiert, wenn man sich gehen lässt, die Selbstdisziplin verliert: Die sonst durchtrainierten Profiboxer Wladimir und Vitali Klitschko begegnen uns plötzlich als schlaffes, deprimiertes Geschwisterpaar, das nur davon träumt, wieder die alte Form zu erlangen. Eine unterhaltsame und zugleich aufrüttelnde Aufforderung: »Gib dich niemals auf«.

This film shows World heavyweight boxing champions Wladimir and Vitali Klitschko terribly out of shape – showing what happens if you let yourself go. The brothers, normally famous for their impressive physiques appear as oversized blobs. Fat and dejected they dream of recovering their former shape. An entertaining and at the same time compelling call: "Never give up".

● BRONZE
KLASSISCHE MEDIEN
CLASSICAL MEDIA
Film
On-air-Design
Film
On-Air Design

● NOMINATION
KLASSISCHE MEDIEN
CLASSICAL MEDIA
Film
TV-On-air-Promotion
Film
TV On-Air Promotion

VIVA
"ReBrand 2011 'Reel'"

Lead Agency
  MTV Networks
  Advertising Unit
Client
  MTV Networks Germany
  GmbH
Marketing Direction
  Imke Deigner
Creative Direction
  Dinko Lacic
Art Direction
  Dinko Lacic,
  Robert Brodmüller,
  Justin Kruse,
  Joffrey Jans
Strategic Planning
  Vivien Hucke
Agency Production
  Christina Chlapek,
  Helen Wembacher,
  Maxim Zhestkov
Animation/Visual Effects/
Special Effects
  Maxim Zhestkov
Computer Animation
  Maxim Zhestkov
Concept
  Dinko Lacic,
  Robert Bode Brodmüller,
  Justin Kruse,
  Maxim Zhestkov
Consulting
  Vivien Hucke,
  Imke Deigner
Cutting
  Robert Bode Brodmüller,
  Maxim Zhestkov
Film Direction
  Laurence Ellis,
  Dinko Lacic,
  Robert Bode Brodmüller,
  Maxim Zhestkov
Film Production
  Good Guys Entertainment
Graphic Design
  Robert Bode Brodmüller,
  Justin Kruse,
  Joffrey Jans,
  Bureau Lombardo
Idea
  Dinko Lacic,
  Justin Kruse,
  Robert Bode Brodmüller,
  Maxim Zhestkov
Motion Graphics and 3D
  Justin Kruse,
  Robert Bode Brodmüller,
  Maxim Zhestkov
Postproduction
  Justin Kruse,
  Robert Bode Brodmüller,
  Christopher Rieke,
  Tobias Lamp
Production
  Patrick Skerlec,
  Maxim Zhestkov
Screen Design
  Robert Bode Brodmüller,
  Justin Kruse
Sound Design
  Hofkapellmeister,
  Sebastian Müller
Other
  umeric,
  les televreateurs,
  ufo,
  maxim Zhestkov,
  zeitguised

Rebrand Musik- und Entertainmentsender Viva. Senderidentität. On Air. Off Air. Neues Logo. Design auf Basis des Viva Logos. Alles neu. Immer Dreieck. Immer in der Mitte. Immer im Herzen des Senders. All Eyes on. Echte Menschen. Echte Momente. Echte Gefühle. Generische Hausschrift. Showverpackungen. Musikstreckenverpackungen. Zuschauer-Flow. Echtzeit-Senderlogo. Echtzeit-Bauchbinde. Promo-Ending. Informationssystem. IDs. Werbetrenner.

Rebrand music and entertainment channel Viva. Redesign music format packagings Channel identity on air. Off air. New logo. Design based on the shape of the Viva logo. Always the triangle. Always in the middle. At the channel's heart. All eyes on. Real people. Real situations. Real feelings. Corporate generic font. Show packagings. Music-format packagings. Audience flow. Real-time channel bug. Real-time cliptitling. Endboards. On-screen programme guide. IDs. Breakbumper.

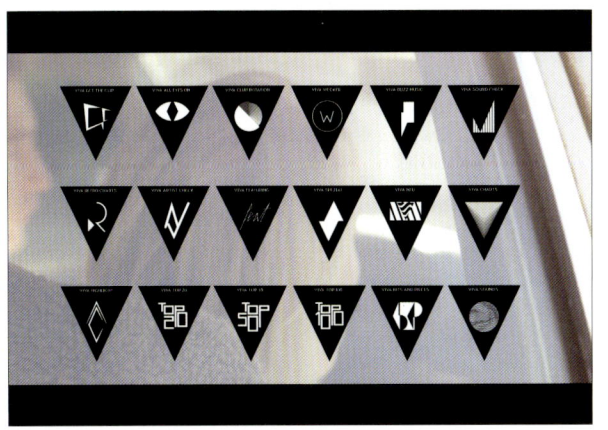

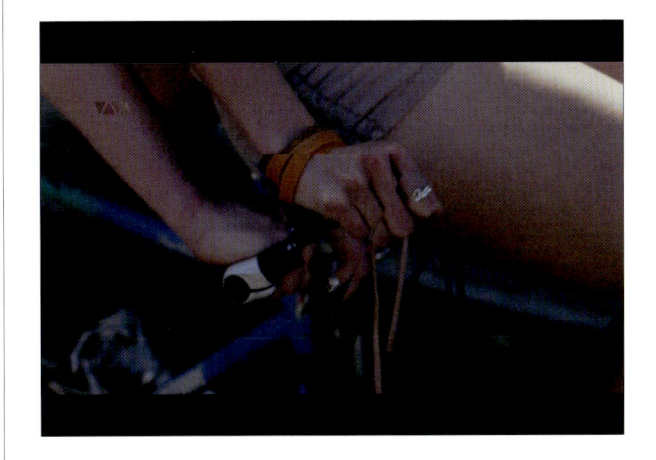

● BRONZE
DIGITALE MEDIEN
DIGITAL MEDIA
  Digitale Medien
  Mobile
  Digital Media
  Mobile

● NOMINATION
DIALOGMARKETING/
PROMOTION/MEDIA
DIALOG MARKETING/
PROMOTION/MEDIA
  Promotion
  Mittel
  Promotion
  Means

TUI
  »Donnerwetter Jetter«

Lead Agency
  Jung von Matt AG
Contributing Agencies
  Jung von Matt/next GmbH,
  Clanmo
Client
  TUI interactive GmbH
Marketing Direction
  Roland Müller-Buchner
Executive Creative Direction
  Götz Ulmer
Creative Direction
  Michael Ploj
Art Direction
  Andres Maldonado,
  Tommy Norin
Client Consulting
  Alexander Kerkow,
  René Requardt,
  Frederike Wasserkampf
Animation/Visual Effects/
Special Effects
  Lucas Zanotto
Audio Production
  David Kamp
Concept
  Salvatore Russomanno
Copy
  Salvatore Russomanno,
  Georg Muehl,
  Christina Jurgeit
Design
  Andres Maldonado,
  Tommy Norin
Idea
  Andres Maldonado,
  Tommy Norin,
  Salvatore Russomanno
Motion Graphics and 3D
  Lucas Zanotto
Programming
  Christian Roeingh
Screen Design
  Andres Maldonado,
  Tommy Norin
Sound Design
  David Kamp
Other
  Film Animation: Lucas Zanotto

Entwicklung einer Mobile App, die TUIs Position als Qualitäts- und Innovationsleader stärkt. Und zugleich die TUI Sommergarantie des Fernreiseangebots kommuniziert.

Development of a mobile app to strengthen TUI's leading position as an innovative travel service and in addition to communicate the »TUI Sommergarantie« (TUI summer guarantee) for every long-distance trip.

BRONZE
DIGITALE MEDIEN
DIGITAL MEDIA
 Digitale Medien
 Online-Werbemaßnahmen
 Digital Media
 Online Advertising

NOMINATION
DIGITALE MEDIEN
DIGITAL MEDIA
 Digitale Medien
 Social Media
 Digital Media
 Social Media

EDDING
 "Digital Highlighter"

Lead Agency
 kempertrautmann gmbh
Client
 edding International AG
Marketing Direction
 Per Ledermann
Advertising Direction
 Angelika Schumacher
Creative Direction
 Heiko Freyland, Stefan Walz
Art Direction
 Bastian Adam
Client Consulting
 Elisabeth Einhaus,
 Niklas Kruchten
Consulting
 Dorothea Feurer
Copy
 Heiko Freyland
Interactive Production
 Larissa Hube (BlueMars)
Production
 Matthias Muck (BlueMars)
Programming
 Andreas Seebald (BlueMars)
Technical Direction
 Tobias Kirchhofer (BlueMars)
Technical Installation
 Sebastian Maus (BlueMars)

 Der erste Digital Highlighter seiner Art, mit dem sich Texte im Internet bearbeiten, anschließend via Social-Media-Plattformen und E-Mail verbreiten oder als PDF speichern lassen. Durch eine Bookmarklet-Lösung funktioniert der Digital Highlighter browserunabhängig auf sämtlichen Websites mit textlichem Content.

 The first digital highlighter of its kind allows users to highlight texts online, share them via social media sites and e-mail or save them as PDF files. A bookmarklet solution allows the digital highlighter to work on any website with text, regardless of which browser is being used.

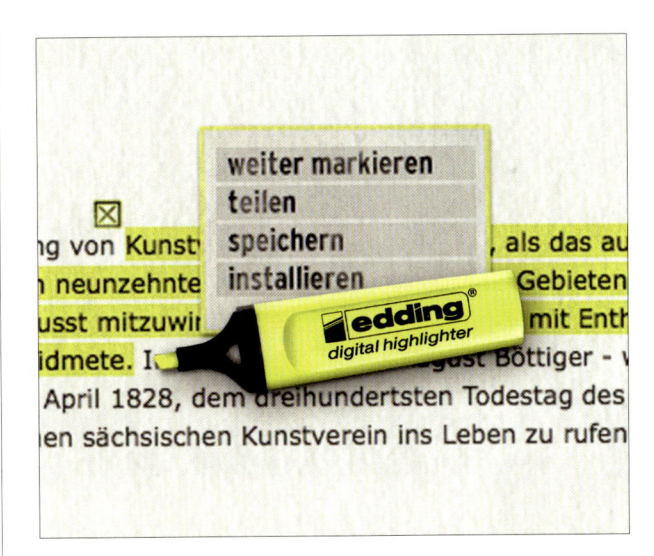

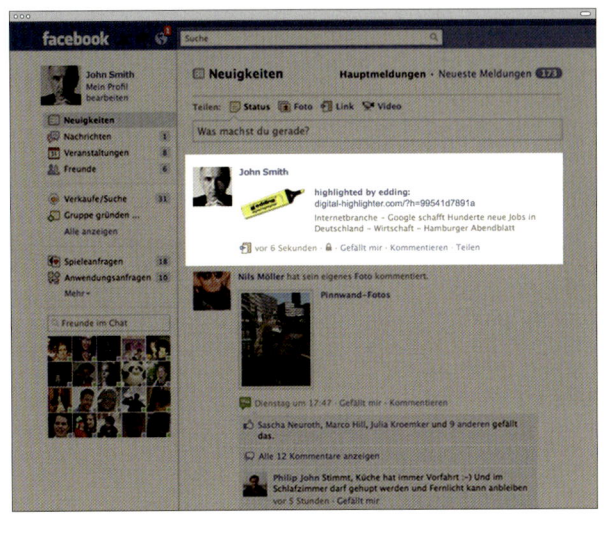

219

BRONZE
DIGITALE MEDIEN
DIGITAL MEDIA
   Digitale Medien
   Viral
   Digital Media
   Viral

NOMINATION
DIALOGMARKETING/
PROMOTION/MEDIA
DIALOG MARKETING/
PROMOTION/MEDIA
   Dialogmarketing
   Dialog Social Media
   Kampagnen
   Dialog Marketing
   Dialog Social Media
   Campaigns

VEGETARIERBUND
DEUTSCHLAND
   »Das Kannibalen Restaurant«

Lead Agency
   Serviceplan
Client
   Vegetarierbund Deutschland
   e.V. (VEBU)
Marketing Direction
   Sebastian Zösch
Advertising Direction
   Sebastian Zösch
Executive Creative Direction
   Alexander Schill
Creative Direction
   Christoph Everke
Art Direction
   Basma Attalla
Client Consulting
   Michaela Krietsch,
   Andrea Killinger,
   Valerie Simon
Copy
   Janne Sachse,
   Daniel Gassner
Graphic Design
   Matthäus Frost,
   Sascha Franz
Production
   Parasol Island,
   Sara Dadras,
   Moritz von Schröter
Programming
   Cosimo Chirico
Sound Design
   Instant Records München

Alle drei Sekunden verhungert ein Mensch, während Unmengen Wasser und Getreide für die Fleischproduktion verschwendet werden. Diesen Widerspruch machen wir zum Gesprächsthema – durch die angebliche Eröffnung eines Kannibalen-Restaurants. Mehr als 700 Artikel in über 60 Ländern und unzählige Beiträge im Web erreichen 50.000.000 Menschen und entfachen eine nachhaltige Diskussion über Fleischkonsum.

Every three seconds a person dies of starvation, while water and crops are wasted on meat production. To raise attention to this conflict we announced the opening of a cannibal restaurant. The overwhelming reactions made meat consumption into an internationally discussed issue: 700 reports in over 60 countries, 50,000,000 sight contacts and numerous comments in blogs, forums and social media.

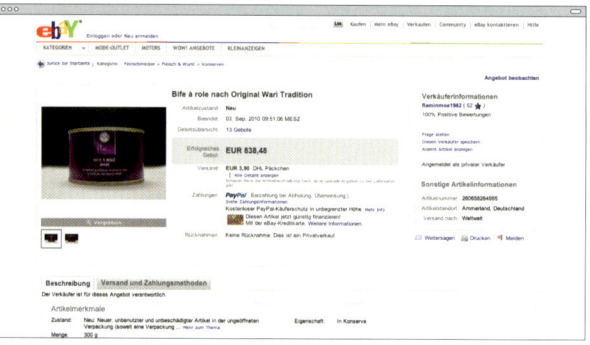

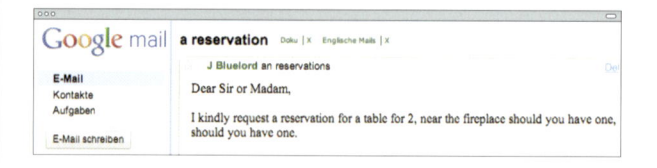

BRONZE
DIGITALE MEDIEN
DIGITAL MEDIA
  Digitale Medien
  Viral
  Digital Media
  Viral

NOMINATION
DIALOGMARKETING/
PROMOTION/MEDIA
DIALOG MARKETING/
PROMOTION/MEDIA
  Promotion
  Aktivitäten
  Promotion
  Activities

ERNTEDANK
KREATIVSPEZIALISTEN
  »Streetview Geburt«

Lead Agency
  Die Brandenburgs GmbH/
  Werbeagentur
Client
  Erntedank Kreativspezialisten
Marketing Direction
  Olaf Brandenburg
Advertising Direction
  Harald Heinen
Creative Direction
  Harald Heinen
Art Direction
  Andy Wyeth,
  Niko Willborn
Strategic Planning
  Olaf Brandenburg
Casting
  Harald Heinen
Concept
  Andy Wyeth
Copy
  Harald Heinen
Film Production
  55 Films GmbH
Idea
  Andy Wyeth,
  Harald Heinen
Image Processing
  Andy Wyeth
Photography
  Claudia Frickemeier

Wir nutzten die Berichterstattung über die heißdiskutierte Einführung von Google Street View in Deutschland, um die Geburt der Kreativagentur Erntedank zu verkünden. Dazu inszenierten wir ein Foto einer echten Geburt vor der Agenturtür im Street View Stil. Nach zwei Tagen im Netz hatten das Bild über 100 Mio. Menschen weltweit gesehen, es führte 85.000 Besucher auf unsere Webseite.

We leveraged the media hype over the Google Street View launch in Germany to announce the birth of the creative agency Erntedank. We created a photo in the typical Street View style of a woman giving birth on the foot path in front of the agency. In just two days, our picture went around the world, was exposed to over 100 million people and led to over 85,000 unique visits to our website.

**BRONZE
DIALOGMARKETING/
PROMOTION/MEDIA
DIALOG MARKETING/
PROMOTION/MEDIA**
  Promotion
  Mittel
  Promotion
  Means

**NOMINATION
CRAFT
CRAFT**
  Typografie
  Typography

**BISCHÖFLICHES HILFSWERK
MISEREOR**
  »Buchstabenmailing«

Lead Agency
  Kolle Rebbe
Client
  Bischöfliches Hilfswerk
  MISEREOR e.V.
Marketing Direction
  Michael Kleine
Executive Creative Direction
  Stefan Kolle
Creative Direction
  Ales Polcar,
  Heiko Schmidt
Art Direction
  Susanne Möbius,
  Reinhard Krug
Client Consulting
  Jessica Gustafsson
Copy
  Henning Flohr
Idea
  Susanne Möbius,
  Reinhard Krug
Production
  Franziska Ziegler
Typography
  Susanne Möbius,
  Reinhard Krug

Die Erdbebenkatastrophe auf Haiti war in allen Medien. Misereor wollte Deutschlands Topjournalisten dazu bewegen, nicht nur über das Elend zu berichten, sondern selbst mit einer Spende zu helfen. Dazu verschickten wir ein ungewöhnliches Mailing. Wir reduzierten den Text des Anschreibens auf die provokante Aufforderung: Taten statt Worte!

The relief organization Misereor wanted to send a mailing to journalists persuading them to do more than just report on the earthquake in Haiti. They wanted reporters to help out with a donation. Our idea: we reduced the call for donations to a single sentence: "Deeds, not words." And enclosed all of the redundant phrases in the mailing as loose letters.

**BRONZE
DIALOGMARKETING/
PROMOTION/MEDIA
DIALOG MARKETING/
PROMOTION/MEDIA**
    Media
    Media

**NOMINATION
DIALOGMARKETING/
PROMOTION/MEDIA
DIALOG MARKETING/
PROMOTION/MEDIA**
    Dialogmarketing
    Dialog Alternative
    Dialog Marketing
    Dialog Alternative

JOBS BEI JUNG VON MATT
    »Trojanisches Recruiting«

Lead Agency
    Jung von Matt AG
Client
    Jung von Matt AG
Marketing Direction
    Inka Wittmann
Creative Direction
    Philipp Barth,
    Holger Oehrlich
Art Direction
    Matthias Grotter
Copy
    Gert Schilling,
    Holger Diesinger
Graphic Design
    Matthias Grotter,
    Robert Jedam
Idea
    Matthias Grotter
Image Processing
    Recom Berlin/bildgudt
Photography
    Uwe Düttmann,
    Emir Haveric,
    Achim Lippoth,
    Anke Luckmann,
    Igor Panitz,
    Staudinger & Franke,
    Alexandra Klever,
    Ralph Baiker,
    Jörg Rothhaar,
    Joe Hoelzl,
    Jan van Endert,
    Martijn Oort,
    Alex Rank

Jung von Matt sucht Artdirektoren. Um Kreative bei großen Agenturen gezielt anzusprechen, sind wir nach dem Prinzip des Trojanischen Pferds vorgegangen. In Zusammenarbeit mit bekannten Fotografen haben wir ihre Mappen als Medium genutzt: In einige Bilder wurden Stellenanzeigen integriert. Die Fotografen präsentierten ihre Mappen bei den Agenturen und trugen so die Botschaft direkt zur Zielgruppe.

Jung von Matt was looking for art directors. To headhunt them from big creative agencies, we employed 15 of Germany's best photographers as Trojan horses. Their portfolios were used as a new medium. Small job ads were integrated into the photographs. The photographers presented their portfolios at the agencies – and in doing so, they took our message directly to the target group.

BRONZE
DESIGN
DESIGN
  Literatur
  Produkt-/Werbebroschüren
  Literature
  Advertising Brochures

NOMINATION
CRAFT
CRAFT
  Typografie
  Typography

———
BILD
  »Das Jahr in Bildern«

Lead Agency
  Jung von Matt AG
Client
  Axel Springer AG
Advertising Direction
  Tanja Hackner
Executive Creative Direction
  Armin Jochum
Art Direction
  Tilman Gossner
Client Consulting
  Ines Jurijczuk
Strategic Planning
  Graphics:
  Derya Ormantji
Copy
  Torben Otten,
  Georg Baur
Final Artwork
  Thomas Thiessen
Graphic Design
  Derya Ormantji
Production
  Philipp Wenhold
Publishing House
  Axel Springer AG
Typography
  Tilman Gossner,
  Derya Ormantji

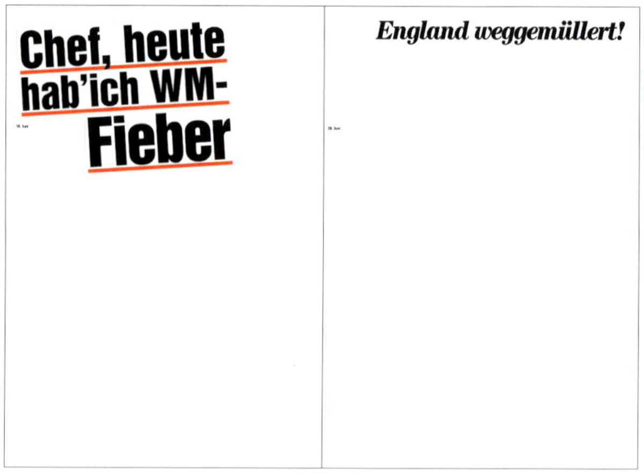

BRONZE
DESIGN
DESIGN
  Design
    Corporate Design
  Design
    Corporate Design

NOMINATION
DESIGN
DESIGN
  Design
    Packaging
  Design
    Packaging

RELAUNCH
  »Cafe Luitpold«

Lead Agency
  Rose Pistola GmbH
Contributing Agencies
  B612 GmbH
Client
  Luitpoldblock GbR,
  Cafe Luitpold
Marketing Direction
  Tina Schmitz,
  Karsten Schmitz,
  Dr. Stephan Meier,
  Barbara Weber
Advertising Direction
  Tina Schmitz
Executive Creative Direction
  Prof. Karin Hoefling,
  Prof. Holger Felten/
  Rose Pistola GmbH
Creative Direction
  Prof. Karin Hoefling,
  Prof. Holger Felten,
  Dr. Christoph Häberle
Art Direction
  Christoph Kienzle,
  Sabine Kraus,
  Frank von Grafenstein,
  Frank Weidenfelder
Client Consulting
  Prof. Holger Felten,
  Rose Pistola GmbH,
  Dr. Christoph Häberle,
  Julia Stephan/B612 GmbH
Strategic Planning
  Prof. Holger Felten,
  Prof. Dr. Christoph Häberle
Concept
  Rose Pistola GmbH,
  B612 GmbH
Copy
  Prof. Karin Hoefling,
  Dr. Sabine Felten,
  Barbara Weber,
  Dr. Jutta Göricke
Design
  Prof. Karin Hoefling,
  Christoph Kienzle,
  Sabine Kraus,
  Frank von Grafenstein,
  Frank Weidenfelder/
  Rose Pistola GmbH,
  Julia Stephan/B612 GmbH

Final Artwork
  Rose Pistola GmbH,
  B612 GmbH
Graphic Design
  Rose Pistola GmbH, Prof. Karin
  Hoefling, Sabine Kraus,
  Christoph Kienzle, Maria
  Fischer, Frank Weidenfelder
Idea
  Rose Pistola GmbH, B612
  GmbH
Illustration
  Rose Pistola GmbH
Image Editing
  Rose Pistola GmbH
Image Processing
  Rose Pistola GmbH
Photography
  Holger Albrich,
  Matthias Haslauer,
  Prof. Holger Felten
Printing
  Spiegel Kartonagenfabrik
  GmbH & Co. KG
Production
  Christoph Kienzle,
  Rose Pistola GmbH,
  Julia Stephan, B612 GmbH
Typography
  Prof. Karin Hoefling,
  Sabine Kraus,
  Christoph Kienzle/
  Rose Pistola GmbH

Aufgabe war die konzeptionelle Neuausrichtung des Münchener Traditionscafés für eine Klientel, die Kaffeehaus-Charme und Konditorenhandwerk schätzt. Durch behutsame Überarbeitung entstand eine elegante Systematik aller Kommunikationsmittel, die auf dem Zusammenspiel eines starken Zeichens – dem »L«, alleinstehend in Gold oder als Rapport –, feiner Haptik und poetisch-skurriler Illustration beruht. Neue Verpackungen übersetzen das Potential der Vergangenheit des Cafés in die Gegenwart: kombinierbare, elegante Papierkonstruktionen verbinden emotionale Ansprache, Stabilität und nachhaltigem Materialeinsatz.

Our principal task was the conceptual reorientation of this traditional Munich café for a clientele that appreciates a coffee house's charm and confectionery handcraft. Our gentle redesign resulted in an elegant system comprising all means of communication, based upon the interplay of the strong emblem "L" standing alone in gold or as a pattern, with fine haptics and poetic, bizarre illustrations. The new packaging brings the full potential of the café's past into the present: a variety of combinable double-walled paper constructions join elegance to stability and sustainable materials.

BRONZE
DESIGN
DESIGN
　Design
　　Kalender
　Design
　　Calendars

● NOMINATION
DIALOGMARKETING/
PROMOTION/MEDIA
DIALOG MARKETING/
PROMOTION/MEDIA
　Dialogmarketing
　　Dialog Mail
　Dialog Marketing
　　Dialog Mail

———
KRAFT FOODS
»Kaffee Kategorie«

Lead Agency
　JWT Germany GmbH
Client
　Kraft Foods Europe GmbH
Marketing Direction
　Stephanie Wilkes
Executive Creative Direction
　Till Hohmann
Creative Direction
　Petra Sievers
Art Direction
　Jens Klaar,
　Cathrin Hoffmann
Client Consulting
　Kara Henry,
　Samantha Yeowell
Strategic Planning
　Stefan Reitz
Agency Production
　Transmission Advertising
　Services GmbH,
　Claudia Klein
Copy
　Tina Krahne
Graphic Design
　Jens Klaar,
　Cathrin Hoffmann
Idea
　Oliver Ramm,
　Alexander Rötterink
Illustration
　Jens Klaar,
　Cathrin Hoffmann
Printing
　Hammesfahr Vertriebs GmbH
Typography
　Jens Klaar,
　Cathrin Hoffmann

Ein VIP-Mailing für 100 Entscheider der Kraft Foods Kaffee-Kategorie. Per Kurier zugestellt oder persönlich übergeben. Es soll Menschen, die alles über Kaffee wissen, begeistern, Produktinteraktion auslösen und die Markenbindung erhöhen. Das Mittel: ein »leerer« Kalender, der mit Kaffee bestreut wird. Das Pulver haftet am Klebedruck und enthüllt Kaffee-»Geheimnisse«, die sogar Experten überraschen.

A VIP mailing for the 100 stakeholders of the Kraft Foods coffee category, delivered via courier. The goal: inspire category experts, create product interaction and increase brand loyalty. The medium: a seemingly blank calendar. The content becomes visible only after coffee powder is spread over the pages and sticks to the glue print – revealing the most surprising coffee secrets. The result: an aromatic calendar about coffee made visible with coffee.

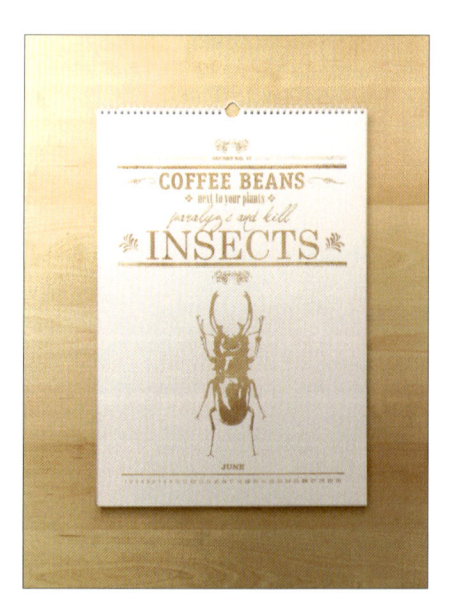

● BRONZE
EDITORIAL
EDITORIAL
  Editorial
  Print/Einzelleistung
  Editorial
  Print/Individual Work

● NOMINATION
EDITORIAL
EDITORIAL
  Editorial
  Print/Jahrgang
  Editorial
  Print/Year's Issue

DU – DAS KULTURMAGAZIN
2010
  »Reportage Dezember 2010
  Tomi Ungerer«

Lead Agency
  Du – Das Kulturmagazin
Client
  Du – Das Kulturmagazin
Marketing Direction
  Oliver Prange
Advertising Direction
  Oliver Burger
Executive Creative Direction
  Oliver Prange
Art Direction
  Franziska Neugebauer
Client Consulting
  Oliver Burger
Chief Editing
  Stefan Kaiser
Image Editing
  Lars Willumeit
Publishing House
  Du – Das Kulturmagazin

227

● **BRONZE**
RÄUMLICHE INSZENIERUNG
SPATIAL SCENE-SETTING
Kommunikation im Raum
Environmental Design

● **NOMINATION**
DIGITALE MEDIEN
DIGITAL MEDIA
Digitale Medien
Digitale Medienformate
im Raum
Digital Media
Digital Media Environment
Design

MOBILITY
"Reflective Kinematronic"

Lead Agency
  ART+COM
Client
  Otto Bock HealthCare GmbH
Creative Direction
  Joachim Sauter
Art Direction
  Hermann Klöckner
Concept
  Joachim Sauter,
  Hermann Klöckner
Idea
  Joachim Sauter,
  Hermann Klöckner
Media Systems
  Jürgen Pietruska
Motion Design
  Hermann Klöckner
Motion Graphics and 3D
  Susanne Traeger,
  Simon Häcker
Programming
  David Siegel
Technical Implementation
  ict AG
Other
  Computative Choreography:
  Hermann Klöckner

Beauftragt mit einer Ausstellung zum Thema Bewegung, sollte Mobility die Aufmerksamkeit der Besucher erregen und sie poetisch-emotional einstimmen. 100 motorbewegte Prothesenhände halten Spiegel, die das Licht eines Scheinwerfers reflektieren. Die Lichtpunkte gleiten, einer komputativen Choreografie folgend, auf der Wand gegenüber immer wieder zum chinesischen Schriftzeichen für Mobilität zusammen.

Mobility was commissioned for the entrée of an exhibition to focus visitors' attention on the theme of movement in a poetic-metaphorical manner. 100 motor-operated prosthetic hands hold small mirrors which reflect the light of a spotlight. The spots of light follow a computer-generated choreography, moving on the wall opposite to repeatedly form the Chinese character for mobility.

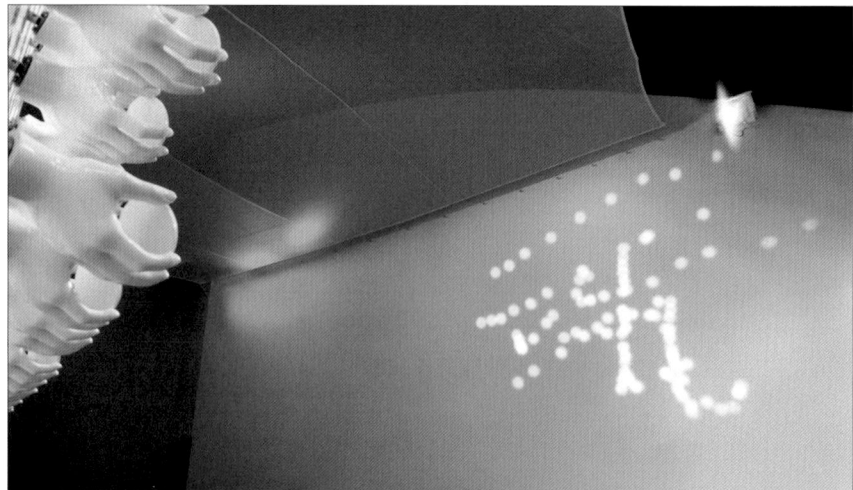

BRONZE
RÄUMLICHE INSZENIERUNG
SPATIAL SCENE-SETTING
    Kommunikation im Raum Craft
    Medienbespielung &
     -integration
    Environmental Design Craft
    Media Design and Integration

NOMINATION
RÄUMLICHE INSZENIERUNG
SPATIAL SCENE-SETTING
    Events Craft
    Medienbespielung &
     -integration
    Events Craft
    Media Design and Integration

MERCEDES-BENZ
»Interaktives Präsentationstool
– CLS Show Paris 2010«

Lead Agency
    Atelier Markgraph
    (Concept, Design, Realisation)
Contributing Agencies
    MESO Digital Interiors
    (vvvv-Programming)
Client
    Daimler AG
Media Design and Integration
    Atelier Markgraph
    (Concept, Design and
    Realisation),
    MESO Digital Interiors
    (vvvv-Programming)

Autosalon Paris: Mit einem interaktiven Präsentationstool wird die Technologie des CLS sichtbar. In Echtzeit interagieren Moderatoren mit dem Fahrzeug, den dahinter gelegenen LED-Flächen und dem Publikum. Durch Bewegungen in sensitiven Feldern können die Moderatoren Begriffe, Grafiken und Bildfenster erzeugen, bewegen und vergrößern. Den Showablauf bestimmen die Zuschauer selbst über Touchpads.

Autosalon Paris: An interactive presentation tool makes the technology of the CLS visible. In real time, presenters interact with the vehicle, the LED panels behind it, and the audience. By making movements in sensitive fields on stage, presenters can create, move and enlarge terms, graphics and image windows. The viewers themselves create the programme proactively by using a touch pad.

BRONZE
CRAFT
CRAFT
  Text
  Copy

NOMINATION
KLASSISCHE MEDIEN
CLASSICAL MEDIA
  Out-of-Home
  Klassisch Kampagne
  Out-of-Home
  Classic Campaign

WELT KOMPAKT
  »Statusmeldungen«

Lead Agency
  Scholz & Friends
Client
  DIE WELT/WELT KOMPAKT,
  Axel Springer AG
Marketing Direction
  Kai-H. Riese
Executive Creative Direction
  Martin Pross,
  Matthias Spaetgens
Creative Direction
  Mathias Rebmann,
  Florian Schwalme
Art Direction
  Michael Schmidt
Client Consulting
  Uli Schuppach
Copy
  Caspar Heuss,
  Momme Clausen,
  Viktoria Grünewald
Graphic Design
  Franziska Boemer

Irland hat begonnen Rettungspaket zu verwenden.
Portugal und Griechenland verwenden das ebenfalls.

Eyjafjallajökull ist seit 2 Monaten Nichtraucher!
Lufthansa, Air France und 27 anderen gefällt das.

Nordkorea hat Südkorea angestupst.

Sepp Blatter Katar!
Sepp Blatter und Katar gefällt das.
Alle 8.036.226 Kommentare anzeigen

VfB Stuttgart wird an Abstiegskampf teilnehmen.
Karlsruher SC gefällt das.

Nicolas Sarkozy gefällt Nicolas Sarkozy.
Nicolas Sarkozy gefällt das.

WELT KOMPAKT
KURZ. ANDERS. GEDRUCKT.

**BRONZE
GANZHEITLICHE
KOMMUNIKATION
INTEGRATED CAMPAIGNS**
  Ganzheitliche Kommunikation
  Integrated Campaigns

**NOMINATION
DIALOGMARKETING/
PROMOTION/MEDIA
DIALOG MARKETING/
PROMOTION/MEDIA**
  Dialogmarketing
  Dialog Crossmediale
  Kampagnen
  Dialog Marketing
  Dialog Cross-Media
  Campaigns

GREENPEACE SCHWEIZ
 »Der Zonen Plan«

Lead Agency
  walker Werbeagentur
Client
  Greenpeace Schweiz
Creative Direction
  Pius Walker
Art Direction
  Stefanie Huber
Client Consulting
  Cornelia Nünlist
Camera
  Manuel Mack,
  Matthias Huser,
  Daniel Kladiva,
  Götz Hudelmaier,
  Michael Kindermann
Copy
  Martin Arnold,
  Heinz Helle
Cutting
  Alex Kut
Film Direction
  Alain Gsponer
Film Production
  Cobblestone/Pumpkin Film
Graphic Design
  Rahel Witschi,
  Signe Fleischmann
Music Composition
  Malte Hagemeister
Postproduction
  Daniel Kladiva
Production
  Pieter Lony (Cobblestone),
  Caro Büchel (Pumpkin Film)

Die Schweiz über die Gefahren von Atomkraft aufklären, damit die Volksabstimmung gegen den Neubau von drei neuen Atomkraftwerken gewonnen wird. 300 verschiedene Plakate, 142.000 Mailings, ein landesweiter Flashmob mit Hunderten zu Boden fallenden Menschen und bald darauf das meistgesehene Viral der Schweiz. Die Bevölkerung ist wachgerüttelt. Die Volksabstimmung kann kommen.

The campaign objective was to create awareness of the risks associated with nuclear energy. The aim was to encourage people to vote against more nuclear power plants being built in the future. 300 different posters, 142,000 mailings, a country-wide flashmob with hundreds of people falling to the ground, followed by the most viewed viral in Switzerland. The public was now awake and ready to vote.

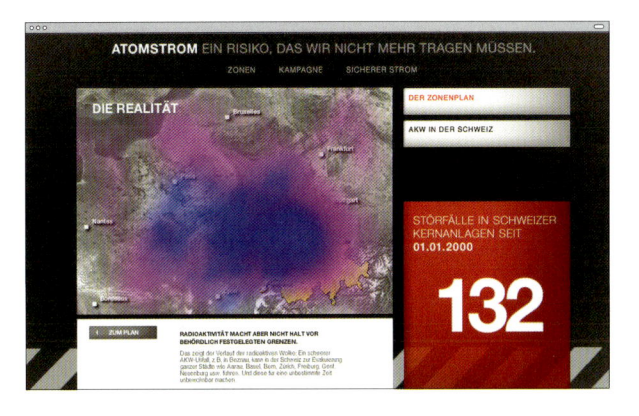

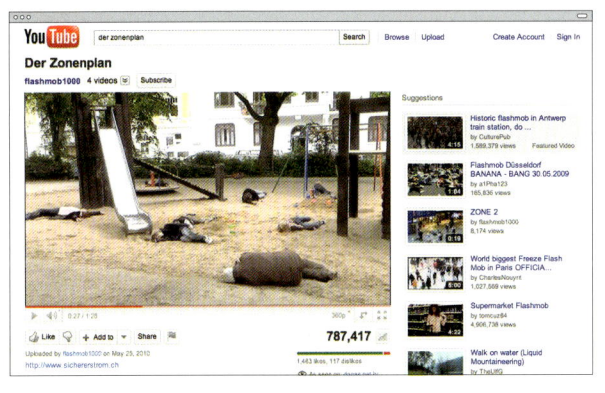

3

PUNKTE
POINTS

BRONZE
KLASSISCHE MEDIEN
CLASSICAL MEDIA
  Print
  Einzelmotiv
  Print
  Single Motif

FRANKFURTER ALLGEMEINE ZEITUNG
  »Dahinter steckt immer ein kluger Kopf – Haneke«

Lead Agency
  Scholz & Friends
Client
  Frankfurter Allgemeine Zeitung GmbH
Marketing Direction
  Josef Krieg
Executive Creative Direction
  Sebastian Turner,
  Martin Pross,
  Matthias Spaetgens
Creative Direction
  Mathias Rebmann,
  Florian Schwalme,
  Oliver Handlos
Art Direction
  Michael Johne
Client Consulting
  Katrin Seegers,
  Marie Toya Gaillard,
  Eva Verena Schmidt
Art Buying
  Dominique Steiner
Copy
  Marco Müller,
  Farid Baslam,
  Felix Heine
Graphic Design
  Till Hohmann
Image Processing
  Appel Grafik,
  Digitales Leben
Photography
  Hans Starck,
  Oliver Rolf

**BRONZE
KLASSISCHE MEDIEN
CLASSICAL MEDIA**
  Print
  Einzelmotiv
  Print
  Single Motif

SCHOLZ & FRIENDS
  »WERU Abschluss-Anzeige«

Lead Agency
  Scholz & Friends
Client
  Scholz & Friends Berlin GmbH
Advertising Direction
  Matthias Spaetgens
Executive Creative Direction
  Martin Pross,
  Matthias Spaetgens
Creative Direction
  Michael Winterhagen,
  Jan Leube
Art Direction
  Wulf Rechtacek,
  Kay Lübke,
  Anatolij Pickmann
Copy
  Michael Häußler

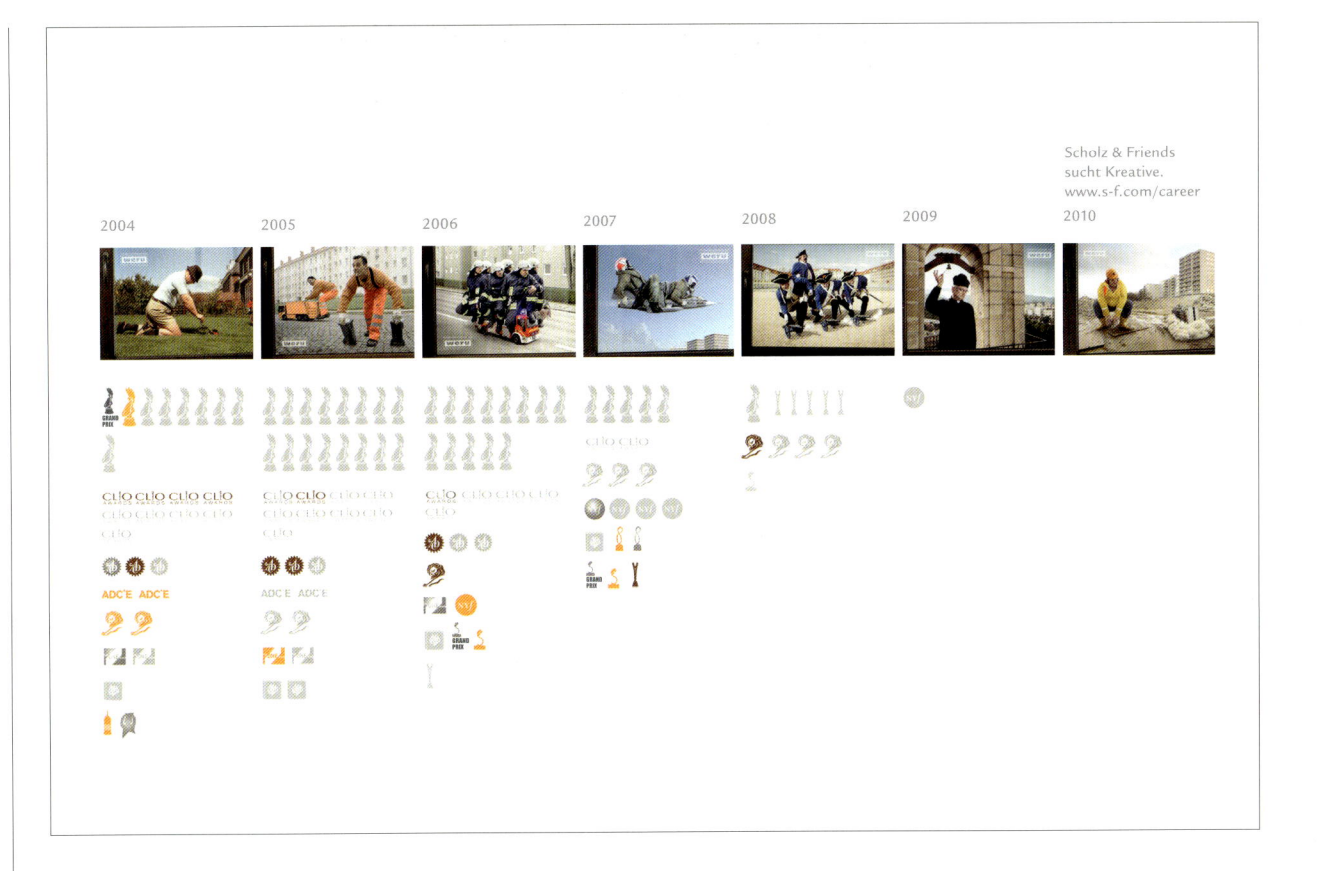

235

BRONZE
KLASSISCHE MEDIEN
CLASSICAL MEDIA
  Print
  Kampagne
  Print
  Campaign

BEATE UHSE TV
»Kindersicherung«

Lead Agency
  kempertrautmann gmbh
Client
  Beate Uhse TV
Marketing Direction
  Ulrich Kuhnt
Creative Direction
  Gerrit Zinke,
  Christian Fritsche
Art Direction
  Simon Jasper Philipp
Client Consulting
  Jan Rütten,
  Joana Gläscher
Art Buying
  Lina Eggers
Copy
  Christoph Gähwiler
Illustration
  Julia Schonlau
Photography
  Lisa Krechting
Postproduction
  retouched-fba OHG,
  Daniel Steinbrück

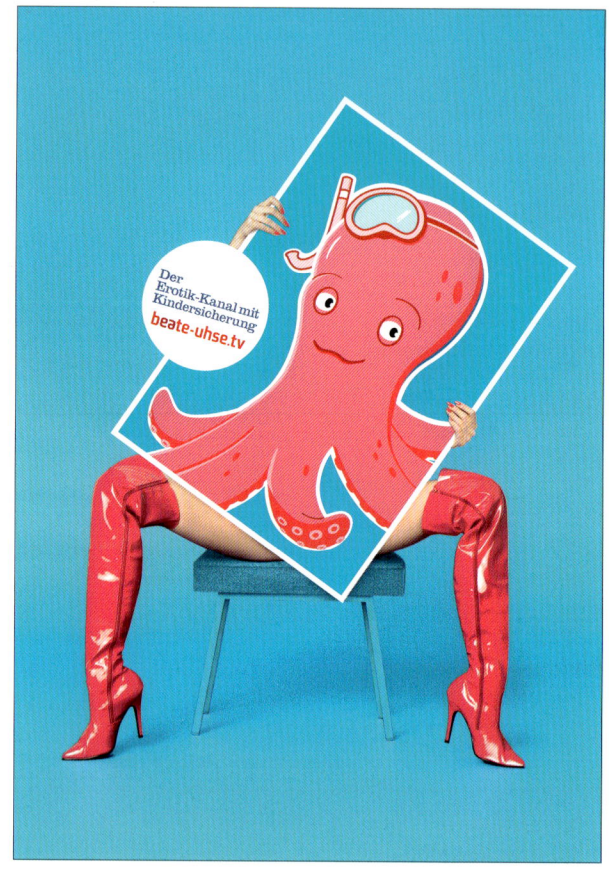

BRONZE
KLASSISCHE MEDIEN
CLASSICAL MEDIA
Print
Kampagne
Print
Campaign

BILD
»Bekennerkampagne«

Lead Agency
　Jung von Matt AG
Client
　Axel Springer AG
Marketing Direction
　Tanja Hackner
Advertising Direction
　Ingo Webecke
Executive Creative Direction
　Armin Jochum
Creative Direction
　Christian Fritsche,
　David Leinweber,
　Sören Porst
Art Direction
　Sabrina Patzek,
　Tilman Gossner,
　Sebastian Schnell,
　Florian Barthelmess
Client Consulting
　Julia Figur,
　Nina Krüger,
　Ines Jurijczuk
Art Buying
　Karen Blome
Concept
　Tobias Feige,
　Torben Otten,
　Georg Baur
Copy
　Franz Beckenbauer,
　Mesut Özil,
　Kai Diekmann,
　Armin Rohde,
　Arthur Abraham,
　Mike Krüger,
　H. P. Baxxter,
　Eva Padberg
Graphic Design
　Daniel Gumbert
Photography
　Mathias Bothor
Postproduction
　Jens Rosendahl

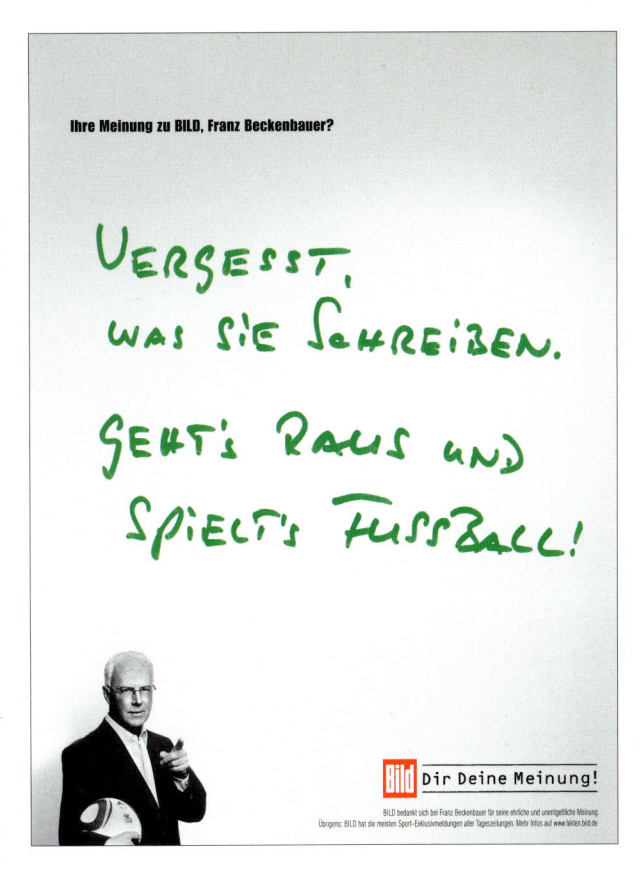

BRONZE
KLASSISCHE MEDIEN
CLASSICAL MEDIA
  Print
  Kampagne
  Print
  Campaign

WELT AM SONNTAG
»Sonntagskampagne«

Lead Agency
  Oliver Voss GmbH
Client
  Axel Springer AG
Marketing Direction
  Johannes Boege,
  Anja Häse
Creative Direction
  Oliver Voss,
  Till Monshausen
Art Direction
  Florian Zwinge
Art Buying
  Katja Sluyter
Illustration
  Florian Zwinge

BRONZE
KLASSISCHE MEDIEN
CLASSICAL MEDIA
 Film
 TV/Kino Einzelspot
 Film
 TV/Cinema Commercial

GOOGLE
 »Deutsch-Französische Liebe«

Lead Agency
 Kolle Rebbe GmbH
Client
 Google Germany GmbH
Marketing Direction
 Barbara Daliri Freyduni
Advertising Direction
 Fabian Teichmueller
 (Product Management)
Executive Creative Direction
 Stefan Kolle
Creative Direction
 Stefan Wübbe,
 Rolf Leger
Art Direction
 Michael Füsslin
Client Consulting
 Katrin Becker
Agency Production
 Nina Svechtarov
Art Buying
 Emanuel Mugrauer
Copy
 Caroline Schmidt
Film Direction
 Christian Reimann
Film Production
 Infected Postproduction GmbH
Idea
 Google Creative Labs
 (New York)/Kolle Rebbe
Sound Design
 Analogue Muse (New York)
 Composer: Jeremy Turner
Sound Engineering
 Composer: Jeremy Turner
Other
 Producers:
 Henrik von Müller,
 Tatjana Morgenthal
 Compositing:
 Moritz Gläsle

Jeden Tag werden auf Google Millionen von Suchanfragen gestellt. Mit eben diesen Suchbegriffen und den entsprechenden Ergebnissen, die die Websuche, Google Maps, Youtube und Co. dazu liefern, erzählt der Film Suchgeschichten, wie sie das Leben schreibt. Egal, ob man sein Herz oder sein Zelt verloren hat, ob man den Mann im Mond sucht oder das passende Outfit zur WM.

Every day, Google receives millions of search requests. Based on these search terms and the corresponding results from the web search, Google Maps, Youtube and others, the film tells the stories behind the searches – the sort you couldn't make up. No matter whether you've lost your heart or your tent, are looking for the man in the moon or for the perfect outfit for the World Cup.

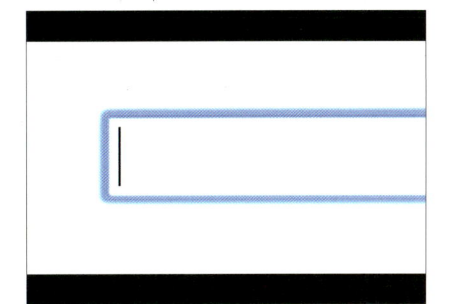

BRONZE
KLASSISCHE MEDIEN
CLASSICAL MEDIA
    Film
    TV/Kino Kampagne
    Film
    TV/Cinema Campaign

GOOGLE KAMPAGNE
»Das Leben ist eine Suche«

Lead Agency
    Kolle Rebbe GmbH
Client
    Google Germany GmbH
Marketing Direction
    Barbara Daliri Freyduni
Advertising Direction
    Fabian Teichmueller
    (Product Management)
Executive Creative Direction
    Stefan Kolle
Creative Direction
    Stefan Wübbe,
    Rolf Leger
Art Direction
    Michael Füsslin
Client Consulting
    Katrin Becker
Agency Production
    Lars Wiepking,
    Nina Svechtarov
Art Buying
    Emanuel Mugrauer
Copy
    Peter Quester,
    Caroline Schmidt,
    Sandra Eichner,
    Kolja Rinne,
    Marko Werth
Film Direction
    Christian Reimann
Film Production
    Infected Postproduction GmbH
Idea
    Google Creative Labs
    (New York)/Kolle Rebbe
Sound Design
    Analogue Muse (New York)
    Composer:
    Jeremy Turner;
    Mikis Meyer,
    Ralf Götzenberger,
    Hans-Ulrich Hönemann
Other
    Producers:
    Henrik von Müller,
    Tatjana Morgenthal,
    Ulrike Kramer,
    Stevie Daniel

Jeden Tag werden auf Google Millionen von Suchanfragen gestellt. Mit eben diesen Suchbegriffen und den entsprechenden Ergebnissen, die die Websuche, Google Maps, Youtube und Co. dazu liefern, erzählt der Film Suchgeschichten, wie sie das Leben schreibt. Egal, ob man sein Herz oder sein Zelt verloren hat, ob man den Mann im Mond sucht oder das passende Outfit zur WM.

Every day, Google receives millions of search requests. Based on these search terms and the corresponding results from the web search, Google Maps, Youtube and others, the film tells the stories behind the searches – the sort you couldn't make up. No matter whether you've lost your heart or your tent, are looking for the man in the moon or for the perfect outfit for the World Cup.

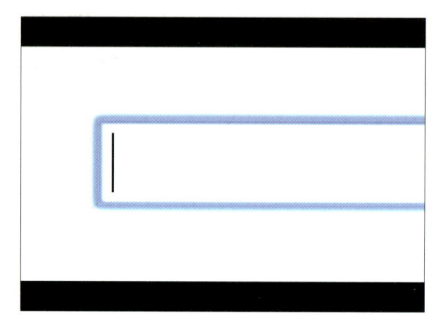

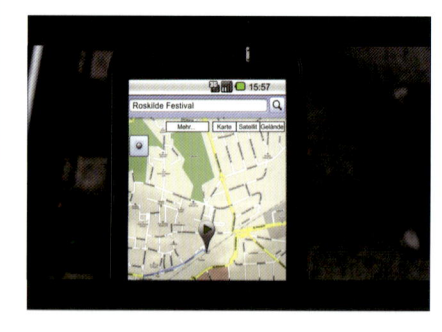

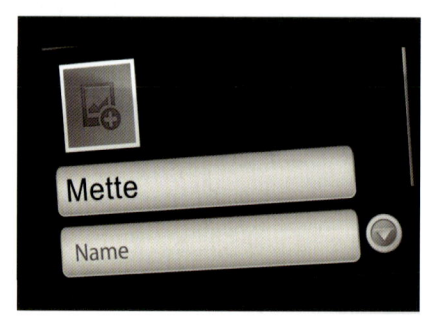

BRONZE
KLASSISCHE MEDIEN
CLASSICAL MEDIA
 Film
 TV/Kino Kampagne
 Film
 TV/Cinema Campaign

SPARKASSE KAMPAGNE
»08/15«

Lead Agency
 Jung von Matt AG
Client
 DSGV
Marketing Direction
 Dr. Lothar Weissenberger
Advertising Direction
 Dr. Lothar Weissenberger
Executive Creative Direction
 Mathias Stiller,
 Wolfgang Schneider
Creative Direction
 Maximilian Millies,
 Marius Lohmann,
 Jan Harbeck,
 David Mously
Art Direction
 Daniel Haschtmann,
 Duc Nguyen
Client Consulting
 Helen Seiffe,
 Jennifer Doubek,
 Philip Rother
Agency Production
 Julia Cramer
Camera
 Frank Griebe
Casting
 Suse Marquardt
Copy
 David Missing,
 Nicolas Linde
Cutting
 Alex Jurkat
Film Direction
 Sebastian Schipper
Film Production
 radical.media GmbH
Music Composition
 Audioforce
Postproduction
 nhb studios berlin GmbH,
 PICTORION das werk GmbH
Production
 Caroline Kousidonis,
 Andre Bause
Sound Engineering
 nhb studios berlin GmbH,
 Studio Funk GmbH & Co. KG
Speaker
 Frank Schlabritz

Das Sparkassen-Finanzkonzept ist mit seiner einzigartigen Beratungsqualität anderen Banken um Längen voraus. Das zeigt die Kampagne rund um die fiktive 08/15-Bank, deren Führungsriege immer wieder versucht, die Leistungen der Sparkasse zu erreichen. Natürlich scheitert sie jedes Mal aufs Neue an diesen hohen Zielen.

The »Sparkassen-Finanzkonzept« offers better financial consultation than any other bank. To convey this message in an entertaining way, we created the fictional »08/15 Bank« (ordinary bank). In a series of TV ads, the board members of the „08/15-Bank" develop different schemes to outdo the Sparkasse. But, of course, all efforts are in vain.

BRONZE
KLASSISCHE MEDIEN
CLASSICAL MEDIA
Film
On-air-Design
Film
On-Air Design

ZDF DAS KLEINE FERNSEHSPIEL
»Vorspann ‹Shahada›«

Lead Agency
  weareflink GmbH
Client
  Bittersuess Pictures with ZDF
  »Das kleine Fernsehspiel«
  and Filmakademie Baden-
  Württemberg
Executive Creative Direction
  Niko Tziopanos
Creative Direction
  Alexander Hanowski
Art Direction
  Alexander Hanowski
Client Consulting
  Andreas Lampe
Agency Production
  Andreas Lampe
Animation/Visual Effects/
Special Effects
  Alexander Hanowski
Computer Animation
  Alexander Hanowski
Concept
  Alexander Hanowski
Film Direction
  Alexander Hanowski
Film Production
  weareflink GmbH
Graphic Design
  Alexander Hanowski
Idea
  Alexander Hanowski
Motion Graphics and 3D
  Alexander Hanowski
Music Composition
  Daniel Sus
Postproduction
  weareflink GmbH
Production
  weareflink GmbH

Shahada erzählt die Geschichte von drei Muslimen in Berlin, deren Werte und Glaube durch persönliche Krisen ins Wanken geraten. Die Titelsequenz verwebt Symbole des Film zu einer metaphorischen Montage. Die Illustrationen verschmelzen zu immer neuen Bildern. Die Kamera, verkohlte Texturen und verblasste Farben erzeugen eine beklemmende Atmosphäre.

Shahada is about three Muslims, whose belief and ethical values start to struggle due to personal crises. The title sequence uses symbols from the movie to create a metaphoric composition, and the camera, charred textures and faded colors produce an oppressive atmosphere.

BRONZE
KLASSISCHE MEDIEN
CLASSICAL MEDIA
Film
Kurzfilme/Sonderformate
für Bewegtbild
Film
Shorts/Special Formats
for Moving Pictures

WM DOKUMENTATION
»Jeder Glaube hat seine
Rituale – die Dokumentation«

Lead Agency
  Jung von Matt AG
Client
  Daimler AG
Marketing Direction
  Anders-Sundt Jensen,
  Lüder Fromm
Advertising Direction
  Damir Maric,
  Jochen Schmidt
Executive Creative Direction
  Mathias Stiller
Creative Direction
  Maximilian Millies,
  Marius Lohmann
Art Direction
  Marius Lohmann,
  Ricardo Distefano
Client Consulting
  Sven Dörrenbächer,
  Stefanie Gombert,
  Marcus Bank,
  Niko Thielsch
Agency Production
  Julia Cramer
Camera
  Wouter Westendorp
Casting
  Trigger Happy Productions
  GmbH
Copy
  Maximilian Millies,
  Thomas Rendel
Cutting
  Hannes Andresen
Film Direction
  Johan Kramer
Film Production
  Trigger Happy Productions
  GmbH
Music Composition
  Moser Meyer
Postproduction
  Media City Lab, PICTORION
  das werk Berlin GmbH,
  FX factory, Condor Post
  Production, Trigger Happy
  Productions
Production
  Trigger Happy Productions
  GmbH
Sound Engineering
  Steffen Graubaum,
  Gunar Voigt
Styling
  Susanne Kreyenfeld, Markus
  Müller, Barbara Hilmes

Zur Fußball-WM starteten Mercedes und der DFB die Faninitiative »Der 4. Stern für Deutschland«. Um Team und Fans im Glauben an den vierten Titel zu vereinen, riefen wir ein dokumentarisches Interviewprojekt ins Leben. In Kooperation mit »11 Freunde« befragten wir über 30 Spieler, Betreuer und Fans. Das Thema: Rituale – charmante Marotten und Aberglaube, die in der Fußballwelt weit verbreitet sind.

During the World Cup 2010, Mercedes and the German Football Association (DFB) initiated »Der 4. Stern für Deutschland« – a campaign that united team and fans in spirit. To achieve this, we started a documentary film project and interviewed over 30 players and fans in cooperation with the football magazine »11 Freunde«. The topic: rituals, quirks and superstitions that fans and players have in common.

**BRONZE
KLASSISCHE MEDIEN
CLASSICAL MEDIA**
Audio
Radio Einzelspot
Audio
Radio Commercial

CBM SPENDENAUFRUF
»Spenden«

Lead Agency
  BBDO Proximity GmbH, Duesseldorf
Client
  Christoffel Blindenmission Deutschland e.V.
Executive Creative Direction
  Sebastian Hardieck,
  Toygar Bazarkaya
Creative Direction
  Sebastian Hardieck
Client Consulting
  Dirk Bittermann,
  Liselotte Schwenkert,
  Katrin Spiegel
Audio Production
  Studio Funk, Duesseldorf
Copy
  Florian Birkner
Sound Engineering
  Arne Schultze
Speaker
  Daniel Schüssler

AUDIO

»SPENDEN« 45″

SFX: MUSIK

SPRECHER:
  Spenden sie Knöpfe.
  Spenden sie Hosen, Stühle und Türklinken.
  Spenden Sie Vögel, Frisuren, Hunde, Steine und Bücher.
  Spenden Sie Schmetterlinge, Hände, Telefonnummern, Schilder, Ohrringe, Kühe, Blumen, Lachen, Farben und Gesichter.
  Spenden Sie Bäume, Sonnenstrahlen, Wiesen, Flugzeuge, Flüsse, Brücken, Wälder, Wasserfälle, Städte, Wolken, Ozeane, Berge und Sterne.

  Spenden Sie Augenlicht.
  Auf christoffel-blindenmission.de

BRONZE
KLASSISCHE MEDIEN
CLASSICAL MEDIA
  Audio
  Radio Kampagne
  Audio
  Radio Campaign

1&1 ALL-NET-FLAT KAMPAGNE
»Spontan verbunden«

Lead Agency
  Jung von Matt AG
Client
  1&1 Internet AG
Marketing Direction
  Karin Eickmeyer
Advertising Direction
  Melanie Wolf
Executive Creative Direction
  Sascha Hanke
Creative Direction
  Jo Marie Farwick,
  Tobias Grimm
Client Consulting
  Sarah Moser,
  Jörg-Peter Dressel
Audio Production
  Hastings Audio
Copy
  Henning Robert,
  Jan-Hendrik Scholz
Radio Production
  Hastings Audio
Speaker
  Jannik Endemann

AUDIO

»SCHÖN & HÄSSLICH«

OFF-SPRECHER:
  1&1 verbindet. Heute: Familie Schön mit Familie Hässlich.

ORIGINAL-TELEFONAT ZWISCHEN DEN VERBUNDENEN:
  »Schön.«
  »Hallo?«
  »Wer ist da?«
  »Ich, Frau Hässlich.«
  »Frau Hässlich?«
  »Ja.«
  »Wer ist denn das? Frau Hässlich.« (Gibt das Telefon an ihren Mann weiter.)
  »Was ist los. Frau Hässlich? Wer ist Frau Hässlich?«
  »Ja.«
  »Ja, also wen wollen Sie denn sprechen bitte?«
  »Ich weiß ja nicht wer dort ist. Wer ist denn da am Ende?«
  »Mein Name ist Schön! Schön! Wie „schön"!«
  »Schön?«
  »Ja.«
  »Und ich bin hässlich.«
  »Sie sind hässlich.«
  »Ja.«
  »Ja, das tut mir leid.«
  »Ja, mir auch. Tschüß!«

OFF-SPRECHER:
  So günstig, da lohnt sich jedes Gespräch.
  Mit der 1&1 All-Net-Flat – für nur 29,90 im Monat unbegrenzt telefonieren.

BRONZE
KLASSISCHE MEDIEN
CLASSICAL MEDIA
  Audio
  Radio Kampagne
  Audio
  Radio Campaign

ANTIK- & TRÖDELMARKT GARE DU NEUSS KAMPAGNE
  »An diesem Bahnhof hält die Zeit.«

Lead Agency
  Scholz & Friends
Client
  Gare du Neuss GmbH
  Antik- & Trödelmarkt
Marketing Direction
  Kay Schlossmacher
Executive Creative Direction
  Niels Alzen
Client Consulting
  Melanie Stein
Audio Production
  Hastings Music GmbH
Copy
  Niels Alzen
Radio Direction
  Lukas Walter
Other
  Music: Tonschneiderei, Hamburg

AUDIO

»DINGE«

NOSTALGISCHE, RUHIGE KLAVIERMUSIK.
EINE ALTE MÄRCHENERZÄHLERSTIMME:
  In Neuss gibt es einen Trödelmarkt.
  Mit Uhren, die schon viele Tage gezählt haben.
  Mit Lampen, die sich an lange Abende erinnern.
  Mit Spiegeln, die Helles und Dunkles kennen.
  Er ist im alten Güterbahnhof.
  Denn die Dinge, die dort warten, sind nur auf der Durchreise.

  Gare Du Neuss.

  An diesem Bahnhof hält die Zeit.

»KOFFER«

NOSTALGISCHE, RUHIGE KLAVIERMUSIK.
EINE ALTE MÄRCHENERZÄHLERSTIMME:
  In einem Bahnhof steht ein Koffer.
  Er ist gefüllt mit Erinnerungen.
  So sehr, dass seine alten Lederriemen fast reißen.
  Er hat eine Herkunft, aber noch kein Ziel.
  Wer rechtzeitig da ist, kann ihn mitnehmen.
  Antik- und Trödelmarkt im alten Güterbahnhof Neuss.

  Gare Du Neuss.

  An diesem Bahnhof hält die Zeit.

»FAHRKARTE«

NOSTALGISCHE, RUHIGE KLAVIERMUSIK.
EINE ALTE MÄRCHENERZÄHLERSTIMME:
  Es gibt einen Bahnhof, an dem man keine Fahrkarte braucht.
  Und es gibt nur ein Ziel.
  Ob man nach Indien reist, in die Kolonialzeit.
  Oder nach England zur Jahrhundertwende.
  Vielleicht nur in die Straße, in der man wohnte.
  Die Endstation ist immer: Gestern.
  Antik- und Trödelmarkt im alten Güterbahnhof Neuss.

  Gare Du Neuss.

  An diesem Bahnhof hält die Zeit.

BRONZE
DIGITALE MEDIEN
DIGITAL MEDIA
Digitale Medien
Digitale Kampagnen
Digital Media
Digital Campaigns

VERGISS AIDS NICHT
"Cock out"

Lead Agency
  Philipp und Keuntje GmbH
Client
  Vergiss Aids nicht e.V.
Advertising Direction
  Jan Schwertner,
  Heiko Schueßling
Executive Creative Direction
  Hartwig Keuntje
Creative Direction
  Diether Kerner,
  Constantin Kaloff
Art Direction
  Mario Zaradic,
  Sönke Schmidt,
  Jens Erasmus Schröder
Client Consulting
  Steffen Schwab,
  Sabrina Bohnacker
Agency Production
  Sandra Niessen,
  Axel Leyck
Audio Production
  Hastings Music GmbH
Casting
  Birgit Eipper
Computer Animation
  Parasol Island GmbH
Consulting
  Steffen Schwab,
  Sabrina Bohnacker
Copy
  Adrienne Tonner,
  René Ewert
Cutting
  Hendryk Press,
  Michael Palfi
Design
  Charles Bals,
  Philip Hansen,
  Dino Figuera
Film Production
  Ziggy Mediahouse
Idea
  Adrienne Tonner,
  René Ewert
Image Processing
  Maud Moerstedt
Interactive Production
  Arne Broich
Motion Graphics and 3D
  Waldemar Fast,
  Sven Klimm,
  Bardia Marco Afchar,
  Joschka Herrlich,
  Christian Wallmeier
Postproduction
  Ziggy Mediahouse

Programming
  Manuel Rodriguez,
  Jeremias Dombrowsky
Sound Design
  Jonathan Wulfes
Technical Direction
  Holger Norden
Technical Implementation
  Manuel Rodriguez

Um Teenager auf humorvolle Weise zum Safer Sex zu animieren, haben wir den Kampf gegen HIV wörtlich genommen. In "Cock out" kann man(n) gegen den HI-Virus boxen – nicht mit Tastatur oder Controller, sondern mit dem eigenen Penis und einem speziellen Kondom, das von der Webcam erkannt wird. TV-Spot, Poster, Virals, Banner, Social Media und eine Kondom-Verteilaktion bewarben das Game zum Welt-Aids-Tag.

In order to encourage teenagers in a fun way to practice safer sex, we took the fight against HIV literally. In "Cock Out", you can box against HIV – not using a keyboard or joystick but your own penis and a special condom that's detected by a webcam. In the run-up to World AIDS Day, we promoted the game with a TV ad, posters, virals, banners, social media and a condom distribution initiative.

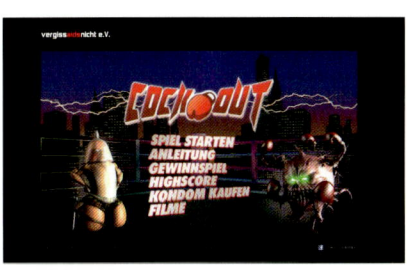

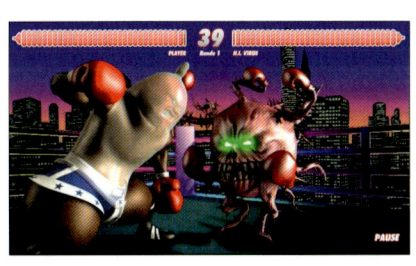

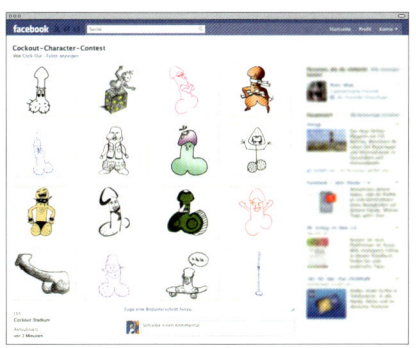

**BRONZE
DIALOGMARKETING/
PROMOTION/MEDIA
DIALOG MARKETING/
PROMOTION/MEDIA**
  Dialogmarketing
  Dialog Broadcast
  Dialog Marketing
  Dialog Broadcast

BVB TRIKOT
  »Kloppo dreht ab«

Lead Agency
  Grimm Gallun Holtappels
  Werbeagentur GmbH & Co. KG
Client
  Kappa Deutschland GmbH
Marketing Direction
  Tobias Blick
Executive Creative Direction
  Florian Grimm,
  Nils Gallun
Creative Direction
  Matthias M. Müller,
  Florian Grimm
Art Direction
  Phillip Eggers
Client Consulting
  Birgit Heikamp
Camera
  Timo Schwarz
Casting
  BVB Dortmund
Copy
  Stefan Geschke,
  Stefan Grahl,
  Jürgen Klopp
Cutting
  Kurt Brown
Film Direction
  Florian Grimm
Film Production
  BM8
Idea
  Stefan Geschke,
  Phillip Eggers
Postproduction
  BM8

Beim BVB, dem »größten Kader der Welt«, gehören alle zur Mannschaft. Deshalb erhalten auch die Berichterstatter eine persönliche Einladung zur Pressekonferenz der Trikotvorstellung. So kann sich jeder Schreiberling einmal fühlen wie ein echter Spieler, der von Herrn Klopp ganz persönlich in der Kabine eins auf die Mütze bekommt. Natürlich ist dies die Einladung zur Pressekonferenz.

At the BVB, everybody belongs to the team. For this reason, the reporters also received an appropriate personal invitation to the press conference to mark the launch of the new team shirts. In this way, every writer can feel what it's like to be a real player being told off personally in the dressing room by Mr Klopp himself. Of course, it's the invitation to the press conference.

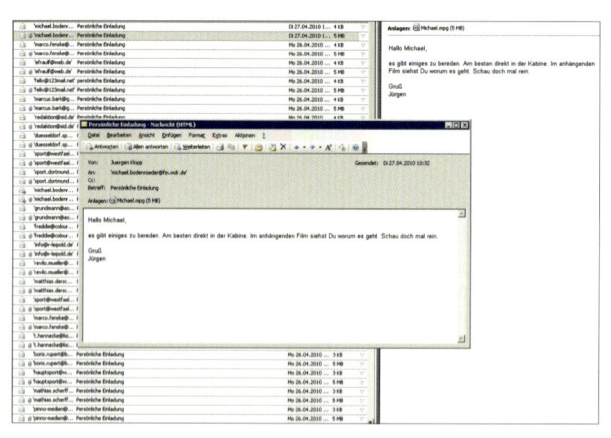

BRONZE
DIALOGMARKETING/PROMOTION/MEDIA
DIALOG MARKETING/PROMOTION/MEDIA
Media
Media

MCCAFÉ
»Anna und die Liebe«

Lead Agency
  TBWA Berlin
Contributing Agencies
  Heye OMD GmbH
Client
  McDonald's Deutschland Inc.
Marketing Direction
  Rainer Saborny
Advertising Direction
  Susan Schramm,
  Thomas Ostermeier
Executive Creative Direction
  Stefan Schmidt,
  Kurt Georg Dieckert
Creative Direction
  Vesna Koselj,
  Tomas Tulinius,
  Frederik Frede
Art Direction
  Lucio Regner,
  Tomas Tulinius
Client Consulting
  David Barton,
  Daniel Münch,
  Alexis Mardon
Strategic Planning
  Simon Walter, Sonia Lago,
  Matthew Gentile
Art Buying
  Martina Kersten
Copy
  Vesna Koselj
Design
  Veit Möller, Andrew Morgan
Image Processing
  TBWA Berlin
Interactive Production
  Elin Svegsjö
Media
  Heye OMD GmbH,
  Jan Dreyer
  (Deputy Managing Director),
  Mareen Naupert
  (Group Head Planning),
  Bjoern Deuter
  (Director Planning)
Photography
  Tom Wagner
Postproduction
  Heye & Partner GmbH
Production
  AprilMay,
  Kristina Tulinius
Programming
  Thomas Michelbach,
  Torsten Bergler,
  Kay Siegert
Other
  Katrin Dettmann
  (Print Production)

744 McCafés in Deutschland sind nicht genug: Zum Start der Markenidee »Alles Gute beginnt mit einem guten Kaffee« wurden Fans der TV-Soap »Anna und die Liebe« emotional aktiviert. Ziel: Werde ein McCafé Fan. Die Idee: Campaign-Placement. Die fiktive Werbeagentur Broda&Broda entwickelte eine Kampagne. Parallel posteten Fans auf Facebook eigene Werbeideen. Davon sah man kurz darauf in Berlin Plakate.

744 McCafés in Germany are not enough. While launching the brand belief "Everything good starts with a good cup of coffee", fans of the TV soap „Anna und die Liebe" were emotionally activated. Goal: become a McCafé fan. The idea: campaign placement. The fictitious agency Broda&Broda developed a campaign. At the same time, fans posted ideas on Facebook. Instantly, posters were seen throughout Berlin.

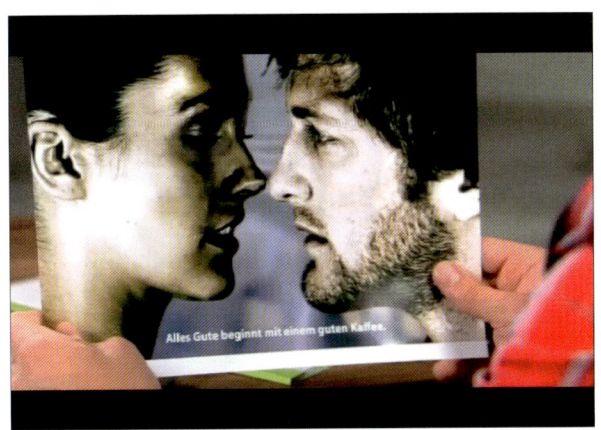

BRONZE
DESIGN
DESIGN
Literatur
Kataloge
Literature
Catalogs

AUSSTELLUNGSPUBLIKATION
»Zur Nachahmung empfohlen!
Expeditionen in Ästhetik und
Nachhaltigkeit«

Lead Agency
    anschlaege.de
Client
    Adrienne Goehler
Executive Creative Direction
    Christian Lagé
Creative Direction
    Axel Watzke
Art Direction
    Steffen Schuhmann
Client Consulting
    Axel Watzke
Concept
    Axel Watzke
Copy
    Adrienne Goehler (Ed.)
Design
    Steffen Schuhmann
Editing
    Anna Maier,
    Hanna Gersmann,
    Beate Willms,
    Adrienne Goehler,
    Nora Kronemeyer
Final Artwork
    Evelin Fuhrmann
Graphic Design
    Axel Watzke
Image Editing
    Adrienne Goehler
Image Processing
    Evelin Fuhrmann
Printing
    Oktoberdruck AG
Production
    Evelin Fuhrmann
Publishing House
    Hatje Cantz Verlag
Typography
    Steffen Schuhmann

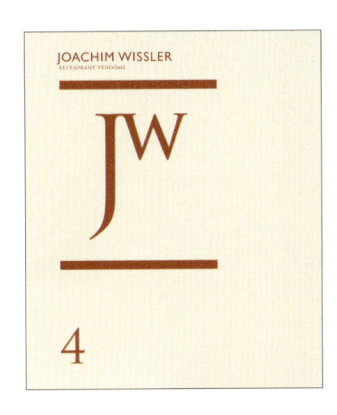

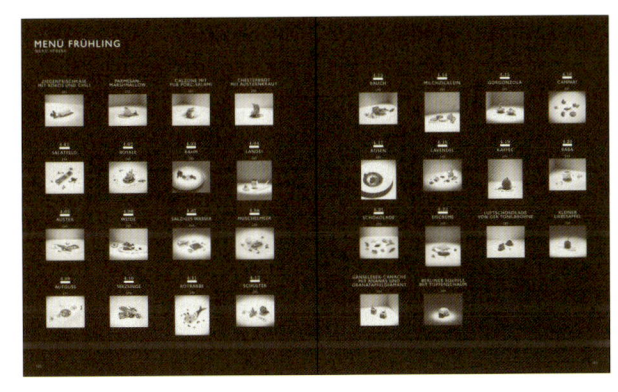

BRONZE
DESIGN
DESIGN
Literatur
Bücher
Literature
Books

KOCHBUCH, JOACHIM
WISSLER GROUP
"JW 4"

Lead Agency
   häfelinger + wagner design
Client
   Joachim Wissler Group GmbH
Executive Creative Direction
   häfelinger + wagner design:
   Frank Wagner
Creative Direction
   häfelinger + wagner design:
   Frank Wagner
Art Direction
   häfelinger + wagner design:
   Veronika Kinczli
Agency Production
   häfelinger + wagner design:
   Melanie Sauer
Concept
   häfelinger + wagner design:
   Frank Wagner,
   Veronika Kinczli
Copy
   Christoph Teuner
Design
   häfelinger + wagner design:
   Veronika Kinczli,
   Nils Jaedicke,
   Dominik Pander
Final Artwork
   häfelinger + wagner design:
   Sebastian Lehnert
Image Processing
   chmil.: Jörg Klein and
   häfelinger + wagner design:
   Adelgund Janik
Photography
   Erik Chmil
Printing
   Druckerei Fritz Kriechbaumer
Publishing House
   Joachim Wissler Group

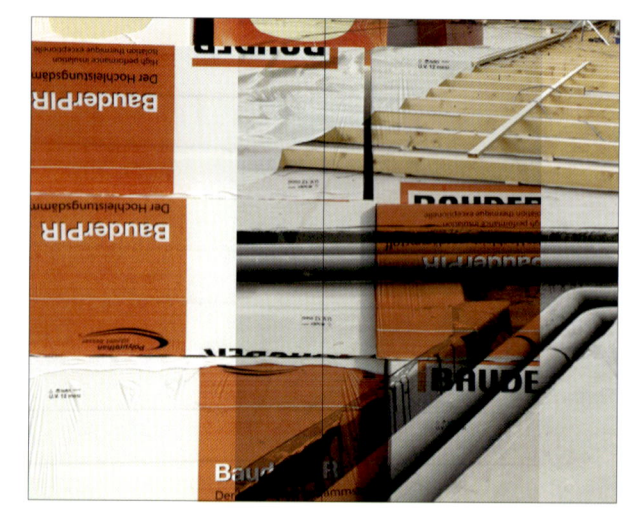

BRONZE
DESIGN
DESIGN
  Literatur
  Bücher
  Literature
  Books

TYPOTRON-HEFT 28
»Lokremise«

Lead Agency
  TGG Hafen Senn Stieger
Client
  Typotron AG
Copy
  Liana Ruckstuhl
Photography
  das digitale bild GmbH
Printing
  Typotron AG
Publishing House
  Typotron AG

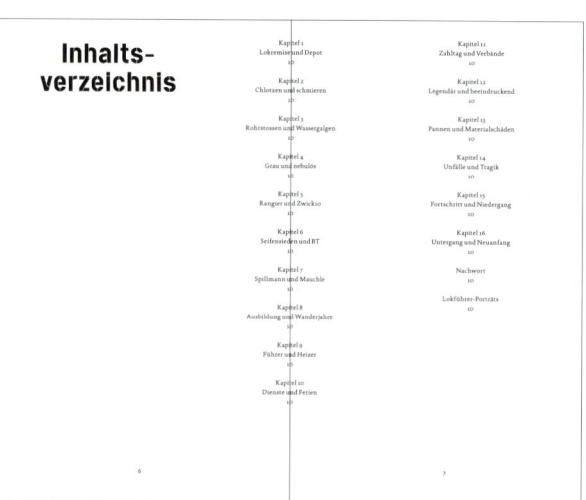

BRONZE
DESIGN
DESIGN
 Design
 Kalender
 Design
 Calendars

WAXHOUSE
 »Waxingkalender«

Lead Agency
 Jung von Matt AG
Client
 WaXhouse Betriebs GmbH
Marketing Direction
 Patrick Doerks
Advertising Direction
 Patrick Doerks
Executive Creative Direction
 Wolf Heumann
Creative Direction
 Peter Kirchhoff,
 Andreas Ottensmeier
Art Direction
 Sébastien Stabenau
Client Consulting
 Birte Helmert,
 Sina Rollfing
Art Buying
 Karen Blome
Copy
 Peter Kirchhoff,
 Michael Okun
Final Artwork
 Sandra Grötsch
Graphic Design
 Gereon Stratmann
Photography
 Marc van Dalen
Production
 Philipp Wenhold

Ein Kalender, der Kunden und Geschäftspartner täglich an die Mission von Waxhouse erinnert: besonders professionell und schonend Körperbehaarung entfernen.

This is a calendar designed to remind Waxhouse's clients and business partners on a daily basis of the company's mission of providing gentle and highly professional hair removal services.

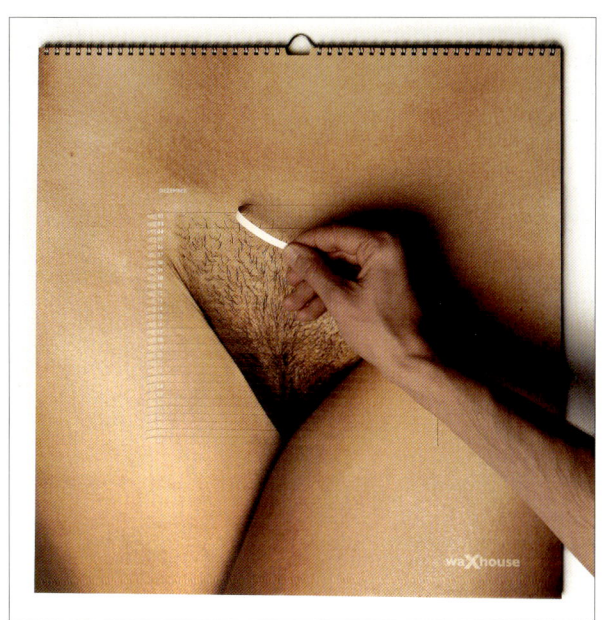

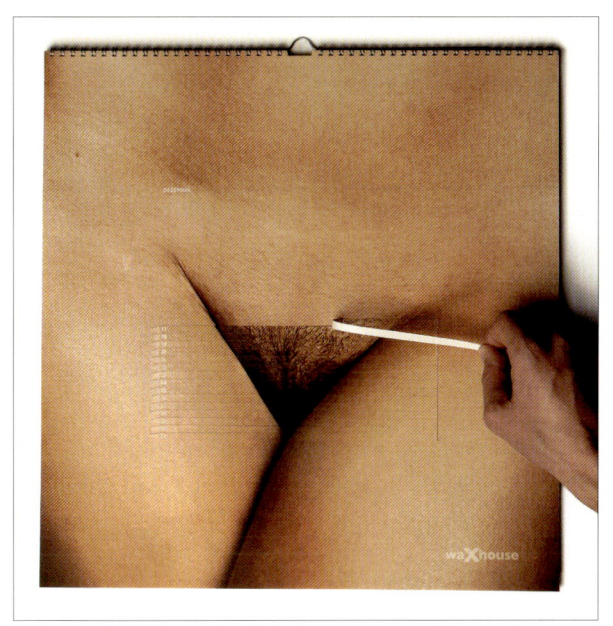

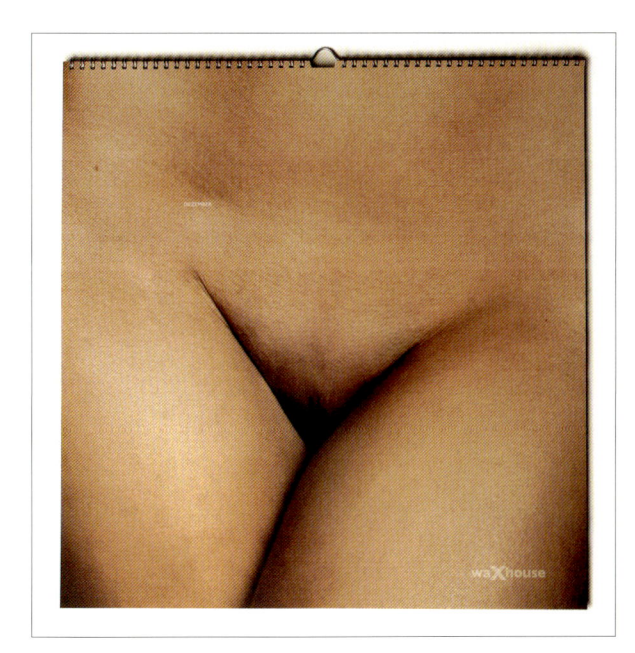

BRONZE
DESIGN
DESIGN
　Design
　Kunst-/Kultur-/
　Veranstaltungsplakate
　Design
　Art/Culture/Event Posters

**PETER BEHRENS SCHULE
DUESSELDORF**
　»Rundgang«

Lead Agency
　herzogenrathsaxler design
Client
　pbsa peter behrens school of
　architecture, Duesseldorf
Design
　margarethe saxler,
　matthias herzogenrath

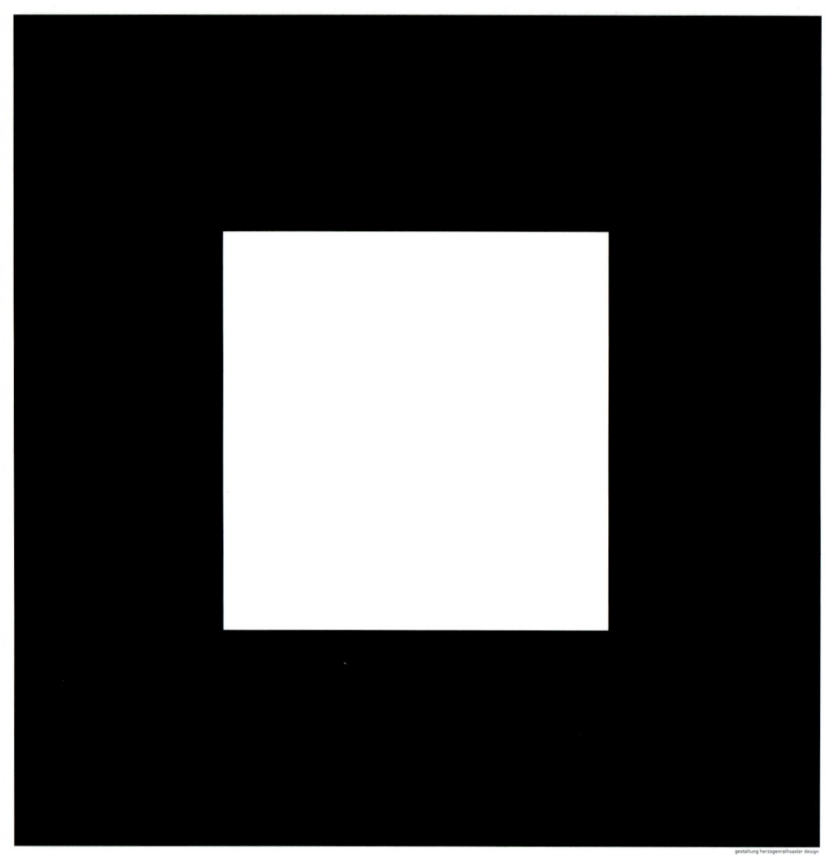

**BRONZE
DESIGN
DESIGN**
Design
Packaging
Design
Packaging

FESTINA PROFUNDO
»Die wasserverpackte Taucheruhr«

Lead Agency
  Scholz & Friends
Client
  Festina Uhren GmbH
Marketing Direction
  Stéphane Gordon
Advertising Direction
  Stéphane Gordon
Executive Creative Direction
  Martin Pross,
  Matthias Spaetgens,
  Wolf Schneider
Creative Direction
  Mathias Rebmann,
  Florian Schwalme
Art Direction
  Michael Hess,
  Juergen Krugsperger,
  Ralf Schröder,
  Ksenia Slavcheva
Client Consulting
  Albert Petzold,
  David von Hilchen
Graphic Design
  Sebastian Frese
Image Processing
  Maren Boerner
Photography
  Attila Hartwig
Production
  Sandro Buschke,
  Nelly Sedlanic

Wie lassen sich Vertrauenswürdigkeit und die Vorzüge einer Taucheruhr sportbegeisterten Menschen kommunizieren? Durch ein überzeugendes Packaging Design. Denn die Festina Profundo 6692 hält, was sie verspricht: nämlich dicht. Den Beweis liefert ihre Verpackung. Sie präsentiert die Uhr in ihrem Element – tauchend im Wasser. Dazu wurde die Uhr in mit Wasser gefüllte Klarsichtbeutel eingeschweißt.

How can we communicate the reliability of a waterproof diver's watch to people with an enthusiasm for sports? The solution: through convincing packaging design. The Festina Profundo 6692 lives up to its promise: it is entirely waterproof. The packaging presents the watch in its natural environment: submerged in water. To this end, the watch has been sealed in a transparent bag filled with water.

BRONZE
DESIGN
DESIGN
  Design
  Produktdesign
  Design
  Product Design

THE DELI GARAGE
»Backsteine«

Lead Agency
  Kolle Rebbe/KOREFE
Client
  T.D.G. Vertriebs GmbH &
  Co. KG
Marketing Direction
  Felix Negwer
Creative Direction
  Katrin Oeding
Art Direction
  Reginald Wagner
Client Consulting
  Marie Steinhoff
Copy
  Till Grabsch,
  Thomas Völker
Final Artwork
  Maik Spreen
Graphic Design
  Derya Sevim,
  Marko Grewe
Photography
  Ulrike Kirmse
Production
  Produktionsbüro Romey von
  Malottky GmbH

Backsteine – die erste Backmischung in Mini-Zementsäcken. Anstelle von Muffins, Cupcakes oder Donuts kommen jetzt Ziegelsteine auf den Tisch. Mit den Backsteinen aus sechs beiliegenden Gussformen lassen sich leckere Kuchenbauwerke errichten.

Brickstones – the world's first cake mix in miniature cement bags. Instead of muffins, cupcakes or donuts, bricks are now served on the table. The six cake moulds for the brickstones let cooks create delicious cake structures.

BRONZE
EDITORIAL
EDITORIAL
Editorial
Print/Ausgabe
Editorial
Print/Issue

FELD HOMMES MAGAZIN
»Finale«

Lead Agency
  loved gmbh
Client
  Feld Verlag
Marketing Direction
  Markus Lenz,
  Kai Maier
Creative Direction
  Mieke Haase
Art Direction
  Oliver Griep
Chief Editing
  Sabine Cole,
  Mieke Haase,
  Oliver Wurm
Editing
  Martina Behrens,
  Michael Beutinger,
  Philip Bittner,
  Penélope Toro,
  Isabelle Thiry,
  Jan Schlüter,
  Harald Braun
Final Artwork
  Appel Grafik
Graphic Design
  Pascal Constanty,
  Inga Detlow,
  Christine Eckart,
  Kathrin Frey,
  Julia Holtz,
  Herr Müller,
  Thilo Pentzin,
  Jan Spading,
  Johanna Swistowski
Idea
  Oliver Griep,
  Sabine Cole
Postproduction
  Appel Grafik,
  Primate Postproduction
Production
  Markus Lenz
Publishing House
  FELD Verlag
Other
  Film Direction:
  Zhoi Hy,
  Judith Stoletzky

BRONZE
EDITORIAL
EDITORIAL
    Editorial
    Print/Ausgabe
    Editorial
    Print/Issue

GOLDEN SECTION GRAPHICS
"In Graphics"

Lead Agency
    Golden Section Graphics
Client
    Golden Section Graphics
Executive Creative Direction
    Jan Schwochow
Creative Direction
    Jan Schwochow
Art Direction
    Paul Blickle
Chief Editing
    Jan Schwochow
Infographics
    Jan Schwochow,
    Katharina Schwochow,
    Paul Blickle,
    Katja Günther,
    Bernd Riedel,
    Katharina Stipp,
    Rafael Vicente,
    Lukas Engelhardt,
    Maria Thiele,
    David Weinberg,
    Simon Wimmer
Printing
    Druckerei Rüss
Publishing House
    Golden Section Graphics GmbH

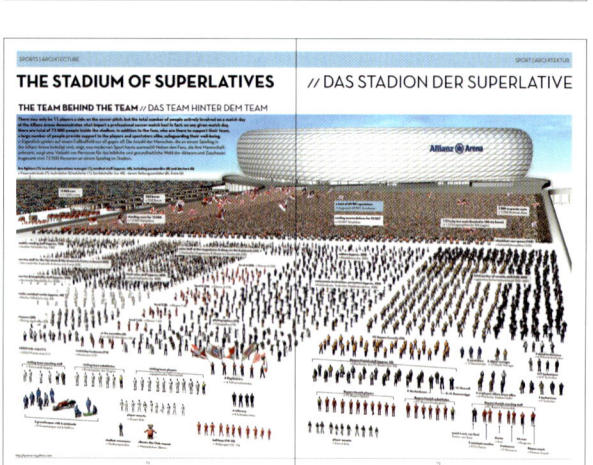

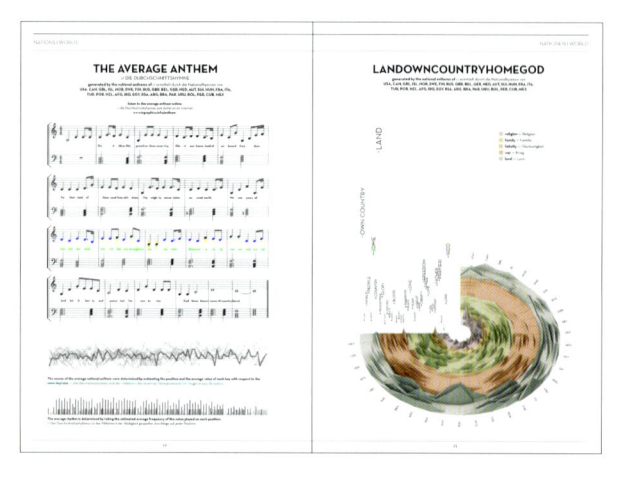

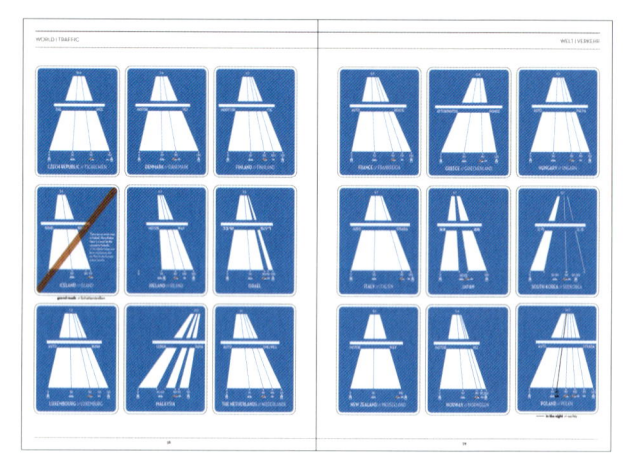

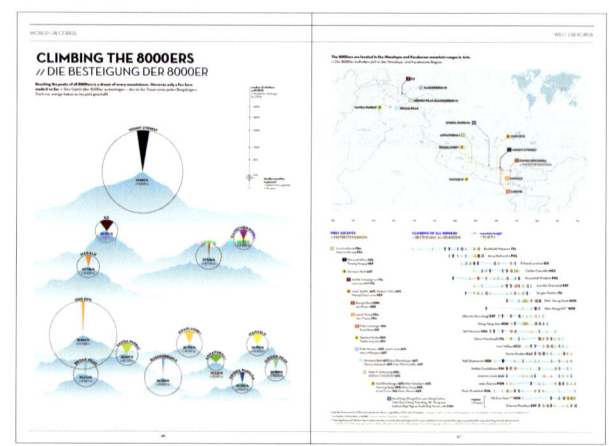

BRONZE
EDITORIAL
EDITORIAL
Editorial
Print/Ausgabe
Editorial
Print/Issue

MAGAZIN DER BAYERISCHEN STAATSFORSTEN
»Bayernwald«

Lead Agency
    Anzinger | Wüschner | Rasp
    Agentur für Kommunikation GmbH
Client
    Bayerische Staatsforsten AöR
Marketing Direction
    Dr. Hermann S. Walter,
    Head of the Office of the Board
    of Directors
Executive Creative Direction
    Markus Rasp
Creative Direction
    Markus Rasp
Art Direction
    Regina Baierl
Client Consulting
    Claudia Anzinger
Strategic Planning
    Gernot Wüschner
Agency Production
    Martina Jacoby
Chief Editing
    Gernot Wüschner
Consulting
    Martina Jacoby
Copy
    Gernot Wüschner
Editing
    Gernot Wüschner,
    Jan Berndorff,
    Tobias Moorstedt,
    Jan Kirsten Biener,
    Hans Gerlach,
    Peter Laufmann
Final Artwork
    Sabine Düe
Illustration
    Eva Hillreiner
Image Processing
    MXM Digital Service, Munich
Photography
    Barbara Bonisolli,
    Robert Fischer,
    Bert Heinzlmeier,
    Matthias Ziegler
Printing
    Gerber Druck+Medien,
    Kirchheim
Publishing House
    Self-published

BRONZE
EDITORIAL
EDITORIAL
 Editorial
 Print/Ausgabe
 Editorial
 Print/Issue

ZEITMAGAZIN
»Es lebe die Einfachheit!«

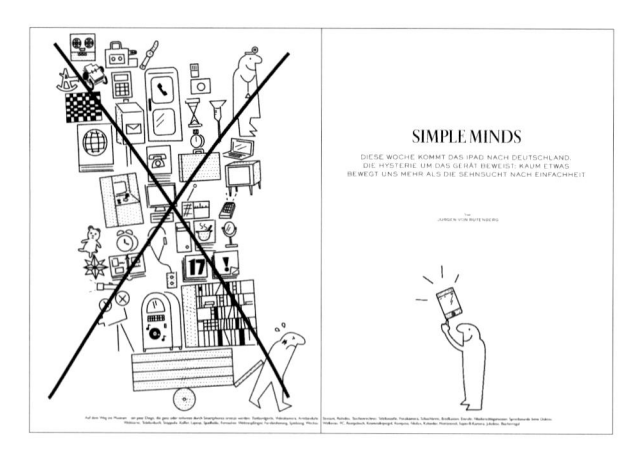

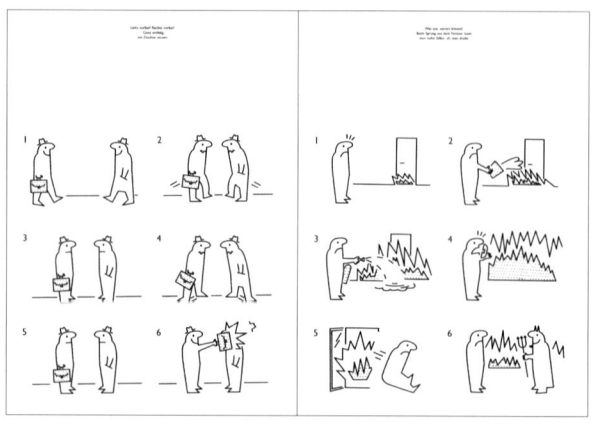

Lead Agency
 ZEITmagazin
Client
 DIE ZEIT
Creative Direction
 Mirko Borsche
Art Direction
 Katja Kollmann
Chief Editing
 Christoph Amend
Graphic Design
 Nina Bengtson,
 Jasmin Müller-Stoy
Illustration
 SANY
Image Editing
 Michael Biedowicz,
 Andreas Wellnitz
Image Processing
 Twentyfour Seven Creative
 Media Services GmbH
Publishing House
 Zeitverlag Gerd Bucerius
 GmbH & Co. KG

BRONZE
EDITORIAL
EDITORIAL
 Editorial
  Print/Ausgabe
 Editorial
  Print/Issue

ZEITMAGAZIN
 »Wir machen das Beste aus Ihren Texten«

Lead Agency
 ZEITmagazin
Client
 DIE ZEIT
Creative Direction
 Mirko Borsche
Art Direction
 Katja Kollmann
Chief Editing
 Christoph Amend
Graphic Design
 Nina Bengtson,
 Jasmin Müller-Stoy,
 Mirko Merkel
Image Editing
 Michael Biedowicz,
 Andreas Wellnitz
Image Processing
 Twentyfour Seven Creative
 Media Services GmbH
Publishing House
 Zeitverlag Gerd Bucerius
 GmbH & Co. KG

BRONZE
EDITORIAL
EDITORIAL
　Editorial
　　Print/Jahrgang
　Editorial
　　Print/Year's Issue

VICE MAGAZINE
»Jahrgang 2010«

Lead Agency
　VICE Deutschland GmbH
Client
　VICE Deutschland GmbH
Marketing Direction
　Benjamin Ruth
Advertising Direction
　Benny Eichelmann
Chief Editing
　Tom Littlewood
Editing
　Barbara Dabrowska,
　Felix Nicklas,
　Andreas Richter,
　Stefan Lauer
Publishing House
　VICE Deutschland GmbH

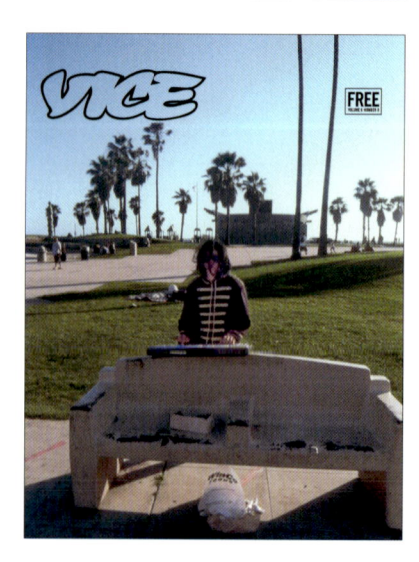

BRONZE
EDITORIAL
EDITORIAL
Editorial
Print/Einzelleistung
Editorial
Print/Individual Work

NEON MAGAZIN
»Jetzt ist aber Schluss!«

Lead Agency
  NEON Magazin
Client
  NEON Magazin GmbH
Marketing Direction
  Antje Schlünder
Executive Creative Direction
  Thomas Lindner,
  Andreas Petzold
Art Direction
  Jonas Natterer
Chief Editing
  Michael Ebert,
  Timm Klotzek
Copy
  Patrick Bauer,
  Frank Höhne
Graphic Design
  Ji-Young Ahn
  (Deputy Art Direction),
  Sandra Stolle
  (Deputy Art Direction),
  Enite Hoffmann,
  Manuel Kostrzynski
Illustration
  Frank Höhne
Image Editing
  Jakob Feigl (Director of
  Photography),
  Kristin Ahlring,
  Amélie Schneider
Printing
  Mohn Media GmbH, Gütersloh
Publishing House
  Gruner + Jahr

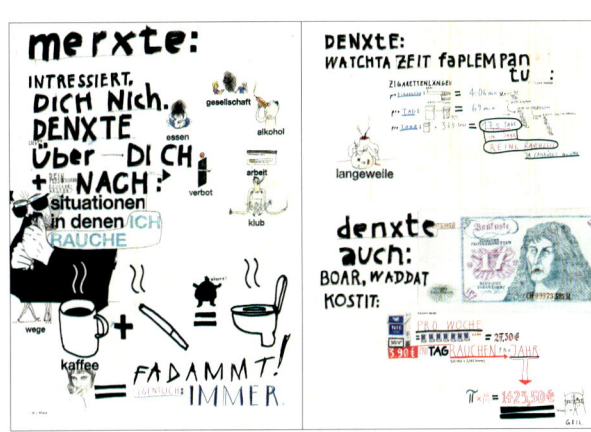

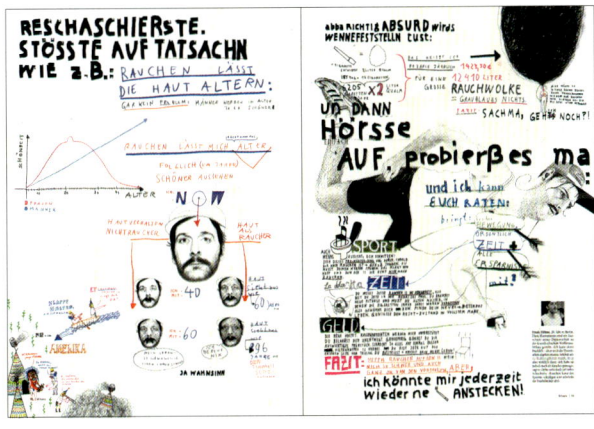

BRONZE
EDITORIAL
EDITORIAL
 Editorial
 Print/Einzelleistung
 Editorial
 Print/Individual Work

STERN MAGAZIN
»Das Beben…«

Lead Agency
 stern Magazin
Client
 Gruner + Jahr AG & Co. KG
Art Direction
 Donald Schneider,
 Mark Ernsting (Deputy)
Design
 Susanne Gräfe
Image Editing
 Harald Menk
Photography
 Various
Publishing House
 Gruner + Jahr AG & Co. KG

BRONZE
EDITORIAL
EDITORIAL
   Editorial
   Print/Einzelleistung
   Editorial
   Print/Individual Work

SÜDDEUTSCHE ZEITUNG
MAGAZIN
   »Nur ankommen ist schöner«

Lead Agency
   Süddeutsche Zeitung Magazin
Client
   Süddeutsche Zeitung Magazin
Art Direction
   Daniel Bognár
Chief Editing
   Dr. Dominik Wichmann
Copy
   Max Fellmann
Illustration
   Christoph Niemann
Image Editing
   Eva Fischer,
   Ralf Zimmermann
Image Processing
   Esther Matusche
Publishing House
   Magazin Verlagsgesellschaft
   Süddeutsche Zeitung mbH

Nur ankommen ist schöner Von wegen grenzenlose Freiheit. Dass der Himmel auch zur Hölle werden kann, weiß keiner so gut wie unser Illustrator Christoph Niemann – er fliegt regelmäßig von New York nach Berlin. Ein Reisebericht

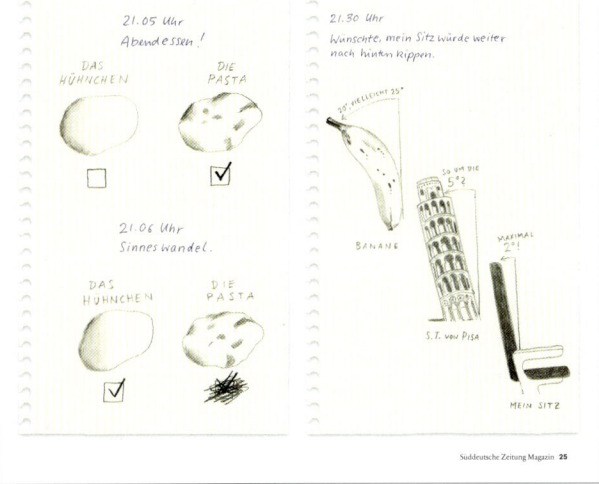

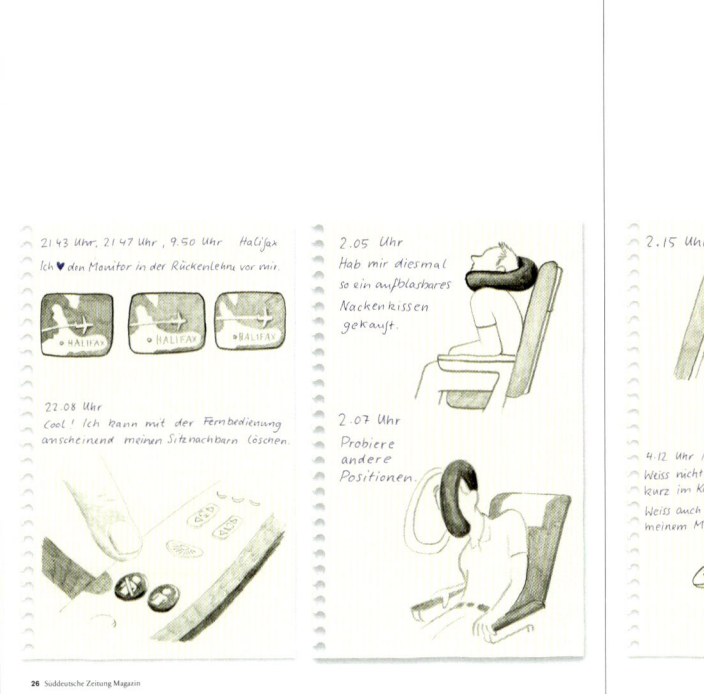

BRONZE
EDITORIAL
EDITORIAL
    Editorial
    Print/Einzelleistung
    Editorial
    Print/Individual Work

SÜDDEUTSCHE ZEITUNG
MAGAZIN
»Schloss mit lustig«

Lead Agency
    Süddeutsche Zeitung Magazin
Client
    Süddeutsche Zeitung Magazin
Art Direction
    Daniel Bognár
Chief Editing
    Dr. Dominik Wichmann
Copy
    Marc Baumann
Graphic Design
    Anne Blaschke,
    Thomas Kartsolis,
    Birthe Steinbeck,
    Dirk Schmidt
Image Editing
    Eva Fischer,
    Ralf Zimmermann
Image Processing
    Esther Matusche
Photography
    Christopher Thomas
Publishing House
    Magazin Verlagsgesellschaft
    Süddeutsche Zeitung mbH

Schloss mit lustig Punk? Hip-Hop? Indie? Von wegen – neuerdings wollen deutsche Jugendliche am liebsten aussehen wie der Bundesverteidigungsminister (und seine Frau)

Fotos: Christopher Thomas

BRONZE
EDITORIAL
EDITORIAL
  Editorial
  Print/Einzelleistung
  Editorial
  Print/Individual Work

SÜDDEUTSCHE ZEITUNG MAGAZIN
  »Sieben auf einem Strich«

Lead Agency
  Süddeutsche Zeitung Magazin
Client
  Süddeutsche Zeitung Magazin
Art Direction
  Daniel Bognár
Chief Editing
  Dr. Dominik Wichmann
Graphic Design
  Anne Blaschke,
  Thomas Kartsolis,
  Birthe Steinbeck,
  Dirk Schmidt
Image Editing
  Eva Fischer,
  Ralf Zimmermann
Image Processing
  Esther Matusche
Photography
  Magnus Muhr
Publishing House
  Magazin Verlagsgesellschaft
  Süddeutsche Zeitung mbH

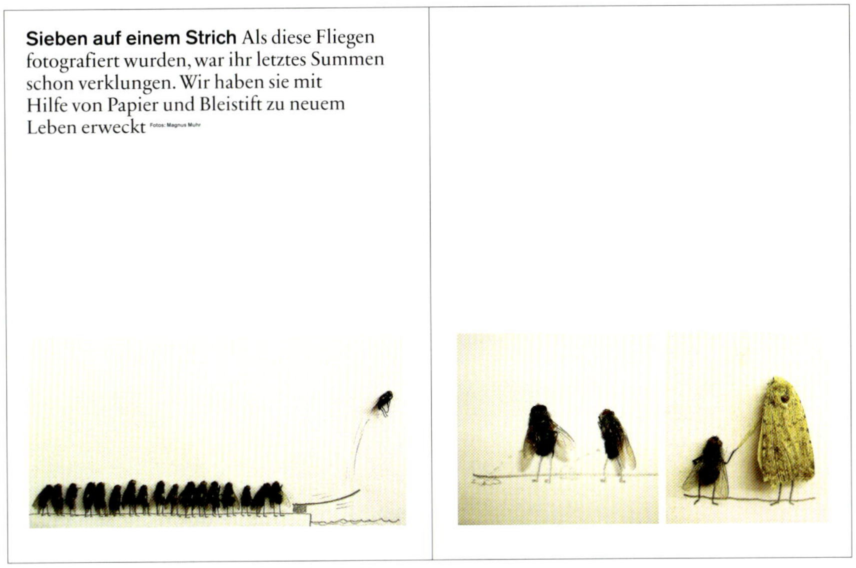

267

BRONZE
EDITORIAL
EDITORIAL
Editorial
Print/Einzelleistung
Editorial
Print/Individual Work

—
ZEITMAGAZIN
»Leanne Shapton/Was von der Liebe übrig bleibt«

Lead Agency
  ZEITmagazin
Client
  DIE ZEIT
Creative Direction
  Mirko Borsche
Art Direction
  Katja Kollmann
Chief Editing
  Christoph Amend
Graphic Design
  Nina Bengtson,
  Jasmin Müller-Stoy
Image Editing
  Michael Biedowicz,
  Andreas Wellnitz
Image Processing
  Twentyfour Seven Creative
  Media Services GmbH
Photography
  Leanne Shapton and
  Michael Schmelling,
  Jason Fulford
Publishing House
  Zeitverlag Gerd Bucerius
  GmbH & Co. KG

268

BRONZE
EDITORIAL
EDITORIAL

Editorial
Multimedia/Gesamtkonzept
Editorial
Multimedia/Integrated
Concept

WELTGRUPPE
»Gesamtauftritt«

Lead Agency
  WELT-Gruppe
Client
  WELT-Gruppe
Chief Editing
  Jan-Eric Peters
Publishing House
  Axel Springer AG

BRONZE
RÄUMLICHE INSZENIERUNG
SPATIAL SCENE-SETTING
Kommunikation im Raum
Environmental Design

EXPO PAVILLON 2010
"Urban Planet"

Lead Agency
  Triad Berlin
  Projektgesellschaft mbH
Client
  Bureau of Shanghai World Expo
  Coordination

Als Besuchermagnet der ersten Stunde war der Urban Planet mit 8 Mio. Besuchern einer der erfolgreichsten Pavillons der Expo Shanghai 2010. Eindrucksvoll vermittelte er die komplexen Prozesse der weltweiten Urbanisierung. Jeder neunte Expo-Besucher begab sich auf die visuelle und akustische Reise und erlebte das Höllenszenario, das die Welt erwartet, wenn nicht bald konkrete Lösungen umgesetzt werden.

A magnet for visitors from the very beginning, the theme pavilion Urban Planet became one of the most successful pavilions of Expo Shanghai 2010, attracting more than 8 million visitors. One in nine Expo visitors embarked on a visual and acoustic journey through the exhibition and experienced the scenario of hell that is upon the world if concrete and future-oriented solutions are not adopted soon.

BRONZE
RÄUMLICHE INSZENIERUNG
SPATIAL SCENE-SETTING
Kommunikation im Raum Craft
Medienbespielung &
-integration
Environmental Design Craft
Media Design and Integration

E. BREUNINGER
»Weiße Weihnachten 2010«

Lead Agency
 Tim John –
 Atelier für Szenografie
Client
 E. Breuninger GmbH & Co.
Marketing Direction
 Carsten Hendrich
Advertising Direction
 Marion Strecker
Executive Creative Direction
 Tim John
Creative Direction
 Tim John
Art Direction
 Tim John
Client Consulting
 Tim John
Strategic Planning
 Tim John
Media Design and Integration
 Markus de Seriis,
 Tim John

Für das Kaufhaus Breuninger in Stuttgart entwickelten wir Weihnachten 2010 einen Gesamtauftritt, der von der Fassade über Schaufenster bis hin zu Einkaufstaschen ging. Höhepunkt waren zwei mechanisch interaktiv-bewegte Schaufenster sowie ein lebensgroßer, mechanischer Knabenchor auf dem Vordach, der am Abend zu jeder vollen Stunde auffuhr und, vom Weihnachtsmann dirigiert, ein Weihnachtslied sang.

On behalf of the Stuttgart-based department store Breuninger, we developed a holistic scenographic performance on the occasion of Christmas 2010. The room-spanning concept involved the store's facade and shop windows, delivering a unique visual design, which was applied to seasonal shopping bags. Two mechanical and interactively steerable shop windows marked one of the installations' highlights.

**BRONZE
RÄUMLICHE INSZENIERUNG
SPATIAL SCENE-SETTING**
　Events
　Events

RUHR.2010 GMBH
»Still-Leben Ruhrschnellweg«

Lead Agency
　TAS Emotional Marketing
　GmbH
Client
　RUHR.2010 GmbH,
　Dr. h.c. Fritz Pleitgen,
　Prof. Dr. Oliver Scheytt
Marketing Direction
　Jürgen Fischer,
　Ralph Kindel
Executive Creative Direction
　Thomas Siepmann
Client Consulting
　Sonja Peger,
　Gundula Beck
Strategic Planning
　Sonja Peger,
　Gundula Beck
Technical Direction
　Mike Brockmann
Other
　Peter Mohnhaupt,
　Meike Nykamp (Sponsoring),
　Stefan Lohrberg,
　Yvonne Lünzmann
　(PR & Internet)

Ein solches Event gab es noch nie: ein Fest der Alltagskulturen auf einer Autobahn. Schauplatz war die A40, sie führt durch eine Region mit 53 Städten und 5,3 Millionen Menschen. Gesperrt für einen Tag machten 3 Millionen Menschen diesen Event zum Leuchtturmprojekt des Kulturhauptstadtjahres 2010. Ein Projekt der Superlative, veranstaltet mit zahlreichen Organisationen, Städten und etwa 12.000 Helfern.

This was a one-of-a-kind event: a festival of everyday culture on a highway – the A40, which runs through a region with 53 cities and 5.3 million residents. On the day of the event, it was closed to traffic, with three million visitors helping to make this event into a flagship project for the European Capital of Culture 2010. A project of superlatives hosted by numerous organizations, cities and some 12,000 helpers.

BRONZE
RÄUMLICHE INSZENIERUNG
SPATIAL SCENE-SETTING
Events
Events

SCHAUSPIEL FRANKFURT
»Licht am Ende des Tunnels –
Beitrag zur Luminale 2010«

Lead Agency
   Atelier Markgraph
   (Concept, Design, Realisation)
Contributing Agencies
   In Cooperation with MESO
   Digital Interiors,
   Ströer Deutsche Städte Medien
   and HELI-Showequipment
Client
   A Co-operation of Schauspiel
   Frankfurt,
   Verkehrsgesellschaft Frankfurt
   (VGF) and Atelier Markgraph
Other
   Martin Professional
   (Sponsor Light and Media
   Systems)

Zur Luminale verwandelt sich die U-Bahn-Station Willy-Brandt-Platz in eine unterirdische Bühne für ein interaktives Text-Schauspiel. Passanten können durch ihre Bewegungen Zitate aus Stücken des Schauspiels Frankfurt abrufen. Betritt ein Akteur eines der »Rollenfelder« auf dem Boden, aktiviert er Licht, LED und Ton. Über die Bespielung der LEDs kann er mit anderen Akteuren in Dialog treten.

At Luminale, the Willy-Brandt-Platz underground station becomes a stage for an interactive text-based play with passers-by as actors. They can activate quotes taken from the plays in Schauspiel Frankfurt's current program. By stepping on one of the "role fields" on the floor, they can trigger lighting, LEDs and sound. Via the LEDs, it's possible to enter into dialog with their fellow participants.

BRONZE
RÄUMLICHE INSZENIERUNG
SPATIAL SCENE-SETTING
Events
Events

SWISSCOM URBAN HACKING
»Wir für die Schweiz«

Lead Agency
   VOK DAMS Agentur für Events und Live-Marketing
Contributing Agencies
   Adcom Group
Client
   Swisscom AG
Marketing Direction
   Roland Trabadelo,
   Head of Sales Communication Private Customers
Executive Creative Direction
   Birgit Kriesche
Creative Direction
   David Korte
Art Direction
   Matthias Koller
Camera
   Philipp Zumbrun
Cutting
   Condor Films
Film Direction
   Thomas Sabel
Film Production
   Condor Films
Speaker
   David Brockelmanns

Ziel war es, die Swisscom zur Love Brand zu machen. Im Rahmen der Olympischen Winterspiele in Vancouver ließ Vok Dams eine Gruppe junger Menschen den Züricher Hauptbahnhof einnehmen. Sie bejubelten Passanten und feierten diese mit Schweizer Fahnen. Die komplette Aktion zahlte auf das Überthema "Swissness" ein und wurde via Youtube sowie Online-Fanbuch kommuniziert.

The event aimed at turning Swisscom into a "love brand". During the Olympic Games in Vancouver, Vok Dams had young people occupy Zurich's central station to cheer on random passers-by and wave Swiss flags. The entire action contributed to the motto of "Swissness" and was communicated via Youtube and a fan book created specially for this project.

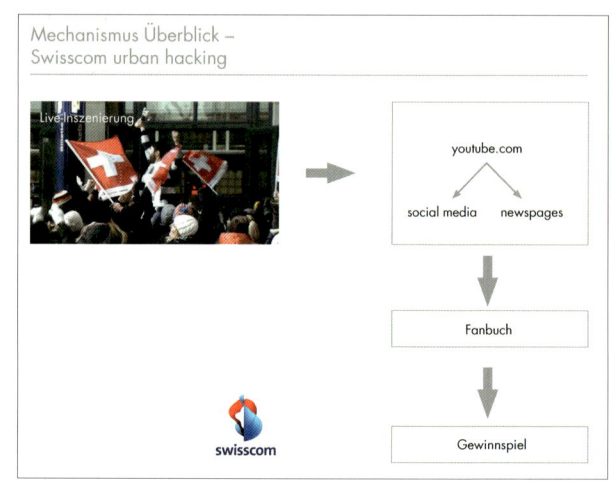

274

**BRONZE
RÄUMLICHE INSZENIERUNG
SPATIAL SCENE-SETTING**
  Events Craft
  Setdesign/Architektur
  Events Craft
  Set Design/Architecture

SMART
  "urban stage"

Lead Agency
  BRAUNWAGNER, K-MB
Contributing Agencies
  mu:d
Client
  Daimler AG
Marketing Direction
  Nicole Israng
Executive Creative Direction
  Manfred Wagner,
  Marina Franke
Creative Direction
  Manfred Wagner
Set Design/Architecture
  Braunwagner

"smart urban stage" ist eine temporäre Kommunikationsplattform für die Themen Elektromobilität und Nachhaltigkeit. Intelligente Hightech-Materialien, neueste Medientechnik und individuelle Gestaltungsoptionen verkörpern das Energie- und Trendbewusstsein der Marke Smart. Das modulare Leichtbaukonzept lässt sich schnell und flexibel in Freiräume europäischer Metropolen einfügen und rückstandslos abbauen.

"smart urban stage" is a temporary communication platform for the topics electric mobility and sustainability. Intelligent high-tech materials, the latest media technology and individual configuration options represent the energy and trend consciousness of the brand Smart. The modular light weight construction can be easily fit into empty spaces of European metropolises and removed free of residues.

275

BRONZE
CRAFT
CRAFT
Text
Copy

DKV REISEKRANKEN-
VERSICHERUNG
»Reiseartikel aus Absurdistan«

Lead Agency
　Ogilvy Frankfurt
Client
　DKV Deutsche Kranken-
　versicherung
Marketing Direction
　Wolfgang Kroul
Advertising Direction
　Peter Baumann
Executive Creative Direction
　Dr. Stephan Vogel
Creative Direction
　Peter Römmelt,
　Simon Oppmann,
　Matthias Storath
Art Direction
　Daniel Schweinzer
Client Consulting
　Carola Romanus,
　Daniela Lösch
Copy
　Lukas Liske

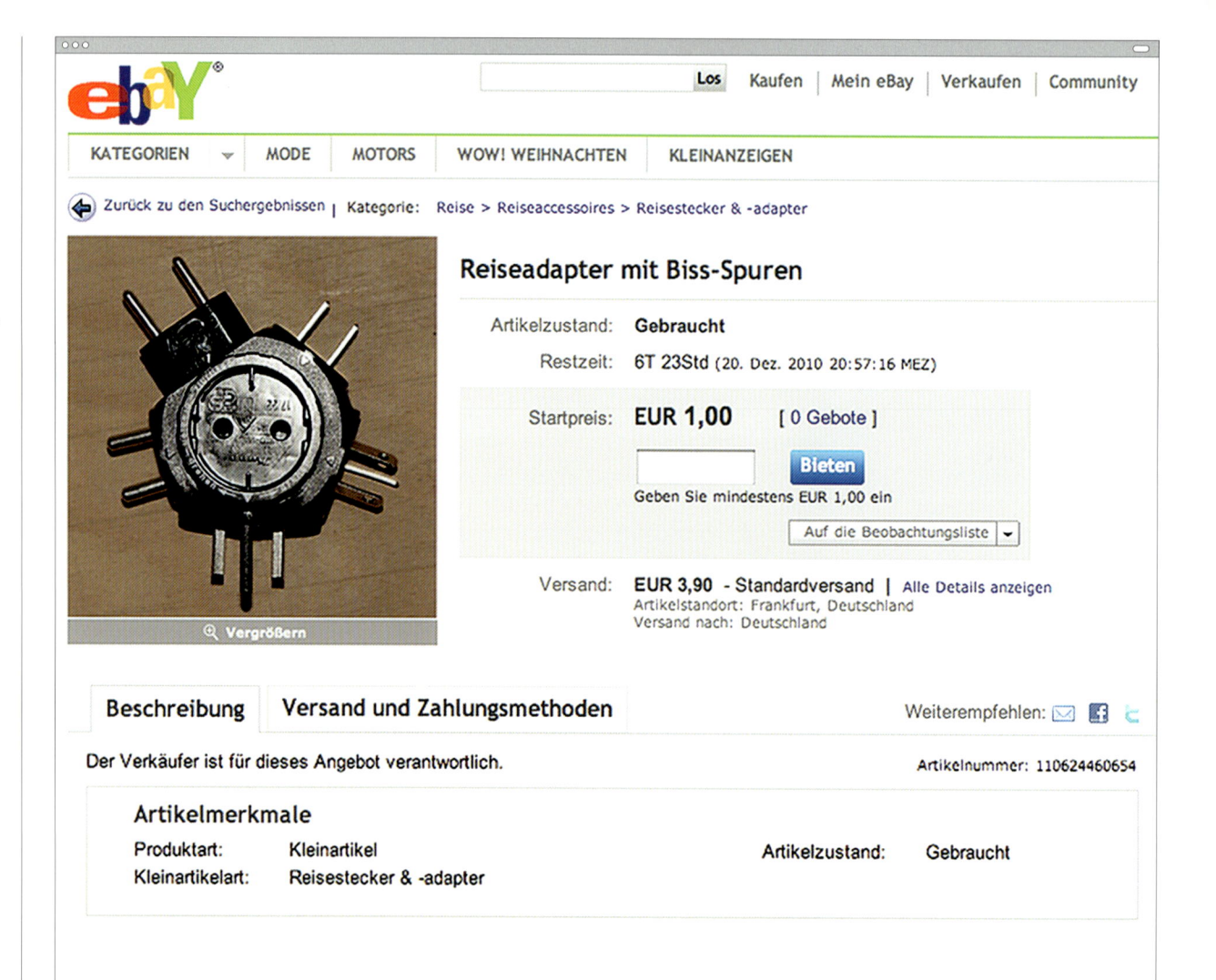

BRONZE
CRAFT
CRAFT
    Typografie
    Typography

LOEWE KAMPAGNE
"Individual 3 D"

Lead Agency
    Scholz & Friends
Client
    Loewe Opta GmbH
Marketing Direction
    Henrik Rutenbeck
Advertising Direction
    Thorsten Bald
Executive Creative Direction
    Martin Pross,
    Matthias Spaetgens,
    Wolf Schneider
Creative Direction
    Matthias Spaetgens,
    Wolf Schneider
Art Direction
    Gito Lima,
    Juergen Krugsperger
Client Consulting
    Stefanie Wurst,
    Joris Jonker
Copy
    Gito Lima
Typography
    Gito Lima

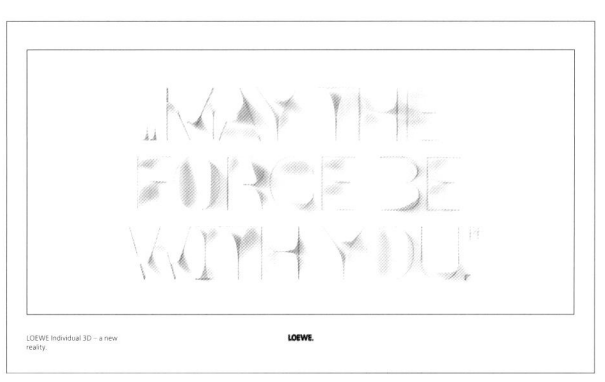

BRONZE
CRAFT
CRAFT
Fotografie
Photography

AERNOUT OVERBEEKE SERIE
"Ndoto, Lengai – Mountain Of God"

Lead Agency
 Jung von Matt AG
Client
 Aernout Overbeeke
Executive Creative Direction
 Armin Jochum
Creative Direction
 Armin Jochum
Art Direction
 Tilman Gossner
Client Consulting
 Eike Voss
Copy
 Torben Otten,
 Georg Baur
Image Processing
 Aernout Overbeeke
Photography
 Aernout Overbeeke

BRONZE
CRAFT
CRAFT
Fotografie
Photography

EIGENWERBUNG SERIE
"Lightsounds"

Lead Agency
  Uwe Düttmann
Client
  Uwe Düttmann
Photography
  Uwe Düttmann

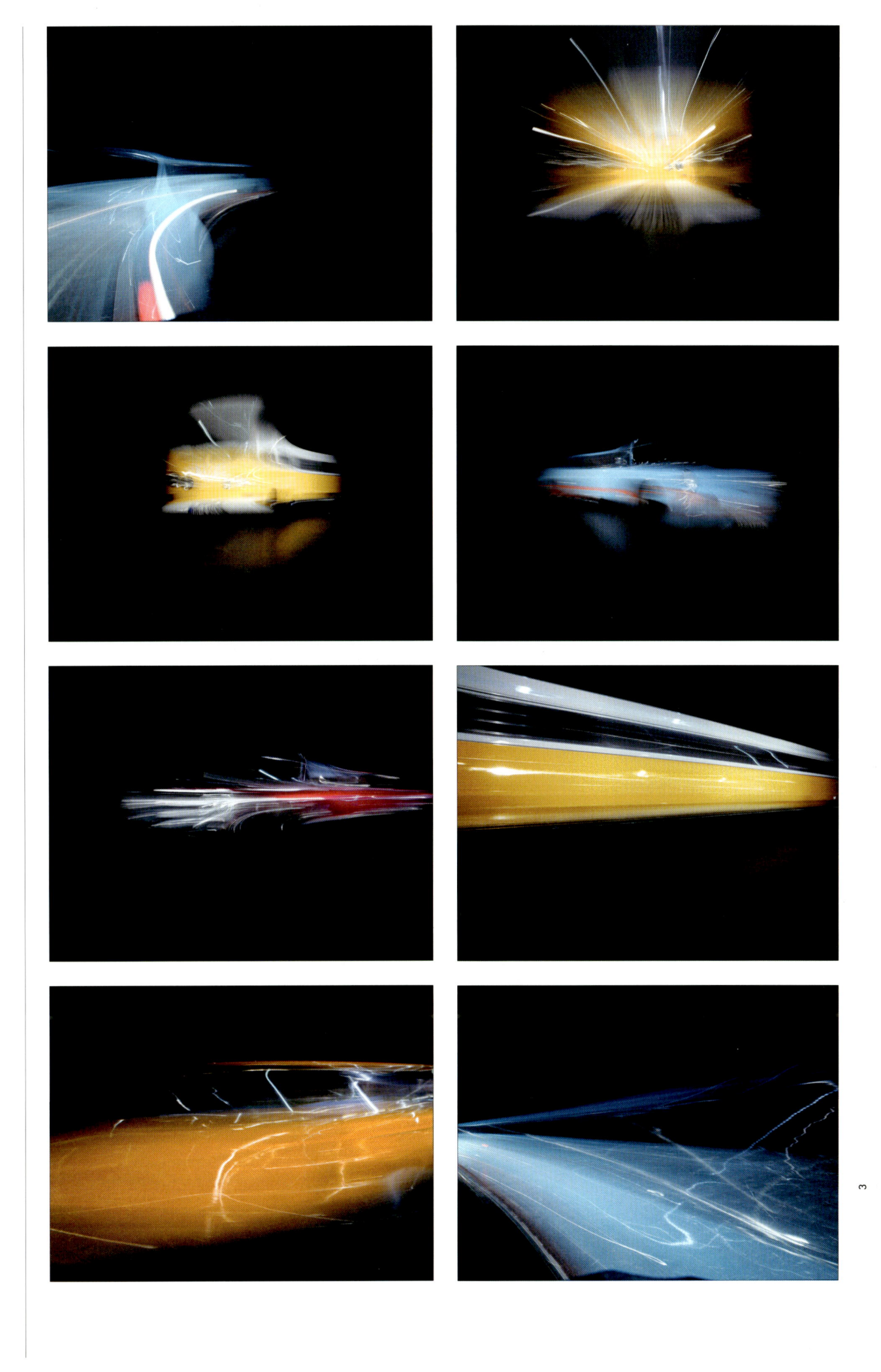

**BRONZE
CRAFT
CRAFT**
Fotografie
Photography

EIGENWERBUNG SERIE
»Torso«

Lead Agency
   Alex Rank Photography
Client
   Alex Rank Photography
Photography
   Alex Rank Photography

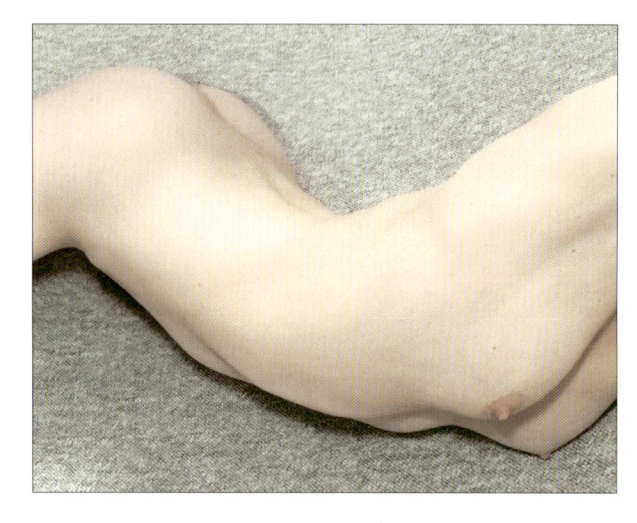

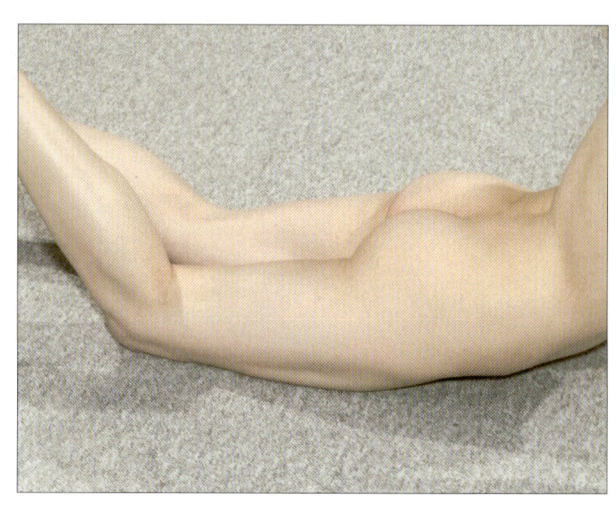

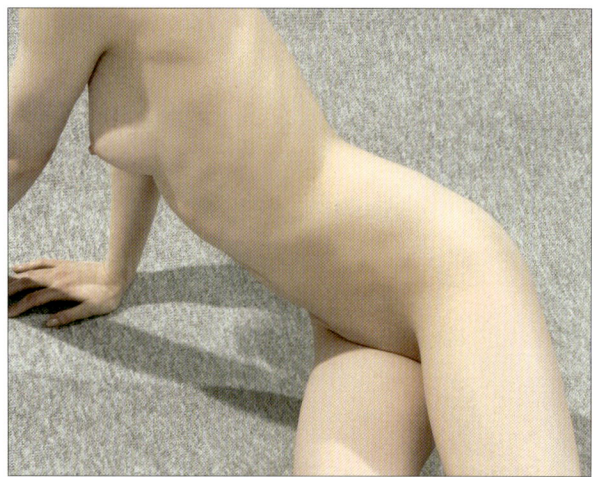

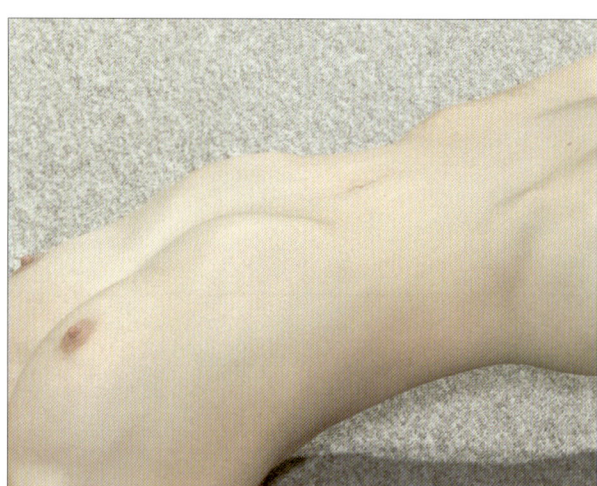

BRONZE
CRAFT
CRAFT
Fotografie
Photography

MERCEDES-BENZ SERIE
»Gesichter der Marke«

Lead Agency
 Jung von Matt AG
Client
 Daimler AG
Marketing Direction
 Anders-Sundt Jensen,
 Lüder Fromm
Advertising Direction
 Damir Maric,
 Lena Ernst
Executive Creative Direction
 Armin Jochum
Creative Direction
 Thimoteus Wagner
Art Direction
 Andreas Wagner
Client Consulting
 Sven Dörrenbächer,
 Sonja Stockmann,
 Yves Rosengart,
 Nicole Drabsch
Copy
 Luca Rescheleit
Image Processing
 Frank Kirchhoff,
 Micha Kühn
Photography
 Kai-Uwe Gundlach

281

● BRONZE
CRAFT
CRAFT
 Illustration
 Illustration

MOTOCROSS ENDURO
MAGAZIN SERIE
 "Enduro Untamed"

Lead Agency
 Serviceplan
Client
 Ziegler Verlags GmbH
Marketing Direction
 Ralf Ziegler
Executive Creative Direction
 Matthias Harbeck,
 Alex Schill
Creative Direction
 Oliver Palmer
Art Direction
 Therese Stüssel,
 Frank Gräfe
Client Consulting
 Amelie Wenzel
Copy
 Martin Magnet,
 Sebastian Wolf
Illustration
 Eat. Sleep + Design.
 Frank Gräfe. Berlin.

282

2

PUNKTE
POINTS

● **NOMINATION
KLASSISCHE MEDIEN
CLASSICAL MEDIA**
   Print
   Einzelmotiv
   Print
   Single Motif

● **NOMINATION
KLASSISCHE MEDIEN
CLASSICAL MEDIA**
   Out-of-Home
   Klassisch Einzelmotiv
   Out-of-Home
   Classic Single Motif

VW POLO
   »Die Recycling-Anzeige«

Lead Agency
   DDB Tribal Group
Client
   Volkswagen AG
Marketing Direction
   Luca de Meo
Advertising Direction
   Hartmut Seeger,
   Veronika Ziegaus
Executive Creative Direction
   Stefan Schulte
Creative Direction
   Birgit van den Valentyn,
   Tim Stuebane
Art Direction
   David Stadtmüller
Client Consulting
   Marie-Louise Jakob
Art Buying
   Kerstin Kraus,
   Susanne Kreft
Copy
   Manuel Wenzel
Graphic Design
   Philipp Bertisch,
   Ron Zander

● **NOMINATION
KLASSISCHE MEDIEN
CLASSICAL MEDIA**
   Print
   Einzelmotiv
   Print
   Single Motif

● **NOMINATION
KLASSISCHE MEDIEN
CLASSICAL MEDIA**
   Out-of-Home
   Klassisch Einzelmotiv
   Out-of-Home
   Classic Single Motif

VW POLO BLUEMOTION
»Meer«

Lead Agency
   Grabarz & Partner
Client
   Volkswagen AG
Marketing Direction
   Luca de Meo,
   Director Marketing
   Communication:
   Martina Berg
Advertising Direction
   Achim Glogowski
Executive Creative Direction
   Ralf Heuel
Creative Direction
   Timm Weber,
   Christoph Stricker,
   Christoph Breitbach
Art Direction
   Jasmin Remmers
Client Consulting
   Reinhard Patzschke,
   Katja Fredriksen,
   Anna Christiane Roth
Art Buying
   Indra Hohns
Copy
   Leander Schmalfuß
Graphic Design
   Barbara Dirscherl
Photography
   Tom Mennemann
   c/o Christa Klubert

●
NOMINATION
KLASSISCHE MEDIEN
CLASSICAL MEDIA
  Print
  Kampagne
  Print
  Campaign

●
NOMINATION
CRAFT
CRAFT
  Illustration
  Illustration

DER SPIEGEL
  »Perspektiven«

Lead Agency
  Jung von Matt AG
Client
  SPIEGEL-Verlag Rudolf
  Augstein GmbH & Co. KG
Advertising Direction
  Ms. zum Hingst
Executive Creative Direction
  Doerte Spengler-Ahrens,
  Jan Rexhausen
Creative Direction
  Doerte Spengler-Ahrens,
  Jan Rexhausen
Art Direction
  Gustavo Nardini
Client Consulting
  Rabea Huthmann,
  Jose Luis Carretero Lopez,
  Natalie Martens
Art Buying
  Susanne Nagel
Consulting
  Rabea Huthmann,
  Jose Luis Carretero Lopez,
  Natalie Martens
Copy
  Fabio Straccia
Illustration
  Noma Bar

● **NOMINATION
KLASSISCHE MEDIEN
CLASSICAL MEDIA**
   Out-of-Home
   Klassisch Einzelmotiv
   Out-of-Home
   Classic Single Motif

● **NOMINATION
KLASSISCHE MEDIEN
CLASSICAL MEDIA**
   Out-of-Home
   Nicht-Klassisch
   Out-of-Home
   Non-Classic

MAD MAGAZIN
  »Glühbirne«

Lead Agency
  Serviceplan
Client
  Panini Verlags GmbH
Executive Creative Direction
  Alex Schill,
  Henning Patzner
Creative Direction
  Ekki Frenkler
Art Direction
  Jan Kromka,
  Stefanie Paulus
Client Consulting
  Dorle Mietzner,
  Annmarie Möller,
  Chris Kunzendorf
Copy
  Valerie Koch
Graphic Design
  Andreas Kienle
Photography
  Alan Grund
Production
  Colin Patterson

● **NOMINATION
KLASSISCHE MEDIEN
CLASSICAL MEDIA**
  Out-of-Home
  Klassisch Kampagne
  Out-of-Home
  Classic Campaign

● **NOMINATION
CRAFT
CRAFT**
  Illustration
  Illustration

MCDONALD'S KAMPAGNE
»Morgenkaffee«

Lead Agency
  DDB Tribal Group
Client
  McDonald's
Marketing Direction
  Andreas Schmidlechner
Executive Creative Direction
  Eric Schoeffler
Creative Direction
  Hannes Böker,
  Werner Celand,
  Sebastian Kainz
Art Direction
  Dian Warsosumarto
Client Consulting
  Philipp Krumpel
Agency Production
  Beate Hinterreither
Copy
  Lukas Grossebner
Illustration
  Karen Caldicott
Image Processing
  Kai Weyer,
  Gabriel Haberl,
  Beate Hinterreither
Photography
  David Hamsley

●
**NOMINATION
KLASSISCHE MEDIEN
CLASSICAL MEDIA**
Out-of-Home
Nicht-Klassisch
Out-of-Home
Non-Classic

●
**NOMINATION
GANZHEITLICHE KOMMUNI-
KATION
INTEGRATED CAMPAIGNS**
Ganzheitliche Kommunikation
Integrated Campaigns

ABSOLUT VODKA
"Made"

Lead Agency
   TBWA Berlin, CHE*CHE
Client
   Pernod Ricard Deutschland GmbH
Marketing Direction
   Alain Dufossé,
   Bernhard Eisheuer
Advertising Direction
   Katja Borsetzky,
   Christina Elste,
   Catherina Zeman
Executive Creative Direction
   Nico Zeh, Tatjana Stein, Kurt Georg Dieckert, Stefan Schmidt
Creative Direction
   Dirk Henkelmann,
   Philip Borchardt
Art Direction
   Philip Borchardt,
   Philipp Migeod
Client Consulting
   Richard Breaux, David Barton, Alexis Mardon, Philip Gaedicke
Strategic Planning
   Christina Keller, Sonia Lago
Architecture
   M AD Ltd. – Alexis Dornier
Art Buying
   Katrin Hermuth
Artist
   Hermann August Weizenegger, Miki, Ebon Heath, Max Herre, Tita von Hardenberg, Talib Kweli
Audio Production
   Miki, Valerie Goodman, Crada
Camera
   Matthias Maercks, Niki Drakos
Casting
   Luise Biesalski
Concept
   Dirk Henkelmann,
   Philip Borchardt, Nico Zeh,
   Tatjana Stein
Consulting
   Luise Biesalski, Philip Gaedicke, Alexis Dornier
Copy
   Dirk Henkelmann,
   Felicitas Olschewski,
   Philip Löffel
Design
   Veit Möller,
   Andrew Morgan,
   Ricardo Müller,
   Chehad Abdallah,
   Benedikt Gansczyk,
   Thomas Kohl
Film Production
   Matthias Maercks,
   Niki Drakos,
   Johannes von Liebenstein
Idea
   Tatjana Stein, Nico Zeh, Dirk Henkelmann, Philip Borchardt
Innovative Technologies
   Wolf Deiss, Artis
Interface Navigation
   Artis
IT Direction
   Erik Scholz
Lighting Design
   M AD Ltd. – Alexis Dornier
Media
   Lioneye
Music Composition
   Miki, Valerie Goodman, Crada
Music Selection
   Nico Zeh
Photography
   Niels Krüger, Robert Wunsch, Ricardo Müller
Production
   Luise Biesalski, Philip Gaedicke, Katrin Dettmann
Technical Conception
   Alexis Dornier
Technical Direction
   Alexis Dornier
Technical Implementation
   Alexis Dornier
Technical Installation
   Alexis Dornier
Other
   tadi–Rock – CHE*CHE (Curator)

"Made" ist eine Institution, die von Absolut Vodka für Kunstinteressierte geschaffen wurde, um kreative Zusammenarbeit zu fördern. Dafür kommen regelmäßig unterschiedliche kreative Visionäre zusammen, um Neues zu erschaffen (A + B = ?). Kommuniziert wurden die "Made"-Projekte durch Poster, Trailer, Kunstinstallationen, einen Blog und über die teilnehmenden Künstler, die für einen internationalen Ruf sorgten.

"Made", an institution founded by Absolut Vodka, is dedicated to all art-savoury people. It fosters creative collaborations by bringing different creative minds together to create new and unseen things (A + B = ?). "Made" and its projects were communicated through posters, trailers, art installations and a blog, as well as the participating artists who quickly gave "Made" an international reputation.

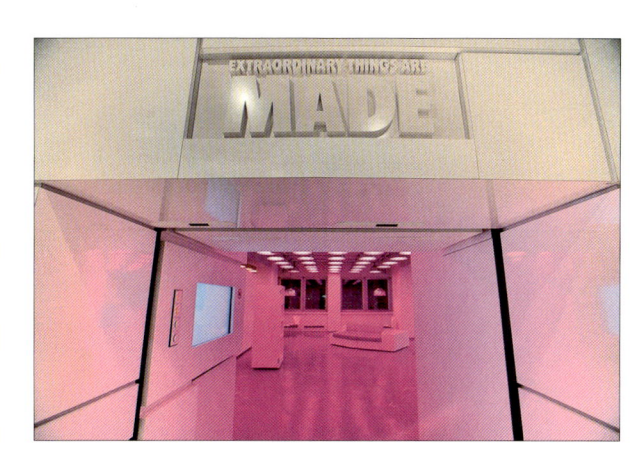

● **NOMINATION**
KLASSISCHE MEDIEN
CLASSICAL MEDIA
  Film
    TV/Kino Einzelspot
  Film
    TV/Cinema Commercial

● **NOMINATION**
CRAFT
CRAFT
  Musik und Sound
  Music and Sound

MERCEDES-BENZ ALLRAD
»Sonntagsfahrer«

Lead Agency
  Jung von Matt AG
Client
  Daimler AG
Marketing Direction
  Anders-Sundt Jensen,
  Lüder Fromm
Advertising Direction
  Damir Maric, Jochen Schmidt
Creative Direction
  Michael Ohanian, Jacques Pense
Art Direction
  Andreas Jeutter
Client Consulting
  Sven Dörrenbacher,
  Yves Rosengart, Julia Körte,
  Nina Jahns
Strategic Planning
  Daniel Adolph
Agency Production
  Meike van Meegen,
  Thomas Nabbelfeld
Animation/Visual Effects/
Special Effects
  nhb Hamburg
Audio Production
  nhb Hamburg
Camera
  Brendan Galvin
Copy
  Norman Scholl
Cutting
  Alexander Jurkat
Film Direction
  Tarsem
Film Production
  radical Berlin
Graphic Design
  Benjamin Beck,
  Alexander Wagner
Idea
  Michael Ohanian,
  Norman Scholl
Music Selection
  Jung von Matt AG,
  nhb Hamburg
Postproduction
  The Mill
Production
  Christiane Dressler
Sound Design
  nhb Hamburg

Passend zur kalten Jahreszeit sollte mit einem aufmerksamkeitsstarken TV-Spot die Überlegenheit des permanenten Allradantriebs von Mercedes-Benz inszeniert werden. Zielgruppe war die breite Öffentlichkeit mit dem Fokus auf Autointeressierten.

To accompany the cold season, a high-profile TV commercial designed to illustrate the superiority of Mercedes-Benz's permanent all-wheel drive. The target group was the general public, with a focus on people with an interest in cars.

● **NOMINATION**
KLASSISCHE MEDIEN
CLASSICAL MEDIA
　Film
　Internetfilme
　Film
　Internet Films

● **NOMINATION**
DIGITALE MEDIEN
DIGITAL MEDIA
　Digitale Medien
　Digitale Kampagnen
　Digital Media
　Digital Campaigns

VW POLO GTI
"Fast Lane – Driven By Fun"

Lead Agency
　DDB Tribal Group
Client
　Volkswagen AG
Executive Creative Direction
　Hartmut Kozok,
　Andreas Dalquist
Creative Direction
　Thomas Bober
Art Direction
　Philip Simon
Client Consulting
　Andreas Kiesel,
　Claus Jacobsen,
　Katrin Steineke,
　Simone Stammen
Strategic Planning
　Kathrin Stieler,
　Patrick Wassel,
　Finn Reddig,
　Thorsten Kremser
Art Buying
　Boris Schepker
Audio Production
　Rainer Schaller/Escape Route,
　Duesseldorf, M-Sound, Munich
Camera
　Jenny Bräuer
Copy
　Jan Hertel, Judith Krüger,
　Simon Marschall,
　Regina Pichler
Cutting
　Henrik Raufmann,
　Thomas Hanser
Film Direction
　Torben Liebrecht
Film Production
　Nerdfilms Berlin
Graphic Design
　Alexandra Spirat,
　Nuno Marcelino,
　Matthes Scheinhardt,
　Tonya Dinter
Other
　IT Direction: Marco Struck
　Flash: Markus Schwarze,
　André Wischnewski
　Programming: Martin Schmid,
　Hauke Schulz, Jan Engelhardt,
　Daniel Knobloch, Ralf Schwarze

Ob U-Bahn-Rutsche, Skateboard-Einkaufswagen oder Turbolift: Die "Fast Lane – Driven by Fun" zeigt in Alltagssituationen, was den Polo GTI ausmacht: Spaß und Geschwindigkeit. Die Reaktionen der Menschen wurden mit versteckten Kameras festgehalten und viral verbreitet. Die Filme wurden von den Usern 3.272.000 Mal angesehen; dazu kommen mehr als 725.000 Page Views und über 34.822 neue Facebook-Fans.

A slide to the underground trains, a shopping cart with an integrated skateboard or a turbolift: the "Fast Lane – Driven by Fun" emphasizes the characteristics of the Polo GTI in everyday situations. The people's reactions were filmed by hidden cameras und spreaded virally. The short clips were watched more than 3,272,000 times, accompanied by over 725,000 page views and 34,822 new facebook fans.

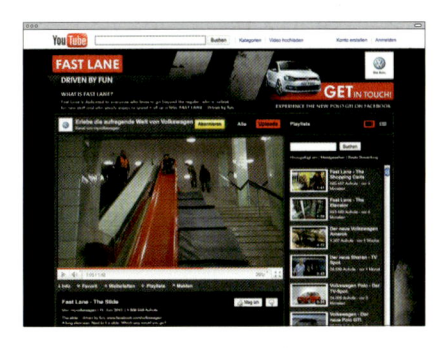

● NOMINATION
KLASSISCHE MEDIEN
CLASSICAL MEDIA
  Audio
    Innovative Nutzung von Audio
  Audio
    Innovative Use of Audio

● NOMINATION
CRAFT
CRAFT
  Text
  Copy

DIE SAHNESCHNITTE
»Ein paar Seiten Radio-
werbung für Radiowerbung«

Lead Agency
  Grabarz & Partner
Client
  Verlag Hermann Schmidt
  Mainz,
  ReinsClassen, Hamburg
Marketing Direction
  Karin Schmidt-Friderichs,
  Armin Reins,
  Veronika Classen
Executive Creative Direction
  Ralf Heuel
Creative Direction
  Ralf Heuel
Art Direction
  Fedja Kehl
Client Consulting
  Franziska Mattes,
  Denise Ewald
Art Buying
  Anna Simdon
Audio Production
  Studio Funk, Hamburg
Copy
  Ralf Heuel
Production
  Studio Funk, Hamburg
Other
  Sound Engineering/
  Co Direction:
  Torsten Hennings

AUDIO

SAHNESCHNITTE. AUFMERKSAMKEIT:

SFX: BEWERBUNGSGESPRÄCH, GEDÄMPFTES BÜRO, TICKEN EINER STANDUHR.
FRAU, RUHIG:

»So, Herr Schneider, schön, dass Sie sich für eine Anstellung in unserem Unternehmen interessieren. Das ist ja ein ganz vielversprechender Lebenslauf. Wie würden Sie denn Ihre Stärken beschreiben?«

SFX: MANN RÄUSPERT SICH UND FÄNGT IRRE LAUT AN ZU SCHREIEN.
MANN:

»ICH BIN HERBERT SCHNEIDER, SO FLEISSIG WIE SONST KEINER. ICH SCHUFTE MORGENS, ABENDS, NACHTS! ICH RACKER VOLLE PULLE, MITTAGS NUR 'NE STULLE, WENN SCHNEIDER KOMMT, DANN KRACHT'S!«

SFX: PAUSE, TICKEN DER STANDUHR.
FRAU, RUHIG:

»Nehmen Sie Ihren Lebenslauf mit, wenn Sie gehen? Danke.«

OFF:

»Tipp 5: Nicht der Lauteste kriegt Aufmerksamkeit und Sympathie, sondern der Interessanteste. Belohne die Menschen fürs Zuhören, indem Du ihnen etwas Spannendes erzählst. Nicht, indem Du sie anschreist.«

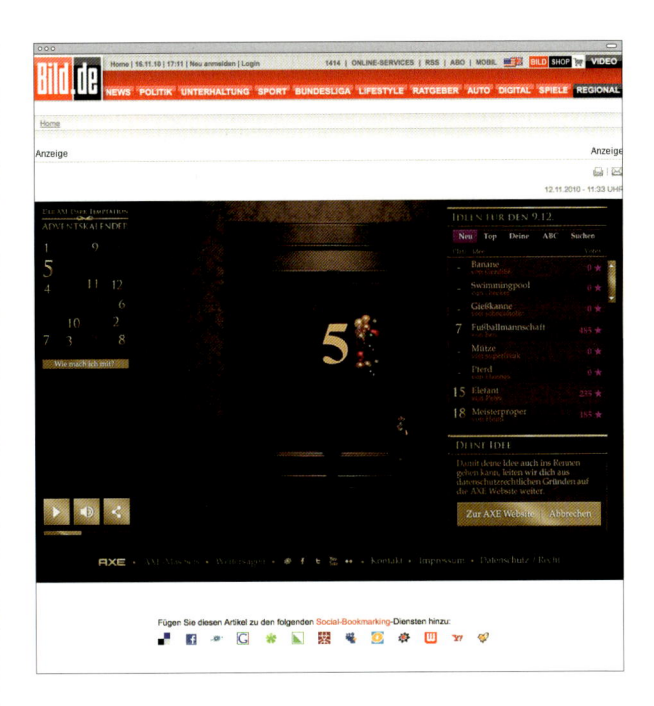

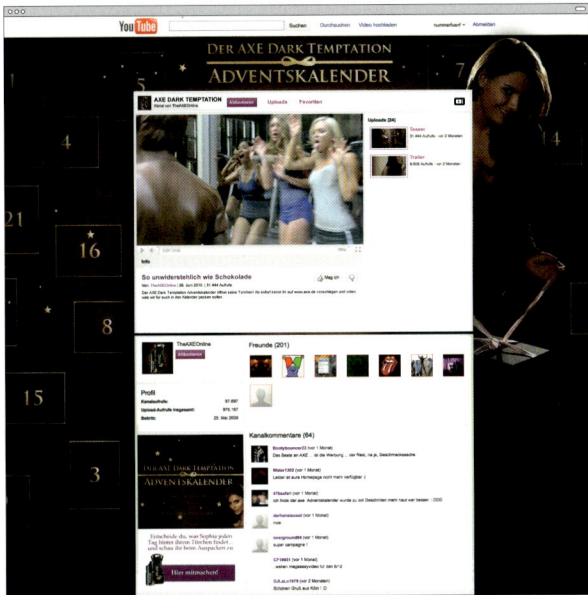

● **NOMINATION
DIGITALE MEDIEN
DIGITAL MEDIA**
　Digitale Medien
　Microsites
　Digital Media
　Microsites

● **NOMINATION
DESIGN
DESIGN**
　Design
　Kalender
　Design
　Calendars

**AXE DARK TEMPTATION,
UNILEVER DEUTSCHLAND**
　»Adventskalender, 24 mal
　so unwiderstehlich wie
　Schokolade«

Lead Agency
　DOKYO GmbH
Contributing Agencies
　La Red GmbH
Client
　Unilever Deutschland GmbH
Executive Creative Direction
　Frank Berning
Creative Direction
　Gerrit Asmus,
　Sönke Busch
Art Direction
　Sönke Busch
Client Consulting
　Christian Leihner
Agency Production
　Christine-Marie Gardeweg
Concept
　Tibor Glage,
　Jens Hellwig,
　Daniel Pieracci,
　Chris Knipping,
　Jochen Sendel,
　Henning Müller-Dannhausen,
　Jessica Hoppe,
　Arnd Lettmann,
　Rudolf Rüssmann,
　Tobias Wortmann
Consulting
　Sven Heckmann
Design
　Margit Schröder
Film Production
　Markenfilm Crossing
Graphic Design
　Torben Cording
Interactive Production
　Gregory Jacobs
IT Direction
　Till Kubelke,
　Jan van Randenborgh
Technical Implementation
　Kuborgh GmbH

295

● NOMINATION
DIGITALE MEDIEN
DIGITAL MEDIA
　Digitale Medien
　Online-Werbemaßnahmen
　Digital Media
　Online Advertising

● NOMINATION
DIALOGMARKETING/
PROMOTION/MEDIA
DIALOG MARKETING/
PROMOTION/MEDIA
　Promotion
　Aktivitäten
　Promotion
　Activities

BIC
"Prank"

Lead Agency
　Jung von Matt AG
Client
　BIC Deutschland GmbH & Co. KG
Marketing Direction
　Sophie Schneider
Advertising Direction
　Katja Görler
Executive Creative Direction
　Mathias Stiller,
　Wolfgang Schneider
Creative Direction
　Florian Kitzing,
　Arndt Poguntke,
　Michael Häußler
Art Direction
　Armand Lidtke
Client Consulting
　Jan-Hendrik Oelckers,
　Alexandra Coenen
Copy
　Manuel Wenzel,
　Jin Woo-Bae,
　Sebastian Flemmig
Idea
　Manuel Wenzel,
　Michael Häußler
Illustration
　Matthias Preuss
Postproduction
　Christoph von Bartkowski,
　Anja Bierau
Production
　Sven Hannemann

Unter dem Motto »Mit BIC unterschreibt man alles« holten wir uns mit dem BIC Stift Autogramme von Promis. Und ließen sie dabei Dinge unterschreiben, die sie normalerweise niemals unterschreiben würden. Youtube-Videos unserer Aktion inspirierten User zu eigenen BIC Pranks und sorgten in Foren, Blogs und Communities für Furore.

True to the motto, "With BIC you'll sign anything", we let celebrities give us their autographs using BIC pens. In the process, we let them sign things they would normally never sign. We put videos of these pranks on Youtube, which inspired users to upload their own. Thereby we caused a great stir among online forums, blogs and communities.

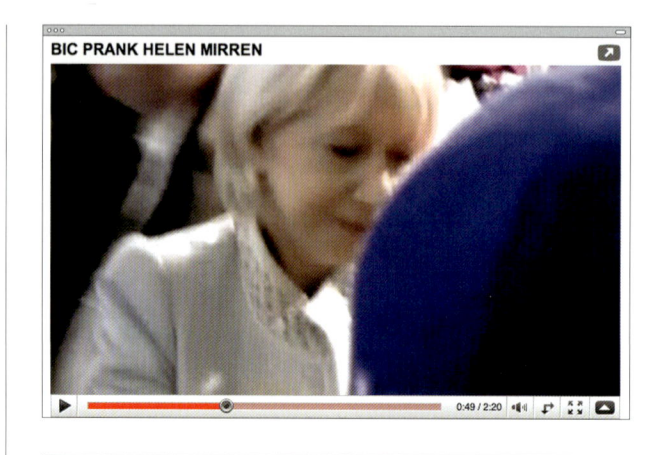

● NOMINATION
DESIGN
DESIGN
  Literatur
  Produkt-/Werbebroschüren
  Literature
  Advertising Brochures

● NOMINATION
DESIGN
DESIGN
  Literatur
  Bücher
  Literature
  Books

GÖRTZ SNEAKER-
SCHNÜRSENKEL
»Vogelhausbuch«

Lead Agency
  gürtlerbachmann GmbH
Client
  Görtz GmbH
Marketing Direction
  Michael Jacobs
Advertising Direction
  Evelyn Chroust
Executive Creative Direction
  Uli Gürtler
Creative Direction
  Uli Gürtler
Art Direction
  Veronika Kieneke
Client Consulting
  Anne Kukereit
Consulting
  Anne Kukereit
Copy
  Claudia Oltmann
Design
  Veronika Kieneke
Final Artwork
  Tobias Langkamp
Idea
  Veronika Kieneke
Illustration
  Veronika Kieneke
Printing
  Müllerditzen AG,
  P.O.P. Werbeteam GmbH,
  Buchbinderei Karen Begemann
  GmbH
Production
  Produktionsbüro Romey von
  Malottky GmbH

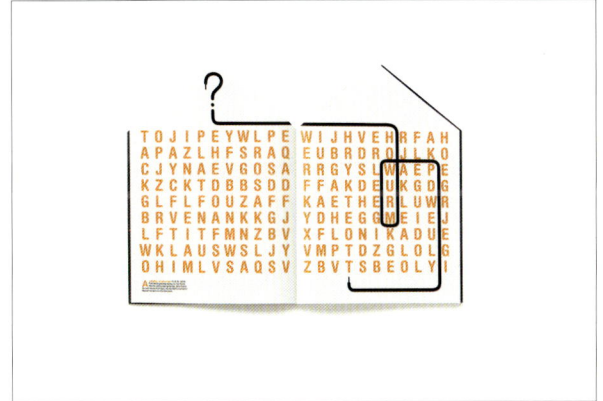

● NOMINATION
DESIGN
DESIGN
   Literatur
   Image-/Informations-
   broschüren
   Literature
   Image/Information Brochures

● NOMINATION
CRAFT
CRAFT
   Typografie
   Typography

GSK ABTEI
   »Das Rote-Faden-Buch«

Lead Agency
   Ogilvy & Mather Advertising
   GmbH
Client
   GlaxoSmithKline Consumer
   Healthcare GmbH & Co. KG
Marketing Direction
   Dr. Gabriele Schiebel-Schlosser
Advertising Direction
   Dr. Gabriele Schiebel-Schlosser
Executive Creative Direction
   Rainer Maass
Creative Direction
   Rob Brünig
Art Direction
   Sandra Prescher
Client Consulting
   Bernd Böhnke
Art Buying
   Carol Redfield
Consulting
   Bernd Böhnke
Copy
   Markus Bredenbals,
   Katharina Kiklas
Idea
   Sandra Prescher
Production
   Markus Jaeger
Publishing House
   Ogilvy & Mather Advertising
   GmbH
Typography
   Eleonore Boppert
Other
   Buchbinderei Mergemeier

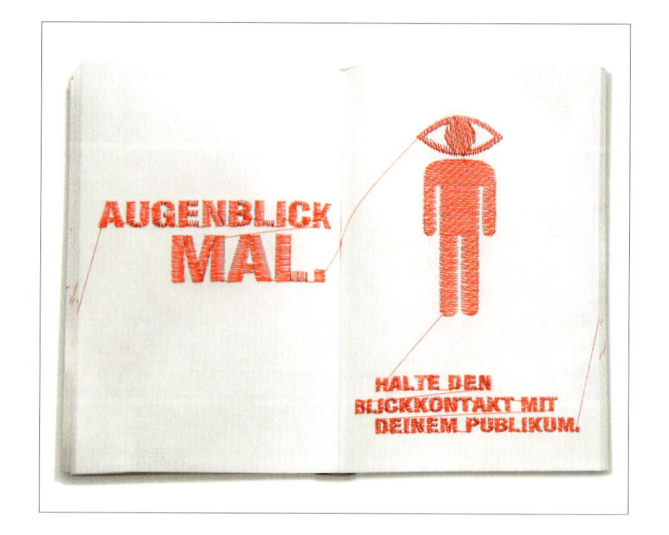

● NOMINATION
DESIGN
DESIGN
  Design
  Kalender
  Design
  Calendars

● NOMINATION
CRAFT
CRAFT
  Text
  Copy

STIHL MOTORSÄGE MS 261
»Die Vorfreude wächst.«

Lead Agency
  Scholz & Friends
Client
  ANDREAS STIHL
  AG & Co. KG
Marketing Direction
  Jürgen Fitting
Advertising Direction
  Norbert Blania
Executive Creative Direction
  Martin Pross,
  Matthias Spaetgens
Creative Direction
  Mathias Rebmann,
  Florian Schwalme
Art Direction
  Patrick Vogel
Client Consulting
  Benjamin Baader,
  Sven Weiche,
  Albert Petzold,
  David von Hilchen
Agency Production
  Nelly Sedlanic
Copy
  Momme Clausen,
  Viktoria Grünewald
Graphic Design
  Franziska Boemer

Der Adventskalender von Stihl verlängert die Vorfreude von Motorsägen-Fans bis ins Jahr 2042: Denn hinter den Türchen befinden sich Nadelbaumsamen für die Weihnachtsbäume von morgen. Auf den Innenseiten der Türchen werden die Bäume fachkundig und amüsant vorgestellt. Nur hinter Türchen 24 findet man keine Samen, sondern Dünger. Denn Vorfreude ist am schönsten, wenn sie nicht so lange dauert.

With conifer seeds in each door, Stihl's Advent calendar extends the anticipation of chainsaw fans until the year 2042. On the reverse side of the doors, the future Christmas trees were introduced in an entertaining yet competent way. Only the door of Christmas Eve held no seeds but fertilizer. Because anticipation is enjoyed most when it does not last too long.

Weihnachten 2034. Mit der Schlangenhautkiefer.

Die Schlangenhautkiefer kommt schon klar. Mit extremer Trockenheit zum Beispiel. Mit ihrem Namen, der sie mit hinterlistigen Tieren in Verbindung bringt, obwohl sie lediglich eine weißlich graue, rautenförmige Schuppenborke hat. Besonders gut kommt sie in ihrer typischen Vegetationseinheit klar: dem Schlangenhautkiefer-Bergwald (Pinion heldreichii). Diese azonale und xerobasiphile Waldgesellschaft ist zusammen mit dem Dinarischen Karst-Blockhalden-Tannenwald (Oreoherzogio-Abietetum illyricae Fuk.) auf Felspartien und windbeeinflussten Graten skelettreicher Standorte wie z.B. im Orjen in Montenegro idealtypisch ausgebildet. Mit extrem trockenen Texten kommt die Schlangenhautkiefer übrigens auch klar. Nur mit der extrem starken **MS 261** nicht, weshalb wir Ihnen ein extrem starkes Weihnachtsfest 2034 wünschen.

**Weihnachten 2041.
Mit dem Virginischen Wacholder.**

Ob Glühwein, Grog oder Eierpunsch – zur Weihnachtszeit kommt bei dem einen oder anderen die rote Nase nicht nur von der Kälte. Wenn Sie sich jetzt wiedererkennen, hätten wir hier genau den richtigen Weihnachtsbaum für Sie: den Virginischen Wacholder. Denn dieser Nadelbaum ist der Quell unendlicher Freude. Immerhin hat er uns Menschen nichts Geringeres geschenkt als die Wacholderbeere – und aus der wird bekanntlich Gin gewonnen. Durch die vierfache Destillation in Kupferkesseln erreicht dieser Schnaps nicht nur seinen runden Geschmack, sondern auch mindestens 37,5 Volumprozent. Ordentlich Umdrehungen hat übrigens auch die **MS 261**. 3200 pro Minute, um genau zu sein. Da fällt selbst der Virginische Wacholder ins Delirium. Und darauf würden wir gerne jetzt schon mit Ihnen anstoßen. Also: Auf feucht-fröhliche Weihnachten 2041!

NOMINATION
EDITORIAL
EDITORIAL
 Editorial
 Print/Einzelleistung
 Editorial
 Print/Individual Work

NOMINATION
CRAFT
CRAFT
 Fotografie
 Photography

STERN MAGAZIN
 »Abschied von Vibe«

Lead Agency
 stern Magazin
Client
 Gruner + Jahr AG & Co. KG
Creative Direction
 Andrea Gothe
Art Direction
 Donald Schneider,
 Mark Ernsting (Deputy)
Graphic Design
 Susanne Soeffker
Image Editing
 Andrea Gothe
Photography
 Thomas Lekfeldt
Publishing House
 Gruner + Jahr AG & Co. KG

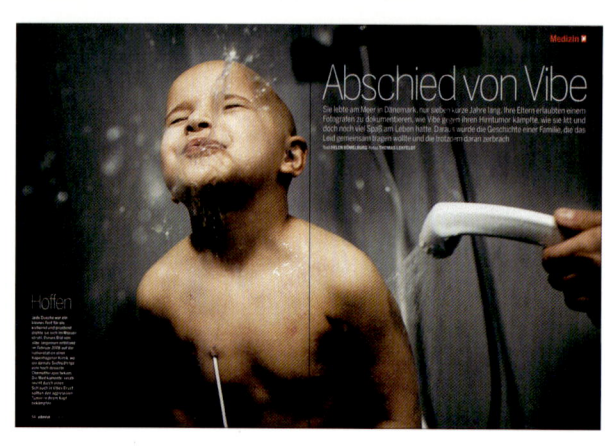

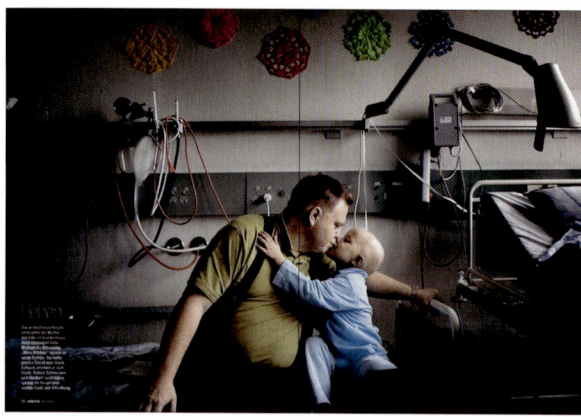

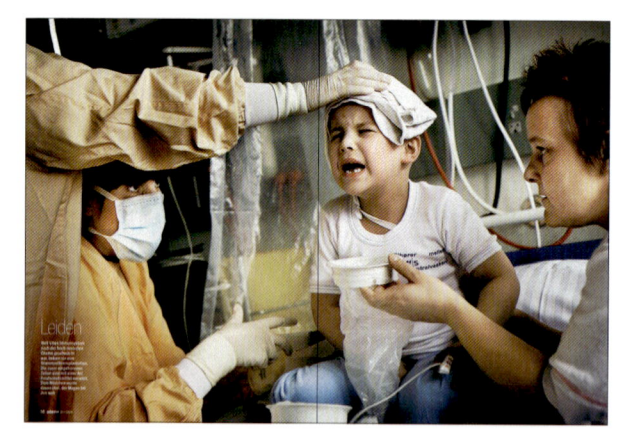

1

PUNKT
POINT

NOMINATION
KLASSISCHE MEDIEN
CLASSICAL MEDIA
  Print
  Einzelmotiv
  Print
  Single Motif

DEUTSCHE BAHN
FERNVERKEHR
  »Deutschland wird kleiner«

Lead Agency
  Ogilvy Frankfurt
Client
  DB Mobility Logistics AG
Marketing Direction
  Ulrich Klenke
  (Head of Corporate Marketing)
Advertising Direction
  Gabriele Handel-Jung,
  Gina P. Roeder
Executive Creative Direction
  Dr. Stephan Vogel
Creative Direction
  Dr. Stephan Vogel
Art Direction
  Daniel Schweinzer
Client Consulting
  Martina Huschka
Copy
  Marcus Pfeiffer

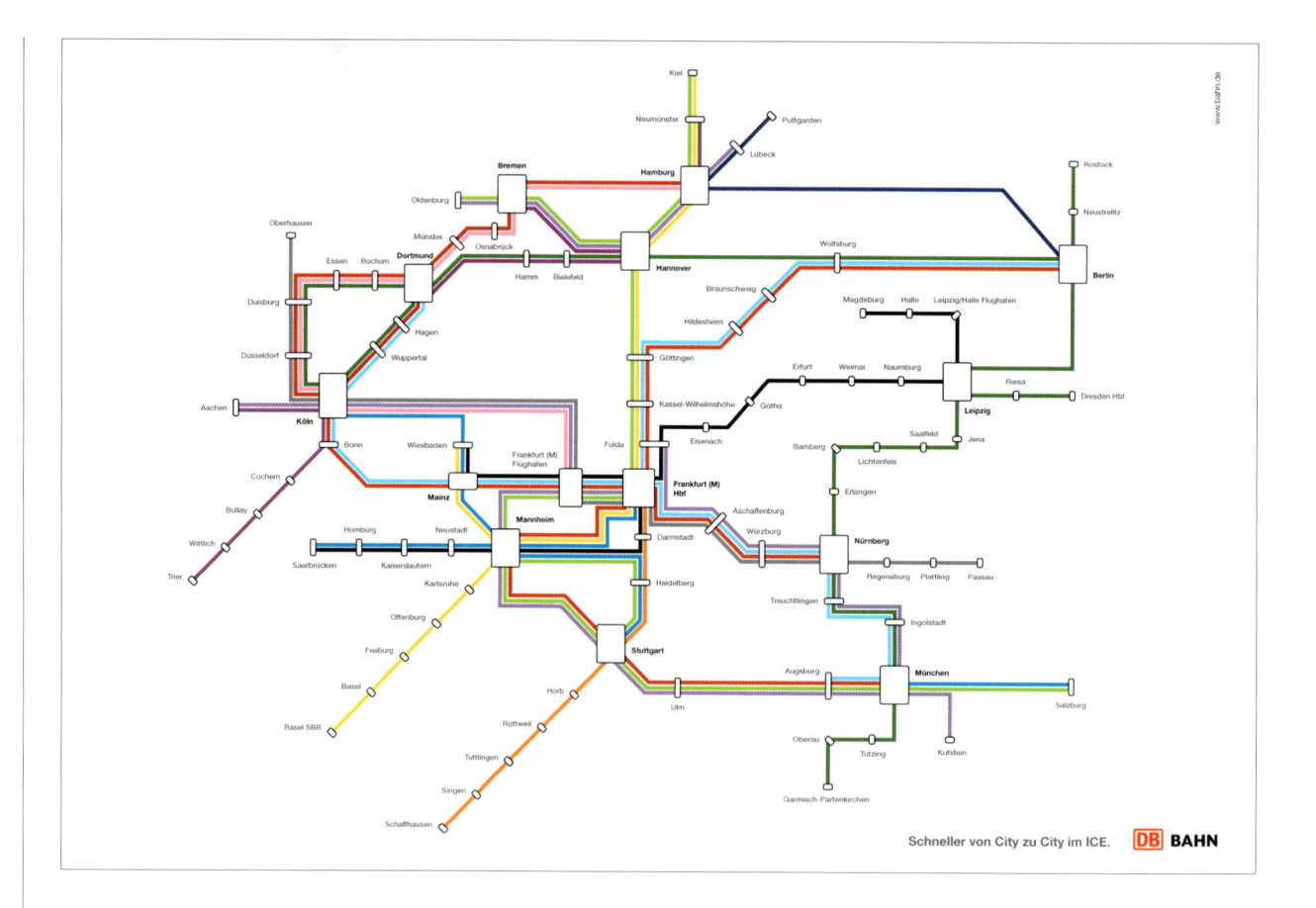

**NOMINATION
KLASSISCHE MEDIEN
CLASSICAL MEDIA**
  Print
  Einzelmotiv
  Print
  Single Motif

IGLO DEL MAR CALAMARES
  »Wo ist eigentlich Paul«

Lead Agency
  BBDO Proximity GmbH,
  Duesseldorf
Client
  Iglo GmbH
Marketing Direction
  Dieter Hartmann
Executive Creative Direction
  Christian Mommertz,
  Wolfgang Schneider
Creative Direction
  Christian Mommertz
Art Direction
  Caroline Kunsemüller
Client Consulting
  Sabine Oomkens,
  Bianca Scheiwe
Copy
  Martin Knipprath
Production
  Schaufler GmbH & Co. KG,
  Duesseldorf

305

NOMINATION
KLASSISCHE MEDIEN
CLASSICAL MEDIA
　Print
　Einzelmotiv
　Print
　Single Motif

SIXT
　«Bruni»

Lead Agency
　Jung von Matt AG
Client
　Sixt GmbH & Co.
　Autovermietung KG
Executive Creative Direction
　Doerte Spengler-Ahrens,
　Jan Rexhausen
Creative Direction
　Doerte Spengler-Ahrens,
　Jan Rexhausen
Art Direction
　Dina Ruewe
Client Consulting
　Miriam Paneth,
　Rabea Huthmann
Copy
　Joshua Mackowiak
Final Artwork
　Silke Fleischhauer
　(Jung von Matt)
Image Processing
　PX2

**Machen Sie es wie Madame Bruni.
Nehmen Sie sich einen kleinen Franzosen.**
(Zum Beispiel den Citroën C3 Picasso für € 29,–/Tag* bei Sixt)

*Mindestanmietung 7 Tage, inkl. 300 km, 48 Std. Vorausbuchungsfrist, zzgl. 20 % an Flughäfen und Bahnhöfen.

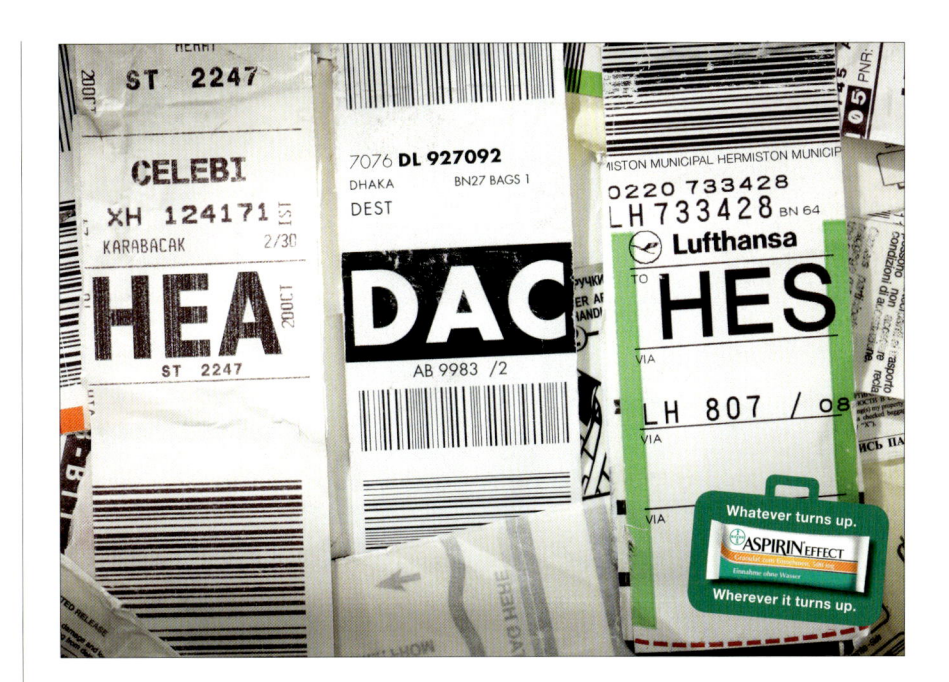

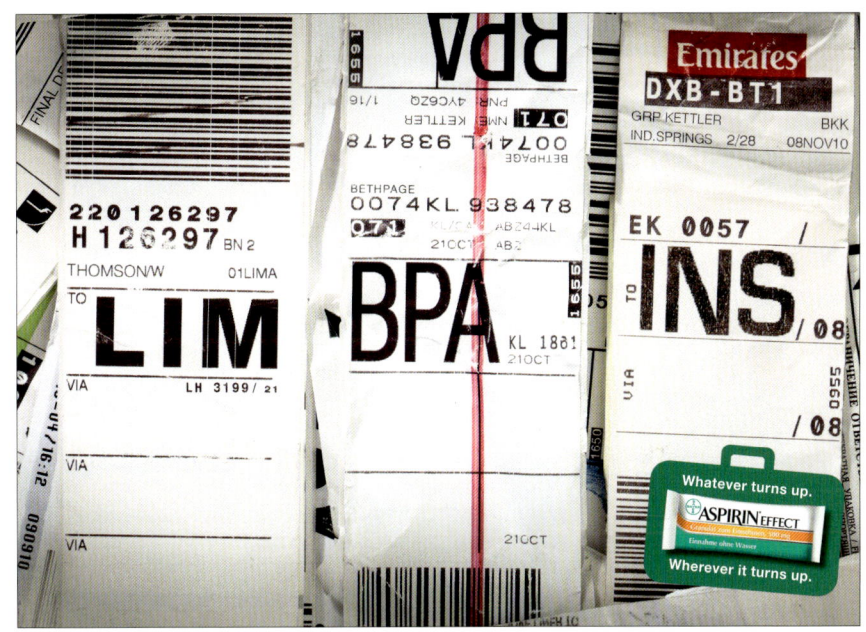

**NOMINATION
KLASSISCHE MEDIEN
CLASSICAL MEDIA**
Print
Kampagne
Print
Campaign

**ASPIRIN EFFECT
»Flughafenkürzel«**

Lead Agency
  BBDO Proximity GmbH,
  Duesseldorf
Client
  Bayer Vital GmbH
Executive Creative Direction
  Christian Mommertz,
  Wolfgang Schneider
Creative Direction
  Veikko Hille
Art Direction
  Fabian Pensel
Client Consulting
  Cécile Maasch,
  Susan Dietrich
Agency Production
  Bernhard Burg,
  Mathias Schöpflin
Art Buying
  Birgit Paulat
Copy
  Ramón Scheffer
Photography
  Oliver Lippert
Production
  ORT Medienverbund GmbH,
  Duesseldorf

**NOMINATION
KLASSISCHE MEDIEN
CLASSICAL MEDIA**
  Print
  Kampagne
  Print
  Campaign

BERLINER MORGENPOST
»Das ist Berlin«

Lead Agency
  Römer Wildberger
  Werbeagentur GmbH
Client
  Ullstein GmH,
  Berliner Morgenpost
Marketing Direction
  André Keeve
Executive Creative Direction
  Alex Römer,
  Thomas Wildberger
Art Direction
  Michael Brauchli,
  Tanja Kirschner
Client Consulting
  Katja Metz
Art Buying
  Katja Metz
Copy
  Stese Wagner,
  Chris Knipping,
  Jessica Hoppe,
  Jonas Wolff
Final Artwork
  Axel Springer, Inhouse
Graphic Design
  Steve Voigt
Image Processing
  PX 1
Media
  Carat
Photography
  Michael Heinsen
Typography
  Michael Brauchli

● **NOMINATION
KLASSISCHE MEDIEN
CLASSICAL MEDIA**
  Print
  Kampagne
  Print
  Campaign

FRITZ-KOLA
»Koffein hochkonzentriert«

Lead Agency
  Red Rabbit
Client
  fritz-kola GmbH
Marketing Direction
  Lorenz Hampl
Creative Direction
  Andreas Geyer
Art Direction
  Meike Grosch,
  Daniel Thaung
Client Consulting
  Christian Neumann-Semerow
Consulting
  Christian Neumann-Semerow
Copy
  Meike Grosch,
  Daniel Thaung
Final Artwork
  Hannah Harders
Idea
  Meike Grosch,
  Daniel Thaung
Illustration
  Meike Grosch,
  Daniel Thaung

NOMINATION
KLASSISCHE MEDIEN
CLASSICAL MEDIA
  Print
  Kampagne
  Print
  Campaign

MERCEDES-BENZ
  »Gefahren ohne Schrecken«

Lead Agency
  Jung von Matt AG
Client
  Daimler AG
Marketing Direction
  Anders-Sundt Jensen,
  Lüder Fromm
Advertising Direction
  Damir Maric,
  Lena Ernst
Creative Direction
  Michael Ohanian,
  Jacques Pense
Art Direction
  Andreas Jeutter,
  Benjamin Beck,
  Marcus Weiss
Client Consulting
  Verena Vogt
Art Buying
  Bianca Winter
Copy
  Oliver Flohrs,
  Robert Herter,
  Norman Scholl
Final Artwork
  Jung von Matt AG
Photography
  Dirk Kittelberger/
  Maground.com Bildagentur
Postproduction
  Bildgudt, Stuttgart

**NOMINATION
KLASSISCHE MEDIEN
CLASSICAL MEDIA**
 Print
 Kampagne
 Print
 Campaign

**MERCEDES-BENZ
TRANSPORTER**
 »Die 4x4 Verkehrszeichen«

Lead Agency
 Scholz & Friends
Client
 Daimler AG
Marketing Direction
 Nicole Baldisweiler
Advertising Direction
 Lutz Wienstroth
Executive Creative Direction
 Martin Pross,
 Matthias Spaetgens
Creative Direction
 Robert Krause,
 David Fischer,
 Philipp Wöhler
Art Direction
 Melanie Specht
Client Consulting
 Stefanie Wurst,
 Anna Gabriel
Art Buying
 Kirsten Rendtel
Copy
 Stefan Sohlau
Image Editing
 Appel Grafik
Photography
 maground.com,
 goZOOMA.de

311

NOMINATION
KLASSISCHE MEDIEN
CLASSICAL MEDIA
  Print
  Kampagne
  Print
  Campaign

VOLKSWAGEN CLASSIC PARTS
  »Nur ein Volkswagen bleibt ein Volkswagen«

Lead Agency
  DDB Tribal Group
Client
  VOLKSWAGEN AG
Marketing Direction
  Dirk Zimmer
Advertising Direction
  Philipp Benzler
Executive Creative Direction
  CCO: Eric Schoeffler,
  ECD: Till Eckel
Creative Direction
  Johannes Hicks
Art Direction
  Gabriel Mattar
Client Consulting
  Silke Lagodny
Copy
  Philip Bolland,
  Andres Blumenthal
Graphic Design
  Bruno Luglio
Image Processing
  Digitales Leben
Photography
  Hans Stark
Other
  Technical Account Director:
  Sascha Mehn

Schade, dass nicht jeder ein Volkswagen ist.
Volkswagen Classic Parts.

Schade, dass nicht jeder ein Volkswagen ist.
Volkswagen Classic Parts.

● **NOMINATION
KLASSISCHE MEDIEN
CLASSICAL MEDIA**
   Print
   Kampagne
   Print
   Campaign

**VORWERK STAUBSAUGER
KOBOLD 140**
   »Teller«

Lead Agency
   Kolle Rebbe GmbH
Client
   Vorwerk Deutschland Stiftung
   & Co. KG
Marketing Direction
   Felix Withöft
Executive Creative Direction
   Stefan Kolle
Creative Direction
   Holger Bultmann,
   Lorenz Ritter
Art Direction
   Alexander Schmid
Client Consulting
   Jessica Gustafsson,
   Arne Trost
Art Buying
   Katrin Grün
Copy
   Sascha Petersen
Final Artwork
   Maik Spreen
Idea
   Sascha Petersen,
   Alexander Schmid
Illustration
   The Scope
Photography
   Norimichi Inoguchi/
   The Scope
Printing
   Mediengruppe Klambt
Production
   Franziska Ziegler

**NOMINATION
KLASSISCHE MEDIEN
CLASSICAL MEDIA**
Print
Innovative Nutzung von Print
Print
Innovative Use of Print

LAND BADEN-WÜRTTEMBERG
»Die erste Anzeige mit Benzingeruch«

Lead Agency
　Scholz & Friends
Client
　Staatsministerium Baden-Württemberg
Marketing Direction
　Dr. Angela Kalous
Advertising Direction
　Andreas Schüle,
　Valerie Bechtler
Executive Creative Direction
　Martin Pross,
　Matthias Spaetgens
Creative Direction
　Robert Krause,
　Philipp Wöhler
Art Direction
　Jens Stein
Client Consulting
　Alexander Wittner,
　Catrin Schmid
Agency Production
　Diana Wuttge
Copy
　Christian Brandes

Verrückt: Autos riechen nach Strom und Anzeigen nach Benzin.

Baden-Württemberg entwickelt die elektromobile Zukunft.

(HIER REIBEN, RIECHEN UND NOCH EINMAL PURE NOSTALGIE ATMEN.)

Als vor 125 Jahren bei uns die ersten Automotoren angelassen wurden, rümpften Kutscher und andere Pferdeliebhaber noch mitleidig lächelnd die Nase. Damals waren Autofahrer eben noch tollkühne Männer in stinkenden Kisten. Doch der Erfolg unserer Erfindung war nicht zu bremsen – der Duft von Schmieröl und Benzin ging schon bald von Baden-Württemberg um die ganze Welt. Der Rest ist eine einmalige Erfolgsgeschichte, die wir jeden Tag fleißig weiterschreiben. Das neueste Kapitel: das erste Hybrid-Serienfahrzeug der Welt mit Lithium-Ionen-Technologie. Das kommt von Mercedes-Benz und riecht ganz klar nach Zukunft. Ingenieure aus Baden-Württemberg haben eben nicht nur Benzin im Blut, sondern auch jede Menge Ideen im Kopf. Das liegt nicht zuletzt daran, dass wir mehr als jedes andere Bundesland in Forschung und Entwicklung investieren. Um die Arbeit am geruchlosen Auto weiter voranzutreiben, haben wir sogar eine eigene Landesagentur für Elektromobilität und Brennstoffzellentechnologie, die e-mobil BW GmbH, gegründet. Damit ist es jetzt im wahrsten Sinne des Wortes amtlich: Die Antriebstechnologie der Zukunft kommt aus Baden-Württemberg. Mal wieder. Und Benzingeruch ist bald nur noch etwas für Nostalgiker – die mit dieser Anzeige noch einmal automobile Historie schnuppern können. Wenn Sie andererseits gerne in Zukunftsvisionen schwelgen, besuchen Sie uns: unter www.e-mobilbw.de oder

Baden-Württemberg
Wir können alles. Außer Hochdeutsch.

**NOMINATION
KLASSISCHE MEDIEN
CLASSICAL MEDIA**
 Out-of-Home
 Klassisch Einzelmotiv
 Out-of-Home
 Classic Single Motif

DEUTSCHE POST
 »Alles beginnt mit einem Brief«

Lead Agency
 Jung von Matt AG
Client
 Deutsche Post AG
Marketing Direction
 Axel Wursthorn
Advertising Direction
 Ekkehard Menzel
Executive Creative Direction
 Mathias Stiller
Creative Direction
 Boris Schwiedrzik,
 Markus Ewertz,
 David Mously,
 Jan Harbeck
Art Direction
 Daniel Haschtmann
Client Consulting
 Julia Kottowski,
 Kathleen von der Eltz
Art Buying
 Marjorie Jorrot
Copy
 David Missing
Final Artwork
 Anja Bierau,
 Christoph von Bartkowski
Idea
 David Missing,
 Daniel Haschtmann
Production
 Sven Hannemann

315

● NOMINATION
KLASSISCHE MEDIEN
CLASSICAL MEDIA
 Out-of-Home
  Klassisch Einzelmotiv
 Out-of-Home
  Classic Single Motif

MERCEDES-BENZ
 »Wackelkontakt«

Lead Agency
 Lukas Lindemann Rosinski
 GmbH
Client
 Mercedes-Benz
Marketing Direction
 Ulrike Mönnich
Advertising Direction
 Till Wartenberg
Executive Creative Direction
 Arno Lindemann,
 Bernhard Lukas
Creative Direction
 Thomas Heyen,
 Markus Kremer
Art Direction
 Dennis Mensching
Client Consulting
 Jascha Oevermann,
 Konstanze Kievenheim
Copy
 Jan Hoffmeister
Photography
 Tom Grammerstorf
Production
 Star Publishing GmbH
Other
 Stefan Kubach (Puppet Maker)

NOMINATION
KLASSISCHE MEDIEN
CLASSICAL MEDIA
Out-of-Home
Klassisch Einzelmotiv
Out-of-Home
Classic Single Motif

SNICKERS
»Du bist nicht du, wenn du hungrig bist/'Peacelord'«

Lead Agency
 BBDO Proximity GmbH, Duesseldorf
Client
 Mars GmbH
Executive Creative Direction
 Sebastian Hardieck,
 Christian Mommertz,
 Wolfgang Schneider
Art Direction
 Achim Metzdorf
Client Consulting
 Sonja Struß,
 Silke Joosten,
 Marilen Kurtz
Copy
 Martin Knipprath,
 Sebastian Steller

**NOMINATION
KLASSISCHE MEDIEN
CLASSICAL MEDIA**
Out-of-Home
Klassisch Kampagne
Out-of-Home
Classic Campaign

SMART FORTWO
»360°«

Lead Agency
  BBDO Proximity GmbH,
  Duesseldorf
Client
  Daimler AG,
  smart MBVD
Executive Creative Direction
  Sebastian Hardieck,
  Toygar Bazarkaya
Creative Direction
  Sebastian Hardieck
Art Direction
  Karolina Bukowiecka,
  Gustavo Vieira Dias
Client Consulting
  Dirk Spakowski,
  Sebastian Schlosser,
  Gülcan Demir,
  Michaela Hünlein
Art Buying
  Joana Uhlaczky
Copy
  Peter Engelbrecht
Photography
  Robert Eikelpoth
Production
  Zerone, Tom Stein

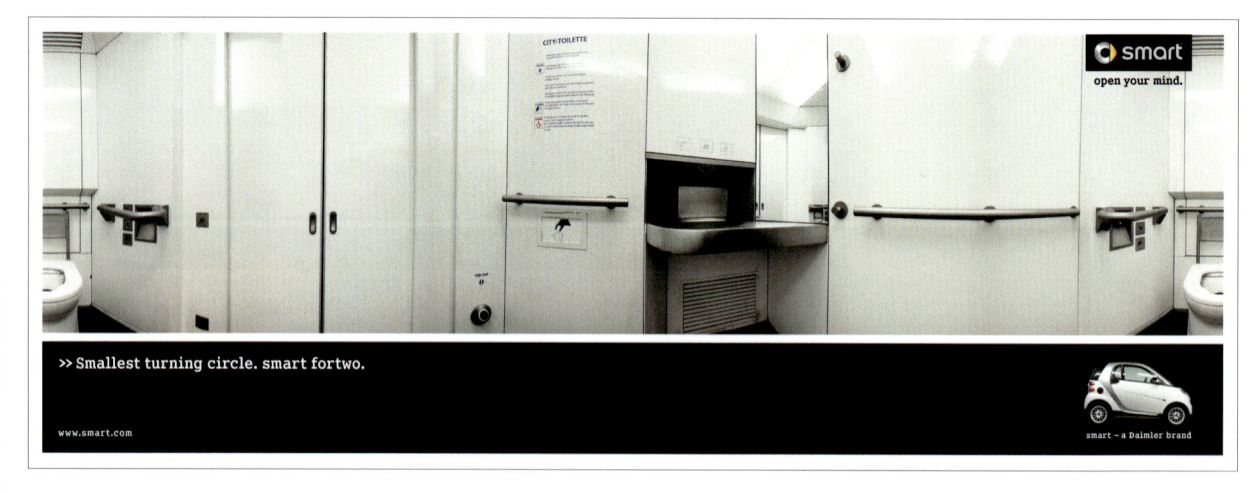

318

NOMINATION
KLASSISCHE MEDIEN
CLASSICAL MEDIA
 Out-of-Home
 Nicht-Klassisch
 Out-of-Home
 Non-Classic

MERCEDES-BENZ
 "The Intelligent Light Billboard"

Lead Agency
 Jung von Matt AG
Client
 Daimler AG
Marketing Direction
 Anders-Sundt Jensen,
 Lüder Fromm
Advertising Direction
 Damir Maric
Executive Creative Direction
 Mathias Stiller
Creative Direction
 Jan Harbeck,
 David Mously
Art Direction
 Oskar Strauss
Client Consulting
 Sven Dörrenbächer,
 Stefanie Gombert
Copy
 Carmen Riemer
Graphic Design
 Stephanie Volkmer
Production
 Sven Hannemann

319

**NOMINATION
KLASSISCHE MEDIEN
CLASSICAL MEDIA**
 Out-of-Home
 Nicht-Klassisch
 Out-of-Home
 Non-Classic

**SMART FORTWO
ELECTRIC DRIVE**
 »Das unsichtbarste Plakat
 der Welt«

Lead Agency
 BBDO Proximity GmbH,
 Duesseldorf
Client
 Daimler AG,
 Mercedes-Benz Vertrieb
 Deutschland
Executive Creative Direction
 Sebastian Hardieck,
 Wolfgang Schneider
Creative Direction
 Ton Hollander,
 Jens Ringena
Art Direction
 Claudia Janus
Client Consulting
 Dirk Spakowski,
 Thanh Vu Tran
Copy
 Dominique Becker

NOMINATION
KLASSISCHE MEDIEN
CLASSICAL MEDIA
Film
TV/Kino Einzelspot
Film
TV/Cinema Commercial

GOOGLE
»Kindertraum«

Lead Agency
  Kolle Rebbe GmbH
Client
  Google Germany GmbH
Marketing Direction
  Barbara Daliri Freyduni
Advertising Direction
  Fabian Teichmueller
  (Product Management)
Executive Creative Direction
  Stefan Kolle
Creative Direction
  Stefan Wübbe,
  Rolf Leger
Art Direction
  Michael Füsslin
Client Consulting
  Katrin Becker
Agency Production
  Lars Wiepking
Art Buying
  Emanuel Mugrauer
Copy
  Caroline Schmidt,
  Sandra Eichner,
  Kolja Rinne,
  Marko Werth
Film Direction
  Christian Reimann
Film Production
  Infected Postproduction GmbH
Idea
  Google Creative Labs (New York), Kolle Rebbe
Sound Design
  Mikis Meyer,
  Ralf Götzenberger,
  Hans-Ulrich Hönemann
Other
  Producers:
  Ulrike Kramer,
  Stevie Daniel
  Compositing:
  Moritz Gläsle

Jeden Tag werden auf Google Millionen von Suchanfragen gestellt. Mit eben diesen Suchbegriffen und den entsprechenden Ergebnissen, die die Websuche, Google Maps, Youtube und Co. dazu liefert, erzählt der Film Suchgeschichten, wie sie das Leben schreibt. Egal, ob man sein Herz oder sein Zelt verloren hat, ob man den Mann im Mond sucht oder das passende Outfit zur WM.

Every day, Google receives millions of search requests. Based on these search terms and the corresponding results from the web search, Google Maps, Youtube and others, the film tells the stories behind the searches – the sort you couldn't make up. No matter whether you've lost your heart or your tent, are looking for the man in the moon or for the perfect outfit for the World Cup.

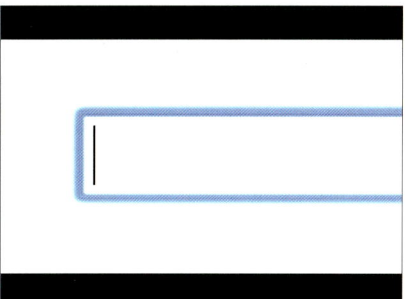

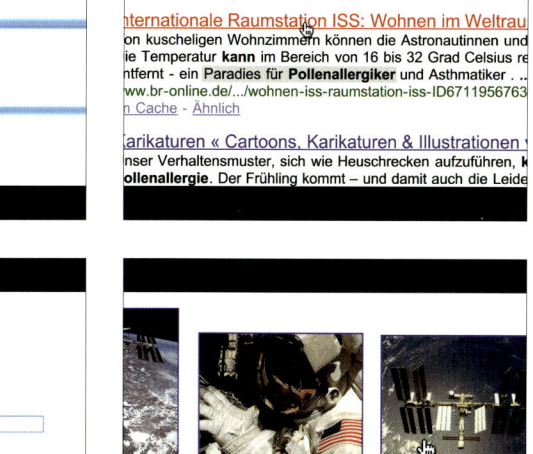

NOMINATION
KLASSISCHE MEDIEN
CLASSICAL MEDIA
Film
TV/Kino Einzelspot
Film
TV/Cinema Commercial

JOBSINTOWN.DE
»Fischer«

Lead Agency
  Grabarz & Partner
Client
  jobsintown.de GmbH
Marketing Direction
  Frank Esbach
Advertising Direction
  Stefan Kraft
  (Managing Director)
Executive Creative Direction
  Ralf Heuel
Creative Direction
  Timm Weber,
  Gösta Diehl,
  Oliver Heidorn
Art Direction
  Thomas Schmiegel
Client Consulting
  Reinhard Patzschke,
  Julica Hauke,
  Jennifer Fabian
Agency Production
  Alexa Schäfer
Animation/Visual Effects/
Special Effects
  Giant Milk Can
Camera
  Mathias Schöningh
Copy
  Kerstin Correll
Film Direction/Radio Direction
  Robert Nylund
Film Production
  Cobblestone Filmproduktion
  GmbH
Graphic Design
  Milena Pfannkuche
Music Composition
  Max Olowinsky,
  Felix Müller,
  Florian Lakenmacher
Sound Engineering
  Recording Studio:
  Studio Funk, Hamburg
Other
  Producer:
  Philipp Schmalriede
  Music:
  Supreme Music

Ein Fischer preist die Schönheit und Romantik seines Berufs. Und doch fühlt er sich zu Höherem berufen und verarbeitet den Fang nicht zu Filets, sondern verknotet ihn kunstvoll wie ein Ballontier. »Falscher Job?« fragt daraufhin das Stellenportal jobsintown.de den Fischer. Und den Zuschauer.

A fisherman praises the beauty and romance of his job. Yet, at the same time, he feels he is destined for greater things and instead of filetting the catch, he craftily shapes it like a balloon animal. "Wrong job?" is the question put to the fisherman and the audience by career website jobsintown.de

● NOMINATION
**KLASSISCHE MEDIEN
CLASSICAL MEDIA**
Film
TV/Kino Einzelspot
Film
TV/Cinema Commercial

**MERCEDES-BENZ
»Weihnachtsgruß«**

Lead Agency
  Jung von Matt AG
Client
  Daimler AG
Marketing Direction
  Anders-Sundt Jensen,
  Lüder Fromm
Advertising Direction
  Alexandra Süß,
  Wolfgang Würth
Executive Creative Direction
  Sascha Hanke
Creative Direction
  Tobias Grimm, Jens Pfau
Art Direction
  Jonathan Schupp
Client Consulting
  Sven Dörrenbächer,
  Jochen Schwarz,
  Isabell Poschadel
Agency Production
  Jannik Endemann
Copy
  Marian Goetz, Tobias Grimm
Film Direction/Radio Direction
  Aleksander Bach
Film Production
  Erste Liebe Filmproduktion
  GmbH
Music Composition
  Peter Gromer
Postproduction
  Slaughterhouse
Sound Design
  Hahn Nitzsche Studios

Der diesjährige Weihnachtsgruß von Mercedes-Benz war ein eigens gedrehter Film. Hauptfigur darin war eine Gans, die nicht als Weihnachtsbraten enden wollte. Der Film wurde international an Kunden, Partner und Freunde des Hauses digital verschickt. Außerdem wurde der Film auf allen Social-Media-Kanälen von Mercedes-Benz platziert.

This year's Mercedes-Benz Christmas greeting was a short film, shot specially for this purpose. The main character was a goose, who did not want to end up on the Christmas dinner table. Customers, suppliers and friends of the brand were sent a link to the film. It was also accessible via the Mercedes-Benz pages on social media sites.

● **NOMINATION**
KLASSISCHE MEDIEN
CLASSICAL MEDIA
  Film
  TV/Kino Einzelspot
  Film
  TV/Cinema Commercial

TOSHIBA
  "Paper 3D"

Lead Agency
  Grey Worldwide GmbH
Client
  Toshiba
Marketing Direction
  Sascha Lange
Advertising Direction
  Thomas French
Executive Creative Direction
  Andreas Henke,
  Sacha Reeb
Creative Direction
  Moritz Grub,
  Regner Lotz
Art Direction
  Moritz Grub,
  Regner Lotz
Client Consulting
  Christian Hupertz,
  Marco Köditz
Agency Production
  Christian Käutner
Camera
  Jim Lacy
Copy
  Moritz Grub,
  Regner Lotz
Cutting
  Tobias Suhm,
  Josch Kretzschmar
Film Direction/Radio Direction
  Hauke Hilberg,
  Kathrin Albers
Film Production
  Bakery Films Filmproduktion
  GmbH & Stoptrick Animation
  Studios
Music Composition
  Fritz Rating
Postproduction
  Slaughterhouse GmbH
  Visual Manufacturing
  (Gwen Teichmann)
Production
  Christian Gemeiner
Sound Design
  BLUWI Edition GmbH &
  Studio Funk GmbH & Co. KG
Sound Engineering
  Christof Weische,
  Arne Schultze
Speaker
  Julia Haacke
Other
  Award Management:
  Felicitas Katzemich
  Photography:
  Moritz Grub

Die neuen Toshiba 3D TVs machen aus 2D-Content 3D-Fernsehen. Diese Message wird im 60-sekündigen Film auf sehr ungewöhnliche Weise umgesetzt. Die Idee begann auf einem weißen Blatt Papier. So auch der Film. Aus einem flachen Papier wird eine detailverliebte dreidimensionale Origami-Welt. Eine faszinierende Reise von 2D zu 3D. Und außerdem: der weltweit erste Stopptrickfilm in 3D.

The new Toshiba 3D TVs turn 2D content into 3D entertainment. The 60 second film conveys this simple message in a very unconventional way. The idea started on a blank sheet of paper. And so does the film. A flat piece of paper turns into an origami landscape. A fascinating journey from 2D to 3D. The film was shot stereoscopically and is the world's first stop motion film in real 3D.

● **NOMINATION**
KLASSISCHE MEDIEN
CLASSICAL MEDIA
  Film
  TV/Kino Einzelspot
  Film
  TV/Cinema Commercial

VOLKSWAGEN LANE ASSIST
  »Linien«

Lead Agency
  DDB Tribal Group
Client
  VOLKSWAGEN AG
Marketing Direction
  Luca de Meo
Advertising Direction
  Hartmut Seeger,
  Veronika Ziegaus
Executive Creative Direction
  Stefan Schulte
Creative Direction
  Till Eckel,
  Johannes Hicks
Art Direction
  Lisa Berger
Client Consulting
  Marie-Louise Jakob
Agency Production
  Bernd Bluhme
Copy
  Ingo Isabettini,
  Manuel Wenzel
Cutting
  Walter Mauriot
Film Direction
  Wilfrid Brimo
Film Production
  Wanda Productions Berlin
Postproduction
  Mikros Paris
Production
  Fabian Barz
Sound Design
  The, Paris

Bei langen Fahrten ein Problem: der Sekundenschlaf. Man wird müde und schweift in Gedanken schnell in eine andere Welt ab. Deshalb sollen Volkswagenfahrer wissen, dass sie ihr Fahrzeug in solchen Momenten mit dem Assistenzsystem Lane Assist warnt, um das Auto zurück auf die Spur und sicher ans Ziel zu bringen.

Always a problem on long rides: microsleep. People get tired and drift off easily in other dimensions. We want Volkswagen drivers to know that the Lane Assist keeps attention to the road. It warns the occupants and helps to get the car back on track and safely to its destination.

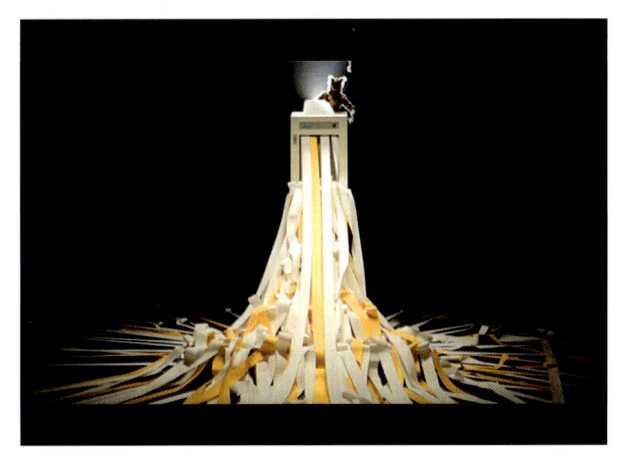

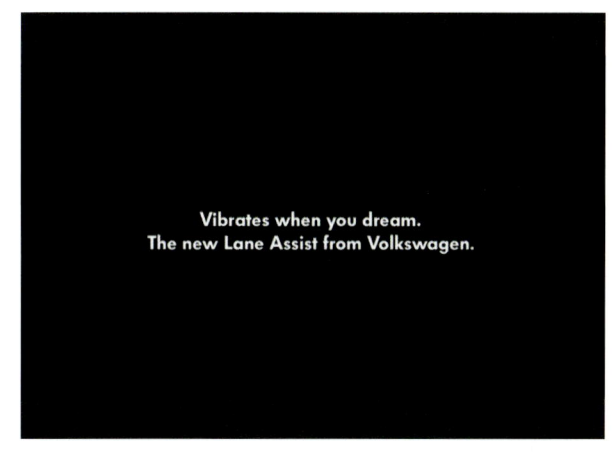

● NOMINATION
KLASSISCHE MEDIEN
CLASSICAL MEDIA
  Film
    TV/Kino Kampagne
  Film
    TV/Cinema Campaign

KURZFILMAGENTUR HAMBURG
  »Kurz vor Film –
  Mehr Vorfilme ins Kino!«

Lead Agency
  WE DO communication GmbH
  GWA
Client
  KurzFilmAgentur Hamburg e.V.
Executive Creative Direction
  Prof. Christoph M. Scheller
Creative Direction
  Thomas Avenhaus
Art Direction
  Martin Itter,
  Lisa Rübel,
  Pia Marecki
Client Consulting
  Cécile Engelen
Strategic Planning
  Tilman Dachselt
Agency Production
  Cécile Engelen
Audio Production
  cine plus Media Service GmbH
  & Co. KG
Camera
  Annabelle Handke
Concept
  Clara Berger
Consulting
  gregor c. blach
Copy
  Clara Berger
Cutting
  Michael Dörfler
Film Direction/Radio Direction
  Michael Dörfler
Film Production
  cine plus Media Service GmbH
  & Co. KG
Graphic Design
  Pia Marecki
Idea
  Thomas Avenhaus,
  Clara Berger
Production
  Christian Bestmann,
  Jasmin Rothenbücher,
  Liane Wagner
Sound Design
  Jan Cziharz
Sound Engineering
  Leschek Faber
Styling
  Katharina de Malotki

Die integrierte Kampagne »Kurz vor Film – Mehr Vorfilme ins Kino!« kämpft für ein Comeback des Kurzfilms als Vorfilm. Prominente Unterstützung kommt von den Schauspieler/-innen Jana Pallaske, Anna Thalbach und Ulrich Matthes. In Spots rufen sie dazu auf, Kinobetreibern im Rahmen einer Unterschriftenaktion auf Festivals und im Netz zu zeigen, dass sich ihr Publikum mehr Vorfilme im Kino wünscht.

The integrated campaign »Kurz vor Film – Mehr Vorfilme ins Kino!« advocates bringing short films as prefilms back into cinemas. In short (!) spots, actors such as Jana Pallaske, Anna Thalbach or Ulrich Matthes call for the support of the movie-going public. Within an integrated campaign online and at film festivals, they can sign for regularly programmed prefilms.

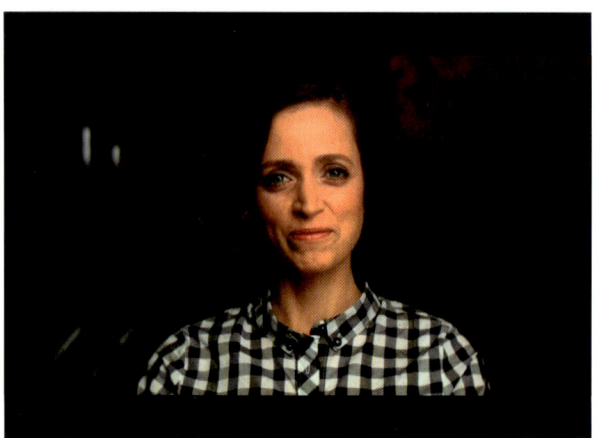

● NOMINATION
KLASSISCHE MEDIEN
CLASSICAL MEDIA
   Film
   TV/Kino Kampagne
   Film
   TV/Cinema Campaign

MEDIA MARKT KAMPAGNE
»Billiger geht so!«

Lead Agency
   kempertrautmann gmbh berlin
Client
   redblue Marketing GmbH
Marketing Direction
   Michael Rook
Advertising Direction
   Klaus Wäcker
Creative Direction
   Alexander Weber-Grün,
   Lennart Witting
Art Direction
   Matthias Walter
Client Consulting
   Marcus Bank,
   Julia Braun
Agency Production
   Ruth Jansen
Audio Production
   Studio Funk Berlin
Camera
   Frank Blau
Copy
   Filiz Tasdan,
   Siyamak Seyedasgari
Film Direction
   Sebastian Schipper
Film Production
   radical media gmbh
Graphic Design
   Sebastian Schmidt,
   Christine Gillmeister,
   Christoph Stender
Music Composition
   Stephan Moritz
Postproduction
   Pictorion das werk GmbH
Production
   radical media gmbh:
   Christiane Dressler,
   Maren Reisner
Sound Design
   Nima Gholiagha

Die erfolgreiche Weiterführung der Kampagne um Deutschlands erfolgreichsten Comedian und Media Markt Liebhaber Mario Barth steht dieses Mal unter dem Motto »Billiger geht so!«. Mario Barth beobachtet und kommentiert das Einkaufsverhalten der Kunden auf seine gewohnt humorvolle Art. Und zwar direkt dort, wo man sie antrifft: im Media Markt.

The prosperous continuation of the campaign around Germany's most successful comedian and Media Markt enthusiast Mario Barth this time is called »Billiger geht so!« (Cheaper – works like this!). Mario Barth is observing and commenting the shopping behavior of the customers in his well-known humorous kind of way. Right there where you encounter them: at the Media Markt.

NOMINATION
KLASSISCHE MEDIEN
CLASSICAL MEDIA
Film
Internetfilme
Film
Internet Films

AUDI
"The Next Big Thing"

Lead Agency
 HEIMAT, Berlin
Contributing Agencies
 Neue Digitale/razorfish GmbH,
 Mutabor Design GmbH
Client
 AUDI AG
Marketing Direction
 Lothar Korn
Advertising Direction
 Michael Finke,
 Tobias Seitz
Executive Creative Direction
 Guido Heffels,
 Jürgen Vossen
Creative Direction
 Guido Heffels,
 Myles Lord,
 Jürgen Vossen
Art Direction
 Carsten Schubert,
 Michael Dunlap,
 Jue Alt
Client Consulting
 Frank Ricken,
 Vivien Ott
Strategic Planning
 Andreas Mengele,
 Sebastian Marx
Animation/Visual Effects/
Special Effects
 Neue Digitale/razorfish GmbH
Camera
 Crille Forsberg
Casting
 Tempomedia Filmproduktion
 GmbH
Copy
 Guido Heffels,
 Ole Vinck,
 Nikolai Diepenbrock,
 Stephen Quell
Cutting
 Joakim Pietras
Film Direction
 Henrik Sundgren@ACNE
Film Production
 Tempomedia Filmproduktion
 GmbH
Motion Graphics and 3D
 Neue Digitale/razorfish GmbH:
 Florian Stumpe
Music Composition
 Torpedo
Screen Design
 Neue Digitale/razorfish GmbH:
 Bartek Elsner
Sound Design
 Plop Production, Sweden

Die Einführung des Audi A1 erfolgte im Internet mit einem sechsteiligen interaktiven Film. John Frank – ein IT-Spezialist – gerät unerwartet in das größte Abenteuer seines Lebens und schützt eine wunderschöne Frau vor dem Zugriff der Mafia. "The Next Big Thing" ist nicht nur der ultimative Showcase für den Audi A1, sondern nimmt den Zuschauer mit auf eine rasante Fahrt durchs Web.

The Audi A1 makes a grand entrance on the Internet with a six-part interactive film. John Frank – an IT specialist – who is thrown into the adventure of his life, helping a girl to escape from a dangerous mafia. "The Next Big Thing" not only is the ultimate showcase for the Audi A1, but also takes the viewer on a thrill ride through the web.

● NOMINATION
**KLASSISCHE MEDIEN
CLASSICAL MEDIA**
Film
Internetfilme
Film
Internet Films

DIGITAL BOMB
"Tron Rap"

Lead Agency
   Hermann Vaske's Emotional
   Network
Client
   ZDF/ARTE
Executive Creative Direction
   Hermann Vaske
Creative Direction
   Hermann Vaske
Art Direction
   Felix Andrew
Agency Production
   Hermann Vaske's Emotional
   Network
Audio Production
   Bernd Thurig Tonstudio
Camera
   Felix Andrew
Copy
   Mark Williams, Hermann Vaske
Cutting
   Carsten Jaeger
Film Direction
   Hermann Vaske
Film Production
   Hermann Vaske's Emotional
   Network
Graphic Design
   Stephan Krtsch
Idea
   Hermann Vaske
Postproduction
   Hermann Vaske's Emotional
   Network

Im Juli 2010 strahlte ARTE den Dokumentarfilm "Digital Bomb" von Hermann Vaske aus. In "Digital Bomb" präsentiert "Tron Guy" die Vergangenheit, Gegenwart und Zukunft des Internets. Eine Achterbahnfahrt durch das Land der digitalen Kreativität im Zeitalter der Amateure. Einige Wochen vor der Ausstrahlung machten wir mit "Tron Guy Rap" im Internet auf den Sendetermin aufmerksam.

In July 2010 Arte broadcasted Hermann Vaske's "Digital Bomb". In the documentary, "Tron Guy" presented the past, present and future of the Internet. A rollercoaster ride through the land of digital creativity in the age of the amateur. A couple of weeks before the premiere, we launched "Tron Guy Rap" to bring attention to the broadcast.

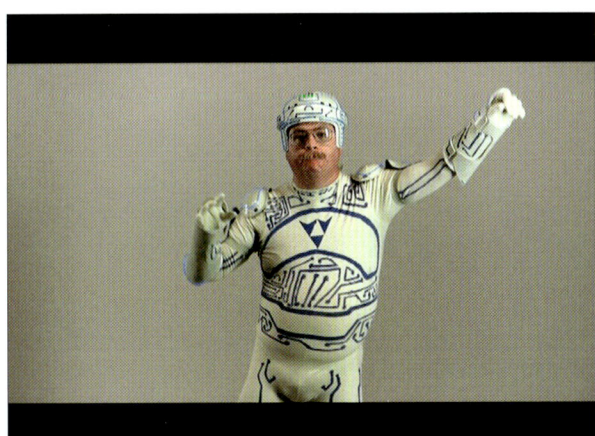

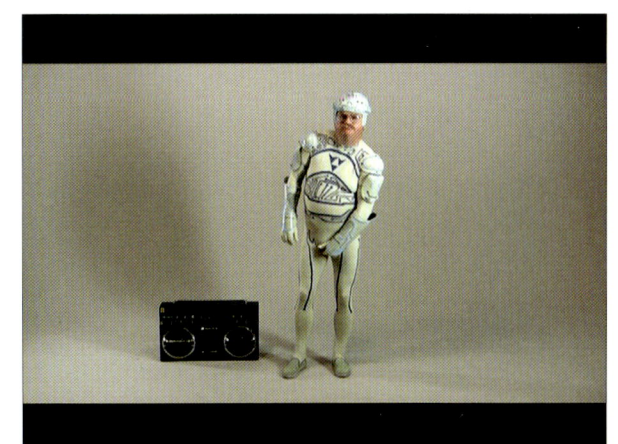

● **NOMINATION**
KLASSISCHE MEDIEN
CLASSICAL MEDIA
　Film
　Internetfilme
　Film
　Internet Films

MARSHMALLOW FLUFF
"Sticky"

Lead Agency
　VIRAL LAB
Client
　Genuport Trade AG
Marketing Direction
　Dr. Uwe Lebens
Advertising Direction
　Anne Kelhetter
Creative Direction
　Andi Knaup
Client Consulting
　Sven Czöppan
Strategic Planning
　Tino Kanzler
Agency Production
　Marcus »Becko« Beck
Animation/Visual Effects/
Special Effects
　Stunt & Wireworks Haeger,
　Leo Plank
Camera
　Jens Harms
Casting
　Andi Knaup
Concept
　Andi Knaup
Consulting
　Sven Czöppan,
　Tino Kanzler
Copy
　Andi Knaup
Cutting
　Jan Gerold
Film Direction
　Andi Knaup
Film Production
　Viral Lab
Idea
　Andi Knaup
Media
　Viral Lab
Postproduction
　Christian Schrills
Production
　Viral Lab
Styling
　Andi Knaup,
　Donia Bdeir
Other
　Cast: Anton Grzesiewski,
　Vincent Edusei,
　Benedict Jacob,
　Constantijn Jonas
　Production Assistance:
　Joshua Groth,
　Sarah Raith

Der US-Kult-Brotaufstrich "Marshmallow Fluff" hat auch in Deutschland immer mehr Fans. Vier von ihnen lernen wir in "Sticky" kennen. Sie erklären die Features so, dass sie beim Betrachter auf jeden Fall hängen bleiben. Und ist die süße Sache erst einmal in aller Munde, heißt es bald überall "I fluff you". Speziell bei Kindern und Familien, bei denen diese Maßnahme die "Fluff"-Bekanntheit gesteigert hat.

Marshmallow Fluff, a true American spread, gains evermore German fans. In "Sticky", four of them explain its features in a way that they get stuck in the viewer's mind. Once having tasted its sweetness everyone will say "I fluff you". The video was uploaded on YouTube and other video sites and spread in German communities where it especially increased the brand awareness with children and families.

NOMINATION
KLASSISCHE MEDIEN
CLASSICAL MEDIA
Film
Internetfilme
Film
Internet Films

MERCEDES-BENZ FEUERWEHR-FAHRZEUGE
»Sirene«

Lead Agency
  Scholz & Friends
Client
  Daimler AG
Marketing Direction
  Peer Näher
Executive Creative Direction
  Martin Pross,
  Matthias Spaetgens
Creative Direction
  Robert Krause,
  Philipp Wöhler
Art Direction
  Robert Bilz,
  Ratko Cindric
Client Consulting
  Stefanie Wurst,
  Anna Gabriel,
  Anna Mrozyk
Agency Production
  Benito Schumacher
Camera
  Esther Dittmann,
  Kalle Klein,
  Dennis Vocke
Copy
  Kanak Mehra
Cutting
  Tobias Suhm
Film Direction
  Daniel Warwick
Film Production
  Czar-Film GmbH
Postproduction
  Slaughterhouse Berlin
Production
  Producer:
  Christian Wegehenkel
Other
  Operator:
  Benedikt Hugendubel
  Music:
  David Arnold, Loft

Mercedes-Benz Rettungsfahrzeuge. »Klingt gut, wenn man in Not ist.« Wenn man schnelle Hilfe braucht, klingt die Sirene der Feuerwehr wie Musik in den Ohren. In unserem Film schmettern daher zwei echte Opernsänger das Tatütata mit voller Inbrunst durch die Straßen. Natürlich aus einem Mercedes-Benz, dem langjährigen und zuverlässigen Partner der Feuerwehr.

Mercedes-Benz Rescue Vehicles. "Sounds good when you need help." When you need help fast, the firefighters' siren sounds like music. Therefore, in our film two real opera singers sing out loud the woo-woo through the streets. Of course out of a Mercedes-Benz, the longtime and reliable partner of the firefighters.

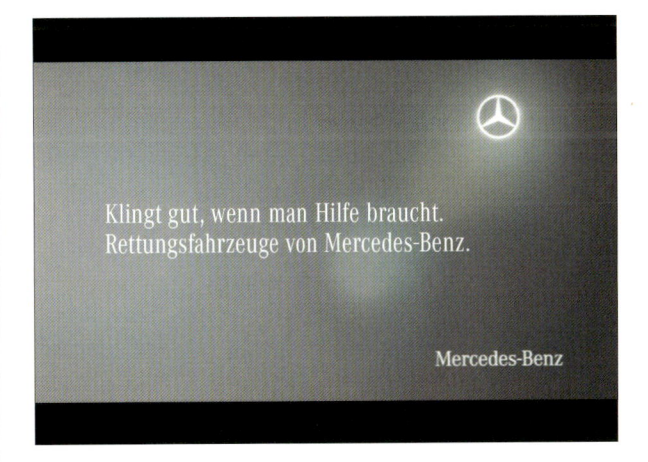

**NOMINATION
KLASSISCHE MEDIEN
CLASSICAL MEDIA**
 Film
 TV-On-air-Promotion
 Film
 TV On-Air Promotion

SKY HD
»Ameisen«

Lead Agency
 Heye & Partner GmbH
Client
 Sky Deutschland
 GmbH & Co. KG
Marketing Direction
 Anthony Liow
Advertising Direction
 Michael Jaeger
Executive Creative Direction
 Alexander Bartel,
 Martin Kießling
Creative Direction
 Ulrich Lützenkirchen,
 Jan Okusluk
Art Direction
 Justin Pettit
Client Consulting
 Dirk Kartes,
 Daniel Hartmann
Agency Production
 Milena Milic
Camera
 Philipp Geigel
Copy
 Thomas Schwarz
Cutting
 Mikel Tischner,
 Rico Reitz
Film Direction
 Rico Reitz
Film Production
 ARRI Commercial
Media
 Tobias Hoffmann
Production
 Phil Decker
Sound Design
 M-Sound, Robert Miller
Other
 Flame Artists:
 Rico Reitz,
 Max Gründl

Wir wurden beauftragt, die Zahl der Sky-Abonnenten sowie das Interesse an Sky-HD-Programmen zu steigern, indem wir die Leistung eines High-Definition-Bildes verdeutlichen. Um dies zu erreichen, entwickelten wir einen TV-Spot, der mit einem klassischen »Störbild«-Effekt spielt. Bei näherem Hinsehen verwandelt sich dieses zur Überraschung des Betrachters in eine hochauflösende Tierdokumentation.

We were asked to develop a TV ad with the goal to increase the number of Sky subscribers as well as the interest in Sky HD programmes by showing what a high-definition picture has to offer. To highlight the advantage of Sky HD, we used a classic noise image, which more and more turns into a high-resolution documentary the closer the camera gets to the picture. The camera zooms up to a single ant holding the Sky logo.

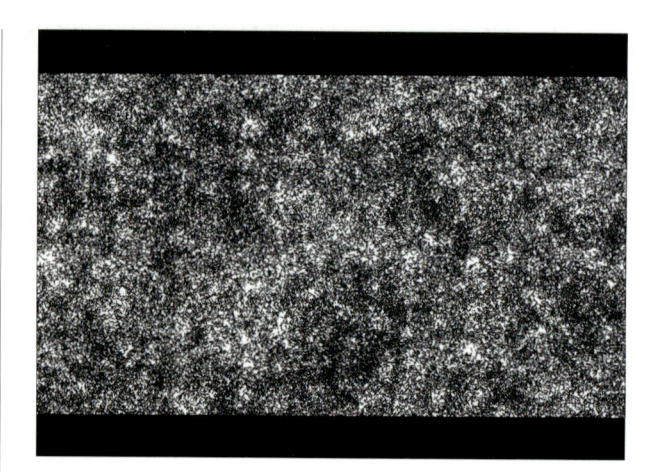

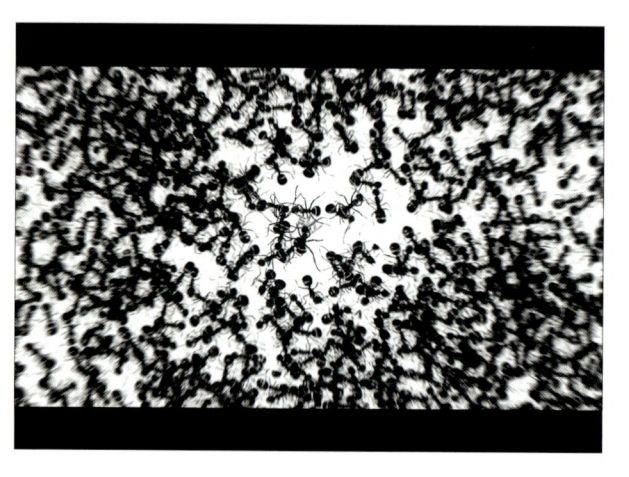

NOMINATION
KLASSISCHE MEDIEN
CLASSICAL MEDIA
Film Craft
Casting
Film Craft
Casting

PARSHIP
»Amor«

Lead Agency
   Leagas Delaney Hamburg GmbH
Client
   PARSHIP GmbH
Marketing Direction
   Oliver Busch
Advertising Direction
   Herbert Murschenhofer
Executive Creative Direction
   Hermann Waterkamp, Stefan Zschaler
Creative Direction
   Oliver Grandt, Willy Kaussen
Client Consulting
   Tjarko Horstmann, Niels Overmeyer
Casting
   Felipe Ascacibar, Jakob Eckstein
Film Production
   element e gmbh

2011 feiert Parship als führende Partnervermittlung ihr zehnjähriges Bestehen. Zehn Jahre, in denen sie unzählige Paare zusammengeführt hat. Jedoch ist dieses Jubiläum nicht für jeden ein Grund zur Freude.

In 2011, Parship celebrates its 10th anniversary as a leading online dating agency. Ten years that have brought many couples together. But not everyone is celebrating our anniversary.

333

NOMINATION
KLASSISCHE MEDIEN
CLASSICAL MEDIA
   Audio
   Radio Einzelspot
   Audio
   Radio Commercial

DUMMY MAGAZIN
   «Khowf»

Lead Agency
   Aimaq & Stolle Creative Brand
   Consulting GmbH
Client
   DUMMY Verlag GmbH
Marketing Direction
   Oliver Gehrs
Advertising Direction
   Oliver Gehrs
Executive Creative Direction
   André Aimaq
Creative Direction
   Uwe Venus
Audio Production
   Dummy
Copy
   Shahir Sirry
Idea
   Shahir Sirry
Speaker
   Shahir Sirry

AUDIO

DER FUNKSPOT «KHOWF»

SFX: RAUSCHEN – GEQUIETSCHE.

Sprecher (auf Arabisch):
«Izhab al'aan illa dokaan al magalaat we eshterri megallat 'Dummy'. Mowdoo3 al shahr al 7aly howa Al-Khowf. Assalamu-Alaikum-wa rahmatu allah we barakatu.»

Derselbe Sprecher (auf Deutsch):
»Noch mal auf Deutsch: Angst – das Thema des neuen Dummy Magazin. Jetzt am Kiosk. Friede sei mit euch und die Barmherzigkeit Gottes und sein Segen.«

NOMINATION
DIGITALE MEDIEN
DIGITAL MEDIA
  Digitale Medien
  Websites
  Digital Media
  Websites

SPORTJUGEND HESSEN
»Helfen ist in Mode«

Lead Agency
  Ogilvy Frankfurt
Client
  Sportjugend Hessen im
  Landessportbund Hessen e.V.
Marketing Direction
  Sabine Rathmann, Gabriele
  Cowlan
Executive Creative Direction
  Michael Kutschinski
Creative Direction
  Petra Berghäuser, Uwe Jakob
Art Direction
  Klaus-Martin Michaelis
Client Consulting
  Sophia Berhe
Casting
  Julia Wehmeyer, Klaus-Martin
  Michaelis, Martina Diederichs,
  Magdalena Ignatowski, Knut
  Wörner, Petra Berghäuser
Concept
  Klaus-Martin Michaelis,
  Hans-Peter Junius, Uwe Jakob,
  Petra Berghäuser
Copy
  Hans-Peter Junius
Cutting
  Klaus-Martin Michaelis
Design
  Klaus-Martin Michaelis
Film Production
  Mathias Köhler,
  Matthias Czeikowitz
Graphic Design
  Klaus-Martin Michaelis
Idea
  Julia Wehmeyer, Klaus-Martin
  Michaelis, Hans-Peter Junius,
  Petra Berghäuser, Uwe Jakob
Interface Navigation
  Klaus-Martin Michaelis,
  Jens Steffen
Motion Design
  Klaus-Martin Michaelis
Motion Graphics and 3D
  Klaus-Martin Michaelis
Photography
  Knut Wörner
Programming
  Jens Steffen
Screen Design
  Klaus-Martin Michaelis
Technical Conception
  Klaus-Martin Michaelis,
  Jens Steffen
Technical Direction
  Jens Steffen
Technical Implementation
  Jens Steffen

Immer mehr Geld in Deutschland wird für luxuriöse Kinder-Sportmode ausgegeben. Gleichzeitig leben immer mehr Kinder in Armut – sogar Sport wird zum Luxus. Die Folge: soziale Ausgrenzung. Um auf diesen Missstand hinzuweisen, inszenieren wir ihn als exklusive Modenschau. Bedürftige Kinder präsentieren auf dem Laufsteg abgenutzte Sportkleidung. Man kann sofort spenden und sehen, wie man hilft.

While in Germany more and more money is spent on kids' luxurious athletic apparel, more and more kids live in poverty – sports themselves become luxury. The result: social exclusion. To generate donations, we stage the sad reality as an exclusive fashion show where needy children present their threadbare sports clothing. And our donation module makes you see right away what your donation does.

NOMINATION
DIGITALE MEDIEN
DIGITAL MEDIA
   Digitale Medien
   Websites
   Digital Media
   Websites

STEPHAN SCHNEIDER
'COLLECTION SS2011'
»www.stephanschneider.be«

Lead Agency
   Chewing the Sun
Client
   Stephan Schneider
Creative Direction
   Chewing the Sun
Casting
   Tomorrow Is Another Day
Cutting
   David Gödel
Photography
   Stefan Heinrichs,
   Camera Moving Stills:
   Stefan Heinrichs,
   Samuel Perriard

Die Kollektion Spring/Summer 2011 des Modedesigners Stephan Schneider wird online mit Moving Stills statt statischen Fotos gezeigt. Jeder Look wird von einem anderen Model präsentiert.

For presenting the Stephan Schneider spring/summer 2011 collection online, we use moving stills instead of static images. The collection is presented by a number of models, each of which is wearing a different look.

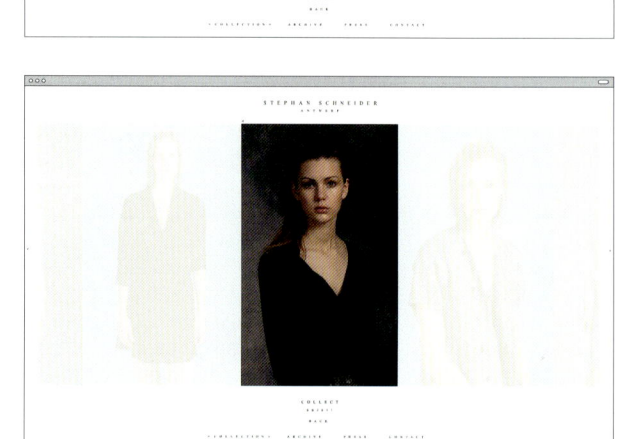

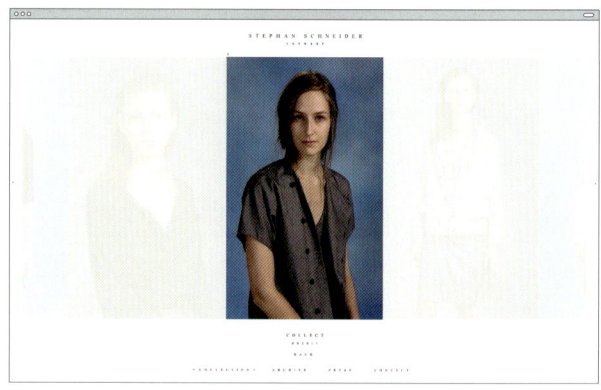

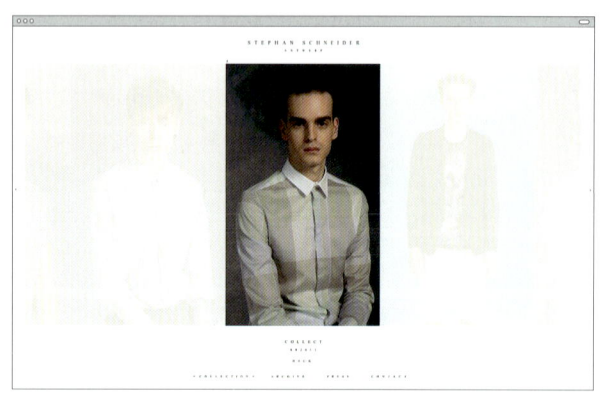

● NOMINATION
DIGITALE MEDIEN
DIGITAL MEDIA
 Digitale Medien
 Social Media
 Digital Media
 Social Media

IKEA
 »Billygramm«

Lead Agency
 Ogilvy Frankfurt
Client
 IKEA Deutschland GmbH & Co. KG
Advertising Direction
 Katja Sottmeier
Executive Creative Direction
 Dr. Stephan Vogel
Creative Direction
 Michael Kutschinski,
 Dr. Ulf Schmidt,
 Uwe Jakob
Art Direction
 Daniel Schweinzer
Client Consulting
 Frank Apel,
 Christian Thiel
Computer Animation
 Valentina Kusmin,
 Sebastian Hilbert
Copy
 Marcus Pfeiffer
Idea
 Daniel Schweinzer,
 Marcus Pfeiffer
Motion Graphics and 3D
 Klaus-Martin Michaelis
Technical Direction
 Jens Steffen
Typography
 Daniel Schweinzer,
 Tanja Oppel

Inhalte ändern sich, Billy bleibt. Seit 30 Jahren. Und weil das auch in Zukunft so sein wird, entwickelten wir etwas ganz Besonderes: die Facebook Application Billygramm. User konnten sich gegenseitig animierte Botschaften aus Billy-Regalen auf die Pinnwand posten. Sie füllten die Regale mit ihrem Inhalt und erlebten, wie die Billys ihre Botschaft transportierten.

Content changes – Billy stays the same. For 30 years. And because that will also be the case in the future, we developed something special: a Facebook App called Billygram. Users were able to post animated messages written with Billy storage racks on each other's walls. They created content out of racks and saw how Billy transmitted the message.

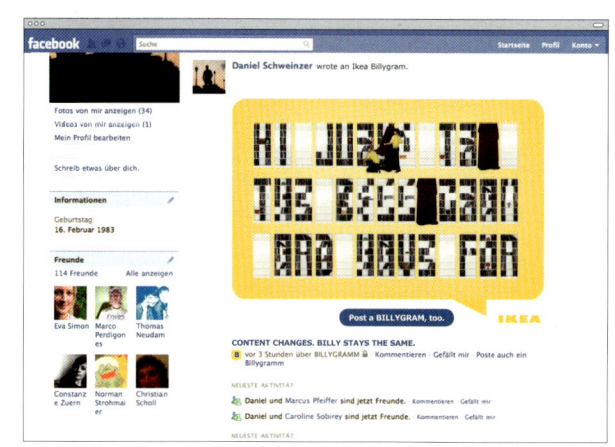

**NOMINATION
DIGITALE MEDIEN
DIGITAL MEDIA**
   Digitale Medien
   Social Media
   Digital Media
   Social Media

—

SONY PLAYSTATION GT5
»Tragt es auf der Strecke aus«

Lead Agency
   Ogilvy Frankfurt
Client
   Sony Computer Entertainment Deutschland GmbH
Marketing Direction
   Ulrich Barbian
Executive Creative Direction
   Michael Kutschinski
Creative Direction
   Uwe Jakob,
   Matthias Storath
Art Direction
   Uwe Jakob,
   Andre Bourguignon,
   Jan Schulz,
   Markus Müller,
   Marco Weber
Client Consulting
   Martin Molter,
   Felix Rompis
Strategic Planning
   Frank Tavidde,
   Benjamin Ringwald
Agency Production
   Jennifer Porst
Audio Production
   Sinus AV Tonstudio
Computer Animation
   Virtual Republic
Concept
   Benjamin Ringwald
Copy
   Nico Schneider,
   Christian Urbanski
Cutting
   Felipe Ascacibar
Film Production
   Doity Production
Innovative Technologies
   Jens Steffen,
   Ralf Zimmermann
Motion Design
   Klaus-Martin Michaelis
Screen Design
   Markus Müller
Other
   Film Direction:
   Felipe Ascacibar
   Animation:
   Matthias Czeikowitz

Als erstes Rennspiel wird GT5 mit dem Echtzeit-Online-Multiplayer-Modus zum sozialen Netzwerk. Deswegen muss das Spiel auch im sozialen Netzwerk beworben werden. Idee: "Challenge your Friends." Eine Facebook-Kampagne, in der die Spieler sich auf provokative Art und Weise gegenseitig heiß auf das Spiel machen.

The task is to make a live experience of the battle feeling of the unique GT5 multi-player mode and to get players excited to race against friends on PS3. The perfect platform for an online face-off is facebook. But their ad spaces are too small and they didn't allow us a profile takeover. So, we rebuilt the profile pages as a replica. Users had the impression that they were still on Facebook.

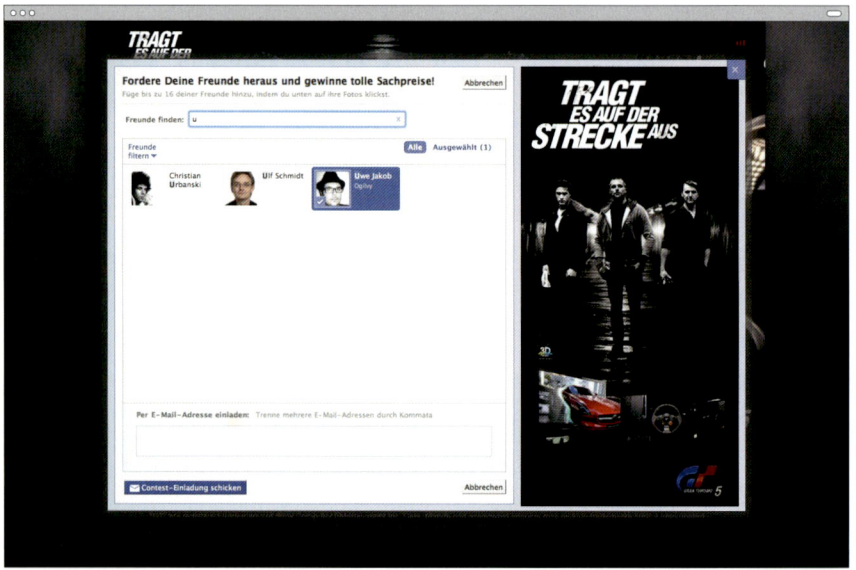

● NOMINATION
DIGITALE MEDIEN
DIGITAL MEDIA
 Digitale Medien
 Mobile
 Digital Media
 Mobile

AUDI
 "Augmented Reality Kalender"

Lead Agency
 Neue Digitale/Razorfish GmbH
Client
 Audi AG
Marketing Direction
 Tim Gotthardt
Executive Creative Direction
 Sven Küster
Creative Direction
 René Lamberti,
 Fabian Roser
Art Direction
 Kathrin Laser
Client Consulting
 Sascha Martini (MD),
 Kristina Klein,
 Dorte Lücker
Computer Animation
 David Löhr
Concept
 Alexander Ardelean
Consulting
 Kristina Klein,
 Dorte Lücker
Copy
 Stephan Deisenhofer,
 Steffen Stäuber
Design
 Bartosz Elsner,
 Florian Uihlein,
 Jens Lembke,
 Julien Pietri
Production
 Commsult AG
Programming
 Dennis Hantke,
 Dirk Tech (Commsult AG)
Sound Design
 Powder & Louder,
 Echo & Gold,
 Benecke & Preisendörfer GbR
Technical Direction
 Paul Schmidt
Technical Implementation
 Mathis Moder
Other
 Printing: Storck Druckerei
 GmbH & Co. KG

Ein Autokalender ohne Autos! Im Kalender selbst waren nur hochwertige Landschaftsfotos zu sehen. Um die Autos zu erleben, musste man zusätzlich eine iPhone App herunterladen. Mit Hilfe der Technik "Augmented Reality" konnte man die Autos dann vor dem passenden Hintergrund zum Leben erwecken – inklusive Animation und Sound! Ein perfektes Beispiel für »Vorsprung durch Technik«.

A car calendar without cars! The calendar showed only beautiful landscapes. In order to experience the cars, the user had to download an iPhone application. Using the augmented reality technology, one could then bring out the cars onto the landscapes. With sounds, animations and all! The perfect illustration of »Vorsprung durch Technik«.

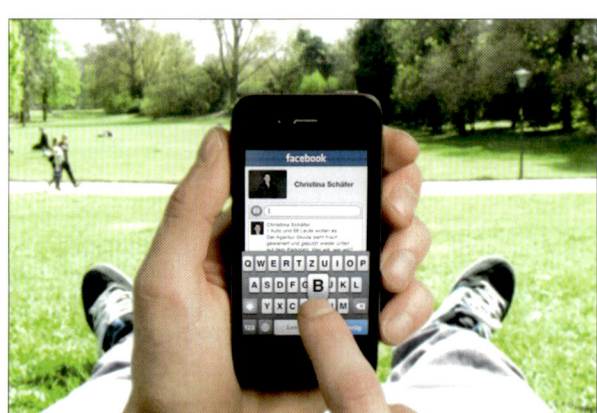

NOMINATION
DIGITALE MEDIEN
DIGITAL MEDIA
　Digitale Medien
　Mobile
　Digital Media
　Mobile

LEAGAS DELANEY
»Die Copytest App«

Lead Agency
　Leagas Delaney Hamburg
　GmbH
Client
　Leagas Delaney Hamburg
　GmbH
Marketing Direction
　Stefan Zschaler
Executive Creative Direction
　Hermann Waterkamp,
　Stefan Zschaler
Creative Direction
　Oliver Grandt
Art Direction
　Ole Kleinhans
Client Consulting
　Sandra Kurth
Strategic Planning
　Mareike Boddin
Copy
　Björn Neugebauer,
　Jakob Eckstein
Graphic Design
　Markus Schmidt
Idea
　Björn Neugebauer,
　Ole Kleinhans
Illustration
　Ole Kleinhans,
　Markus Schmidt
Interactive Production
　Sven Schmiede
Programming
　Cranberry Production GmbH
Technical Conception
　Sven Schmiede
Technical Implementation
　Leagas Delaney Integrated
　Productions

　Wie rekrutiert man kreativen Nachwuchs aus der Generation Facebook? Indem man einen zeitgemäßen Copytest entwickelt – als App.

　How should the copytest be redesigned if an advertising agency wants to recruit fresh talent from Generation Facebook? As an app, of course.

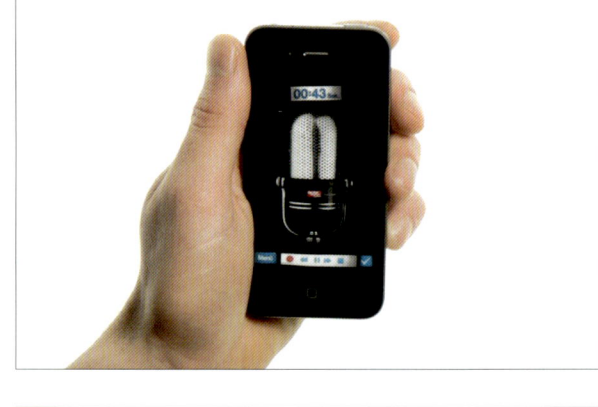

340

NOMINATION
DIGITALE MEDIEN
DIGITAL MEDIA
   Digitale Medien
   Online-Werbemaßnahmen
   Digital Media
   Online Advertising

MERCEDES-BENZ SLS AMG
»Stuttgarter Sportwagen«

Lead Agency
   Elephant Seven Hamburg GmbH
Client
   Mercedes-Benz Vertrieb Deutschland
Executive Creative Direction
   Oliver Viets
Creative Direction
   Kai Becker
Art Direction
   Oliver Baus,
   Lana Bragina
Client Consulting
   Söhnke Wulff,
   Jost Thedens
Agency Production
   Elephant Seven Hamburg GmbH
Computer Animation
   Oleg Friesen
Consulting
   Söhnke Wulff,
   Jost Thedens
Copy
   Benjamin Bruno,
   Julia Molina
Motion Design
   Oleg Friesen,
   Christopher Remmers
Programming
   Tobias Ruprecht (Flash)

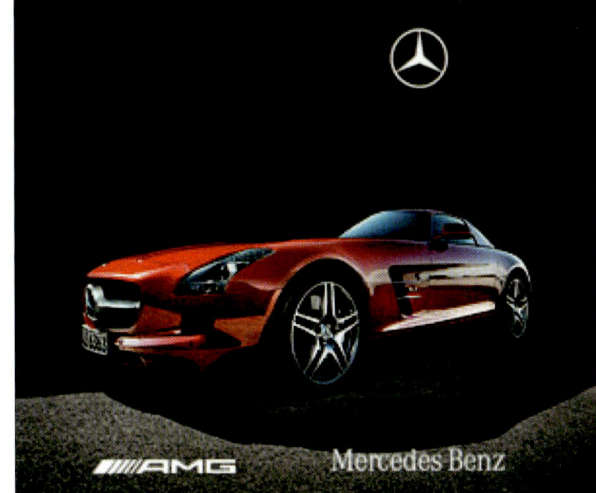

NOMINATION
DIGITALE MEDIEN
DIGITAL MEDIA
  Digitale Medien
  Online-Werbemaßnahmen
  Digital Media
  Online Advertising

SCHÜLER COMMUNITY-CENTER
»Schüler Surprise Images«

Lead Agency
  Jung von Matt AG
Client
  Schueler.CC
Marketing Direction
  Steffen Presse
Executive Creative Direction
  Sascha Hanke
Creative Direction
  Jo Marie Farwick,
  Nicole Holzenkamp
Art Direction
  Daniel Breining
Client Consulting
  André Martens
Concept
  Ali Antzar,
  Daniel Breining
Copy
  Ali Antzar
Graphic Design
  Daniel Breining
Production
    Supercomm Data Marketing,
    Bonn – Sven Nobereit

Pop-ups und Banner haben ausgedient. Gerade Jugendliche nehmen sie kaum noch wahr. Um diese Zielgruppe im Netz trotzdem zu erreichen, gibt es jetzt die Schüler-Surprise-Images: Banner, die hinter dem Text versteckt sind und erst dann sichtbar werden, wenn man den Text markiert. Genau das macht sich Schueler.cc zunutze und holt die Kids dort ab, wo sie es nie erwarten würden: hinter dem Referat!

Pop-ups und banner ads have run their course. Young people barely notice them anymore. But now "Schüler Surprise Images" have been created to reach them online anyway. Banners that are hidden behind text, and only become visible when the text is highlighted. The website Schüler.cc is using this to its advantage, and grabbing kids' attention where they would never expect it: behind an essay!

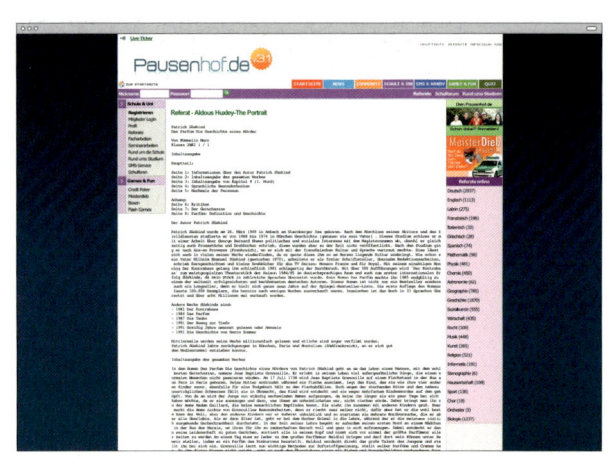

342

NOMINATION
DIGITALE MEDIEN
DIGITAL MEDIA
Digitale Medien
Digitale Medienformate
im Raum
Digital Media
Digital Media Environment
Design

IHK FRANKFURT – LICHTSKULPTUR
»Puls der Stadt«

Lead Agency
  BlueMars – Gesellschaft für digitale Kommunikation mbH in Cooperation with shift GmbH
Client
  Industrie- und Handelskammer Frankfurt
Executive Creative Direction
  Tobias Kirchhofer (BlueMars), Stefan Walz (shift)
Creative Direction
  Stefan Walz
Art Direction
  Natalya Etaryan, Marcus Goldemann
Client Consulting
  Frank Auth
Strategic Planning
  Dorothea Feurer
Agency Production
  Matthias Muck
Audio Production
  Sara Walz
Computer Animation
  Sebastian Maus
Consulting
  Timm Nüchter
Design
  Natalya Etaryan
Film Production
  Sara Walz
Idea
  Tobias Kirchhofer, Stefan Walz
Image Processing
  Matthias Muck, Natalya Etaryan
IT Direction
  Sebastian Maus
Photography
  Timm Nüchter
Postproduction
  Sara Walz
Programming
  Daniel Seebald, Rene Kermici
Sound Design
  Robert Heel
Technical Direction
  Ted Markson, Edmundas Balciunas
Technical Installation
  Ted Markson, Edmundas Balciunas
Other
  Nicole Wiegand, Sandra Reiß, Alexander Scherf, Anja Pontoriero

»Puls der Stadt« macht den Herzschlag von Frankfurt sichtbar. Gemessen wird er an den digitalen Schlagadern der Metropole: den Online-Daten zum Flugverkehr, den Börsennotierungen, der Verkehrsdichte, Konversationen in sozialen Netzwerken usw. Die aufgezeichneten Daten der vergangenen 24 Stunden steuern 16 LED-Kuben, die den Puls der Stadt in dreidimensionalen Animationen sicht- und hörbar machen.

The digital installation "Pulse of the City" makes the heartbeat of Frankfurt visible. It measures the digital arteries of the city: online data for air traffic, stock market quotations, traffic density, conversations in social networks, etc. The recorded data of the past 24 hours controls 16 LED cubes, which make the pulse of the city visible and audible in three-dimensional animations.

NOMINATION
DIGITALE MEDIEN
DIGITAL MEDIA
   Digitale Medien
   Digitale Kampagnen
   Digital Media
   Digital Campaigns

IKEA KATALOGEINFÜHRUNG 2010/2011
   »Der IKEA Katalog kommt nicht allein.«

Lead Agency
   Grimm Gallun Holtappels
Client
   IKEA Deutschland GmbH & Co. KG
Marketing Direction
   Claudia Wilvonseder
Advertising Direction
   Hendrik Zimmer
Executive Creative Direction
   Nils Gallun, Florian Grimm
Creative Direction
   Nils Gallun, Florian Grimm, Matthias M. Müller
Art Direction
   Tobias Mausolf
Client Consulting
   Torben Erhorn, Chris Wind
Agency Production
   Hermann Krug CFS,
   Marcella Wegener,
   Antje von Zitzewitz
Audio Production
   Studio Funk
Copy
   Imke Hemig, Nina Puri
Cutting
   Christian Auerswald,
   Erfan Moniri, Rodian Stiehl
Design
   Tobias Mausolf
Editing
   Lennart Reip,
   Andrea Afflerbach,
   Carla Dropkewitz,
   Oliver Dütschke,
   Wiebke Heygster,
   Marc Jägermann,
   Beatrice Möller,
   Nicole Schreiber,
   Maik Vukan,
   Carolin Otterbach
Film Production
   539090, VCC, SEED
Idea
   IKEA
Interface Navigation
   Tobias Mausolf
Motion Design
   Mario Korb
Programming
   Mario Korb,
   Michael Kneib,
   Michael Sturm,
   Frank Butenhoff,
   Martin Thielicke
Screen Design
   Tobias Mausolf

Der IKEA Katalog 2010/2011 kommt nicht allein. Schwedische Einrichtungsexperten bringen ihn persönlich nach Deutschland und verschönern über 100 Haushalte.

The 2010/2011 IKEA catalog won't be coming alone. Swedish furnishing experts will be bringing it to Germany in person, and transforming over 100 households.

NOMINATION
DIGITALE MEDIEN
DIGITAL MEDIA
  Digitale Medien
  Digitale Kampagnen
  Digital Media
  Digital Campaigns

MCDONALD'S
  »Nürnburger«

Lead Agency
  Neue Digitale/Razorfish GmbH
Client
  McDonald's Deutschland
Marketing Direction
  Rainer Saborny,
  Birte Teufel
Executive Creative Direction
  Sven Küster
Creative Direction
  René Lamberti
Art Direction
  Sanjay Gill,
  Sebastian Skowronek
Client Consulting
  Mathias Sinn,
  Norman Rockmann,
  Lukas Kammerer
Strategic Planning
  Alina Hückelkamp
Concept
  Alexander Ardelean,
  Ramona Stöcker
Film Production
  Stink GmbH, Berlin
Graphic Design
  Kathrina Vogel,
  Julia Weidemann
Production
  Nils Schwemer,
  Christian Brochot
Other
  Technical Director:
  Paul Schmidt
  Senior Technical Architect:
  Mathis Moder
  Application Developer:
  Pieter Snoeck

McDonald's plante in Kooperation mit Uli Hoeneß ein Produkt namens »Nürnburger« herauszubringen. Die Zutaten für den skurrilen Burger: drei Original Nürnburger Rostbratwürstchen (aus Uli Hoeneß' Wurst-Fabrik, einer der größten in Deutschland) in einer Semmel – dazu Senf und Röstzwiebeln. Die Herausforderung: das Aktionsprodukt sollte ohne traditionelle Medien beworben werden.

In cooperation with the former German football star Uli Hoeneß, McDonald's planned to launch a product named »Nürnburger«. The ingredients: three original »Nürnberger Rostbratwürstchen« (a small, thin variety of the German Bratwurst, sourced from Uli Hoeneß's sausage factory) in a bread bun – with mustard and roasted onions. The challenge was to promote the burger without traditional media.

● NOMINATION
DIGITALE MEDIEN
DIGITAL MEDIA
    Digitale Medien
    Digitale Kampagnen
    Digital Media
    Digital Campaigns

PRITT
    "Paper Gang"

Lead Agency
    Syzygy Deutschland GmbH
Contributing Agencies
    uniquedigital GmbH (Media)
Client
    Henkel AG & Co. KGaA
Creative Direction
    Dominik Lammer
Art Direction
    Alexander Meinhardt,
    Christina Metzler,
    Wolfgang Schröder
Client Consulting
    Susanne Lehr
Copy
    Dorothee Zoll,
    Sarah Winkler
Design
    Thorsten Binder,
    Sonja Johnke
Programming
    Eric Hofmann,
    Leonardo Paredes

Kinder kennen Pritt. Erwachsene auch. Teens nicht. Die sind, wo Pritt nicht ist: online. Sie zu erreichen, erforderte die Vereinigung von Digital und Analog im Zeichen des Bastelns – und im Namen von Pritt. Die Paper Gang hat, was bei Digital Natives punktet: Web-Credibility. Ihre Social Profiles und Bannerkampagne promoteten den Stop-Motion-Contest, der »selbstgebastelt« in "user-gen" verwandelte.

Kids know Pritt. As do adults. Teens don't – they are where Pritt isn't: online. Reaching them required unifying digital and analog in the spirit of crafting – and in the name of Pritt. The Paper Gang has digital native's currency: web credibility. Their social profiles and banner campaign promoted the Gang-starring stop motion contest that showed what happens when "self-made" becomes "user-gen".

● NOMINATION
**DIALOGMARKETING/
PROMOTION/MEDIA
DIALOG MARKETING/
PROMOTION/MEDIA**
 Dialogmarketing
 Dialog Mail
 Dialog Marketing
 Dialog Mail

ALL4FAMILY
 »Memory für Eltern«

Lead Agency
 DDB Tribal Group
Client
 all4family
Marketing Direction
 Martina Krenn
Executive Creative Direction
 Eric Schoeffler
Creative Direction
 Hannes Böker,
 Werner Celand,
 Sebastian Kainz
Art Direction
 Dietmar Kreil
Client Consulting
 Lele Grasl
Agency Production
 Beate Hinterreither
Copy
 Stefan Friedrich

Das Elternmagazin All4family schickte ein Mailing an Leser, deren Abo vor dem Auslaufen stand. Mit dabei: ein Memory-Spiel, bei dem der Text auf der Kartenrückseite das Motiv der Vorderseite verrät! Durch diesen Trick gewinnen die Eltern garantiert gegen ihre Kinder. Zumindest, solange diese noch nicht lesen können. Was beweist: in Familienangelegenheiten können Eltern auf All4family vertrauen!

All4family parents magazine sent a direct mail to subscribers whose standing order was about to expire. Attached as a loyalty gift: a special Pairs game with a text on the back of each card revealing the motif! Thanks to this clever detail, parents are guaranteed to win against their kids – until they learn to read. The game proved to subscribers that All4family is truly the parents' best friend.

● NOMINATION
DIALOGMARKETING/
PROMOTION/MEDIA
DIALOG MARKETING/
PROMOTION/MEDIA
  Dialogmarketing
  Dialog Mail
  Dialog Marketing
  Dialog Mail

MENSCHENRECHTE (REPORTER OHNE GRENZEN)
»Sonderstempel«

Lead Agency
  Serviceplan
Client
  Reporter ohne Grenzen
  Österreich
Marketing Direction
  Mag. Hanna Ronzheimer
Executive Creative Direction
  Alexander Schill
Creative Direction
  Christoph Everke,
  Cosimo Möller,
  Alexander Nagel
Client Consulting
  Nadine Wintrich
Graphic Design
  Elena Ressel,
  Annalena Bottmann

Die internationale Organisation Reporter ohne Grenzen kämpft weltweit für die Freilassung unschuldig inhaftierter Journalisten. Zum Internationalen Tag der Menschenrechte 2010 eröffneten wir ein Postamt mit einem eigens gestalteten Poststempel und Sondermarken, welche die Portraits inhaftierter Journalisten zeigten. Das Stempeln der Briefmarke setzte das Portrait sozusagen »hinter Gitter«.

The international organization Reporters without Borders fights worldwide for the discharge of innocently detained journalists. On the International Day of Human Rights, we opened our own post-office having an own post-mark and stamps showing the portraits of detained journalists. Through marking the stamp, the portrait got figuratively put behind bars.

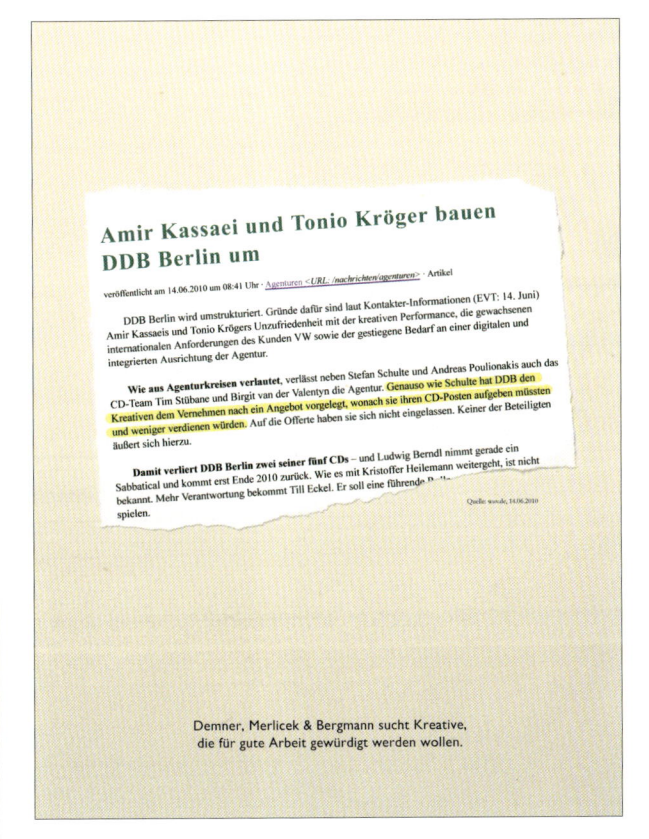

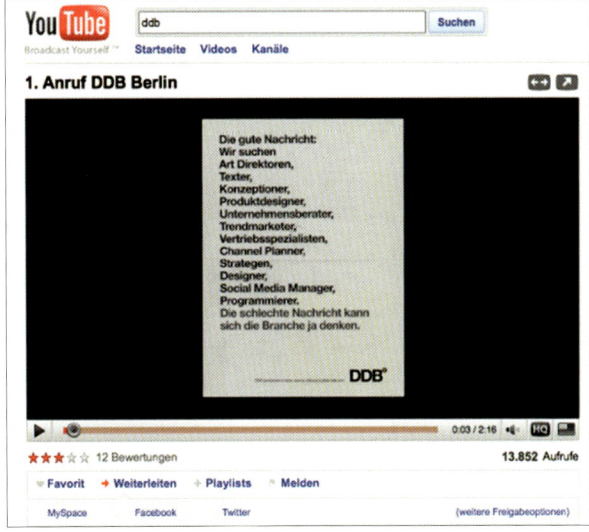

NOMINATION
DIALOGMARKETING/
PROMOTION/MEDIA
DIALOG MARKETING/
PROMOTION/MEDIA
  Dialogmarketing
  Dialog Crossmediale
  Kampagnen
  Dialog Marketing
  Dialog Cross-Media
  Campaigns

DEMNER, MERLICEK &
BERGMANN
"DMB vs. DDB"

Lead Agency
  Demner, Merlicek & Bergmann
Client
  Demner, Merlicek & Bergmann
Creative Direction
  Francesco Bestagno,
  Alexander Hofmann,
  Mariusz Jan Demner
Art Direction
  Francesco Bestagno
Client Consulting
  Siegfried Kaufmann
Copy
  Alexander Hofmann
Interactive Production
  Albert Waaijenberg
Other
  Graphics: Claudia Strauß

DDB Wien suchte 2009 u.a. Social Media Manager. Wir fragten bei DDBs in Deutschland nach. Doch gab es diese Positionen nirgends. Die Anrufe wurden via Youtube zum Branchengespräch. DDB revanchierte sich 2010 durch konzertierte Abwerbungen. Obwohl gerade exzellente Köpfe bei DDB Berlin frei wurden. Also suchten wir dort mit Bannern und Anzeigen nach neuen Mitarbeitern und wurden "Talk of Town".

2009 DDB Vienna looked for "Social Media Managers", among others. We inquired further at German DDB offices. However, no such jobs were known there. Through Youtube, these phone calls soon became the talk of the ad industry. DDB's revenge in 2010: concerted enticements. Even though brilliant minds had just left DDB Berlin. With banners and ads we looked for new employees there – becoming the talk of the town.

**NOMINATION
DIALOGMARKETING/
PROMOTION/MEDIA
DIALOG MARKETING/
PROMOTION/MEDIA**
　Dialogmarketing
　Dialog Crossmediale
　Kampagnen
　Dialog Marketing
　Dialog Cross-Media
　Campaigns

STÄDEL MUSEUM
　»Frankfurt baut das neue
　Städel«

Lead Agency
　Ogilvy Frankfurt
Client
　Städel Museum
Advertising Direction
　Kerstin Schultheis
Executive Creative Direction
　Dr. Stephan Vogel
Creative Direction
　Dr. Stephan Vogel,
　Christian Mommertz,
　Helmut Meyer
Art Direction
　Daniel Schweinzer,
　Helmut Meyer
Client Consulting
　Sabina Pal
Strategic Planning
　Ralph Poser,
　Anna Höhn
Copy
　Dr. Stephan Vogel,
　Marcus Pfeiffer,
　Lukas Liske

　Für seine Sammlung moderner Kunst baut das Städel Museum eine Erweiterung. Dafür fehlten 5 Mio. Euro an Spendengeldern. Aber: Es ist schwierig, Spenden zu sammeln, wenn man kein Mediabuget hat und keine süßen Tiere zeigen kann, sondern moderne Kunst. Deshalb entwickelten wir keine Werbekampagne, sondern erklärten das neue Städel zu einem Projekt für ganz Frankfurt: Alle Einwohner können Botschafter des Museums werden.

　The Städel Museum Frankfurt builds an extension for its vast collection of modern art. But they are still short of 5 million euros and fund raising is tough. Especially, when there is no media budget and no cute animal to open donators' wallets. So, instead of advertising, we turned the new Städel into a project for the whole city: All Frankfurt citizens can become ambassadors of their museum.

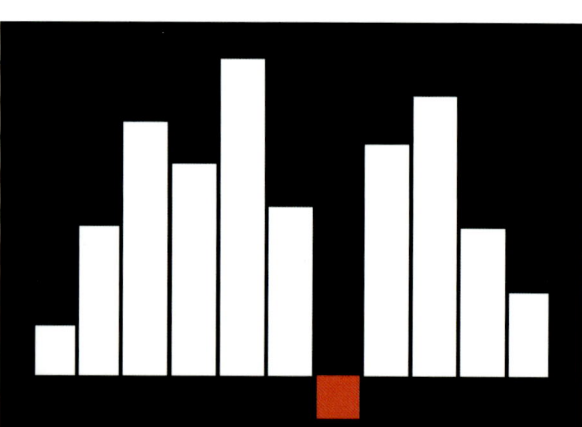

**NOMINATION
DIALOGMARKETING/
PROMOTION/MEDIA DIALOG
MARKETING/PROMOTION/
MEDIA**

Dialogmarketing
Dialog Social Media
Kampagnen
Dialog Marketing
Dialog Social Media
Campaigns

FC ST. PAULI
»Schädelgenerator«

Lead Agency
  Jung von Matt AG
Contributing Agencies
  Jung von Matt/Elbe GmbH
Client
  FC St. Pauli
Marketing Direction
  Thomas Wegmann
Executive Creative Direction
  Sascha Hanke
Creative Direction
  Jo Marie Farwick,
  Nicole Holzenkamp,
  Tobias Grimm,
  Jens Pfau
Art Direction
  Julia Stoffer,
  Benjamin Busse,
  Sven Gabriel
Client Consulting
  Sascha Kurfiss
Concept
  Björn A. Lange
Copy
  Florian Hoffmann
Cutting
  Niels Münter
Production
  Markenfilm Crossing
Screen Design
  David Aufdembrinke
Sound Design
  Audioforce

Zum 100. Geburtstag des FC St. Pauli gaben wir Fans die Möglichkeit, auf Schaedelgenerator.de ein Foto von sich hochzuladen. Aus diesem Bild wurde dann automatisch ein individualisierbarer Totenschädel generiert. So entstand das wohl persönlichste Logo, das es jemals für einen Bundesligaclub gab. Und egal, wie die Saison gelaufen ist: Wir glauben an euren Wiederaufstieg, Jungs!

To mark the 100th birthday of FC St. Pauli, we gave fans the opportunity to upload their picture to skullgenerator.com. A skull and crossbones were automatically generated from the photo, which could subsequently be personalized. Thus, we created the most individual football-club logo ever. And no matter how the season turned out – we believe you'll return to the Bundesliga, guys!

NOMINATION
DIALOGMARKETING/
PROMOTION/MEDIADIALOG
MARKETING/PROMOTION/
MEDIA
  Dialogmarketing
  Dialog Alternative
  Dialog Marketing
  Dialog Alternative

KOLLE REBBE
"The Damn-Hot-Lovely-Christmas-Store"

Lead Agency
  Kolle Rebbe/KOREFE
Client
  Kolle Rebbe GmbH
Marketing Direction
  Stefan Kolle
Creative Direction
  Katrin Oeding
Art Direction
  Christian Doering
Client Consulting
  Marie Steinhoff
Copy
  Fabian Bill,
  Gereon Klug,
  Thomas Völker
Final Artwork
  Maik Spreen
Graphic Design
  Saara Järvinen,
  Derya Sevim,
  Marko Grewe
Production
  Franziska Ziegler

Kolle Rebbe eröffnet zum Nikolaustag ein Kaufhaus voller Weihnachtsgeschenke exklusiv für seine Mitarbeiter: den Damn-Hot-Lovely-Christmas-Store. Dort gibt es 80 Geschenke in vier verschiedenen Preiskategorien, die man sich mit der eigens entwickelten Währung »Kolle Rebbe Kronen« kaufen kann.

On St. Nicolas day, Kolle Rebbe opened a department store exclusively for employees: the Damn-Hot-Lovely-Christmas-Store. There, 80 Christmas presents were available in four price categories, and could be bought with "Kolle Rebbe Crowns".

352

**NOMINATION
DIALOGMARKETING/
PROMOTION/MEDIADIALOG
MARKETING/PROMOTION/
MEDIA**
  Dialogmarketing
  Dialog Alternative
  Dialog Marketing
  Dialog Alternative

**SCHOLZ & FRIENDS
RECRUITING**
  «Pizza Digitale»

Lead Agency
  Scholz & Friends
Client
  Scholz & Friends Hamburg
Executive Creative Direction
  Matthias Schmidt
Creative Direction
  Marc Kittel,
  Pedro Sydow
Art Direction
  Stefan Schabenberger
Client Consulting
  Jessica Modschiedler
Copy
  Christopher Nothegger
Graphic Design
  Kathrin Fach
Image Processing
  Alireza Rashidi
Programming
  Aleksandr Lossenko
Technical Direction
  Andreas Maser

Zusammen mit Croque Master entwickelte Scholz & Friends die Pizza Digitale, die vier Wochen lang kostenlos ausgeliefert wurde – an Agenturen, in denen potenzielle Bewerber Überstunden schieben. Das Rezept war einfach: Pizzateig mit Tomatensauce in Form eines QR-Codes, der direkt auf eine mobile Landingpage führte. So erreichten wir genau die, die wir haben wollten: digitale Kreative.

Scholz & Friends and Croque Master created the Pizza Digitale, which was delivered free of charge for a period of four weeks – to agencies where potential applicants were working overtime. A pizza base topped with a tomato-sauce QR-code, which redirected the user directly to a mobile landing page. This ensured that our message was targeted at exactly the right kind of people: at digital creatives.

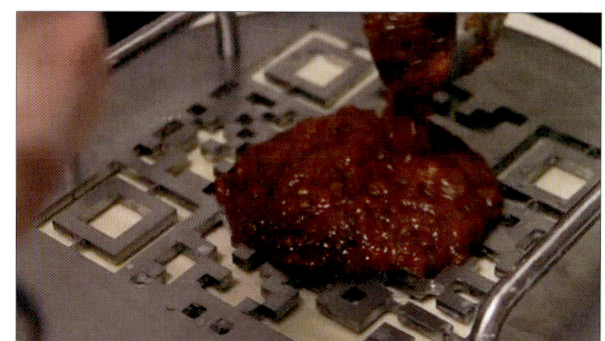

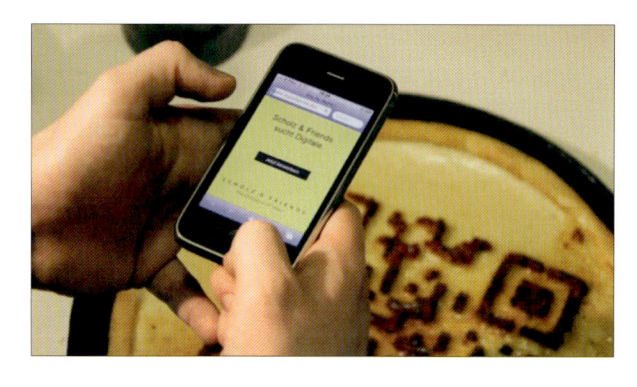

353

**NOMINATION
DIALOGMARKETING/
PROMOTION/MEDIA** **DIALOG
MARKETING/PROMOTION/
MEDIA**
    Promotion
    Aktivitäten
    Promotion
    Activities

SPORTSCHECK – WIR MACHEN SPORT
    "Sporty Vouchers"

Lead Agency
    Ogilvy Frankfurt
Client
    SportScheck GmbH
Marketing Direction
    Carsten Schürg
Advertising Direction
    Claudia Schneider
Executive Creative Direction
    Michael Kutschinski,
    Dr. Stephan Vogel
Creative Direction
    Uwe Jakob
Art Direction
    Christian Urbanski
Client Consulting
    Frank Apel,
    Katharina Marsenger
Copy
    Christian Urbanski,
    Petra Berghäuser
Photography
    Mathias Köhler

Zur Mitte der Wintersaison möchte Sportscheck in Frankfurt am Main mit einer starken Aktion den Abverkauf seiner Wintersportartikel steigern und Kunden für den Spaß im Schnee begeistern. Miniatur-Snowboarder und -Skifahrer machen zugeschneite Autos in Frankfurt zu abgefahrenen Skipisten. Sie wecken Lust auf Wintersport und sind gleichzeitig Aktionsgutscheine für die neue Wintersportausrüstung.

Midway through the winter sports season, Sportscheck in Frankfurt asked for an impactful promotional idea to drive sales of winter sports equipment and to remind people that snow can be great fun. Miniature snowboarders and skiers turned cars covered in snow into skid-marked ski-slopes. They showed the fun side of winter sports – and were also discount vouchers for winter sports equipment.

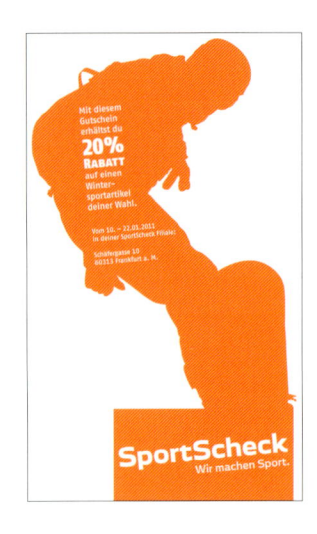

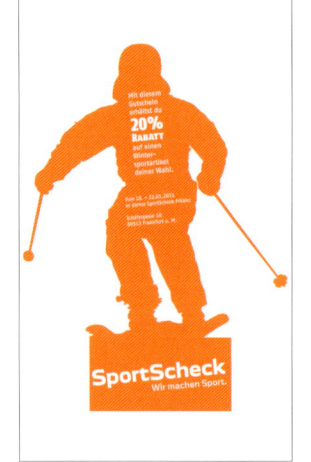

NOMINATION
DIALOGMARKETING/
PROMOTION/MEDIA DIALOG
MARKETING/PROMOTION/
MEDIA
 Promotion
 Aktivitäten
 Promotion
 Activities

TAGES ANZEIGER
»Dranbleiben 2.0«

Lead Agency
 Spillmann/Felser/Leo Burnett
Client
 Tages Anzeiger,
 Tamedia
Marketing Direction
 Marcel Tappeiner
Advertising Direction
 Cyril Hänggi
Executive Creative Direction
 Martin Spillmann
Creative Direction
 Peter Brönnimann
Art Direction
 Dana Wirz
Client Consulting
 Andy Stäheli
Copy
 Peter Brönnimann

Seit 15 Jahren geht es bei der Tages-Anzeiger-Werbung ums Dranbleiben. 2010 wurden erstmals die Leserinnen und Leser eingeladen, zu zeigen, an welchen Themen der Tages-Anzeiger dranbleiben soll.

For 15 years, the Tages-Anzeiger adverts have been all about keeping up to date. In 2010, for the first time readers were invited to show which topics they wanted the Tages-Anzeiger to stick to.

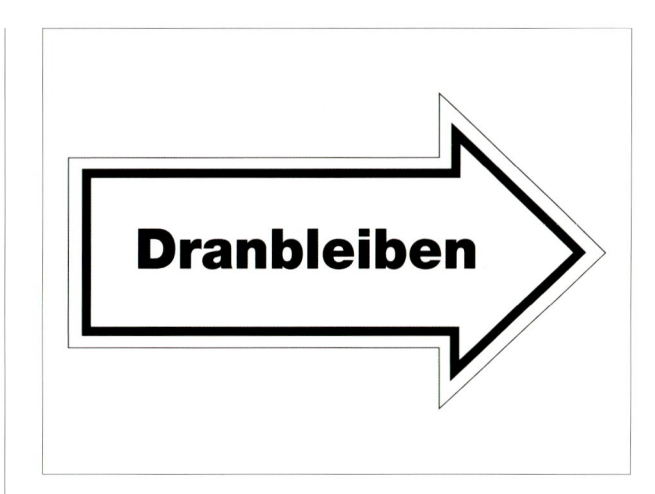

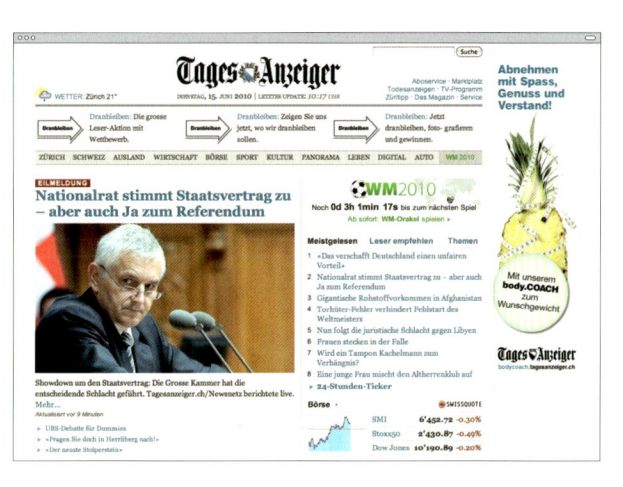

**NOMINATION
DIALOGMARKETING/
PROMOTION/MEDIADIALOG
MARKETING/PROMOTION/
MEDIA**
    Promotion
    Mittel
    Promotion
    Means

**EXTRA PROFESSIONAL
POLAR-FRESH**
    »Minz Tickets«

Lead Agency
    BBDO Proximity GmbH,
    Duesseldorf
Client
    Wrigley GmbH
Executive Creative Direction
    Sebastian Hardieck,
    Wolfgang Schneider
Creative Direction
    Carsten Bolk (ECD)
Art Direction
    Michael Plückhahn,
    Gustavo Vieria Dias
Client Consulting
    Sonja Struss,
    Silke Joosten
Agency Production
    Steffen Gentis (Head of TV)
Audio Production
    Studio Funk GmbH,
    Duesseldorf
Copy
    Isabel Campagna
Film Production
    Sytwala tv, Duesseldorf
Postproduction
    Sytwala tv, Duesseldorf
Speaker
    Stephan Schleberger
Other
    Sound Engineering:
    Marco Manzo

Jeder kennt den Moment: Man fährt ins Parkhaus und hat keine Hand für das Parkticket frei. Automatisch steckt man es sich zwischen die Lippen, während man sich in Richtung Parklücke manövriert. Genau das wollte Wrigley zu einer angenehmeren Erfahrung machen – und entwickelte deshalb das erste Parkticket mit Minz-Geschmack. Passend zur Markensaussage: Mundpflege für unterwegs.

Every driver knows the situation when you drive into the parking lot: you haven't got a free hand for the parking ticket. Automatically, you put it between your lips and drive to a parking space. Based on this observation, Wrigley decided to make that a more pleasant experience. By creating the first mint flavored parking ticket and thus strengthens the brand message: oral care to go.

● NOMINATION
DIALOGMARKETING/
PROMOTION/MEDIA DIALOG
MARKETING/PROMOTION/
MEDIA
  Promotion
  Mittel
  Promotion
  Means

IWC SCHAFFHAUSEN
»Das erste Bewerbungsbogen-puzzle«

Lead Agency
  Jung von Matt AG
Client
  IWC International Watch Co. AG
Marketing Direction
  Karoline Huber
Advertising Direction
  Thomas Scheuring
Executive Creative Direction
  Armin Jochum,
  Fabian Frese
Creative Direction
  Daniel Frericks
Art Direction
  Sebastian Schnell
Client Consulting
  Nils Frommann,
  Maurice Moitroux
Art Buying
  Karen Blome
Concept
  Tobias Feige,
  Sebastian Schnell
Copy
  Tobias Feige
Design
  Sebastian Schnell
Graphic Design
  Christopher Brinkmann
Idea
  Sebastian Schnell,
  Tobias Feige,
  Christopher Brinkmann
Production
  Philipp Wenhold
Technical Conception
  Philipp Wenhold
Technical Implementation
  Richard Romminger
  Edelstahltechnik

Mit dem ersten Bewerbungsbogen-Puzzle haben wir ein gezieltes Recruiting-Tool entwickelt, das Talente für unseren Kunden IWC Schaffhausen anwerben soll. Ob man das Zeug für den Job als Uhrmacher im Luxus-Segment hat, zeigt sich schon beim Zusammensetzen des Response-Elements: eines Uhrwerkpuzzles aus 660 Kleinstteilen.

The Recruiting Puzzle was created for our client IWC Schaffhausen as a unique tool for discovering young talents at watchmaking fairs. You'll easily see if you have what it takes to make it as a luxury watchmaker as you try to assemble the response mechanism: a clockwork puzzle made of 660 tiny pieces.

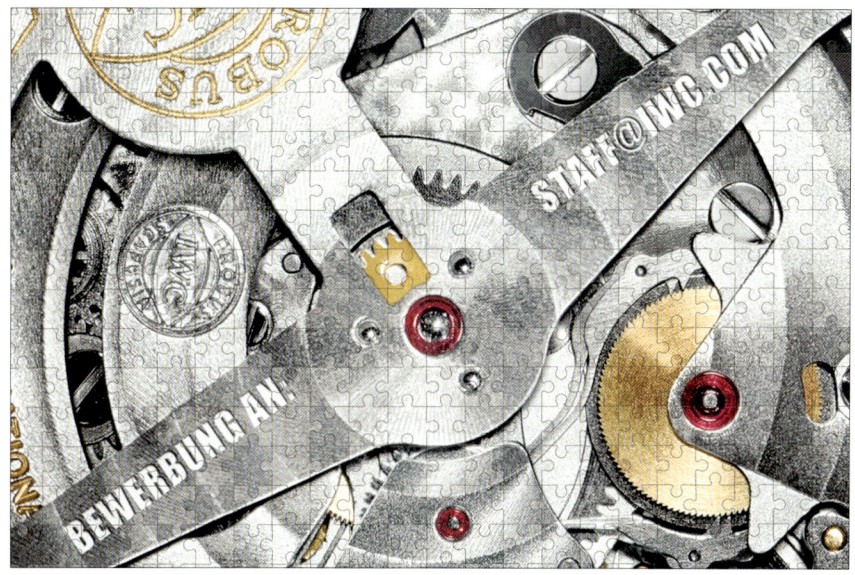

357

NOMINATION
DIALOGMARKETING/
PROMOTION/MEDIA DIALOG
MARKETING/PROMOTION/
MEDIA
  Media
  Media

FRIEDRICHS & FRIENDS
"Proofreading Facebook"

Lead Agency
  Jung von Matt AG
Client
  Friedrichs & Friends
Executive Creative Direction
  Mathias Stiller,
  Wolfgang Schneider
Creative Direction
  Jan Harbeck,
  David Mously
Art Direction
  Oskar Strauss
Client Consulting
  Alexandra Coenen
Copy
  Alescha Lechner

Friedrichs & Friends ist ein Lektorat, das auf die Korrektur von Werbetexten spezialisiert ist. Unsere Aufgabe war es, Friedrichs & Friends in der deutschen Werbelandschaft bekannter zu machen. Deshalb haben wir uns dort angemeldet, wo fast alle Werber zu finden sind: auf Facebook. Hier haben wir die Posts potenzieller Kunden verbessert und die Korrektur zusammen mit einer kleinen Botschaft veröffentlicht.

Friedrichs & Friends is a proofreading agency which is specialized in the communication industry. Our task was to strengthen and to increase the popularity of Friedrichs & Friends among the German advertising scene. That's why we went to a place where almost all advertising people can be found: Facebook. Here, we read and – in case we found mistakes – corrected the posts of our potential clients.

NOMINATION
DIALOGMARKETING/
PROMOTION/MEDIADIALOG
MARKETING/PROMOTION/
MEDIA
  Media
  Media

PATTEX KLEBER CLASSIC
  »Kran«

Lead Agency
  Serviceplan
Client
  Henkel AG & Co. KGaA
Marketing Direction
  Cedric Schupp
Executive Creative Direction
  Alex Schill,
  Matthias Harbeck
Creative Direction
  Alexander Rehm
Art Direction
  Andreas Balog
Client Consulting
  Stefan Schütte,
  Sandra Robert
Agency Production
  Simon Feichtl
Copy
  Nicolas Becker,
  Lorenz Langgartner
Film Production
  Saurus Filmbauten
Graphic Design
  Marijo Sanje,
  Fabian Halder
Production
  Michael Gruber,
  Thorsten Huth,
  Markus Rössler

Wir bauten eine überdimensionale Pattex Klebstofftube und montierten sie an Kräne exponierter Baustellen. Es sah so aus, als würden die Baumaterialien nicht mit einem Haken, sondern mit einer Klebstofftube transportiert.

We assembled a huge Pattex Power Glue tube at a construction crane and, during normal operation, transported extremely heavy objects on the construction site.

359

NOMINATION
DIALOGMARKETING/
PROMOTION/MEDIA DIALOG
MARKETING/PROMOTION/
MEDIA
  Media
  Media

SAW 3D
»Kino-Promotion«

Lead Agency
  Saatchi & Saatchi Duesseldorf
Client
  UFA-Palast
Marketing Direction
  Frederic Riech
Executive Creative Direction
  Stephan Zilges
Creative Direction
  Marco Obermann
Art Direction
  Jean-Pierre Gregor,
  Thomas Demeter
Client Consulting
  Marco Golbach,
  Nora Hetzelt
Agency Production
  Alexandra Beck,
  Reiner Hunfeld
Copy
  Till Koester,
  Philipp Hentges

In 3D wirkt "Saw" realer als je zuvor. Und darauf gaben wir Kinobesuchern einen kleinen Vorgeschmack. Mit einem einfachen Wobbler. Der zeigt auf der Vorderseite Jigsaws Gesicht und kündigt auf der Rückseite den Kinostart an. Direkt vor der Rückfahrkamera der Autos im UFA-Parkhaus angebracht, erschien Jigsaws gruselige Fratze auf dem Monitor im Armaturenbrett, sobald der Rückwärtsgang eingelegt wurde.

Thanks to 3D, the "Saw" movie is closer to the audience than ever before. To give the target audience a little foretaste, we created wobblers with Jigsaw's face on the front and the release date on the back. In the UFA-Palast's parking garage, promoters attached wobblers to the cars' rearview cameras. When the movie-goers put in the reverse gear, Jigsaw's scary grimace could be seen on the screen.

● **NOMINATION DIALOGMARKETING/ PROMOTION/MEDIADIALOG MARKETING/PROMOTION/ MEDIA**
 Media
 Media

TEXTERSCHMIEDE
 »Guerilla-Funk«

Lead Agency
 Jung von Matt AG
Client
 Texterschmiede e.V.
Marketing Direction
 Gabriela Friedrich
Advertising Direction
 Gabriela Friedrich
Executive Creative Direction
 Armin Jochum
Creative Direction
 Fabian Frese, Jan-Florian Ege
Art Direction
 Raphael Schils, Martin Strutz
Audio Production
 Hastings Hamburg
Consulting
 Matthias Luehrsen
Copy
 Christian Meyer
Programming
 Boris Fründt,
 Christian Passarge
Radio Production
 Hastings Hamburg
Other
 (Speakers and Copywriters):
 Niklas Schachtebeck,
 Georg Mühl, Lilian Das,
 Christian Hansmann,
 Sebstian Weber,
 Markus Günther,
 Philip Steck, Toby Schroeder,
 Michael Weißflog,
 Steffi Askemper

Der erste Guerilla-Funkspot der Welt: Um Absolventen der Texterschmiede auf innovative Weise ein Vorstellungsgespräch zu verschaffen, schmuggelten wir ihre Funkspots in die Sprecher-Castings des Tonstudios Hasting. Diese gingen an CDs und Texter der wichtigsten Agenturen. Und damit punktgenau ins Ohr der Zielgruppe.

The first guerilla radio commercial in the world: to get job interviews for graduates of the Texterschmiede, we smuggled their radio ads into e-mails of the sound studio Hastings. E-mails in which Hastings sends out casting tapes of professional speakers to creative directors in ad agencies. Thus, we caught the target group's attention right away. And they were all ears.

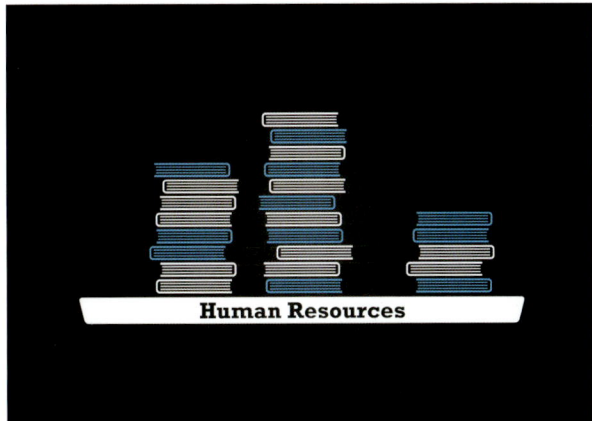

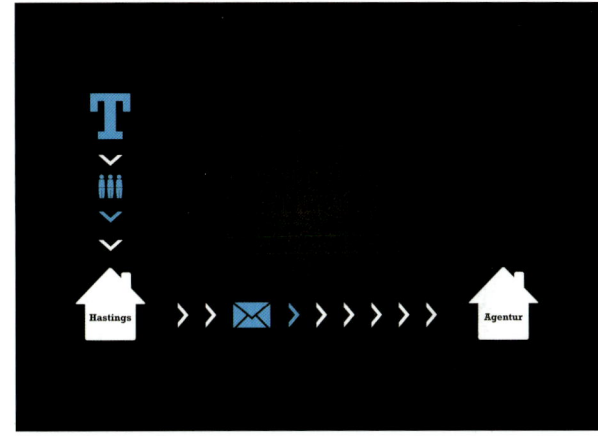

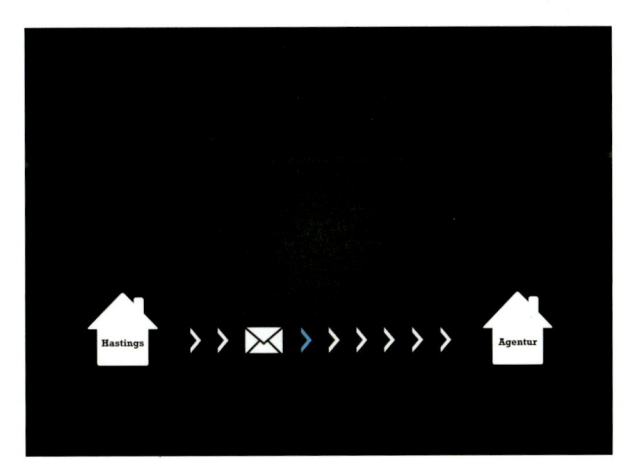

361

● NOMINATION
DESIGN
DESIGN
   Literatur
   Produkt-/Werbebroschüren
   Literature
   Advertising Brochures

MOORMANN BROSCHÜRE
2010
»In einfachen Verhältnissen«

Lead Agency
   Jäger & Jäger
Client
   Nils Holger Moormann GmbH
Marketing Direction
   Nicole Christof
Publishing House
   Verlag Hermann Schmidt Mainz

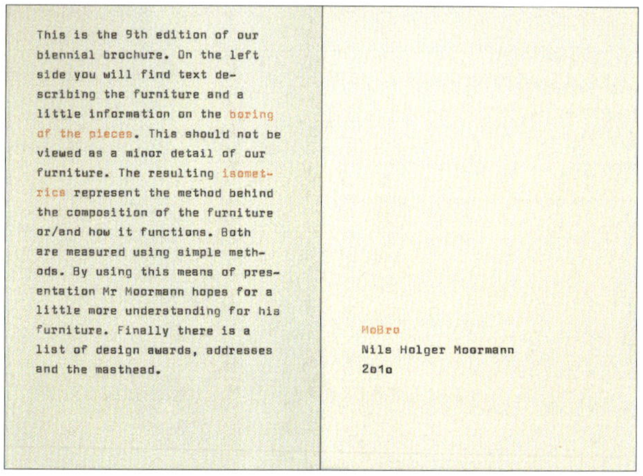

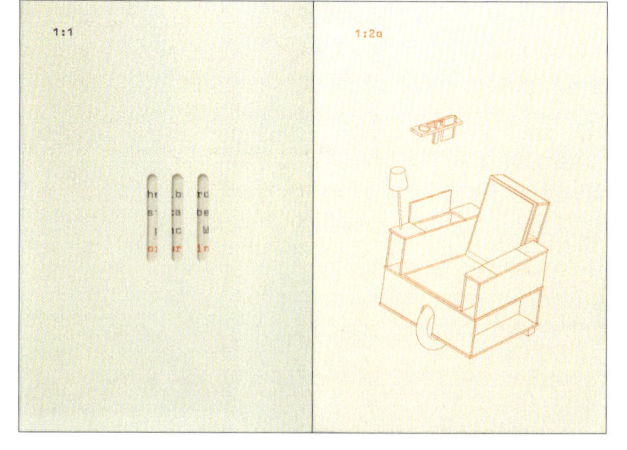

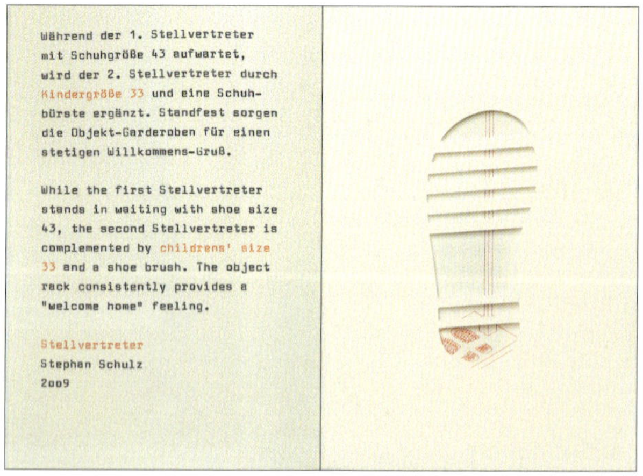

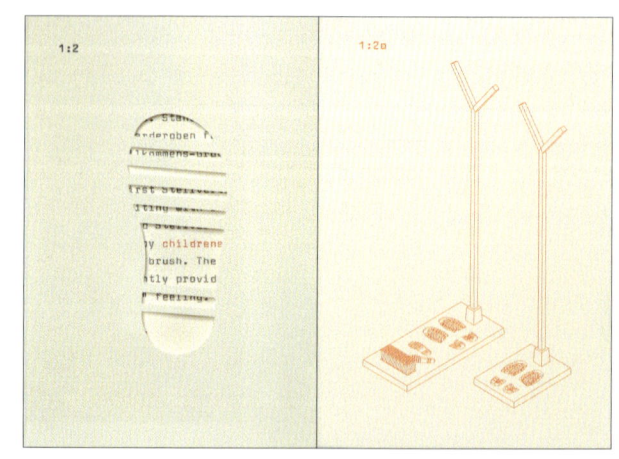

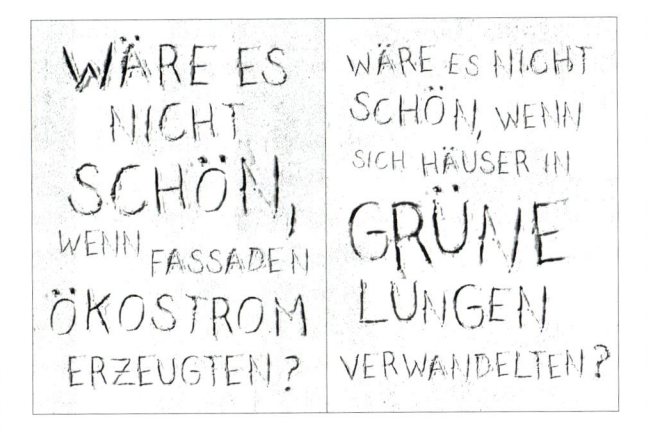

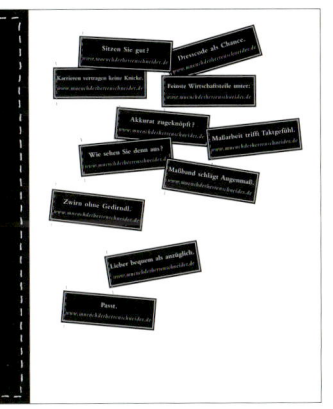

NOMINATION
DESIGN
DESIGN
  Literatur
  Image-/Informations-
  broschüren
  Literature
  Image/Information Brochures

BILEKJAEGER
»Hier spricht der Text.«

Lead Agency
  bilekjaeger
Client
  bilekjaeger
Executive Creative Direction
  Maurice Jäger
Creative Direction
  Uli Weber
Design
  Jasmin Beham
Printing
  Gress-Druck GmbH
Publishing House
  bilekjaeger
Typography
  Franz Geis

Eigenwerbung mal anders: Wir verzichten konsequent auf die Darstellung der üblichen Arbeitsbeispiele. Und lassen dagegen allein diverse Texte sprechen – mit aller visueller Kraft.

Self-promotion of a different kind: we consciously dispense with showing the usual examples of our work. And, instead, just let various texts speak – with full visual power.

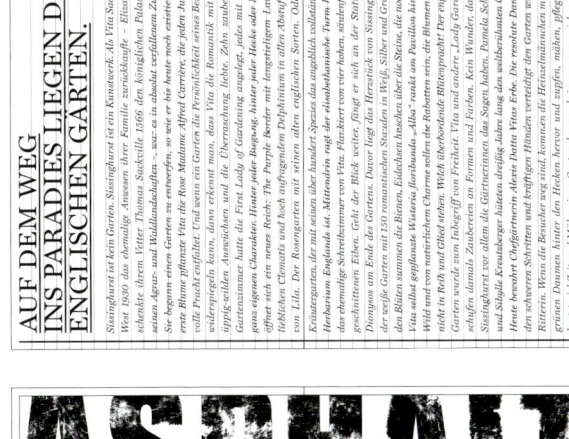

363

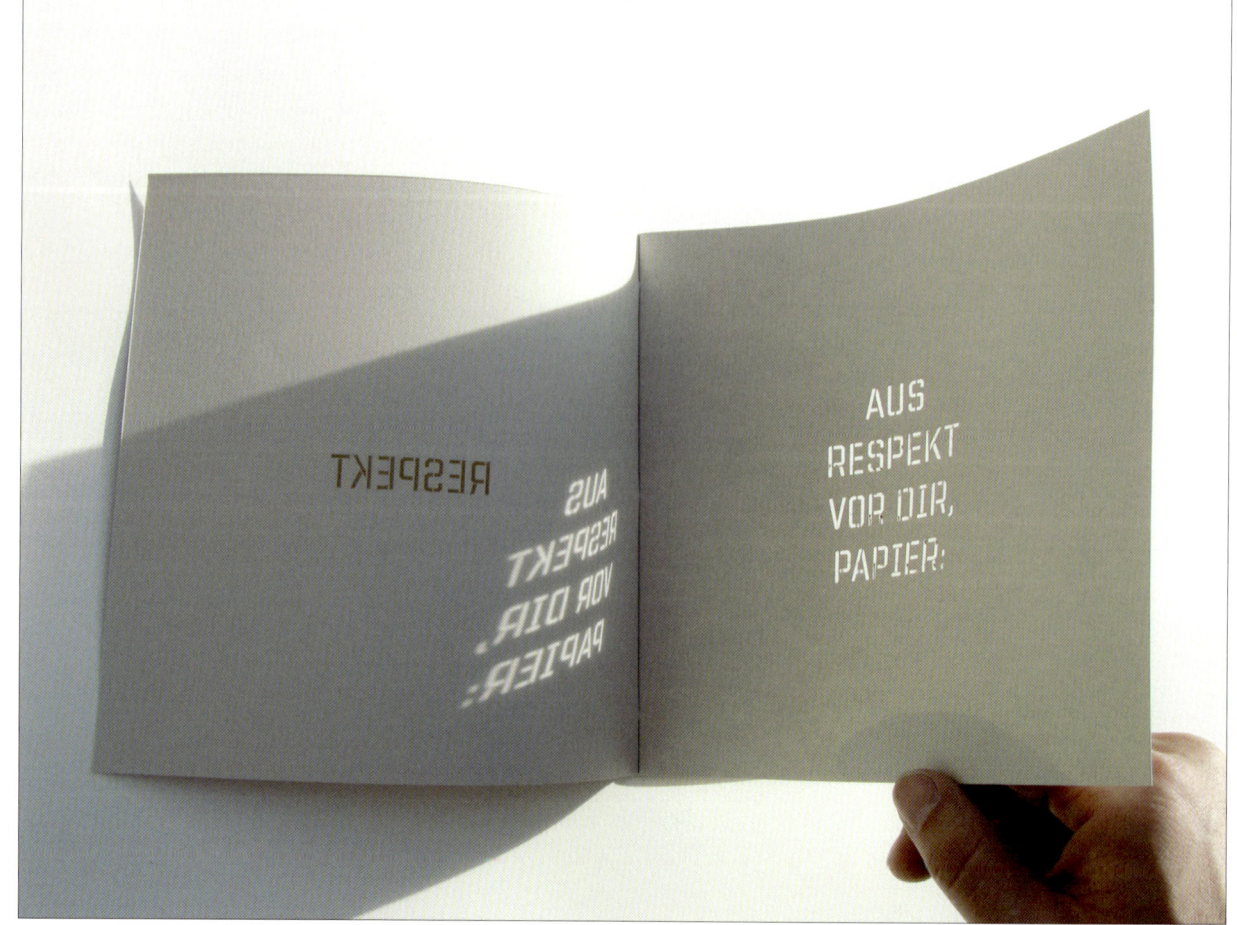

● NOMINATION
DESIGN
DESIGN
   Literatur
   Image-/Informations-
   broschüren
   Literature
   Image/Information Brochures

HEIDELBERGER
DRUCKMASCHINEN
   »Aus Respekt vor Dir, Papier.«

Lead Agency
   FREIE RADIKALE Werbung
Client
   HEIDELBERGER DRUCK-
   MASCHINEN AG
Marketing Direction
   Adriana Nuneva
Advertising Direction
   Claudia Cischek
Executive Creative Direction
   Karlheinz Müller,
   Paul Wagner
Creative Direction
   Karlheinz Müller,
   Paul Wagner
Art Direction
   Karlheinz Müller
Client Consulting
   Karlheinz Müller,
   Paul Wagner
Strategic Planning
   Karlheinz Müller,
   Paul Wagner
Agency Production
   Claudia Geyer G2
Consulting
   Karlheinz Müller,
   Paul Wagner
Copy
   Paul Wagner
Final Artwork
   Claudia Geyer G2
Printing
   Pinsker Druck + Medien GmbH
Publishing House
   Heidelberger Druckmaschinen
   AG

NOMINATION
DESIGN
DESIGN
Literatur
Kataloge
Literature
Catalogs

LEGO
"Signs"

Lead Agency
  serviceplan
Contributing Agencies
  plan.net
Client
  LEGO GmbH
Marketing Direction
  Katharina Sutch
Executive Creative Direction
  Alexander Schill
Creative Direction
  Christoph Nann,
  Maik Kaehler
Art Direction
  Till Diestel
Client Consulting
  Tim Schnabel,
  Patrick Stehle
Copy
  Rudolf Novotny
Publishing House
  www.lego-signs.com
Other
  Programming:
  Markus Mrugalla,
  Benjamin Heeb,
  Florian Feiler

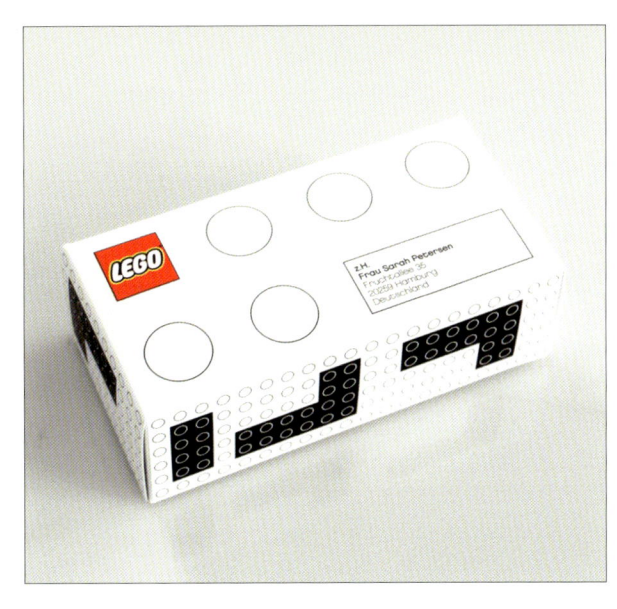

NOMINATION
DESIGN
DESIGN
Literatur
Berichte
Literature
Reports

OBI MITARBEITERBUCH
»40 Jahre OBI«

Lead Agency
  KircherBurkhardt GmbH
Client
  OBI Group Holding GmbH
Executive Creative Direction
  Lukas Kircher
Creative Direction
  Sebastian Eick
Client Consulting
  Andreas Schulte,
  Catrin Ehlert
Art Buying
  Tana Budde
Concept
  Tom Levine
Copy
  Tom Levine
Image Editing
  Tana Budde
Printing
  Raff GmbH, Riederich
Publishing House
  KircherBurkhardt GmbH

NOMINATION
DESIGN
DESIGN
  Literatur
  Bücher
  Literature
  Books

BIRKHÄUSER
  "TypoLyrics – The Sound of Fonts"

Lead Agency
  MAGMA Brand Design
Client
  Birkhäuser GmbH
Art Direction
  Lars Harmsen,
  Flo Gaertner
Editing
  Jan Kiesswetter,
  Julia Kahl
Graphic Design
  Jan Kiesswetter
Illustration
  Various
Printing
  E&B engelhardt und bauer
Publishing House
  Birkhäuser GmbH
Typography
  Diverse
Other
  Project Management:
  Berit Liedtke,
  Ulrike Ruh

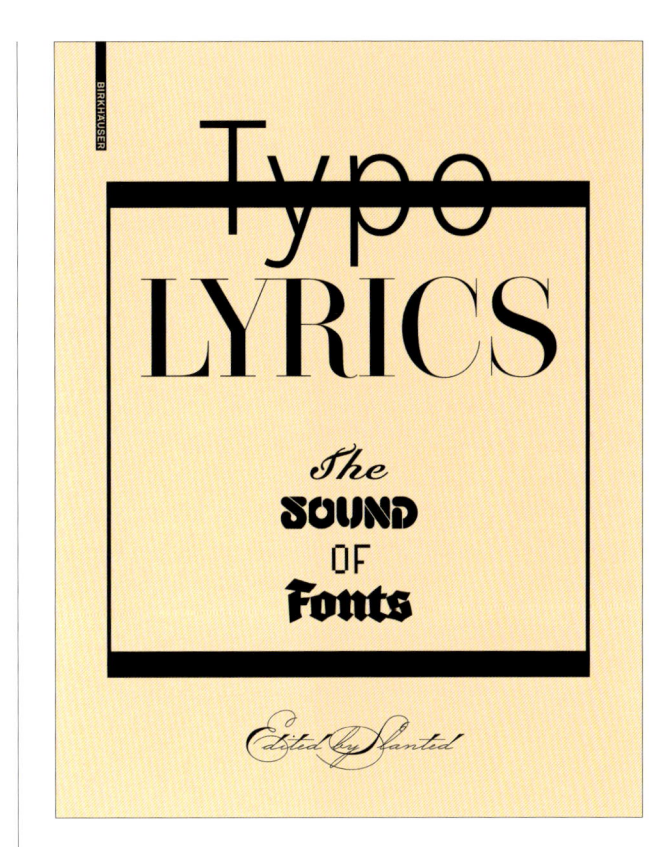

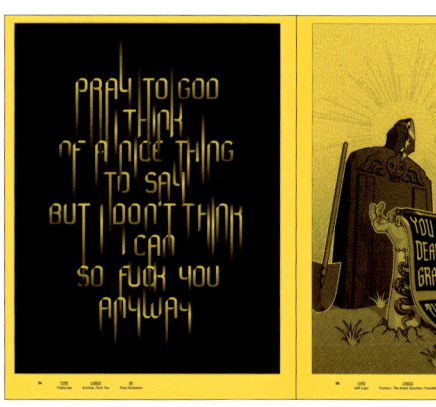

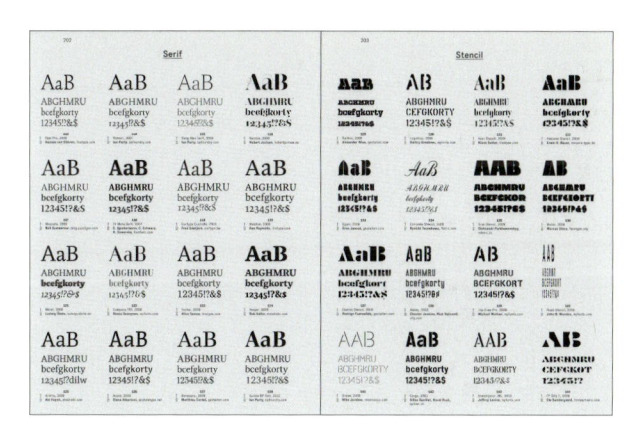

367

NOMINATION
DESIGN
DESIGN
Literatur
Bücher
Literature
Books

CHRISTOPHER THOMAS
»Passion«

Lead Agency
  Anzinger | Wüschner | Rasp
  Agentur für Kommunikation GmbH
Client
  Christopher Thomas
Executive Creative Direction
  Markus Rasp
Creative Direction
  Markus Rasp
Art Direction
  Daniel Pietsch
Image Processing
  Tobias Winkler
Photography
  Christopher Thomas
Publishing House
  Prestel Verlag

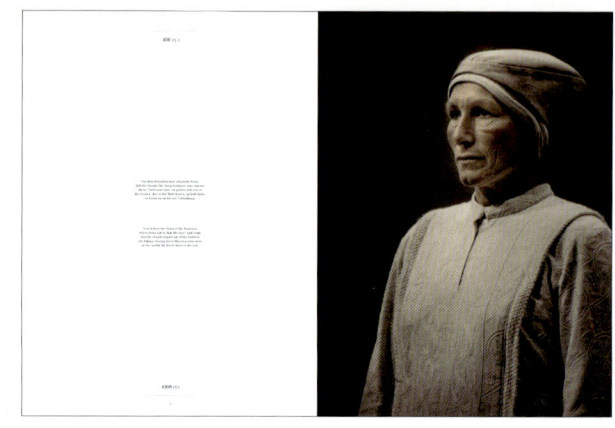

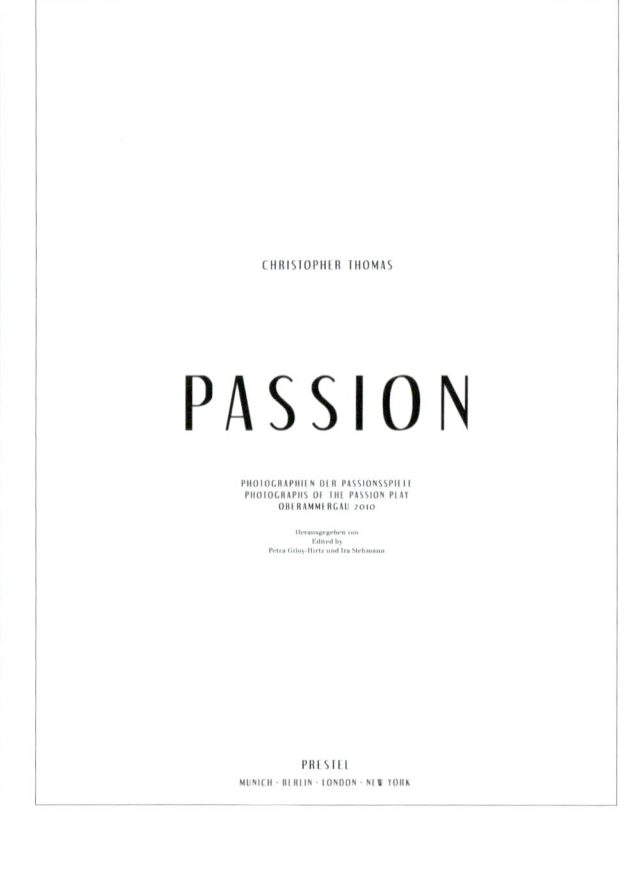

**NOMINATION
DESIGN
DESIGN**
Literatur
Bücher
Literature
Books

COSMIC COLLECTION
»Soirée graphique –
Ausgabe No.1«

Lead Agency
   KOMET Werbeagentur AG
   BSW
Client
   Soirée graphique
Marketing Direction
   Gabriela Fust
Advertising Direction
   Marcel Durst
Executive Creative Direction
   Thom Pfister
Creative Direction
   Thom Pfister
Art Direction
   Roland Zenger,
   Tamara Janes
Client Consulting
   Simon Schatzmann
Concept
   Thom Pfister
Consulting
   Bettina Ammann,
   Emma Isolini
Copy
   Isabella Jungo,
   Antonia Bekiaris
Design
   Sarah Pia
Final Artwork
   Rahel Alder
Graphic Design
   Roland Zenger,
   Tamara Janes,
   Sarah Pia,
   Thom Pfister
Idea
   Thom Pfister
Image Processing
   Rahel Alder
Printing
   Ast Fischer
Production
   Ast Fischer
Publishing House
   Self-published
Typography
   Roland Zenger,
   Tamara Janes,
   Sarah Pia

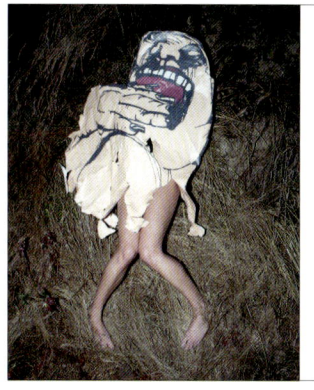

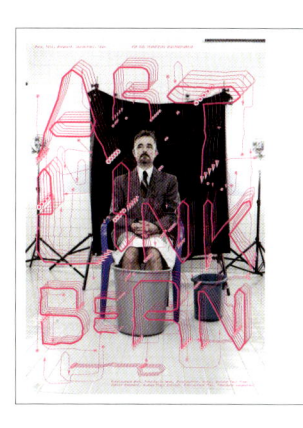

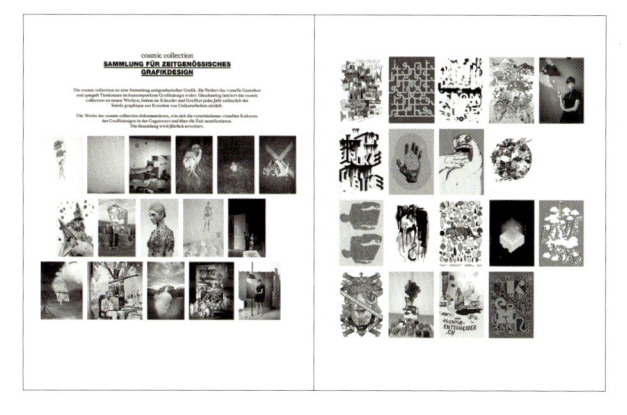

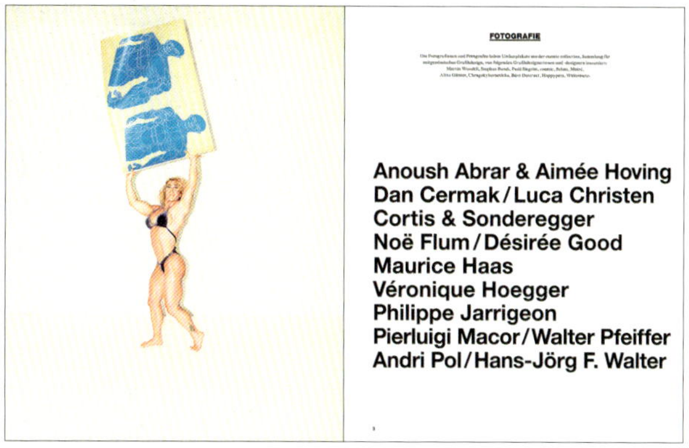

NOMINATION
DESIGN
DESIGN
  Literatur
  Bücher
  Literature
  Books

DESIGNFORUM
»Wien 2006–2010«

Lead Agency
  Alexander Egger,
  Isolde Fitzel
Client
  designforum Wien
Creative Direction
  Alexander Egger
Art Direction
  Alexander Egger,
  Isolde Fitzel
Concept
  Alexander Egger
Consulting
  Katharina Baumann,
  Susanna Fichta
Copy
  die jungs kommunikation –
  Martin Lengauer,
  Katharina Baumann
Design
  Alexander Egger,
  Isolde Fitzel
Editing
  die jungs kommunikation –
  Martin Lengauer,
  Katharina Baumann
Final Artwork
  Isolde Fitzel
Graphic Design
  Alexander Egger,
  Isolde Fitzel
Idea
  Alexander Egger
Photography
  Images from designforum Wien,
  except for images from exhibitions and lectures,
  Lisa Fleck
Printing
  Ueberreuter Print GmbH,
  Korneuburg, Austria
Production
  Isolde Fitzel
Publishing House
  designforum Wien

NOMINATION
DESIGN
DESIGN
　Literatur
　Bücher
　Literature
　Books

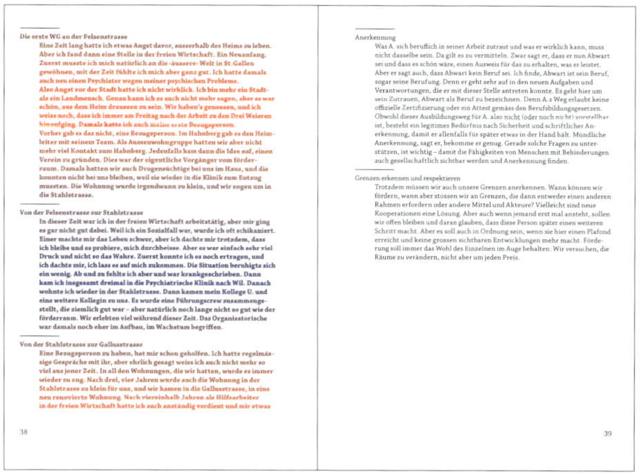

FÖRDERRAUMGESCHICHTEN
»Wollen wir einen Raum bieten, in dem man auch scheitern darf?«

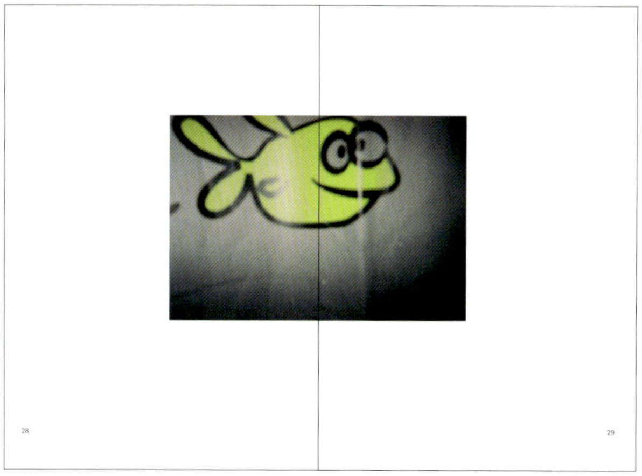

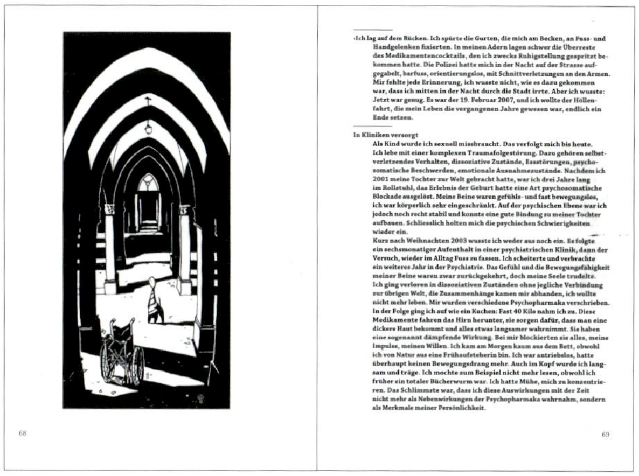

Lead Agency
　TGG Hafen Senn Stieger
Client
　förderraum
Copy
　Andreas Heller,
　Michel Mettler
Illustration
　Silvia Gogesch,
　grafixon
Photography
　förderraum Residents and Staff
Printing
　Typotron AG
Publishing House
　förderraum

NOMINATION
DESIGN
DESIGN
Literatur
Bücher
Literature
Books

GUM
»Magazin für konzeptionelles
Gestalten. Ausgabe 11.«

Lead Agency
  GUM-Projektgruppe,
  FH Bielefeld
Client
  Fachhochschule Bielefeld,
  Fachbereich Gestaltung
Marketing Direction
  Project Management:
  Martin Deppner,
  Dirk Fütterer
Art Direction
  Dirk Fütterer
Concept
  Martin Deppner,
  Dirk Fütterer,
  Marc Jakubowski,
  Philip Reinartz,
  Lukas Timmer
Copy
  Various Authors
Design
  Marc Jakubowski, Philip
  Reinartz, Lukas Timmer
Editing
  Marc Jakubowski, Philip
  Reinartz, Lukas Timmer
Final Artwork
  Marc Jakubowski, Philip
  Reinartz, Lukas Timmer
Image Editing
  Steffen Bunte,
  Marc Jakubowski,
  Philip Reinartz,
  Lukas Timmer
Image Processing
  Steffen Bunte,
  Wolfgang Kraatz,
  Druckgrafische Werkstätten
  der FH Bielefeld
Photography
  Steffen Bunte,
  Various Photographers
Printing
  Engelhardt und Bauer,
  Karlsruhe
Production
  Kehrer Design Heidelberg,
  Druckgrafische Werkstätten
  der FH Bielefeld
Publishing House
  Kehrer Verlag Heidelberg
Typography
  Marc Jakubowski, Philip
  Reinartz, Lukas Timmer
Other
  Bookbinding:
  Großbuchbinderei Spinner,
  Ottersweier

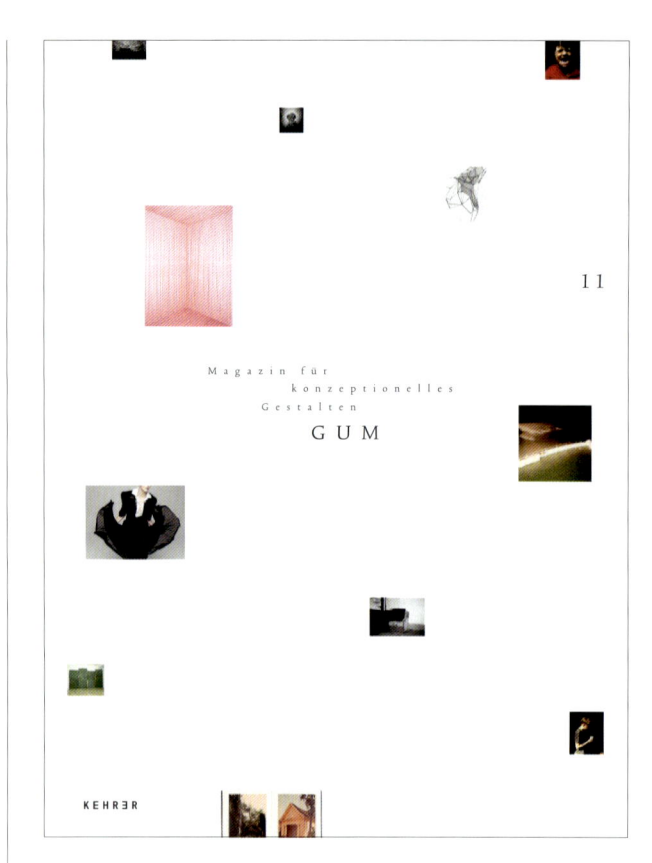

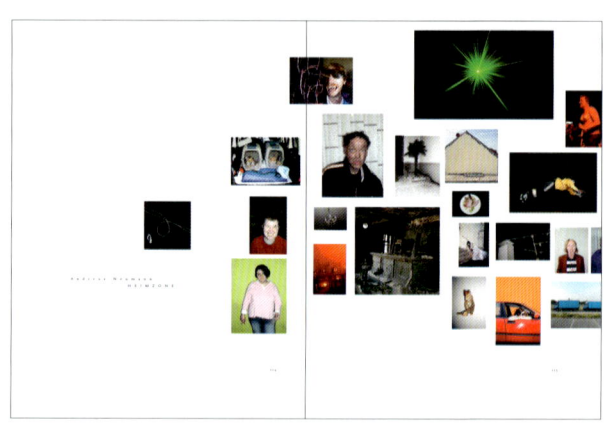

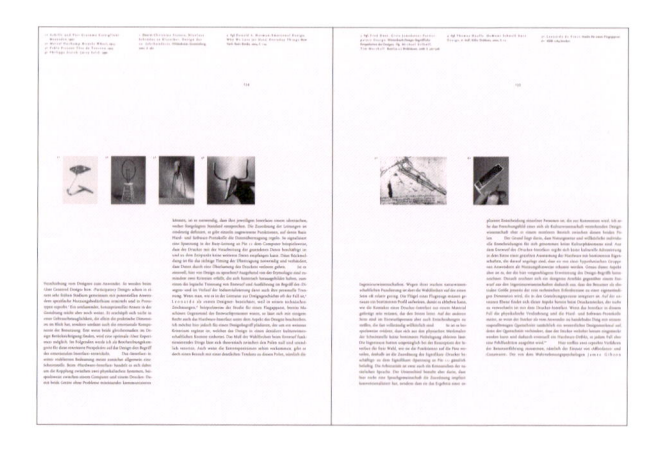

372

NOMINATION
DESIGN
DESIGN
Literatur
Bücher
Literature
Books

JULI GUDEHUS
»Das Lesikon der visuellen Kommunikation«

Lead Agency
  Verlag Hermann Schmidt Mainz
Client
  Verlag Hermann Schmidt Mainz
Marketing Direction
  Karin Schmidt-Friderichs
Advertising Direction
  Karin Schmidt-Friderichs
Creative Direction
  Juli Gudehus
Art Direction
  Juli Gudehus
Design
  Juli Gudehus
Graphic Design
  Juli Gudehus
Idea
  Juli Gudehus
Printing
  C.H. Beck, Nördlingen
Publishing House
  Verlag Hermann Schmidt Mainz
Typography
  Juli Gudehus,
  Andreas Trogisch

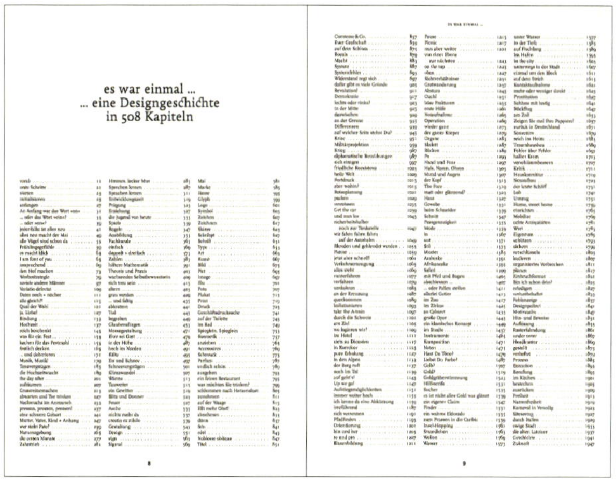

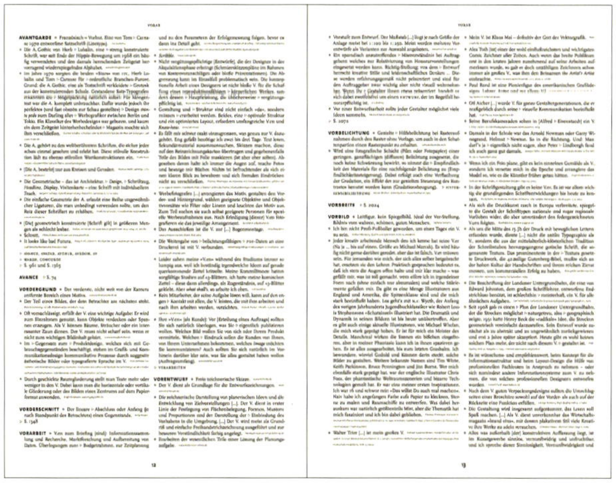

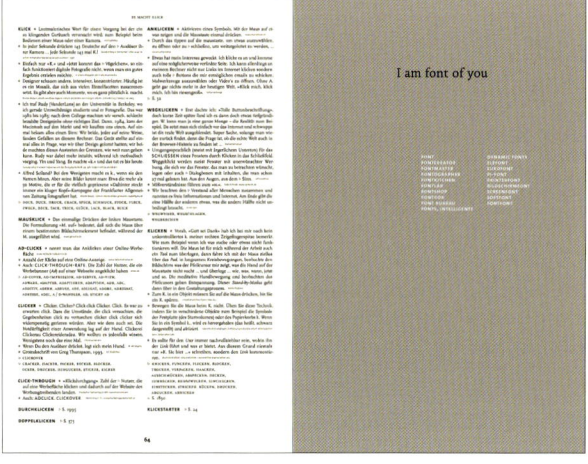

● NOMINATION
DESIGN
DESIGN
　Literatur
　Bücher
　Literature
　Books

STRICHPUNKT DESIGN
"It's A Boy – It's A Girl"

Lead Agency
　Strichpunkt Design
Client
　Strichpunkt Design
Executive Creative Direction
　Kirsten Dietz,
　Jochen Rädeker
Creative Direction
　Kirsten Dietz
Art Direction
　Kirsten Dietz
Design
　Kirsten Dietz
Publishing House
　Taschen GmbH

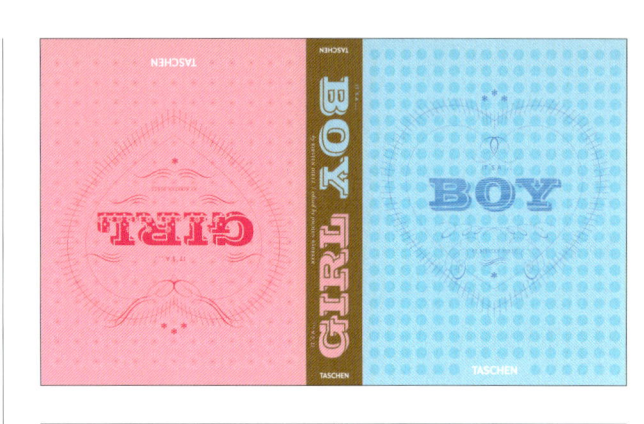

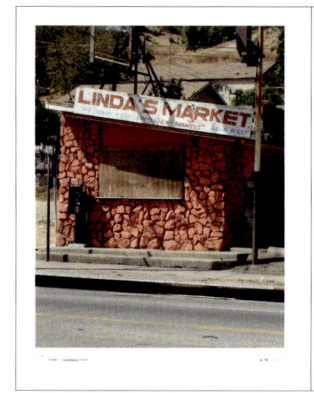

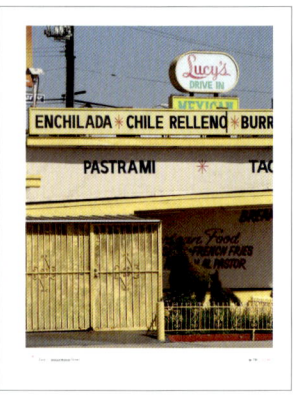

374

● NOMINATION
DESIGN
DESIGN
  Literatur
  Buchumschläge/-titel
  Literature
  Book Jackets/Covers

SUHRKAMP VERLAG
  »›Das Weisse Buch‹
  von Rafael Horzon«

Lead Agency
  STUDIO94
Client
  Suhrkamp Verlag
Creative Direction
  Patricia Woerler-Horzon
Design
  Patricia Woerler-Horzon
Publishing House
  Suhrkamp Verlag

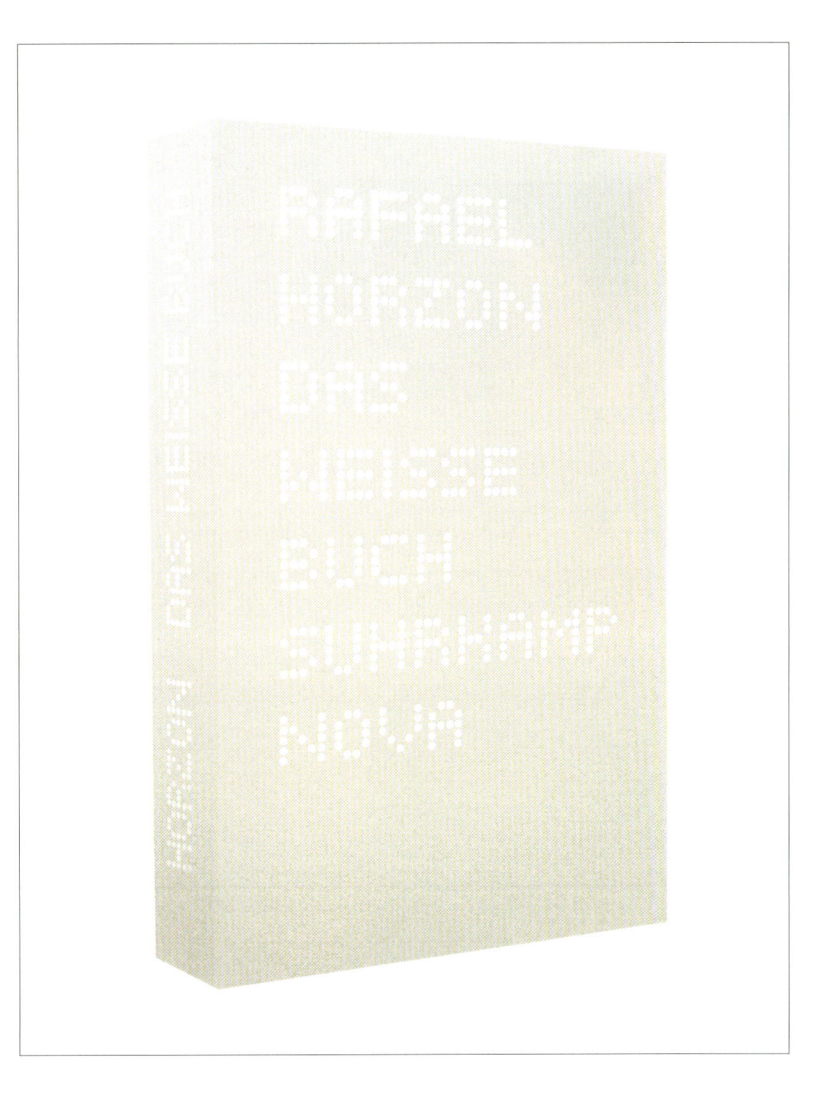

NOMINATION
DESIGN
DESIGN
  Design
  Corporate Design
  Design
  Corporate Design

CORPORATE DESIGN
»Altes Kloster«

Lead Agency
  Halle34 OG f. zeitgenössische Kommunikation
Client
  Hotel Altes Kloster GmbH
Marketing Direction
  Michaela Gansterer-Zaminer
Advertising Direction
  Michaela Gansterer-Zaminer
Creative Direction
  Sigi Mayer
Art Direction
  Emanuela Sarac
Client Consulting
  Marcus Arige
Agency Production
  Marcus Arige
Final Artwork
  Andreas Ehrenberger
Illustration
  Thomas Paster

Für das in Hainburg a.d. Donau neu errichtete Hotel Altes Kloster wurde ein völlig neues Corporate Design geschaffen. Der Name war vorgegeben und bezog sich auf ein Kloster, das an selber Stelle im Jahr 1235 von den Minoriten gegründet wurde. Es stand daher fest, dass wir ein schlichtes, modernes Corporate Design schaffen wollten, das den Anforderungen des Hotels gerecht werden sollte.

On historical grounds in Hainburg, where in the year 1235 a monastery was founded, a new hotel, therefore named »Altes Kloster«, was established. For us, it was clear to design a plain but modern corporate design, which should match the new hotel perfectly.

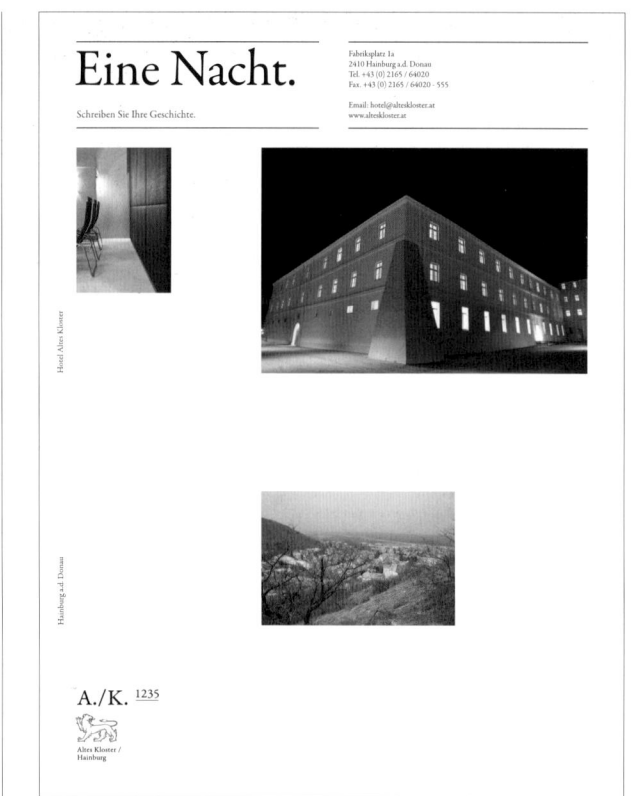

NOMINATION
DESIGN
DESIGN
  Design
  Corporate Design
  Design
  Corporate Design

CORPORATE DESIGN
»Beisser«

Lead Agency
  Mutabor Design GmbH
Client
  Beisser GmbH & Co. KG
Marketing Direction
  Claas Rudolf Habben
Creative Direction
  Sven Ritterhoff
Art Direction
  Nils Zimmermann
Copy
  Jan Knopp
Design
  Silvia Bubel,
  Stefan Mückner,
  Karina Schoffro,
  Kirsten Kaselow,
  Nils Zimmermann,
  Martin Oberhäuser
Final Artwork
  Susanne Weber

Mutabor kommt aus dem Lateinischen und bedeutet »ich werde verwandelt werden«. Die Designagentur steht für den permanenten Wandel durch Innovation. Als Ausdruck von Verwandlung wurde Veränderung durch Farbe als Grundprinzip gewählt, welches auf das gesamte Corporate Design angewandt wurde.

Mutabor is derived from Latin and means "I will be changed". The design agency stands for permanent change through innovation. As an expression of transformation, change through color was chosen as the basic principle and was applied throughout the entire corporate design.

● NOMINATION
DESIGN
DESIGN
  Design
  Corporate Design
  Design
  Corporate Design

CORPORATE DESIGN
"Community Film"

Lead Agency
  gürtlerbachmann GmbH
Client
  Community Film GmbH
Marketing Direction
  Acki Heldens
Executive Creative Direction
  Uli Gürtler
Creative Direction
  Reiner Fiedler
Art Direction
  Reiner Fiedler
Client Consulting
  Sharifa Hawari
Consulting
  Sharifa Hawari
Design
  Reiner Fiedler
Idea
  Reiner Fiedler
Illustration
  Julian Hets

Das Corporate Design für die Filmproduktion Community Film, Spezialist für Filmformate im Internet, greift gestalterische Elemente der ersten Generation von PCs auf und grenzt sich so von der hochglanzpolierten Welt aktueller Internetseiten und -dienstleistungen ab. Mit Mut zur Selbstironie wird die Wortmarke aus »antiken« Computertasten gebildet. Einfachheit und Klarheit bestimmen somit das Design.

The corporate design for the film production Community Film, specialized in online design, picks up design elements from the first generation of PCs and distinguishes itself from the high-gloss world of prevailing websites and web providers. With courage for self-mockery, the word mark is formed from antiquated computer keyboards. Simplicity and clarity characterize the entire design.

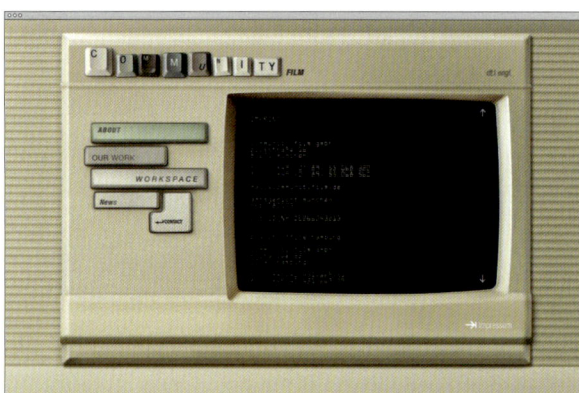

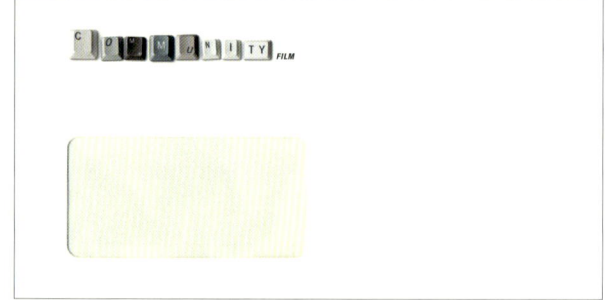

NOMINATION
DESIGN
DESIGN
  Design
  Corporate Design
  Design
  Corporate Design

CORPORATE DESIGN
»Mutabor«

Lead Agency
  Mutabor Design GmbH
Client
  Mutabor Design GmbH
Creative Direction
  Sven Ritterhoff
Art Direction
  Kirsten Kaselow
Design
  Kirsten Kaselow,
  Rasmus Bruning,
  Alexandra Fukazawa
Final Artwork
  Susanne Weber

Mutabor kommt aus dem Lateinischen und bedeutet »ich werde verwandelt werden«. Die Designagentur steht für den permanenten Wandel durch Innovation. Als Ausdruck von Verwandlung wurde Veränderung durch Farbe als Grundprinzip gewählt, welches auf das gesamte Corporate Design angewandt wurde.

Mutabor is derived from Latin and means "I will be changed". The design agency stands for permanent change through innovation. As an expression of transformation, change through color was chosen as the basic principle and was applied throughout the entire corporate design.

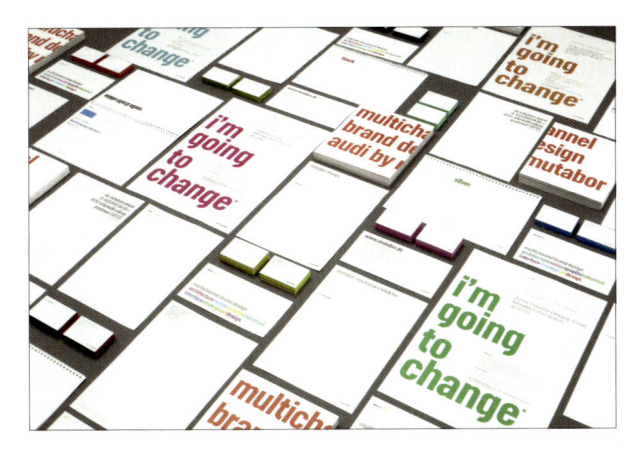

NOMINATION
DESIGN
DESIGN
 Design
 Corporate Design
 Design
 Corporate Design

CORPORATE DESIGN
»Restaurant Hoch III
Hamburg«

Lead Agency
 weissraum.de(sign)°
Client
 HCBC zwei UG & Co. KG
Executive Creative Direction
 Bernd Brink,
 Lucas Buchholz
Art Direction
 Nils Zimmermann
Graphic Design
 Aggi Berg
Photography
 Hannes Cunze
Production
 Susann Buchholz and
 Christoph Schmidt
 (alvons design),
 Karlo Mertens (Mertens
 Company)

Aufgabe: Entwicklung des Corporate Designs für einen neuen Hotspot in Hamburgs Szeneviertel St. Pauli. Die Location erstreckt sich über drei Etagen und beinhaltet Café, Bar und Club. Lösung: Das Hoch III hat viele Gesichter, aber nur ein zentrales Gestaltungselement, das sich durch den gesamten Auftritt zieht. Von Print über Web bis hin zum Raumkonzept – das markante Hoch-III-Zeichen ist allgegenwärtig.

Task: To develop the corporate design for a new hotspot within the vibrant quarter of Hamburg's St. Pauli. Over three floors, the venue is café, bar and club. Solution: »Hoch III« has many different faces, but one essential design language, that spreads its wings throughout the whole concept. From print to web to environment, the striking »Hoch III« logo becomes the grid and major key element.

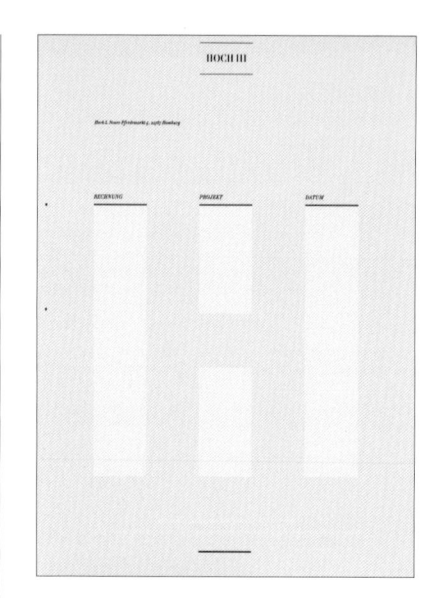

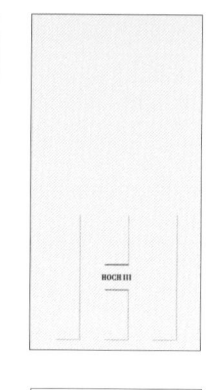

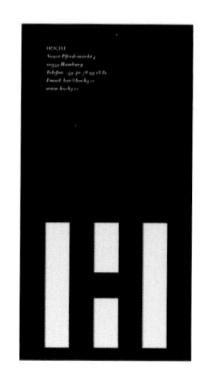

**NOMINATION
DESIGN
DESIGN**
  Design
  Kalender
  Design
  Calendars

**AD FONTES –
ZU DEN QUELLEN**
»Jahreskalender 2011«

Lead Agency
  Clormann Design GmbH
Client
  Clormann Design GmbH
Executive Creative Direction
  Marc M. Clormann
Creative Direction
  Marc M. Clormann
Art Direction
  Beatrix Béres
Strategic Planning
  Marc M. Clormann
Concept
  Marc M. Clormann
Graphic Design
  Beatrix Béres
Idea
  Marc M. Clormann
Illustration
  Beatrix Béres
Printing
  Hauff Druck Art GmbH
Production
  Hauff Druck Art GmbH

Das Deckblatt und die 12 Monate lassen sich an perforierten Linien in je 8 Segmenten auffalten. Im Jahresverlauf verwandelt sich der Kalender in eine dreidimensionale Blüte. 12 verschiedene Papierprägungen korrespondieren mit der jeweiligen Illustration. Auf der Rückseite befindet sich ein integrierter Fuß zum Aufstellen des Kalenders.

Each month can be opened in 8 segments on perforated lines. The 12 different embossings of the paper correspond to the plant illustrations of each month. After opening the 12th month, the calendar becomes a three-dimensional flower and can be placed in different positions with the integrated frame on the reverse side.

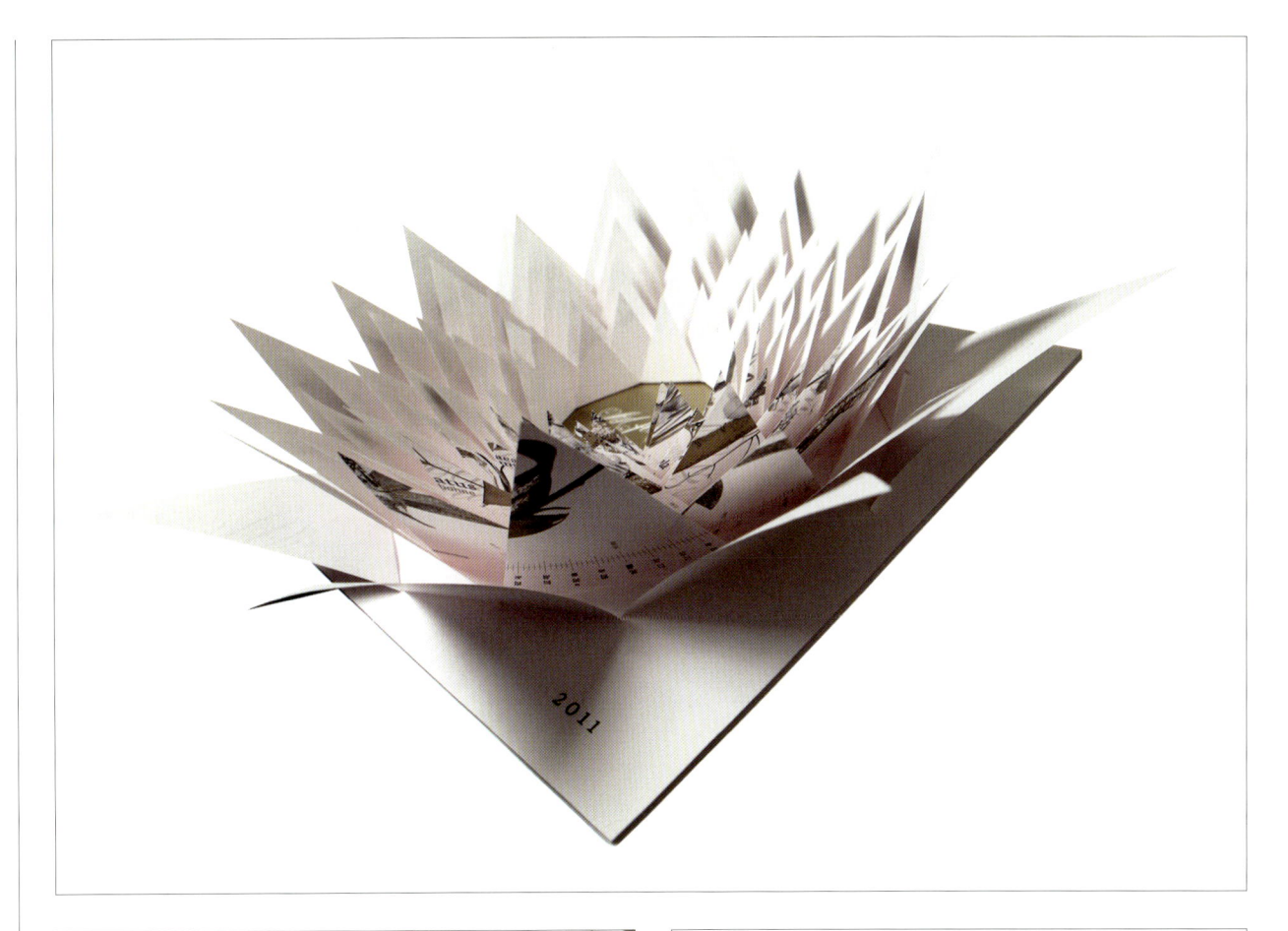

381

NOMINATION
DESIGN
DESIGN
  Design
  Kalender
  Design
  Calendars

F.A.Z., F.A.S
»Der Erste Seite-Kalender«

Lead Agency
  Scholz & Friends
Client
  Frankfurter Allgemeine Zeitung GmbH
Marketing Direction
  Josef Krieg
Executive Creative Direction
  Martin Pross,
  Matthias Spaetgens
Creative Direction
  Mathias Rebmann,
  Florian Schwalme
Art Direction
  Johannes Stoll
Client Consulting
  Marie Toya Gaillard,
  Eva Verena Schmidt
Agency Production
  Franziska Ibe
Copy
  Nils Tscharnke
Graphic Design
  Sebastian Haus

Seit über 60 Jahren ist die F.A.Z. Garant für Qualitätsjournalismus. Das beweist der Abreiß-Kalender eindrucksvoll. Denn mit 365 F.A.Z.-Titelseiten im Originalformat dokumentiert er die tiefgründige Berichterstattung über das Weltgeschehen seit 1949. Der Clou: Die Datums- und Wochentagspaare der alten, teils historischen Titelseiten stimmen exakt mit den Kalenderdaten 2011 überein.

For more than 60 years, the F.A.Z. has been synonymous with quality journalism – an achievement that is proven impressively by this tear-off calendar. Composed of 365 full-size front pages, it documents the thorough news coverage of the F.A.Z. since 1949. Best of all, the front pages have been selected so as to match exactly the date and weekday combinations of 2011.

NOMINATION
DESIGN
DESIGN
  Design
  Kunst-/Kultur-/
  Veranstaltungsplakate
  Design
  Art/Culture/Event Posters

FIFTYFIFTY EDITION
  »Galerie Plakate«

Lead Agency
  Euro RSCG Duesseldorf
Client
  fiftyfifty
Marketing Direction
  Hubert Ostendorf
Executive Creative Direction
  Felix Glauner
Creative Direction
  Martin Breuer,
  Martin Venn
Art Direction
  Ingmar Krannich
Graphic Design
  Michael Becker,
  Franziska Lopau

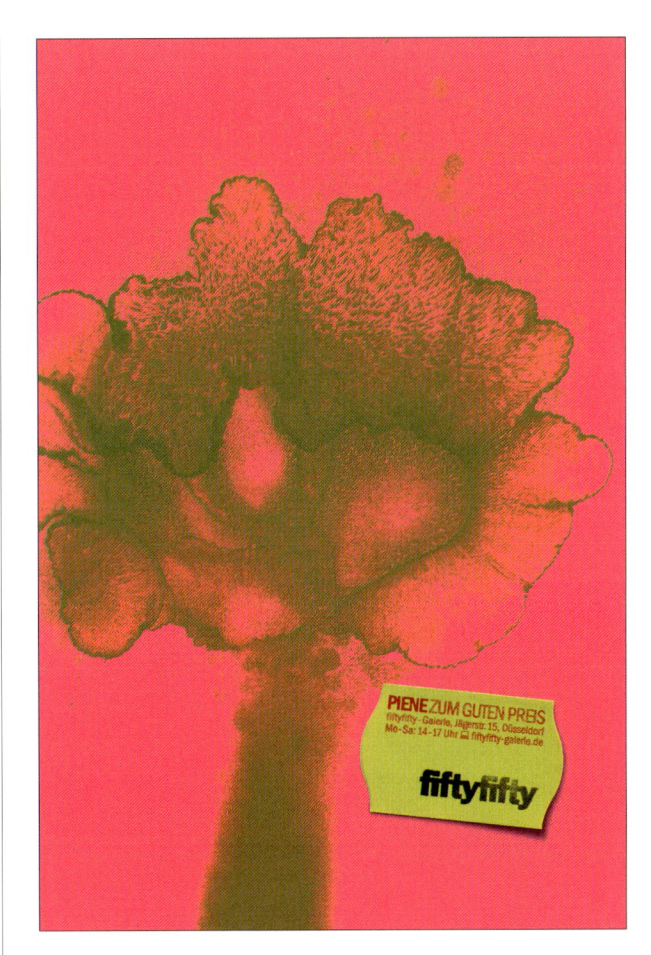

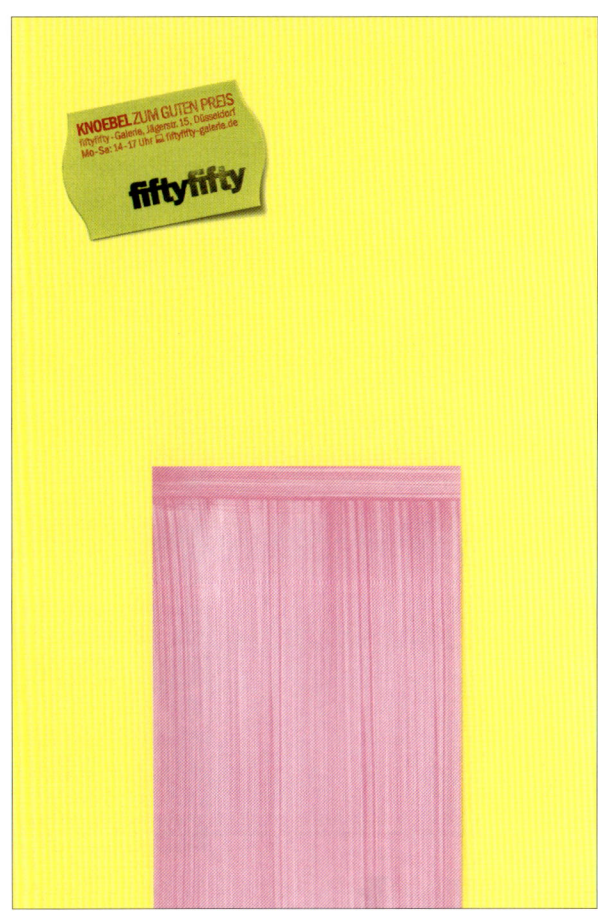

● NOMINATION
DESIGN
DESIGN
 Design
 Kunst-/Kultur-/
 Veranstaltungsplakate
 Design
 Art/Culture/Event Posters

———

SCHAUSPIELHAUS BOCHUM
 »Einführungskampagne«

Lead Agency
 Scheer
Client
 Schauspielhaus Bochum –
 Anstalt des öffentlichen Rechts
Marketing Direction
 Christine Hoenmanns
Advertising Direction
 Janna Rohden
Creative Direction
 Stefan Scheer
Art Direction
 Christian Frenssen
Client Consulting
 Florian Müller
Copy
 Stefan Scheer
Illustration
 Philipp Lemm

384

● NOMINATION
DESIGN
DESIGN
　Design
　Packaging
　Design
　Packaging

**PANASONIC EVOIA
AA-ALKALI-BATTERIE**
　»Die langlebigste Batterie«

Lead Agency
　Scholz & Friends
Client
　Panasonic Energy Europe N.V.
Marketing Direction
　Lars Schimming
Executive Creative Direction
　Martin Pross,
　Matthias Spaetgens
Creative Direction
　Michael Winterhagen
Art Direction
　Walter Ziegler
Client Consulting
　Salvatore Amato
Agency Production
　Diana Wuttge
Copy
　Michael Schöpf

　Evoia AA von Panasonic halten den Guinness-Rekord als langlebigste Alkali-Batterien der Welt. Ihre Lebensdauer ist doppelt so lang wie die vergleichbarer Produkte. Die neue Verpackung zeigt dies auf einfache Weise: In der für acht Batterien ausgelegten Verpackung befinden sich nur vier Batterien.

　Evoia AA alkaline batteries from Panasonic hold the Guinness Record as the longest lasting alkaline batteries in the world. In fact, they last twice as long as comparable products. The new packaging shows this in a simple way: Designed for eight batteries, the packaging carries only four batteries.

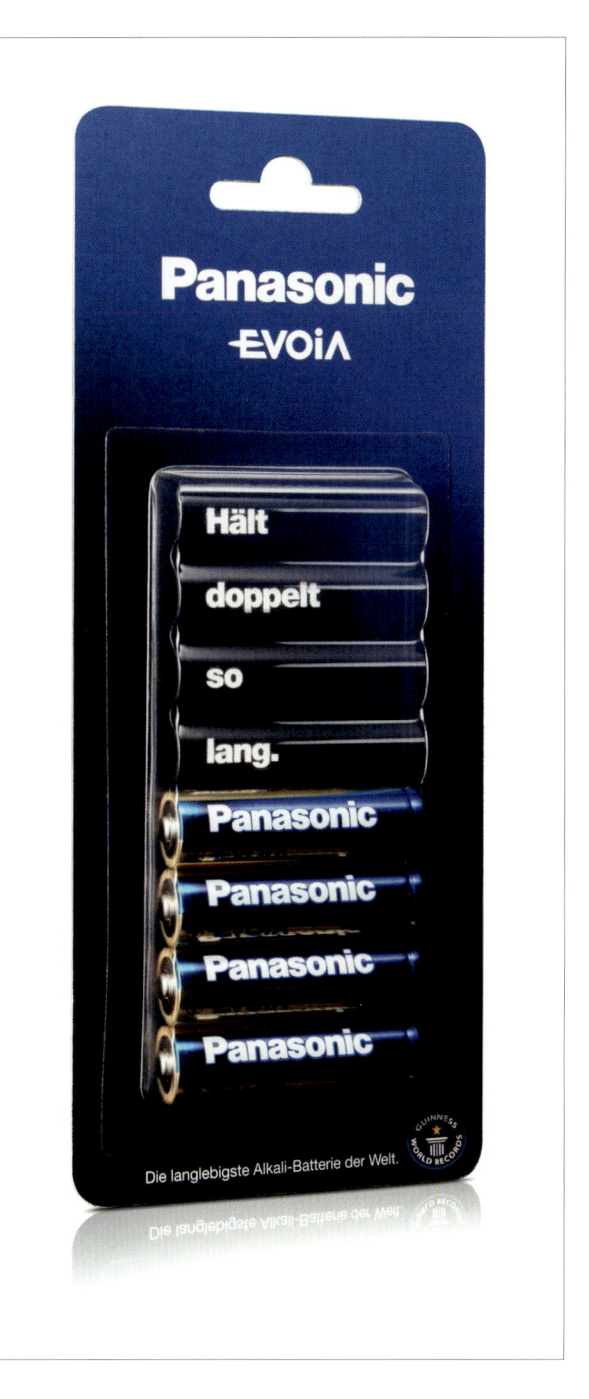

385

NOMINATION
DESIGN
DESIGN
　Design
　Packaging
　Design
　Packaging

**ROGGENKAMP ORGANICS
FRISCHE SUPPEN**
　»Suppentöpfe,
　›Hausmacher Art‹«

Lead Agency
　Scholz & Friends
Client
　Roggenkamp Organics AG
Marketing Direction
　Stefan Roggenkamp
Advertising Direction
　Stefan Roggenkamp
Executive Creative Direction
　Martin Pross, Wolf Schneider,
　Matthias Spaetgens
Creative Direction
　Wolf Schneider,
　Michael Winterhagen
Art Direction
　Maja Cerning, Ralf Schroeder,
　Esther Schwarz,
　Maria-Michaela Tonn
Client Consulting
　Anna Kubitza
Copy
　Lina Jachmann, Doerte Schuetz
Final Artwork
　Appel Grafik
Image Processing
　Maren Boerner
Photography
　Attila Hartwig
Production
　Sandro Buschke

　Roggenkamp Organics entdeckt eines der ältesten Zivilisationsgüter neu: Der Kochtopf schafft als nachhaltige, langlebige Verpackung den Sprung ins 21. Jahrhundert. Und er ist gekommen, um zu bleiben: Nach dem Gebrauch ist er einfach auszuspülen und kann beliebig oft mit Roggenkamps Frischer Suppe aufgefüllt werden. So etabliert sich die Marke nachhaltig in deutschen Kühl- und Küchenschränken.

　Roggenkamp Frische Suppe »Hausmacher Art« ("homemade-style" fresh soup) is rediscovering one of our civilization's oldest goods: the stockpot. With sustainable packaging that can be used again and again, it has managed the leap forward into the 21st century. And it is here to stay: after use it can be rinsed and refilled. The brand becomes a permanent fixture in cupboards and fridges.

**NOMINATION
DESIGN
DESIGN**
　Design
　Packaging
　Design
　Packaging

**WILD BAG® BOX
"Out_Of_Ark"**

Lead Agency
　identis GmbH,
　design-gruppe
　joseph pölzelbauer
Client
　winwood48 KG
Marketing Direction
　Svenja Schneppe
Creative Direction
　Joseph Pölzelbauer
Design
　Joseph Pölzelbauer,
　Simone Pölzelbauer
Graphic Design
　Simone Pölzelbauer

Die Wild Bag Box ist die Verpackung für "out_of_ark", eine Taschenkollektion mit 15 verschiedenen Tiermotiven aus fünf Kontinenten. Die Crossoverbags werden in der ausbruchssicheren Wild Bag Box transportiert – wie es sich für wilde Taschen gehört. Die Wild Bag Box ist mehr als eine Verpackung. Sie ist Teil der Story und bestätigt die Lebendigkeit der Produkte. Das Innenleben wird Teil des Packungsbildes.

The Wild Bag Box is the packaging for "out_of_ark", a bag collection with 15 different motifs featuring animals from five continents. The crossover bags are transported in an escape-proof Wild Bag Box – as is befitting of wild bags. This makes the Wild Bag Box so much more than just packaging. It becomes part of the story and affirms the vitality of the products. What's inside becomes part of the packaging.

NOMINATION
DESIGN
DESIGN
　Design
　Produktdesign
　Design
　Product Design

THE DELI GARAGE
»Lutschwerkzeug«

Lead Agency
　Kolle Rebbe/KOREFE
Client
　T.D.G. Vertriebs GmbH
　& Co. KG
Marketing Direction
　Felix Negwer
Creative Direction
　Katrin Oeding
Art Direction
　Reginald Wagner
Client Consulting
　Kristina Wulf
Copy
　Till Grabsch,
　Gereon Klug
Graphic Design
　Paul Svoboda,
　Sarah Gossner
Production
　Produktionsbüro
　Romey von Malottky GmbH

Lutschwerkzeug sind sechs Lollis mit verschiedenen Geschmacksrichtungen in der Form von Schraubendrehern, verpackt in einer Werkzeugtasche aus Leder. Der Schraubendreherlook verändert die Wahrnehmung: Hier ist der Griff nicht der Stiel, sondern die Lutschfläche.

By reversing the normal lollipop form, screwdrivers are turned into lollipops. The edible part is turned into a handle, the tip into a lollipop stick. The Lollitool is packaged in a classic tool bag made of leather and is only available in a limited edition.

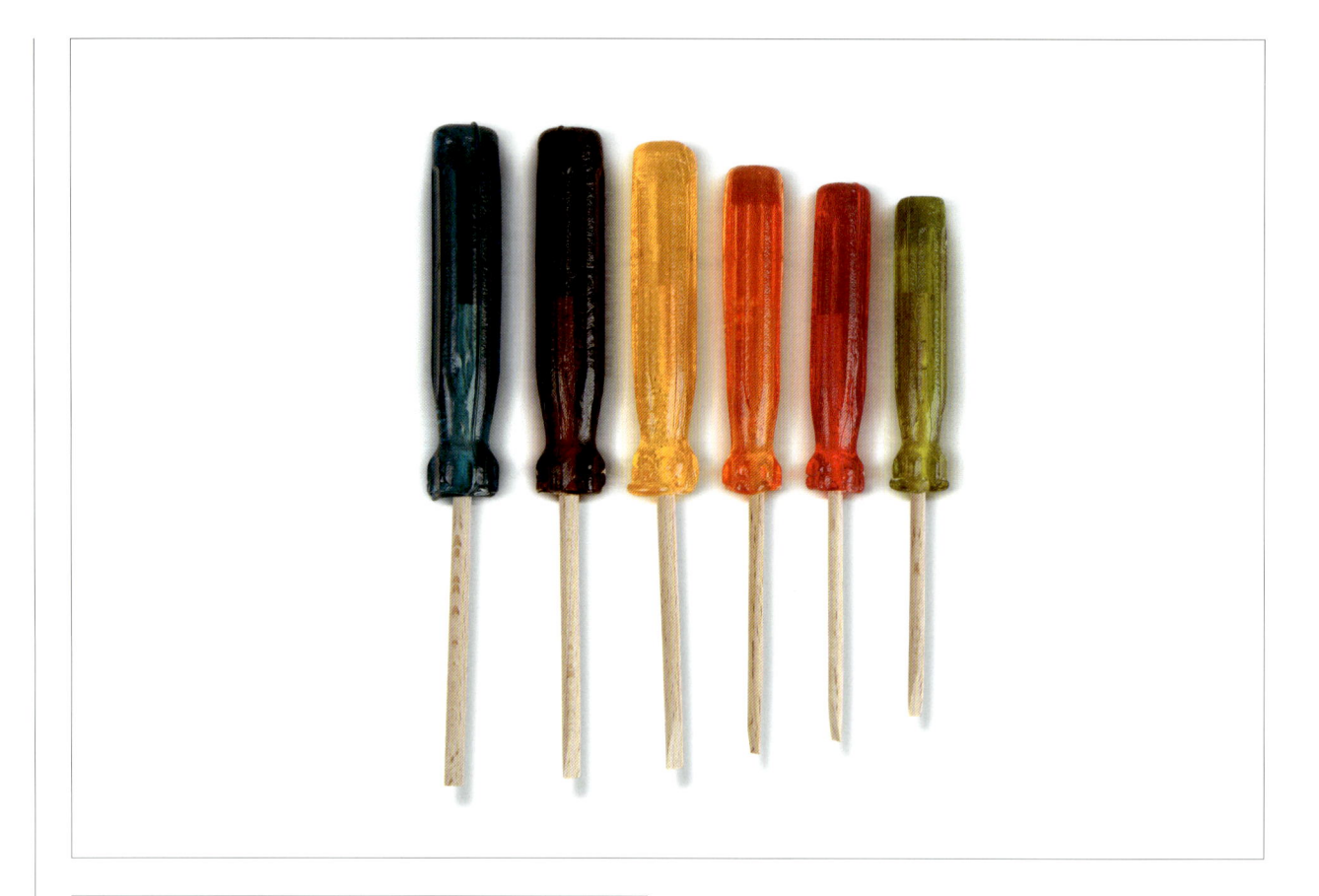

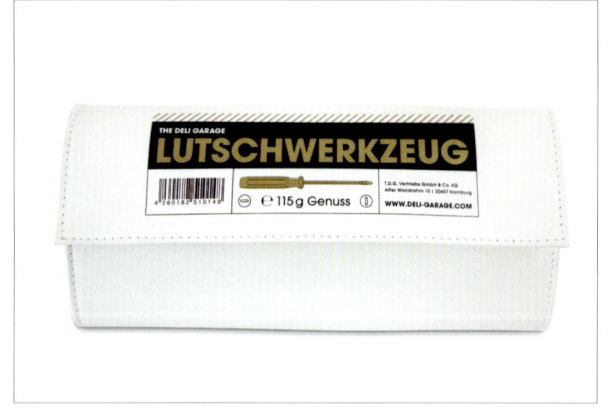

NOMINATION
EDITORIAL
EDITORIAL
Editorial
Print/Ausgabe
Editorial
Print/Issue

DAS NEUE TESTAMENT
ALS MAGAZIN
»Ausgabe 1/2010«

Lead Agency
    Neubau Editorial Design &
    Medienbüro Oliver Wurm
Client
    Neubau Editorial Design &
    Medienbüro Oliver Wurm
Executive Creative Direction
    Andreas Volleritsch,
    Oliver Wurm
Art Direction
    Andreas Volleritsch
Strategic Planning
    Oliver Wurm
Copy
    Oliver Wurm
Publishing House
    Bibelmagazin Gbr,
    Volleritsch & Wurm

● NOMINATION
EDITORIAL
EDITORIAL
Editorial
Print/Ausgabe
Editorial
Print/Issue

—
INTERKANTONALER RÜCK-
VERSICHERUNGSVERBAND
»100 Jahre IRV«

Lead Agency
    KOMET Werbeagentur AG
    BSW
Client
    Interkantonaler
    Rückversicherungsverband IRV
Marketing Direction
    Martin Kamber
Advertising Direction
    Rolf Meier
Executive Creative Direction
    Thom Pfister
Creative Direction
    Thom Pfister
Art Direction
    Roland Zenger,
    Tamara Janes
Client Consulting
    Simon Schatzmann
Strategic Planning
    Kurt Schori
Chief Editing
    Rolf Meier
Concept
    Thom Pfister
Consulting
    Emma Isolini
Copy
    Isabella Jungo,
    Antonia Bekiaris
Design
    Tamara Janes
Final Artwork
    Rahel Alder
Graphic Design
    Roland Zenger,
    Tamara Janes
Idea
    Thom Pfister
Illustration
    Marc Zehnhäusern
Image Processing
    Rahel Alder
Infographics
    Reto Eckert
Photography
    Beat Schweizer
Printing
    Rickli & Wyss
Production
    Ast Fischer
Publishing House
    In-house Production
Typography
    Tamara Janes

– DER IRV IM
WANDEL DER ZEIT
– L'UIR AU FIL
DU TEMPS

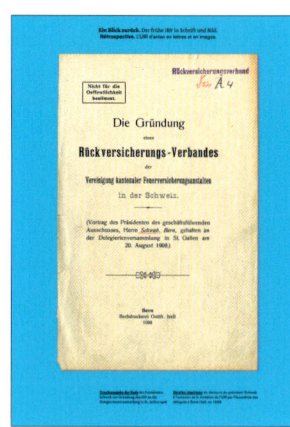

NOMINATION
EDITORIAL
EDITORIAL
 Editorial
  Print/Ausgabe
 Editorial
  Print/Issue

KID'S WEAR MAGAZINE
»Vol. 31 Herbst/Winter 2010/11«

Lead Agency
 Meiré&Meiré
Client
 Achim Lippoth
Art Direction
 Mike Meiré
Editing
 Ann-Katrin Weiner
Publishing House
 kid's wear Verlag

NOMINATION
EDITORIAL
EDITORIAL
- Editorial
- Print/Ausgabe
- Editorial
- Print/Issue

MAGAZIN DER BAYERISCHEN STAATSFORSTEN
»Waldfest«

Lead Agency
  Anzinger|Wüschner|Rasp
  Agentur für Kommunikation GmbH
Client
  Bayerische Staatsforsten AöR
Marketing Direction
  Dr. Hermann S. Walter,
  Head of the Office
  of the Board of Directors
Executive Creative Direction
  Markus Rasp
Creative Direction
  Markus Rasp
Art Direction
  Olaf Zimmermann
Client Consulting
  Claudia Anzinger
Strategic Planning
  Gernot Wüschner
Agency Production
  Martina Jacoby
Chief Editing
  Gernot Wüschner
Consulting
  Martina Jacoby
Copy
  Gernot Wüschner
Editing
  Gernot Wüschner,
  Jan Kirsten Biener,
  Hanno Charisius,
  Jan Füchtjohann,
  Hans Gerlach
Final Artwork
  Sabine Düe
Illustration
  Roman Klonek,
  Eva Hillreiner,
  Doc Robert
Image Processing
  MXM Digital Services, Munich
Photography
  Marion Blomeyer,
  Barbara Bonisolli,
  Bert Heinzlmeier,
  Peter Jacoby,
  Matthias Ziegler
Printing
  Gerber Druck+Medien,
  Kirchheim
Publishing House
  Self-published

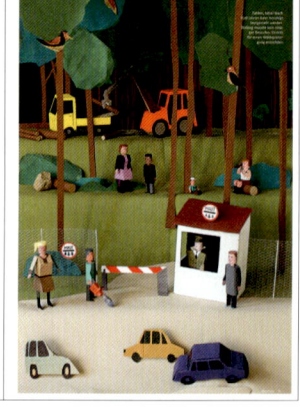

NOMINATION
EDITORIAL
EDITORIAL
Editorial
Print/Ausgabe
Editorial
Print/Issue

NEON MAGAZIN
»XXL-Ausgabe –
Was bin ich wirklich wert?«

Lead Agency
  NEON Magazin
Client
  Gruner + Jahr
Advertising Direction
  Antje Schlünder
Executive Creative Direction
  Thomas Lindner,
  Andreas Petzold
Art Direction
  Jonas Natterer
Chief Editing
  Michael Ebert,
  Timm Klotzek
Copy
  Various
Editing
  Various
Graphic Design
  Ji-Young Ahn (Deputy Art Direction),
  Sandra Stolle (Deputy Art Direction),
  Enite Hoffmann,
  Manuel Kostrzynski
Illustration
  Various
Image Editing
  Jakob Feigl (Director of Photography),
  Kristin Ahlring,
  Amélie Schneider
Photography
  Various
Printing
  Mohn Media GmbH, Gütersloh
Publishing House
  Gruner + Jahr

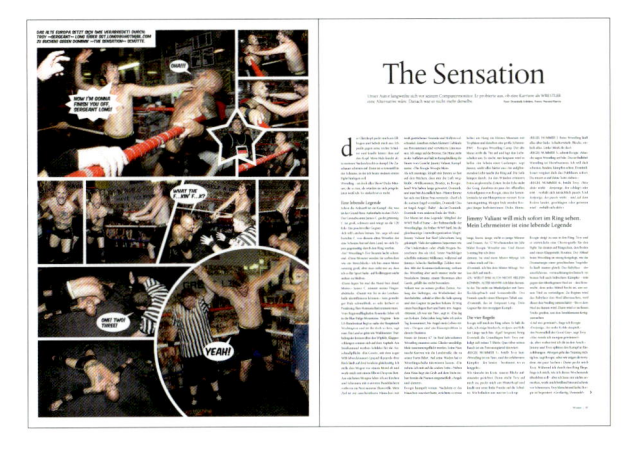

393

NOMINATION
EDITORIAL
EDITORIAL
  Editorial
  Print/Ausgabe
  Editorial
  Print/Issue

SLEEK – MAGAZINE FOR ART AND FASHION
»#26 ›Flora|Fauna‹«

Lead Agency
  B|BE Branded Entertainment GmbH
Client
  Christian Bracht
Marketing Direction
  Iris Gräbner
Creative Direction
  Christian Küpker
Chief Editing
  Annika von Taube
Printing
  Buch- und Offsetdruckerei H. Heenemann, Berlin
Publishing House
  B|BE Branded Entertainment GmbH

394

NOMINATION
EDITORIAL
EDITORIAL
Editorial
Print/Ausgabe
Editorial
Print/Issue

SÜDDEUTSCHE ZEITUNG MAGAZIN
»Edition 46/Menschen. Ein Bilderzyklus von Hans-Peter Feldmann«

Lead Agency
  Süddeutsche Zeitung Magazin
Client
  Süddeutsche Zeitung Magazin
Art Direction
  Daniel Bognár
Chief Editing
  Dr. Dominik Wichmann
Graphic Design
  Anne Blaschke,
  Thomas Kartsolis,
  Birthe Steinbeck,
  Dirk Schmidt
Image Editing
  Eva Fischer,
  Ralf Zimmermann
Image Processing
  Esther Matusche
Publishing House
  Magazin Verlagsgesellschaft
  Süddeutsche Zeitung mbH

Süddeutsche Zeitung Magazin

Edition 46 19. November 2010

Menschen
Ein Bilderzyklus von *Hans-Peter Feldmann* für das *Magazin der Süddeutschen Zeitung*

NOMINATION
EDITORIAL
EDITORIAL
Editorial
Print/Ausgabe
Editorial
Print/Issue

SÜDDEUTSCHE ZEITUNG
MAGAZIN
»Hoffnung?«

Lead Agency
 Süddeutsche Zeitung Magazin
Client
 Süddeutsche Zeitung Magazin
Art Direction
 Daniel Bognár
Chief Editing
 Dr. Dominik Wichmann
Graphic Design
 Anne Blaschke,
 Thomas Kartsolis,
 Birthe Steinbeck,
 Dirk Schmidt
Illustration
 Daniel Richter,
 Josephine Meckseper,
 Kiki Smith,
 Thomas Schütte
Image Editing
 Eva Fischer,
 Ralf Zimmermann
Image Processing
 Esther Matusche
Publishing House
 Magazin Verlagsgesellschaft
 Süddeutsche Zeitung mbH

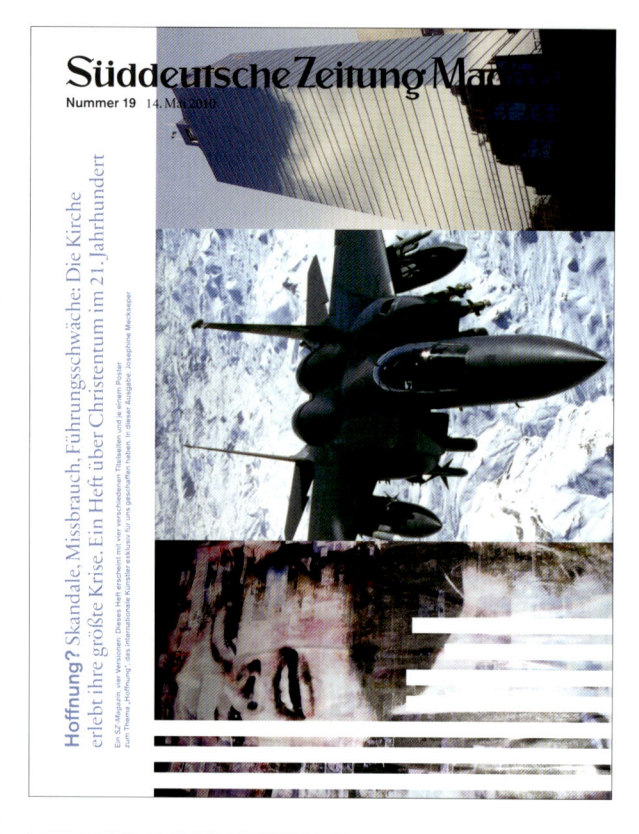

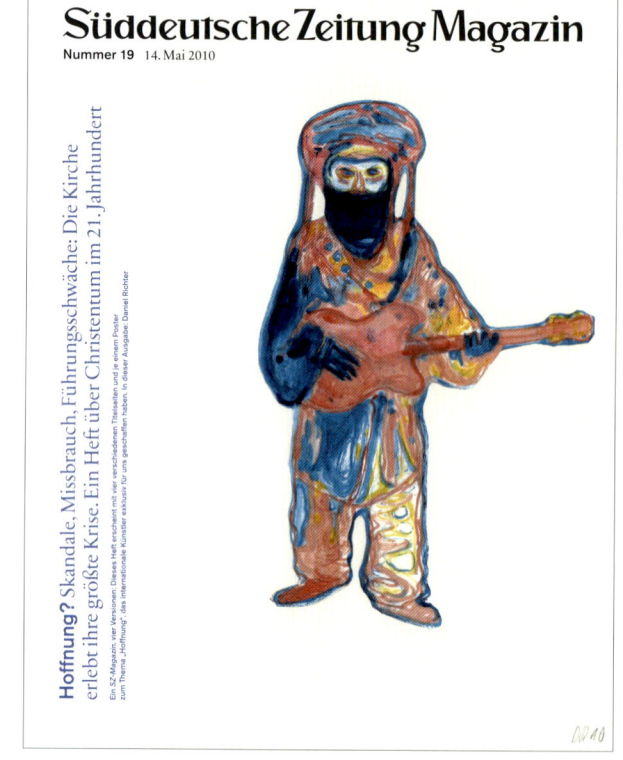

NOMINATION
EDITORIAL
EDITORIAL
 Editorial
 Print/Ausgabe
 Editorial
 Print/Issue

SÜDDEUTSCHE ZEITUNG
MAGAZIN
 »Solange sie noch leben«

Lead Agency
 Süddeutsche Zeitung Magazin
Client
 Süddeutsche Zeitung Magazin
Art Direction
 Daniel Bognár
Chief Editing
 Dr. Dominik Wichmann
Graphic Design
 Anne Blaschke,
 Thomas Kartsolis,
 Birthe Steinbeck,
 Dirk Schmidt
Illustration
 Reinhard Kleist
Image Editing
 Eva Fischer,
 Ralf Zimmermann
Image Processing
 Esther Matusche
Publishing House
 Magazin Verlagsgesellschaft
 Süddeutsche Zeitung mbH

Süddeutsche Zeitung Magazin

Nummer 16   23. April 2010

Solange sie noch leben 65 Jahre nach dem Ende des Zweiten Weltkriegs stehen sich die letzten lebenden Täter und Zeugen des Holocausts vor Gericht gegenüber. Wenn sie sterben, wird alles nur noch Geschichte sein. Deswegen dieses *SZ-Magazin*

NOMINATION
EDITORIAL
EDITORIAL
Editorial
Print/Ausgabe
Editorial
Print/Issue

VICE MAGAZINE
"v7n1 –
The Barking Dog Issue"

Lead Agency
 VICE Deutschland GmbH
Client
 VICE Deutschland GmbH
Marketing Direction
 Benjamin Ruth
Advertising Direction
 Benny Eichelmann
Chief Editing
 Tom Littlewood
Copy
 Mark Allen,
 Suroosh Alvi,
 Andy Capper,
 Rocco Castoro,
 Harry Cheadle,
 Ryan Duffy,
 Alex Dunbar,
 Amy Kellner,
 Michael Lutz,
 Chris Nieratko,
 André Pluskwa,
 Andreas Richter,
 Alistair Savage,
 Benjamin Seibe
Editing
 Barbara Dabrowska,
 Felix Nicklas,
 Andreas Richter,
 Stefan Lauer
Photography
 Ayman Oghanna,
 Thorne Anderson,
 Timur Civan,
 Patrick Duncan,
 Will Fairman,
 A. M. Goraya,
 Jerry Hsu,
 Sandy Kim,
 Henry Langston,
 Muir Vidler,
 Christoph Voy,
 Karlheinz Weinberger,
 Ed Zipco
Publishing House
 VICE Deutschland GmbH

NOMINATION
EDITORIAL
EDITORIAL

Editorial
Print/Jahrgang
Editorial
Print/Year's Issue

DER FREITAG
»Nr. 2, 5, 6, 16, 22, 28, 39, 46, 47, 51/52«

Lead Agency
 der Freitag
Client
 der Freitag
Art Direction
 Janine Sack,
 Andine Müller (Consulting)
Chief Editing
 Philip Grassmann,
 Jörn Kabisch (Deputy)
Graphic Design
 Jana Schnell
Image Editing
 Corinna Koch,
 Internship:
 Antje Berghäuser,
 Jan Wirdeier,
 Erik Irmer,
 Eva Olibet,
 Johannes Stein,
 Kevin Mertens
Publishing House
 der Freitag Mediengesellschaft mbH & Co Kg

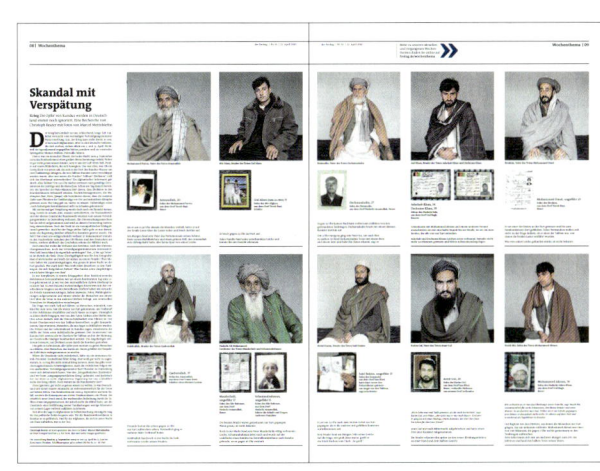

NOMINATION
EDITORIAL
EDITORIAL
 Editorial
 Print/Einzelleistung
 Editorial
 Print/Individual Work

———

BERLINER ILLUSTRIRTE ZEITUNG
 »Kinohauptstadt Berlin:
 Das Netzwerk«

Lead Agency
 Berliner Morgenpost
Client
 Berliner Illustrirte Zeitung
Chief Editing
 Carsten Erdmann
Editing
 Sandra Garbers,
 Felix Müller
Infographics
 Babette Ackermann-Reiche
Printing
 Druckhaus Spandau
Publishing House
 Axel Springer AG

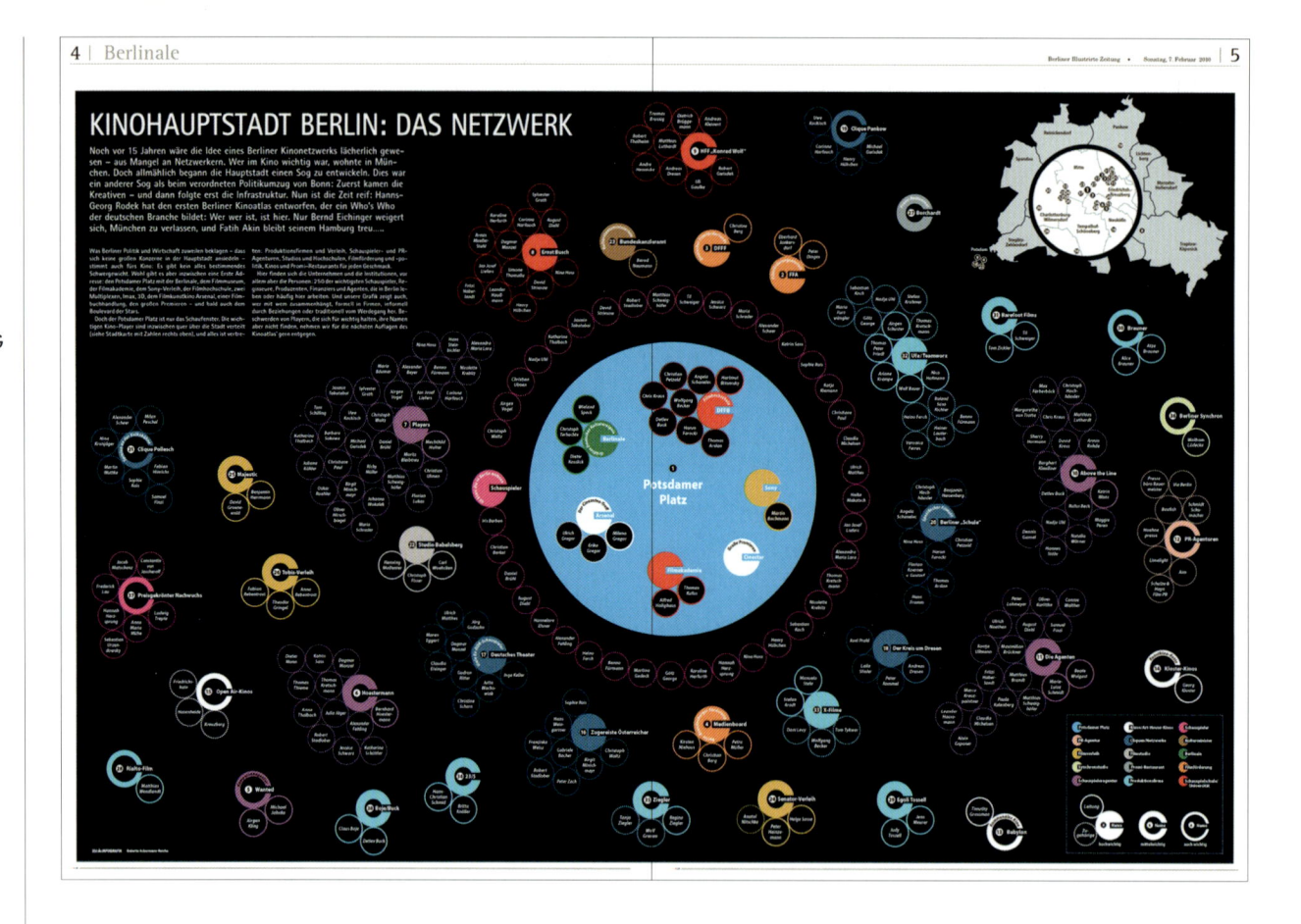

NOMINATION
EDITORIAL
EDITORIAL
  Editorial
  Print/Einzelleistung
  Editorial
  Print/Individual Work

BERLINER ILLUSTRIRTE ZEITUNG
  »Kleine Menschen,
  große Welt«

Lead Agency
  Berliner Morgenpost
Client
  Berliner Illustrirte Zeitung
Chief Editing
  Carsten Erdmann
Copy
  Jan Draeger
Design
  Ralf Jacob
Editing
  Sandra Garbers
Photography
  Andreas Mühe
Printing
  Druckhaus Spandau
Publishing House
  Axel Springer AG

401

NOMINATION
EDITORIAL
EDITORIAL

Editorial
Print/Einzelleistung
Editorial
Print/Individual Work

BERLINER MORGENPOST
»Ein einzigartiges Orchester«

Lead Agency
 Berliner Morgenpost
Client
 Berliner Morgenpost
Art Direction
 Hans-Jürgen Polster
Chief Editing
 Carsten Erdmann
Copy
 Susan Mücke,
 Hajo Schumacher
Design
 Layoutteam
 Berliner Morgenpost
Editing
 Berlin-Ressort
Infographics
 Berliner Morgenpost
Photography
 Reto Klar,
 Martin Lengemann,
 Jim Rakete
Printing
 Druckhaus Spandau
Publishing House
 Axel Springer AG

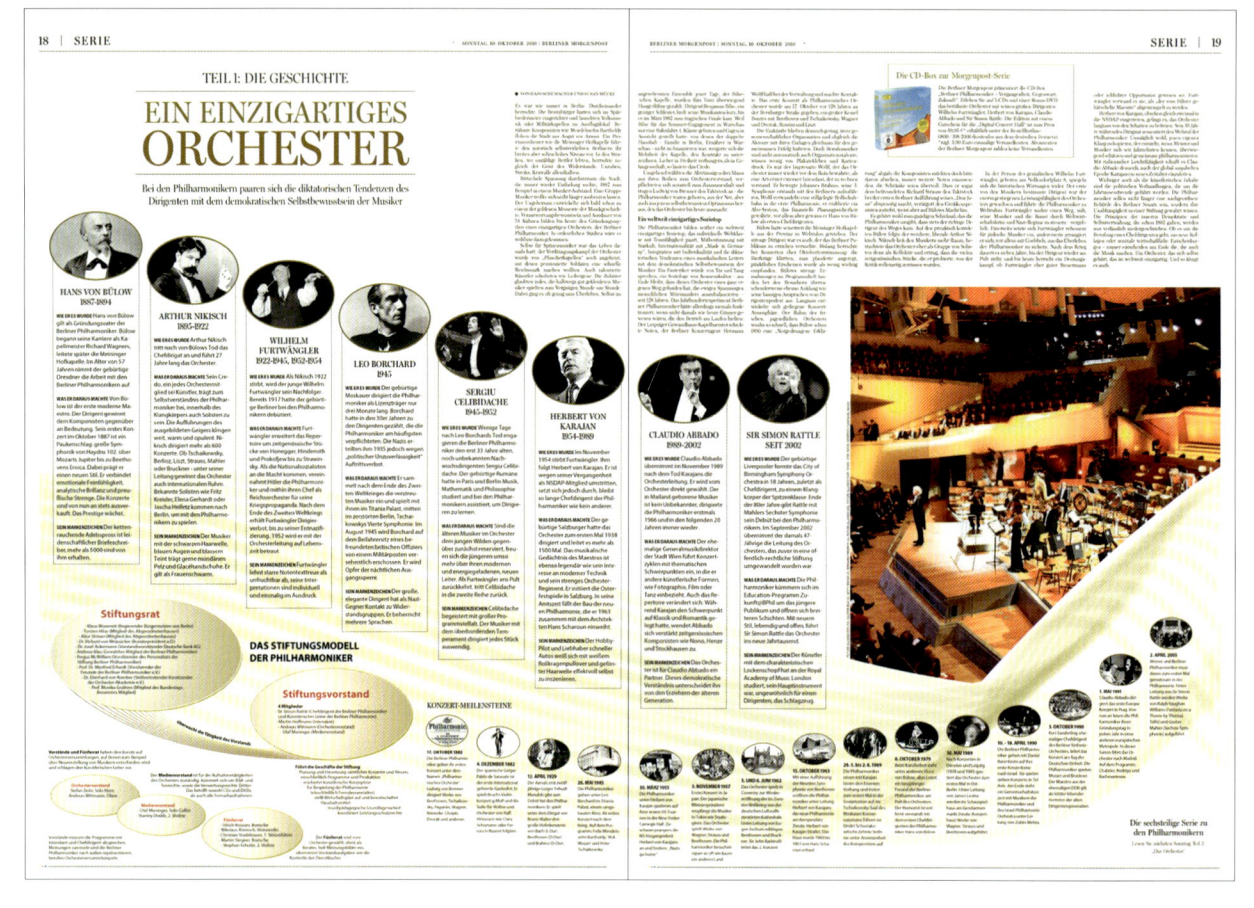

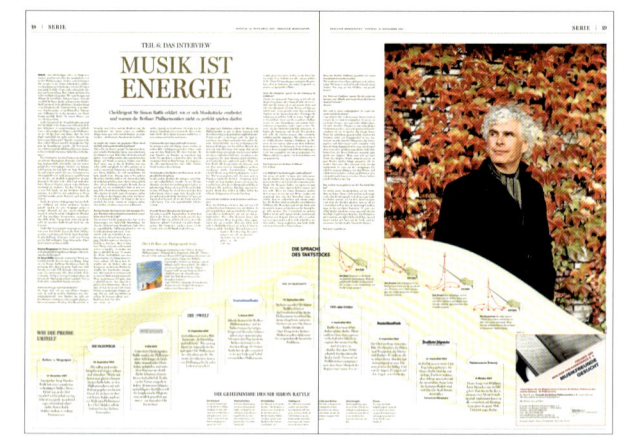

NOMINATION
EDITORIAL
EDITORIAL
    Editorial
    Print/Einzelleistung
    Editorial
    Print/Individual Work

DIE ZEIT
»Wer wird Präsident?«

Lead Agency
    Golden Section Graphics
Client
    DIE ZEIT
Creative Direction
    Jan Schwochow
Infographics
    Paul Blickle,
    Katharina Stipp,
    Jan Schwochow
Publishing House
    Zeitverlag Gerd Bucerius
Other
    Research: Bernd Riedel

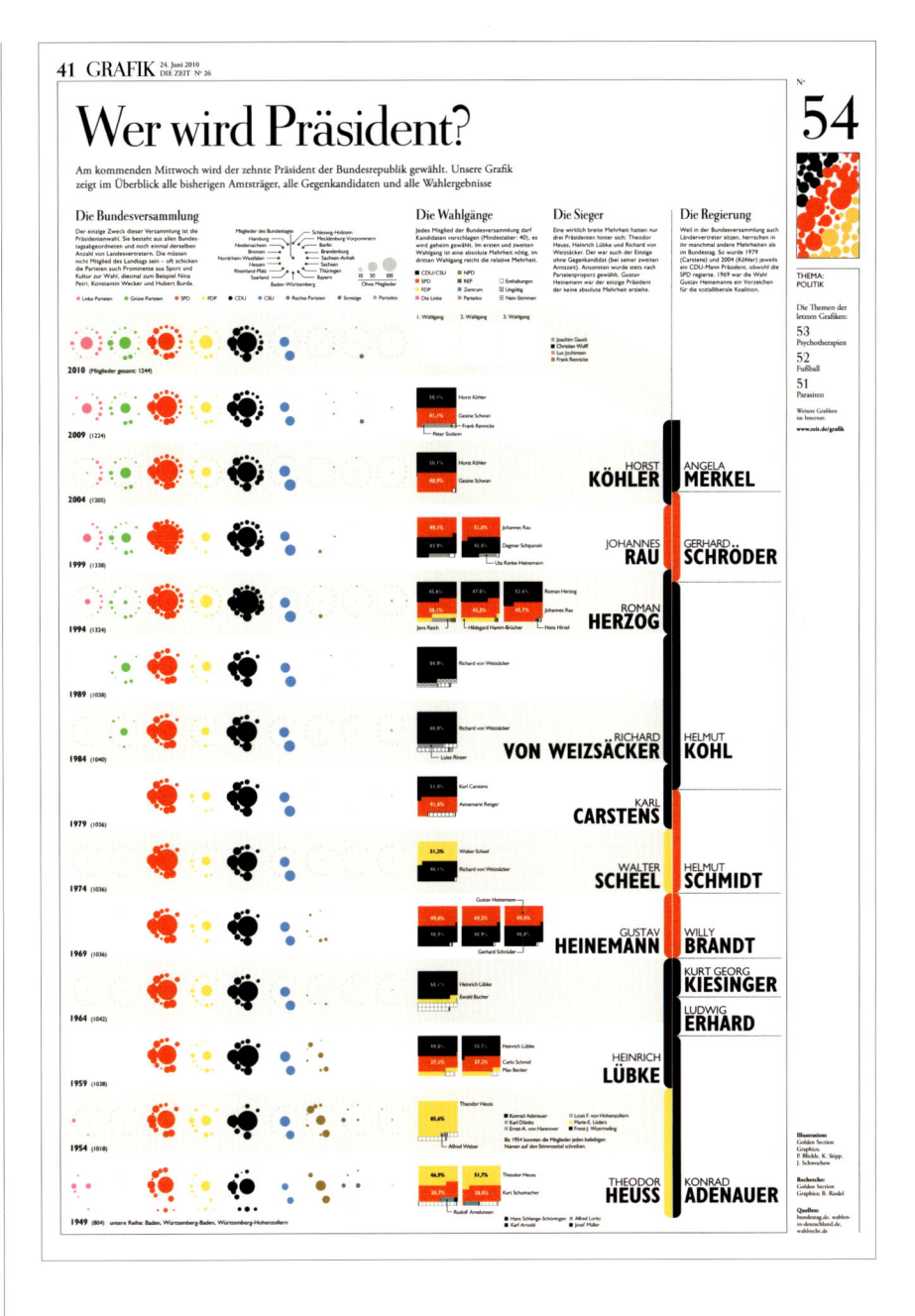

NOMINATION
EDITORIAL
EDITORIAL
  Editorial
  Print/Einzelleistung
  Editorial
  Print/Individual Work

IN GRAPHICS
 "Transfer Calligraphy"

Lead Agency
  Golden Section Graphics
Client
  Golden Section Graphics
Creative Direction
  Jan Schwochow
Infographics
  Katja Günther,
  Bernd Riedel
Publishing House
  Golden Section Graphics GmbH

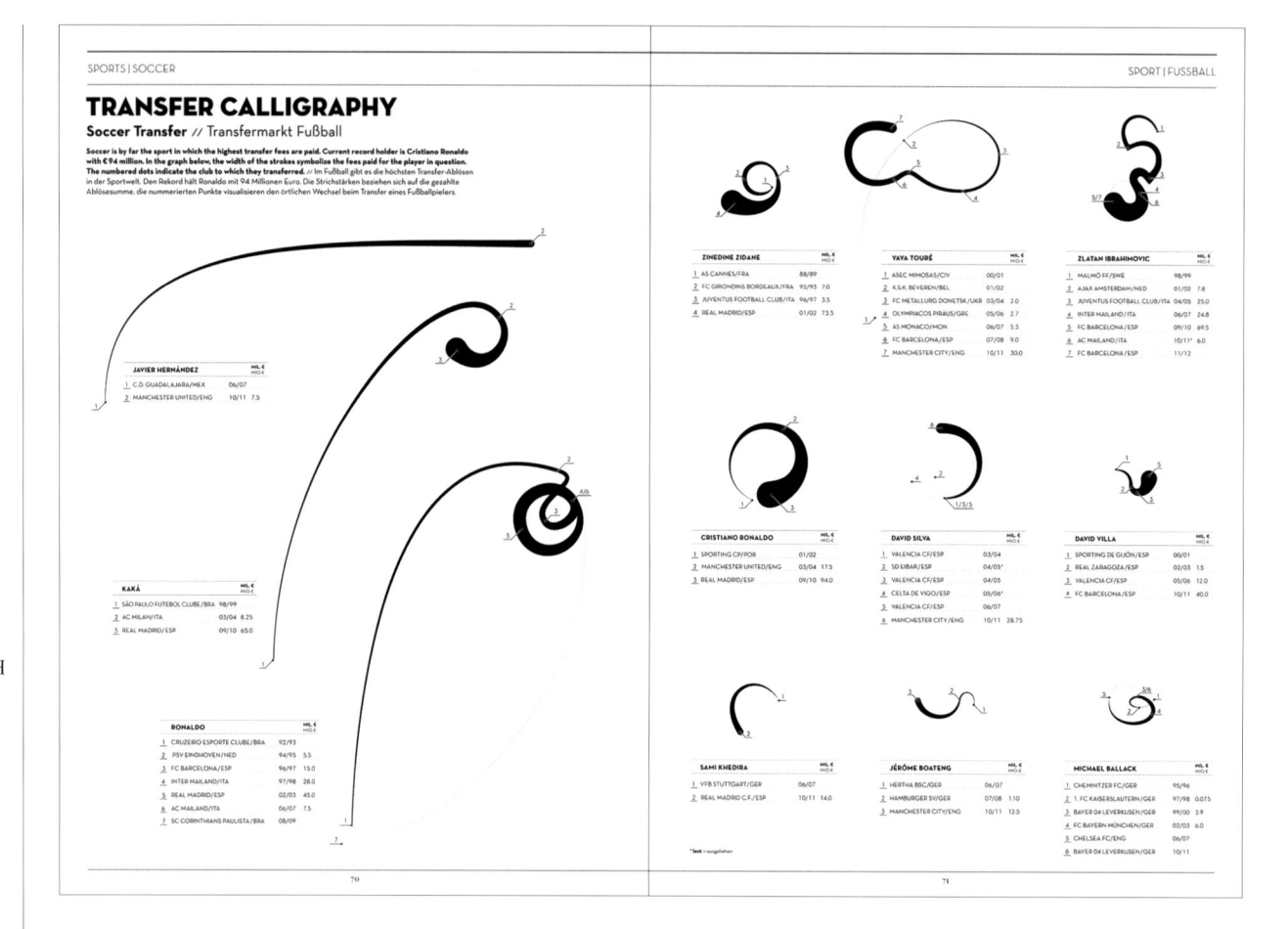

NOMINATION
EDITORIAL
EDITORIAL
Editorial
Print/Einzelleistung
Editorial
Print/Individual Work

—
NEON MAGAZIN FEBRUAR 2010
»Lasst sie heulen!«

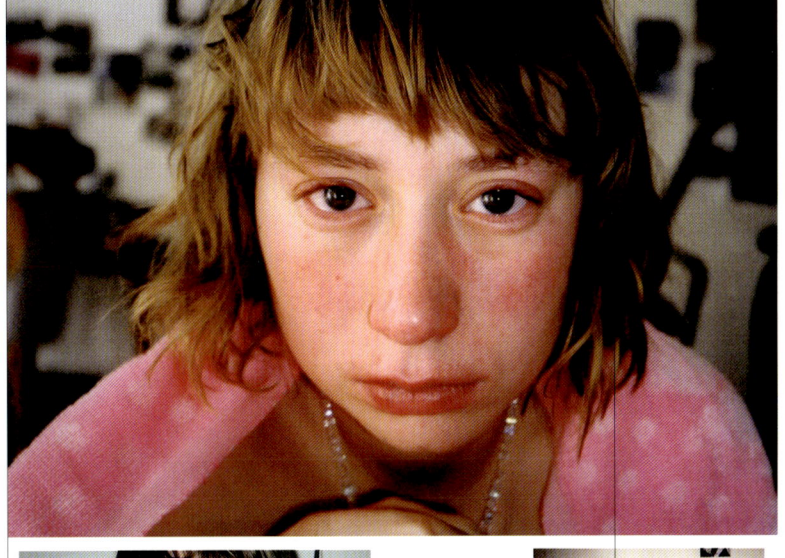

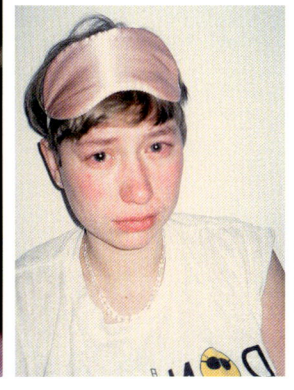

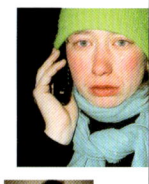

Lead Agency
 NEON Magazin
Client
 NEON Magazin GmbH
Advertising Direction
 Antje Schlünder
Executive Creative Direction
 Thomas Lindner,
 Andreas Petzold
Art Direction
 Jonas Natterer
Chief Editing
 Michael Ebert,
 Timm Klotzek
Copy
 David Pfeifer
Graphic Design
 Sandra Stolle
  (Deputy Art Direction),
 Ji-Young Ahn,
 Enite Hoffmann,
 Manuel Kostrzynski
Image Editing
 Jakob Feigl
  (Director of Photography),
 Kristin Ahlring,
 Amélie Schneider
Photography
 Melanie Bonajo
Printing
 Mohn Media GmbH, Gütersloh
Publishing House
 Gruner + Jahr

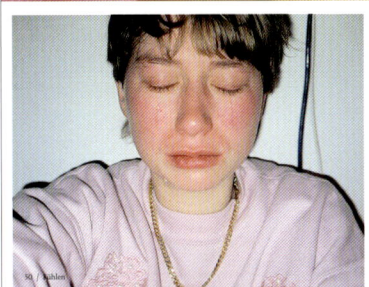

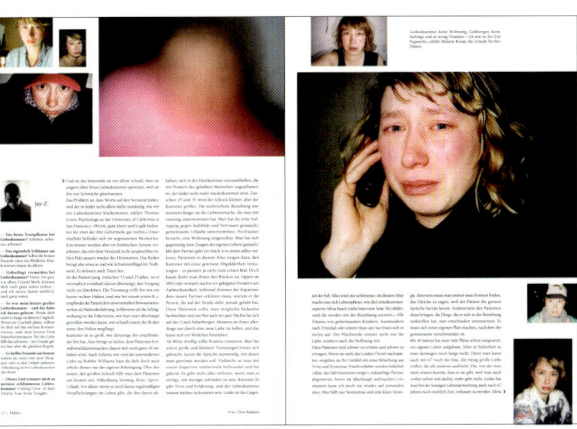

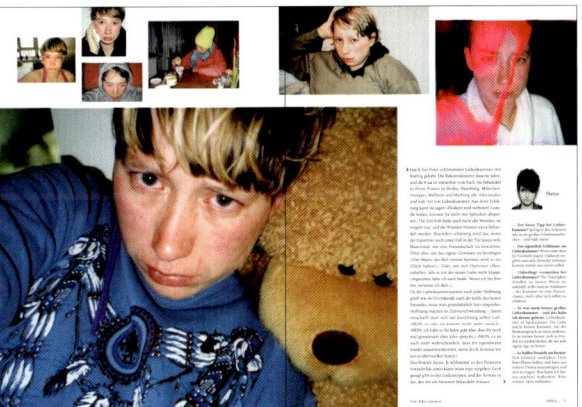

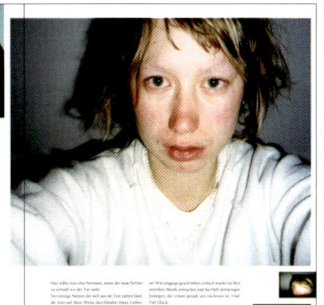

NOMINATION
EDITORIAL
EDITORIAL
　Editorial
　　Print/Einzelleistung
　Editorial
　　Print/Individual Work

STERN MAGAZIN
»Ausbruch ins Leben«

Lead Agency
　stern Magazin
Client
　Gruner + Jahr AG & Co. KG
Art Direction
　Donald Schneider,
　Mark Ernsting (Deputy)
Graphic Design
　John Skudra
Image Editing
　Andrea Gothe
Photography
　Heidi & Hans-Jürgen Koch
Publishing House
　Gruner + Jahr AG & Co. KG

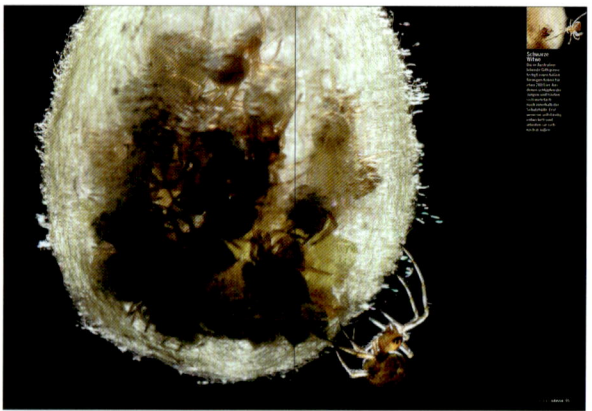

NOMINATION
EDITORIAL
EDITORIAL
Editorial
Print/Einzelleistung
Editorial
Print/Individual Work

STERN MAGAZIN
»Der endlose Krieg«

Lead Agency
  stern Magazin
Client
  Gruner + Jahr AG & Co. KG
Art Direction
  Donald Schneider,
  Mark Ernsting (Deputy)
Graphic Design
  Corinna Sobek
Image Editing
  Harald Menk
Photography
  João Pina
Publishing House
  Gruner + Jahr AG & Co. KG

NOMINATION
EDITORIAL
EDITORIAL
 Editorial
 Print/Einzelleistung
 Editorial
 Print/Individual Work

SÜDDEUTSCHE ZEITUNG MAGAZIN
»80 Jahre Helmut Kohl«

Lead Agency
 Süddeutsche Zeitung Magazin
Client
 Süddeutsche Zeitung Magazin
Art Direction
 Daniel Bognár
Chief Editing
 Dr. Dominik Wichmann
Copy
 Max Fellmann
Graphic Design
 Anne Blaschke,
 Thomas Kartsolis,
 Birthe Steinbeck,
 Dirk Schmidt
Image Editing
 Eva Fischer,
 Ralf Zimmermann
Image Processing
 Esther Matusche
Photography
 Andrew Zuckerman
Publishing House
 Magazin Verlagsgesellschaft
 Süddeutsche Zeitung mbH

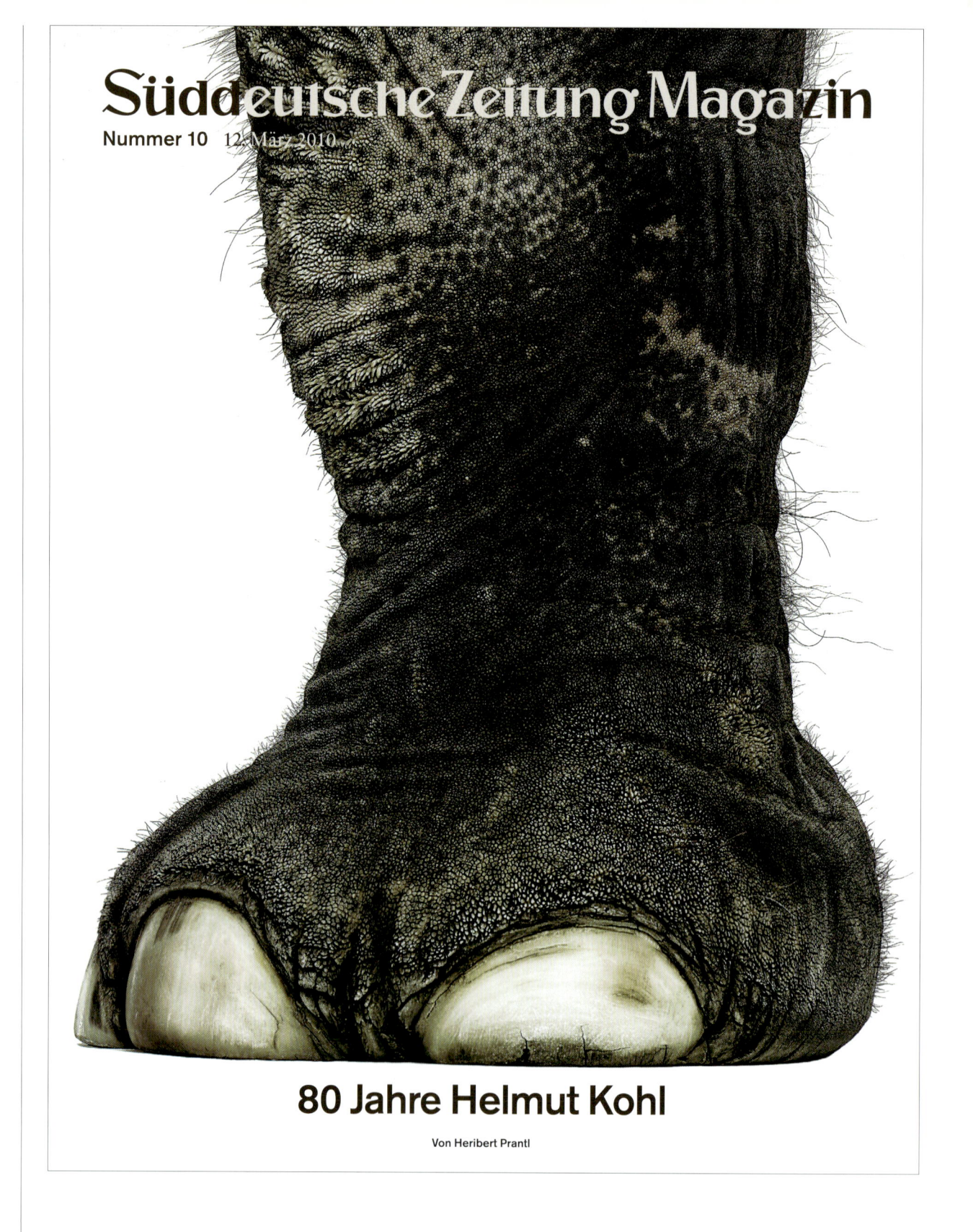

Süddeutsche Zeitung Magazin
Nummer 10 12. März 2010

80 Jahre Helmut Kohl

Von Heribert Prantl

NOMINATION
EDITORIAL
EDITORIAL
Editorial
Print/Einzelleistung
Editorial
Print/Individual Work

SÜDDEUTSCHE ZEITUNG MAGAZIN
»Alle zusammen und jeder für sich«

Lead Agency
  Süddeutsche Zeitung Magazin
Client
  Süddeutsche Zeitung Magazin
Art Direction
  Daniel Bognár
Chief Editing
  Dr. Dominik Wichmann
Copy
  Max Fellmann
Graphic Design
  Anne Blaschke,
  Thomas Kartsolis,
  Birthe Steinbeck,
  Dirk Schmidt
Image Editing
  Eva Fischer,
  Ralf Zimmermann
Image Processing
  Esther Matusche
Photography
  Kai-Uwe Gundlach
Publishing House
  Magazin Verlagsgesellschaft
  Süddeutsche Zeitung mbH

Alle zusammen und jeder für sich Der Fotograf Kai-Uwe Gundlach hat Menschen in Japan fotografiert, auf der belebtesten Kreuzung der Welt. Dann hat er das Treiben der Straße aus seinen Bildern entfernt. Was dabei herauskommt, ist ein völlig neuer Blick ins Herz der Menschen, ein Blick, der von ihrer Einsamkeit erzählt, inmitten der Masse

NOMINATION
EDITORIAL
EDITORIAL
   Editorial
   Print/Einzelleistung
   Editorial
   Print/Individual Work

SÜDDEUTSCHE ZEITUNG
MAGAZIN
   »Da fällt mir Einstein
   vom Herzen«

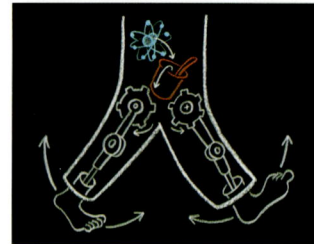

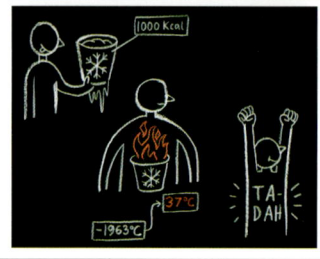

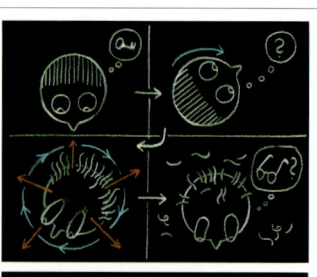

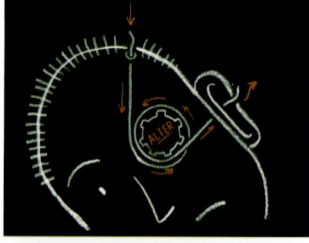

Lead Agency
   Süddeutsche Zeitung Magazin
Client
   Süddeutsche Zeitung Magazin
Art Direction
   Daniel Bognár
Chief Editing
   Dr. Dominik Wichmann
Copy
   Max Fellmann
Graphic Design
   Anne Blaschke,
   Thomas Kartsolis,
   Birthe Steinbeck,
   Dirk Schmidt
Illustration
   Christoph Niemann
Image Editing
   Eva Fischer,
   Ralf Zimmermann
Image Processing
   Esther Matusche
Publishing House
   Magazin Verlagsgesellschaft
   Süddeutsche Zeitung mbH

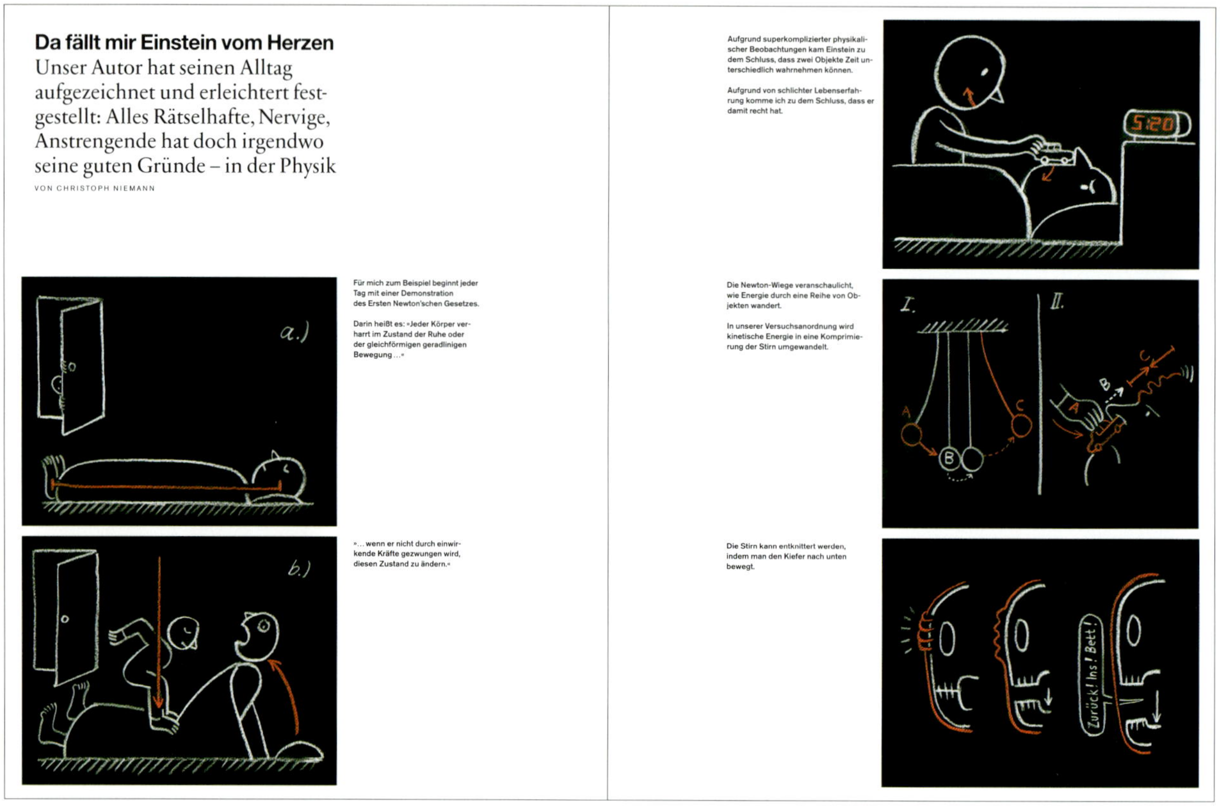

410

NOMINATION
EDITORIAL
EDITORIAL
    Editorial
    Print/Einzelleistung
    Editorial
    Print/Individual Work

SÜDDEUTSCHE ZEITUNG
MAGAZIN
»Kunstschuss«

Lead Agency
    Süddeutsche Zeitung Magazin
Client
    Süddeutsche Zeitung Magazin
Art Direction
    Daniel Bognár
Chief Editing
    Dr. Dominik Wichmann
Copy
    Max Fellmann
Graphic Design
    Anne Blaschke,
    Thomas Kartsolis,
    Birthe Steinbeck,
    Dirk Schmidt
Image Editing
    Eva Fischer,
    Ralf Zimmermann
Image Processing
    Esther Matusche
Publishing House
    Magazin Verlagsgesellschaft
    Süddeutsche Zeitung mbH

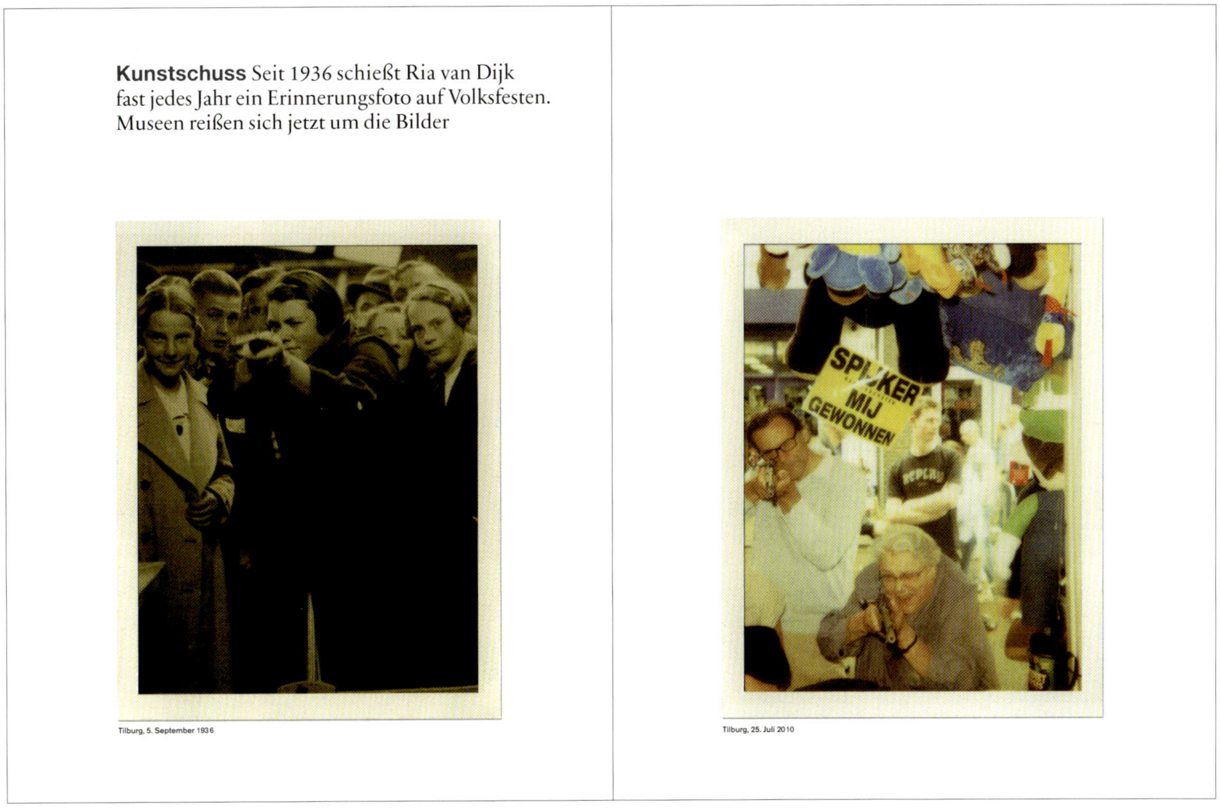

411

NOMINATION
EDITORIAL
EDITORIAL
Editorial
Print/Einzelleistung
Editorial
Print/Individual Work

ZEITMAGAZIN
»Fuchs, du hast die Uhr gestohlen«

Lead Agency
 ZEITmagazin
Client
 DIE ZEIT
Creative Direction
 Mirko Borsche
Art Direction
 Katja Kollmann
Chief Editing
 Christoph Amend
Graphic Design
 Nina Bengtson,
 Jasmin Müller-Stoy
Image Editing
 Michael Biedowicz,
 Andreas Wellnitz
Image Processing
 Twentyfour Seven Creative
 Media Services GmbH
Photography
 Henry Leutwyler
 Animation of Dolls:
 Payton Curtis
 Photos of Watches:
 Ragnar Schmuck
Publishing House
 Zeitverlag Gerd Bucerius
 GmbH & Co. KG
Other
 Selection of Watches:
 Gisbert L. Brunner

NOMINATION
EDITORIAL
EDITORIAL
    Editorial
    Print/Einzelleistung
    Editorial
    Print/Individual Work

ZEITMAGAZIN
    »Ich habe einen Traum/
    Queen Elizabeth II«

Lead Agency
    ZEITmagazin
Client
    DIE ZEIT
Creative Direction
    Mirko Borsche
Art Direction
    Katja Kollmann
Chief Editing
    Christoph Amend
Graphic Design
    Nina Bengtson,
    Jasmin Müller-Stoy
Image Editing
    Michael Biedowicz,
    Andreas Wellnitz
Image Processing
    Twentyfour Seven Creative
    Media Services GmbH
Photography
    "The Lightness of Being"
    by Chris Levine
Publishing House
    Zeitverlag Gerd Bucerius
    GmbH & Co. KG

ZEIT MAGAZIN

ICH HABE EINEN TRAUM

QUEEN ELIZABETH II

»THE LIGHTNESS OF BEING« BY CHRIS LEVINE

NOMINATION
EDITORIAL
EDITORIAL
Editorial
Print/Einzelleistung
Editorial
Print/Individual Work

ZEITMAGAZIN
»Ölbilder«

Lead Agency
  ZEITmagazin
Client
  DIE ZEIT
Creative Direction
  Mirko Borsche
Art Direction
  Katja Kollmann
Chief Editing
  Christoph Amend
Graphic Design
  Nina Bengtson,
  Jasmin Müller-Stoy,
  Mirko Merkel
Image Editing
  Michael Biedowicz,
  Andreas Wellnitz
Image Processing
  Twentyfour Seven Creative
  Media Services GmbH
Photography
  Benjamin Lowy
Publishing House
  Zeitverlag Gerd Bucerius
  GmbH & Co. KG

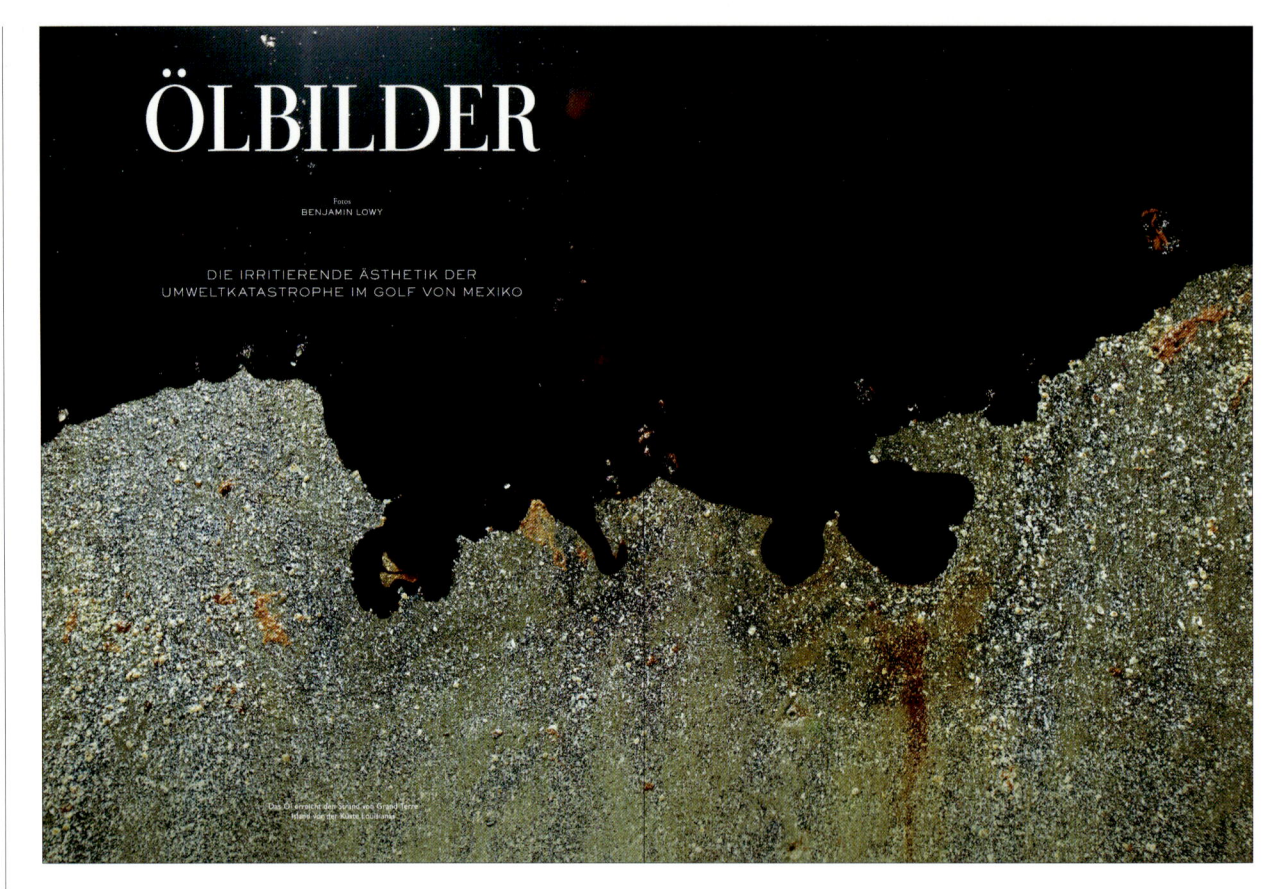

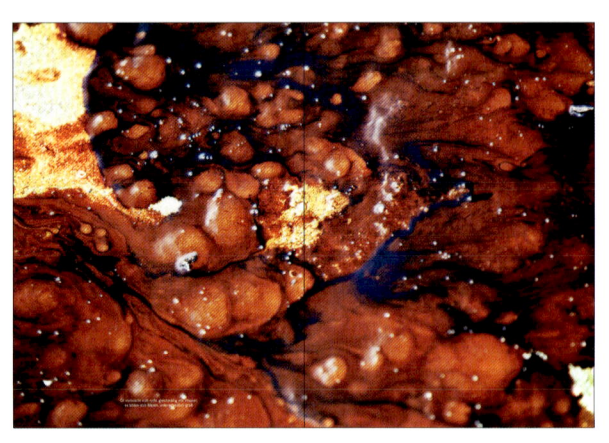

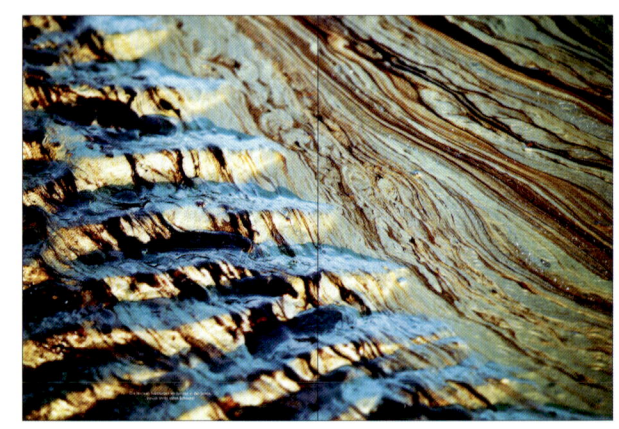

● NOMINATION
EDITORIAL
EDITORIAL
 Editorial
 Print/Einzelleistung
 Editorial
 Print/Individual Work

ZEITMAGAZIN
 »Schwarz ist das neue Weiß«

Lead Agency
 ZEITmagazin
Client
 DIE ZEIT
Creative Direction
 Mirko Borsche
Art Direction
 Katja Kollmann
Graphic Design
 Nina Bengtson,
 Jasmin Müller-Stoy
Image Processing
 delta E, Twentyfour Seven
 Creative Media Services GmbH
Photography
 Hubertus Hamm
Publishing House
 Zeitverlag Gerd Bucerius
 GmbH & Co. KG

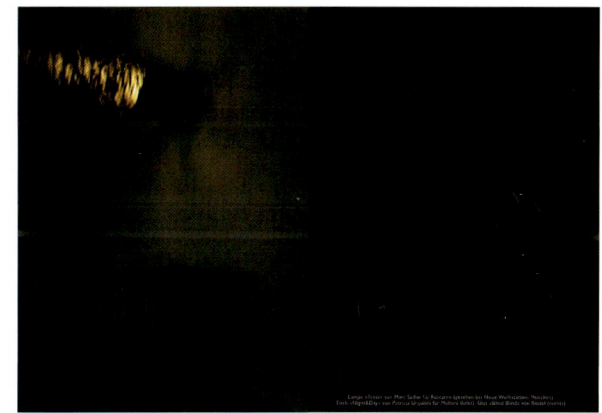

415

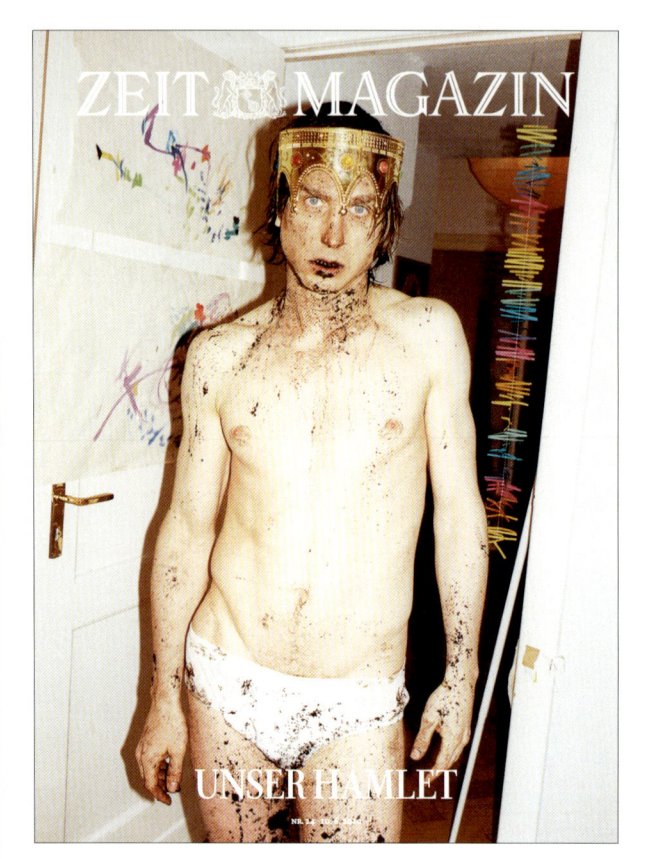

NOMINATION
EDITORIAL
EDITORIAL
   Editorial
   Print/Einzelleistung
   Editorial
   Print/Individual Work

ZEITMAGAZIN
   »Unser Hamlet«

Lead Agency
   ZEITmagazin
Client
   DIE ZEIT
Creative Direction
   Mirko Borsche
Art Direction
   Katja Kollmann
Chief Editing
   Christoph Amend
Graphic Design
   Nina Bengtson,
   Jasmin Müller-Stoy,
   Mirko Merkel
Image Editing
   Michael Biedowicz,
   Andreas Wellnitz
Image Processing
   Twentyfour Seven
   Creative Media Services GmbH
Photography
   Juergen Teller
Publishing House
   Zeitverlag Gerd Bucerius
   GmbH & Co. KG

● NOMINATION
**EDITORIAL
EDITORIAL**
Editorial
Multimedia/Gesamtkonzept
Editorial
Multimedia/
Integrated Concept

AUDI MAGAZIN
"iPad App"

Lead Agency
  loved gmbh
Contributing Agencies
  Programming:
  Otterbach IT GmbH &
  e-production42 gmbh
Client
  AUDI AG (I/VM-4)
Marketing Direction
  Ralf Maltzen
Advertising Direction
  Tanja Quenzler
Executive Creative Direction
  Mieke Haase
Creative Direction
  Rouven Steinke
Art Direction
  Julia-Christin Holtz,
  Pascal Constanty,
  Alexandra Michels
Client Consulting
  Peter Matz
Strategic Planning
  Peter Matz
Chief Editing
  Sabine Cole
Concept
  loved gmbh
Editing
  Jan Strahl,
  Hermann J. Müller,
  Oliver Wurm,
  Timo Ahrens,
  Harald Braun,
  Dorothea Sundergeld,
  Tom Vanderbilt,
  Okka Rohd,
  Steffan Heuer,
  Thilo Komma-Pöllath,
  Katahrina Lotter,
  Thomas Wirth,
  Roland Huschk
Image Editing
  Penélope Toro
Image Processing
  Otterbach Medien KG
  GmbH & Co.
IT Direction
  Otterbach IT GmbH
Programming
  e-production42 gmbh
Publishing House
  Programming:
  Otterbach IT GmbH &
  e-production42 gmbh

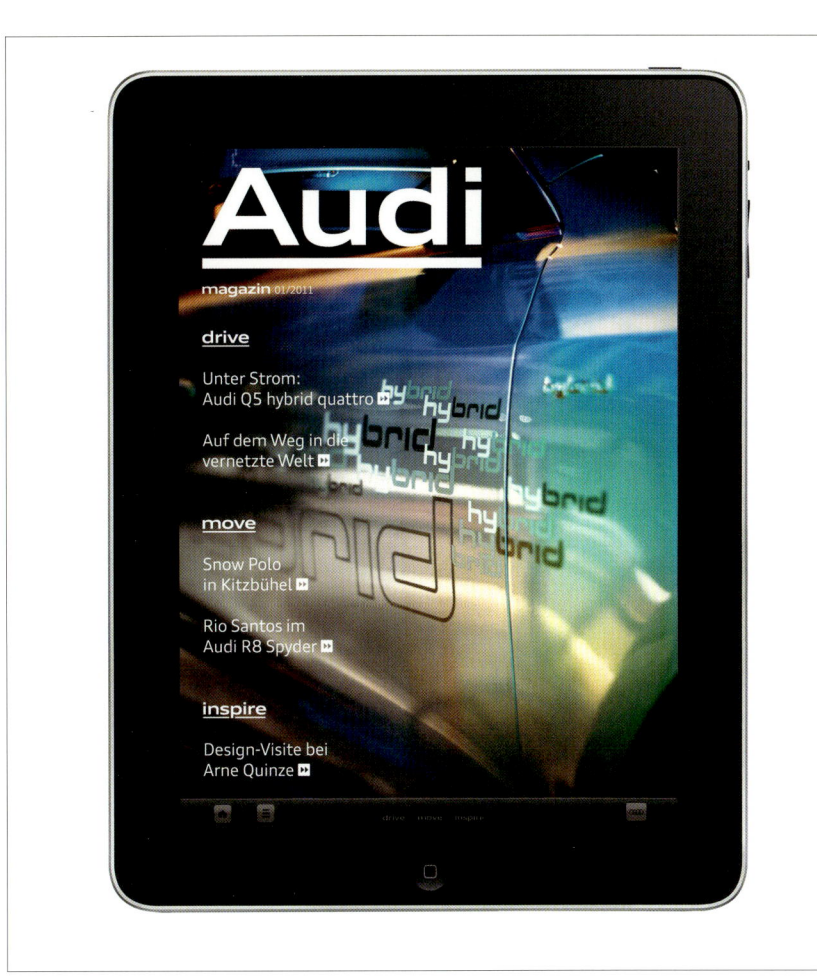

● **NOMINATION**
RÄUMLICHE INSZENIERUNG
SPATIAL SCENE-SETTING
Kommunikation im Raum
Environmental Design

AUDI MESSAUFTRITT
«Mondial de L'Automobile Paris 2010»

Lead Agency
   Schmidhuber + Partner/
   Mutabor Design
Contributing Agencies
   Schmidhuber + Partner/
   Mutabor Design
Client
   AUDI AG, Ingolstadt
Executive Creative Direction
   Michael Ostertag-Henning (S+P),
   Johannes Plass (Mutabor)
Creative Direction
   Michael Ostertag-Henning
Architecture
   Schmidhuber + Partner
Lighting Design
   Light Planning:
   Four to one:
   scale design, Hürth
Media
   Media Planning:
   NIYU® media projects, Berlin
Media Systems
   CT Creative Technology
   GmbH & Co. KG, Nürtingen
Scenography
   Schmidhuber + Partner
Trade Fair Construction
   Ernst F. Ambrosius & Sohn
   gegr. 1872 GmbH, Frankfurt

Wie inszeniert man den Erfolg einer Marke? Die Antwort: Über das Raumerlebnis. Dynamisch fließende Freiformen brechen mit Sehgewohnheiten. Fahrzeuge und Architektur sprechen eine gemeinsame Sprache. Ein Kommunikationsboulevard zur Besucherführung: vom A1 zum A8, von technologischen Effizienzbausteinen zur »Beweisführung« in der Fahrzeugflotte. Die Dynamik der Marke als 360°-Erlebnis.

How do you stage success? The solution: By the three-dimensional spatial experience itself! With free forms and doubly-curved surfaces, car design and architecture speak the same language. A communication boulevard leads through the topics: from A1 to A8 and concept studies; from new technologies to the proof by the vehicle fleet. The "art of progress" brand value is translated into dynamics in space.

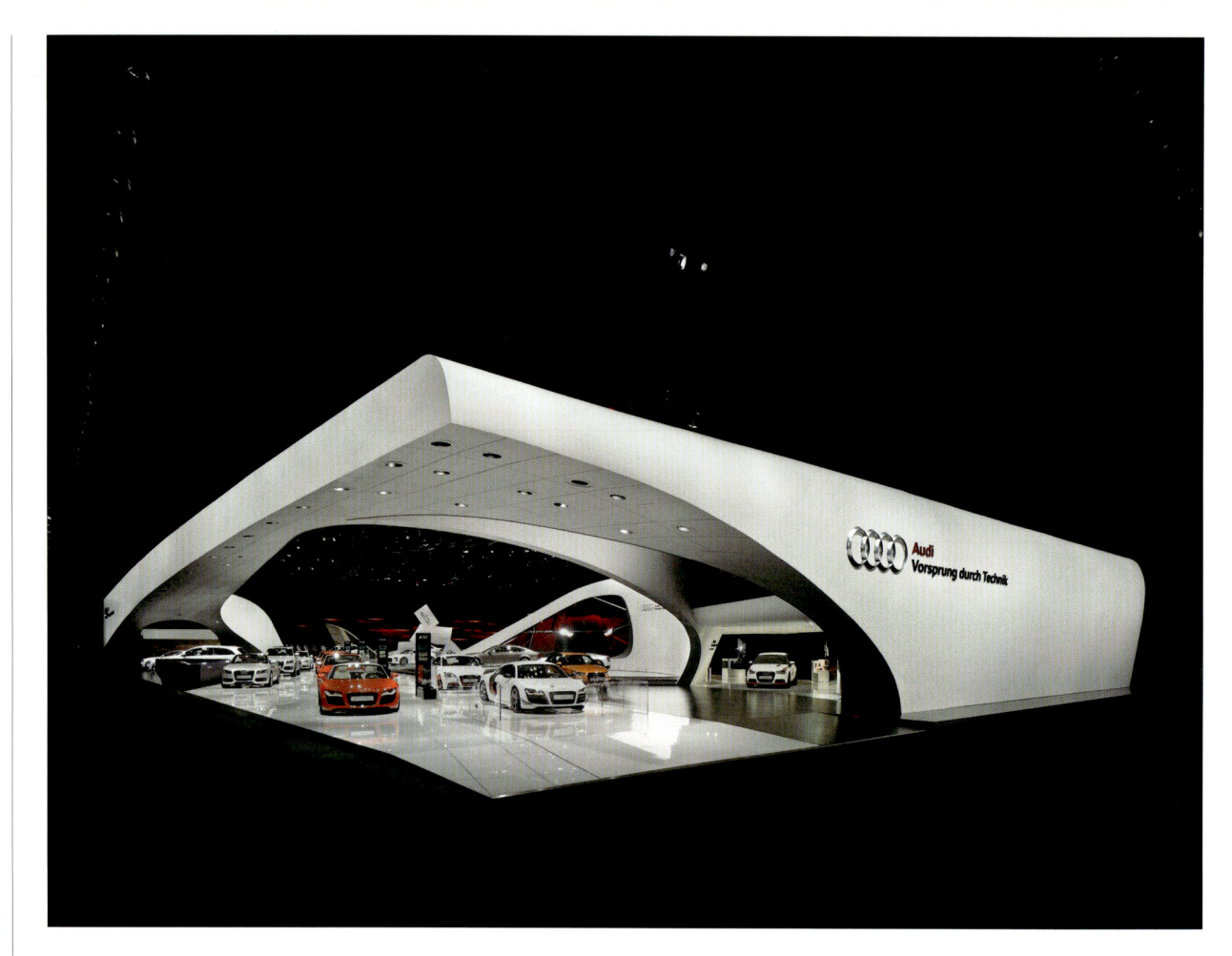

NOMINATION
RÄUMLICHE INSZENIERUNG
SPATIAL SCENE-SETTING
Kommunikation im Raum
Environmental Design

AUDI MESSESTAND CES
"Open for the future"

Lead Agency
  tisch13 GmbH
Client
  AUDI AG
Marketing Direction
  Bernhard Neumann
Executive Creative Direction
  Carsten Röhr
Creative Direction
  Nina Wiemer
Art Direction
  Paul Gonzalez
Architecture
  Bathke Geisel Architekten
Architecture/Scenography
  Lutz Geisel
Lighting Design
  Four to one
Photography
  Gabor Ekecs
Trade Fair Construction
  A&A Expo International B.V.

NOMINATION
RÄUMLICHE INSZENIERUNG
SPATIAL SCENE-SETTING
 Kommunikation im Raum
 Environmental Design

DESSO, MESSESTAND
"Circulation"

Lead Agency
 TULP DESIGN GmbH
Client
 DESSO BV
Executive Creative Direction
 Maik Schober,
 Alexander Striegl,
 Michael Zanin
Design
 Maik Schober,
 Alexander Striegl,
 Michael Zanin
Trade Fair Construction
 Ulff & Ulff GmbH & Co. KG

Der Messestand, inspiriert von M. C. Eschers unendlicher Treppe, lässt Dessos Teppich zur Architektur werden. Die im Fokus stehende Cradle-to-Cradle-Rückenbeschichtung Ecobase bedeckt die gesamte Außenfläche des Stands. Erst im Inneren werden die farbigen Teppichfliesen für den Besucher sichtbar und fühlbar.

The fair stand inspired by M. C. Escher's never-ending stairs makes Desso's carpet become the architecture. The stand design focuses on the Cradle-to-Cradle carpet backing Ecobase, which completely covers the outer surface of the stand. Only on the inside, the colored carpet tiles become visible and palpable for the visitor.

● NOMINATION
RÄUMLICHE INSZENIERUNG
SPATIAL SCENE-SETTING
Kommunikation im Raum
Environmental Design

HASENKOPF MESSESTAND
»Hasenkopf entdeckt das Ei des Kolumbus«

Lead Agency
　Martin et Karczinski GmbH
Contributing Agencies
　Drändle 70|30 GmbH
Client
　Hasenkopf GmbH & Co. KG
Creative Direction
　Peter Martin
Art Direction
　Jürgen Drändle,
　Patrick Wachner
Design
　Johannes Kemnitzer

Ein überdimensionales Ei aus Corian bildet den Mittelpunkt des Messeauftritts der Industrie-Manufaktur Hasenkopf. In Anlehnung an die Redewendung »Das Ei des Kolumbus«, der Lösung eines vermeintlich unlösbaren Problems, illustriert es auf einzigartige Weise den Pioniergeist und die Kompetenz des Zuliefererspezialisten auf dem Feld der thermischen Verformung.

An oversized egg made of Corian is at the center of the exhibition presence of Industrie-Manufaktur Hasenkopf. Based on the saying »Das Ei des Kolumbus« (That's just the thing), the solution to a seemingly insolvable problem, the egg uniquely illustrates the pioneering spirit and expertise of the supplier specialist in the area of thermal forming.

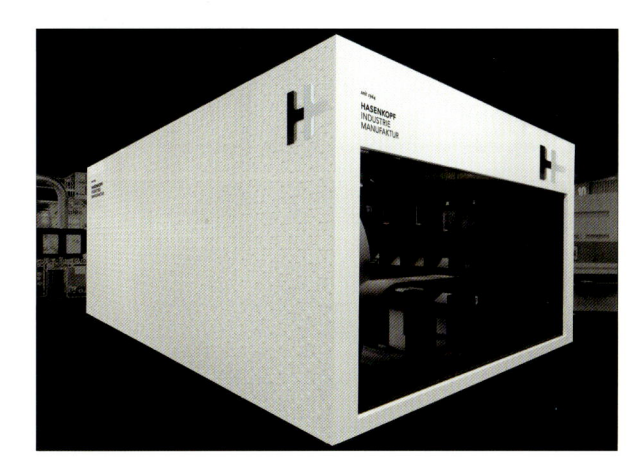

421

● **NOMINATION
RÄUMLICHE INSZENIERUNG
SPATIAL SCENE-SETTING**
Kommunikation im Raum
Environmental Design

**PERGAMONMUSEUM BERLIN
SONDERAUSSTELLUNG**
»Die geretteten Götter aus dem Palast vom Tell Halaf«

Lead Agency
  neo.studio | neumann schneider architekten
Client
  Vorderasiatisches Museum – Staatliche Museen zu Berlin
Executive Creative Direction
  Moritz Schneider,
  Tobias Neumann
Architecture/Scenography
  Anne Binder,
  Christian Lemmer,
  Max Wasserkampf,
  Thordis Jonsdottier,
  Marie Märgner
Graphic Design
  Marlen Hähle,
  Nora Tanner
Lighting Design
  Torsten Rullmann
Media
  Eva-Maria Heinrich,
  David Schwager

Die fremdartigen Großskulpturen aus dem Palast vom Tell Halaf und ihre außergewöhnliche Geschichte sind Gegenstand dieser Ausstellung aus elf Einzelinszenierungen. Mit ihrer Entdeckung nach 3.000 Jahren beginnt auch das Drama ihrer Zerstörung und Wiederauferstehung. Nach ihrer scheinbar endgültigen Vernichtung 1943 in Berlin sind die Bildwerke aus 27.000 Fragmenten wieder erstanden.

The sculptures from the palace of Tell Halaf and their extraordinary history are the subject of this exhibition in eleven chapters. Their discovery after 3,000 years in the desert is the beginning of a drama of destruction and resurrection. Completely destroyed in 1943 in Berlin, the sculptures were miraculously restored from 27,000 pieces during the last ten years.

**NOMINATION
RÄUMLICHE INSZENIERUNG
SPATIAL SCENE-SETTING**
  Events
  Events

AUDI A7 SPORTBACK
»Weltpremiere«

Lead Agency
  Mutabor Design GmbH
Client
  AUDI AG
Marketing Direction
  Thomas Behres
Creative Direction
  Frederike Putz
Client Consulting
  Holger Fischer
Design
  Lennard Niemann
  Silvia Bubel

Das leere Blatt Papier als Raum für kreative Ideen war omnipräsentes und überdimensionales Gestaltungselement sowie visuelles Superzeichen der Weltpremiere des Audi A7 Sportback, der neuen Designikone aus dem Hause Audi. Das Event war zugleich Auftakt für die Marketingkampagne zur Markteinführung des neuen Modells mit der Kampagnenidee »Nichts ist inspirierender als ein weißes Blatt Papier«.

The blank sheet of paper as a space for creative ideas was a huge omnipresent design element, and the overarching visual element in the world premiere of the Audi A7 Sportback, the new design icon from Audi. The event was also the prelude to the subsequent marketing campaign for the market launch of the new model, with "Nothing is more inspiring than a blank sheet of paper" as the campaign idea.

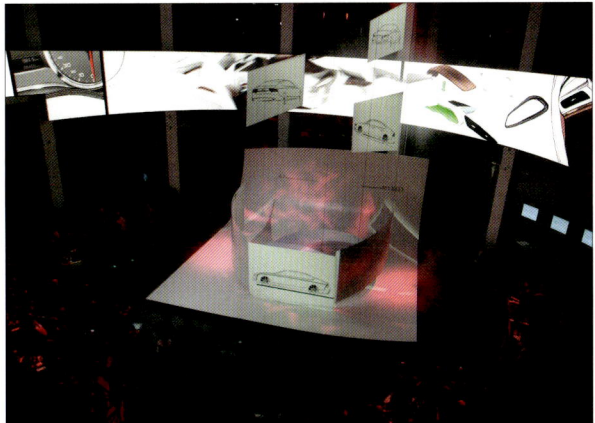

**NOMINATION
RÄUMLICHE INSZENIERUNG
SPATIAL SCENE-SETTING**
  Events
  Events

EMMI SCHWEIZ
  "Lightshow"

Lead Agency
  Scholz & Friends Zürich
Client
  Emmi Schweiz AG
Marketing Direction
  Robin A. Barraclough,
  Marco Peter
Advertising Direction
  Katharina Müller,
  Melanie Muri
Executive Creative Direction
  Suze Barrett,
  Dennis Lück
Creative Direction
  Joerg Jahn,
  Christian Sommer
Art Direction
  Ivo Hlavac,
  Andreas Villing
Client Consulting
  Mathias Rösch
Lighting/Music/Sound
  Hofstetter Marketing

Als Datum für den Launch des neuen Dachmarken-Designs wurde der 1. August gewählt – der Nationalfeiertag der Schweiz. Emmi machte an diesem Tag der Schweiz ein Geschenk – ein spektakuläres Lichtevent, welches die Grenze zwischen Werbung und Kultur aufhob. So wurde aus einem Corporate Event ein nationales Ereignis, dessen Reichweite das neue Design der Dachmarke Emmi unübersehbar platzierte.

We scheduled the launch of the new umbrella brand design for August 1st, the Swiss national holiday. On this day, Emmi gave a present to Switzerland – a spectacular light event that eliminated the boundary between advertising and art. This sleight of hand instantly turned a brand event into a national event by placing the package design conspicuously in full view of an entire country.

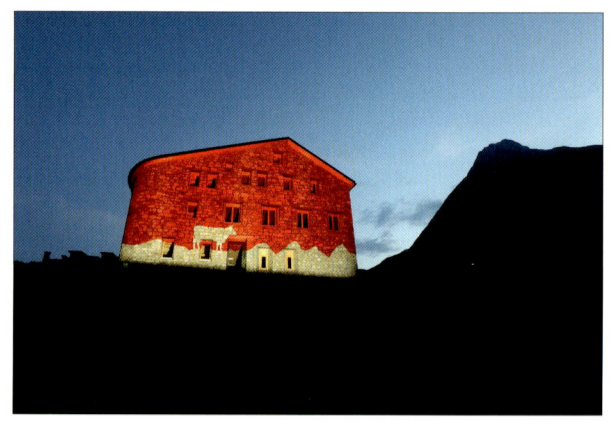

🔴 NOMINATION
RÄUMLICHE INSZENIERUNG
SPATIAL SCENE-SETTING
　Events
　Events

PANASONIC
»Barterlass«

Lead Agency
　Jung von Matt AG
Contributing Agencies
　Jung von Matt/relations GmbH
Client
　Panasonic Marketing
　Europe GmbH
Marketing Direction
　Rainer Engel
Advertising Direction
　Ralf Hansen,
　Rainer Tschepe
Executive Creative Direction
　Armin Jochum,
　Jung von Matt/relations:
　Joachim Kortlepel
Creative Direction
　Fabian Frese,
　Thimoteus Wagner
Art Direction
　Jonas Keller,
　Andreas Wagner
Client Consulting
　Melanie von der Dovenmühle,
　Peter Plambeck,
　Patrick Hammer
Agency Production
　Jannik Endemann
Camera
　Viviane Blumenschein,
　Nikolai von Graevenitz
Consulting
　Sandra Wirt,
　Albertina Inselmann,
　Tim Scholz
Copy
　Luca Rescheleit
Cutting
　Florian Panier,
　Daniel Wunderer
Film Direction
　Viviane Blumenschein
Film Production
　Tony Petersen Film –
　Anke Petersen
Idea
　Jonas Keller,
　Andreas Wagner,
　Luca Rescheleit,
　Armin Jochum
Postproduction
　Tony Petersen Film,
　Benni Grüner,
　Jung von Matt
Production
　Marcus Loick
Other
　Team Assistance:
　Nina Rahn

Alle zehn Jahre finden in Oberammergau die berühmtesten Passionsspiele der Welt statt. Dazu gibt es eine kuriose Tradition: den Barterlass. Die über 2.000 Oberammergauer, die in den Spielen auftreten, dürfen sich ein ganzes Jahr vorher weder Haar noch Bart schneiden. Oberammergau wird zum haarigsten Dorf der Welt! Mit Panasonic Bart- und Haarschneidern erlösten wir Oberammergau von seinen Haarmassen.

Every ten years, the Bavarian village of Oberammergau stages the world's most famous Passion play. Over 2,000 villagers take part in the play – and in the bizarre tradition called the »Barterlass« (beard decree). For one year before the play, the performers must not cut their hair or beard. Oberammergau becomes the hairiest village in the world! And Panasonic hair and beard shavers become their salvation.

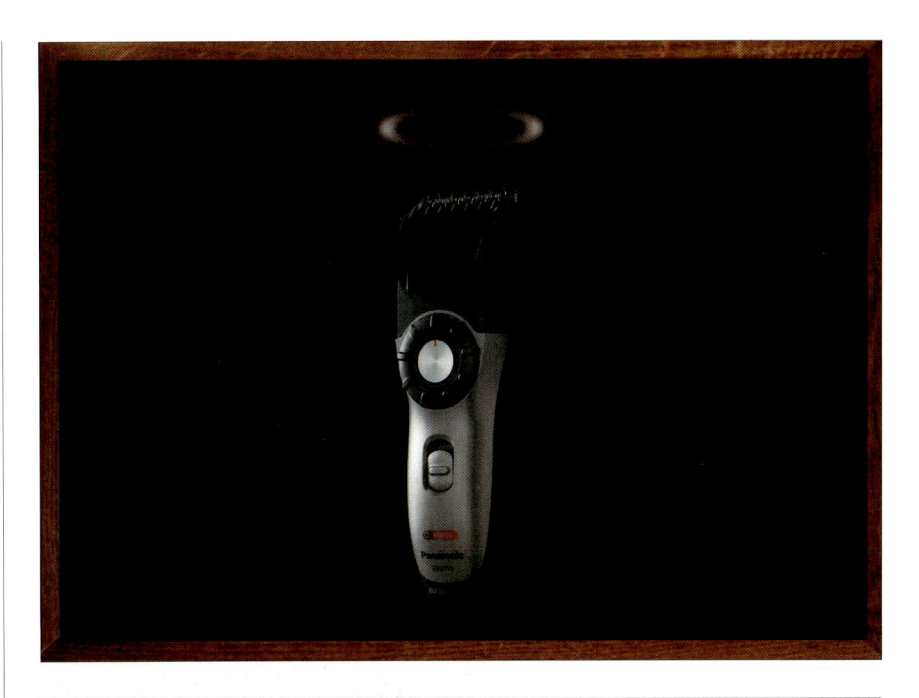

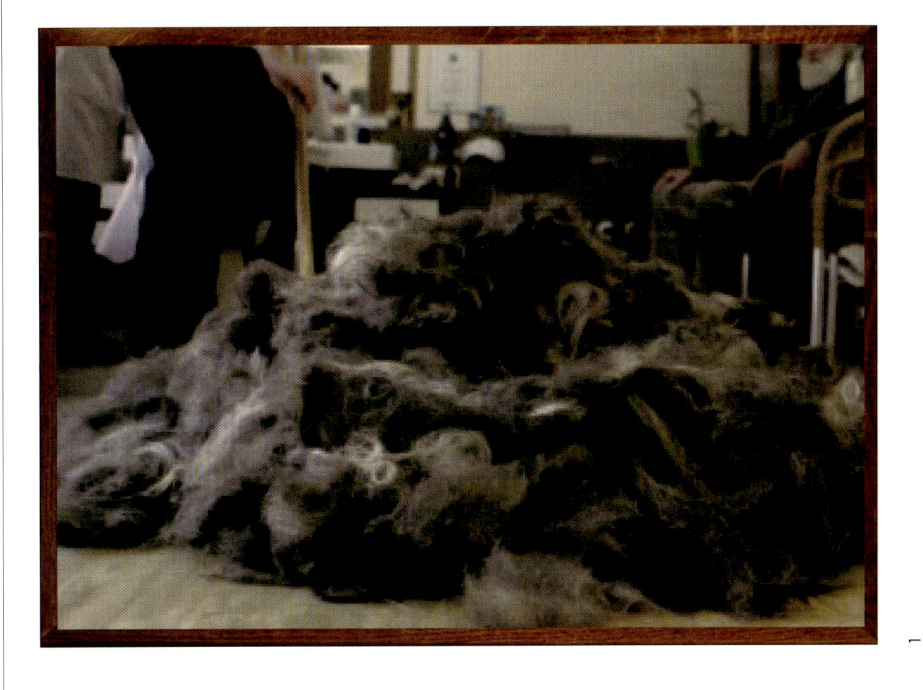

NOMINATION
RÄUMLICHE INSZENIERUNG
SPATIAL SCENE-SETTING
Events Craft
Dramaturgie
Events Craft
Dramaturgy

ADC
»46. Awards Show 2010«

Lead Agency
  CE+Co GmbH
Contributing Agencies
  Syzygy,
  Groves Sound Communications,
  360 Grad
Client
  Art Directors Club
  für Deutschland (ADC) e.V.
Marketing Direction
  Susann Schronen
Advertising Direction
  Doris Balke,
  Verena Moll
Executive Creative Direction
  Cedric Ebener (CE+Co)
Creative Direction
  Cedric Ebener (CE+Co)
Art Direction
  Dominik Lammer (Syzygy),
  John Groves (Groves Sound Communications)
Client Consulting
  Annika Jungclaus (CE+Co)
Strategic Planning
  Helena Henneken (CE+Co)
Dramaturgy
  Cedric Ebener (CE+Co)

Herausforderung: mehr Kategorien als zuvor, keine dramaturgische Steigerungsmöglichkeit innerhalb der Show, einige Kategorien nutzen Gäste für Pausen, wenige Highlights stehlen der kreativen Masse die Show. Lösung: eine Awardverleihung mit Medaillenspiegel – mehr kreative Exzellenz auf der Bühne, sichtbare Vernetzung der Kommunikationsbranche, neuer Spannungsbogen! Resonanz: Begeisterung!

Challenges: increased amount of categories, weak dramaturgy within the course of show, some categories are used for breaks by the guests, diversity of creative ideas pales besides a few highlights. Solution: an award show on the basis of a medal table: more creative excellence on stage, visible linking of communication channels, novel dramaturgy! Response: enthusiasm!

● NOMINATION
CRAFT
CRAFT
  Text
  Copy

---

75 JAHRE ARAG
»Die Geschichte
der Versicherung«

Lead Agency
  BUTTER.
Client
  ARAG Allgemeine Rechts-
  schutz-Versicherungs-AG
Advertising Direction
  Connie Peters
Executive Creative Direction
  Frank Stauss
Creative Direction
  Matthias Eickmeyer,
  Reinhard Henke,
  Nadine Schlichte
Art Direction
  Nicole Hoffeins (Illustration)
Client Consulting
  Anna Dankert,
  Rolf Schrickel,
  Dorota Schupke
Copy
  Reinhard Henke

427

NOMINATION
CRAFT
CRAFT
Text
Copy

AUGSBURGER ALLGEMEINE
KAMPAGNE
»Weltnachrichten aus der Region«

Lead Agency
　Scholz & Friends
Client
　Augsburger Allgemeine
Marketing Direction
　Rüdiger Hoebel
Executive Creative Direction
　Martin Pross,
　Matthias Spaetgens
Creative Direction
　Mathias Rebmann,
　Florian Schwalme
Art Direction
　Michael Schmidt
Client Consulting
　Salvatore Amato
Strategic Planning
　Graphics:
　Franziska Boemer
Copy
　Caspar Heuss,
　Momme Clausen,
　Viktoria Grünewald

Obama zapft is!

Washington. Der US-Präsident vergnügte sich heute in Olching, **um zwischen der Hamas und de**m Chor der Meringer Trachten**truppe zu vermitteln. Beide Seit**en freuen sich auf ein gutes Ge**fecht im hügeligen Norden des** Festgeländes, und bereiten eine **Invasion auf strategisch wichtige** Bierzelte vor. Es stehen 8000 **Soldaten an der Grenze, die auf** eine Wurst und ein paar Gläser **Erdöl warten. Im Februar steht** ein Shuttle-Bus bereit, der die **erschöpften Truppen zurück an** den Augsburger Bahnhof fährt.

Augsburger Allgemeine
Nachrichten aus aller Welt. Und der Region.

NOMINATION
CRAFT
CRAFT
Text
Copy

DYNAUDIO
»Die Nahhörerlebnis-Plakate.«

Lead Agency
   Geschke Pufe Berlin
Client
   Dynaudio
Marketing Direction
   Wilfried Ehrenholz
Advertising Direction
   Torsten Morisse,
   Eike-Peter Frost,
   Roland Hoffmann
Executive Creative Direction
   Jan Geschke,
   Stefan Pufe
Creative Direction
   Jan Geschke,
   Stefan Pufe
Art Direction
   Jan Geschke,
   Stefan Pufe,
   Marcus Weiss,
   Till Heinke
Client Consulting
   Jan Geschke,
   Stefan Pufe
Strategic Planning
   Jan Geschke,
   Stefan Pufe
Copy
   Jan Geschke,
   Stefan Pufe

„In dieser unglaublichen Liveaufnahme aus dem Village Vanguard, Heroes, 1980, am Beginn des 6.Stücks, das atemberaubende Lee Konitz Solo in c-moll, die Kellnerin stellt Drinks vor ein paar Gäste vorne links, während Gil Evans die Intro spielt, die Gläser klirren, die Löffel, sogar die Eiswürfel, und Miles, mein Labrador, er setzt sich vor meine neuen Focus 160 und er begreift ums Leben nicht, dass er nicht sieht, was er hört, er sucht, er guckt, er schnüffelt hinter den Boxen, er gräbt mit der Pfote nach der Kellnerin. Das hat er früher nie gemacht, und wir lachen, daß uns die Tränen kommen, noch vor denen von der Musik."

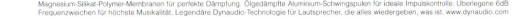

„Von links kommen diese drei tadschikischen Clowns mit den Kalaschnikows, sie laufen auf McClane zu und feuern in kurzen Stößen takatakk takatakk takatakk, von rechts fliegt eine Handgranate und kullert gegen seinen Stiefel klackk, und die Glock in seiner Hand hat plötzlich Ladehemmung, ein extrem unappetitliches krrrrk, und er schnappt sich diesen Kerosinkanister und schmeißt ihn direkt ins Feuer katschuung, und einen Sekundenbruchteil später bläst den ganzen Saustall ins Nirwana wwwwwwwwoooooooosshhhhhhhhhhhhhhhhhhhh. Das Beste daran ist sein Lachen."

NOMINATION
CRAFT
CRAFT
Text
Copy

FESTOOL PENDELSTICHSÄGE
CARVEX PS 400
»Stuttgart 21«

Lead Agency
    Scholz & Friends
Client
    Festool GmbH
Advertising Direction
    Klaus Danner
Executive Creative Direction
    Martin Pross,
    Matthias Spaetgens
Creative Direction
    David Fischer,
    Philipp Wöhler,
    Robert Krause
Art Direction
    Jörg Waschescio
Client Consulting
    Uli Schuppach,
    Susanne Kieck
Copy
    Christian Brandes

NOMINATION
CRAFT
CRAFT
Text
Copy

FTD
»Kampagne«

Lead Agency
 KNSK Werbeagentur GmbH
Client
 FTD G+J Wirtschaftsmedien
Marketing Direction
 Antje Fitzner
Advertising Direction
 Maike Bernhardt
Creative Direction
 Tim Krink,
 Ulrike Wegert
Art Direction
 Thomas Thiele
Client Consulting
 Olaf Uthmann
Copy
 Ulrike Wegert,
 Steffen Steffens,
 Felix Lemcke

„Krise" kommt aus dem Griechischen. Warum sind wir jetzt nicht überrascht?

FINANCIAL TIMES DEUTSCHLAND
Wissen, was wichtig wird. Immer und überall.

NOMINATION
CRAFT
CRAFT
Text
Copy

RITTER SPORT
»Kampagne 2010«

Lead Agency
　Kolle Rebbe GmbH
Client
　Alfred Ritter GmbH & Co. KG
Marketing Direction
　Jürgen Herrmann
Advertising Direction
　Holger Henck
Executive Creative Direction
　Stefan Kolle
Creative Direction
　Stefan Wübbe,
　Rolf Leger
Art Direction
　Jörg Dittmann,
　Nadine Nolting
Client Consulting
　Katrin Becker,
　Saskia Merz
Copy
　Florian Ludwig,
　Fabian Bill

● NOMINATION
CRAFT
CRAFT
   Typografie
   Typography

SCHEUFELEN
»Höchstleistungen«

Lead Agency
   Strichpunkt Design
Client
   Papierfabrik Scheufelen
   GmbH & Co. KG
Marketing Direction
   Irmgard Glanz
Executive Creative Direction
   Kirsten Dietz,
   Jochen Rädeker
Creative Direction
   Kirsten Dietz
Art Direction
   Julia Ochsenhirt,
   Agnetha Wohlert
Client Consulting
   Jochen Rädeker
Typography
   Julia Ochsenhirt,
   Agnetha Wohlert

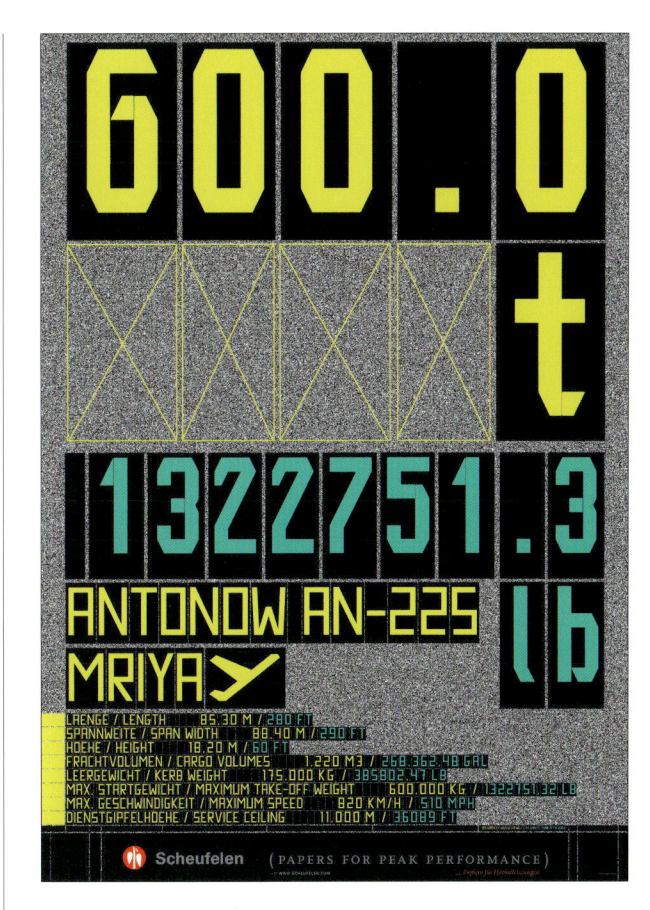

NOMINATION
CRAFT
CRAFT
  Fotografie
  Photography

DAS BRUSTKREBSPROJEKT
»Amazonen«

Lead Agency
  Dorland Werbeagentur GmbH
Client
  Dorland Werbeagentur GmbH
Executive Creative Direction
  Hendrick Melle
Creative Direction
  Esther Haase,
  Hendrick Melle,
  Uta Melle
Image Processing
  Esther Haase
Photography
  Esther Haase

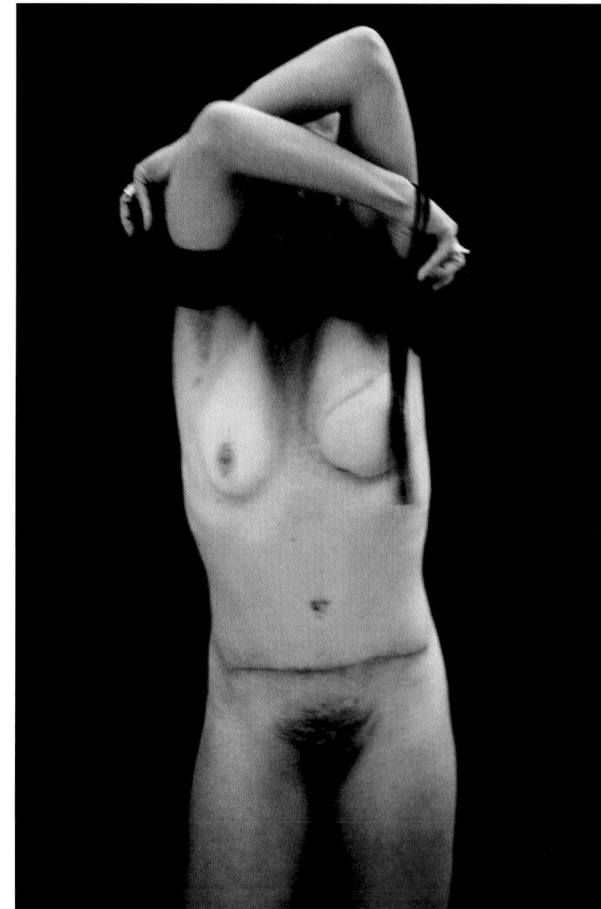

NOMINATION
CRAFT
CRAFT
  Fotografie
  Photography

EIGENWERBUNG SERIE
»Kulissenbauer«

Lead Agency
  michael haegele
Client
  michael haegele
Image Processing
  Jan Wengenroth
Photography
  Michael Haegele

NOMINATION
CRAFT
CRAFT
Fotografie
Photography

EIGENWERBUNG SERIE
»Seneca tanzt den Ovid«

Lead Agency
 Uwe Düttmann
Client
 Uwe Düttmann
Photography
 Uwe Düttmann

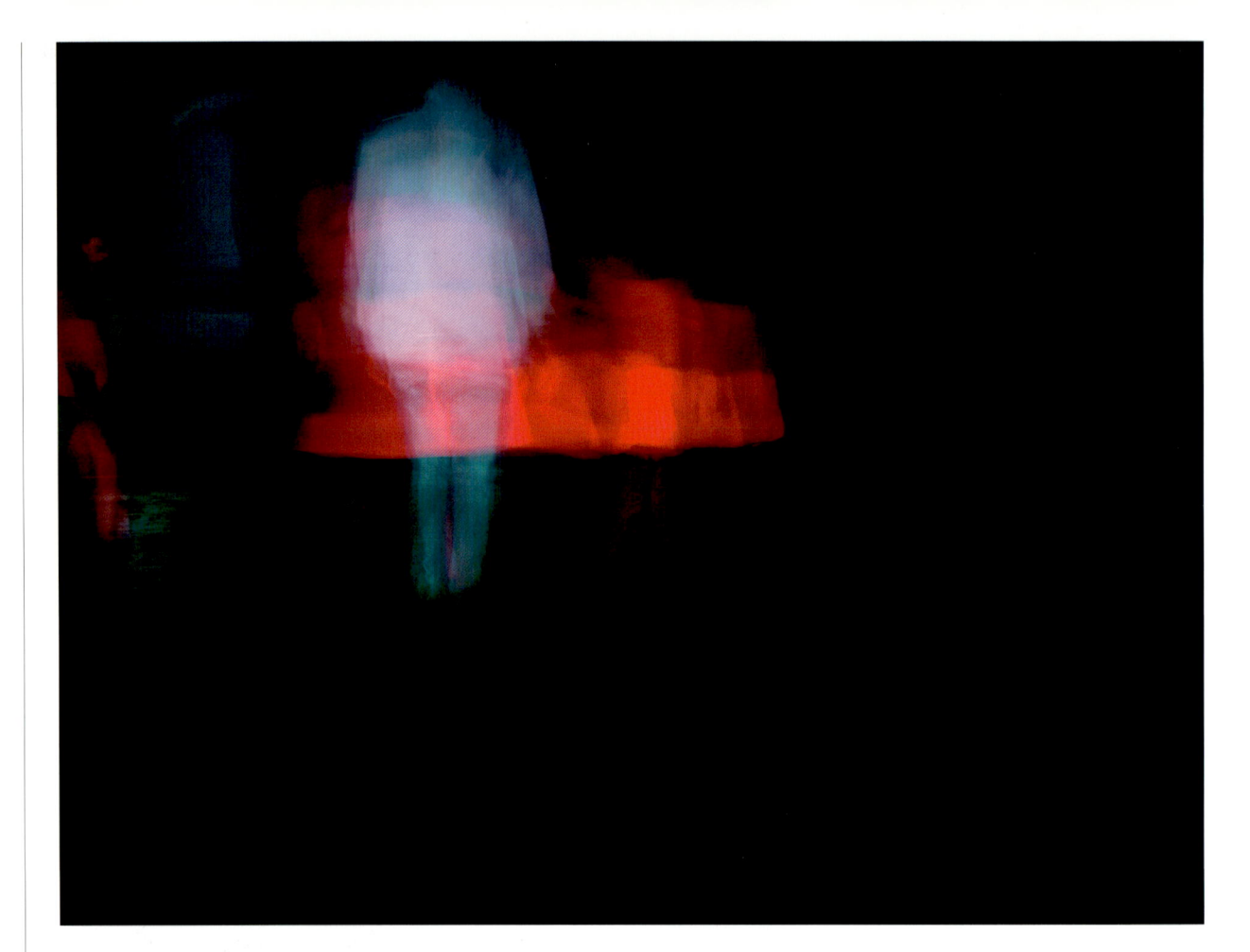

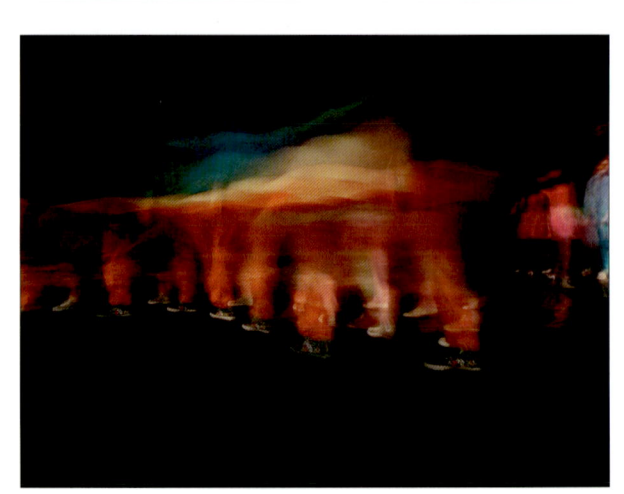

**NOMINATION
CRAFT
CRAFT**
Fotografie
Photography

**EIGENWERBUNG SERIE
»SLS«**

Lead Agency
  Alex Rank Photography
Client
  Alex Rank Photography
Photography
  Alex Rank Photography

**NOMINATION
CRAFT
CRAFT**
Fotografie
Photography

**FELD HOMMES MAGAZIN
SERIE**
»Sex Maschine«

Lead Agency
  loved gmbh
Client
  Feld Hommes Magazin
Creative Direction
  Mieke Haase
Art Direction
  Mieke Haase
Image Processing
  Primate Postproduction
Photography
  Robert Grischek

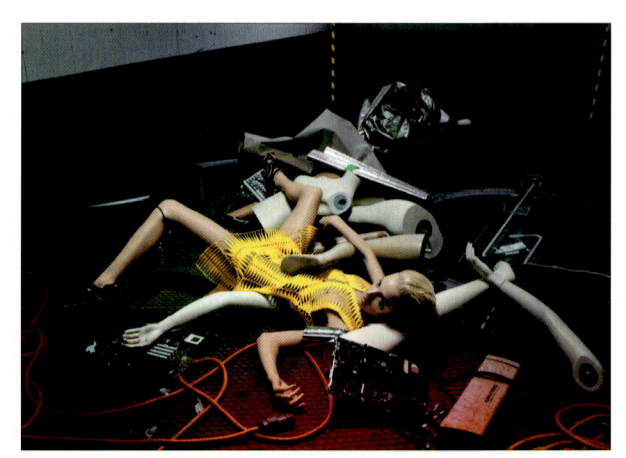

**NOMINATION
CRAFT
CRAFT**
Fotografie
Photography

ROBERTO SAVIANO, AUTOR
GEGEN DIE CAMORRA. SERIE
»Ich habe in allen Winkeln
der Erde geschrieben…«

Lead Agency
  stern Magazin
Client
  Gruner + Jahr AG & Co. KG
Creative Direction
  Andrea Gothe
Art Direction
  Donald Schneider,
  Mark Ernsting (Deputy)
Photography
  Hans-Jürgen Burkard

439

● NOMINATION
CRAFT
CRAFT
　Fotografie
　Photography

STERN MAGAZIN SERIE
»Eine verwehte Welt«

Lead Agency
　stern Magazin
Client
　Gruner+Jahr AG & Co. KG
Creative Direction
　Andrea Gothe
Art Direction
　Donald Schneider,
　Mark Ernsting (Deputy)
Photography
　Ragnar Axelsson

NOMINATION
CRAFT
CRAFT
Fotografie
Photography

TOYOTA AURIS HYBRID SERIE
»Perspektivwechsel«

Lead Agency
  Saatchi & Saatchi Duesseldorf
Client
  Toyota Deutschland GmbH
Advertising Direction
  Sabine Sageb/Toyota
Executive Creative Direction
  Stephan Zilges
Creative Direction
  Marco Obermann,
  Thorsten Altmann
Art Direction
  Jean-Pierre Gregor
Client Consulting
  Julia Stark
Strategic Planning
  Art Buying:
  Bettina Tetens
  Production:
  Add Pictures
Copy
  Till Koester
Image Processing
  Recom
Photography
  Christian Schmidt

441

**NOMINATION
CRAFT
CRAFT**
  Illustration
  Illustration

AUDI QUATTRO SERIE
  »Mechanik und Elektronik
  innovativ kombiniert«

Lead Agency
  kempertrautmann GmbH
Client
  AUDI AG
Marketing Direction
  Lothar Korn
Advertising Direction
  Michael Finke,
  Rainer Denninger
Creative Direction
  Heiko Freyland,
  Mathias Lamken,
  Gerrit Zinke,
  Tobias Ahrens
Art Direction
  Mathias Lamken,
  Maria Sommer
Client Consulting
  Andrea Bison,
  Niklas Kruchten,
  Elisabeth Einhaus
Copy
  Heiko Freyland,
  Sven Nagel
Illustration
  Liga_01 Computerfilm GmbH
Image Processing
  Liga_01 Computerfilm GmbH

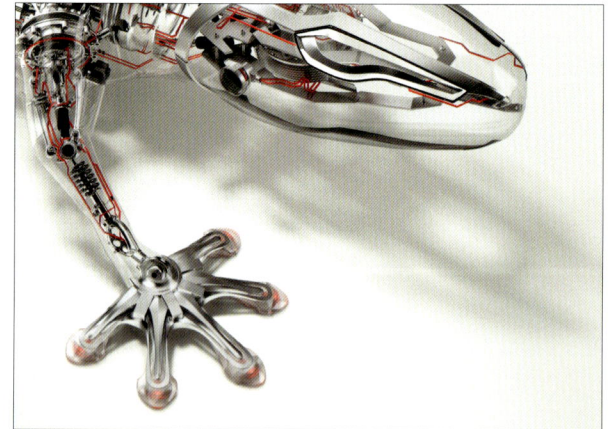

**NOMINATION
CRAFT
CRAFT**
Illustration
Illustration

**BUND FÜR UMWELT UND
NATURSCHUTZ DEUTSCHLAND
SERIE**
»5 vor 12«

Lead Agency
  Scholz & Friends
Client
  BUND e.V.
Marketing Direction
  Norbert Franck
Advertising Direction
  Mark Hörstermann
Executive Creative Direction
  Martin Pross,
  Matthias Spaetgens
Creative Direction
  Florian Schwalme,
  Mathias Rebmann
Art Direction
  Ksenia Slavcheva,
  René Gebhardt,
  Björn Kernspeckt,
  Sebastian Frese
Client Consulting
  Christine Scharney,
  Susanne Kieck
Illustration
  Peppermill Berlin

● NOMINATION
CRAFT
CRAFT
  Illustration
  Illustration

KULTURSPIEGEL SERIE
  "Simon Spilsbury"

Lead Agency
  KulturSPIEGEL
Client
  KulturSPIEGEL,
  Marianne Wellershoff
Art Direction
  Jens Kuppi
Copy
  Redaktion KulturSPIEGEL
Illustration
  Simon Spilsbury

● NOMINATION
CRAFT
CRAFT
   Illustration
   Illustration

RADIO MEPHISTO 97.6 SERIE
"Heads"

Lead Agency
   Preuss und Preuss GmbH
Client
   Mephisto 97.6
Marketing Direction
   Ben Hänchen
Executive Creative Direction
   Michael Preuss
Creative Direction
   Michael Preuss,
   Timm Holm
Art Direction
   Zuzana Havelcova,
   Björn von Buchholtz
Client Consulting
   Nina Preuss
Copy
   Michael Preuss,
   Till Grabsch
Illustration
   Zuzana Havelcova,
   Andrey Gordeev
Image Processing
   Zuzana Havelcova

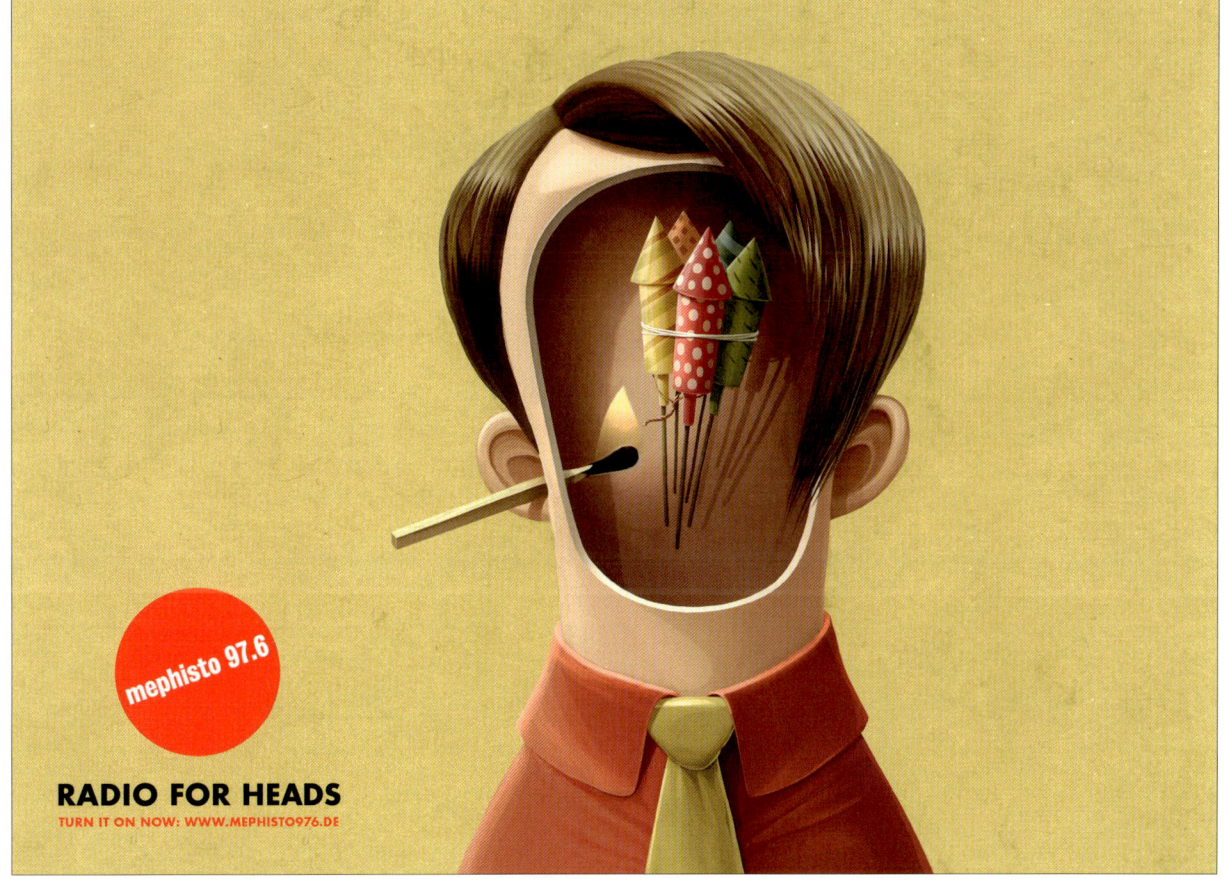

● NOMINATION
CRAFT
CRAFT
  Illustration
  Illustration

STERN MAGAZIN SERIE
»Drunter-Welt«

Lead Agency
  stern Magazin
Client
  Gruner + Jahr AG & Co. KG
Creative Direction
  Donald Schneider
Art Direction
  Donald Schneider,
  Mark Ernsting (Deputy)
Illustration
  Wolfgang Joop

NOMINATION
CRAFT
CRAFT
 Illustration
 Illustration

VW GOLF SERIE
 »Kein Weg vorbei«

Lead Agency
 DDB Tribal Group
Client
 Volkswagen AG
Marketing Direction
 Luca de Meo
Advertising Direction
 Martina Berg
Executive Creative Direction
 CCO: Eric Schoeffler
 ECD: Till Eckel
Creative Direction
 Johannes Hicks
Art Direction
 Marc Isken
Client Consulting
 Jan Isterling,
 Silke Lagodny
Copy
 Andres Blumenthal
Illustration
 Mathis Rekowski

447

● NOMINATION
CRAFT
CRAFT
   Musik und Sound
   Music and Sound

BFF ORIGINALKOMPOSITION
»Treppe«

Lead Agency
   Young & Rubicam GmbH
Client
   BFF
Marketing Direction
   Katja Grieger
Advertising Direction
   Katja Grieger
Executive Creative Direction
   Jan Leube
Creative Direction
   Uwe Marquardt
Art Direction
   Helge Kniess
Client Consulting
   Lennart Wittgen
Audio Production
   Tinseltown Music
Copy
   Manuel Rentz
Music Composition
   Claudio Pagonis

»Ich bin die Treppe runtergefallen« ist die wohl bekannteste Ausrede, mit der Opfer häuslicher Gewalt ihre Verletzungen erklären. In unserem TV-Spot führen wir dem Zuschauer durch eine übertriebene Darstellung von Treppenstürzen vor Augen, wie absurd diese Ausrede in ihrer Häufigkeit ist – und fordern auf, sich im Zweifel an den BFF zu wenden.

"I fell down the stairs" is the most common excuse that is used by the victims of domestic violence. Our TV commercial broaches this issue by showing many women falling down the stairs, with the pictures getting more and more drastic. At the end of our commercial, we ask the audience to question this excuse – and not to hesitate to contact the BFF.

● NOMINATION
CRAFT
CRAFT
   Musik und Sound
   Music and Sound

MERCEDES-BENZ E-KLASSE LANG ORIGINALKOMPOSITION
   "Shadows"

Lead Agency
   Jung von Matt AG
Client
   Beijing Benz Automotive Co., Ltd.
Marketing Direction
   Mark Si
Advertising Direction
   Henry Li,
   Jane Liu
Executive Creative Direction
   Sascha Hanke
Creative Direction
   Michael Matthiass,
   Andreas Summ
Art Direction
   Jan Berg
Client Consulting
   Thilo Hecht,
   Daniel Kießling,
   Lisa Zhang,
   Magdalena Klein
Strategic Planning
   Malte Lenze
Audio Production
   audioforce, Berlin
Copy
   Oliver Kohtz
Music Composition
   Robert "Robster" Henke,
   Thomas Wagner
Sound Design
   audioforce, Berlin

Wächterlöwen stehen in China für Kraft und Macht. Ihr Wettlauf mit der E-Klasse Lang demonstriert, dass das Fahrzeug für dieselben Attribute steht: Der Wagen besteht den »Initiationsritus« der Löwen. Der Film wurde (beinahe vollständig) mit CGI umgesetzt: Die Schattenlöwen, das Fahrzeug und auch die Stadtszenerie sind computergeneriert.

Guardian lions are Chinese symbols for strength and power. Their race against the long-wheelbase E-Class demonstrates that the vehicle stands for the same attributes: the car passes the "initiation rite" of the lions. The footage was created (almost completely) with CGI: the lion shadows, the car, even the city itself is computer-generated.

● NOMINATION
CRAFT
CRAFT
   Musik und Sound
   Music and Sound

VODAFONE MUSIKAUSWAHL
"Where are you?"

Lead Agency
   Jung von Matt AG
Contributing Agencies
   White Horse Music GmbH
Client
   Vodafone D2 GmbH
Marketing Direction
   Gregor Gründgens
Advertising Direction
   Anne Stilling
Executive Creative Direction
   Götz Ulmer,
   Fabian Frese,
   Armin Jochum
Creative Direction
   David Leinweber,
   Sören Porst
Art Direction
   David Leinweber,
   Sören Porst
Client Consulting
   Henner Blömer,
   Anke Göbber,
   Victoria Lackner
Strategic Planning
   Henner Blömer
Audio Production
   White Horse Music GmbH,
   Studio Funk Hamburg
Music Selection
   Sebastian Strasser,
   Götz Ulmer,
   Gerrit Winterstein

Der ausgewählte Song unterstützt perfekt die Sound-CI von Vodafone und ist gleichzeitig eingängig und einprägsam. Inhaltlich harmoniert er mit der emotionalen Story des Spots und treibt diese voran. Zudem beweist er großes Ausdauerpotential: "We are the people" wird Nr. 1 in den Media Control Single Top 100. Und zehn Wochen nach Kampagnenstart ist er noch immer in den Top 3 der Charts.

The selected song has the perfect sound to enhance Vodafone's corporate identity – catchy, memorable and in tune with the campaign's heart-warming stories, even pulling the story along. And the song seems to be here to stay: "We are the people" reached no. 1 in the Media Control top 100 single charts and, ten weeks after the start of the campaign, it is still among the top 3.

NOMINATION
GANZHEITLICHE KOMMUNIKATION
INTEGRATED CAMPAIGNS
Ganzheitliche Kommunikation
Integrated Campaigns

SP ZÜRICH
»Was Zürich braucht.«

Lead Agency
 walker
Client
 SP Zürich
Executive Creative Direction
 Pius Walker
Creative Direction
 Pius Walker,
 Nikolaus Ronacher
Art Direction
 Signe Prince Fleischmann,
 Andrea Bissig
Client Consulting
 Cornelia Nünlist
Copy
 Martin Arnold,
 Heinz Helle
Idea
 Nikolaus Ronacher,
 Martin Arnold

Mit der Facebook Gruppe »Was Zürich braucht« startete die SP Zürich ihre Wahlkampagne. Die Ideen der Zürcher wurden auf FB diskutiert und via "Like"-Funktion gevotet. Aus FB Vorschlägen wurden Banner und Poster. Gemeinsam mit den SP-Kandidaten und den Ideengebern wurde im Netz, auf der Straße, in der Presse und im Radio diskutiert. Die SP hat die Wahl gewonnen und die Zürcher bekommen u.a. freies Wi-Fi.

With the Facebook group "What Zurich needs", SP Zürich launched its election campaign. Ideas posted by locals were discussed on FB and were then voted for via the "like" button. The FB ideas were then converted into banners and posters. The creators of the ideas, along with the SP candidates, fueled discussions on the streets, online and in the press. As a result, the SP won the elections in Zurich.

www.adc.de

Alle Filme und Spots der folgenden Kategorien finden Sie unter: www.adc.de
For all films and audio commercials of the following categories visit: www.adc.de

Film
  Film

Film Craft
  Film Craft

Audio
  Audio

Audio Craft
  Audio Craft

Digitale Medien
  Digital Media

Digitale Medien Craft
  Digital Media Craft

Dialogmarketing
  Dialog Marketing

Promotion
  Promotion

Media
  Media

Kommunikation im Raum
  Environmental Design

Kommunikation im Raum Craft
  Environmental Design Craft

Events
  Events

Events Craft
  Events Craft

Musik und Sound
  Music and Sound

Ganzheitliche Kommunikation
  Integrated Campaigns

Nehmen Sie die Herausforderung an?

360 GRAD

Schnell anmelden bis
15. August 2011
Nur noch wenige Plätze!

Der Fight geht in die nächste Runde! Die Absolventen des ersten Jahrgangs haben sich erfolgreich durchgeboxt – und jetzt sind Sie dran. Steigen Sie in den Ring und stellen Sie sich Ihrer Herausforderung. Groß, mächtig, unübersichtlich, schwer einzuschätzen, immer für eine Überraschung gut. Ihr Name: „360 Grad Kommunikation". Sie werden sich wohl mit ihr auseinandersetzen müssen. Wenn Sie dann nicht richtig reagieren, zeigen Ihre Budgets nur wenig Wirkung, und Sie werden unweigerlich auf die Bretter geschickt. Bringen Sie sich lieber als Mitglied im Kommunikationsverband richtig in Form. Mit der Ausbildung zum 360° Kommunikationsberater(KV)® werden Sie dann bestens vorbereitet antreten und den Ring als Gewinner verlassen. Verschaffen Sie sich den Durchblick. Werden Sie jetzt Mitglied im Kommunikationsverband, und das 360 Grad Schwergewicht wird zum Fliegengewicht. www.kommunikationsverband.de

kommunikations verband
Kommunikation professionalisieren.

AFTER EFFECTS, PHOTOSHOP, CINEMA 4D UND INDESIGN. DA TUT ES DOCH GUT, WIEDER ECHTE HANDARBEIT ZU SEHEN.

www.volkswagen.de

Der Phaeton.

Das Auto.

Jürgen Schröder
Ruhrorter Straße 24
47059 Duisburg

Telefon: (02 03) 43 46 37
Handy: (01 72) 9 43 69 11

Grabarz & Partner Werbeagentur
z. Hd. Herrn Ralf Heuel
Lilienstraße 11

20095 Hamburg

Duisburg, den 12.9.1998

Bewerbung als Texter

Lieber Ralf,

von Kopf bis Fuß, vom Scheitel bis zur Sohle, vom Wirbel bis zum Zeh bin ich mit Haut und Haaren der geborene Texter. Ich liebe das Wort, und die Worte lieben mich. Ich habe Buchstaben im Blut und Headlines im Kopf.

Für euch will ich – vom Briefing bis zum Dreh, vom Neger vor der Hütte bis zur großen Fallhöhe, von „ins Boot geholt" bis „einfach mal in die Tüte gesprochen", vom luxuriösen Timing bis zum engen Höschen, von der knackigen Line über die intelligente Longcopy bis hin zum aktivierenden Call to Action, von 0 auf 100, von der Klassik bis in die Postmoderne – die eierlegende Wollmilchsau im Copywriting sein.

Ich bin ein stressresistenter Teamplayer, gebe immer 110 % und freue mich sehr auf ein persöhnliches Gespräch.

Viele Grüße

Jürgen Schröder

Jürgen Schröder
Rissener Dorfstraße 23
22559 Hamburg

Telefon: 040 47222190
Mobil: 01577 72786370
E-Mail: j.schroe@web.de

Grabarz & Partner Werbeagentur
Nina Batze
Alter Wall 55
20457 Hamburg

Hamburg, den 17.6.2011

Bewerbung als Senior-Projektmanager

Liebe Nina,

von Kopf bis Fuß, vom Scheitel bis zur Sohle, vom Wirbel bis zum Zeh bin ich mit Haut und Haaren der geborene Projektmanager. Ich liebe Zahlen, und schwarze Zahlen lieben mich. Ich habe den Erfolg im Blut und Timings im Kopf.

Für euch will ich – vom Pitch bis zur Implementation, vom roughen Draft bis zur Strategy Keynote, von der Stakeholder Analysis bis zum Channel Monitoring, vom Flyer bis zur 360°-Kampagne, vom Mission Statement bis zur Brand Architecture, vom B2B-Mittelständler bis zum internationalen B2C-Marktführer, von der Kaltakquise bis zum Input-Output-Review, von ATL bis BTL, von der Klassik bis in die Postmoderne – die eierlegende Wollmilchsau im Projektmanagement sein.

Ich bin ein stressresistenter Teamplayer, gebe immer 110 % und freue mich sehr auf ein persöhnliches Gespräch.

Viele Grüße
Jürgen Schröder

Die Zeiten ändern sich, die Fehler nicht.

WIENERS+WIENERS
Übersetzen · Adaptieren · Korrigieren

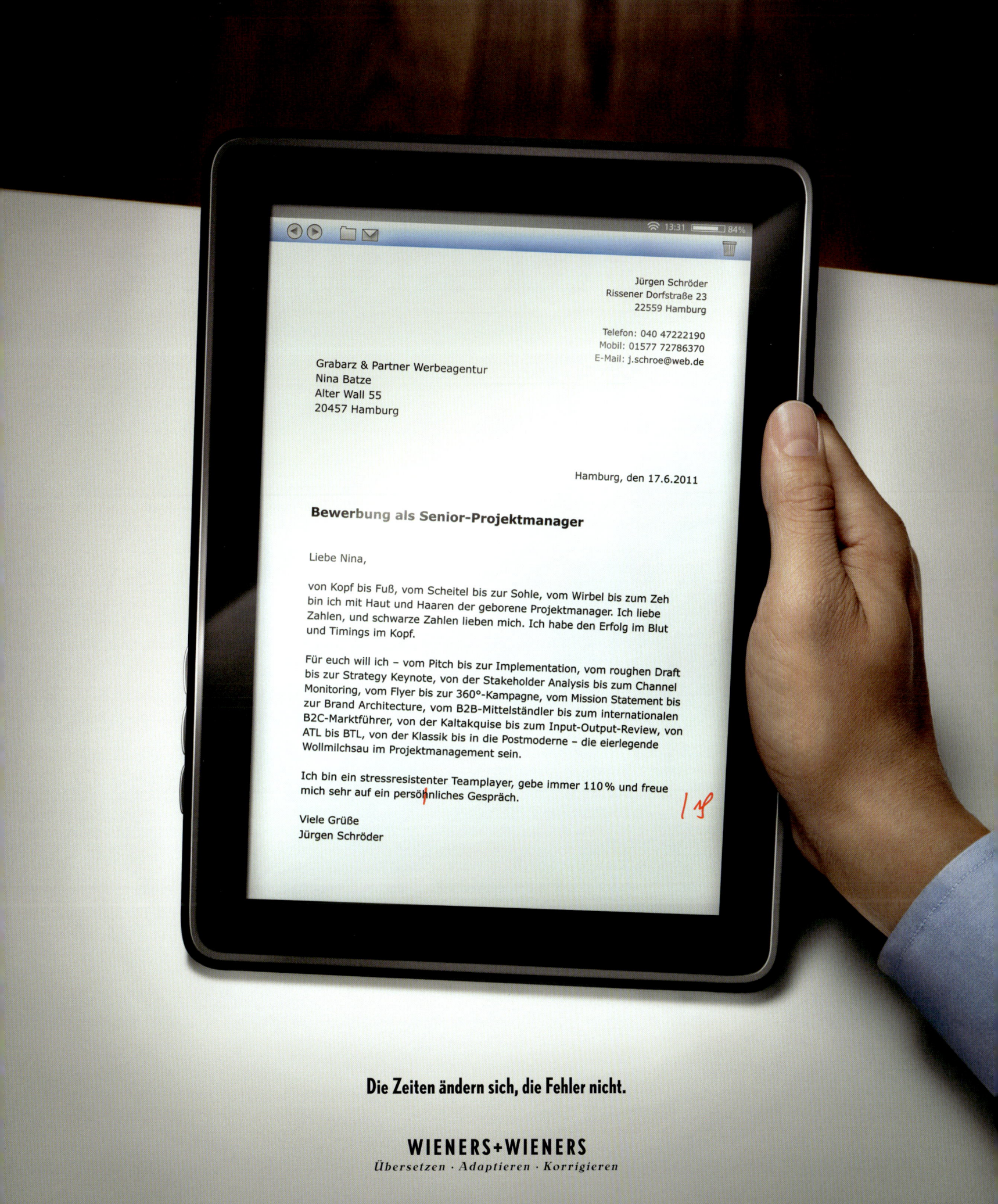

Ideen. Durchgesetzt.

Idee: Packende **Bilder** internationaler Top-Fotografen, kommentiert von prominenten Autoren.

Idee: Ein ganz neues Ressort für **Menschen**, die etwas (und uns) bewegen.

Idee: Mehr Platz für die **Wirtschaft** – und das Beste aus „The Economist" exklusiv.

Idee: Großer **Debattenteil** für den Schlagabtausch von Vor- und Querdenkern.

Idee: Analysen, die das **politische Geschehen** auf den Punkt bringen und die größeren Zusammenhänge sichtbar machen.

Idee: Investigativ recherchierte **Reportagen**, die Partei ergreifen und auch unbequemen Stimmen Gehör verschaffen.

FOCUS ist ein Magazin für Macher. Für alle, die sich lieber für ihre Leistung kritisieren lassen, als sich aus lauter Vorsicht und vorauseilendem Gehorsam jede Initiative zu verkneifen. Aus dieser Haltung heraus haben wir in den letzten Monaten viele neue Ideen im FOCUS umgesetzt. Aus dieser Haltung heraus bewundern wir alle, die für und um ihre Ideen kämpfen. Deshalb unterstützen wir den ADC.

Wir gratulieren allen Siegern des ADC Wettbewerbs 2011.

HORIZONT

**Exklusives Angebot:
4 Wochen HORIZONT
- gratis -**

Ideengeber.
Erfolgreiche Markenführung braucht gute Ideen und außergewöhnliche Kreation. Was in Marketing, Werbung und Medien wirklich läuft, zeigt Ihnen jede Woche HORIZONT. Holen Sie sich den richtigen Input für Ihre Kreativideen aus HORIZONT. Am besten gleich vier Wochen gratis.

www.horizont.net/ideengeber

HORIZONT
ZEITUNG FÜR MARKETING, WERBUNG UND MEDIEN

ALLE 60 SEKUNDEN STIRBT EINE ART AUS.
JEDE MINUTE ZÄHLT, JEDE SPENDE HILFT: BUND.NET

BUND
FREUNDE DER ERDE

KATEGORIE:
LEIDENSCHAFT
Der Publikumspreis der Deutschen Bank

Die Ausstellungsbesucher auf dem ADC Festival 2011 in Frankfurt am Main hatten nicht nur die Möglichkeit, leidenschaftlich über gute Kreation und exzellente Ideen zu diskutieren. Zum ersten Mal konnten sie auch selbst abstimmen, um den Gewinner des Publikumspreises der Deutschen Bank zu küren. Die Besucher bekamen hierzu jeweils ein Exemplar des „pass on your passion"-Stickers ausgehändigt, mit dem sie in der Ausstellung die für sie leidenschaftlichste und kreativste Arbeit markierten.

Nach der Auszählung des Publikumsvotings am Ende des ADC Festivals stand ein eindeutiger Sieger fest: die Arbeit „5 vor 12" für den Bund für Umwelt und Naturschutz Deutschland von Scholz & Friends Berlin.

Auftraggeber: BUND e.V.
Kommunikationsleitung: Dr. Norbert Franck
Projektleitung: Mark Hörstermann
Lead-Agentur: Scholz & Friends
Kreativgeschäftsführer: Martin Pross, Matthias Spaetgens
Creative Direction: Florian Schwalme, Mathias Rebmann
Art Direction: Ksenia Slavcheva, René Gebhardt, Björn Kernspeckt, Sebastian Frese
Kundenberatung: Christine Scharney, Susanne Kieck
Illustration: Peppermill Berlin
Grafikdesign: Sebastian Frese

In association with
Deutsche Bank

Passion to Perform

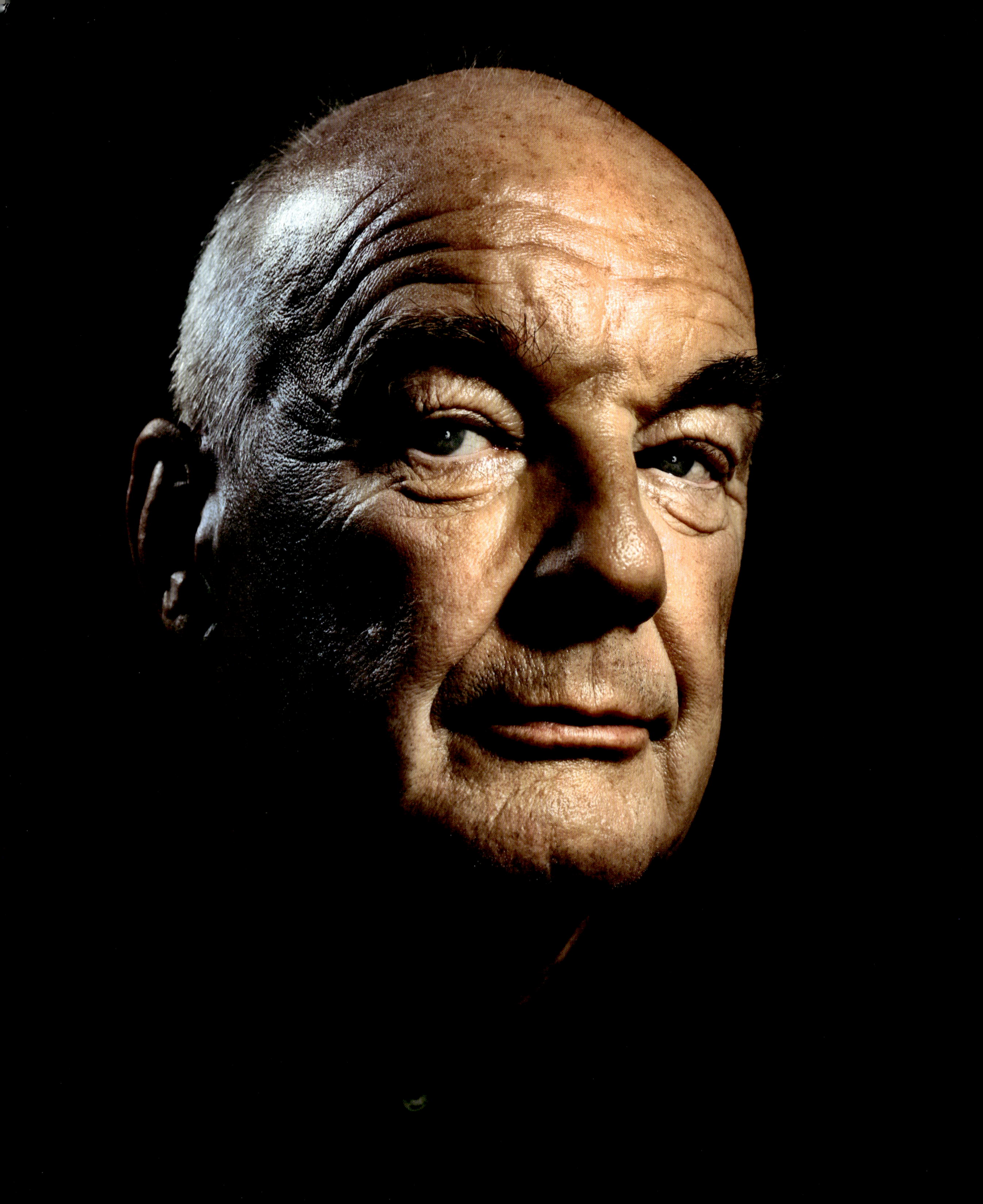

„**Also von mir hat er das nicht.**"
Gerrit Gründgens, 69, Kaufmann, Vater von Gregor Gründgens
(Brand & Marketing Director Vodafone und W&V-Leser)

W&V
Werben & Verkaufen

corporate design, branding, digital media in frankfurt – seit 2000

hauser lacour

pa • picture alliance
Ein Unternehmen der dpa-Gruppe

Die Nägel warten voller Vorfreude auf ihre Verleihung. Sie genießen das Rampenlicht. Gleich werden sie jemanden sehr glücklich machen - und wir halten diesen Moment fest.

www.picture-alliance.com - Fotopartner des ADC-Festivals 2011

DER ADC SAGT DANKE.

IDEEN.DURCHSETZEN.

DER ART DIRECTORS CLUB DANKT DEN PARTNERN, FÖRDERERN UND SPONSOREN DES ADC FESTIVALS 2011.

PARTNER
- Stadt Frankfurt am Main
- Frankfurt — Wirtschaftsförderung Frankfurt — Frankfurt Economic Development GmbH

FÖRDERER
- Tourismus+Congress GmbH Frankfurt am Main
- FrankfurtRheinMain GmbH — International Marketing of the Region
- Europäische Union: Investition in Ihre Zukunft – Europäischer Fonds für regionale Entwicklung
- Hessisches Ministerium für Wirtschaft, Verkehr und Landesentwicklung / Hessisches Ministerium für Wissenschaft und Kunst — HESSEN
- Regionalverband FrankfurtRheinMain
- Stadt Offenbach am Main — Magistrat der Stadt Offenbach am Main, Wirtschaftsförderung
- Frankfurt Rhein Main — Die Wirtschaftsinitiative

OFFIZIELLE SPONSOREN DES ADC
- In association with Deutsche Bank
- FOCUS
- entega
- messe frankfurt

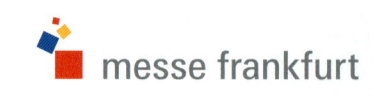

Passion to Perform

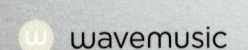

- AMBER MEDIA
- amiando — event registration & ticketing
- APPEL GROUP. — Berlin Düsseldorf Frankfurt Hamburg München Stuttgart
- Lürzer's Int'l ARCHIVE — Ads, TV and Posters world-wide
- artlife — messe events specials
- AS&S RADIO
- Bayão
- beef
- brandbook.de
- DAILYPLACES
- DELI PICTURES
- DESIGNERDOCK — only good staff make good stuff
- FRANKEN \ ARCHITEKTEN GMBH — ARCHITECTURE BRANDSPACE CONSULTING
- FAW — FACHVERBAND AUSSENWERBUNG E.V.
- Frankfurter Allgemeine Zeitung für Deutschland
- Frankfurter Rundschau
- GoSee
- GROUP.IE — Identity Engineering
- GROVES SOUND COMMUNICATIONS
- hauser lacour
- HORIZONT — Zeitung für Marketing, Werbung und Medien
- Jägermeister
- Linotype by Monotype Imaging
- LUKAS LINDEMANN ROSINSKI
- Media Frankfurt — Excellence in airport advertising
- NEUMANN & MÜLLER VERANSTALTUNGSTECHNIK
- Ogilvy
- ORGATECH — Mietmobiliar + Accessoires
- PAGE
- pa·picture alliance
- Rotkäppchen
- Scheufelen — PREMIUM WHITE SINCE 1855
- S+ seltmann+söhne
- Südliche Weinstrasse — Zum Wohl. Die Pfalz.
- Touchmore — Haptische Werbemedien
- TRAFFIC
- 25h TWENTY FIVE HOURS HOTEL FRANKFURT — TAILORED BY LEVI'S
- VELTINS
- VOSS+FISCHER
- VW
- W&V — Werben & Verkaufen
- wavemusic
- weave
- WERBEWEISCHER — WERBUNG IM KINO
- Wertheim Village — Outlet Shopping
- WIENERS+WIENERS — Übersetzen · Adaptieren · Korrigieren
- ZMG — ZEITUNGS MARKETING GESELLSCHAFT

ADC KUNDE DES JAHRES
ADC CUSTOMER OF THE YEAR
YVONNE ZIMMERMANN
MARC WEEGEN

**BRITTA STEFFEN
SCHWIMM-OLYMPIA-
SIEGERIN UND -WELT-
MEISTERIN 2009
OLYMPIC CHAMPION
AND WORLD
CHAMPION 2009
IN SWIMMING**

**ADC NIGHT OF HONOR
9. DEZEMBER 2010, BERLIN
9 DECEMBER 2010, BERLIN**

Im Frühsommer 2008 wartet der bisher eher als altehrwürdig bekannte Bankenverbund der Volksbanken Raiffeisenbanken mit einer Werbekampagne auf, die … sagen wir es mal so … ganz und gar nicht Werbung sein will.

»Drang« heißt die Dokumentation, die das Herzstück des Kommunikationsauftritts darstellt. »Drang« – eine Dokumentation, knapp eine Stunde lang. Praktisch ohne werblichen Hinweis auf den Initiator.

Einer der Protagonisten, Siegfried Müller, stellt darin eine Frage, die ihm einerseits wohl gegönnt, den Auftritt in unserem Kommunikationszeitalter aber bestens beschreibt. Dazu muss man wissen: Siegfried Müller ist Fleischermeister im Ruhestand, kurz vor der Abreise nach Ruanda, wo er Schwarzafrikanern die Kunst der deutschen Wurstherstellung beibringen soll. Er fragt sich, so rein rhetorisch, irgendwo zwischen Köln und Ruanda: »Was ist denn schon normal?«

Normal für die Welt des normalen Werbeverantwortlichen ist offenbar Folgendes: zwei bis drei Jahre in der Position verharren, nach Möglichkeit nichts wirklich verändern (lief ja immer schon irgendwie), bloß nichts wagen … und dann – als wäre es der natürliche Gang der Dinge – in die nächste höhere Position rutschen, aufsteigen. Man nennt das Karriere. Begründung: Hat ja nichts falsch gemacht. (Wenn man ehrlich ist, hat derjenige auch nichts wirklich richtig gemacht.)

Yvonne Zimmermann und Marc Weegen, die Kommunikationsverantwortlichen des Bundesverbands der Volksbanken Raiffeisenbanken, wollen diesem Klischee partout nicht entsprechen. Das könnte Zufall sein, ist aber eher schon historisch bedingt. Sie sind Kinder der ihnen anvertrauten Marke. Und das seit ihrem Geburtsjahr, dem Beginn ihrer Mitgliedschaft in der genossenschaftlichen Vereinigung.

So sind sie Teil ebendieser Marke und konnten letzten Endes gar nicht anders als … sich verantwortlich fühlen. Auch wenn das unter Umständen bedeutete, den alles andere als mehrheitsfähigen Weg zu wählen.

Der mehrheitsfähige Weg … Sie (werte Anwesende) wissen schon. Den (mehrheitsfähigen) Weg gehen mit den "shiny happy people", Mann und Frau Mitte 30, frisch verheiratet, im Cabrio, im Frühjahr, in der Toskana, die Grinsmaske aufgesetzt … Dazu irgendeine Schlagzeile mit dem Wort »Zukunft«, alternativ »Kompetenz« oder besser beides.

Das passt. Nicht unbedingt falsch, aber nein – nie und nimmer richtig. Stattdessen: Yvonne Zimmermann und Marc Weegen stellen das scheinbar gängige Klischee der Finanzkommunikation in Frage … und besinnen sich auf die ureigenen Wurzeln der genossenschaftlich organisierten Volksbanken Raiffeisenbanken: Die erklärte Nähe zum Menschen, seiner Individualität und seinem ureigenen Bestreben.

Dazu versuchen sie den jovialen Schulterschluss erst gar nicht. Sie versuchen sich nicht in gängigen Pauschalantworten, nein, sie machen genau das Gegenteil. Sie stellen eine Frage: Was treibt dich an? Yvonne Zimmermann und Marc Weegen hören den Antworten zu. Dabei lassen sie ausreden, quatschen, resümieren, in Frage stellen, meckern, berichten. Nicht notwendigerweise über Geld, nicht über Banken, nicht mal über die Volksbanken Raiffeisenbanken, sondern über Beweggründe, Ängste, Lasten, Ziele.

Sie wagen damit etwas, das in der Bankenkommunikation eigentlich normal sein sollte, aber gerne vergessen wird: Das Geld bzw. das Bankprodukt folgt dem Menschen, nicht umgekehrt. In Werbung übersetzt heißt das: »Jeder Mensch hat etwas, das ihn antreibt. Wir machen den Weg frei.« Eine Leitidee, die sich multimedial über das Land legt und die vor allem durch ihre Unaufdringlichkeit eindringlich wird.

Sie lassen dazu keine Werbewelt erfinden, sie nehmen einfach die, in der wir leben. (Bei genauerem Betrachten gibt es auch keine andere.) Sie legen ihren sorgsam ausgewählten Protagonisten keine Worte in den Mund. Sie führen sie nicht als Testimonials vor.

Es gibt kein Skript, keine im Test gewonnenen Erkenntnisse, es gibt keine Angst – nein, es gibt nur eine Frage. So sieht »echt« nicht nach »Knoppers« aus, sondern ist es einfach: wahrhaftig und echt. Die Protagonisten müssen nicht einmal Kunden der Volksbanken Raiffeisenbanken sein.

Yvonne Zimmermann und Marc Weegen wagen ein Experiment. Und haben dabei einen der elementar wichtigsten Fürsprecher. Uwe Fröhlich, den Präsidenten des Bundesverbands der Volksbanken Raiffeisenbanken, einen, der ebenfalls zulässt. Nur so ist das unendliche Vertrauen zu erklären, das ein Projekt wie dieses braucht. Wenn man ein erklärtes Ziel hat – statt eines müden Briefingformulars, generiert aus den Standards der Werbeindustrie. Sie vertrauen. Ja, sie vertrauen. All denen, die an der Konzeption und Umsetzung der Kampagne beteiligt sind. Und weil sie vertrauen, lassen sie auch zu.

Sie lassen zu, dass Menschen sagen, was sie denken. Sie lassen zu, dass überaus Wohlhabende neben weniger Wohlhabenden zu Wort kommen. Sie lassen zu, dass ein Dokumentarfilm entsteht, der wie ein ganz normaler Kinofilm vermarktet wird. Inklusive DVD-Release. Sie lassen zu, dass alles – ob Print oder Film – ohne ihr Beisein realisiert wird. Sie lassen zu, dass Prominente wie Dettmar Cramer wie normale Menschen behandelt werden. Ohne Extrawurst.

Am Ende schaffen sie einen Präzedenzfall, der mittlerweile Standard für Finanzdienstleistungen geworden ist. Eine Kampagne, eine Herangehensweise, die zur Referenz wurde. Auch innerhalb der eigenen Reihen: Yvonne Zimmermann und Marc Weegen schwören rund 87 Prozent des aus rund 1.200 Banken bestehenden Bankenverbunds auf die Kampagne ein. Eine bis dato unerreichte Zustimmung.

Ein Präzedenzfall aber auch, der sich nicht an Worthülsen wie »360 Grad« oder "integrated" orientiert. Sondern nur an der absoluten Relevanz des Notwendigen und Glaubhaften. Trotzdem schaffte es ihre Arbeit von null auf Platz 1 der am häufigsten ausgezeichneten Kampagnen des ADC Festivals 2010. Über alle Kommunikationskategorien hinweg. Dahin, wo es am wichtigsten ist: wahrhaftig, ehrlich und mit Anstand – in die Herzen der Menschen.

Alleine dafür verdienen Yvonne Zimmermann und Marc Weegen den Ehrentitel »Kunde des Jahres«.

In the early summer of 2008, the Federal Association of German »Volksbanken und Raiffeisenbanken« Co-operative Banks came up with an advertising campaign that … let's put it this way … doesn't want to be advertising.

»Drang« is the name of the documentary that represents the heart of the communication strategy. »Drang« – a documentary, almost an hour long. Almost completely free of any advertising-related reference to its initiator.

In the documentary, one of the protagonists, Siegfried Müller, poses a question that in a way perfectly describes the strategy in our age of communication. One thing you need to know: Siegfried Müller is a retired butcher, about to leave for Rwanda where he is supposed to teach native Africans the art of German sausage-making. Somewhere between Cologne and Rwanda, he asks himself the purely rhetorical question: "What's normal nowadays anyway?"

Normal for the world of normal advertising executives is obviously the following: biding your time for two to three years in one position, if possible not really changing anything (everything's always worked out somehow), definitely not trying anything new … and then – as if it were the natural order of things – sliding into the next higher position, climbing the ladder. That's what's called a career. The reason for the promotion: Didn't do anything wrong. (In all honesty, they didn't really do anything right either.)

Yvonne Zimmermann and Marc Weegen, responsible for the Federal Association of German »Volksbanken und Raiffeisenbanken« Co-operative Banks communications wanted to avoid this cliché in every way possible. That could be a coincidence, but is more likely based on historical reasons. They are children of the brand they're now responsible for. And have been since their birth, the beginning of their membership in the cooperative association.

Which means they are truly part of this brand, and in the end, couldn't have done anything else other than … feel responsible. Even if that might also mean having to choose the exact opposite of the path acceptable for the majority of people.

The path acceptable for the majority … you (dear guests) know what I mean. Going the way acceptable for the majority, together with the "shiny happy people", husband and wife, mid-thirties, just married, in a convertible, in the spring, in Tuscany, smiling from ear to ear … Add a random headline with the word "future," or maybe "expertise," or better yet, both.

That fits. Not really wrong, but no – never ever right either. Instead: Yvonne Zimmermann and Marc Weegen call what appears to be the standard cliché in financial marketing into question … and go back to their own roots in the cooperatively organized Volksbanken Raiffeisenbanken: The declared closeness to real people, their individuality, and their own aspirations.

In doing this, they don't even begin to try and use the friendly "arm around the shoulders" shtick. They don't try to use conventional one-size-fits-all answers, … no … they do the exact opposite. They ask a question: what drives you? Yvonne Zimmermann and Marc Weegen listened to the answers. They let people finish speaking, shoot the breeze, summarize, question, complain, report. Not necessarily about money, not even about banks, and not about the Volksbanken Raiffeisenbanken, but about motives, fears, pressures, and goals.

They dare to do something that actually should be a normal part of banks' communication, but is often forgotten: Money and banking products follow the people, and not the other way around. Translated into advertising, that means: "Each and every person has something that drives them. We clear the obstacles from their path." A central idea that spreads out across the country in multimedia form and becomes poignant as a result of its unobtrusiveness.

And they don't create an advertising world to accomplish this, they simply use the one we live in. (When you look closely, there really is no other.) They don't put any words in the mouths of their carefully selected protagonists. They don't use them for testimonials.

There's no script, no findings gained from a test, no fear – no, just one question. So, "real" doesn't look like "Knoppers," instead it really is: truthful and real. The protagonists don't even have to be customers of the Volksbanken Raiffeisenbanken.

Yvonne Zimmermann and Marc Weegen dare to conduct an experiment. And in doing so, have one of the most fundamentally important advocates. Uwe Fröhlich, the President of the Federal Association of German »Volksbanken und Raiffeisenbanken« Co-operative Banks, someone that also allows things to happen. That's the only way to explain the infinite trust that a project like this requires. When you have a stated goal – instead of a tired briefing form, generated from advertising industry standards. They trust. Yes, they trust. All those that are involved in designing and implementing the campaign. And because they trust, they also allow.

They allow people to say what they think. They allow extremely wealthy people to speak right next to those less wealthy. They allow a documentary to be created that is marketed exactly like a normal movie. Which includes a DVD release. They allow for everything – whether print or film – to be carried out without their presence. They allow celebrities like Dettmar Cramer to be treated like normal people. Without any special treatment.

In the end, they set a precedent that has, in the meantime, become the standard for financial services. A campaign, an approach, that has become a reference case. And that also applies to their own ranks: Yvonne Zimmermann and Marc Weegen get about 87 percent of the banking association, which consists of around

1,200 banks, to commit to the campaign. An approval rating which has never been seen since.

And it's also a precedent that isn't oriented around empty phrases like "360-degree" or "integrated," but instead only around the absolute relevance of what's necessary and believable. And yet, their work still manages to go from zero to the campaign which received the most awards at the 2010 ADC Festival. Across all communications categories. Right to the most important place of all: truthful, honest, and with integrity – into the hearts of the people.

And for this alone, Yvonne Zimmermann and Marc Weegen deserve the honorary title of "Customer of the Year."

ADC EHRENMITGLIED
DES JAHRES
ADC HONORARY MEMBER
OF THE YEAR
 RAINER BRANDT

LUTZ WILDE
JOURNALIST

ADC NIGHT OF HONOR
9. DEZEMBER 2010, BERLIN
9 DECEMBER 2010, BERLIN

Sehr geehrte Damen und Herren, lieber Rainer Brandt,

eine kurze Vorbemerkung: Sie werden mich in Ihrem werbetreibenden Kreis sicher nicht kennen. Das liegt einfach daran: ich arbeite als Redakteur bei der Stiftung Warentest – und die Medien dieser Einrichtung sind traditionell völlig werbefrei. Einen gemeinsamen *Werbe*hintergrund haben wir – Sie und ich – also nicht. Eines aber eint uns doch: die gebotene Bewunderung für das Werk von Rainer Brandt.

Als Kind bin ich auf Rainer Brandts Schaffen gewissermaßen »über Bande« aufmerksam geworden. Immer wenn mein Vater eine ganz bestimmte Sendung im Fernsehen sah, schlug seine Mimik um in ein glückliches, fast grenzwertiges Dauergrinsen. Er schaute dann eine Folge von »Die Zwei«. Dass nicht *wirklich* Roger Moore und Tony Curtis – wir haben sie eben im Einspielfilm gesehen – für das Gekicher im Wohnzimmer verantwortlich waren, das erkannte ich erst viel später. Die schnellen Gags verdanken wir Rainer Brandt. Die schnoddrigen Sprüche waren im Originalskript der Serie ja gar nicht vorhanden.

Was hat Rainer Brandt da mit seiner Bearbeitung von so vielen Filmen und Serien gemacht? Zunächst einmal hat er uns jede Menge Spaß bereitet. Rainer Brandt produzierte und produziert gute Laune, und die ist Öl für die Lebenslampe. Und ein Weiteres ist klar: Mit seinem Mut zur Außergewöhnlichkeit und seinem Talent hat er dem Publikum, sicher mehr aber noch seinen Film- und Fernsehkollegen klargemacht: Traut euch was! Und er hat gezeigt, dass die Arbeit in den Synchronstudios mehr Wertschätzung verdient! Rainer Brandt hat das mit dem großen Erfolg der von ihm bearbeiteten Filme und Serien unter Beweis gestellt. Vor allem große Kinofilme, die seine unverwechselbare Handschrift trugen, machten die Produzenten reich – und wurden in der Regel mit dem »Goldenen Vorhang« ausgezeichnet. Das ist der Preis der Branche für wirtschaftlichen Erfolg.

Paradebeispiel ist natürlich die vielgepriesene Serie »Die Zwei«. In anderen Ländern, in denen sie im Original gezeigt wurde, kam sie nur mäßig an. In den USA war sie sogar ein Flop. Bis Anfang der 70er-Jahre wurden ausländische Filme hierzulande nach dem Motto »Am Besten nichts Neues« bearbeitet. Mit Rainer Brandt wurde das dann anders. Endlich schaute man darauf, was die Macher eines Films mit den Dialogen *ausdrücken* wollten – und nicht mehr nur auf den Wortlaut der Originalfassung.

Den unverwechselbaren schnoddrigen Witz von Rainer Brandt haben seine Kollegen – soweit ich sehe – allerdings nicht kopiert. Wahrscheinlich haben sie das Aussichtslose des Versuchs erkannt. Rainer Brandt hat – ich benutze das hässliche, aber treffende Wort – ein Alleinstellungsmerkmal.

Natürlich habe ich für diese Lobrede nach Vergleichbarem gesucht, wohl wissend, dass nicht alles, was hinkt, ein Vergleich ist. In der Welt des Zelluloids aber: Fehlanzeige. In den Sinn kam mir am Ende nur ein Beispiel aus meiner eigenen Arbeitswelt. Der Journalist Hunter Thompson ist mir eingefallen. Der war zwar nicht so witzig wie Rainer Brandt, doch auch er hatte den Mut, mit den Traditionen seiner Branche zu brechen. So hat er sich bei seinen Reportagen fast nie mit einer schlichten Darstellung des *Vor*gefundenen begnügt, sondern die Stories mit *Er*fundenem angereichert, um so – paradoxerweise – ein noch klareres Bild der Wirklichkeit zu zeichnen und – wie Rainer Brandt – eine viel größere Wirkung zu erzielen.

Rainer Brandt hat solche kreativen Leistungen dauerhaft und nachhaltig vollbracht – und dafür ehren Sie ihn heute Abend völlig zu Recht.

Sicher hätte er mit seinem Einfallsreichtum und seinem Sprachtalent auch in Ihrer Branche erfolgreich arbeiten können. Aber das hat er gottlob vermieden. Ich sage »gottlob«, weil wir sonst nicht in den Genuss herzhaft synchronisierter Genreklassiker wie Belmondos »Der Profi« oder »Das große Fressen« gekommen wären und auch Werke wie der Film »Wild trieben es die alten Hunnen« nicht die Aufmerksamkeit bekommen hätten, die sie verdienen.

Säße Rainer Brandt in Ihren Reihen, würde uns auch seine Schauspielkunst fehlen. Tatsächlich ist dieser Mann nicht nur Text und Stimme, sondern er agiert – als klassisch ausgebildeter Schauspieler – auch *vor* dem Publikum. Zuletzt spielte, sang und tanzte er – gemeinsam mit seiner Frau Ursula Heyer – im Musical "Dirty Dancing". Jetzt steckt er in den Proben für das Lindenberg-Musical »Hinterm Horizont«. Seine Rolle: Stasichef Mielke. Die Premiere ist im Januar.

Rainer Brandt kann mehr als lustig-anzügliche Sprüche klopfen und weiß offenbar stets, wann ein zu bearbeitendes Werk ausnahmsweise mal keine Formulierungen wie »Hallöchen Popöchen« verträgt, denn er kennt die Grenzen seines Geschäfts. Nur geeigneten Filmen drückt er seinen Stempel auf. Kinoklassiker wie »Der Nachtportier« oder die »Reise nach Indien« hat er höchst erfolgreich bearbeitet, ohne auf das bewährte »Schnodder-Deutsch« zurückzugreifen.

Rainer Brandt ist mit Fantasie gesegnet. Ihm gelingt scheinbar spielend das Leichte, das – wie Sie wohl am besten wissen – *so* schwer zu machen ist. Sein witziger Jargon ist dabei nicht nur der Straße, der Halbwelt, dem Jiddischen und dem Berlinerischen abgelauscht, wie Rainer Brandt das schon häufig erzählt hat. Er beruht weitgehend auf zahllosen »Ausnahmeeinfällen«, die hoffentlich niemals zu »Einnahmeausfällen« geführt haben.

Ob Rainer Brandt ein Künstler ist, mag jeder selbst beurteilen. Berufen kann er sich jedenfalls auf den großen William Shakespeare. Der hat im Stück »Was ihr wollt« getextet: »Denn kluge Blödelei ist niemals öde, doch öder Tiefsinn immer blöde«.

Lieber Rainer Brandt,

als Fan Deiner Arbeit beglückwünsche ich Dich ganz herzlich zur Ehrenmitgliedschaft im Art Directors Club. Ein Spruch, den Du bitte als Ausdruck meiner Bewunderung ansehen mögest, lautet: »Wer sich durchs Leben schlägt als Mann, den ficht kein Greisenalter an«.

Ihnen, liebe »Normal-Mitglieder« des Art Directors Club, danke ich für die kluge Preis-Entscheidung. Als Mitarbeiter der Stiftung Warentest vergebe ich dafür heute Abend das Qualitätsurteil »sehr gut«.

Vielen Dank.

Ladies and Gentlemen, Mr. Rainer Brandt,

Before I begin, I'd like to make a brief preliminary remark – I'm positive none of you will recognize me from your advertising world. That's simply because I work as an editor for the Stiftung Warentest magazine, and the media channels we use have traditionally been completely free of advertising. Which means you and I don't share a mutual *advertising* background. But we do have one thing in common: an admiration for Rainer Brandt's handiwork.

As a child I became aware of Rainer Brandt's work sort of indirectly. Whenever my father watched this one specific TV show, his facial expression changed into a happy, almost non-stop grin. He was watching an episode of "The Persuaders!". I only realized much later that it wasn't *really* Roger Moore und Tony Curtis – who we just saw in the video clip – that were responsible for the giggling in the living room. Here in Germany, we owed the quick-lipped gags to Rainer Brandt. He added these brash expressions in himself – they weren't actually in the series' original scripts.

What did Rainer Brandt do by being a part of so many movies and series? Well for starters, he gave us a lot of fun times. Rainer Brandt produced and produces a good mood, which is oil for life's lamp. And another thing is clear: thanks to his courage to be different and his talent, he told the audience, and more so his colleagues from movies and television: believe in yourself and go out on a limb!

And he showed us that work in a dubbing studio deserves more recognition! Rainer Brandt proved this with the huge success seen by the movies and series he worked on. Above all, the blockbuster movies, which clearly bear his unmistakable signature, made the producers rich – and were usually awarded the »Goldene Vorhang.« That's the industry's award for commercial success.

A prime example is, of course, the highly-praised series "The Persuaders!". In other countries where the original was shown, it got a lukewarm reception. In the US it actually flopped. Until the early 70s, foreign movies were dubbed here in Germany based on the premise that "the best thing to do is to not change anything." But with Rainer Brandt, that all changed. Finally, people began to focus on what the filmmakers were trying to *express* with the dialog – and not on the exact wording of the original script.

But, as far as I can tell, Rainer Brandt's colleagues never copied his unmistakable, brash style. They probably realized just how hopeless the effort would be. Rainer Brandt had – I'll use the ugly, but applicable phrase – a USP.

When preparing this speech, I obviously looked for something comparable, knowing full well that for some things, there simply is no comparison. And in the end, I didn't find anything similar in the entire world of moving pictures. Ultimately, the only thing I could think of was an example from my own working environment. I thought of the journalist Hunter Thompson. Now, he may not have been as funny as Rainer Brandt. But he did have the courage to break with his industry's traditions. You see, in his reports he was never satisfied with simply presenting what he *found out*, but instead, he enriched his stories with things he *made up* in order to – paradoxically – create a clearer picture of reality and – just like Rainer Brandt – have a much larger impact.

Rainer Brandt performed such creative wonders continuously and effectively – which is why you are absolutely correct in your decision to honor him this evening.

With his creativity and linguistic talent, he surely could have worked successfully in your industry. But thank heavens, he avoided it. I say "thank heavens," because if he hadn't, we would never have had the pleasure of enjoying superbly dubbed classics of the genre such as Belmondo's «Le Professionnel» or "The Big Feast," and works such as the movie «Attila flagello di Dio» would have never gotten the attention they deserve.

If Rainer Brandt was one of you guys, we would all miss his acting talent. Because this man is not only text and voice, but he also performs – as a classically trained actor – *in front* of an audience. He last acted, sang, and danced – together with his wife Ursula Heyer – in the musical "Dirty Dancing." He's currently rehearsing for the Udo Lindenberg musical »Hinterm Horizont.« His role: Erich Mielke, head of the DDR's secret police. The première is in January.

Rainer Brandt can do more than just make funny, lewd wisecracks, and obviously always knows when phrases like »Hallöchen Popöchen« are, for once, not appropriate for something he's dubbing. The man knows the limits of his business. He only puts his signature on the movies that qualify. He successfully dubbed movie classics such as "The Night Porter" or "A Passage to India" without falling back on his time-tested »Schnodder-Deutsch.«

Rainer Brandt has been blessed with imagination. He seems to be able to do with absolute ease that which – as you all know best – is *so* hard to do. His funny jargon is not only taken from the street, the underworld, Yiddish, and Berliner slang, as Rainer Brandt has often said. It's primarily based on numerous "exceptional ideas" that hopefully never led to "losses of income."

Everyone has to decide for themselves whether or not Rainer Brandt is an artist. But in any case, he can invoke the words of the great William Shakespeare, who wrote in the play "Twelfth Night": "For folly that he wisely shows is fit; But wise men, folly-fall'n, quite taint their wit."

Dear Rainer Brandt,

As a fan of your work, I would like to congratulate you on your honorary membership in the Art Directors Club. The following is a saying that you can take as an expression of my admiration: "Old age is the badge of honor you wear for making your way through life as a man."

And I would like to thank you, dear "normal members" of the Art Directors Club, for this wise award decision. As an employee of Stiftung Warentest, I give the overall quality of this evening a rating of "excellent."

Thank you.

ADC LEBENSWERK DES JAHRES
ADC LIFETIME ACHIEVEMENT
REINHARD SIEMES

REINHARD SIEMES*
WERBETEXTER, EHEMALIGER ADC PRÄSIDENT UND LANGJÄHRIGES ADC VORSTANDSMITGLIED
COPYWRITER, FORMER ADC PRESIDENT AND ADC MEMBER OF THE BOARD FOR MANY YEARS

ADC NIGHT OF HONOR
9. DEZEMBER 2010, BERLIN
9 DECEMBER 2010, BERLIN

Anfang September schickte ich eine Mail an Reinhard Siemes mit dem Betreff »Tach, Ehrenmitglied« und informierte ihn über seine Wahl zum Ehrenrentner, wie er sich selbst nennt. Nach drei Stunden bekam ich diese Antwort: »Im ersten Moment dachte ich: Das ist nicht mehr mein ADC. Die sollen lieber Verona Pooth für ihr Lebenswerk ehren. Dank ihr weiß ich, was eine Spinatwachtel ist. Dann las ich Deinen Bewerbungstext für mich. Wenn der dazu geführt hat, dass sich der extrem progressive ADC auf seine Vergangenheit besinnt, sind vielleicht doch noch einige der Nasen mit dem Atem an der Normalität.«

Was gibt es über Siemes zu sagen?

Dass er die ADC Nachwuchsseminare ins Leben rief, an der LMU in München und der HdK in Berlin lehrte, dass er die Texterschule im Internet gründete, 25 Jahre lang in W&V als Nestbeschmutzer auftrat und dass er um die 80 Preise gewann, mag dem einen oder anderen von Ihnen noch in Erinnerung sein.

Es gibt aber auch Leistungen, die weitgehend unbekannt sind. So hat er gemeinsam mit Otti Severin auf den ADC Empfängen in Cannes mindestens zehn Fördermitglieder aufgerissen. Die beiden guckten sich ein ganz bestimmtes Opfer aus, machten es betrunken und pressten ihm dann auf liebenswürdige Weise die Fördermitgliedschaft ab. Das ging insofern problemlos, als Otti und Siemes seit vier Tagen im Training waren. Das Opfer hatte nicht die geringste Chance und war nach einer Stunde platt.

Er hat in seiner Zeit als Präsident den »Kunden des Jahres« eingeführt und zum ersten Mal geehrt, Francois Pommerau von der Sopexa. Gleichzeitig brachte er den ADC in argen Misskredit. Ein W&V-Redakteur hatte ihn während der Jurierung gefragt: »Wenn es eine Blechmedaille für die schlechteste Kampagne gäbe, wem würden Sie die als ADC Präsident verleihen?« »Ganz klar, den BWM-Anzeigen von der Düsseldorfer Agentur Spießig und Ärmlich. Die Texte sind nichts als sprachlicher Schleim.« Die Folge war schrilles Geschrei in vielen deutschen Marketing-Etagen.

Er drückte Philip Morris eine Zigaretten-Kampagne mit rauchenden Tieren aufs Auge, wobei er die Süchtigen selbst zeichnete. Etwa einen Seehund, der sagte: »Sie schmeckt wunderbar. Wenn sie nur beim Baden besser brennen würde.« Heute gäbe es wütende Proteste von Tierschutzvereinen. Damals ging die Marke sang- und klanglos unter.

Für ein New-York-Heft der Zeitschrift Holiday empfahl er einen Siebendollarschein als Werbegeschenk – für den nächtlichen Spaziergang durch Harlem und die Bronx. Die Idee wurde leider abgelehnt.

Den Anbieter von gebrauchten Klavieren trieb er mit winzigen Kleinanzeigen in den Ruin. Ende November, als das Weihnachtsgeschäft anlaufen sollte, hatte der gute Mann nur noch einen unverkäuflichen Hobel in seinem Geschäft herumstehen. Einmal überredete er eine W&V-Redakteurin, sich mit sieben seiner Arbeiten, die in Deutschland unbekannt waren, bei deutschen Agenturen zu bewerben. Dabei auch eine Anzeige mit Gold vom ADC of New York. Die Redakteurin hörte von neun Agenturen gar nichts, wurde 18 Mal mit Standardbriefen abgelehnt und bekam von fünf Agenturen eine Einladung zum Gespräch. Siemes nahm sich trotzdem nicht das Leben.

Soviel steht fest: Er war sowohl in seiner Zeit als ADC Vorstand als auch in seinen Texterjahren alles andere als ein Harfenspieler. Er bevorzugte die Triangel, am liebsten gegen den Takt.

Vielleicht fragen Sie sich, was macht ein ewiger Texter mit 70 Jahren in der selbst gewählten slowenischen Pampa. Dazu ein paar Bilder:

So sieht es da aus. (Scan Postkarte)
Das ist sein Laden, in dem er ahnungslosen Touristen Antiquitäten verkauft.
Die meisten sogar echt. (Foto Laden)
Das ist die Besitzerin des Ladens. (Foto Katze)

* VON IHM SELBST VERFASST UND GESPROCHEN
WRITTEN AND SPOKEN BY HIMSELF

Das sind die slowenischen Kastanienkreise, die er entdeckt hat. Sie sind ähnlich rätselhaft wie englischen Kornkreise. (Foto Kastanien)
Das ist die Tür auf dem Hof des k. u. k. Gemäuers, in dem er wohnt – womit ich bei einer seiner Tätigkeiten bin. Er malt und macht Bildobjekte, ohne Konzept und vor allem ohne Anspruch. (Foto Tür)
Mal mit Stockfotos. (Kasten mit Busen-Kaffeetasse)
Mal mit Bildern von Ebay. (Kasten mit Landschaftsgemälde)
Mal mit eigenen Bildern. (Kasten mit Karnevalszug) (Kasten mit Bäumen)
Und mal mit Text. (Kasten mit »nichts«)

Alles in allem lebt Siemes entspannt vor sich hin, zappt im Fernsehen alle Werbeblöcke weg, hofft, dass Guido Westerwelle nach Tschetschenien fährt und in einer Rede vor der Achmat-Kadyrow-Moschee auf die islamischen Rebellen schimpft und freut sich, wenn er mal wieder in Berlin ist. Zum Beispiel, um ADC Ehrenrentner zu werden.

At the beginning of September, I sent an e-mail to Reinhard Siemes with the subject line "Hi there, honorary member" and informed him that he had been voted an honorary pensioner, as he calls himself. After three hours I received this reply: "At first I thought: It's no longer the ADC I know. I would rather they honored Verona Pooth for her lifework. Thanks to her, I know what an old crank is. Then I read the candidacy text you'd written for me. If that led to the extremely progressive ADC reflecting on its past, then maybe a few of them still have their heads screwed on the right way."

What can you say about Siemes?

One or two of you may remember that he initiated the ADC seminars for emerging talent; lectured at the LMU in Munich and the HdK in Berlin; that he founded a school for copywriters on the Internet; spent 25 years at W&V fouling his own nest; and won around 80 prizes.
    Yet, there are other feats that aren't so well-known. Like the time when, together with Otti Severin, he persuaded at least ten people at the ADC reception in Cannes to become supporting members. The two men spied their victims, got them drunk and forced them, in the nicest possible way, to sign up for supporting membership. It all went without a hitch, seeing as Otti and Siemes had been in training for four days. The victims didn't stand a chance and raised the white flag after an hour.
    During his time as president, he introduced the "Customer of the Year" and on the first occasion, he honored Francois Pommerau from Sopexa. At the same time, he brought the ADC into disrepute. During the judging, a W&V editor asked him, "If there were a wooden spoon for the worst campaign, as ADC President, who would you award it to?" "Without question: the BWM advertisements by the agency Stuffy and Poor in Duesseldorf. The texts are nothing but verbal gunk." There followed many a shrill outcry from various German marketing departments.
    He dropped a cigarette campaign with smoking animals into the lap of Philip Morris, in which he drew the addicts himself. I think it was a seal saying: "It tastes fantastic; if only it would burn better when I'm swimming." Today, there would be angry protests from animal rights groups. Back then, nobody passed any remarks.
    For a New York issue of the magazine Holiday, he suggested giving away a seven-dollar bill as a free gift – for the evening stroll through Harlem and the Bronx. The idea was unfortunately rejected. He drove the seller of used pianos to ruin with tiny classified advertisements. At the end of November, as the Christmas sales

period was due to begin, the good man had only one unsellable wreck left standing around in his shop.

Once, he convinced a W&V editor to apply to various German agencies with seven examples of his work that were unknown in Germany, among them an advertisement that had been awarded gold by the ADC of New York. The editor heard nothing at all from nine agencies, was turned down 18 times with a standard letter and was invited to interview by five agencies. Nonetheless, Siemes didn't kill himself.

This much is clear: during his time as ADC Member of the Board and during his years as a copywriter, he was anything but a harpist. He preferred the triangle, with a predilection for playing against the beat.

Maybe you are asking yourselves, what does a 70-year-old copywriter do in the Slovenian backwoods of his own choosing? Here are a few pictures:

This is what it looks like there. (Scan postcard)
This is his shop, where he sells antiques to unsuspecting tourists. Most of them are even genuine. (Photo of shop)
That is the owner of the shop. (Photo of cat)
These are the Slovenian chestnut circles that he has discovered. They are just as mysterious as the English crop circles. (Photo of chestnuts)
This is the door to the court of the Imperial and Royal ruins where he lives – which brings me to one of his activities. He paints and makes visual objects, with no concept and definitely no standards. (Photo of the doors)
Sometimes with stock photos. (Box with "breasts" coffee cup)
Sometimes with pictures from Ebay. (Box with landscape paintings)
Sometimes with his own pictures. (Box with a carnival procession) (Box with trees)
And sometimes with text. (Box with "nothing")

All in all, Siemes drifts leisurely through life, switches over all the commercial breaks, hopes that Guido Westerwelle will travel to Chechnya and rail against the Islamic rebels in a speech given in front of the Akhmad Kadyrov Mosque, and looks forward to being back in Berlin – to become ADC honorary pensioner for example.

NACHRUF ZUM TOD VON WALTER LÜRZER
OBITUARY ON THE PASSING OF WALTER LÜRZER

HANS-PETER ALBRECHT
ADC VORSTAND
ADC MEMBER OF THE BOARD

Habe die Ehre, Walter Lürzer.

letzten Donnerstag, am 14. April 2011, ist Walter Lürzer gestorben. Mit Walter Lürzer verliert die Branche einen sehr, sehr Großen, der ADC ein Ehrenmitglied, wie es nur ein Werber zu erfinden wagen würde.

Was der Mann angepackt hat, wurde was. Am liebsten "against all odds". Sogar dem Sensenmann ist er schon spektakulär von der Schaufel gesprungen. Mittels selbstgesteuertem Flugzeugabsturz und anschließendem Stromausfall im gesamten Rhein-Main-Gebiet. Strommast umgenietet, überlebt. Großartige G'schicht.

Aber der verdammte Krebs hat jetzt gewonnen. Erheblich zu früh. 68! Da hätte er locker noch zwei Generationen Werber beeinflussen können. Wie viele Agenturen hat er aufgemacht, zum Erfolg geführt, gierigen Käufern für ordentlich Kohle überlassen? »Raster bringt Zaster«, Walter Lürzer. TBWA Deutschland; Lürzer, Conrad; aus Campbell-Ewald mach Lowe Deutschland. Immer erste Liga, immer mindestens ein Pokal. Oder ein Löwe.

Dann die Sensationsidee »Lürzers Archiv« aus a) Langeweile und b) Verärgerung, weil ihn die Art Direktorin Doris Lacerte nicht an ihr legendäres Archiv ließ. Auf der Zielgeraden schließlich die Professur an der Angewandten in Wien. Seine Lebensrolle.

Eine Urgewalt. Ein sensationeller Ausbeuter. Wenn man den Begriff mal positiv begreift. Der hat aus Bergen Gold rausgeholt, diese Berge wussten vorher gar nicht, was Metall ist. O.K. Da war nicht nur positive Motivation dabei. Aber wer fragt danach, wenn Sie mit einem Esel ein Springreiten gewinnen. Auch der Esel ist danach happy, gibt ja viele Karotten extra. Selbst wenn Sie für den Sieg öfter mal zur Gerte griffen. Lürzer hat aus ungezählten Eseln hochdekorierte Kreative gemacht. (Und umgekehrt. Er hat auch gerne mal gezeigt, wie das ist mit dem Kaiser und den Kleidern.)

Mit vulkanhafter Kreativität, mit Witz, Frechheit und Fortune haben er und Michael Conrad es geschafft, Anfang der 80er in Deutschland die GGK-Allmacht und -Herrschaft zu brechen. Mit dem Cointreau-Mann und Margret Astor und »Dies war ein Präzisionsinstrument mit 0,00000000001% Genauigkeit: ein Bosch-Scheinwerfer.« Mit Fiat.

Lürzer hat sowas von präzise hingeschaut und hingehört. Und diese chirurgische Analyse-Präzision mit dem österreichischen Schmäh sauber getarnt. »Wir fliegen nur brave Kinder« – eine Anzeige für die Lufthansa. Bild: ein heulendes Kind.

Weit vor der »Erfindung« vernetzter Kommunikation haben Lürzer und Conrad einen Protagonisten begleitet, der für eine Kampagne quer durch Deutschland lief, haben Paul Breitner für Pitralon den Bart abgenommen und per Flugzeug-Banner »MC&LB suchen Texter & AD« Personal gesucht. Grenzen? Barrieren? Einreißen.

Fiat meckert am Fiat-Kreativen Klaus E. Küster herum. Lürzer: »Na, gehns. Da such ich mia lieber einen neuen Kunden als wie so einen Kreativen zu finden.« Da ist sie wieder, die Urgewalt. Durchaus zum Wohle des Kunden. Kommentar Küster: »Der Lürzer geht Dir nicht auf den Sack, der geht auf die Knochen.«

Lürzer »überzieht« die Mittagspause, weil er mit seinem Pudel Gassi geht. Sein Chef, Alex Peabody, stellt ihn zur Rede. Lürzer: »Zahlen Sie mich für mein Hirn? Oder für mein' Oarsch?« So gesehen verliert die Welt einen wirklich genialen ... Dings, äh ... Kopf.

Lürzer und der ADC? Eine typische Lürzer-Karriere. Mitglied. Unter Protest ausgetreten. Ehrenmitglied. Jury-Präsident.

Jetzt zeigt er dem Ogilvy und dem Bernbach und dem Gossage, wo der Bartel den Most holt. Mist. Dass man das nicht auf Youtube sehen kann.

Schlusswort Walter Lürzer: »Schwafeln Sie nicht.«

It's an honor, Walter Lürzer.

Last Thursday, Walter Lürzer passed away. With his passing, the industry loses one of the greats and the ADC an honorary member that only an advertiser could dream of creating.

Whatever the man touched turned to gold. Preferably against all odds. He even spectacularly escaped the Reaper's grasp, after crashing a plane he was flying and subsequently causing a power outage throughout the entire Rhine/Main region. Knocked over a transmission tower, survived. An amazing story.

But goddamn cancer won the battle. Way to early. 68! He would have easily been able to influence another two generations of advertisers. How many agencies did he open, lead to success, and then sell to greedy buyers for loads of dough? "Patterns bring paychecks," said Walter Lürzer. TBWA Deutschland; Lürzer, Conrad; turn Campbell-Ewald into Lowe Deutschland. Always in the major leagues, always at least one trophy. Or a lion.

Then the sensational idea for "Lürzer's Archive," which stemmed from a) boredom and b) infuriation that art director Doris Lacerte didn't let him use her legendary archive. And on the home stretch, finally the professorship at the University of Applied Sciences in Vienna. His life role.

An elemental force. A sensational exploiter. When you view the term in a positive light. He got gold out of mountains, and beforehand these mountains didn't even know what metal was. O.K. There was more than just positive motivation there. But who asks about it when you win a showjumping competition with a donkey. And the donkey is also happy afterwards, he gets a lot of extra carrots. Even if they often used the crop to get the win. Lürzer turned countless donkeys into highly decorated creative folks. (And vice versa. He also like to show how it is with the emperor and his clothes.)

With volcano-like creativity, with humor, brashness, and fortune, he and Michael Conrad succeeded in destroying the GGK's omnipotence and dominance in Germany during the early 80s. With the Cointreau man and Margret Astor and "This was a precision instrument with 0.00000000001% accuracy: a Bosch headlight." With Fiat.

Lürzer watched and listened ever so closely. And masked this surgical, analytical precision with Austrian sarcasm. "We only fly well-behaved children" read a Lufthansa ad. The picture: a crying child.

Long before the "invention" of integrated marketing, Lürzer (and Conrad) followed a protagonist that walked across Germany for a campaign, shaved Paul Breitner's beard for Pitralon, and looked for new staff using an airplane banner that read: "MC&LB looking for copywriters and art directors." Limits? Barriers? Tear them down.

Fiat complained about Fiat's creative mind Klaus E. Küster. Lürzer: "Oh, come on. I'd rather look for a new client than for such a creative guy." There it is again, that elemental force. By all means for the good of the client. Küster's statement: "Lürzer isn't just annoying, he's back-breaking."

Lürzer gets back late from his lunch break because he was taking his poodle for a walk. His boss, Alex Peabody, confronts him about it. Lürzer: "Do you pay me for my brain? Or for my ass?" When you look at it that way, the world has lost a truly brilliant … umm … mind.

Lürzer and the ADC? A typical Lürzer career. Member. Left in protest. Honorary Member. Jury President.

Now he's showing Ogilvy and Bernbach and Gossage which side his bread is buttered on. Damn. And we can't watch it on Youtube.

Walter Lürzer's closing remarks: "Don't waffle."

NACHRUF
ZUM TOD VON REINHARD SIEMES
OBITUARY
ON THE PASSING OF REINHARD SIEMES

SEBASTIAN TURNER
ADC VORSTAND
1998–2010
ADC MEMBER OF THE
BOARD 1998–2010

Liebe Mitglieder,

Reinhard Siemes ist vergangenen Samstag, am 16. April 2011, im Alter von 70 Jahren gestorben.

Unter den großen Kreativen ragte Reinhard Siemes heraus als der, der sich kümmert. So schreiben wie er konnten wenige, sich dabei auch noch für andere einzusetzen, das tat wohl keiner so wie er. Es ist eine verbreitete berufliche Deformation unter herausragenden Kreativen, dass sie ihre Anfänge vergessen und alle Anfänger gleich mit. Reinhard Siemes hat darunter gelitten und das Gegenteil getan. Er hat seine Begabung an den Nachwuchs verschwendet und mit seiner Begeisterung zwei oder wohl eher drei Werbergenerationen angesteckt.

Für viele – auch mich – war er eine der ersten beruflichen Begegnungen mit der kreativen Exzellenz. Dabei pflegte er nicht die übliche Leier von der Qualität, die von der Qual kommt und vor allem den Referenten selbst anpreist und seine Rücksichtslosigkeit entschuldigt. Er sprach von Sensibilität und Menschlichkeit. Dabei sprach er auch über sich, was er nicht zugegeben hätte. Der Branche hat er den Spiegel vorgehalten, wie schlecht sie ihre eigene Zukunft behandelt. Viele Kreative haben mit ihm gelitten, wenn sie sahen, wie er mit sich selbst umging. Er kämpfte den längsten Teil seines Lebens mit seinem Todfreund, wie er sagte, dem Alkohol.

Der ADC hatte in ihm seinen Motor und sein Gewissen für eine kleine Ewigkeit. Er war Präsident, Vorstand, Seminarleiter, Programmgestalter, Buch-Macher, Geldbesorger, Organisator und unerreichter Redner. Seine Ansprachen im Springer-Journalistenclub am Vorabend der Preisverleihung waren die Krönungsmessen der Kreativgemeinde. Wenn je ein Kreativer für den ADC gelebt hat, dann er. Voriges Wochenende ging dieses Leben zu Ende. Erst letztes Jahr wurde er für sein Lebenswerk geehrt. In der Urkunde steht: »Der ADC dankt Reinhard Siemes für alles.«

Dear Members,

Reinhard Siemes passed away last Saturday, on 16 April 2011. He was 70 years old.

Out of all the great creative minds, Reinhard Siemes stands out as the one that cared. Only a small few could write like him, and basically no one stood up for others the way he did. It is a widespread professional deformity among outstanding creative minds that they forget where they came from and everybody else starting out along with it. Reinhard Siemes suffered because of this, and as a result, did the exact opposite. He wasted his gift on aspiring talents and passed on his enthusiasm to two or probably even three generations of advertisers.

For many – including myself – he was one of the first professional encounters with creative excellence. But his wasn't the usual story of quality that comes from agony and above all praises the contributor himself and excuses the fact that he's inconsiderate. He spoke of sensibility and humanity. And in doing so, he also spoke about himself, which is something he wouldn't have admitted. He held a mirror up to the industry, and how badly it treats its own future. And many creative minds suffered with him when they saw how he treated himself. He spent a large part of his life battling his deadly friend, as he called it, namely alcohol.

He was the engine and conscience of the ADC for a short eternity. He was president, CEO, seminar leader, program designer, bookmaker, fundraiser, organizer, and unrivalled speaker. His speeches at the Springer Journalist Club on the night before the award ceremony were an absolute highlight for the creative community. If ever a creative mind lived for the ADC, he did. Last weekend, this life came to a close. Just last year he was honored for his life's work. The certificate reads: "The ADC thanks Reinhard Siemes for everything."

NACHRUF
ZUM TOD VON KURT WEIDEMANN
OBITUARY
ON THE PASSING OF KURT WEIDEMANN

JOCHEN RÄDEKER
VORSTANDSSPRECHER
DES ADC
ADC SPOKESMAN OF
THE BOARD

Liebe Mitglieder,

unser Ehrenmitglied Kurt Weidemann ist gestern, am 30. März 2011, verstorben.

Das ist für uns alle, für den ADC, ein ganz großer Verlust. Er war mit 88 Jahren unser ältestes Mitglied, er war einer der ganz wenigen Weltstars des Designs. Es gibt kaum jemanden, vielleicht keinen, der die Design- und Kommunikationslandschaft in Deutschland in den letzten 60 Jahren so geprägt hat wie er.

Edzard Reuter hatte ihn 2005 in seiner Laudatio bei der Ernennung zum ADC Ehrenmitglied so beschrieben: »Er ist Designer genau wie Typograf, Lehrer genau wie Kommunikator, unbestechlicher Mahner genau wie streng objektiver Berater.«

Er war der Gestalter unzähliger Konzernauftritte von Bahn über Coop und Mercedes bis Porsche. Als Typograf hat er den Umfang der Bibel um 150 Seiten reduziert und Schriften geschaffen, die aus unserem täglichen Leben nicht wegzudenken sind. Als Hochschulgründer, Professor, Redner und Autor hat er uns oft begeistert – manchmal laut, manchmal leise, stets mit Intelligenz, Witz und Weisheit. Wer seine Kriegstagebücher gelesen hat, weiß um ein Leben, das mehr als außergewöhnlich war – und um eine unbedingte Ehrlichkeit mit sich selbst und anderen. Um einen Menschen, der seinen Beruf nie als Job, sondern immer als Berufung gesehen hat. Um einen Menschen, der keine Einstellung, sondern stets eine Haltung hatte.

Für mich und für viele von uns war er noch weit mehr als das alles. Ein Forderer. Ein Förderer. Ein Freund. Ein Großteil der deutschen Kreativen hat von Kurt gelernt, mit Kurt diskutiert, mit Kurt gefeiert. Kurt war bis zu seinem letzten Tag aktiv. Er hat weit mehr als nur ein erfülltes Leben gelebt in diesen 88 Jahren. Ich habe ihm ganz persönlich, wir alle haben ihm als Kollegen und Freunde unendlich viel zu verdanken.

Wir nehmen mit allergrößter Hochachtung Abschied von Kurt Weidemann.

Dear Members,

Our honorary member Kurt Weidemann passed away yesterday.

This a huge loss for us all, and for the ADC. At 88 years old, he was our oldest member, and he was one of the very few design superstars. There aren't many people, maybe no one at all, that shaped the design and advertising landscape in Germany during the past 60 years more than he did.

In 2005, Edzard Reuter described him as follows in his speech honoring Kurt Weidemann upon being named an honorary member of ADC: "He is a designer as well as a typographer, a teacher as well as a communicator, an incorruptible critic as well as a strict, objective advisor."

He designed numerous corporate identities, from Deutsche Bahn to Coop to Mercedes and Porsche. As a typographer, he reduced the length of the Bible to 150 pages and created fonts that today we can't begin to imagine living without. As founder of a university, professor, speaker, and author, he often wowed us – sometimes loud, sometimes quiet, but always with intelligence, wit, and wisdom. Those that read his war diaries know about a life that was more than extraordinary – and about his absolute honesty with himself and others. About a person that never viewed his profession as a job, but always as a calling. About a person that didn't have an attitude, but instead always had a position.

To me and many of us, he was way more than all that. A promoter. A challenger. A friend. A large share of Germany's creative minds learned from Kurt, discussed with Kurt, celebrated with Kurt. Kurt was active right up until his last day. He lived far more than a fulfilling life in these 88 years. Myself personally, and all of us as colleagues and friends, owe so much to him.

Today, holding him in the utmost regard, we bid farewell to Kurt Weidemann.

ADC DEUTSCHLAND MITGLIEDER
ADC GERMANY MEMBERS

A

Jury Member/Rookie
Jeremy Abbett
 Managing Director, Partner
Truth Dare Double Dare
www.truthdaredoubledare.com
jeremy.abbett@adc.de

Jury Member
Tobias Ahrens
 Freelance Creative Director,
 Copywriter
tobias.ahrens@adc.de

Jury Member
Monika Aichele
 Illustrator
Studio Monika Aichele c/o
schoenere welt
www.monikaaichele.com
monika.aichele@adc.de

Marietta Albinus
 Art Direction
Euro RSCG Zürich Eurad AG
www.euroscg.ch
marietta.albinus@adc.de

Jury Member/Member of the Board
Hans-Peter Albrecht
 Copywriter
hp albrecht werbeagentur gmbh
www.hpalbrecht.de
hanspeter.albrecht@adc.de

Jury Member
Niels Alzen
 Managing Director Creation
Scholz & Friends
www.s-f.com
niels.alzen@adc.de

Jury Member
Christoph Amend
 Editor in Chief
ZEITmagazin
christoph.amend@adc.de

Paul Apostolou
Elephant Seven GmbH
paul.apostolou@adc.de

Ulf Armbrust
 Creative Director
ulf.armbrust@adc.de

Christiane Arp
 Editor in Chief
Condé Nast Verlag GmbH Vogue
christiane.arp@adc.de

Jury Member
Simone Ashoff
 Owner
Good School
www.good-school.de
simone.ashoff@adc.de

Jürgen Assmann
 Creative Director
JA Creative-Consulting
www.ja-creative-consulting.com
juergen.assmann@adc.de

Jakob Augstein
Der Freitag
jakob.augstein@adc.de

B

Fred Baader
 Creative Consultant
fred.baader@adc.de

Jury Member
Stefan Baggen
 Managing Director, Creative
 Director
BaggenDesign GmbH
www.baggendesign.de
stefan.baggen@adc.de

Jury Member
Frank Bannöhr
 Creative Director
neues aus hamburg
frank.bannoehr@adc.de

Jury Member
Michael Barche
 Managing Director Creation
gudella, barche. Werbeagentur
GmbH & Co KG
www.gudellabarche.de
michael.barche@adc.de

Jury Member/Rookie
Suze Barrett
 Executive Creative Director
Scholz & Friends Schweiz GmbH
suze.barrett@adc.de

Alexander Bartel
 Managing Director Creation
Wunderhaus
www.wunderhaus.com
alexander.bartel@adc.de

Jury Member
Philipp Barth
 Creative Director Text
Jung von Matt/Neckar GmbH
www.jvm-neckar.de
philipp.barth@adc.de

Jury Member
Dirk Bartos
 Creative Director, Managing
 Director
Bartos Kersten Editorial
Printmediendesign OHG
www.bartoskersten.de
dirk.bartos@adc.de

Tom Batoy
 Composer, Music Producer
Mona Davis Beat GmbH
www.monadavis.com
tom.batoy@adc.de

Jury Member
Asta Baumöller
 Owner, Managing Director
MELT.MEDIA RECRUITMENT
Personalberatung Medien
www.melt-media.biz
asta.baumoeller@adc.de

Toygar Bazarkaya
 Chief Creative Officer
BBDO Düsseldorf
toygar.bazarkaya@adc.de

Jan Bazing
 Illustrator
Jan Bazing Illustrationsatelier
jan.bazing@adc.de

Jury Member
Wolfgang Behnken
 Art Director
Behnken&Prinz
wolfgang1.behnken@adc.de

Jochen Beithan
 Creative Director
JBCC Jochen Beithan Corporate
Communication
jochen.beithan@adc.de

Bernd Beitz
 Managing Director
Beitz Kommunikation
bernd.beitz@adc.de

Arwed Berendts
 Managing Director Creation,
 Partner
Saint Elmo's Campaign GmbH
www.saint-elmos.com
arwed.berendts@adc.de

Jury Member
Matthias Berg
 Creative Director, Consultant
MATTHIAS BERG arbeitet.
www.matthiasberg.com
matthias.berg@adc.de

Jury Member
Kathrin BergerGley
 Freelance Art Director,
 Creative Director
www.kathrinberger.com
kathrin.berger@adc.de

Rookie
Kai Bergmann
 Professor of Visual
 Communication
Hochschule Augsburg
www.bergmannstudios.com
kai.bergmann@adc.de

Jury Member
Ludwig Berndl
 Freelance Creative
ludwig.berndl@adc.de

Jury Member
Prof. Hans-Joachim Berndt
 Managing Director, Director
FILMHAUS Duck Soup GmbH
Film- und Fernsehproduktion
www.filmhaus.de
hansjoachim.berndt@adc.de

Michi Besler
 Artist, Composer
www.eardrum.de
michi.besler@adc.de

Jury Member
Reinhard Besser
 Composer, Music Producer
BesserMusic
www.bessermusic.com
reinhard.besser@adc.de

Joachim Beutler
 Creative Director
Communication network
joachim.beutler@adc.de

Marco Bezerra
 Creative Director
Crispin Porter + Bogusky Europe
marco.bezerra@adc.de

Jury Member
Matthias Birkenbach
 Managing Director Creation
SIGNUM communication GmbH
www.signum-web.de
matthias.birkenbach@adc.de

Manfred Bissinger
HOFFMANN UND CAMPE
VERLAG Corporate Publishing
www.hoffmann-und-campe.de
manfred.bissinger@adc.de

Prof. Lars Uwe Bleher
 Managing Director Creation
Atelier Markgraph GmbH
www.markgraph.de
larsuwe.bleher@adc.de

Helge Blöck
 Creative Director, Partner
Fosbury Luther Lindbergh
Werbeagentur GmbH & Co. KG
www.F-L-L.com
helge.bloeck@adc.de

Jury Member
Timo Blunck
 Composer
BLUWI – Blunck, Will & Denker
GbR
www.bluwi.com
timo.blunck@adc.de

Rookie
Hannes Böker
 Creative Director
DDB
www.ddb.at
hannes.boeker@adc.de

🟥 Jury Member
Carsten Bolk
 Executive Creative Director
BBDO Düsseldorf
www.bbdo.de
carsten.bolk@adc.de

Michael Borch
 Managing Director
Michael Borch Werbung GmbH
michael.borch@adc.de

🟥 Jury Member
Philip Borchardt
 Creative Director
TBWA Werbeagentur GmbH
www.tbwa.com
philip.borchardt@adc.de

🟥 Jury Member
Mirko Borsche
 Art Director
mirko.borsche@adc.de

🟥 Jury Member
Frank Brammer
 Managing Director, Partner
Franken Architekten GmbH
www.franken-architekten.de
frank.brammer@adc.de

🟥 Jury Member
Prof. Lo Breier
 Creative Director Art
Axel Springer AG Bild am Sonntag
Chefredaktion
lo.breier@adc.de

Peter Breul
 Art Director
Frankfurter Allgemeine Zeitung GmbH
peter.breul@adc.de

Heike Brockmann
 Creative Director
heimoto
www.heimoto.com
heike.brockmann@adc.de

🟥 Jury Member
Felix Bruchmann
 Creative Director
Bruchmann, Schneider.
felix.bruchmann@adc.de

🟥 Jury Member
Prof. Uwe R. Brückner
 Creative Director
ATELIER BRÜCKNER GmbH
www.atelier-brueckner.com
uwe.brueckner@adc.de

🟥 Jury Member
Rob Brünig
 Executive Creative Director
schoepfung GmbH
robert.bruenig@adc.de

Reto Brunner
 Creative Director, Co-Owner
BRUNNER BEKKER
www.brunnerbekker.com
reto.brunner@adc.de

Carsten Buck
 Graphic Designer
Mutter
www.mutter.de
carsten.buck@adc.de

🟥 Jury Member
Holger Bultmann
 Creative Director
Kolle Rebbe
holger.bultmann@adc.de

🟥 Jury Member
Hans-Jürgen Burkard
 Photographer
hansjuergen.burkard@adc.de

Sönke Busch
 Freelance Art Director
www.buschwork.com
soenke.busch@adc.de

Uwe Buschkötter
 Owner
UBM RECORDS GMBH
Musikproduktion
www.ubm-records.com
uwe.buschkoetter@adc.de

C

🟥 Jury Member
Wolf-Peter Camphausen
 Freelance Creative Director, Creative Consultant
wolfpeter.camphausen@adc.de

Thomas Caspari
 Director, Photographer
Casparifilm Produktions GmbH
www.tcaspari.de
thomas.caspari@adc.de

Thomas Chudalla
 Creative Director
thomas.chudalla@adc.de

Veronika Classen
 Creative Director, Co-Owner
REINSCLASSEN GmbH&Co.KG
www.reinsclassen.de
veronika.classen@adc.de

Mats Cordt
 Photographer
Mats Cordt Photography
www.matscordt.com
mats.cordt@adc.de

🟥 Jury Member
Olaf Czeschner
 Freelance Creative Director
olaf.czeschner@adc.de

D

🟥 Jury Member
Dietmar Dahmen
 Creative Director, Freelancer
Dietmar Dahmen
dietmar.dahmen@adc.de

Arndt Dallmann
 Director Operations
Atletico International Advertising
www.atleticointernational.com
arndt.dallmann@adc.de

🟥 Jury Member
Mark Daniels
 Creative Director
neues handeln GmbH
www.neueshandeln.de
mark.daniels@adc.de

Christian Daul
 Creative Director, Managing Director
Scholz & Volkmer GmbH
www.s-v.de
christian.daul@adc.de

Martien Delfgaauw
 Creative Director
HEIMAT Berlin
www.heimat-berlin.com
martien.delfgaauw@adc.de

🟥 Jury Member
Mariusz Jan Demner
 Managing Partner, CEO
Demner, Merlicek & Bergmann Werbegesellschaft mbH
www.dmb.at
mariuszjan.demner@adc.de

🟥 Jury Member
Hajo Depper
 Managing Director Creation
hajo.depper@adc.de

🟥 Jury Member
Feico Derschow
 Headmaster
MCAD MasterClass e.V.
www.mcad-school.de
feico.derschow@adc.de

🟥 Jury Member
Kurt Georg Dieckert
 Chief Creative Officer
TBWA Werbeagentur GmbH
www.tbwa.de
kurtgeorg.dieckert@adc.de

Oliver Diehr
 Creative Director Art
Oliver Diehr
oliver.diehr@adc.de

Kai Diekmann
 Editor in Chief
BILD Chefredaktion
kai.diekmann@adc.de

🟥 Jury Member
Kirsten Dietz
 Creative Director, Managing Partner
Strichpunkt Agentur für visuelle Kommunikation GmbH
www.strichpunkt-design.de
kirsten.dietz@adc.de

Prof. Tanja Diezmann
 Managing Partner
pReview digital design GmbH
www.preview-design.com
tanja.diezmann@adc.de

🟥 Jury Member/Rookie
Axel Domke
 Creative Director
MUTABOR Design GmbH
www.mutabor.de
axel.domke@adc.de

🟥 Jury Member
Frank Dovidat
 Managing Partner
Publicis Hamburg GmbH
www.publicis-hamburg.de
frank.dovidat@adc.de

🟥 Jury Member
Martin Drust
 Managing Director Creation, Partner
kempertrautmann change GmbH
martin.drust@adc.de

Uwe Düttmann
 Photographer
Studio Uwe Düttmann
uwe.duettmann@adc.de

E

Cedric Ebener
 Managing Director
CE+Co GmbH
www.ceundco.com
cedric.ebener@adc.de

Lars Eberle
 Managing Director
LESS RAIN GMBH
www.lessrain.com
lars.eberle@adc.de

🟥 Jury Member
Till Eckel
 Creative Director
DDB Berlin GmbH
www.de.ddb.com
till.eckel@adc.de

🟥 Jury Member
Axel Eckstein
 Managing Director, Creative Director
Euro RSCG Zürich
axel.eckstein@adc.de

Jury Member
Tobias Eichinger
Creative Director
Heye & Partner GmbH
tobias.eichinger@adc.de

Jury Member
Kay Eichner
Creative Director Text
KNSK Werbeagentur GmbH
www.knsk.de
kay.eichner@adc.de

Matthias Eickmeyer
Executive Creative Director
Butter GmbH
matthias.eickmeyer@adc.de

Lutz Engelke
Managing Partner
Triad Berlin Projektgesellschaft mbH
www.triad.de
lutz.engelke@adc.de

Jury Member/Member of the Board
Johannes Erler
Partner
Bureau Johannes Erler
johannes.erler@adc.de

Jury Member
Christoph Everke
Managing Director Creation
Serviceplan Campaign
www.serviceplan.de
christoph.everke@adc.de

F

Jury Member
Jo Marie Farwick
Creative Director
Jung von Matt/Elbe
jo.farwick@adc.de

Dr. Kai Fehse
Institute for Cognition and Communication
kai.fehse@adc.de

Klaus Fehsenfeld
Managing Director, Creative Director
W.A.F. Werbegesellschaft mbH
www.waf-werbung.de
klaus.fehsenfeld@adc.de

Jury Member
Thomas Feicht
Managing Director
INSTANT Corporate Culture
www.e-instant.de
thomas.feicht@adc.de

Alex Feil
Director
ELEMENT E
alex.feil@adc.de

Jury Member/Member of the Board
Claus Fischer
Managing Director
VOSS + FISCHER gmbh
www.voss-fischer.de
claus.fischer@adc.de

Jury Member
David Fischer
Creative Director
Scholz & Friends Berlin
www.s-f.com/berlin
david.fischer@adc.de

Georg Fischer
Photographer
www.georg-fischer.com
georg.fischer@adc.de

Jury Member
Catrin Florenz
Creative Director
DDB Tribal
www.ddb-tribal.com
catrin.florenz@adc.de

Jury Member
Heico Forster
Creative Director
Verlagsgruppe Milchstrasse GmbH
www.milchstrasse.de
heico.forster@adc.de

Jury Member
Heike Frank
Copywriter
heike.frank@adc.de

Jury Member
Oliver Frank
Creative
vccp Berlin
oliver.frank@adc.de

Jury Member
Ekki Frenkler
Creative Director, Managing Director Creation
mediaplus gruppe für innovative media co. kg Gruppe für innovative Kommunikation GmbH & Co. KG
www.mediaplus.de
ekkehard.frenkler@adc.de

Jury Member
Daniel Frericks
Creative Director, Managing Director
neues aus hamburg werbeagentur
daniel.frericks@adc.de

Jury Member
Fabian Frese
Managing Director Creation
Jung von Matt/Alster Werbeagentur GmbH
fabian.frese@adc.de

Jury Member
Heiko Freyland
Creative Director
kempertrautmann gmbh
www.kempertrautmann.com
heiko.freyland@adc.de

Jury Member
Niklas Frings-Rupp
Partner, Managing Director
niklas.fringsrupp@adc.de

Jury Member
Christian Fritsche
kempertrautmann
www.christianfritsche.com
christian.fritsche@adc.de

Jan Fröscher
Freelance Creative Director, Copywriter
jan.froescher@adc.de

Jury Member
Thomas Fuchs
Illustrator
www.thomasfuchs.com
thomas.fuchs@adc.de

Jury Member
Klaus Funk
Managing Director, Concept Creator
Studio Funk GmbH & Co. KG
www.studiofunk.de
www.vcc.de
klaus.funk@adc.de

G

Jury Member
Stephan Ganser
Executive Creative Officer
Publicis München Publicis Modem Deutschland
stephan.ganser@adc.de

Martin Gassner
Executive Creative Director
martin.gassner@adc.de

Oliver Gehrs
DUMMY Verlag Magazin und Entwicklung
www.dummy-magazin.de
oliver.gehrs@adc.de

Jury Member
Florian Geiss
Photographer
Florian Geiss Photography
www.floriangeiss.com
florian.geiss@adc.de

Jury Member
Jan Geschke
Copywriter, Managing Director Creation
Geschke Pufe Berlin
janhendrik.geschke@adc.de

Jury Member
Andreas Geyer
Creative Director, Co-Owner
andreas.geyer@adc.de

Michel Girardin
Creative Director, Owner
Girardin Creative Consulting
www.girardin.ch
michel.girardin@adc.de

Prof. Friederike Girst
Professor of Visual Communication
www.friederikegirst.de
friederike.girst@adc.de

Felix Glauner
Chief Creative Officer
Euro RSCG Worldwide
www.eurorscg.com
felix.glauner@adc.de

Jury Member
Joachim Glawion
Creative Director
Demner, Merlicek & Bergmann
joachim.glawion@adc.de

Jury Member
Ove Gley
Creative Director
Heimat Werbeagentur
ove.gley@adc.de

Rookie
Tom Gläser
Managing Director
Neue Sentimental Film AG
www.neuesentimentalfilm.com
tom.glaeser@adc.de

Prof. Rüdiger Goetz
Managing Director Creation
KW43 BRANDDESIGN
www.kw43.de
ruediger.goetz@adc.de

Jury Member
Lothar Gorris
Head of Culture Section
Spiegel-Verlag Rudolf Augstein GmbH & Co. KG
lothar.gorris@adc.de

Andreas Grabarz
Managing Director
GRABARZ & PARTNER Werbeagentur GmbH
www.grabarzundpartner.de
andreas.grabarz@adc.de

Rookie
Oliver Grandt
Creative Director
Leagas Delaney Hamburg GmbH
www.leagasdelaney.de
oliver.grandt@adc.de

Martin Graß
Creative Director Text, Freelancer
www.martingrass.com
martin.grass@adc.de

Tobias Gremmler
    Freelance Art Director
www.syncon-d.com
tobias.gremmler@adc.de

* Jury Member
Florian Grimm
    Creative Director, Managing
    Director Creation
Grimm Gallun Holtappels
Werbeagentur GmbH & Co. KG
www.2gh.de
florian.grimm@adc.de

* Jury Member
Ole Grönwoldt
    Industrial Designer
HANSASTRASSE GBR
www.hansastrasse.com
ole.groenwoldt@adc.de

Prof. Luc(as) de Groot
    Typography, Design
LucasFonts GmbH
www.fontfabrik.com
lucasde.groot@adc.de

* Jury Member
John Groves
    Composer, Music Producer
Groves Sound Communications
www.groves.de
john.groves@adc.de

* Jury Member
Hartmut Grün
    Creative Director
Grün Communication
hartmut.gruen@adc.de

Kai-Uwe Gundlach
    Photographer
Studio Gundlach
www.studiogundlach.de
kaiuwe.gundlach@adc.de

Uli Gürtler
    Creative Director
gürtlerbachmann Werbung GmbH
uli.guertler@adc.de

H

* Jury Member
Esther Haase
    Photo Designer
Esther Haase Photography
www.estherhaase.com
esther.haase@adc.de

* Jury Member
Fritz Haase
    Creative Director, Owner
Haase & Knels Atelier für
Gestaltung
www.haase-und-knels.de
fritz.haase@adc.de

* Jury Member
Mieke Haase
    Creative Director, Co-Owner
loved GmbH/Feld Hommes
www.feldhommes.de
mieke.haase@adc.de

Sibylle Haase
    Creative Director, Owner
Haase & Knels Atelier für
Gestaltung
www.haase-und-knels.de
sibylle.haase@adc.de

* Jury Member
Nadim Habib
    Designer
DDB Tribal
nadim.habib@adc.de

* Jury Member
Dirk Haeusermann
    Executive Creative Director
Draftfcb Deutschland GmbH
www.draftfcb.de
dirk.haeusermann@adc.de

* Jury Member
Helen Haeusermann
    Creative Director Text
www.helenhaeusermann.de
helen.haeusermann@adc.de

Nikolaus Hafermaas
    Dean Faculty Design
Art Center College of Design
Dean of Special Programs, Chair
Graphic Design
www.artcenter.edu
www.uebersee.us
nikolaus.hafermaas@adc.de

Heiko Hagemann
    Director, Director of
    Photography
heiko.hagemann@adc.de

* Jury Member
Rosa Haider-Merlicek
    Creative Director
Demner, Merlicek & Bergmann
www.dmb.at
rosa.haider@adc.de

Hubertus Hamm
    Photographer
Hubertus Hamm
www.hubertushamm.de
hubertus.hamm@adc.de

* Jury Member
Oliver Handlos
    Creative Director
BBDO New York
oliver.handlos@adc.de

* Jury Member
Timm Hanebeck
    Managing Director Creation
timm.hanebeck@adc.de

Sascha Hanke
    Creative Director, Managing
    Director Creation
HEIMAT Hamburg
sascha.hanke@adc.de

* Jury Member
Jan Harbeck
    Managing Director Creation
BBDO Proximity Berlin GmbH
jan.harbeck@adc.de

* Jury Member
Matthias Harbeck
    Managing Director Creation,
    Partner
Serviceplan Campaign
matthias.harbeck@adc.de

* Jury Member
Sebastian Hardieck
    Chief Creative Officer
BBDO Proximity Düsseldorf
GmbH
www.bbdo.de
sebastian.hardieck@adc.de

Lars Harmsen
    Creative Director, Managing
    Director
Magma Brand Design GmbH &
Co. KG/Slanted.de/Volcano-Type.
de
www.magmabranddesign.com
lars.harmsen@adc.de

Felix Harnickell
    Creative Director
Harnickell Design
felix.harnickell@adc.de

* Jury Member
Joachim Hauser
    Freelance Creative Director
joachim.hauser@adc.de

* Rookie
Stefan Hauser
    Managing Director
hauser lacour
kommunikationsgestaltung gmbh
www.hauserlacour.de
stefan.hauser@adc.de

Tom Hauser
    Creative Director
Crispin Porter + Bogusky
tom.hauser@adc.de

Irene Hecht
    Creative Director Art
Lecturer IMK Wiesbaden
irene.hecht@adc.de

Uli Heckmann
    Photo Designer
www.uliheckmann.com
uli.heckmann@adc.de

* Jury Member
Guido Heffels
    Creative Director, Managing
    Director Creation
HEIMAT, Berlin
www.heimat-berlin.com
guido.heffels@adc.de

* Jury Member
Kristoffer Heilemann
    Creative Director
BBDO Germany
kristoffer.heilemann@adc.de

Prof. Achim Heine
    Managing Partner
Heine/Lenz/Zizka Projekte GmbH
www.hlz.de
achim.heine@adc.de

Gerald Heinemann
    Chief Creative Officer
www.abbeyroad-networks.de
gerald.heinemann@adc.de

Carsten Heintzsch
    Creative Director, Partner
Agentur Carsten Heintzsch
carsten.heintzsch@adc.de

Erik Heitmann
    Creative Director, Managing
    Director
Kreativgenossenschaft eG
erik.heitmann@adc.de

Rainer Hellmann
    Creative Director
rainer.hellmann@adc.de

Andreas Henke
    Chief Creative Officer
GREY Worldwide
andreas.henke@adc.de

* Jury Member
Dirk Henkelmann
    Creative Director
TBWA Werbeagentur GmbH
dirk.henkelmann@adc.de

* Jury Member
Dietmar Henneka
    Photographer
Studio Dietmar Henneka
www.henneka.com
dietmar.henneka@adc.de

* Jury Member
Torsten Hennings
    Director, Producer, Audio
    Engineer
Studio Funk GmbH & Co. KG
www.studiofunk.de
torsten.hennings@adc.de

* Jury Member
Klaus-Jürgen Hergert
    Art Director, Creative
    Director
klausjuergen.hergert@adc.de

Thorsten Herken
 Director
www.pulk-berlin.com
thorsten.herken@adc.de

🌸 Jury Member
Christoph Herold
 Creative Director Text
christoph.herold@adc.de

🌸 Jury Member
Norbert Herold
 Creative Director
norbert.herold@adc.de

🌸 Jury Member
Klaus Hesse
 Design Director
Hesse Design GmbH
www.klassehesse.com
klaus.hesse@adc.de

Ralf Heuel
 Managing Director Creation, Partner
GRABARZ & PARTNER Werbeagentur GmbH
www.grabarzundpartner.de
ralf.heuel@adc.de

🌸 Jury Member
Wolf Heumann
 Managing Director Creation
Jung von Matt/Elbe GmbH
www.jvm.de
wolf.heumann@adc.de

🌸 Rookie
Kai Heuser
 Creative Director
Jung von Matt/Neckar
kai.heuser@adc.de

Prof. Fons M. Hickmann
 Professor of Graphic Design
Fons Hickmann m23
www.fonshickmann.com
fons.hickmann@adc.de

🌸 Jury Member
Christoph Hildebrand
 Creative Director
Kolle Rebbe GmbH
christoph.hildebrand@adc.de

Christoph Himmel
 Conception, Art Direction
christoph.himmel@adc.de

Oliver Hinrichs
 Interactive Designer, Freelance Creative Director, digital
www.oliverhinrichs.de
oliver.hinrichs@adc.de

🌸 Jury Member
Gepa Hinrichsen
 Copywriter
gepa.hinrichsen@adc.de

Volker Hinz
 Photographer
volker.hinz@adc.de

🌸 Jury Member
Peter Hirrlinger
 Freelance Creative Director, Copywriter
Peter Hirrlinger
www.peterhirrlinger.de
peter.hirrlinger@adc.de

Wilbert Hirsch
 Managing Director, Composer
complete audio GmbH
www.completeaudio.com
wilbert.hirsch@adc.de

🌸 Jury Member
Nicole Hoefer-Wirwas
 Freelance Creative Director
BOOST
www.boost-seminare.de
nicole.hoefer@adc.de

🌸 Jury Member
Niels van Hoek
 Creative Director
Berger Baader Hermes
www.bergerbaaderhermes.de
niels.vanhoek@adc.de

🌸 Jury Member
Thomas Hofbeck
 Creative Director
Ogilvy & Mather Werbeagentur GmbH
www.ogilvy-frankfurt.de
thomas.hofbeck@adc.de

Caspar-Jan Hogerzeil
 Director
www.hogerzeil.de
casparjan.hogerzeil@adc.de

🌸 Jury Member
Till Hohmann
 Chief Creative Officer
JWT Germany JWT Hamburg GmbH
www.jwt.de
till.hohmann@adc.de

Ton Hollander
 Creative Director
BBDO GmbH
ton.hollander@adc.de

🌸 Jury Member
Judith Homoki
 Freelance Creative Director, Copywriter
www.judithhomoki.de
judith.homoki@adc.de

Ingo Höntschke
 Freelance Creative Director, Copywriter
www.ingohoentschke.de
ingo.hoentschke@adc.de

🌸 Jury Member
Andreas Horbelt
 Chief Creative Officer
Uniplan
www.uniplan.com
andreas.horbelt@adc.de

Helmut Huber
 Managing Director Creation
Euro RSCG München
helmut.huber@adc.de

🌸 Jury Member
Reinhard Hunger
 Photographer
reinhard.hunger@adc.de

🌸 Jury Member/Rookie
Lars Huvart
 Creative Director
Ogilvy & Mather Werbeagentur GmbH
lars.huvart@adc.de

Andreas Hykade
 Animated Film Maker
Andreas Hykade
andreas.hykade@adc.de

J

Tom Jacobi
 Member of the Board, Marketing Director
Engel & Völkers AG
www.engelvoelkers.com
tom.jacobi@adc.de

Tim Jacobs
 Creative Director
DDB Tribal
tim.jacobs@adc.de

Achim Jäger
 Managing Director
Jung von Matt/Neckar GmbH
www.jvm.de
achim.jaeger@adc.de

Alexander Jaggy
 Managing Director Creation
Jung von Matt/Limmat AG, Werbeagentur BSW
www.jvm.ch
alexander.jaggy@adc.de

🌸 Jury Member
Joerg Jahn
 Creative Director
Jung von Matt/Neckar GmbH
www.jvm.de
joerg.jahn@adc.de

🌸 Jury Member/Member of the Board
Mathias Jahn
 Chief Creative Officer
Heye, Group
www.heye.de
mathias.jahn@adc.de

Wolf Jaiser
 Director, Managing Director
VIDEOTAPE, THE MEMORY COLLECTIVE
www.videotape.tv
wolfgang.jaiser@adc.de

🌸 Rookie
Uwe Jakob
 Creative Director
Ogilvy One
uwe.jakob@adc.de

🌸 Jury Member
Armin Jochum
 Member of the Board
Jung von Matt/AG
www.jvm.de
armin.jochum@adc.de

Peter Jooß
 Managing Director Creation
Wire Advertising GmbH
peter.jooss@adc.de

Daniel Josefsohn
 Photographer, Director
www.danieljosefsohn.com
daniel.josefsohn@adc.de

🌸 Jury Member
Eva Jung
 Creative Director, Managing Director
gobasil GmbH
www.gobasil.com
eva.jung@adc.de

🌸 Jury Member
Richard Jung
 Professor of Communication Design & Corporate Identity
Hochschule Niederrhein Fachbereich Design
richard.jung@adc.de

Gabi Junklewitz
 Freelance Creative Director, Copywriter
gabi.junklewitz@adc.de

K

Laszlo Kadar
 Managing Director, Director, Director of Photography
Laszlo Kadar Film GmbH & Co. KG
www.kadar.de
laszlo.kadar@adc.de

🌸 Jury Member
Florian Kähler
 Freelance Copywriter
www.florian-kaehler.de
florian.kaehler@adc.de

🌸 Jury Member
Maik Kähler
 Creative Director
Serviceplan Hamburg GmbH&Co.KG
www.serviceplan.de
maik.kaehler@adc.de

Sebastian Kainz
  Creative Director
DDB Wien
sebastian.kainz@adc.de

Constantin Kaloff
  Copywriter
constantin.kaloff@adc.de

Hans-Jürgen Kämmerer
  Creative Director
Leo Burnett GmbH
hansjuergen.kaemmerer@adc.de

Christian Kämmerling
  Creative Consultant
Contrix GmbH Media Consulting
christian.kaemmerling@adc.de

Florian Käppler
  Managing Director, Composer
KLANGERFINDER GmbH & Co KG
www.klangerfinder.de
florian.kaeppler@adc.de

Oliver Kapusta
  Executive Creative Director
Saatchi & Saatchi Berlin
oliver.kapusta@adc.de

✱ Jury Member
Stefan Karl
  Partner, Managing Director
SHANGHAI BERLIN Neue Marken-Kommunikation GmbH + Co. KG
www.shanghai-berlin.de
stefan.karl@adc.de

✱ Jury Member
Nikolai Karo
  Director, Author
Soulmate
www.nikokaro.de
nikolai.karo@adc.de

✱ Jury Member
Detmar Karpinski
  Copywriter
KNSK Werbeagentur GmbH
www.knsk.de
detmar.karpinski@adc.de

Amir Kassaei
  Chief Creative Officer
DDB Worldwide
www.ddb.com
amir.kassaei@adc.de

✱ Jury Member
Willy Kaussen
  Creative Director Text
Scholz & Friends Hamburg GmbH
www.s-f.com
willy.kaussen@adc.de

✱ Jury Member
Christoph Keese
Axel Springer AG
christoph.keese@adc.de

✱ Jury Member/Rookie
Jonas Keller
  Creative Director
Jung von Matt/Alster
www.jvm.de
jonas.keller@adc.de

Michael Keller
  Managing Director
KMS TEAM GmbH
www.kms-team.de
michael.keller@adc.de

✱ Jury Member
André Kemper
  Owner, Managing Director
kempertrautmann gmbh
www.kempertrautmann.com
andre.kemper@adc.de

✱ Jury Member
Claudia Kempf
  Photo Designer
www.claudiakempf.com
claudia.kempf@adc.de

✱ Jury Member
Diether Kerner
  Head of Creation
Philipp und Keuntje GmbH
www.philippundkeuntje.de
diether.kerner@adc.de

Oliver Kessler
  Freelance Creative Director, Copywriter
oliver.kessler@adc.de

Hartwig Keuntje
  Managing Director
Philipp und Keuntje GmbH
www.philippundkeuntje.de
hartwig.keuntje@adc.de

✱ Jury Member/Rookie
Pit Kho
  Chief Creative Officer
Euro RSCG 4D
pit.kho@adc.de

✱ Jury Member
Doris Kiermeier
  Freelance Copywriter
TOUCHÉ Text + Konzeption
Doris Kiermeier
doris.kiermeier@adc.de

✱ Jury Member
Martin Kießling
  Managing Director, Creative Director
Heye & Partner Werbeagentur GmbH
www.heye.de
martin.kiessling@adc.de

✱ Jury Member
Matthias Kindler
  Managing Director
THE COMPANIES Marken.Erlebnisse.Ergebnisse.GmbH
www.thecompanies.de
matthias.kindler@adc.de

Lukas Kircher
  Creative Director, Co-Owner
KircherBurkhardt GmbH
www.kircher-burkhardt.com
lukas.kircher@adc.de

✱ Jury Member
Peter Kirchhoff
  Creative Director Text
Jung von Matt/Elbe
www.jvm.de
peter.kirchhoff@adc.de

✱ Jury Member
Fabian Kirner
  Creative Director
kt west
fabian.kirner@adc.de

✱ Rookie
Wenke Kleine-Benne
nhb Studio Hamburg GmbH
www.nhb.de
wenke.kleine-benne@adc.de

✱ Jury Member
Andreas Klemp
  Executive Creative Director, Managing Director
Red Urban GmbH, Heye & Partner
andreas.klemp@adc.de

✱ Jury Member
Elke Klinkhammer
  Executive Creative Director
Neue Digitale/Razorfish GmbH
elke.klinkhammer@adc.de

✱ Jury Member
Sven Klohk
  Creative Director
www.kolle-rebbe.de
sven.klohk@adc.de

✱ Jury Member
Timm Klotzek
  Editor in Chief
NEON Magazin GmbH
www.neon.de
timm.klotzek@adc.de

Georg Knichel
  Creative Director
Schnelle Brüter
www.schnelle-brueter.de
hansgeorg.knichel@adc.de

Werner Knopf
  Managing Director
KNSK Werbeagentur GmbH
www.knsk.de
werner.knopf@adc.de

Claus Koch
  Owner, Managing Director
Claus Koch™
www.clauskoch.com
claus.koch@adc.de

✱ Jury Member
Michael Koch
  Executive Creative Director
gkk DialogGroup
www.gkk.de
michael.koch@adc.de

Christian Kohlmann
  Concept, Director
www.christiankohlmann.de
christian.kohlmann@adc.de

✱ Jury Member
Stefan Kolle
  Managing Director Creation
Kolle Rebbe GmbH
www.kolle-rebbe.de
stefan.kolle@adc.de

✱ Jury Member
Dagmar König
  Freelance Creative Director, Copywriter
dagmar.koenig@adc.de

✱ Jury Member
Daniel Könnecke
  Creative Director, Managing Director
PLAN.NET campaign Hamburg GmbH & CO. KG Haus der Kommunikation
daniel.koennecke@adc.de

Wilfried Korfmacher
  Creative Director
www.fh-duesseldorf.de
wilfried.korfmacher@adc.de

✱ Jury Member
Joachim Kortlepel
  Managing Director, Creation
Jung von Matt/relations GmbH
joachim.kortlepel@adc.de

✱ Rookie
Bernd Kracke
  President
Hochschule für Gestaltung Offenbach am Main
www.hfg-offenbach.de
bernd.kracke@adc.de

Bernd Krämer
  Owner
Cream Colored Ponies
www.cream-colored-ponies.com
bernd.kraemer@adc.de

✱ Jury Member
Thorsten Kraus
  Professor of Digital Communication Design
Hochschule Niederrhein Fachbereich Design
Scholz&Friends NRW
www.designkrefeld.de
thorsten.kraus@adc.de

* Jury Member
Delle Krause
  Creative Chairman
Ogilvy & Mather Werbeagentur GmbH
www.ogilvy-frankfurt.de
delle.krause@adc.de

* Jury Member
Robert Krause
  Creative Director
Scholz&Friends Berlin GmbH
robert.krause@adc.de

Jörg Krauthäuser
  Managing Partner
facts+fiction GmbH
www.factsfiction.com
joerg.krauthaeuser@adc.de

* Jury Member/Rookie
Markus Kremer
  Creative Director Art
Lukas Lindemann Rosinski
www.llr-hamburg.de
markus.kremer@adc.de

* Jury Member
Johannes Krempl
  Owner, Managing Director
glow GmbH
Agentur für Kommunikation
www.glow-berlin.de
johannes.krempl@adc.de

Stephanie Krink
  Freelance Creative Director, Copywriter
stephanie.krink@adc.de

Tim Krink
  Creative Director, Partner
KNSK Werbeagentur GmbH
www.knsk.de
tim.krink@adc.de

Henner Kronenberg
  Creative Director, Partner
GRABARZ & PARTNER Werbeagentur GmbH
www.grabarzundpartner.de
henner.kronenberg@adc.de

Lars Kruse
  Managing Partner
Puschert & Kruse GmbH
Werbeagentur und Meisterbetrieb für Werbetechnik
lars.kruse@adc.de

* Jury Member
Detlef Krüger
  Creative Director
KNSK Werbeagentur GmbH
www.knsk.de
detlef.krueger@adc.de

Mike Krüll
  Creative Director Text
Krüllkonzept
michael-kruell@tele2.ch
mike.kruell@adc.de

Irene Kugelmann
  Creative Director Art
irene.kugelmann@adc.de

* Jury Member
Bastian Kuhn
  Freelance Creative Director
www.bastiankuhn.com
bastian.kuhn@adc.de

Stephanie Kurz
  Designer
Stan Hema GmbH
www.stanhema.com
stephanie.kurz@adc.de

Thomas Kurzawski
  Creative Director, Partner
Fosbury Luther Lindbergh Werbeagentur GmbH & Co.KG
www.f-l-l.com
thomas.kurzawski@adc.de

* Jury Member
Michael Kutschinski
  Managing Director Creation
OgilvyOne
www.ogilvy.com
michael.kutschinski@adc.de

L

* Rookie
Prof. Laurent Lacour
  Managing Director
hauser lacour kommunikationsgestaltung
www.hauserlacour.de
laurent.lacour@adc.de

* Jury Member
Roland Lambrette
  Managing Director
Atelier Markgraph GmbH
www.markgraph.de
roland.lambrette@adc.de

Mathias Lamken
  Group Creative Director
GRABARZ & PARTNER
mathias.lamken@adc.de

Dominik Lammer
  Creative Director
Syzygy Deutschland GmbH
www.syzygy.net
dominik.lammer@adc.de

* Jury Member/Rookie
Justin Landon
  Creative Director
Kolle Rebbe GmbH
www.about.me/justinlandon
justin.landon@adc.de

Petra Langhammer
  Art Director
Petra Langhammer
petra.langhammer@adc.de

* Jury Member
Rolf Leger
  Creative Director
Kolle Rebbe Werbeagentur GmbH
www.kolle-rebbe.de
rolf.leger@adc.de

* Jury Member
Jochen Leisewitz
  Managing Director Creation
BrawandRieken Werbeagentur GmbH
www.brawandrieken.de
jochen.leisewitz@adc.de

* Rookie
Felix Lemcke
GRABARZ & PARTNER Werbeagentur GmbH
www.grabarzundpartner.de
felix.lemcke@adc.de

Bruce Leonard
  Managing Director, Director
Dowsing & Leonard Filmproduktion GmbH
www.dowsing-leonard.de
bruce.leonard@adc.de

Andreas Leonhard
  Partner, Managing Director
Social Media Akademie webculture GmbH
www.socialmediaakademie.de
andreas.leonhard@adc.de

Charly Leske
  Director, Director of Photography
www.charlyleske.com
charly.leske@adc.de

* Jury Member
Sebastian Letz
  Creative Director
Milla & Partner
sebastian.letz@adc.de

* Jury Member
Jan Leube
  Managing Director Creation
Young & Rubicam GmbH
www.young-rubicam.de
jan.leube@adc.de

* Jury Member/Rookie
Andreas Liedtke
  Graphic Designer
HORIZONT/beef Magazin Verlagsgruppe Deutscher Fachverlag
andreas.liedtke@adc.de

Alfred Limbach
  Creative Director
Limbach Concept GmbH
alfred.limbach@adc.de

* Jury Member
Arno Lindemann
  Owner, Creative Director
Lukas Lindemann Rosinski GmbH
www.llr-hamburg.de
arno.lindemann@adc.de

David Linderman
  Designer for Interactive Media
Hi-Res! London
www.hi-res.net
david.linderman@adc.de

Holger Lindhardt
  Creative Director
Philipp und Keuntje GmbH
www.philippundkeuntje.de
holger.lindhardt@adc.de

Dirk Linke
  Creative Director, Owner
ringzwei Dirk Linke
www.ringzwei.com
dirk.linke@adc.de

* Jury Member
Harald Linsenmeier
  Freelance Creative Director, Copywriter
www.hlfreelance.de
harald.linsenmeier@adc.de

Werner Lippert
projects GmbH
werner.lippert@adc.de

Sascha Lobe
  Managing Director
L2M3 Kommunikationsdesign GmbH
www.L2M3.com
sascha.lobe@adc.de

Marcus Loeber
  Composer, Producer
KCM Marcus Loeber
www.marcusloeber.com
marcus.loeber@adc.de

Uwe Loesch
  Managing Director, Art Director
Uwe Loesch Arbeitsgemeinschaft für visuelle und verbale Kommunikation
www.uweloesch.de
uwe.loesch@adc.de

* Jury Member
Benjamin Lommel
  Partner, Managing Director
LommelLudwig GmbH & Co KG
www.lommelludwig.de
benjamin.lommel@adc.de

* Jury Member/Rookie
Myles Lord
  Creative Director Art
HEIMAT, Berlin
myles.lord@adc.de

Giovanni di Lorenzo
DIE ZEIT
www.zeit.de
giovanni.dilorenzo@adc.de

Sven Loskill
　Creative Director
Jung von Matt/next GmbH
www.jvm.de
sven.loskill@adc.de

🌟 Jury Member
Frank Lübke
　Creative Director, Owner
www.ideawanted.de
frank.luebke@adc.de

🌟 Jury Member
Matthias Lührsen
　Managing Partner
HASTINGS MUSIC Gesellschaft f.
Musikproduktion Rundfunk- und
Fernsehwerbung mbH
www.hastings.de
matthias.luehrsen@adc.de

🌟 Jury Member
Bernhard Lukas
　Managing Director Creation
Lukas Lindemann Rosinski GmbH
www.lukaslindemannrosinski.de
bernhard.lukas@adc.de

Jens Ulrich Lützenkirchen
　Creative Director
jensulrich.luetzenkirchen@adc.de

M

Markus Maczey
　Managing Director Creation
Plan.Net Campaign Zweite
GmbH&Co.KG
www.plan-net.de
markus.maczey@adc.de

🌟 Rookie
Knut Maierhofer
　Managing Partner
KMS Team GmbH
www.kms-team.com
knut.maierhofer@adc.de

🌟 Jury Member
Prof. Ivica Maksimovic
　Creative Director
Maksimovic & Partners Agentur
für Werbung und Design GmbH
www.maksimovic.de
ivica.maksimovic@adc.de

Jürgen Mandel
　Creative Director
juergen.mandel@adc.de

🌟 Jury Member
Andreas Manthey
　Creative Director
HEIMAT, Berlin
andreas.manthey@adc.de

Oliver Mark
　Photographer
oliver.mark@adc.de

🌟 Jury Member
Uwe Marquardt
　Executive Creative Director
Young & Rubicam GmbH
www.yr-germany.de
uwe.marquardt@adc.de

Olaf Martens
　Photographer
olaf.martens@adc.de

Michael Matthiass
　Freelance Creative Director
　Text
Quantentext
www.quantenschokolade.de
michael.matthiass@adc.de

Dennis May
　Group Creative Director
DDB Düsseldorf
dennis.may@adc.de

🌟 Jury Member
Chris Mayrhofer
　Creative Director, Managing
　Director Creation
Hello AG Agentur für
Kommunikation
www.hello-muenchen.de
chris.mayrhofer@adc.de

Jan van Meel
　Creative Director
janvan.meel@adc.de

🌟 Jury Member
Marco Mehrwald
　CCO
Interone GmbH
www.interone.de
marco.mehrwald@adc.de

🌟 Rookie
Florian Meimberg
　Director, Author
www.florian-meimberg.com
florian.meimberg@adc.de

🌟 Jury Member
Oscar Meixner
　Sound Engineer, Composer
Hastings Music GmbH
www.hastings.de
oscar.meixner@adc.de

Fritz Hendrick Melle
　Managing Director Creation
Dorland Werbeagentur GmbH
www.dorland.de
fritzhendrick.melle@adc.de

Prof. HG Merz
　Architect, Museum Designer
hg merz architekten
museumsgestalter
www.hgmerz.com
hg.merz@adc.de

🌟 Jury Member
Stefan Meske
　Managing Director, Creation
Scholz & Friends NeuMarkt
GmbH
www.s-f.com
stefan.meske@adc.de

🌟 Jury Member
Helmut Meyer
　Creative Director
helmut.meyer@adc.de

Michael „Much" Meyer
　Managing Director, Creative
　Director
19:13 Werbeagentur GmbH
www.19h13.com
michael.meyer@adc.de

Thomas Meyer-Hermann
　Director, Producer
Studio Film Bilder
www.filmbilder.de
thomas.meyerhermann@adc.de

Raphael Milczarek
　Creative
Goodby, Silverstein & Partners
raphael.milczarek@adc.de

🌟 Jury Member/Member of the Board
Johannes Milla
　Managing Director, Creative
　Director
Milla & Partner
www.milla.de
johannes.milla@adc.de

Bernd Misske
　Creative Director
bernd.misske@adc.de

🌟 Jury Member/Rookie
Matthias Mittermüller
　Creative Director
Serviceplan Dritte Werbeagentur
GmbH
Haus der Kommunikation
matthias.mittermueller@adc.de

🌟 Jury Member
Jana Mohr
　Creative Director Text
Liebig Werke
jana.liebig@adc.de

🌟 Jury Member
Cosimo Möller
　Creative Director Text
Serviceplan Dritte Werbeagentur
cosimo.moeller@adc.de

🌟 Jury Member
Christian Mommertz
　Chief Creative Officer
BBDO Proximity Düsseldorf
GmbH
christian.mommertz@adc.de

🌟 Rookie
Till Monshausen
Oliver Voss GmbH c/o Miami Ad
School Europe
www.olivervoss.com
till.monshausen@adc.de

🌟 Jury Member
Stephan Moritz
　Studio Manager, Composer
Studio Funk GmbH & Co. KG
www.studiofunk.de
stephan.moritz@adc.de

Boris Mosner
　Director, Director of
　Photography
boris.mosner@adc.de

🌟 Jury Member
Ono Mothwurf
　Freelance Copywriter
www.mothwurf.de
ono.mothwurf@adc.de

🌟 Jury Member
David Mously
　Managing Director Creation
BBDO Proximity Berlin GmbH
david.mously@adc.de

🌟 Jury Member
Prof. Gudrun Müllner
　Professor of Visual
　Communication
Hochschule Augsburg
Fakultät für Gestaltung
www.hs-augsburg.de
gudrun.muellner@adc.de

N

🌟 Jury Member
Alexander Nagel
　Art Director
Serviceplan
alexander.nagel@adc.de

🌟 Jury Member
Britta Nagel
　Art Direction
ATELIER BRÜCKNER GmbH
britta.nagel@adc.de

Beat Nägeli
　Creative Consultant, Lecturer
beat.naegeli@adc.de

🌟 Jury Member/Rookie
Christoph Nann
　Creative Director
Serviceplan Hamburg
GmbH&Co.KG
christoph.nann@adc.de

Marco Antonio do Nascimento
　Art Director
marcoantonio.donascimento@
adc.de

🟥 Jury Member
Kerrin Nausch
  Executive Creative Director
Burda Creative Group Creative Works
www.hubert-burda-media.com
kerrin.nausch@adc.de

🟥 Jury Member/Member of the Board
Lutz Nebelin
  Managing Director, Creation
Jung von Matt/relations GmbH
www.jvm.com
lutz.nebelin@adc.de

🟥 Jury Member
Hans Neubert
  Freelance Creative Director, Copywriter
www.hans-neubert.de
hans.neubert@adc.de

🟥 Jury Member
Gerd Neumann
  International Executive Creative Director
Ogilvy & Mather Werbeagentur GmbH
www.ogilvy.com
gerd.neumann@adc.de

Sylvia Neuner
  Illustrator
Sylvia Neuner Illustration
www.sylvianeuner.de
sylvia.neuner@adc.de

Christoph Niemann
  Designer, Illustrator, Animator
Christoph Niemann, Inc.
christoph.niemann@adc.de

🟥 Jury Member
Ralf Nolting
  Creative Director
GRABARZ & PARTNER Werbeagentur GmbH
www.grabarzundpartner.de
ralf.nolting@adc.de

O

Carlos Obers
  Copywriter
carlos.obers@adc.de

🟥 Jury Member
Katrin Oeding
  Creative Director
www.katrinoeding.com
katrin.oeding@adc.de

Lars Oehlschlaeger
  Creative Director
Robot Werbeagentur GmbH & Co KG
www.robot-berlin.com
lars.oehlschlaeger@adc.de

🟥 Jury Member
Holger Oehrlich
  Creative Director
Jung von Matt/Neckar GmbH
holger.oehrlich@adc.de

Oliver Oelkers
  Advertisement, Managing Director
OLIVER OELKERS WERBUNG/DESIGN
oliver.oelkers@adc.de

🟥 Jury Member
Michael Ohanian
  Managing Director Creation
Jung von Matt/Alster
www.jvm.de
michael.ohanian@adc.de

🟥 Jury Member
Jan Okusluk
  Freelance Creative Director
jan.okusluk@adc.de

🟥 Jury Member
Olaf Oldigs
  Managing Director Creation
Kolle Rebbe GmbH
www.kolle-rebbe.de
olaf.oldigs@adc.de

Bettina Olf
  Creative Director
Kempertrautmann Werbeagentur
bettina.olf@adc.de

🟥 Jury Member
Simon Oppmann
  Creative Director Art
Ogilvy & Mather Werbeagentur GmbH
www.ogilvy.com
simon.oppmann@adc.de

Peter Oprach
  Creative Director Text
peter.oprach@adc.de

🟥 Rookie
Michael Ostertag-Henning
  Managing Partner
Schmidhuber + Partner corporate architecture
michael.ostertaghenning@adc.de

Mike John Otto
  Managing Director, Creative Director
BlackBeltMonkey, my next agency GmbH
www.blackbeltmonkey.com
mikejohn.otto@adc.de

P

Thomas Pakull
  Managing Creative Director
Interone GmbH
www.interone.de
thomas.pakull@adc.de

🟥 Jury Member
Heinrich Paravicini
  Creative Director, Owner
Mutabor Design GmbH
www.mutabor.de
heinrich.paravicini@adc.de

🟥 Jury Member
Henning Patzner
  Managing Director Creation
Serviceplan Campaign
www.creativeexplosion.de
henning.patzner@adc.de

🟥 Jury Member
Patricia Pätzold
  Group Creative Director
kempertrautmann gmbh
patricia.paetzold@adc.de

Markus Peichl
  Editorial Director
Fifteen Minutes GmbH
www.liebling-zeitung.com
markus.peichl@adc.de

🟥 Jury Member/Rookie
Jacques Pense
  Creative Director
Jung von Matt/Neckar GmbH
jacques.pense@adc.de

🟥 Jury Member
Ole Peters
  Managing Director Creation, Partner
Sehsucht GmbH
www.sehsucht.de
ole.peters@adc.de

🟥 Jury Member
Bert Peulecke
  Chief Creative Officer
kempertrautmann gmbh
bert.peulecke@adc.de

🟥 Jury Member
Johannes Plass
  Managing Director
Mutabor Design GmbH
www.mutabor.com
johannes.plass@adc.de

🟥 Jury Member/Member of the Board
Britta Poetzsch
  Chief Creative Officer
M.E.C.H. McCann-Erickson Communications House Berlin GmbH
britta.poetzsch@adc.de

🟥 Jury Member
Torsten Pollmann
  Creative Director
Euro RSCG GmbH
www.eurorscg.de
torsten.pollmann@adc.de

Dr. Ulf Poschardt
  Deputy Editor in Chief
Axel Springer AG
WELT am SONNTAG
www.welt.de
ulf.poschardt@adc.de

Prof. Hans-Georg Pospischil
  Art Director
Lettera GmbH
www.letteradesign.de
hansgeorg.pospischil@adc.de

Michael Preiswerk
  Creative Director, Managing Director
Brandplatform GmbH
michael.preiswerk@adc.de

🟥 Jury Member
Martin Pross
  Member of the Board
Scholz & Friends Berlin GmbH
www.s-f.com
martin.pross@adc.de

Marco Pupella
  Executive Vice President
Saatchi & Saatchi Milan
www.saatchi.com
marco.pupella@adc.de

Nina Puri
  Freelance Creative Director, Copywriter
Puri & Söhne
www.ninapuri.de
nina.puri@adc.de

Raphael Püttmann
  Freelance Art Director, Creative Director
raphael.puettmann@adc.de

Q

Peter Quester
  Freelance Copywriter
peter.quester@adc.de

R

🟥 Jury Member/Member of the Board/Spokesman of the Board
Jochen Rädeker
  Creative Director, Managing Partner
Strichpunkt Agentur für visuelle Kommunikation GmbH
www.strichpunkt-design.de
jochen.raedeker@adc.de

Prof. Diddo Ramm
  Creative Director
DRDCC MEDIA GmbH
www.drdccmedia.com
diddo.ramm@adc.de

🟥 Jury Member
Oliver Ramm
  Freelance Creative Director, Copywriter
www.oliver-ramm.de
oliver.ramm@adc.de

Alex Rank
   Photographer
www.alexrank.com
alex.rank@adc.de

❋ Jury Member
Markus Rasp
   Creative Director, Partner
Anzinger | Wüschner | Rasp
Agentur für Kommunikation
GmbH
www.agentur-awr.de
markus.rasp@adc.de

❋ Jury Member/Rookie
Mathias Rebmann
   Head of Creation
Scholz & Friends Berlin GmbH
www.s-f.com
mathias.rebmann@adc.de

❋ Jury Member
Peter Redlin
   Managing Director Creation
Milla & Partner
www.milla.de
peter.redlin@adc.de

❋ Jury Member
Petra Reichenbach
   Art Direction
reichenbach-design
petra.reichenbach@adc.de

Cosima Reif
   Copywriter, Illustrator
www.zufallsproduktion.at
cosima.reif@adc.de

❋ Jury Member
Dietmar Reinhard
   Freelance Creative
www.reinhardillustration.de
dietmar.reinhard@adc.de

Armin Reins
   Creative Director, Co-Owner
REINSCLASSEN GmbH &
Co. KG
www.reinsclassen.de
armin.reins@adc.de

❋ Jury Member
Alexander Reiss
   Group Creative Director
DDB Düsseldorf GmbH
alexander.reiss@adc.de

❋ Jury Member
Michael Reissinger
   Director, Managing Director
PIXELBUTIK by DELI PICTURES
GmbH
www.pixelbutik.de
michael.reissinger@adc.de

Prof. Thomas Rempen
   Creative Consultant
Büro Rempen GmbH
www.rempen.com
thomas.rempen@adc.de

Ivo von Renner
   Photographer
ivovon.renner@adc.de

Daniel Requardt
   Composer, Music Producer
audio-video-disco soundagent
www.audio-video-disco.de
daniel.requardt@adc.de

Matthias Rewig
   Managing Director, Owner
nhb studios berlin GmbH
www.nhb.de
matthias.rewig@adc.de

❋ Jury Member
Jan Rexhausen
   Creative Director, Managing
   Director
Jung von Matt/fleet GmbH
www.jvm.de
jan.rexhausen@adc.de

Brigitte Richter
   Photographer
brigitte.richter@adc.de

❋ Jury Member
Katja Rickert
   Creative Director
SCHOLZ & VOLKMER GmbH
www.s-v.de
katja.rickert@adc.de

❋ Jury Member
Torsten Rieken
   Managing Director Creation
BrawandRieken Werbeagentur
GmbH
www.brawandrieken.de
torsten.rieken@adc.de

Manfred Rieker
   Photographer
Manfred Rieker GmbH & Co. KG
manfred.rieker@adc.de

Manfred Riemel
   Creative Consultant
www.riemel.com
manfred.riemel@adc.de

Mike Ries
   Executive Creative Director
Euro RSCG
mike.ries@adc.de

Jan Ritter
   Owner, Creative Director
Ritterslagman Werbeagentur
GmbH & Co. KG
www.ritterslagman.com
jan.ritter@adc.de

❋ Jury Member
Kai Röffen
   Executive Creative Director,
   Managing Director
kt west (kempertrautmann)
kai.roeffen@adc.de

❋ Jury Member
Heiner Baptist Rogge
   Creative Director, Partner
SHANGHAI BERLIN
Neue Marken-Kommunikation
GmbH + Co. KG
www.shanghai-berlin.de
heinerbaptist.rogge@adc.de

❋ Jury Member
Alex Römer
   Managing Director Creation
Römer Wildberger Werbeagentur
GmbH
alex.roemer@adc.de

❋ Jury Member
Peter Römmelt
   Executive Creative Director
Ogilvy & Mather Werbeagentur
GmbH
www.ogilvy.de
peter.roemmelt@adc.de

Nikolaus Ronacher
   Art Director, Creative
   Director
www.nikolausronacher.de
nikolaus.ronacher@adc.de

Christine de Rooy
   Creative Director
christinede.rooy@adc.de

❋ Jury Member
Thilo Rothacker
   Illustrator
thilo rothacker illustration
www.thilo-rothacker.com
thilo.rothacker@adc.de

Constantin Rothenburg
   Creative Director
constantin.rothenburg@adc.de

❋ Jury Member/Rookie
Alexander Rötterink
   Designer
HHDC Hamburg Design Center
www.hhdc.de
alexander.roetterink@adc.de

❋ Jury Member
Raban Ruddigkeit
   Art Director
® ruddigkeit corporate ideas
www.ruddigkeit.de
raban.ruddigkeit@adc.de

❋ Jury Member
Detlef Rump
   Creative Director, Managing
   Director Creation
Proximity Germany GmbH
www.proximity.de
detlef.rump@adc.de

S

Kersten Sachse
   Managing Director Creation
Heuer & Sachse Werbeagentur
GmbH
www.heuer-sachse.de
kersten.sachse@adc.de

Leigh Sachwitz
   Creative Director, Managing
   Director
flora&faunavisions GmbH
www.florafaunavisions.de
leigh.haas@adc.de

Prof. Wolfgang Sasse
   Freelance Creative Director,
   Copywriter
Büro für persuasive
Kommunikation
www.wolfgangsasse.com
wolfgang.sasse@adc.de

Prof. Joachim Sauter
   Member of the Board, Chief
   Creative Officer
ART+COM AG
www.artcom.de
joachim.sauter@adc.de

Simon Schäfer
   Managing Director
Paperclip GmbH
simon.schaefer@adc.de

❋ Jury Member
Stephan Schäfer-Mehdi
   Freelance Creative Director,
   Creative Consultant
stephan.schaefermehdi@adc.de

Wolfram Schäffer
   Creative Director, Owner
design hoch drei GmbH & Co.KG
wolfram.schaeffer@adc.de

Reinhold Scheer
   Freelance Creative Director
reinhold.scheer@adc.de

❋ Jury Member/Member of the Board
Stefan Scheer
   Creative Director
Scheer Werbeagentur
www.scheer.tv
stefan.scheer@adc.de

❋ Jury Member
Burkhart von Scheven
   Managing Director Creation
Saatchi & Saatchi GmbH
www.saatchi.de
burkhartvon.scheven@adc.de

Sebastian Schier
   Creative Director
Saatchi & Saatchi GmbH
sebastian.schier@adc.de

★ Jury Member
Alexander Schill
Partner
Serviceplan Gruppe
alexander.schill@adc.de

★ Jury Member
Sandra Schilling
Freelance Creative Director
www.sandraschilling.com
sandra.schilling@adc.de

Andreas Schimmelpfennig
Creative Director, Managing Director
Elastique. GmbH
www.elastique.de
andreas.schimmelpfennig@adc.de

Prof. Michael Schirner
Managing Partner
michael.schirner@adc.de

★ Jury Member
Christian Schmachtenberg
Creative Director
Jung von Matt/relations GmbH
christian.schmachtenberg@adc.de

Ralf Schmerberg
Director, Photographer
Atelier Ralf Schmerberg
www.ralfschmerberg.com
ralf.schmerberg@adc.de

Martin Schmid
Director, Managing Director
JO!SCHMID Filmproduktion GmbH
www.joschmid.de
martin.schmid@adc.de

★ Jury Member
Susanne Schmidhuber
Interior Architect, Managing Director
Schmidhuber + Partner corporate architecture
www.schmidhuber.de
susanne.schmidhuber@adc.de

★ Jury Member
Heiko Schmidt
Creative Director Art
Kolle Rebbe GmbH
www.kolle-rebbe.de
heiko.schmidt@adc.de

★ Jury Member/Member of the Board
Jens Schmidt
Creative Director
Moccu GmbH & Co. KG
Kreativagentur für Digitale Medien
www.moccu.com
jens.schmidt@adc.de

★ Jury Member
Julia Schmidt
Creative Director Art
julia.schmidt@adc.de

Matthias Schmidt
Member of the Board
Scholz & Friends Group GmbH
www.s-f.com
matthias.schmidt@adc.de

Stefan Schmidt
Creative at large, Europe
TBWA\ Germany
www.tbwa.de
stefan.schmidt@adc.de

★ Rookie
Dr. Ulf Schmidt
Creative Director
ulf.schmidt@adc.de

★ Jury Member/Rookie
Bertram Schmidt-Friderichs
Publisher
Verlag Hermann Schmidt Mainz GmbH & Co. KG
www.typografie.de
bertram.schmidtfriderichs@adc.de

★ Jury Member/Rookie
Karin Schmidt-Friderichs
Publisher
Verlag Hermann Schmidt Mainz GmbH & Co KG
www.typografie.de
karin.schmidtfriderichs@adc.de

Harald Schmitt
Creative Director
schmittiliger
harald.schmitt@adc.de

★ Jury Member
Michael Schnabel
Photographer
Studio Michael Schnabel
www.michaelschnabel.com
michael.schnabel@adc.de

★ Jury Member
Christian Schneider
Composer, Music Producer
pearls° Gesellschaft für Acoustic Identity mbH
www.pearls-music.com
christian.schneider@adc.de

Donald Schneider
Art Director
Gruner & Jahr AG & Co. KG
Stern Art Director
donald.schneider@adc.de

Frank Schneider
Creative Director
frank.schneider@adc.de

Günther Schneider
Creative Director Text
Heye & Partner GmbH
www.heye-hh.de
guenther.schneider@adc.de

★ Jury Member
Manfred Schneider
Managing Director Creation
SCHNEIDERS" Kommunikation für Lebensart
www.schneiders-kommunikation.de
manfred.schneider@adc.de

★ Jury Member
Tim Schneider
Creative Director
HEIMAT, Berlin
www.heimat-berlin.com
tim.schneider@adc.de

★ Jury Member
Wolf Schneider
Managing Director Creation
SCHOLZ & FRIENDS Identify
www.s-f.com
wolf.schneider@adc.de

★ Jury Member
Wolfgang Schneider
CCO
BBDO Germany GmbH
www.bbdo.de
wolfgang.schneider@adc.de

Cordt Schnibben
Head of Department
Spiegel-Verlag Rudolf Augstein GmbH & Co. KG Der Spiegel
cordt.schnibben@adc.de

Eric Schoeffler
Chief Creative Officer
DDB Tribal Group
www.ddb-tribal.com
eric.schoeffler@adc.de

★ Jury Member
Marc Schölermann
Director
MARKENFILM
marc.schoelermann@adc.de

Bernd Schöll
Managing Director
Instant Records GmbH
www.instant-records.de
bernd.schoell@adc.de

★ Jury Member
Joachim Schöpfer
Partner
Serviceplan Public Opinion GmbH & Co.KG
joachim.schoepfer@adc.de

★ Jury Member
Volker Schrader
Chief Creative Officer
Publicis
volker.schrader@adc.de

Patrick Schrag
Freelance Copywriter
www.patrickschrag.com
www.patrickschrag.tumblr.com
patrick.schrag@adc.de

★ Jury Member
Stefan Schulte
Creative Director, Managing Director Creation
kempertrautmann berlin
www.kempertrautmann.com
stefan.schulte@adc.de

★ Jury Member
Birgit Schuster
Freelance Art Creative
birgit.schuster@adc.de

Klemens Schüttken
Freelance Creative
klemens.schuettken@adc.de

★ Jury Member/Rookie
Florian Schwalme
Creative Director
Scholz & Friends Berlin GmbH
florian.schwalme@adc.de

Christian Schwarm
Owner, Managing Director
Dorten GmbH
www.dorten.com
christian.schwarm@adc.de

Roland A. Schwarz
Managing Partner
schwarzspringer Werbeagentur GmbH
roland.schwarz@adc.de

★ Jury Member
Boris Schwiedrzik
Creative Director
Jung von Matt/Spree GmbH
boris.schwiedrzik@adc.de

Jan Schwochow
Managing Director, Creation
Golden Section Graphics GmbH Informationsdesign
www.golden-section-graphics.com
jan.schwochow@adc.de

Florian Seidel
Director, Photographer
www.studioseidel.de
florian.seidel@adc.de

Claudius Seidl
Frankfurter Allgemeine Zeitung
claudius.seidl@adc.de

★ Jury Member/Rookie
Wolfgang Seidl
Designer
SEIDLDESIGN
www.seidldesign.com
wolfgang.seidl@adc.de

★ Jury Member
Christian Seifert
Composer
www.lowbird.org
christian.seifert@adc.de

* Jury Member
Oliver Seltmann
Publisher, Editor
seltmann+söhne Kunst- und Fotobuchverlag
www.diealben.de
oliver.seltmann@adc.de

Marcello Serpa
Creative Director
Almap BBDO Comunicacoes Ltda.
Edificio Morumbi Office Tower
marcello.serpa@adc.de

* Jury Member
Stefan Setzkorn
Managing Director
Rapp Germany
stefan.setzkorn@adc.de

Othmar Severin
Creative Consultant
othmar.severin@adc.de

* Jury Member
Anna Clea Skoluda
Designer
www.anna-clea.de
annaclea.skoluda@adc.de

* Jury Member
Matthias Spaetgens
Managing Director Creation, Partner
Scholz & Friends Berlin GmbH
www.s-f.com
matthias.spaetgens@adc.de

* Jury Member/Member of the Board
Dörte Spengler-Ahrens
Managing Director Creation
Jung von Matt/Fleet GmbH
www.jvm.de
doerte.spenglerahrens@adc.de

* Jury Member
Reinhard Spieker
Art Director, Owner
WATZMANN Advertising Culture KG
www.watzmann-kg.de
reinhard.spieker@adc.de

Prof. Dr. Erik Spiekermann
Chairman of the Management Board
Edenspiekermann AG
www.edenspiekermann.com
erik.spiekermann@adc.de

Julia Stackmann
Freelance Creative Director, Copywriter
julia.stackmann@adc.de

* Jury Member
Prof. Anja Steinig
Designer
formwechsel
www.formwechsel.de
anja.steinig@adc.de

Graf Michael Stiebel
Managing Director, Director
Downtown Film Productions International Zulassung Hamburg & Dubai
www.downtownfilm.ae
michael.stiebel@adc.de

Mathias Stiller
Managing Director Creation
Jung von Matt/Spree GmbH
www.jvm.de
mathias.stiller@adc.de

Christian Stöppler
Managing Director
DSB&K Werbeagentur GmbH
www.dsbk.net
christian.stoeppler@adc.de

* Jury Member
Matthias Storath
Executive Creative Director
Ogilvy & Mather
matthias.storath@adc.de

* Jury Member
Norman Störl
Managing Director Creation
Jung von Matt/Elbe GmbH
norman.stoerl@adc.de

* Jury Member/Rookie
Tim Strathus
Creative Director Text
Interone GmbH
www.interone.de
tim.strathus@adc.de

* Jury Member
Christoph Stricker
Creative Director Art
GRABARZ & PARTNER
www.grabarz.de
christoph.stricker@adc.de

* Jury Member
Marc Strotmann
Copywriter, Managing Director Creation
Hello AG Agentur für Kommunikation
www.hello-muenchen.de
marc.strotmann@adc.de

* Jury Member
Tim Stübane
Executive Creative Director
Ogilvy & Mather Berlin
www.ogilvy.de
tim.stuebane@adc.de

* Jury Member
Achim Szymanski
Freelance Creative Director, Copywriter
www.achim-szymanski.de
achim.szymanski@adc.de

T

Ralph Taubenberger
Creative Director, Freelancer
www.ralphtaubenberger.de
ralph.taubenberger@adc.de

* Jury Member
Christine Taylor
Design Director
christine.taylor@adc.de

* Jury Member
Jens Theil
Copywriter
Kolle Rebbe GmbH
jens.theil@adc.de

* Jury Member
Patrick They
Illustrator
patrick they illustration
www.patrickthey.com
patrick.they@adc.de

Christopher Thomas
Photographer
Fotostudio Christopher Thomas
christopher.thomas@adc.de

* Jury Member
Axel Thomsen
Creative Director, Managing Director
PLAN.NET Campaign Erste GmbH & Co. KG
www.serviceplan.de
axel.thomsen@adc.de

* Jury Member
Hans-Joachim Timm
Executive Creative Director
guhl/partners.Zürich CH Agentur für Kommunikation
www.guhlpartners.ch
hansjoachim.timm@adc.de

* Jury Member
Franco Tortora
Composer, Music Producer
Mona Davis Beat GmbH
www.monadavis.com
franco.tortora@adc.de

* Jury Member
Christian Traut
Creative Director
KNSK Werbeagentur GmbH
www.knsk.de
christian.traut@adc.de

Emiliano Trierveiler
Creative Director
Crispin Porter + Bogusky Europe
emiliano.trierveiler@adc.de

Tomas Tulinius
Freelance Art Director, Creative Director
www.tomastulinius.com
tomas.tulinius@adc.de

* Jury Member
Sebastian Turner
sebastian.turner@adc.de

U

* Jury Member
Götz Ulmer
Managing Director Creation
Jung von Matt/Alster Werbeagentur GmbH
www.jvm.com
goetz.ulmer@adc.de

* Jury Member
Frank C. Ulrich
Creative Director
frank.ulrich@adc.de

Peter Unfried
Deputy Editor in Chief
TAZ Verlags- und Vertriebs GmbH
www.taz.de
peter.unfried@adc.de

* Jury Member
Eric Urmetzer
Creative Director, Owner
TOMORROW STUDIOS Markenkommunikation
www.tomorrow-studios.com
eric.urmetzer@adc.de

V

* Jury Member
Birgit van den Valentyn
Executive Creative Director
Ogilvy & Mather Berlin
birgit.vandenvalentyn@adc.de

* Jury Member
Mirko Vasata
Copywriter, Managing Director Creation
Vasata Schröder Florenz Werbeagentur GmbH
www.vsfw.de
mirko.vasata@adc.de

* Jury Member
Prof. Hermann Vaske
Creative Director, Director
Hermann Vaske's Emotional Network
www.whyareyoucreative.com
hermann.vaske@adc.de

* Jury Member
Jean-Louis Vidière | ésèpe
Conception, Art Direction
Steiner Sarnen AG für Kommunikation
www.steinersarnen.ch
jeanlouis.vidiere@adc.de

Oliver Viets
  Executive Creative Director
Elephant Seven Hamburg GmbH
www.e-7.com
oliver.viets@adc.de

Gerhard Peter Vogel
  Creative Director, Managing Director
KOPRA GmbH Publicity on demand Agentur für crossmediale Markenbotschaften und Markeninteraktion
www.kopra-network.de
gerhardpeter.vogel@adc.de

🔴 Jury Member/Member of the Board
Dr. Stephan Vogel
  Managing Director, Creation
Ogilvy & Mather Werbeagentur GmbH
www.ogilvy-frankfurt.de
stephan.vogel@adc.de

🔴 Jury Member
Manfred Vogelsänger
  Director, Managing Director
Vogelsänger Film GmbH
www.vogelsaenger.tv
manfred.vogelsaenger@adc.de

Michael Volkmer
  Managing Director, Owner
Scholz & Volkmer GmbH
www.s-v.de
michael.volkmer@adc.de

Stefan Vonderstein
  Managing Director
SteinleMelches
stefan.vonderstein@adc.de

🔴 Jury Member
Oliver Voss
  Owner
Oliver Voss Werbeagentur
www.miamiadschool.de
oliver.voss@adc.de

W

Prof. Manfred Wagner
  Creative Director, Owner
Braun Wagner
www.braunwagner.de
manfred.wagner@adc.de

Martin Wagner
  Director
martin.wagner@adc.de

🔴 Jury Member
Thimoteus Wagner
  Managing Director Creation
Jung von Matt/Alster Werbeagentur GmbH
www.jvm.de
thimoteus.wagner@adc.de

🔴 Jury Member
Peter Waibel
  Managing Director
Jung von Matt/Neckar GmbH
www.jvm.de
peter.waibel@adc.de

🔴 Jury Member
Prof. Jörg Waldschütz
  Professor of Digital Communication Design
Hochschule RheinMain Kommunikationsdesign
joerg.waldschuetz@adc.de

🔴 Jury Member
Pius Walker
  Creative Director, Owner
Walker Werbeagentur
www.walker.ag
pius.walker@adc.de

Thomas Walmrath
  Creative Director
thomas.walmrath@adc.de

Stefan Walz
  Creative Director, Founder
shift GmbH
www.shifthamburg.com
stefan.walz@adc.de

🔴 Jury Member
Tobias Wannieck
  Freelance Creative Director
www.wannieck.com
tobias.wannieck@adc.de

🔴 Jury Member
Manfred Wappenschmidt
  Creative Director Art
Leo Burnett GmbH
www.leoburnett.de
manfred.wappenschmidt@adc.de

🔴 Jury Member
Hermann Waterkamp
  Creative Director, Managing Partner
Leagas Delaney Hamburg GmbH
www.leagasdelaney.com
hermann.waterkamp@adc.de

Reinhold Weber
  Creative Director, Managing Director
Reinhold Werbeagentur AG
www.bueroreinhold.ch
reinhold.weber@adc.de

🔴 Jury Member
Timm Weber
  Group Creative Director
GRABARZ & PARTNER Werbeagentur GmbH
timm.weber@adc.de

Uli Weber
  Creative Director
Uli Weber Creative Consulting
uli.weber@adc.de

🔴 Jury Member
Alexander Weber-Grün
  Creative Director
kempertrautmann Berlin
alexander.webergruen@adc.de

🔴 Jury Member
Ulrike Wegert
  Creative Director Text
KNSK Werbeagentur GmbH
www.knsk.de
ulrike.wegert@adc.de

Michael Weies
  Art Director
A NEW KIND
www.anewkind.de
michael.weies@adc.de

Michael Weigert
  Creative Director, Managing Director
weigertpirouzwolf Werbeagentur GmbH
www.weigertpirouzwolf.de
michael.weigert@adc.de

🔴 Jury Member
Stefan Weil
  Managing Director Creation
Atelier Markgraph GmbH
www.markgraph.de
stefan.weil@adc.de

Jan Weiler
  Conception, Text
www.janweiler.de
jan.weiler@adc.de

Markus Weisbeck
  Designer
Surface-Gesellschaft für Gestaltung mbH
www.surface.de
markus.weisbeck@adc.de

Hans Weishäupl
  Managing Director Creation
das comitee Agentur für Kommunikation
www.das-comitee.de
hans.weishaeupl@adc.de

Arnfried Weiss
  Freelance Creative
Arnfried Weiss Werbung und Projekte
arnfried.weiss@adc.de

Walther Weiss
  Creative Director, Freelancer
Walther Weiss Creative Director
walther.weiss@adc.de

Philipp Welte
Hubert Burda Media Holding GmbH & Co.KG
philipp.welte@adc.de

🔴 Jury Member
Deneke von Weltzien
  Managing Director Creation
Jung von Matt Brand Activation Werbeagentur GmbH
www.jvm.de
denekevon.weltzien@adc.de

Konrad Wenzel
  Creative Director
Huth + Wenzel Agentur für Kommunikation
www.huth-wenzel.de
konrad.wenzel@adc.de

🔴 Jury Member
Matthias Wetzel
  Freelance Creative Director, Copywriter
matthias.wetzel@adc.de

Dr. Dominik Wichmann
  Editor in Chief
Gruner + Jahr AG & Co. KG Stern
www.stern.de
dominik.wichmann@adc.de

Marc Wientzek
  Creative Director
Aimaq & Stolle Creative Brand Consulting GmbH
www.asberlin.com
marc.wientzek@adc.de

Thomas Wildberger
  Creative Director, Co-Owner
Römer Wildberger Werbeagentur GmbH
thomas.wildberger@adc.de

🔴 Rookie
Heike Wilhelm
  Managing Director
Jung von Matt
heike.wilhelm@adc.de

Kai Wilhelm
  Creative Director
Agentur 19. August GmbH
www.a198.de
kai.wilhelm@adc.de

Klaus Wilhelm
  Art Director
klaus.wilhelm@adc.de

Claudia Willvonseder
  Head of Marketing IKEA Germany
IKEA Deutschland GmbH & Co. KG
www.ikea.de
claudia.willvonseder@adc.de

🔴 Jury Member
Mathias Willvonseder
  Composer, Producer
Gutleut GmbH Studio
www.gutleut.eu
mathias.willvonseder@adc.de

Holger Windfuhr
　Art Director
Handelsblatt GmbH
WirtschaftsWoche
www.wiwo.de
holger.windfuhr@adc.de

※ Jury Member
Conny J. Winter
　Photographer, Director
www.connywinter.com
conny.winter@adc.de

※ Jury Member
Michael Winterhagen
　Creative Director
Scholz & Friends Berlin GmbH
michael.winterhagen@adc.de

※ Jury Member
Marc Wirbeleit
　Freelance Creative Director
　Text
www.text.cd
marc.wirbeleit@adc.de

Frieder Wittich
　Director
c/o Esther Kurle Management
www.estherkurle.com
frieder.wittich@adc.de

※ Jury Member
Harald Wittig
　Freelance Creative Director,
　Copywriter
harald.wittig@adc.de

※ Jury Member
Philipp Wöhler
　Creative Director Text
Scholz & Friends Berlin GmbH
philipp.woehler@adc.de

Lars Wohlnick
　Creative Director
VCCP
lars.wohlnick@adc.de

Ewald Wolf
　Managing Director, Creative
　Director
weigertpirouzwolf Werbeagentur
GmbH
www.weigertpirouzwolf.de
ewald.wolf@adc.de

Gregor Wöltje
　Managing Director
WoeltjeKleene
Unternehmensberatung
gregor.woeltje@adc.de

※ Jury Member
Folker Wrage
　Chief Creative Officer
McCann Erickson
www.mccann.ch
folker.wrage@adc.de

Stefan Wübbe
　Creative Director Text
Kolle Rebbe Werbeagentur GmbH
stefan.wuebbe@adc.de

※ Rookie
Fabian Wurm
　Chief Editor
beef – Magazin für kreative
Kommunikation
fabian.wurm@adc.de

※ Jury Member
Paul Würschmidt
　Creative Director
paul.wuerschmidt@adc.de

Z

※ Jury Member
Dietrich Zastrow
　Creative Director, Consultant
dietrich.zastrow@adc.de

※ Jury Member
Julia Ziegler
　Creative Director Art
Jung von Matt/Alster
www.jvm.de
julia.ziegler@adc.de

※ Jury Member
Christoph Zielke
　Professor of Communication
　Design
Hochschule Rhein-Waal
www.hesse-design.com
christoph.zielke@adc.de

※ Jury Member
Ralf Zilligen
　Chairman
Arthur Schlovsky
www.arthurschlovsky.de
ralf.zilligen@adc.de

Jürgen Zimmermann
　Director, Managing Director
FBI Film Bureau International
GmbH
www.fbi-film.com
juergen.zimmermann@adc.de

※ Jury Member
Gerrit Zinke
　Creative Director, Partner
kempertrautmann
gerrit.zinke@adc.de

Ingo Zirngibl
ingo.zirngibl@adc.de

※ Jury Member
Friedrich von Zitzewitz
　Managing Director Creation
Plan.Net Campaign Hamburg
GmbH & Co.KG
friedrich.vonzitzewitz@adc.de

※ Jury Member
Peter Zizka
　Managing Director, Creation
Heine/Lenz/Zizka Projekte GmbH
www.hlz.de
peter.zizka@adc.de

※ Jury Member
Stefan Zschaler
　Managing Partner
Leagas Delaney Hamburg GmbH
www.leagasdelaney.de
stefan.zschaler@adc.de

※ Jury Member
Ulrich Zünkeler
　Copywriter
ulrich.zuenkeler@adc.de

ADC DEUTSCHLAND EHRENMITGLIEDER
ADC GERMANY HONORARY MEMBERS

1979
Hubert Troost (verstorben/died in 1991)

1980
Prof. Dr. h. c. Vicco von Bülow, Loriot

1981
Tomi Ungerer

1982
Prof. Heinz Edelmann (verstorben/died in 2009)

1983
Willi Fleckhaus (verstorben/died in 1983)

1985
Rolf Gillhausen (verstorben/died in 2004)

1986
Jean-Paul Goude

1987
Karl Gerstner

1988
Helmut Krone (verstorben/died in 1996)

1989
Reinhart Wolf (verstorben/died in 1988)

1990
Helmut Schmitz (verstorben/died in 2000)

1991
Günter Gerhard Lange (verstorben/died in 2008)

1992
Paul Gredinger

1993
Prof. Hans Hillmann

1994
Wolf D. Rogosky (verstorben/died in 1996)

1995
Peter Lindbergh

1996
Michael Conrad

1996
Prof. Walter Lürzer (verstorben/died in 2011)

1997
Prof. Dr. Werner Gaede

1998
Prof. Dr. h. c. Dieter Rams

1999
Konstantin Jacoby

2000
Rudolf Augstein (verstorben/died in 2002)

2001
Othmar Severin

2002
Robert Gernhardt (verstorben/died in 2006)

2003
Prof. Michael Schirner

2004
Armin Maiwald

2005
Prof. Kurt Weidemann (verstorben/died in 2011)

2006
Jean-Remy von Matt

2007
Michael Ballhaus

2008
Ellen von Unwerth

2009
Christoph Schlingensief (verstorben/died in 2010)

2010
Rainer Brandt

ADC DEUTSCHLAND VORSTAND
ADC GERMANY BOARD
11.2010–10.2011

Hans-Peter Albrecht

Johannes Erler

Claus Fischer

Mathias Jahn

Johannes Milla

Lutz Nebelin

Britta Poetzsch

Jochen Rädeker
  Vorstandssprecher/Spokesman of the Board

Stefan Scheer

Jens Schmidt

Dörte Spengler-Ahrens

Dr. Stephan Vogel

ADC DEUTSCHLAND FÖRDERMITGLIEDER
ADC GERMANY SUPPORTING MEMBERS

@ Carola Wendt, Hamburg
ACHT FRANKFURT GmbH & Co. KG . digital solutions, Frankfurt/Main
Adobe Systems GmbH, Munich
ARD-Werbung SALES & SERVICES GmbH, Frankfurt/Main
ARRI Film und TV Services GmbH, Munich
Art Directors Club Verlag GmbH, Berlin
Axel Springer AG, Berlin

BASF SE, Ludwigshafen
BBDO Berlin GmbH, Berlin
BBDO Germany GmbH, Duesseldorf
BBDO Stuttgart GmbH, Stuttgart
Burda Community Network GmbH, Munich
BUTTER. GmbH, Duesseldorf

Cobblestone Filmproduktion GmbH, Hamburg
Corbis GmbH, Duesseldorf
CP2 Agentur für Marketing+Werbung, Weiden

DDB Group Germany GmbH, Berlin
DESIGNERDOCK Headquarters Ltd., Berlin
DO IT! GmbH, Duesseldorf
DraftFCB, Hamburg

Eberhard, Raith & Partner GmbH, Munich
Embassy of Dreams Filmproduktion GmbH, Munich
e+p commercial GmbH, Munich
Euro RSCG GmbH Düsseldorf, Duesseldorf

FAW Fachverband Aussenwerbung e. V., Frankfurt/Main
FOCUS Magazin Verlag GmbH, Munich

Getty Images DevCo Deutschland GmbH, Munich
Gramm Werbeagentur GmbH, Duesseldorf
Grey Worldwide GmbH, Duesseldorf
Gruner+Jahr AG & Co. KG stern Marketing Direction, Hamburg

HEAG Südhessische Energie AG (HSE) Entega, Darmstadt
Heinrich Bauer Verlag KG Central Advertising Direction, Hamburg
Heye Group, Unterhaching
Hochkant Film GmbH & Co. KG, Munich
HORIZONT Deutscher Fachverlag GmbH, Frankfurt/Main

Interone GmbH, Munich

Jahreszeiten Verlag GmbH Architektur und Wohnen, Hamburg
J. Walter Thompson GmbH & Co. KG, Frankfurt/Main

Kolle Rebbe Werbeagentur GmbH, Hamburg
Königsdruck Printmedien und digitale Dienste GmbH, Berlin

Laszlo Kadar Film GmbH & Co. KG, Hamburg
Leo Burnett GmbH, Frankfurt/Main

MACROMEDIA Hochschule für Medien und Kommunikation, Munich
Markenfilm GmbH & Co. KG, Wedel
McCann Erickson Frankfurt GmbH, Frankfurt/Main
McCann Erickson Hamburg GmbH, Hamburg
Media Consulta Advertising GmbH, Berlin
media.net berlinbrandenburg e. V., Berlin
MetaDesign AG, Berlin
Museum für Kommunikation, Berlin
Muth, bdc GmbH, Frankfurt/Main

netz98 new media GmbH, Mainz
Neue Sentimental Film Frankfurt GmbH, Frankfurt/Main
New ID Filmproduktion GmbH, Duesseldorf

Ogilvy & Mather Werbeagentur GmbH, Frankfurt/Main

Papierfabrik Scheufelen GmbH & Co. KG, Lenningen
Peek & Cloppenburg KG, Duesseldorf
phocus brand contact GmbH & Co. KG, Nuremberg
PICTORION das werk GmbH Niederlassung Frankfurt, Frankfurt/Main
Pirates'n Paradise Film & Videopostproduction GmbH, Duesseldorf
Plusform Präsentationspappen, Wunstorf

Red Cell Werbeagentur GmbH, Duesseldorf
Reemtsma Cigarettenfabriken GmbH Marketing Director, Hamburg
RMS Radio Marketing Service GmbH & Co. KG, Hamburg

Saatchi & Saatchi GmbH, Frankfurt/Main
Scholz & Friends Group GmbH, Berlin
Scholz & Friends Group GmbH, Hamburg
Serviceplan Gruppe für innovative Kommunikation GmbH & Co. KG, Munich
SPIEGEL-Verlag Rudolf Augstein GmbH & Co. KG, Hamburg
Studio Funk GmbH & Co. KG, Hamburg

TBWA Deutschland Holding GmbH, Berlin
Tony Petersen Film GmbH, Hamburg

Uniplan International GmbH & Co. KG, Cologne

VCC GmbH Agency for Postproduction, Duesseldorf
Verlag Werben & Verkaufen GmbH, Munich
Vogelsänger Studiogruppe Foto-Film-Video-Multimedia-Event, Lage Pottenhausen

WerbeWeischer GmbH & Co. KG, Hamburg
Westiform GmbH & Co. KG, Ortenberg

Young & Rubicam GmbH, Frankfurt/Main

JURYS
JURIES

ADC Jury Chairman 2011: Chuck Porter

Jury 1 – Print
Single Motif, Campaign, Innovative Use of Print, Junior ADC Print All

Presiding Juror: Dörte Spengler-Ahrens

Niklas Frings-Rupp
Matthias Harbeck
Nicole Hoefer-Wirwas
Detmar Karpinski
Dagmar König
Delle Krause
Andreas Manthey
Olaf Oldigs
Alex Römer
Matthias Spaetgens
Oliver Voss
Gerrit Zinke

Jury 2 – Out-of-Home
Classic Single Motif, Classic Campaign, Non-Classic, Junior ADC Out-of-Home All

Presiding Juror: Gepa Hinrichsen

Kathrin BergerGley
Kurt Georg Dieckert
Ove Gley
Bernhard Lukas
Gudrun Müllner
Patricia Pätzold
Mathias Rebmann
Alexander Schill
Sandra Schilling
Hermann Waterkamp
Dietrich Zastrow
Ralf Zilligen

Jury 3 – Film 1 (3D)
TV/Cinema Commercial, TV/Cinema Campaign, Junior ADC Film Practice Works

Presiding Juror: Guido Heffels

Tobias Ahrens
Niels Alzen
Holger Bultmann
Oliver Frank
Daniel Frericks
Matthias Lührsen
Alexander Nagel
Michael Ohanian
Ole Peters
Kai Röffen
Christoph Stricker
Stephan Vogel

Jury 4 – Film 2
Sales Promotion Films, Image Films, Junior ADC Film Semester Works

Presiding Juror: Torsten Hennings

Till Eckel
Bastian Kuhn
Jochen Leisewitz
Benjamin Lommel
Hans Neubert
Torsten Pollmann
Michael Reissinger
Peter Römmelt
Wolfgang Schneider
Marc Schölermann
Marc Strotmann
Deneke von Weltzien

Jury 5 – Film 3
  Internet Films, Film Craft

Presiding Juror: Mirko Vasata

Carsten Bolk
Dietmar Dahmen
Hartmut Grün
Jonas Keller
Robert Krause
Simon Oppmann
Henning Patzner
Tim Schneider
Klemens Schüttken
Christian Traut
Hermann Vaske
Paul Würschmidt

Jury 6 – Film 4
  TV On-Air Promotion, On-Air Design,
  Shorts/Special Formats for Moving
  Pictures, Innovative Use of Film, Junior ADC
  Film Graduation Works

Presiding Juror: Christian Mommertz

Asta Baumöller
Hajo Depper
Stephan Ganser
Nadim Habib
Peter Hirrlinger
Joerg Jahn
Nikolai Karo
Gerd Neumann
Joachim Schöpfer
Hans-Joachim Timm
Manfred Vogelsänger
Thimoteus Wagner

Jury 7 – Audio
  Radio Commercial, Radio Campaign,
  Podcast, Webcast, Sound Logo, Jingle,
  Innovative Use of Audio, Audio Craft,
  Junior ADC Audio All

Presiding Juror: Hans-Peter Albrecht

Frank Bannöhr
Mariusz Jan Demner
Kay Eichner
Fabian Frese
Christian Fritsche
Klaus Funk
Sebastian Hardieck
Lars Huvart
Martin Kießling
Jana Mohr
Oliver Ramm
Ulrich Zünkeler

Jury 8 – Digital Media 1
  Websites, Microsites, Social Media

Presiding Juror: Arno Lindemann

Olaf Czeschner
Martin Drust
Michael Kutschinski
Justin Landon
Jan Leube
Katja Rickert
Jens Schmidt
Birgit Schuster
Peter Waibel
Pius Walker
Timm Weber
Marc Wirbeleit

Jury 9 – Digital Media 2
Mobile, Online Advertising, E-Mail, Viral, Digital Media Environment Design, Digital Campaigns, Digital Media Craft, Junior ADC Digital Media All

Presiding Juror: Simone Ashoff

Philip Borchardt
Jo Marie Farwick
Heike Frank
Florian Grimm
Timm Hanebeck
Judith Homoki
Pit Kho
Elke Klinkhammer
Marco Mehrwald
Nina Puri
Burkhart von Scheven
Friedrich von Zitzewitz

Jury 10 – Dialog Marketing
Dialog Print, Dialog Mail, Dialog Broadcast, Dialog Digital, Dialog Mobile Marketing, Dialog Cross-Media Campaigns, Dialog Social Media Campaigns, Dialog Alternative, Junior ADC Dialog Marketing All

Presiding Juror: Michael Koch

Jeremy Abbett
Michael Barche
Christoph Everke
Wolf Heumann
Andreas Klemp
Stefan Kolle
Uwe Marquardt
Kerrin Nausch
Bert Peulecke
Detlef Rump
Matthias Storath
Folker Wrage

Jury 11 – Promotion
Activities, Means, Junior ADC Promotion All

Presiding Juror: Lutz Nebelin

Catrin Florenz
Joachim Glawion
Christoph Hildebrand
Niels van Hoek
Johannes Krempl
David Mously
Christoph Nann
Jan Okusluk
Britta Poetzsch
Matthias Schmidt
Tim Stübane
Harald Wittig

Jury 12 – Media
Media, Junior ADC Media

Presiding Juror: Armin Jochum

Frank Dovidat
Ekki Frenkler
Helen Haeusermann
Jan Harbeck
Dirk Henkelmann
Florian Kähler
Doris Kiermeier
Markus Kremer
Rolf Leger
Stefan Meske
Alexander Reiss
Alexander Weber-Grün

Jury 13 – Literature 1
  Advertising Brochures, Image/Information Brochures, Catalogs, Reports, Junior ADC Semester Works, Junior ADC Practice Works

Presiding Juror: Volker Schrader

Matthias Birkenbach
Peter Kirchhoff
Dirk Linke
Harald Linsenmeier
Frank Lübke
Chris Mayrhofer
Helmut Meyer
Heiner Baptist Rogge
Manfred Schneider
Reinhard Spieker
Manfred Wappenschmidt
Michael Winterhagen

Jury 14 – Literature 2
  Books, Book Series, Book Jackets/Covers, Book Jacket Series, Junior ADC Graduate Works

Presiding Juror: Klaus Hesse

Monika Aichele
Dirk Bartos
Klaus-Jürgen Hergert
Christoph Herold
Norbert Herold
Andreas Liedtke
Jacques Pense
Petra Reichenbach
Stefan Schulte
Wolfgang Seidl
Anja Steinig
Jean-Louis Vidière | ésèpe

Jury 15 – Design 1
  Corporate Design, Junior ADC Design Graduate Works

Presiding Juror: Stefan Baggen

Wolfgang Behnken
Lo Breier
Axel Domke
Thomas Feicht
Rosa Haider-Merlicek
Irene Hecht
Ivica Maksimovic
Jan Rexhausen
Wolf Schneider
Frank C. Ulrich
Jörg Waldschütz
Christoph Zielke

Jury 16 – Design 2
  Individual Graphics, Art/Culture/Event Posters, Typography (Craft), Junior ADC Design Practice Works, Junior ADC Typography (Craft) All

Presiding Juror: Peter Zizka

Kirsten Dietz
Heico Forster
Fabian Kirner
Daniel Könnecke
Detlef Krüger
Heinrich Paravicini
Alexander Rötterink
Heiko Schmidt
Julia Schmidt
Bertram Schmidt-Friderichs
Stefan Setzkorn
Christine Taylor

Jury 17 – Design 3
Calendars, Packaging, Product Design, Junior ADC Design Semester Works

Presiding Juror: Katrin Oeding

Rob Brünig
David Fischer
Heiko Freyland
Andreas Geyer
Ole Grönwoldt
Uli Gürtler
Thorsten Kraus
Sebastian Letz
Jürgen Mandel
Holger Oehrlich
Jochen Rädeker
Axel Thomsen

Jury 18 – Editorial
Print/Issue, Print/Year's Issues, Print/Individual Work, Multimedia/Integrated Concept, Multimedia/Individual Work, Junior ADC Editorial All

Presiding Juror: Markus Rasp

Christoph Amend
Mirko Borsche
Johannes Erler
Lothar Gorris
Mieke Haase
Christoph Keese
Lukas Kircher
Timm Klotzek
Karin Schmidt-Friderichs
Claudius Seidl
Anna Clea Skoluda
Sebastian Turner

Jury 19 – Environmental Design
Environmental Design, Environmental Design Craft, Junior ADC Environmental Design All

Presiding Juror: Johannes Milla

Timo Blunck
Frank Brammer
Uwe R. Brückner
Tobias Eichinger
Kristoffer Heilemann
Stefan Karl
Sven Klohk
Roland Lambrette
Johannes Plass
Christian Schmachtenberg
Susanne Schmidhuber
Mathias Willvonseder

Jury 20 – Events
Events, Events Craft, Junior ADC Events All

Presiding Juror: Matthias Kindler

Suze Barrett
Mark Daniels
Cedric Ebener
Claus Fischer
Joachim Hauser
Andreas Horbelt
Joachim Kortlepel
Britta Nagel
Peter Redlin
Stephan Schäfer-Mehdi
Tobias Wannieck
Stefan Weil

Jury 21 – Copy
   Copy, Junior ADC Text All

Presiding Juror: Ono Mothwurf

Philipp Barth
Matthias Berg
Felix Bruchmann
Wolf-Peter Camphausen
Jan Geschke
Eva Jung
Cosimo Möller
Achim Szymanski
Birgit van den Valentyn
Ulrike Wegert
Matthias Wetzel
Philipp Wöhler

Jury 22 – Photography
   Photography, Junior ADC Photography All

Presiding Juror: Michael Schnabel

Hans-Jürgen Burkard
Florian Geiss
Esther Haase
Dirk Haeusermann
Dietmar Henneka
Reinhard Hunger
Claudia Kempf
Diether Kerner
Matthias Mittermüller
Oliver Seltmann
Jens Theil
Julia Ziegler

Jury 23 – Illustration
   Illustration, Junior ADC Illustration All

Presiding Juror: Raban Ruddigkeit

Axel Eckstein
Thomas Fuchs
Fritz Haase
Thomas Hofbeck
Maik Kähler
Dietmar Reinhard
Thilo Rothacker
Boris Schwiedrzik
Jan Schwochow
Patrick They
Eric Urmetzer
Conny J. Winter

Jury 24 – Music and Sound
   Music and Sound

Presiding Juror: Reinhard Besser

Ludwig Berndl
John Groves
Willy Kaussen
Oscar Meixner
Stephan Moritz
Torsten Rieken
Christian Schneider
Florian Schwalme
Christian Seifert
Norman Störl
Tim Strathus
Franco Tortora

Jury 25 – Integrated Campaigns
   Integrated Campaigns, Junior ADC
   Integrated Campaigns

Presiding Juror: Till Hohmann

Hans-Joachim Berndt
Feico Derschow
Oliver Handlos
Mathias Jahn
Richard Jung
André Kemper
Myles Lord
Ralf Nolting
Martin Pross
Stefan Scheer
Götz Ulmer
Stefan Zschaler

AGENTUREN UND VERLAGE
AGENCIES AND PUBLISHERS

7 Seas,
46

A

Adcom Group
274
Aimaq & Stolle Creative Brand Consulting GmbH
334
Alexander Egger, Isolde Fitzel
370
Alex Rank Photography
280, 437
anschlaege.de
250
Anzinger | Wüschner | Rasp Agentur für Kommunikation GmbH
202, 259, 368, 392
ART+COM
228
ATELIER BRÜCKNER
197, 200
Atelier Markgraph
198, 229, 273
Axel Springer AG
224, 269, 400ff.

B

B612 GmbH
225
BBDO Proximity GmbH, Duesseldorf
206, 244, 305, 307, 317f., 320, 356
B|BE Branded Entertainment GmbH
394
Berliner Morgenpost
400ff.
Bibelmagazin Gbr, Volleritsch & Wurm
389
bilekjaeger
363
Birkhäuser GmbH
367
BlueMars – Gesellschaft für digitale Kommunikation mbH
96, 343
BLUWI, Hamburg
199
BRAUNWAGNER, K-MB
275
Büro Rempen GmbH
78
BUTTER.
427

C

CE+Co GmbH
426
Chewing the Sun
336
Clormann Design GmbH
381

D

DDB Tribal Group
64, 182, 203, 286, 290, 293, 312, 325, 347, 447
Dederichs Reinecke & Partner, Portrix.net
46
Demner, Merlicek & Bergmann
349
der Freitag
399
der Freitag Mediengesellschaft mbh & Co Kg
399

designforum Wien
370
Die Brandenburgs GmbH/Werbeagentur
221
DIE ZEIT
195
DOKYO GmbH
295
Dorland Werbeagentur GmbH
434
Drändle 70|30 GmbH
421
Du – Das Kulturmagazin
227

E

Elephant Seven Hamburg GmbH
341
Euro RSCG Duesseldorf
383

F

FELD Verlag
257
fischerappelt AG
96
förderraum
371
FREIE RADIKALE Werbung
364

G

GENERAL DE PRODUCCIONES Y DISEÑO, S.A. Sevilla
199
Geschke Pufe Berlin
429
gobasil GmbH
134
Golden Section Graphics GmbH
258, 403f.
Grabarz & Partner
88, 140, 152, 179, 207, 287, 294, 322
Grey Worldwide GmbH
204, 324
Grimm Gallun Holtappels Werbeagentur GmbH & Co. KG
78, 132, 248, 344
Gruner+Jahr AG & Co. KG
170, 263f., 300, 393, 405f.
GUM-Projektgruppe, FH Bielefeld
372
gürtlerbachmann GmbH
297, 378

H

häfelinger+wagner design
251
Halle34 OG f. zeitgenössische Kommunikation
376
Hatje Cantz Verlag
250
Heidelberger Druckmaschinen AG
364
HEIMAT, Berlin
72, 100, 164, 216, 328
Hermann Vaske's Emotional Network
329
herzogenrathsaxler design
254
Heye OMD GmbH
249
Heye & Partner GmbH
332

I

identis GmbH, design-gruppe joseph pölzelbauer
387
In-house Production
390

J

Jack Rouse Associates
148
Jäger & Jäger
190, 362
Joachim Wissler Group
251
Jung von Matt AG
46, 86, 106, 124, 174, 176, 189, 212f., 218, 223f., 237, 241, 243, 245, 253, 278, 281, 288, 292, 296, 306, 310, 315, 319, 323, 342, 351, 357f., 361, 425, 449f.
Jung von Matt/Elbe GmbH
86, 124, 351
Jung von Matt/Fleet,
46
Jung von Matt/Limmat
162
Jung von Matt/next
46
Jung von Matt/next GmbH, Clanmo
218
Jung von Matt/relations GmbH
425
JUNO
144
JWT Germany GmbH
226

K

Kehrer Verlag Heidelberg
372
kempertrautmann gmbh
96, 110, 180, 219, 236, 442
kempertrautmann gmbh berlin
327
kempertrautmann west gmbh
136
kid's wear Verlag
391
KircherBurkhardt GmbH
366f.
KNSK Werbeagentur GmbH
205, 431
Kolle Rebbe GmbH
84, 156, 208, 222, 239f., 313, 321, 432
Kolle Rebbe/KOREFE
192, 256, 352, 388
KOMET Werbeagentur AG BSW
369, 390
KulturSPIEGEL
444

L

La Red GmbH
295
Leagas Delaney Hamburg GmbH
150, 333, 340
loved gmbh
180, 257, 417, 438
Lukas Lindemann Rosinski GmbH
128, 140, 178, 316

M

m box bewegtbild GmbH, Berlin
199
Magazin Verlagsgesellschaft
Süddeutsche Zeitung mbH
265ff., 395ff., 408–411
MAGMA Brand Design
367
Martin et Karczinski GmbH
421
Meiré&Meiré
391
MESO Digital Interiors
229, 273
MFO Berlin, Achter April Stuttgart
118
michael haegele
435
Milla & Partner
108
Mindpirates
64
MTV Networks Advertising Unit
217
mu:d
275
Mutabor Design GmbH
196, 328, 377, 379, 418, 423

N

NEON Magazin GmbH
170, 263, 393, 405
neo.studio | neumann schneider architekten
422
Neubau Editorial Design & Medienbüro Oliver Wurm
389
Neue Digitale/Razorfish GmbH
328, 339, 345
Nowadays GmbH & Co. KG
182
Nüssli (Deutschland) GmbH
108

O

Ogilvy Frankfurt
165, 177, 188, 276, 304, 335, 337f., 350, 354
Ogilvy & Mather Advertising GmbH
298
Oliver Voss GmbH
238

P

Parasol Island GmbH
182
Philipp und Keuntje GmbH
247
plan.net
158, 365
Prestel Verlag
368
Preuss und Preuss GmbH
445

R

Redaktion NIDO
170
Red Rabbit
309
Rocket & Wink
209
Römer Wildberger Werbeagentur GmbH
308
Rose Pistola GmbH
225
® ruddigkeit corporate ideas
118

S

Saatchi & Saatchi Duesseldorf
360, 441
Scheer
384
Schmidhuber+Partner,
108, 418
Schmidhuber und Partner GbR, Munich
196
Scholz & Friends
54, 163, 186, 230, 234f., 246, 255, 277, 299, 311, 314, 331, 353, 382, 385f., 428, 430, 443
Scholz & Friends Zürich
424
Self-published
259, 369, 392
Seltmann+Söhne
100, 209
serviceplan
94, 158, 365
Serviceplan
120, 154, 187, 220, 282, 289, 348, 359
shift GmbH
96, 343
Spillmann/Felser/Leo Burnett
355
stern Magazin
264, 300, 406f., 439f., 446
Stiftung Deutsche Bibelgesellschaft
134
Strichpunkt Design
166, 374, 433
Ströer Deutsche Städte Medien and HELI-Showequipment
273
STUDIO94
375
Stuttgart Citizens
181
Süddeutsche Zeitung Magazin
265ff., 395ff., 408–411
Suhrkamp Verlag
375
Syzygy Deutschland GmbH
346
Syzygy, Groves Sound Communications, 360 Grad
426

T

Tamschick Media+Space GmbH, Berlin
199
Taschen GmbH
374
TAS Emotional Marketing GmbH
272
TBWA Berlin
249
TBWA Berlin, CHE*CHE
291
TBWA Paris
116
TGG Hafen Senn Stieger
252, 371
Tim John – Atelier für Szenografie
271
tisch13 GmbH
419
Triad Berlin Projektgesellschaft mbH
270
trigger happy productions
64
TULP DESIGN GmbH
420
Typotron AG
252

U

uniquedigital GmbH (Media)
346
Universal Music
162
Uwe Düttmann
279, 436

V

Verlag Hermann Schmidt Mainz
190f., 362, 373
VICE Deutschland GmbH
262, 398
VIRAL LAB
330
VOK DAMS Agentur für Events und Live-Marketing
274

W

walker
201, 451
walker Werbeagentur
231
weareflink GmbH
242
WE DO communication GmbH GWA
175, 326
weissraum.de(sign)°
380
WELT-Gruppe
269
White Horse Music GmbH
46, 449
www.lego-signs.com
365

Y

Young & Rubicam GmbH
448

Z

ZEITmagazin
146, 193, 194, 260f., 268, 412–416
Zeitverlag Gerd Bucerius
403
Zeitverlag Gerd Bucerius GmbH & Co. KG
146, 193, 194, 195, 260f., 268, 412–416

FIRMEN CLIENTS

1&1 Internet AG
245

A

Achim Lippoth
391
Adrienne Goehler
250
Aernout Overbeeke
278
ALDAR Properties PJSC + Ferrari SPA
148
Alex Rank Photography
280, 437
Alfred Ritter GmbH & Co. KG
432
all4family
348
Amnesty International France
116
ANDREAS STIHL AG & Co. KG
186, 299
ARAG Allgemeine Rechtsschutz-Versicherungs-AG
427
Arctic Paper
144
Art Directors Club für Deutschland (ADC) e.V.
426
Atelier Markgraph
273
Audi AG
136, 196, 328, 339, 419, 423, 442
AUDI AG, Ingolstadt
418
AUDI AG (I/VM-4)
417
Augsburger Allgemeine
428
A. W. Faber-Castell Vertrieb GmbH
187
Axel Springer AG
224, 237f.
Axel Springer Mediahouse Berlin GmbH
188

B

Bayerische Staatsforsten AöR
259, 392
Bayer Vital GmbH
307
Beate Uhse TV
236
Beijing Benz Automotive Co., Ltd.
449
Beisser GmbH & Co. KG
377
Berliner Illustrirte Zeitung
400f.
Berliner Morgenpost
402
BFF
448
BIC Deutschland GmbH & Co. KG
296
bilekjaeger
363
BIONADE GmbH
84
Birkhäuser GmbH
367
Bischöfliches Hilfswerk MISEREOR e.V.
208, 222
Bittersuess Pictures
242
BMW AG Deutschland
94
Braun GmbH
206

Bundesministerium für Wirtschaft und Technologie represented by Koelnmesse International GmbH
108
BUND e.V.
443
Bureau of Shanghai World Expo Coordination
270

C

Cafe Luitpold
225
Caritas
162
CERN
197
Christian Bracht
394
Christoffel Blindenmission Deutschland e.V.
244
Christopher Thomas
368
Clormann Design GmbH
381
Community Film GmbH
378

D

Daimler AG
54, 174, 178, 212, 229, 243, 275, 281, 292, 310f., 319, 323, 331
Daimler AG, Mercedes-Benz Vertrieb Deutschland
320
Daimler AG, smart MBVD
318
DaWanda GmbH
175
DB Mobility Logistics AG
304
Demner, Merlicek & Bergmann
349
der Freitag
399
designforum Wien
370
DESSO BV
420
Deutsche Post AG
315
Deutscher Handwerkskammertag (DHKT)
163
Deutscher Tierschutzbund e.V. Bundesgeschäftsstelle
204
Deutsches Schauspielhaus in Hamburg
150
Diesel Deutschland GmbH
182
DIE WELT/WELT KOMPAKT, Axel Springer AG
230
DIE ZEIT
146, 193ff., 260f., 268, 403, 412–416
DKV Deutsche Krankenversicherung
276
Dorland Werbeagentur GmbH
434
DSGV
241
DSV
189
Du – Das Kulturmagazin
227
DUMMY Verlag GmbH
334
Dynaudio
429

E

E. Breuninger GmbH & Co.
271
edding International AG
219
edding International GmbH
110
Emmi Schweiz AG
424
ENTEGA VERTRIEB GmbH
64, 203
Erntedank Kreativspezialisten
221

F

Fachhochschule Bielefeld, Fachbereich Gestaltung
372
FC St. Pauli
351
Feld Hommes Magazin
438
Feld Verlag
257
Festina Uhren GmbH
255
Festool GmbH
430
Fey & Co.
213
Filmakademie Baden-Württemberg
242
fiftyfifty
383
förderraum
371
Frankfurter Allgemeine Zeitung GmbH
234, 382
Friedrichs & Friends
358
fritz-kola GmbH
309
FTD G+J Wirtschaftsmedien
431

G

Galaxxy-Pet Food GmbH
207
Gare du Neuss GmbH Antik- & Trödelmarkt
246
Genuport Trade AG
330
Germanwings GmbH
128
GlaxoSmithKline Consumer Healthcare GmbH & Co. KG
298
Golden Section Graphics
258, 404
Google Germany GmbH
239f., 321
Görtz GmbH
297
Görtz GmbH, Görtz 17 GmbH
180
Greenpeace Schweiz
231
Grimm Gallun Holtappels Werbeagentur GmbH & Co. KG
132
Gruner+Jahr
393
Gruner+Jahr AG & Co. KG
264, 300, 406f., 439f., 446

H

Hasenkopf GmbH & Co. KG
421
HCBC zwei UG & Co. KG
380
HEIDELBERGER DRUCKMASCHINEN AG
364
Henkel AG & Co. KGaA
346, 359
Hi-Cone, a division of ITW ESPAÑA, S.A.
78
Hornbach Baumarkt AG
72, 100, 164
Hotel Altes Kloster GmbH
376
Hyposwiss Private Bank
201

I

Iglo GmbH
305
IKEA Deutschland GmbH & Co. KG
140, 152, 337, 344
Industrie- und Handelskammer Frankfurt
343
Initiative vermisste Kinder
96
Institut für Stadtgeschichte Frankfurt
198
Interkantonaler Rückversicherungsverband IRV
390
IWC International Watch Co. AG
357

J

Joachim Wissler Group GmbH
251
jobsintown.de GmbH
322
Jung von Matt AG
176, 223

K

Kappa Deutschland GmbH
248
Kolle Rebbe GmbH
352
Konzerthaus Dortmund
86, 124
Kraft Foods Europe GmbH
226
Kulturprojekte Berlin Transmediale
118
KulturSPIEGEL, Marianne Wellershoff
444
KurzFilmAgentur Hamburg e.V.
326

L

Leagas Delaney Hamburg GmbH
340
LEGO GmbH
154, 365
LemonAid Beverages GmbH
106
Loewe Opta GmbH
277
Luitpoldblock GbR
225

M

Mars GmbH
317
McDonald's
290
McDonald's Deutschland
345
McDonald's Deutschland Inc.
249
McFit GmbH
216
Medienbüro Oliver Wurm
389
Mephisto 97.6
445
Mercedes-Benz
316
Mercedes-Benz Vertrieb Deutschland
341
michael haegele
435
Modern Music School
88
Moto Waganari
177
MTV Networks Germany GmbH
217
Mutabor Design GmbH
379

N

NEON Magazin GmbH
170, 263, 405
Neubau Editorial Design
389
Nike Deutschland
156
Nils Holger Moormann GmbH
190, 362

O

OBI Group Holding GmbH
367
Otto Bock HealthCare GmbH
228

P

Panasonic Energy Europe N.V.
385
Panasonic Marketing Europe GmbH
425
Panini Verlags GmbH
289
Papierfabrik Scheufelen GmbH & Co. KG
433
PARSHIP GmbH
333
Passionsspiele Oberammergau
202
pbsa peter behrens school of architecture, Duesseldorf
254
Pernod Ricard Deutschland GmbH
291
redblue Marketing GmbH
327

R

ReinsClassen, Hamburg
294
Reporter ohne Grenzen Österreich
348
Rocket & Wink
209
Roggenkamp Organics AG
386
RUHR.2010 GmbH
272

S

SAP Deutschland
165
Saudi Expo 2010 Commission, Ministry of Municipal and Rural Affairs, Saudi Arabia
199
Schauspiel Frankfurt
273
Schauspielhaus Bochum – Anstalt des öffentlichen Rechts
384
Scholz & Friends Berlin GmbH
235
Scholz & Friends Hamburg
353
Schueler.CC
342
serviceplan campaign hamburg
158
SGCC (State Grid Corporation of China)
200
Sixt GmbH & Co. Autovermietung KG
306
Sky Deutschland Fernsehen GmbH & Co. KG
120
Sky Deutschland GmbH & Co. KG
332
Soirée graphique
369
Sony Computer Entertainment Deutschland GmbH
338
SPIEGEL-Verlag Rudolf Augstein GmbH & Co. KG
288
Sportjugend Hessen im Landessportbund Hessen e.V.
335
SportScheck GmbH
354
SP Zürich
451
Staatsministerium Baden-Württemberg
314
Staatstheater Stuttgart Schauspiel
166
Städel Museum
350
Stephan Schneider
336
Stiftung Deutsche Bibelgesellschaft
134
Strichpunkt Design
374
Stuttgart Citizens
181
Süddeutsche Zeitung Magazin
265ff., 395ff., 408–411
Suhrkamp Verlag
375
Swisscom AG
274

T

Tages Anzeiger, Tamedia
355
T.D.G. Vertriebs GmbH & Co. KG
192, 256, 388
Texterschmiede e.V.
361
Toshiba
324
Toyota Deutschland GmbH
441
TUI interactive GmbH
218
Typotron AG
252

U

UFA-Palast
360
Ullstein GmH, Berliner Morgenpost
308
Unilever Deutschland GmbH
295
Uwe Düttmann
279, 436

V

Vegetarierbund Deutschland e.V. (VEBU)
220
Vergiss Aids nicht e.V.
247
Verkehrsgesellschaft Frankfurt (VGF)
274
Verlag Hermann Schmidt Mainz
191, 294, 373
VICE Deutschland GmbH
262, 398
Vodafone D2 GmbH
450
Volkswagen AG
286f., 293, 312, 325, 447
Vorderasiatisches Museum – Staatliche Museen zu Berlin
422
Vorwerk Deutschland Stiftung & Co. KG
313

W

WaXhouse Betriebs GmbH
253
WELT-Gruppe
269
WIENERS+WIENERS GmbH
179
winwood48 KG
387
WMF AG
205
Wrigley GmbH
356
WWF Deutschland
46

Z

ZDF/ARTE
329
ZDF »Das kleine Fernsehspiel«
242
Ziegler Verlags GmbH
282

MACHER
MAKERS

A

Abdallah, Chehad 291
Abraham, Arthur 237
Abt, Uta 64
Achenbach, Marc 174
Ackermann-Reiche, Babette 400
Adam, Bastian 110, 136, 219
Adolph, Daniel 292
Afchar, Bardia Marco 247
Afflerbach, Andrea 344
Ahamad, Rafael 150
Ahlring, Kristin 263, 393, 405
Ahn, Ji-Young 263, 393, 405
Ahrens, Timo 417
Ahrens, Tobias 442
Aimaq, André 334
Albers, Kathrin 324
Albrich, Holger 225
Alder, Rahel 369, 390
Alings, Philipp 206
Allen, Mark 398
Aloji, Victor 178
Alt, Florian 206
Alt, Jue 100, 328
Altmann, Julika 195
Altmann, Thorsten 441
Alvi, Suroosh 398
Alzen, Niels 246
Amato, Salvatore 385, 428
Amend, Christoph 146, 193f., 260f., 268, 412ff., 416
Ammann, Bettina 369
Amoa, Kena 189
Anderson, Leroy 206
Anderson, Thorne 398
Andresen, Hannes 243
Andrew, Felix 329
Antzar, Ali 342
Anzinger, Claudia 259, 392
Apel, Frank 337, 354
Ardelean, Alexander 339, 345
Arige, Marcus 376
Armann, Michael 120
Arnold, David 331
Arnold, Jörg 162
Arnold, Martin 201, 231, 451
Ascacibar, Felipe 136, 333, 338
Askemper, Steffi 361
Asmus, Gerrit 295
Attalla, Basma 120, 220
Auerswald, Christian 344
Aufdembrinke, David 213, 351
Auth, Frank 343
Avenhaus, Thomas 175, 326
Axelsson, Ragnar 440
Aydemir, Gün 176

B

Baader, Benjamin 163, 186, 299
Babucke, Svenja 216
Bach, Aleksander 323
Bach, Ina 88, 179
Backens, Peter 205
Baeriswyl, Christina 162
Bähr, Jana 163
Baierl, Regina 259
Baiker, Ralph 223
Balciunas, Edmundas 343
Bald, Thorsten 277
Baldisweiler, Nicole 54, 311
Balke, Doris 426
Balog, Andreas 187, 359
Bals, Charles 247
Bank, Marcus 243, 327
Banneyer, Nina 170
Bar, Noma 288
Barbian, Ulrich 338
Barcelos, Ulé 118
Bargheer, Olaf 150
Barraclough, Robin A. 424
Barrett, Suze 424
Bartel, Alexander 332
Barth, Philipp 223
Barth, Verena 120
Barthelmess, Florian 237
Bartholdt, Verena 88

Bartkowski, Christoph von 296, 315
Barton, David 249, 291
Barz, Fabian 325
Baslam, Farid 234
Bauer, Patrick 170, 263
Bauer, Varhan Orchestrovich 148
Bauer, Yvonne 170
Baumann, Katharina 370
Baumann, Marc 266
Baumann, Peter 276
Baumgartner, Judith 64
Baur, Georg 224, 237, 278
Baus, Oliver 341
Bause, Andre 241
Baxmann, Andreas 110
Baxxter, H. P. 237
Bazarkaya, Toygar 244, 318
Bdeir, Dania 330
Bechtler, Valerie 314
Bechtolsheim, Matthias von 72, 100, 164, 216
Beck, Alexandra 360
Beck, Benjamin 292, 310
Beck, Gundula 272
Beck, Marcus »Becko« 330
Beckenbauer, Franz 237
Becker, Dominique 320
Becker, Hans-Peter 88
Becker, Kai 341
Becker, Katrin 239f., 321, 432
Becker, Laura 140, 152
Becker, Michael 383
Becker, Nicolas 187, 359
Becker, Roman 94
Becker, Sön 128
Beckmann, Jan 124
Beecken, Thomas 178
Beham, Jasmin 363
Behrend, Dirk 64
Behrens, Martina 257
Behrens, Michael 46
Behres, Thomas 423
Bekiaris, Antonia 369, 390
Bellisario, Syria 170
Belser, Tim 180
Benamara, Malik 156, 208
Bengtson, Nina 146, 193f., 260f., 268, 412–416
Benrath, Max 179
Benzler, Philipp 312
Béres, Beatrix 381
Berg, Aggi 380
Berg, Jan 449
Berg, Martina 287, 447
Berger, Clara 326
Berger, Lisa 325
Berghäuser, Antje 399
Berghäuser, Petra 335, 354
Bergler, Torsten 249
Berhe, Sophia 335
Berndl, Ludwig 64, 203
Berndorff, Jan 259
Berndt, Jakob 106
Bernhardt, Maike 431
Berning, Frank 295
Berns, Tina 179
Bertisch, Philipp 286
Bestagno, Francesco 349
Bestmann, Christian 326
Bethke, Marc 178
Beutinger, Michael 257
Beving, Joep 140
Beyeler, Pascal 162
Beyer, Nico 216
Biedowicz, Michael 146, 193f., 260f., 269, 412ff., 416
Biel, Christopher 166
Bieling, Marc 118
Biener, Jan Kirsten 259, 392
Bierau, Anja 296, 315
Biesalski, Luise 291
Bill, Fabian 352, 432
Bilz, Robert 331
Binder, Anne 422
Binder, Thorsten 346
Binkert, Lisa 201
Birkner, Florian 244
Bison, Andrea 110, 442
Bissig, Andrea 451
Bittel, Johannes 86
Bittermann, Dirk 244
Bittner, Philip 257
Bitzer, Simone 46

blach, gregor c. 175, 326
Blania, Norbert 186, 299
Blankenhorn, Nicolas 64
Blaschke, Anne 266f., 395ff., 408–411
Blau, Frank 327
Blendow, Michael 213
Blick, Tobias 248
Blickle, Paul 258, 403
Blineder, Tobias 120
Block, Guido 208
Blome, Karen 237, 253, 357
Blömer, Henner 450
Blomeyer, Marion 392
Bluhme, Bernd 325
Blum, Wolfgang 84
Blümel, Romy 110
Blumenschein, Viviane 425
Blumenthal, Andres 312, 447
Blunck, Timo 150
Bober, Thomas 293
Boddin, Mareike 340
Bode Brodmüller, Robert 217
Boege, Johannes 238
Boemer, Franziska 299f., 428
Boerner, Maren 255, 386
Bognár, Daniel 265ff., 395ff., 408–411
Böhm, Michael 213
Böhme, Ansgar 84
Bohnacker, Sabrina 247
Böhning, Tobias 208
Böhnke, Bernd 298
Boiron, Maxime 116
Böker, Hannes 290
Bolk, Carsten 356
Bolland, Philip 312
Bompoint, Jean Louis 216
Bonajo, Melanie 405
Bonisolli, Barbara 259, 392
Boppert, Eleonore 298
Borchardt, Philip 291
Borsche, Mirko 146, 193f., 260f., 268, 412–416
Borsetzky, Katja 291
Boseckert, Steffen 64
Botarel, Mihai 182
Bothe, Josefine 64
Bothor, Mathias 237
Botsch, Maria 100
Bottmann, Annalena 348
Bourguignon, Andre 338
Bragina, Lana 341
Brandenburg, Olaf 221
Brandes, Christian 54, 314, 430
Branss, Kai 136
Brasseler, Kristina 118
Brauchli, Michael 308
Bräuer, Jenny 293
Braun, Harald 257, 417
Braun, Julia 327
Bräunl, Manfred 94
Breaux, Richard 291
Bredenbals, Markus 298
Breining, Daniel 342
Breitbach, Christoph 287
Breitkreuz, Habib 212
Breuer, Martin 383
Brimo, Wilfrid 325
Brink, Bernd 379
Brinkmann, Christopher 357
Brkitsch, Oliver 140
Brochot, Christian 345
Brockelmanns, David 274
Brockmann, Mike 272
Broich, Arne 247
Brönnimann, Peter 355
Brown, Kurt 248
Brückner, Prof. Uwe R. 197, 200
Bruhn, Tanja 140
Bruhns, Lars 96
Brünig, Rob 298
Bruning, Rasmus 379
Brunner, Anne-Laure 116
Brunner, Gisbert L. 412
Brunner, Remo 162
Bruno, Benjamin 341
Bruns, Maria 54
Bruns, Sönke 182
Buba, Natalie 140
Bubel, Silvia 377, 423
Büchel, Caro 231
Buchholtz, Björn von 445
Buchholz, Lucas 380
Buchholz, Susann 380

528

Budde, Tana 366
Bueltmann, Chris 182
Bugetti, Christophe-Claude 64, 203
Bukowiecka, Karolina 318
Bultmann, Holger 313
Bunte, Steffen 372
Burg, Bernhard 307
Burgdorff, Martin 195
Burger, Oliver 227
Buri, Lars 64, 203
Burkard, Hans-Jürgen 439
Busch, Oliver 333
Busch, Sönke 295
Buschke, Sandro 255, 386
Busse, Benjamin 212, 351
Butenhoff, Frank 344
Bütow, Stefanie 106
Butterbrodt, Andreas 64
Buzelli, Chris 203
Byns, Björn 150

C

Caldicott, Karen 290
Campagna, Isabel 356
Capper, Andy 398
Carretero Lopez, Jose Luis 46, 288
Castoro, Rocco 398
Celand, Werner 290
Cerning, Maja 386
Cerning, Ulf 54
Charisius, Hanno 392
Cheadle, Harry 398
Chirico, Cosimo 220
Chlapek, Christina 217
Chmil, Erik 251
Christof, Nicole 190, 362
Chroust, Evelyn 297
Chudalla, Silvia 136
Cindric, Ratko 331
Cischek, Claudia 364
Ciuraj, Cathrin 64
Civan, Timur 398
Classen, Veronika 294
Clausen, Momme 163, 230, 299, 428
Clormann, Marc M. 381
Coenen, Alexandra 296, 358
Cohrs, Johann 106
Cole, Sabine 257, 417
Comando, Carly 116
Constanty, Pascal 257, 417
Conzen, Alphons 212
Cording, Torben 295
Correll, Kerstin 322
Cowlan, Gabriele 335
Crada 291
Cramer, Julia 189, 241, 243
Crantz, Dajana 86, 124, 212
Cunze, Hannes 380
Curtis, Payton 412
Czeikowitz, Matthias 335, 338
Czerlinski, Pascal 78
Cziharz, Jan 326
Czöppan, Sven 330

D

Dabrowska, Barbara 262, 398
Dachselt, Tilman 326
Dadras, Sara 182, 220
Dainese, Livio 162
Dalen, Marc van 253
Daliri Freyduni, Barbara 239f., 321
Dalquist, Andreas 293
Daniel, Stevie 240, 321
Dankert, Anna 427
Danner, Klaus 430
Das, Lilian 361
Daugherty, Anita 148
Decker, Phil 332
Deckert, Marc 170
Deflorin, Andriu 162
Deigner, Imke 217
Deisenhofer, Stephan 339
Deiss, Wolf 291
Deitert, Tobias 54
Dellert, Andreas 120

Demeter, Thomas 360
Demir, Gülcan 318
Demner, Mariusz Jan 349
Denninger, Rainer 442
Deppner, Martin 372
Detlow, Inga 257
Dettmann, Katrin 249, 291
Deuter, Bjoern 249
Dias, Gustavo Vieira 318, 356
Dieckert, Kurt Georg 249, 291
Diehl, Gösta 322
Diekmann, Kai 237
Diel, Marco 182
Diepenbrock, Nikolai 328
Diesinger, Holger 223
Diestel, Till 365
Dietrich, Ellen 195
Dietrich, Susan 307
Dietz, Kirsten 166, 374, 433
Diezel, Anja 175
Dinter, Tonya 293
Dirfard, Thomas 110
Dirscherl, Barbara 287
Distefano, Ricardo 243
Dittmann, Esther 331
Dittmann, Jörg 84, 156, 432
Dittrich, Susanne 154
Doc Robert 100, 392
Doering, Christian 192, 352
Doerks, Patrick 253
Dombrowsky, Jeremias 247
Dörfler, Michael 326
Dornier, Alexis 291
Dörrenbächer, Sven 174, 212, 243, 281, 292, 319, 323
Doubek, Jennifer 241
Dovenmühle, Melanie von der 425
Drabsch, Nicole 281
Draeger, Jan 401
Drakos, Niki 291
Drändle, Jürgen 421
Dreckkötter, Marco 150
Drescher, Christina 106
Dressel, Jörg-Peter 245
Dressler, Christiane 100, 189, 292, 327
Dressler, Jan 72
Dreyer, Jan 249
Dropkewitz, Carla 344
Drösser, Christoph 195
Druck, Beisner 110
Drühe, Markus 156
Düe, Sabine 202, 259, 392
Duffe, Sybilla 120
Duffy, Ryan 398
Dufossé, Alain 291
Dunbar, Alex 398
Duncan, Patrick 398
Dunlap, Michael 164, 216, 328
Durband, Sebastian 162, 182
Dürr, Dr. Carola 64
Durst, Marcel 369
Dütschke, Oliver 344
Düttmann, Uwe 223, 279, 436

E

Ebener, Cedric 426
Eberhard, Sebastian 154
Ebert, Michael 170, 263, 393, 405
Eckart, Christine 257
Eckart, Oliver 156
Eckel, Till 312, 325, 447
Eckert, Alexander 182
Eckert, Reto 390
Eckhardt, Christiane 180
Eckstein, Jakob 333, 340
Edusei, Vincent 330
Ege, Jan-Florian 361
Egger, Alexander 370
Eggers, Lina 110, 236
Eggers, Phillip 248
Ehlert, Catrin 366
Ehrenberger, Andreas 376
Ehrenholz, Wilfried 429
Eichelmann, Benny 262, 398
Eichler, Stephan 206
Eichner, Sandra 240, 321
Eick, Sebastian 296
Eicken, Susanne zu 46
Eickhoff, Thomas 88, 179

Eickmeyer, Karin 245
Eickmeyer, Matthias 427
Eikelpoth, Robert 318
Einhaus, Elisabeth 110, 219, 442
Eipper, Birgit 247
Eisenberg, Kim-Fabien 150
Eisheuer, Bernhard 291
Ekecs, Gabor 419
Ekrt, Viktor 72
Ellis, Laurence 217
Elsner, Bartek 328
Elsner, Bartosz 339
Elste, Christina 291
Eltz, Kathleen von der 315
Endemann, Jannik 212, 245, 323, 425
Endert, Jan van 223
Engel, Rainer 425
Engelbrecht, Peter 318
Engelen, Cécile 175, 326
Engelhardt, Jan 293
Engelhardt, Lukas 258
Ercan, Taner 188
Erdmann, Carsten 400ff.
Erhorn, Torben 78, 344
Erler, Isabelle 64
Ernst, Lena 212, 281, 310
Ernsting, Mark 264, 300, 406f., 439f., 446
Esbach, Frank 322
Espenschied, Dragan 64
Esser, Tim 128
Etaryan, Natalya 343
Everke, Christoph 120, 220, 348
Ewald, Denise 140, 152, 207, 294
Ewert, René 247
Ewertz, Markus 315

F

Faber, Jallo 100
Faber, Leschek 326
Fabian, Jennifer 322
Fach, Kathrin 353
Fairman, Will 398
Falkensteiner, Michael 94, 158
Farsijani, Bijan 84
Farwick, Jo Marie 86, 124, 212f., 245, 342, 351
Fast, Waldemar 247
Faulhaber, Nina 64, 203
Fechner, Georg 188
Fehler, Peter 208
Feichtl, Simon 359
Feige, Tobias 237, 357
Feigl, Jakob 263, 393, 405
Feil, Alex 174
Feiler, Florian 365
Fellmann, Max 265, 408–411
Felten, Dr. Sabine 225
Felten, Prof. Holger 225
Feurer, Dorothea 96, 110, 219, 343
Fichta, Susanna 370
Fiedler, Reiner 378
Fiedler, Sebastian 179
Fietje, Eike 152
Figuera, Dino 247
Figur, Julia 237
Fill, Susanna 72, 100
Fink, Christopher 206
Finke, Michael 328, 442
Fischbeck, Vanessa 174
Fischer, Carsten 110
Fischer, David 311, 430
Fischer, Eva 265ff., 395ff., 408–411
Fischer, Holger 423
Fischer, Jürgen 272
Fischer, Malte 54
Fischer, Maria 225
Fischer, Robert 259
Fisser, Marijke 86, 124, 212
Fitting, Jürgen 186, 299
Fitzel, Isolde 370
Fitzner, Antje 431
Fleck, Lisa 97
Fleischhauer, Silke 306
Fleischmann, Signe 231
Fleischmann, Signe Prince 451
Flemmig, Sebastian 296
Flohr, Henning 222
Flohrs, Oliver 310

Forsberg, Crille 328
Forstreuter, Emilia 118
Fragstein, Marc 118
Fragstein, Michael 118
Franck, Norbert 443
Francke, Marcell 96
Frank, Lennart 64, 203
Franke, Marina 275
Franz, Sascha 220
Franzgrote, Heiko 110
Frede, Frederik 249
Fredriksen, Katja 287
Frei, Lukas 162
Freier, Matthias 182
French, Thomas 324
Frenkler, Ekki 289
Frenssen, Christian 384
Frericks, Daniel 357
Frese, Fabian 357, 361, 425, 450
Frese, Sebastian 255, 443
Frey, Annika 106
Frey, Kathrin 257
Freyland, Heiko 180, 219, 442
Frickemeier, Claudia 221
Friedrich, Gabriela 361
Friedrich, Sandra 128
Friedrich, Stefan 347
Friesen, Oleg 341
Fritsche, Christian 110, 236f.
Fritsche, Timo 150, 174
Fröhlich, Jana 197
Fromm, Lüder 174, 212, 243, 281, 292, 310, 319, 323
Frommann, Nils 357
Frost, Eike-Peter 429
Frost, Matthäus 220
Fründt, Boris 361
Füchtjohann, Jan 392
Fuhrmann, Evelin 250
Fukazawa, Alexandra 379
Fulford, Jason 268
Fürste, Moritz 96
Füsslin, Michael 84, 239f., 321
Fust, Gabriela 369
Fütterer, Dirk 372

G

Gabriel, Anna 54, 311, 331
Gabriel, Sven 86, 351
Gaedicke, Philip 291
Gaentzsch, Julia 205
Gaertner, Flo 367
Gähwiler, Christoph 110, 236
Gaillard, Marie Toya 234, 382
Galliard, Ilonka 162
Gallun, Nils 78, 132, 248, 344
Galvin, Brendan 292
Gamper, Mario 54
Gansczyk, Benedikt 291
Gansterer-Zaminer, Michaela 376
Garbers, Sandra 400f.
Gardeweg, Christine-Marie 295
Gasparian, Frederico 212
Gassner, Daniel 220
Gebhardt, René 443
Gehrs, Oliver 334
Geigel, Philipp 332
Geis, Franz 363
Geisel, Lutz 419
Geissler, Alexander 120
Gelhausen, Lars 64
Gemeiner, Christian 324
Gentile, Matthew 249
Gentis, Steffen 206, 356
Gerdes, Anne 195
Gerlach, Hans 259, 391
Gerlach, Ines 163
Gerold, Jan 330
Gersmann, Hanna 250
Gerwien, Antje 64, 203
Geschke, Jan 429
Geschke, Stefan 248
Gessler, Stephan 64
Geyer, Claudia 364
Geyer, Andreas 309
Ghini, Antonio 148
Gholiagha, Nima 97
Giannetta, Filippo 118
Gill, Sanjay 345

Gillmeister, Christine 327
Giloy-Hirtz, Petra 202
Glage, Sven 64
Gluge, Tibor 295
Glanz, Irmgard 433
Gläscher, Joana 236
Gläser, Mark 148
Gläsle, Moritz 239, 321
Glauner, Felix 383
Glock, Lisa 46
Glogowski, Achim 287
Gnädinger, Andrea 162
Göbber, Anke 450
Gödel, David 336
Goehler, Adrienne 250
Goetz, Marian 323
Gogesch, Silvia 371
Göhrig, Anna 118
Golbach, Marco 360
Gold, Anne 64
Goldemann, Marcus 343
Gombert, Stefanie 243, 319
Gonzalez, Paul 419
Goodman, Valerie 291
Goraya, A. M. 398
Gordeev, Andrey 445
Gordon, Stéphane 255
Göricke, Dr. Jutta 225
Görler, Katja 296
Gossner, Sarah 196, 388
Gossner, Tilman 224, 237, 278
Gothe, Andrea 300, 406, 439f.
Gotthardt, Tim 339
Götz, Michael 110
Götzenberger, Ralf 240, 321
Grabmayer, Marian 64
Gräbner, Iris 394
Grabsch, Till 192, 356, 388, 445
Graevenitz, Nikolai von 425
Gräfe, Frank 282
Gräfe, Susanne 264
Grafenstein, Frank von 225
Grahl, Stefan 248
Grammerstorf, Tom 316
Grandt, Oliver 150, 333, 340
Grann, Edward 116
Grasl, Lele 347
Grass, Martin 179
Grasshoff, Isabell 177
Grassmann, Philip 399
Graubaum, Steffen 243
Grauel, Ralf 64
Grebert, Johannes 54
Gregor, Jean-Pierre 360, 441
Greter, Wolfgang 144
Grewe, Marko 256, 352
Griebe, Frank 241
Grieger, Katja 448
Griep, Oliver 257
Grimm, Florian 78, 132, 248, 344
Grimm, Tobias 86, 124, 212, 245, 323, 351
Grischek, Robert 438
Grobe, Fabian 124
Gröger, Jens 212
Gromer, Peter 323
Grosch, Meike 309
Grossebner, Lukas 290
Groth, Joshua 330
Grötsch, Sandra 253
Grotter, Matthias 223
Groves, John 426
Grub, Moritz 204, 324
Gruber, Helen 195
Gruber, Michael 359
Grün, Katrin 84, 313
Grund, Alan 289
Gründgens, Gregor 450
Gründl, Max 332
Grüner, Benni 425
Grünewald, Viktoria 230, 299, 428
Grzesiewski, Anton 330
Gsponer, Alain 231
Guddat, Katrin 195
Gudehus, Juli 373
Gulla, Konrad 213
Gumbert, Daniel 237
Günder, Diana 120
Gundlach, Kai-Uwe 281, 409
Günther, Alexa 154
Günther, Katja 258
Günther, Markus 361
Gursch, Philip 54

Gürtler, Uli 297, 378
Gustafsson, Jessica 208, 222, 313
Guth, Dennis 182

H

Haacke, Julia 324
Haase, Esther 434
Haase, Mieke 110, 257, 417, 438
Habben, Claas Rudolf 377
Haberl, Gabriel 290
Häberle, Dr. Christoph 225
Häberle, Prof. Dr. Christoph 225
Habermann, Arne 213
Häcker, Simon 228
Hackner, Tanja 224, 237
Haderer, Dr. Karoline 64, 203
Haegele, Michael 435
Hagemeister, Malte 231
Hähle, Marlen 422
Halder, Fabian 359
Hamm, Hubertus 415
Hammer, Patrick 425
Hampl, Lorenz 309
Hamsley, David 290
Hänchen, Ben 445
Handel-Jung, Gabriele 304
Handke, Annabelle 326
Handlos, Oliver 163, 234
Hänggi, Cyril 355
Hanke, Sascha 86, 124, 212f., 245, 323, 342, 351, 449
Hannemann, Sven 296, 315, 319
Hanowski, Alexander 196, 242
Hansen, Philip 247
Hansen, Ralf 425
Hanser, Thomas 293
Hanske, Paul-Philipp 170
Hansmann, Christian 361
Hanson, Duane 64
Hantke, Dennis 339
Harbeck, Jan 189, 241, 315, 319, 358
Harbeck, Matthias 154, 187, 282, 359
Hardcastle, Paul 100
Hardenberg, Tita von 291
Harders, Hannah 309
Hardieck, Sebastian 244, 317f., 320, 356
Harms, Jens 330
Harmsen, Lars 367
Harrow-Sandmann, Hans 64
Hartmann, Daniel 332
Hartmann, Dieter 305
Hartmann, Patrik 150
Hartwig, Attila 255, 385
Hartwig, Tim 140
Haschtmann, Daniel 189, 241, 315
Häse, Anja 238
Haslauer, Matthias 225
Hassan, Mark 72, 100, 164, 216
Hauke, Julica 322
Haus, Sebastian 382
Hauser, Tom 140, 152, 207
Häußler, Michael 235, 296
Havelcova, Zuzana 445
Haveric, Emir 223
Haverkamp, Johannes 182
Hawari, Sharifa 378
Haydn, Joseph 86
Haye, Dennis De La 64
Heath, Ebon 291
Hecht, Thilo 449
Hecking, Tobias 182
Heckmann, Sven 295
Heeb, Benjamin 365
Heel, Robert 343
Heesch, Martin 212
Heffels, Guido 72, 100, 164, 216, 328
Heffels, Kerstin 72, 100, 216
Hegemann, Dominik 200
Heider, Dirk 118
Heidorn, Oliver 322
Heidt, Julian 205
Heikamp, Birgit 248
Heilemann, Kristoffer 64, 203
Heine, Felix 234
Heine, Hendrik 136
Heinen, Harald 221
Heinke, Till 429
Heinlein, Peter 188
Heinrich, Eva-Maria 422

Heinrichs, Stefan 336
Heinrichs, Uwe 150
Heinsen, Michael 308
Heinz, Tina 164
Heinzlmeier, Bert 259, 392
Helbig, Silvio 86, 140
Heldens, Acki 378
Helle, Heinz 201, 231, 451
Heller, Andreas 371
Hellwig, Jens 295
Helmert, Birte 253
Hemig, Imke 344
Henck, Holger 432
Hendrich, Carsten 271
Henke, Andreas 204, 324
Henke, Reinhard 427
Henke, Robert "Robster" 449
Henkelmann, Dirk 291
Henneken, Helena 426
Hennen, André 140, 207
Hennings, Torsten 88, 207, 294
Henry, Kara 226
Hentges, Philipp 360
Henze, Cornell 64
Henze, Tom 189
Herholz, Benjamin 213
Hermuth, Katrin 291
Herr Müller 257
Herre, Max 291
Herrlich, Joschka 247
Herrmann, Jürgen 431
Hertel, Jan 293
Herter, Robert 174, 310
herzogenrath, matthias 254
Hess, Michael 255
Hesse, Claudia 64
Hesselmann, Nico 54
Hets, Julian 378
Hetzelt, Nora 360
Heuel, Ralf 88, 140, 152, 179, 207, 287, 294, 322
Heuer, Steffan 417
Heumann, Wolf 106, 253
Heuser, Kai 176
Heuss, Caspar 163, 230, 428
Heyen, Thomas 178, 316
Heygster, Wiebke 344
Hicks, Johannes 312, 325, 447
Hilberg, Hauke 324
Hilbert, Sebastian 337
Hilchen, David von 255, 299
Hille, Veikko 307
Hillreiner, Eva 259, 392
Hilmes, Barbara 243
Hinterreither, Beate 290, 347
Hinze, Haika 195
Hirsing, Juliana 120
Hlavac, Ivo 424
Hochberg, Mortimer 212
Hoebel, Rüdiger 428
Hoefflin, Bernd T. 174
Hoefling, Prof. Karin 225
Hoelzl, Joe 223
Hoenmanns, Christine 384
Hoff, Arndt von 140
Hoffeins, Nicole 427
Hoffmann, Cathrin 226
Hoffmann, Enite 263, 393, 405
Hoffmann, Florian 212, 351
Hoffmann, Roland 429
Hoffmann, Tobias 332
Hoffmeister, Jan 128, 316
Hofmann, Alexander 349
Hofmann, Eric 346
Hohmann, Till 226, 234
Höhn, Anna 350
Höhne, Frank 263
Hohns, Indra 287
Holden, Eric 116
Hollander, Ton 320
Holm, Timm 445
Holtz, Julia 257
Holtz, Julia-Christin 417
Holzenkamp, Nicole 213, 342, 351
Hönemann, Hans-Ulrich 240, 321
Hoppe, Jessica 295, 308
Höppler, Isabell 203
Hornich, Grit 208
Horsley, Roby 64
Hörstermann, Mark 443
Horstmann, Tjarko 150, 333
Hose, Frank 100
Hsu, Jerry 398

Hube, Larissa 219
Huber, Karoline 357
Huber, Samuel 212
Huber, Stefanie 201, 231
Huber, Stephan 196
Hucke, Vivien 217
Hückelkamp, Alina 345
Hucker, Florian 54
Hudelmaier, Götz 231
Hufgard, Christina 188
Hugendubel, Benedikt 331
Hunfeld, Reiner 360
Hunger, Reinhard 164
Hünlein, Michaela 318
Hupertz, Christian 324
Huppertz, Jankel 182
Huschk, Roland 417
Huschka, Martina 304
Huser, Matthias 231
Hüskes, Nina 199
Huth, Thorsten 359
Huthmann, Rabea 288, 306
Hy, Zhoi 257

I

Ibe, Franziska 382
Illenberger, Sarah 110
Inoguchi, Norimichi 313
Inselmann, Albertina 425
Irmer, Erik 399
Isabettini, Ingo 325
Isernhagen, Carsten 207
Ising, Tom 170
Isken, Marc 447
Isolini, Emma 369, 390
Israng, Nicole 275
Isterling, Jan 447
Itter, Martin 326

J

Jachmann, Lina 386
Jacob, Benedict 330
Jacob, Ralf 401
Jacobs, Gregory 295
Jacobs, Michael 180, 297
Jacobsen, Claus 293
Jacoby, Martina 259, 392
Jacoby, Peter 392
Jaedicke, Nils 251
Jaeger, Carsten 329
Jaeger, Markus 298
Jaeger, Michael 332
Jäger, Maurice 363
Jägermann, Marc 344
Jaggy, Alexander 162
Jahn, Joerg 424
Jähnert, Robert 156, 208
Jahns, Nina 292
Jakob, Marie-Louise 286, 325
Jakob, Uwe 177, 335, 337f., 354
Jakubowski, Marc 372
Janes, Tamara 369, 390
Janik, Adelgund 251
Janke, Michael 64
Jans, Joffrey 217
Jansen, Imke 192
Jansen, Ruth 327
Janus, Claudia 320
Jaquier, Marielle 182
Järvinen, Saara 352
Jäschke, Markus 206
Jedam, Robert 223
Jensen, Anders-Sundt 174, 212, 243, 281, 292, 310, 319, 323
Jerez, Sebastian 64
Jeutter, Andreas 292, 310
Jochum, Armin 46, 224, 237, 278, 281, 357, 361, 425, 450
Johannsen, Leif 96
John, Felix 186
John, Tim 271
Johne, Michael 234
Johnke, Sonja 346
Johnson Heade, Martin 64
Jonas, Constantijn 330

Jonker, Joris 277
Jonsdottier, Thordis 422
Joode, Rachel de 64
Joop, Wolfgang 446
Joosten, Silke 317, 356
Joppen, Jürgen 140
Jordan, Chris 64
Jorrot, Marjorie 315
Jung, Eva 134
Jung, Fabian 175
Jung, Teresa 72, 100
Jungclaus, Annika 426
Jungo, Isabella 369, 390
Junius, Hans-Peter 335
Jurgeit, Christina 218
Jurijczuk, Ines 224, 237
Jurkat, Alex 241
Jurkat, Alexander 292

K

Kabisch, Jörn 399
Kaehler, Maik 94, 158, 365
Kahl, Julia 367
Kainz, Sebastian 347
Kaiser, Stefan 227
Kaloff, Constantin 247
Kalous, Dr. Angela 314
Kamber, Martin 390
Kammerer, Lukas 345
Kamp, David 218
Kamp, Sebastian 175
Kanzler, Tino 330
Karpinski, Detmar 205
Kartes, Dirk 332
Kartsolis, Thomas 266f., 395ff., 408–411
Kaselow, Kirsten 377, 379
Käßhöfer, Christina 182
Kastner-Linke, Susi 110, 136
Kate, Alexander 96, 180
Kaufmann, Siegfried 349
Kaussen, Willy 150, 333
Käutner, Christian 324
Keeve, André 308
Kehl, Fedja 294
Kelhetter, Anne 330
Keller, Christina 64, 291
Keller, Jonas 425
Kellerer, Stefan 205
Kellner, Amy 398
Kellner, Lars 177
Kemnitzer, Johannes 421
Kencana, Rain 54
Kerkow, Alexander 218
Kermici, Rene 343
Kerner, Diether 247
Kernspeckt, Björn 443
Kersten, Martina 249
Ketterl, Dr. Hans-Peter 94
Keuntje, Hartwig 247
Kieck, Susanne 430, 443
Kieneke, Veronika 297
Kienle, Andreas 289
Kienzle, Christoph 225
Kiesel, Andreas 293
Kiesl, Thomas 96
Kießling, Daniel 449
Kießling, Martin 332
Kiesswetter, Jan 367
Kievenheim, Konstanze 178, 316
Kiklas, Katharina 298
Killinger, Andrea 220
Kim, Sandy 398
Kinczli, Veronika 251
Kindel, Ralph 272
Kindermann, Michael 231
Kircher, Lukas 366
Kircher, Rebecca 54
Kirchhofer, Tobias 219, 343
Kirchhoff, Frank 231
Kirchhoff, Peter 106, 253
Kirchner, Katja 106
Kirmse, Ulrike 256
Kirner, Fabian 136
Kirsamer, Philipp 54
Kirschner, Tanja 308
Kisser, Thomas 136
Kittel, Marc 353
Kittel, Michael 46
Kittelberger, Dirk 310

Kitzing, Florian 296
Klaar, Jens 226
Klaas, Julia 205
Kladiva, Daniel 231
Klar, Reto 402
Kleebinder, Hans-Peter 136
Kleffer, Elisabeth 208
Klein, Claudia 226
Klein, Jörg 251
Klein, Kalle 331
Klein, Kristina 339
Klein, Magdalena 449
Kleine, Michael 208, 222, 344
Kleinhans, Ole 340
Kleist, Reinhard 397
Klemp, Ute 78
Klenke, Ulrich 304
Klessig, Daniel 54
Klever, Alexandra 223
Klimm, Sven 247
Klingenfuß, Monika 154
Klöckner, Hermann 228
Klohk, Sven 208
Klonek, Roman 392
Klopp, Jürgen 248
Klotzek, Timm 170, 263, 393, 405
Klubert, Christa 287
Klug, Gereon 352, 388
Knauer, Holger 152
Knaup, Andi 330
Kniess, Helge 448
Knipping, Chris 295, 308
Knipprath, Martin 305, 317
Knoblich, Steffen 158
Knobloch, Daniel 293
Knopp, Jan 377
Knüwer, Thomas 84
Koch, Corinna 399
Koch, Hans-Jürgen 406
Koch, Heidi 406
Koch, Julia 154
Koch, Valerie 289
Köditz, Marco 324
Koenen, Stefan 163
Koester, Till 360, 441
Köhler, Mathias 335, 354
Kohls, Kirsten 205
Kohtz, Oliver 449
Kolaja, Dieter 205
Kolle, Stefan 156, 208, 222, 239f., 313, 321, 352, 432
Kollender, Johannes 196
Koller, Matthias 274
Kollmann, Katja 146, 193f., 260f., 268, 412–416
Komma-Pöllath, Thilo 417
Köpf, Kai 174
Korb, Mario 344
Korbes, Christian 154
Korn, Lothar 328, 442
Korte, David 274
Körte, Julia 292
Korten, Karola 110
Kortlepel, Joachim 425
Koselj, Vesna 249
Kossatz, Oliver 213
Kostrzynski, Manuel 263, 393, 405
Kottowski, Julia 315
Kousidonis, Caroline 189, 241
Kovats, Stephen 118
Koyama, Joji aka Woof Wan-Bau 100
Kozok, Hartmut 293
Kraack, Heinke 150
Kraatz, Wolfgang 372
Kraft, Stefan 322
Krahne, Tina 226
Kramer, Johan 243
Kramer, Stephanie 158
Kramer, Ulrike 240, 321
Krannich, Ingmar 383
Kraus, Kerstin 286
Kraus, Sabine 225
Krause, Robert 54, 311, 314, 331, 430
Krause, Stephan 182
Krauss, Sandro 54
Krauße, Vera 54
Krawinkel, Sebastian 64
Kray, Oliver 136
Krebs, Annette 213
Krechting, Lisa 236
Kreft, Susanne 286
Kreil, Dietmar 347
Krejci, Martin 72

Kremer, Markus 178, 316
Kremer, Tim 64, 203
Kremser, Thorsten 293
Krenn, Martina 347
Kretzschmar, Josch 140, 324
Kreyenfeld, Susanne 243
Krieg, Josef 234, 382
Kriesche, Birgit 274
Krietsch, Michaela 220
Krink, Tim 205, 431
Kriwat, Jakob 178
Kromka, Jan 289
Kronast, Franziska 170
Kronemeyer, Nora 250
Kroul, Wolfgang 276
Krtsch, Stephan 329
Kruchten, Niklas 110, 136, 442
Krude, Sona 150
Krug, Hermann 344
Krug, Reinhard 222
Krüger, Judith 293
Krüger, Mike 237
Krüger, Niels 291
Krüger, Nina 237
Krugsperger, Juergen 255, 277
Krumpel, Philipp 290
Kruse, Justin 217
Kruse, Tobias 64
Kubach, Stefan 316
Kubelke, Till 295
Kubitza, Anna 386
Kucera, Stepan 72
Kuczmierczyk, Damian 178
Kueckner, Christoph 158
Kühn, Micha 281
Kuhnt, Ulrich 236
Kukereit, Anne 297
Kundt, Mirjam 72, 100, 164
Kunsemüller, Caroline 305
Kunze, Ben 196
Kunzendorf, Chris 289
Küpker, Christian 394
Kuppi, Jens 444
Kurfiss, Sascha 212f., 351
Kurth, Sandra 340
Kurtz, Marilen 317
Kusmin, Valentina 337
Küster, Sven 339, 345
Kut, Alex 231
Kutschinski, Michael 177, 335, 337f., 354
Kweli, Talib 291

L

L'Hoest, Johannes 110
Labonde, Thomas 128
Lacic, Dinko 217
Lackner, Victoria 450
Lacy, Jim 324
Lagé, Christian 250
Lago, Sonia 249, 291
Lagodny, Silke 312, 447
Lakenmacher, Florian 174, 322
Lamberti, René 339, 345
Lamken, Mathias 442
Lammer, Dominik 346, 426
Lamp, Tobias 217
Lampe, Andreas 242
Landon, Justin 156, 208
Landon, Nick 148
Landquist, Martin 100
Langanki, Thomas 166
Langdon, John 110
Lange, Björn A. 351
Lange, Björn-Arne 213
Lange, Jürgen 54
Lange, Sascha 324
Langgartner, Lorenz 187, 359
Langhammer, Petra 64
Langkamp, Tobias 297
Langston, Henry 398
Laser, Kathrin 339
Laß, Torsten 195
Lauer, Axel 170
Lauer, Stefan 262, 398
Laufmann, Peter 259
Lebens, Dr. Uwe 330
Lechner, Bianca 358
Ledermann, Per 110, 219
Leeuwen, Dennis van 150

Leger, Rolf 84, 239f., 321, 432
Lehment, Tobias 110
Lehnert, Sebastian 251
Lehr, Susanne 346
Lehrenfeld, Sandra 204
Leibert, Felix 54
Leihner, Christian 165, 295
Leinweber, David 237, 450
Leiser, Steffen 124
Lekfeldt, Thomas 300
Lembke, Jens 339
Lemcke, Felix 431
Lemm, Philipp 384
Lemmer, Christian 422
Lengauer, Martin 370
Lengemann, Martin 402
Lenz, Alexander 182
Lenz, Markus 257
Lenz, Stefan 54
Lenze, Malte 449
Leroux, Benoît 116
Lettmann, Arnd 295
Leube, Jan 235, 448
Leutner, Maria 64
Leutwyler, Henry 412
Levine, Chris 413
Levine, Tom 366
Leyck, Axel 247
Li, Henry 449
Lidtke, Armand 296
Liebenstein, Johannes von 291
Liebrecht, Torben 293
Liedtke, Berit 367
Ließ, Kristin 156, 208
Lima, Gito 277
Linde, Nicolas 241
Lindemann, Arno 128, 140, 178, 316
Lindenberg, Antje 106
Lindner, Thomas 170, 263, 393, 405
Linscheid, Edgar 64, 163
Liow, Anthony 332
Lipah, Roman 120
Lipp, Alexander 110
Lippert, Johannes 150
Lippert, Oliver 307
Lippoth, Achim 223
Liske, Lukas 276, 350
Littlewood, Tom 262, 398
Liu, Jane 449
Loesslein, Roland 182
Löffel, Philip 291
Löffler, Franziska 46
Lohmann, Marius 241, 243
Löhr, David 339
Lohrberg, Stefan 272
Loibl, Sandra 154
Loick, Marcus 425
Lony, Pieter 231
Lopau, Franziska 383
Lord, Myles 100, 164, 216, 328
Lorenz, Peter 64
Lösch, Daniela 276
Loskill, Sven 46
Lossenko, Aleksandr 353
Lotter, Kathrina 417
Lotz, Regner 204, 324
Lowy, Benjamin 414
Lübke, Kay 235
Lück, Dennis 424
Lücker, Dorte 339
Luckmann, Anke 223
Ludwig, Florian 84, 156, 432
Luebcke, Jan 152
Luehrsen, Matthias 361
Luglio, Bruno 96, 312
Lühe, Martin 84
Lukas, Bernhard 128, 178, 316
Lünzmann, Yvonne 272
Lutz, Michael 398
Lützenkirchen, Ulrich 332
Lux, Björn 144

M

Maasch, Cécile 307
Maass, Rainer 298
Mach, Matthias 152
Mack, Bianca 150
Mack, Manuel 231
Mackens, Michael 128

Mackowiak, Joshua 306
Mäder, Christoph 86
Maercks, Matthias 291
Magalhaes, Ana 192
Magnet, Martin 282
Maier-Schönung, Eva 64
Maier, Anna 250
Maier, Kai 257
Malasek E. C., Filip 148
Maldonado, Andres 218
Mall, Andi 140
Malotki, Katharina de 326
Maltzen, Ralf 417
Mancinone, Denise 154
Manke, Michael 136
Manzo, Marco 356
Marcelino, Nuno 293
Mardon, Alexis 249, 291
Marecki, Pia 175, 326
Märgens, Marie 422
Maric, Damir 174, 212, 243, 281, 292, 310, 319
Markgraf, Dennis 182
Markson, Ted 343
Marquardt, Suse 241
Marquardt, Uwe 448
Marschall, Simon 293
Marsenger, Katharina 354
Martelli, Filippo 64
Martens, André 342
Martens, Natalie 288
Martin, Peter 421
Martini, Sascha 339
Marx, Sebastian 328
Maser, Andreas 175, 353
Matthiesen, Patrick 96
Mattar, Gabriel 312
Mattes, Franziska 140, 152, 294
Matthias, Michael 208
Matthiass, Michael 449
Matthys, Res 64, 203
Matusche, Esther 265ff., 395ff., 408–411
Matz, Peter 417
Mauriot, Walter 325
Maus, Sebastian 219, 343
Mausolf, Tobias 78, 344
May, Dennis 182
Mayer, Sigi 376
Mayet, Frederik 202
Meckseper, Josephine 396
Meegen, Meike van 86, 292
Mehn, Sascha 312
Mehra, Kanak 331
Meier, Dr. Stephan 225
Meier, Rolf 390
Meimeth, Nani Miliane 64
Meinhardt, Alexander 346
Meinhof, Ben 174
Meiré, Mike 391
Meister, Julia 170
Meister, Roman 162
Meligi, Alexander El 110
Melle, Hendrick 434
Melle, Uta 434
Meneses von Arnim, Bastian 64, 203
Mengele, Andreas 328
Menk, Harald 264, 407
Mennemann, Tom 287
Mensching, Dennis 316
Menzel, Ekkehard 315
Meo, Luca de 286f., 325, 447
Merget, Sebastian 96
Merkel, Mirko 146, 194, 261, 414, 416
Merkel, Moritz 216
Mertens, Karlo 380
Mertens, Kevin 399
Merz, Max 64
Merz, Saskia 432
Mette, Holger 64
Mettler, Michel 371
Metz, Katja 308
Metzdorf, Achim 317
Metzler, Christina 346
Meusel, Matthias 64
Meyer, Christian 361
Meyer, Hans-Jürgen 78
Meyer, Helmut 188, 350
Meyer, Katharina 54
Meyer, Mikis 86, 240, 321
Meyer, Thomas 64
Michaelis, Klaus-Martin 335, 337f.
Michelbach, Thomas 249
Michels, Alexandra 417

Micka, Boris 199
Mietzner, Dorle 289
Migeod, Philipp 291
Miki 291
Milde, Alexander 78
Mildner, Florian 54
Milic, Milena 332
Miller, Robert 332
Millies, Maximilian 241, 243
Missing, David 189, 241, 315
Mittermüller, Christoph 120
Mittermüller, Matthias 120
Möbius, Susanne 222
Moder, Mathis 339, 345
Mödl, Ludwig 202
Modschiedler, Jessica 353
Moerstedt, Maud 247
Möhler, Christian 88
Mohnhaupt, Peter 272
Mohr, Benjamin 164
Moitroux, Maurice 357
Mokreva, Savina 94, 158
Molina, Julia 341
Molinari, Patrick 196
Moll, Phoebe 206
Moll, Verena 426
Möller, Annmarie 289
Möller, Beatrice 344
Möller, Cosimo 348
Möller, Veit 249, 291
Molter, Martin 338
Mommertz, Christian 206, 305, 317, 350
Moniri, Erfan 344
Mönnich, Ulrike 316
Monshausen, Till 238
Montag, Alexa 54
Moorstedt, Tobias 259
Morgan, Andrew 249, 291
Morgenthal, Tatjana 239f.
Morisse, Torsten 429
Moritz, Stephan 327
Moser, Sarah 245
Mously, David 189, 241, 315, 319, 358
Mrozyk, Anna 331
Mrugalla, Markus 365
Ms. zum Hingst 288
Muck, Mathias 96
Muck, Matthias 219, 343
Mücke, Susan 402
Mückner, Stefan 377
Muehl, Georg 218
Mugrauer, Emanuel 192, 239f., 321
Mühe, Andreas 401
Mühl, Georg 361
Mühlan, Nico 134
Muhr, Magnus 267
Müller-Buchner, Roland 218
Müller-Dannhausen, Henning 46, 201, 295
Müller-Rossbach, Laura 72
Müller-Stoy, Jasmin 146, 193f., 260f., 268, 412–416
Müller, Andine 399
Müller, Felix 174, 322, 400
Müller, Florian 384
Müller, Henrik von 239f.
Müller, Hermann J. 417
Müller, Karlheinz 364
Müller, Katharina 424
Müller, Knud Alex 46
Müller, Marco 234
Müller, Markus 243, 338
Müller, Matthias M. 78, 132, 248, 344
Müller, Ricardo 291
Müller, Sebastian 217
Münch, Daniel 249
Mundhenke, Justin 212
Münter, Niels 86, 124, 351
Muri, Melanie 424
Murschenhofer, Herbert 333

N

Nabbelfeld, Thomas 292
Nagel, Alexander 348
Nagel, Susanne 288
Nagel, Sven 442
Näher, Peer 331
Nann, Christoph 94, 158, 365
Nardini, Gustavo 288

Natterer, Jonas 263, 393, 405
Naupert, Mareen 249
Navab-Pour, Mitra 196
Negwer, Felix 192, 256, 387
Nessler, Daniel 162
Netzberger, Matthias 132
Neugebauer, Björn 340
Neugebauer, Franziska 227
Neumann-Semerow, Christian 309
Neumann, Bernhard 196, 419
Neumann, Sebastian 64, 203
Neumann, Tobias 422
Nguyen, Duc 241
Nicklas, Felix 262, 398
Niederprüm, Dario 64
Niemann, Christoph 265, 410
Niemann, Lennard 423
Nieratko, Chris 398
Niessen, Sandra 247
Nitsch, Josefine 140
Nitzsche, Thomas 140
Nobereit, Sven 342
Nocken, Klaas 46, 213
Nöding, Wolf 110
Noël, Rémi 116
Noerbaeck, Lasse 118
Nöldge, Juri 64
Nolting, Nadine 432
Norden, Holger 247
Norin, Tommy 218
Norvilas, Alexander 46
Notari, Guido 72
Nothegger, Christopher 353
Notter, Heiko 140
Novotny, Rudolf 365
Nüchter, Timm 343
Nugent, Lana 46
Nuneva, Adriana 364
Nünlist, Cornelia 201, 231, 451
Nuntawat, Golf 201
Nygard, Mattias 64
Nykamp, Meike 272
Nylund, Robert 322

O

Oberhäuser, Martin 196, 377
Obermann, Marco 360, 441
Ochsenhirt, Julia 166, 433
Oeding, Katrin 192, 256, 352, 388
Oehrlich, Holger 223
Oelckers, Jan-Hendrik 296
Oevermann, Jascha 178, 316
Oghanna, Ayman 398
Ohanian, Michael 174, 176, 292, 310
Ohm, Frithjof 54
Okun, Michael 150, 253
Okusluk, Jan 332
Olibet, Eva 399
Olowinsky, Max 322
Olowinsky, Maximilian 174
Olschewski, Felicitas 291
Oltmann, Claudia 297
Oomkens, Sabine 305
Oort, Martijn 223
Oppel, Tanja 337
Oppmann, Simon 276
Orejón, Andrés 178
Ormantji, Derya 224
Orpin, Alan 208
Oßwald, Anke 54
Ostendorf, Hubert 383
Ostermeier, Thomas 249
Ostertag-Henning, Michael 418
Ott, Isabel 64
Ott, Paul 64
Ott, Vivien 328
Otten, Torben 224, 237, 278
Ottensmeier, Andreas 253
Otterbach, Carolin 344
Ouchiian, Djik 179
Overbeeke, Aernout 278
Overmeyer, Niels 333
Ozannat, Jean 116
Özil, Mesut 237

P

Padberg, Eva 237
Pagonis, Claudio 448
Pal, Sabina 350
Palfi, Michael 247
Palmer, Oliver 154, 187, 282
Pander, Dominik 251
Panek, Sabine 140
Paneth, Miriam 46, 306
Panier, Carolin 96
Panier, Florian 46, 425
Panitz, Igor 223
Pantel, Maxie 196
Pappas, Christian 110
Paredes, Leonardo 346
Pasini, Luca 64
Passarge, Christian 361
Paster, Thomas 375
Patalas, Igor 154
Patterson, Colin 289
Patzek, Sabrina 237
Patzner, Henning 289
Patzschke, Reinhard 322
Paul, Florian 46
Paulat, Birgit 307
Paulis, Giovanni de 170
Paulus, Stefanie 289
Peger, Sonja 272
Pense, Jacques 174, 292, 310
Pensel, Fabian 307
Pentzin, Thilo 257
Perez, Fernando 162
Perriard, Samuel 336
Peschman, Konrad 208
Peter, Marco 424
Peters, Anke 64
Peters, Connie 427
Peters, Jan-Eric 269
Petersen, Anke 425
Petersen, Sascha 84, 313
Pettit, Justin 332
Petzenhauser, Christoph 100
Petzold, Albert 186, 255, 299
Petzold, Andreas 170, 263, 393, 405
Pfannkuche, Milena 152, 322
Pfau, Jens 86, 124, 212, 323, 351
Pfeifer, David 405
Pfeifer, Gianna 118
Pfeiffer, Marcus 304, 337, 350
Pfister, Thom 369, 390
Philipp, Simon Jasper 110, 236
Pia, Sarah 368
Pichler, Regina 293
Pickmann, Anatolij 235
Pieracci, Daniel 295
Pietras, Joakim 328
Pietri, Julien 339
Pietruska, Jürgen 228
Pietsch, Daniel 202, 368
Pignatti, Michele 148
Pina, João 407
Piquel, Max 199
Pita, Damjan 86, 212
Plambeck, Peter 425
Plank, Leo 330
Plass, Johannes 196, 418
Plewa, Szymon 64
Plogstedt, Patrick 150
Ploj, Michael 218
Plückhahn, Michael 356
Pluskwa, André 398
Poguntke, Arndt 296
Pohlmann, Tino 54
Polcar, Ales 222
Polster, Hans-Jürgen 402
Pölzelbauer, Joseph 387
Pölzelbauer, Simone 387
Pontoriero, Anja 343
Popke, Oliver 134
Popp, Julius 165
Porst, Jennifer 338
Porst, Sören 237, 450
Poschadel, Isabell 323
Poschauko, Martin 191
Poschauko, Thomas 191
Poser, Ralph 350
Potthoff, Kay 213
Poulionakis, Andreas 64, 203
Prange, Oliver 227
Prescher, Sandra 298

Press, Hendryk 247
Presse, Steffen 342
Preuss, Matthias 296
Preuss, Michael 445
Preuss, Nina 445
Pross, Martin 54, 163, 186, 230, 234f., 255, 277, 299, 311, 314, 331, 382, 385f., 428, 430, 443
Pufe, Stefan 429
Puri, Nina 344
Putz, Frederike 423

Q

Quell, Stephen 216, 328
Quenzler, Tanja 417
Quester, Peter 240

R

Rädeker, Jochen 166, 433
Rahn, Nina 425
Raith, Sarah 330
Rakete, Jim 402
Ramert, Chan-Young 64, 203
Ramm, Oliver 84, 226
Randenborgh, Jan van 295
Rank, Alex 223
Rashidi, Alireza 353
Rasp, Markus 202, 259, 368, 392
Rathmann, Sabine 335
Rating, Fritz 204, 324
Raufmann, Henrik 293
Rebele, Regina 182
Rebmann, Mathias 163, 230, 234, 255, 299, 382, 428, 443
Rechtacek, Wulf 235
Reddig, Finn 293
Redfield, Carol 298
Redlin, Peter 108
Reeb, Sacha 204, 324
Regner, Lucio 249
Rehde, Malte 213
Rehm, Alexander 359
Reichartz, Moritz 118
Reidies, Daniela 189
Reimann, Christian 239f., 321
Reinartz, Philip 372
Reins, Armin 294
Reip, Lennart 344
Reisner, Maren 327
Reiß, Sandra 343
Reisser, Mirko 110
Reissinger, Michael 150
Reitz, Rico 332
Reitz, Stefan 226
Rekowski, Mathis 447
Remmers, Christopher 341
Remmers, Jasmin 287
Rendel, Thomas 243
Rendtel, Kirsten 54, 311
Renken, Folke 54
Renne, Max 124
Renner, Katja 64
Rentz, Manuel 448
Requardt, René 218
Rescheleit, Luca 281, 425
Ressel, Elena 348
Retzlek, Biljana 96
Reuke, Marco 205
Rexhausen, Jan 46, 288, 306
Rhee, Robert 150
Richter, Andreas 262, 398
Richter, Daniel 396
Richter, Maik 72, 100, 164
Ricken, Frank 328
Riebenstahl, Dennis 140
Riech, Frederic 360
Riedel, Bernd 258, 403f.
Rieger, Christian 78
Rieke, Christopher 217
Riemer, Carmen 319
Riemland, Kai 196
Riese, Kai-H. 230
Ringena, Jens 320
Ringwald, Benjamin 338
Rinne, Kolja 240, 321

Ritter, Lorenz 208, 313
Ritterhoff, Sven 377, 379
Robert, Henning 212
Robert, Henning 86, 245
Robert, Sandra 187, 359
Rocketson, Dr. Gerald 209
Rockmann, Norman 345
Röder, Julian 64
Rodriguez, Manuel 247
Roeder, Gina P. 304
Roeingh, Christian 218
Röffen, Kai 136
Roggenkamp, Stefan 386
Rohd, Okka 417
Rohde, Armin 237
Rohden, Janna 383
Rohlfing, Maike 170
Röhm, Anne-Katrin 86, 124
Röhr, Carsten 419
Rolf, Oliver 234
Rollfing, Sina 253
Romanti, Lars 182
Romanus, Carola 276
Römer, Alex 308
Römmelt, Peter 276
Rompis, Felix 338
Ronacher, Nikolaus 451
Ronzheimer, Hanna 348
Rook, Michael 327
Röppischer, Franz 154
Rösch, Mathias 424
Rosendahl, Jens 237
Rosengart, Yves 281, 292
Roser, Fabian 339
Rössler, Markus 359
Rosten, Jesse 46
Roth, Anna Christiane 287
Rothenbücher, Jasmin 326
Rother, Philip 189, 241
Rothhaar, Jörg 223
Rothhaas, Julia 170
Rötterink, Alexander 226
Roy, Felix 163
Rübel, Lisa 326
Ruckstuhl, Liana 252
Ruddigkeit, Raban 118
Ruewe, Dina 306
Rüffer, Stefan 150
Ruh, Ulrike 207
Rullmann, Torsten 422
Ruprecht, Tobias 341
Rüsenberg, Nils 88, 179
Rüssmann, Peter 180
Rüssmann, Rudolf 295
Russomanno, Salvatore 218
Rutenbeck, Henrik 277
Ruth, Benjamin 262, 398
Rütten, Jan 110, 136, 236

S

Sabel, Thomas 274
Saborny, Rainer 249, 345
Sacchetti, Mateo 163
Sachse, Janne 220
Sack, Janine 399
Sageb, Sabine 441
Sahin, Bella 64
Sahler, Frank 72, 100, 164
Salam, Kai Abd-EL 72
Samsel, Martin 162
Sanje, Marijo 187, 359
Sarac, Emanuela 376
Sarnes, Malte 150
Sarreiter, Benedikt 170
Sauer, Melanie 251
Sauer, Tobias 208
Sauter, Joachim 228
Sauvigny, Simone 150
Savage, Alistair 398
saxler, margarethe 254
Schabenberger, Stefan 353
Schachtebeck, Niklas 361
Schäfer, Alexa 322
Schallberger, Tom 46
Schaller, Rainer 293
Schamber, Sandra 64
Scharney, Christine 443
Schatzmann, Simon 369, 390
Scheer, Stefan 384

Scheffer, Ramón 307
Scheinhardt, Matthes 293
Scheiwe, Bianca 305
Schelkmann, Ann-Katrin 64
Scheller, Prof. Christoph M. 175, 326
Schenk, Marty 54
Schepker, Boris 293
Scherer, David 110
Scherf, Alexander 343
Scheuring, Thomas 357
Schiebel-Schlosser, Dr. Gabriele 298
Schill, Alex 282, 289, 359
Schill, Alexander 94, 120, 154, 158, 187, 220, 348, 365
Schilling, Gert 223
Schils, Raphael 361
Schimmer, Florian 110
Schimming, Lars 385
Schindler, Nicolas 54
Schipper, Sebastian 241, 327
Schlabritz, Frank 241
Schleberger, Stephan 356
Schlegel, Andy 189
Schlichte, Nadine 427
Schlingmann, Julia 118
Schlosser, Sebastian 318
Schlossmacher, Kay 246
Schlünder, Antje 170, 263, 393, 405
Schlüter, Jan 257
Schmalfuß, Leander 287
Schmalriede, Philipp 322
Schmelling, Michael 268
Schmerberg-Davila, Greta 64
Schmerberg, Ralf 64
Schmid, Alex 170
Schmid, Alexander 313
Schmid, Catrin 314
Schmid, Martin 293
Schmidlechner, Andreas 290
Schmidt-Burgk, Nikolas 54
Schmidt-Fitzner, Nicolas 86, 124
Schmidt-Friderichs, Bertram 191
Schmidt-Friderichs, Karin 191, 294, 373
Schmidt, Axel 150
Schmidt, Caroline 239f., 321
Schmidt, Christian 441
Schmidt, Christoph 380
Schmidt, Dirk 266f., 395ff., 408–411
Schmidt, Dr. Ulf 177, 337
Schmidt, Eva Verena 234, 382
Schmidt, Heiko 222
Schmidt, Jochen 174, 243, 292
Schmidt, Markus 340
Schmidt, Matthias 353
Schmidt, Michael 163, 230, 428
Schmidt, Paul 339, 345
Schmidt, Rainer 188
Schmidt, Sebastian 327
Schmidt, Sönke 247
Schmidt, Stefan 249, 291
Schmiede, Sven 150, 340
Schmiegel, Thomas 322
Schmitt, Katharina 213
Schmitz, Karsten 225
Schmitz, Tina 225
Schmuck, Ragnar 412
Schnabel, Michael 84
Schnabel, Tim 365
Schneider, Amélie 263, 393, 405
Schneider, Claudia 354
Schneider, Donald 264, 300, 406f., 439f., 446
Schneider, Moritz 422
Schneider, Nico 338
Schneider, Sophie 296
Schneider, Wolf 255, 277, 386
Schneider, Wolfgang 189, 206, 241, 296, 307, 317, 320, 356, 358
Schnell, Jana 399
Schnell, Sebastian 237, 357
Schneppe, Svenja 387
Schobel, Marcel 199
Schober, Maik 420
Schoeffler, Eric 64, 182, 203, 290, 312, 347, 447
Schoffro, Karina 377
Scholl, Norman 292, 310
Scholz, Erik 291
Scholz, Franziska 182
Scholz, Jan-Hendrik 86, 124, 212, 245
Scholz, Tim 425
Schömbs, Stefan 140
Schön, Martin 178

Schöningh, Mathias 322
Schonlau, Julia 236
Schönmann, Sven 140
Schöpf, Michael 385
Schöpflin, Mathias 307
Schori, Kurt 390
Schramm, Florian 163, 174, 230, 234, 255, 443
Schramm, Susan 249
Schrayer, Grover 64
Schreiber, Nicole 344
Schrickel, Rolf 427
Schriewer, Andreas 94, 179
Schrills, Christian 330
Schröder, Jens Erasmus 247
Schröder, Linn 64
Schröder, Margit 295
Schröder, Niels 195
Schröder, Ralf 255
Schröder, Wolfgang 346
Schroeder, Ralf 386
Schroeder, Toby 361
Schroeder, Vera 170
Schroer, Patrick 96
Schronen, Susann 426
Schröter, Moritz von 220
Schubert, Annabel 213
Schubert, Carsten 328
Schubert, Johannes 213
Schueßling, Heiko 247
Schuetz, Doerte 386
Schuhmann, Steffen 250
Schüle, Andreas 314
Schulte, Andreas 366
Schulte, Josef-Konstantin 54
Schulte, Stefan 64, 203, 286, 325
Schultheis, Kerstin 350
Schultheiss, Dr. Björn 216
Schultze, Arne 244, 324
Schulwitz, Silja 213
Schulz, Felix 156, 208
Schulz, Hauke 293
Schulz, Inken 84
Schulz, Jan 338
Schulz, Matthias 78, 132
Schumacher, Angelika 110, 219
Schumacher, Benito 54, 331
Schumacher, Hajo 402
Schupke, Dorota 427
Schupp, Cedric 359
Schupp, Jonathan 323
Schuppach, Uli 230, 430
Schürg, Carsten 354
Schüssler, Daniel 244
Schuster, Stefan 54
Schuster, Stephen 205
Schütte, Stefan 359
Schütte, Thomas 396
Schwab, Matt 197
Schwab, Steffen 247
Schwager, David 422
Schwalme, Florian 299, 382, 428
Schwarz, Esther 386
Schwarz, Jochen 124, 323
Schwarz, Thomas 332
Schwarz, Timo 178, 248
Schwarze, Markus 293
Schwarze, Ralf 293
Schwarzhoff, Frank 177
Schwarzwald, Oliver 84
Schweder, Hendrik 72, 100
Schweers, Malte 196
Schweinzer, Daniel 276, 304, 337, 350
Schweizer, Beat 390
Schwemer, Nils 124, 345
Schwengel, Jens 189
Schwenkert, Liselotte 244
Schwertner, Jan 247
Schwiedrzik, Boris 315
Schwochow, Jan 258, 403f.
Schwochow, Katharina 258
Sciolti, Stefano 136
Sedlanic, Nelly 255, 299
Seebald, Andreas 219
Seebald, Daniel 343
Seeger, Hartmut 286, 325
Seegers, Katrin 234
Seibe, Benjamin 398
Seidel, Kerstin 170
Seife, Helen 189
Seifert, Michael 46
Seiffe, Helen 241
Seil, Tom 216

Seiler, Frank 154
Seitz, Tobias 328
Sendel, Jochen 295
Seriis, Markus de 271
Sevim, Derya 256, 352
Seyedasgari, Siyamak 216, 327
Shapton, Leanne 268
Si, Mark 449
Sibai, Mona 64, 203
Siebenhaar, Liane 86
Siegel, David 228
Siegert, Kay 249
Siepmann, Thomas 272
Sievering, Thorsten 179
Sievers, Petra 226
Sikvolgyi, Veronika 165
Simdon, Anna 294
Simon, Barbara 64
Simon, Philip 293
Simon, Valerie 220
Sinclair, Mike 64
Sinn, Mathias 345
Sirry, Shahir 334
Skerlec, Patrick 217
Skowronek, Sebastian 345
Skudra, John 406
Slavcheva, Ksenia 255, 443
Sluyter, Katja 238
Smetek, Wieslav 195
Smith, Kiki 396
Smith, Randy 148
Snoeck, Pieter 345
Sobek, Corinna 407
Soeffker, Susanne 300
Sohlau, Stefan 311
Sommer, Christian 424
Sommer, Daniel 72
Sommer, Maria 442
Sommer, Matthias 64
Sossidi, Constantin 152
Sottmeier, Katja 337
Soukup, David 128
souziehaas 64
Spading, Jan 257
Spaetgens, Matthias 54, 163, 186, 230, 234f., 255, 277, 299, 311, 314, 331, 382, 385f., 428, 430, 443
Spakowski, Dirk 318, 320
Späthe, Sylvia 72, 100
Specht, Melanie 54, 311
Spengler-Ahrens, Doerte 46, 288, 306
Spiegel, Katrin 244
Spillmann, Martin 355
Spilsbury, Simon 444
Spirat, Alexandra 293
Spitze, Sebastian 150
Spreckley, Sam 118
Spreen, Maik 84, 256, 313, 352
Stabenau, Sébastien 253
Stadtmüller, David 286
Stäheli, Andy 355
Stammen, Simone 293
Stampa, Benedikt 86
Starck, Hans 234
Stark, Hans 312
Stark, Julia 441
Stäuber, Steffen 339
Staudenmayer, Ellen 54
Stauss, Alexander 72
Stauss, Frank 427
Steck, Philip 361
Steffen, Jens 177, 335, 337f.
Steffens, Steffen 431
Stehle, Patrick 365
Stehmann, Ira 202
Steiger, Nina 64
Stein, Jens 54, 314
Stein, Johannes 399
Stein, Melanie 246
Stein, Tatjana 291
Stein, Tom 318
Steinbeck, Birthe 266f., 395ff., 408–411
Steinbrück, Daniel 236
Steineke, Katrin 293
Steiner, Dominique 234
Steiner, Monika 120
Steinert, Alexandra 196
Steinhoff, Marie 192, 256, 352
Steinke, Rouven 417
Steller, Sebastian 317
Stender, Christoph 327
Stephan, Daniela 128
Stephan, Julia 225

Stetefeld, Eva 188
Stiehl, Rodian 344
Stieler, Kathrin 293
Stiller, Mathias 189, 241, 243, 296, 315, 319, 358
Stilling, Anne 450
Stipp, Katharina 258, 403
Stöcker, Ramona 345
Stockmann, Sonja 174, 281
Stoffer, Julia 351
Stoletzky, Judith 257
Stoll, Johannes 382
Stolle, Daniel 64
Stolle, Sandra 170, 263, 393, 405
Stolz, Patricia 54
Stölzl, Philipp 54
Storath, Matthias 72, 100, 164, 276, 338
Störl, Norman 124, 213
Storr, Alexandra 166
Stowasser, Sarah 205
Straccia, Fabio 288
Strahl, Jan 417
Strasser, Dan 182
Strasser, Sebastian 450
Strathus, Tim 120
Stratmann, Gereon 253
Strauss, Daniela 72, 164
Strauss, Oskar 319, 358
Strauss, Peter 165
Strauß, Claudia 349
Strecker, Marion 271
Stricker, Christoph 287
Striegl, Alexander 420
Struck, Marco 293
Strukamp, Christoff 158
Struss, Sonja 356
Struß, Sonja 317
Strutz, Martin 361
Stückl, Christian 202
Stuebane, Tim 286
Stumpe, Florian 328
Sturm, Caroline 64, 203
Sturm, Michael 344
Stüssel, Therese 282
Stuttgart Citizens 181
Suhm, Tobias 86, 324, 331
Summ, Andreas 449
Sundergeld, Dorothea 417
Sundgren, Henrik 328
Sus, Daniel 242
Süß, Alexandra 323
Sutch, Katharina 365
Svechtarov, Nina 239f.
Svegsjö, Elin 249
Svoboda, Paul 387
Swistowski, Johanna 257
Sydow, Pedro 353
tadi-Rock 291

T

Tamschick, Marc 199f.
Tanner, Nora 422
Tappeiner, Marcel 355
Taroux, Philippe 116
Tarsem 292
Tasdan, Filiz 327
Taube, Annika von 394
Tavidde, Frank 338
Tech, Dirk 339
Tehrani, Turan 118
Teichmann, Gwen 324
Teichmueller, Fabian 239f., 321
Teller, Juergen 416
Temelkovski, Ljupcho 64
Tetens, Bettina 441
Teufel, Birte 345
Teuner, Christoph 251
Thaung, Daniel 309
Thedens, Jost 341
Theil, Jens 110
Thesing, Dominik 54
Theuerkauff, Florian 134
Thiel, Christian 337
Thiele, Maria 258
Thiele, Thomas 205, 431
Thielicke, Martin 344
Thielsch, Niko 243
Thiessen, Thomas 224
Thiry, Isabelle 257

Thom, Christiane 175
Thomas, Christopher 202, 266, 368
Tillack, Anja 216
Tiller, Alexander 64
Tiller, Antonio 64
Timmer, Lukas 371
Tischner, Mikel 332
Tolle, Moritz 140
Toneva, Silvana 64
Tonn, Maria-Michaela 386
Tonner, Adrienne 247
Toro, Penélope 257, 417
Trabadelo, Roland 274
Traeger, Susanne 228
Tran, Thanh Vu 64
Trautmann, Dr. Michael 180
Trobitz, Ingrid 166
Trogisch, Andreas 372
Trost, Arne 313
Tscharnke, Nils 163, 382
Tschepe, Rainer 425
Tulinius, Kristina 249
Tulinius, Tomas 249
Tünte, Marius 204
Turner, Jeremy 239f.
Turner, Sebastian 234
Twenhäfel, Heiner 88
Tziopanos, Niko 242

U

Uckert, Silja 174
Uhlaczky, Joana 318
Uihlein, Florian 339
Ulmer, Götz 218, 450
Unger, Jonas 146
Urbanski, Christian 338, 354
Uthmann, Olaf 431

V

Valentin, Alexander 182
Valentyn, Birgit van den 286
Valin, Jessica 72, 100, 164
Vanderbilt, Tom 417
Varga, Nicole 72, 100
Vaske, Hermann 329
Veken, Dominic 84
Velicky, Jan 148
Venn, Martin 383
Vens, Stephan 64
Venus, Uwe 334
Vicente, Rafael 258
Vidler, Muir 398
Viets, Oliver 341
Villing, Andreas 424
Vincent, Anne 116
Vinck, Ole 216, 328
Vocke, Dennis 331
Vogel, Benno 120
Vogel, Christian 118
Vogel, Dr. Stephan 165, 188, 276, 304, 337, 350, 354
Vogel, Jürgen 189
Vogel, Kathrina 345
Vogel, Patrick 163, 299
Vogl, Johannes 54
Vogler, Felix 54
Vogt, Verena 310
Voigt, Gunar 243
Voigt, Steve 308
Volk, Tatjana 182
Völker, Thomas 256, 352
Volkmann, Thomas 150
Volkmer, Stephanie 319
Volleritsch, Andreas 389
Völlmecke, Florian 156
Voss, Eike 278
Voss, Oliver 238
Vossen, Jürgen 328
Voy, Christoph 398
Vukan, Maik 344

W

Waack, Bernhard 212
Waaijenberg, Albert 349
Wache, Frank 144
Wachner, Patrick 421
Wäcker, Klaus 327
Wagner, Alexander 292
Wagner, Andreas 281, 425
Wagner, Frank 251
Wagner, Liane 326
Wagner, Manfred 275
Wagner, Paul 364
Wagner, Reginald 256, 388
Wagner, Stese 308
Wagner, Thimoteus 281, 425
Wagner, Thomas 449
Wagner, Tom 249
Wahl, Christian 54
Walker, Pius 201, 231, 451
Wallmeier, Christian 247
Walter, Dr. Hermann S. 259, 392
Walter, Lukas 64, 246
Walter, Matthias 216, 327
Walter, Simon 249
Walz, Sara 343
Walz, Stefan 96, 110, 219, 343
Wan-Bau, Woof 100
Wandersleben, Maren 158
Wanja, Christoph 175
Warning, Hannelore 187
Warns, Ole 78
Warsosumarto, Dian 290
Wartenberg, Till 178, 316
Warwick, Daniel 331
Waschescio, Jörg 54, 430
Wassel, Patrick 293
Wasserkampf, Frederike 218
Wasserkampf, Max 422
Waterkamp, Hermann 150, 333, 340
Watzke, Axel 250
Webecke, Ingo 237
Weber-Grün, Alexander 327
Weber, Achim 64
Weber, Barbara 225
Weber, Marcel 118
Weber, Marco 338
Weber, Peter 64
Weber, Philipp 186
Weber, Sebstian 361
Weber, Susanne 377, 379
Weber, Timm 287, 322
Weber, Uli 363
Wegehenkel, Christian 331
Wegener, Marcella 344
Wegert, Ulrike 205, 431
Wegmann, Thomas 351
Wehmeyer, Julia 335
Weiche, Sven 163, 186, 299
Weidemann, Julia 345
Weidenfelder, Frank 225
Weinberg, David 258
Weinberger, Karlheinz 398
Weiner, Ann-Katrin 391
Weinsheimer, Silke 170
Weische, Christof 324
Weiss, Marcus 310, 429
Weiß, Samuel 110
Weissenberger, Dr. Lothar 189, 241
Weißflog, Michael 361
Weizenegger, Hermann August 291
Wellnitz, Andreas 146, 193f., 260f., 268, 412ff., 416
Wembacher, Helen 217
Wendt, Marco 120
Wengenroth, Jan 435
Wenhold, Philipp 224, 253, 357
Wenke, Benjamin 46
Wenzel, Amelie 282
Wenzel, Manuel 286, 296, 325
Werne, Rilana von 136
Werth, Marko 240, 321
Westebbe, Mathias 64
Westendorp, Wouter 243
Westermann, Claudia 86
Wetzel, Felix 175
Weyer, Kai 290
Wichmann, Dr. Dominik 265ff., 395ff., 408–411
Widmer, Johannes 208
Wiechell, Lennart 108

Wieg, Benjamin 118
Wiegand, Nicole 343
Wieland, Alex 187
Wiemer, Nina 419
Wieners, Ralf 179
Wienstroth, Lutz 54, 311
Wiepking, Lars 156, 240, 321
Wild, Benjamin 213
Wildberger, Thomas 308
Wilhelm, Gregor 170
Wilken, Katrin 150
Wilkes, Stephanie 226
Will, Christian 106
Will, Stefan 150, 199
Willborn, Niko 221
Williams, Mark 329
Willimski, Gregor 179
Willms, Beate 250
Willumeit, Lars 227
Willvonseder, Claudia 140, 152, 344
Wimmer, Simon 258
Wind, Chris 344
Windisch, Barbara 165
Wink, Petronius Amund 209
Winkler, Sarah 346
Winkler, Tobias 368
Winter, Bianca 310
Winterhagen, Michael 186, 235, 385f.
Winterstein, Gerrit 450
Wintrich, Nadine 348
Wirdeier, Jan 399
Wirt, Sandra 425
Wirth, Thomas 417
Wirz, Dana 355
Wischnewski, André 293
Withöft, Felix 313
Witschi, Rahel 231
Wittgen, Lennart 448
Witting, Lennart 327
Wittkowski, Clemens 124
Wittmann, Inka 223
Wittner, Alexander 314
Woerler-Horzon, Patricia 375
Wögerer, Florian 110
Wöhler, Philipp 54, 311, 314, 331, 430
Wohlert, Agnetha 433
Wolf, Melanie 245
Wolf, Sebastian 282
Wölfel, Jan 140, 207
Wolff, Jonas 308
Wolff, Manuel 94, 158
Wolter, Per 152
Woo-Bae, Jin 296
Wörner, Knut 335
Wortmann, Tobias 156, 295
Wübbe, Stefan 84, 239f., 321, 432
Wulf, Kristina 388
Wulfert, Ole 64
Wulfes, Jonathan 247
Wulff, Söhnke 341
Wunderer, Daniel 425
Wunsch, Robert 291
Wurm, Oliver 257, 389, 417
Wurst, Stefanie 54, 277, 311, 331
Wursthorn, Axel 315
Würth, Wolfgang 323
Wüschner, Gernot 259, 392
Wuttge, Diana 54, 314, 385
Wyeth, Andy 221

Y

Yeowell, Samantha 226

Z

Zacharias, Ivan 148
Zajac, Dominika 182
Zander, Ron 286
Zanin, Michael 420
Zanotto, Lucas 218
Zaradic, Mario 247
Zastrow, Kai 156
Zboralski, Oliver 152
Zeh, Nico 291
Zeh, Yves 213
Zehnhäusern, Marc 390
Zeman, Catherina 291
Zenger, Roland 369, 390
Zhang, Lisa 449
Zhestkov, Maxim 217
Ziegaus, Veronika 286, 325
Ziegler, Franziska 222, 313, 352
Ziegler, Hannah 128
Ziegler, Matthias 259, 392
Ziegler, Ralf 282
Ziegler, Veronika 179
Ziegler, Walter 385
Ziemba, Oskar 175
Zieten, Peter 136
Zilges, Stephan 360, 441
Zimmer, Dirk 312
Zimmer, Hendrik 140, 152, 344
Zimmermann, Nils 377, 380
Zimmermann, Olaf 392
Zimmermann, Ralf 177, 265ff., 338, 395ff., 408–411
Zinke, Gerrit 110, 236, 442
Zipco, Ed 398
Zitzewitz, Antje von 344
Zocholl, Anika 128
Zoll, Dorothee 346
Zösch, Sebastian 220
Zschaler, Stefan 150, 333, 340
Zuckerman, Andrew 408
Zumbrun, Philipp 274
Zwinge, Florian 238

IMPRESSUM
IMPRINT

Herausgeber und verantwortlich für den redaktionellen Inhalt Editor and responsible for editorial contents	Art Directors Club Verlag GmbH Franklinstraße 15 D-10587 Berlin Phone: 0049 30 5900 310 0 www.adc.de
ADC Projektleitung ADC Project Management	Sarah Rempen
ADC Projektkoordination ADC Project Coordination	Lea Bauer
ADC Redaktion ADC Editing	Kathrin Finger, Lea Bauer
ADC Übersetzung ADC Translation	WIENERS+WIENERS GmbH
Organisation avedition Organization avedition	Anja Schrade, Petra Kiedaisch
Projektmanagement avedition Project Management avedition	Anja Schrade
Redaktion avedition Editing avedition	Anja Schrade, Wiebke Ullmann
Übersetzung avedition Translation avedition	Sean McLaughlin
Gestaltungskonzept Design Concept	MAGMA Brand Design GmbH & Co. KG, Karlsruhe www.magmabranddesign.de
Schrift Font	Futura ND Sabon LT
Satz, Reinzeichnung Setting, Artwork	Eva Mokhlis, Oliver Grünberg, Kathrin Romer
Lithografie Lithography	Corinna Rieber Prepress
Druck Printing	Leibfarth & Schwarz GmbH & Co.KG, Dettingen/Erms
Bindung Binding	Verlagsbuchbinderei Karl Dieringer GmbH, Gerlingen
Papier Inhalt Paper Inside Pages	phoenixmotion Xenon, 135g/m², FSC certified, Scheufelen
UV-Relieflack UV Relief Varnish	V4 Veredelung, Leinfelden-Echterdingen
Lesebändchen Ribbon Page Markers	Verlagsbuchbinderei Karl Dieringer GmbH, Gerlingen
Der ADC dankt	Marlene Bücker Nora Bullien Skadi Groh Julian Karnetzky Vivian Katsch Anja Kaun Katharina Schoenauer

avedition GmbH
Koenigsallee 57
D-71638 Ludwigsburg
Phone: 0049 7141 1477 391
Fax: 0049 7141 1477 399
www.avedition.com

ISBN 978-3-89986-152-5

Copyright © 2011 by
Art Directors Club Verlag GmbH, Berlin
avedition GmbH, Ludwigsburg

Nachdruck, auch auszugsweise, nur mit Genehmigung der Art Directors Club Verlag GmbH
Reprint, also in extracts, only with prior approval of the Art Directors Club Verlag GmbH

Alle Rechte, insbesondere das Recht der Vervielfältigung, Verbreitung und Übersetzung, vorbehalten. Kein Teil des Werkes darf in irgendeiner Form (durch Fotokopie, Mikrofilm oder ein anderes Verfahren) ohne schriftliche Genehmigung reproduziert oder unter Verwendung elektronischer Systeme verarbeitet, vervielfältigt oder verbreitet werden.

This work is subject to copyright. All rights are reserved, whether the whole or part of the material is concerned, and specifically but not exclusively the right of translation, reprinting, reuse of illustrations, recitation, broadcasting, reproduction on microfilms or in other ways, and storage in databases or any other media. For use of any kind, the written permission of the copyright owner must be obtained.

Printed in Germany

DANK
ACKNOWLEDGMENTS

Für die freundliche Unterstützung danken wir
For their friendly support we would like to thank

LEIBFARTH & SCHWARZ

KARL DIERINGER VERLAGSBUCHBINDEREI

Scheufelen
PREMIUM WHITE SINCE 1855

V4 VEREDELUNG